MARY IMOGENE BASSETT HOSPITAL

Analytical Biochemistry

An International Journal

VOLUME 20

1967

ACADEMIC PRESS
New York and London

Made in the United States of America

CONTENTS OF VOLUME 20

NUMBER 1, JULY 1967

J. FEENEY AND F. W. HEMMING. Nuclear Magnetic Resonance Spectrometry of Naturally Occurring Polyprenols 1

L. I. GLEBKO, J. I. ULKINA, AND V. E. VASKOVSKY. Spectrophotometrical Method for Determination of Nitrogen in Biological Preparations Based on Thymol-Hypobromite Reaction . . 16

L. INGRAM, M. P. TOMBS, AND A. HURST. Mobility—Molecular Weight Relationships of Small Proteins and Peptides in Acrylamide-Gel Electrophoresis 24

P. L. IPATA. A Coupled Optical Enzyme Assay for 5′-Nucleotidase 30

W. F. BON. Simultaneous Analysis of Different Specimens in the Ultracentrifuge 37

RAYMOND E. HANSEN, THEODORE T. KALAL, AND HELMUT BEINERT. A Gas-Flow System for the Control of the Temperature of an Electron Paramagnetic Resonance Sample at Temperatures Between 80 and 273 Degrees Kelvin 40

J. I. OHMS, J. ZEC, J. V. BENSON, JR., AND J. A. PATTERSON. Column Chromatography of Neutral Sugars: Operating Characteristics and Performance of a Newly Available Anion-Exchange Resin 51

W. A. KHAN, T. BALDWIN, U. BRODBECK, AND K. E. EBNER. A Simple Chemical Synthesis of α-D-Glucose-1,6-Diphosphate . 58

JEAN LUST AND VICTOR RICHARDS. Influence of Buffers on the Phenol Extraction of Liver Microsomal Ribonucleic Acids . 65

B. P. LISBOA AND R. F. PALMER. Application of Thin-Layer Chromatographic Techniques to the Separation of Δ^{16}-C_{19}-Steroids and Related Compounds 77

HERBERT SCHUEL AND REGINA SCHUEL. Automated Determination of Protein in the Presence of Sucrose 86

E. SULKOWSKI AND M. LASKOWSKI, SR. The Separation of Nucleotides and their Derivatives by Continuous Free-Flow Electrophoresis 94

ARTHUR KARMEN. A Combination Membrane-Gas Detector for Monitoring Concentrations of Dissolved Volatiles 102

C. R. MCEWEN. Tables for Estimating Sedimentation through Linear Concentration Gradients of Sucrose Solution 114

A. CHRAMBACH, R. A. REISFELD, M. WYCKOFF, AND J. ZACCARI. A Procedure for Rapid and Sensitive Staining of Protein Fractionated by Polyacrylamide Gel Electrophoresis 150

B. C. Ray Sarkar and U. P. S. Chauhan. A New Method for Determining Micro Quantities of Calcium in Biological Materials 155
K. H. Haraguchi, J. C. Jansen, and B. V. Siegel. A Multiple-Wavelength Selector for a Continuous Spectrophotometric Column Monitoring System 167
D. N. Skilleter and R. G. O. Kekwick. An Improved Ion-Exchange Procedure for the Chromatography of the Metabolites of Mevalonate 171
George W. Rushizky and Warren W. Miller. Activation Analysis of Mono- and Oligonucleotides 181
Martin A. Rizack. Separation of Adenosine 3′,5′-Phosphate Derivatives on Thin Layers of ECTEOLA Cellulose . . . 192

Short Communications

Don M. Carlson. A Simple Quantitative Assay for *N*-Acetylgalactosaminitol 195
Gary J. Nelson and Robert A. Booth. Increasing the Sensitivity of Char Sprays for the Detection of Lipids on Thin-Layer Chromatograms by Viewing under Ultraviolet Light 198
I. Salasoo. Distribution of Rabbit Serum Proteins in Fractionation by the Cold Ethanol Method 200

Addendum 203

Number 2, August 1967

Howard Ko and Max E. Royer. A Submicromolar Assay for Nonpolar Acids in Plasma and Depot Fat 205
Carl Monder and Newell Sells. Influence of Acids on the Determination of Calcium and Magnesium by Atomic Absorption Spectrophotometry 215
B. Stavrić, W. J. Johnson, and A. Chartrand. Use of a Sensitive New Method for Determination of the Urinary-Excretion of Dichlorodiphenylacetic Acid (DDA) by Human Subjects . 224
D. J. Watson, E. B. Romanoff, J. Kato, and D. B. Bartosik. A Method for the Determination of Progesterone in Biological Specimens 233
Albert A. Dietz and Tina Lubrano. Separation and Quantitation of Lactic Dehydrogenase Isoenzymes by Disc Electrophoresis 246
Je. H. Kim, Basudev Shome, Ta-Hsiu Liao, and John G. Pierce. Analysis of Neutral Sugars by Gas-Liquid Chromatography

of Alditol Acetates: Application to Thyrotropic Hormone and Other Glycoproteins 258
Martha A. Ward, Timothy E. McCarthy, and Jonathan S. Nishimura. Gas-Liquid Chromatography and Derivatives of Several Amino Acids that Occur in the Actinomycins . . . 275
W. S. Zaugg and R. J. Knox. Determination of Phosphate in Biological Materials and Reaction Mixtures by Atomic Absorption Spectrophotometry 282
Clinton A. Nerenberg, Dinesh C. Sharma, and Ralph I. Dorfman. An Automatic Device for Adding Solvents to Chromatography Tanks 294
Vivian E. Shih, Mary L. Efron, and Gerald L. Mechanic. Rapid Short Column Chromatography of Amino Acids. A Method for Blood and Urine Specimens in the Diagnosis and Treatment of Metabolic Disease 299
Ronald Bentley and Nancy Botlock. A Gas Chromatographic Method for Analysis of Anomeric Carbohydrates and for the Determination of Mutarotation Coefficients 312
Charles J. Rogers, Cecil W. Chambers, and Norman A. Clarke. Spectrophotofluorometric Determination of Nanogram Amounts of α,ϵ-Diaminopimelic Acid-A Bacterial Cell Wall Constituent 321
Mildred Van De Bogart and Helmut Beinert. Micro Methods for the Quantitative Determination of Iron and Copper in Biological Material 325
Arnold S. Bleiweis, Henry C. Reeves, and Samuel J. Ajl. Rapid Separation of Some Common Intermediates of Microbial Metabolism by Thin-Layer Chromatography 335
Raymond F. Chen. Practical Aspects of the Calibration and Use of the Aminco-Bowman Spectrophotofluorometer 339
Ronald D. Brown and Charles E. Holt. Rapid Separation of Thymine Dimer and Pyrimidines on Ion-Exchange Paper . 358

Short Communications

R. Brentani, M. Brentani, and I. Raw. Zone Sedimentation Analysis of RNA in Angle-Head Rotors 361
John Gorton Davis and Mary B. Siele. Ultrafilter for the Concentration of High Molecular Weight Solutes . . 363
James Winkelman and Gary Slater. Chemiluminescence of Liquid Scintillation Mixture Components 365
C. David Wise. The Fluorometric Determination of Brain Serotonin 369
Erratum 370

Number 3, September 1967

Charles L. Burger. Measurement of Nucleotide, Amino Acid, and DNA Contents of Tissues after Whole-Body X-Irradiation . . . 373

P. Biely and Š. Bauer. Determination of Intracellular 2-Deoxy-D-glucose 6-Phosphate and Uridine Diphosphate-2-deoxy-D-glucose . . . 387

J. Attal, S. M. Hendeles, and K. B. Eik-Nes. Determination of Free Estrone in Blood Plasma by Gas-Phase Chromatography with Electron Capture Detection . . . 394

Volney Wallace. Rapid Automated Analysis Involving Liquid-Liquid Extraction: Atropine by a Prudhomme Method . . . 411

L. A. Veiga and E. L. Chandelier. Detection and Differentiation of Sugars on Paper by *p*-Anisidine/Periodate Reaction . . . 419

Bette L. Hamman and Malcolm M. Martin. Direct Spectrophotometric Quantitation of Steroid Chromatograms. 1. The Measurement of Corticosteroids . . . 423

U Hla-Pe and Aung-Than-Batu. A New Colorimetric Method for the Determination of Formiminoglutamic Acid in Urine . 432

Wesley C. Starbuck, Charles M. Mauritzen, Carolyn McClimans, and Harris Busch. A Computer Program for the Calculation of Amino Acid Analysis Data . . . 439

M. Rowland and S. Riegelman. The Use of Carbon Disulfide as a Solvent for the Silylation of Submicrogram Amounts of Carboxylic Acids . . . 463

Paul W. Hathaway, Laszlo Jakoi, William G. Troyer, Jr., and Morton D. Bogdonoff. A Method for Semiautomatic Differential Analysis of Urinary Catecholamines . . . 466

Gerald Goldstein. Ligand-Exchange Chromatography of Nucleotides, Nucleosides, and Nucleic Acid Bases . . . 477

Claus Grunwald, Miguel Vendrell, and Bruce B. Stowe. Evaluation of Gas and Other Chromatographic Separations of Indolic Methyl Esters . . . 484

Käthi Hunziker and Karl Schmid. A Brief Method for the Identification of the α_1-Acid Glycoprotein Variants . . . 495

Lewis D. Steginк. Microenzymic Method for the Quantitative Analysis of Acetyl Groups in Proteins and Peptides . . . 502

Volney Wallace. Correction for Cross-Contamination in AutoAnalyzer Analysis . . . 517

Hannah E. Rosenthal. A Graphic Method for the Determination and Presentation of Binding Parameters in a Complex System . . . 525

I. B. Rubin, A. D. Kelmers, and G. Goldstein. The Determination of Transfer Ribonucleic Acid by Aminoacylation. I. Leu-

U. Hla-Pe and Aung-Than-Batu. A New Colorimetric Method

cine and Phenylalanine Transfer Ribonucleic Acid from *E. coli* B 533

SHORT COMMUNICATIONS

JOHN G. FORTE, HAROLD HELBOCK, AND PAUL SALTMAN. A Versatile Apparatus for Membrane Transport Studies . 545

B. M. MITRUKA AND M. ALEXANDER. Ultrasensitive Detection of Certain Microbial Metabolites by Gas Chromatography 548

A. V. LEBOUTON. Electrophoretic Separation of Soluble Rat Liver Cell Proteins on Gelatinized Cellulose Acetate . 550

WARREN STECK. On the Identification of Some Naturally Occurring Hydroxycinnamic Acid Derivatives 553

CAREL J. VAN OSS. The Hazards of Knotting Dialysis Bags . 556

ADRIENNE N. WEINSTEIN AND STANTON SEGAL. Thin-Layer Chromatographic Separation of Hexitols and Corresponding Hexoses 558

ERRATA 562

AUTHOR INDEX 563

SUBJECT INDEX 565

INFORMATION FOR AUTHORS

Analytical Biochemistry will publish articles on qualitative and quantitative techniques based on chemical, physical, and biological principles; methods of preparation, purification, characterization, isolation, and separation of biological substances and related materials; and instrumentation.

Address. Manuscripts should be submitted to **Dr. Alvin Nason, Editor, McCollum-Pratt Institute, The Johns Hopkins University, Baltimore, Maryland 21218.**

Manuscripts should be concise and consistent in style, spelling, and use of abbreviations. At least two copies should be submitted, each copy to include all figures and tables. The original copy must be typewritten, double-spaced, on one side of white bond paper, about 8½ × 11 inches in size, with one-inch margins on all sides. Each manuscript should have a separate title page noting title of article, authors' names (without degrees), a running title (not exceeding 35 letters and spaces), and address to which proof should be mailed. Please number all pages of manuscript.

Authors are encouraged to use descriptive subheadings in this order: Methods, Results, Discussion, Summary, Acknowledgments, and References.

Units of weights, measures, etc., when used in conjunction with numerals should be abbreviated and unpunctuated (e.g., 10%, 50 ml, 3 gm, 8 cm).

Figures should be mentioned consecutively with Arabic numerals in order of mention in the text; each figure should have a descriptive legend. Legends should be typed together on a separate sheet, double-spaced. All illustrations should be in finished form ready for the engraver. A convenient size for drawings is 8½ × 11 inches (21 × 27.5 cm). Drawings should be made with India ink on tracing linen, smooth surface white paper, or Bristol board. Graph paper if used should be ruled in blue. Grid lines that are to show in the final engraving should be inked in black.

Photographs must be kept to a minimum and should be glossy prints with strong contrasts; the magnification should be indicated by a scale where possible.

Tables should be typed on separate pages, numbered consecutively with Arabic numerals in order of mention in the text. All tables should have descriptive headings, typed (double-spaced) above the table.

Footnotes should be designated in text by superscript numbers and listed on a separate sheet; in tables, by superscript letters and placed at bottom of page containing table.

References to the literature should be cited in the text by Arabic numerals in parentheses and listed at the end of the paper in consecutive order. Abbreviations of journal titles should follow the style used in *Chemical Abstracts* (Vol. 55, 1961). Please note style of capitalization and punctuation for journal articles and edited books in the following examples:

1. Bishop, N. I., *Biochim. Biophys. Acta* **27**, 205 (1958).
2. Cohen, S. S., *in* "The Chemical Basis of Heredity" (W. D. McElroy and B. Glass, eds.), p. 651. Johns Hopkins Press, Baltimore, Maryland, 1957.

Proofs. Galley proofs will be sent to the authors with reprint order forms. **Fifty reprints** of each article are provided free of charge.

ANALYTICAL BIOCHEMISTRY 20, 1–15 (1967)

Nuclear Magnetic Resonance Spectrometry of Naturally Occurring Polyprenols

J. FEENEY

Varian Research Laboratory, Varian Associates Ltd., Walton-on-Thames, Surrey, England

AND

F. W. HEMMING

The Department of Biochemistry, The University of Liverpool, Liverpool, England

Received October 31, 1966

A number of alcohols with the general formula I, where $n = 1$ to 13, occur in nature. Green leaves of many higher plants yield polyprenols

$$\mathrm{H{-}\left[CH_2{-}\overset{\displaystyle CH_3}{\overset{|}{C}}{=}CH{-}CH_2\right]_{\mathit{n}}{-}OH}$$

(I)

(structure I) in which $n = 9$ to 13 (1–4), while the wood of the silver birch contains polyprenols with from 6 to 9 isoprene residues (1, 5, 6). A series of alcohols in which $n = 16$ to 21 and in which the OH-terminal isoprene residue is saturated (Structure II) have been isolated from mammalian

$$\mathrm{H{-}\left[CH_2{-}\overset{\displaystyle CH_3}{\overset{|}{C}}{=}CH{-}CH_2{-}\right]_{\mathit{n}-1}{-}CH_2{-}\overset{\displaystyle CH_3}{\overset{|}{C}H}{-}CH_2{-}CH_2{-}OH}$$

(II)

tissues and have been termed dolichols (1, 7). Similar alcohols in which n varies from 14 to 18 have been isolated from bakers' yeast (1, 8). Finally, the mould *Aspergillus fumigatus* Fresenius has been shown to contain a family of hexahydropolyprenols (Structure III) containing 18 to 24 isoprene

$$\mathrm{H{-}\left[CH_2{-}\overset{\displaystyle CH_3}{\overset{|}{C}H}{-}CH_2{-}CH_2{-}\right]_{2}{-}\left[CH_2{-}\overset{\displaystyle CH_3}{\overset{|}{C}}{=}CH{-}CH_2{-}\right]_{\mathit{n}-3}{-}CH_2{-}\overset{\displaystyle CH_3}{\overset{|}{C}H}{-}CH_2{-}CH_2{-}OH}$$

(III)

residues of which the OH-terminal isoprene residue, the ω-terminal isoprene residue, and the residue adjacent to the ω-terminal isoprene residue are saturated (9).

While techniques such as mass spectrometry and ozonolytic degradation give useful evidence about the basic structures of these compounds, they give no information on their stereochemistry. Infrared spectrometry provides essentially qualitative stereochemical information and at the most shows the polyprenols to contain predominantly *cis* isoprene residues. Of the techniques normally available, only nuclear magnetic resonance (NMR) spectrometry provides quantitative data on this point. A group of workers led by Bates (10–12) has summarized the stereochemical information to be gained from a study of 60 Mc/sec NMR spectra of solutions of isoprenoid compounds in carbon tetrachloride. A more recent review of this application has also appeared (13). Chen (14) has reported the advantages of using benzene as solvent when determining the *cis* and *trans* contents of 1,4-polyisoprene. In the course of studying the NMR of naturally occurring polyprenols and of suitable reference compounds the present authors have confirmed and extended these findings. Some of the results are reported here.

MATERIALS AND METHODS

Reference Compounds. Phytol and geraniol were commercial samples purchased from Koch-Light (Colnbrook, Bucks, England). Solanesol (natural all-*trans*-nonaprenol from tobacco) and citronellal were gifts from Dr. O. Isler of Hoffmann-LaRoche, Basle, Switzerland. The latter compound was reduced with sodium borohydride to yield citronellol. Nerol was a gift from B. K. Tidd of Natural Rubber Producers Research Association, Welwyn, England. All these alcohols were purified by preparative thin-layer chromatography and their purity was confirmed by infrared spectroscopy and by thin-layer chromatography.

Natural Polyprenols. The polyprenols studied and their sources are as follows. (Details of isolation are to be found in the appropriate references.) The leaves of the common horsechestnut tree (*Aesculus hippocastanum*) yielded a family of polyprenols which were given the trivial names castaprenol-11, castaprenol-12, and castaprenol-13 (2) containing respectively 11, 12, and 13 isoprene residues. Ficaprenols-10, -11, and -12 were obtained from the leaves of the decorative Indiarubber plant (*Ficus elastica*)(3), while the leaves of the beet (*Beta vulgaris* var. *crassa*) provided betaprenols-10, -11, -12, and -13 (15). Betulaprenols-7, -8, and -9 were isolated from the wood and betulaprenols-10, -11, and -12 from the leaves of the European white birch (*Betula pendula,* also known as *B.*

verrucosa) (6). Dolichols-18 to -20 were isolated from pig liver (7), and *Aspergillus fumigatus* Fresenius yielded hexahydroprenols-19 to -23 (9).

Determination of Spectra. Most spectra were determined at 100 Mc/sec with a Varian HA 100 spectrometer but some were obtained using a Varian A60 or A60A spectrometer. Usually, spectra were determined by one of the authors (J. F.) with the help of Miss A. Heinrich at Varian Associates Ltd., Walton-on-Thames. Other spectra were obtained through the courtesy of Dr. R. J. Abraham, J. V. Barkley, and Misses R. Adlard and C. Hale of the Department of Organic Chemistry, The University of Liverpool. Benzene, carbon tetrachloride, and deuterochloroform were used as solvents and tetramethylsilane was the internal standard. Between 3 and 20 mg samples of prenol were studied for each spectrum.

RESULTS AND DISCUSSION

1. *Cis-trans Configuration of Isoprene Residues*

In all, sixteen polyprenols isolated from higher plant tissue have been examined. The positions of resonance peaks in the spectra of these compounds are summarized in Table 1; 100 Mc/sec spectra of castaprenol-12 in benzene and carbon tetrachloride are reproduced in Figure 1. The sub-

TABLE 1
Chemical Shifts and Assignments of Peaks in the Nuclear Magnetic Resonance Spectra at 100 Mc/sec of Polyprenols[a]

Chemical shifts (τ) (±0.01 τ)		
In benzene	In carbon tetrachloride	Assignments[b]
8.5 ↓ 8.2	8.5 ↓ 8.2	R—C(*CH*$_3$)=CH—R [c]
7.95w, 7.87~, 7.83, 7.80~	8.00, 7.97	—*CH*$_2$—C(—)=
6.06, 5.99 d	6.10, 6.02 d	=CH—*CH*$_2$—OH
4.73	4.95	—C(—)=*CH*—CH$_2$
4.66, 4.59, 4.52 t	4.74, 4.66, 4.58 t	—C(—)=*CH*—CH$_2$—OH

[a] w = weak, ~ = shoulder, d = doublet, t = triplet.
[b] The resonating proton is in italics.
[c] See Table 2 for a more detailed analysis of this region.

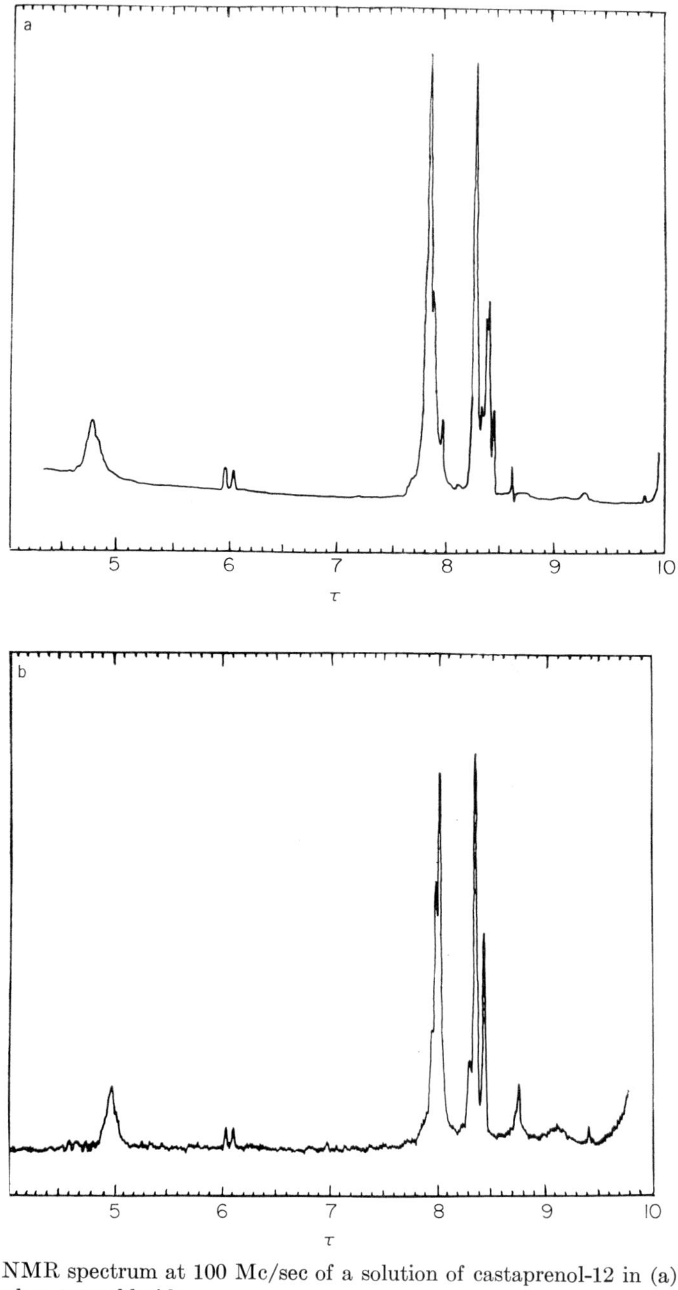

FIG. 1. NMR spectrum at 100 Mc/sec of a solution of castaprenol-12 in (a) benzene and (b) carbon tetrachloride.

stitution of deuterochloroform for carbon tetrachloride as solvent had a negligible effect on the peak positions. Each of these alcohols gave resonance peaks in the region 8.2 to 8.6 τ, which can be assigned to protons of methyl groups on trisubstituted olefinic groups. The precise position of these peaks is summarized in Table 2. When carbon tetrachloride or deuterochloroform was the solvent, each compound gave an intense peak at 8.34 τ with a rather weak peak at 8.28 τ and a peak of medium intensity at 8.42 τ. These positions agree well with those assigned by Bates (10–12) on the basis of 60 Mc/sec spectra to the protons of the methyl groups of a *cis* internal residue (8.34 τ), of a *cis* OH-terminal residue (8.27 τ), and of a *trans* internal residue

TABLE 2
Nuclear Magnetic Resonance of Protons of Methyl Groups of Polyprenols in the Region 8.2–8.5 τ

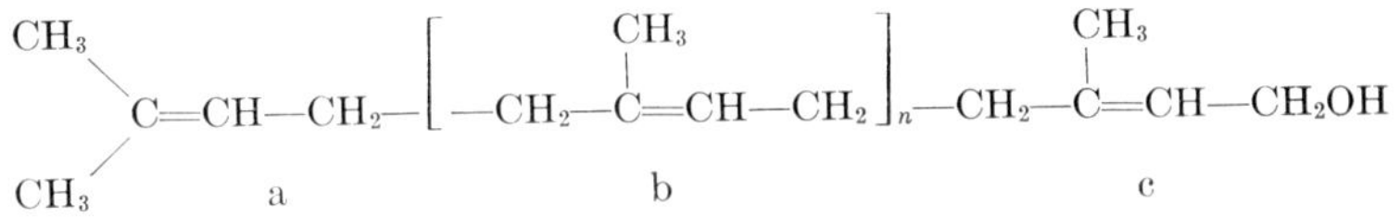

Type of isoprene residue containing the methyl group	Chemical shift (τ)[a] In benzene *cis*	In benzene *trans*	In CCl_4 *cis*	In CCl_4 *trans*
a (ω-terminal)	8.32	8.43	8.34	8.42
b (internal)	8.25	8.38	8.34	8.42
c (OH-terminal)	8.355	8.51	8.28	8.34

[a] $\pm 0.01\ \tau$.

(8.41 τ), respectively. Bates also reported that the methyl groups of an ω-terminal isoprene residue would give peaks at 8.34 τ (methyl group *cis* to the olefinic proton) and at 8.41 τ (methyl group *trans* to the olefinic proton). These assignments were confirmed by the NMR spectra of citronellol, geraniol, nerol, phytol, and solanesol.

One of the problems in using 60 Mc/sec spectra to assay quantitatively the number of *cis* and *trans* isoprene residues in a polyisoprene structure is the incomplete separation of the peaks, with consequential errors in estimating peak areas. Chen (13) has reported the superior resolution of *cis* and *trans* methyl peaks of polyisoprene when benzene (peak separation of 0.14 τ) instead of carbon tetrachloride (peak separation of 0.08 τ) is used as a solvent. In fact, when solutions of polyprenoids in carbon tetrachloride are studied at 100 Mc/sec instead of 60 Mc/sec, the *cis* and *trans* peaks of internal isoprene residues are sufficiently well separated for reasonably accurate area measurements. Unfortunately, the corresponding peaks of any unsaturated terminal isoprene residues still complicate these measurements. For this reason, most of the polyprenols have also been studied as solutions in benzene for it became apparent that useful differences in chemical shifts (peak positions) of protons of methyl groups from different parts of the polyisoprene chain existed. These are summarized in Table 2

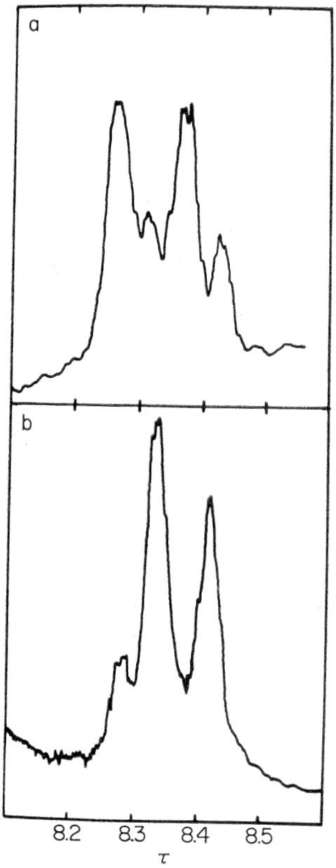

FIG. 2. Methyl-proton region of the 100 Mc/sec NMR spectrum of a solution of betulaprenol-7 in (a) benzene and (b) carbon tetrachloride. Methy groups resonating in this region are 1 *cis* and 1 *trans* ω-terminal, 3 *cis* internal, 2 *trans* internal, and 1 *cis* "OH-terminal" (see Table 2).

(see also Fig. 2 and 3). It can be seen that, whereas in carbon tetrachloride the *cis* "OH-terminal" (8.28 τ) residue peak is separated from the other peaks and the *trans* "OH-terminal" residue peak (8.34 τ) is hidden under the *cis* internal residue peak (8.34 τ), in benzene the *cis* "OH-terminal" residue peak (8.355 τ) is hidden under the *trans* internal residue peak (8.38 τ) and it is the *trans* "OH-terminal" (8.51 τ) residue that is clear of the other peaks. Thus benzene permits a positive identification of a *trans*

"OH-terminal" residue and carbon tetrachloride (or deuterochloroform) a positive identification of a *cis* "OH-terminal" residue. The conclusions regarding the *cis* "OH terminal" residue in benzene are based on the disappearance of the 8.28 τ peak and the increase in relative intensity (by an amount equivalent to three protons) of the 8.38 + 8.355 τ peak when the

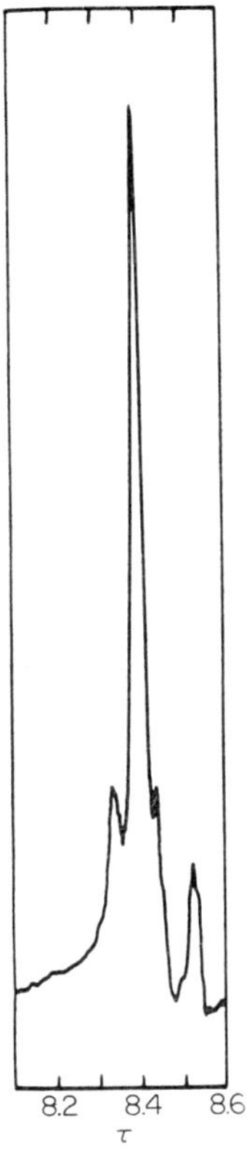

FIG. 3. Methyl-proton region of the 100 Mc/sec NMR spectrum of a solution of solanesol in benzene. Methyl groups resonating in this region are 1 *cis* and 1 *trans* ω-terminal, 7 *trans* internal, and 1 *trans* "OH-terminal" (see Table 2).

natural polyprenols were studied in benzene instead of carbon tetrachloride (Fig. 2). Also, the *cis* "OH terminal" residue of nerol gave a peak at 8.37 τ. The assignment of the *trans* "OH-terminal" residue peak (8.51 τ) is based on the spectra of solanesol (see Fig. 3) and phytol. The spectrum of geraniol in benzene gave its *trans* "OH-terminal" residue peak at 8.49 τ but this value is probably atypically low for this type of residue.

2. *The ω-Terminal Isoprene Residue*

It is clear from Table 2 that in benzene the positions of the peaks of the *cis* (8.32 τ) and *trans* (8.43 τ) methyl groups of ω-terminal isoprene residues no longer coincide with those of the *cis* and *trans* methyl groups (respectively) of internal isoprene residues. With a 100 Mc/sec instrument these ω-residue methyl peaks can be readily identified and their presence or absence in a spectrum offers strong evidence in favor of or against the presence of a normal ω-terminal isoprene residue. Peaks at 8.32 and 8.43 τ, each corresponding in intensity to three protons, were the only peaks in this part of the spectrum of citronellol, whereas they were entirely absent from the spectrum of phytol, confirming the assignments. The spectrum of solanesol was entirely in agreement with this but the spectra of both geraniol and nerol gave corresponding peaks at positions about 0.04 τ higher than expected.

3. *Partially Saturated Polyprenols*

As well as the fully unsaturated polyprenols, there are in nature a number of partially saturated polyprenols. These are the dihydropolyprenols (dolichols) and the hexahydropolyprenols. These compounds have very long molecules containing 14 to 24 isoprene residues. Mass spectrometry and infrared spectroscopy indicate that both series of alcohols contain a saturated "OH-terminal" isoprene residue (7–9). This can be confirmed without question by their nuclear magnetic resonance spectra.

All fully unsaturated prenols have a 2,3 double bond:

$$\begin{array}{l} CH_3 \\ | \\ -C{=}CH{-}CH_2{-}OH \end{array}$$

The protons of the α-methylene group resonate close to 6 τ and because the methylene group is adjacent to a carbon atom carrying one hydrogen the resonance appears as a doublet (Table 1, Fig. 1). The intensity of this doublet is equivalent to two protons. On hydrogenation of the 2,3 double bond the position of resonance of the α-methylene protons moves upfield and since it is now adjacent to a carbon atom carrying two hydrogens it appears as a triplet. Thus citronellol and catalytically hydrogenated prenols give a spectrum containing a triplet close to 6.5 τ (Table 3) instead of a doublet close to 6.0 τ. Similarly the spectra of natural dihydro- and hexahydropolyprenols lack the doublet at 6.0 τ but contain the triplet at 6.5 τ with an area equivalent to two protons. This is shown quite clearly in Figure 4.

That the 2,3 double bond of the dihydropolyprenols has been saturated and has not simply migrated (for example to the 3,4 position) can be shown

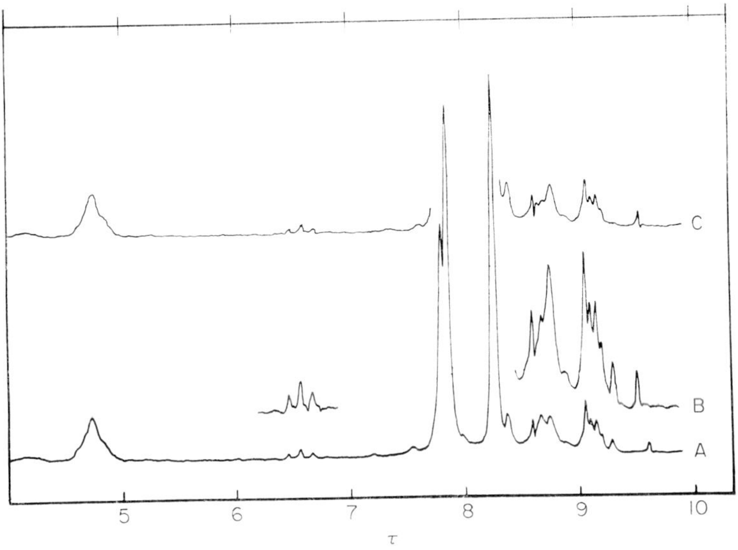

FIG. 4. NMR spectrum at 60 Mc/sec of a solution in benzene of the mixture of hexahydropolyprenols of *Aspergillus fumigatus*. Trace B is an amplified version of trace A. Trace C was recorded after shaking with deuterium oxide.

TABLE 3
Chemical Shifts of Protons of Saturated Isoprene Residues[a]

Peak position (τ)[b]		
In benzene	In CCl_4	Assignment
9.19, 9.09[c] d	9.15, 9.08 d	$-CH_2-\overset{\mathit{CH_3}}{\overset{\vert}{CH}}-CH_2-CH_2OH$
9.12[c], 9.02 d	N.D.	$-CH_2-\overset{\mathit{CH_3}}{\overset{\vert}{CH}}-CH_2-CH_2-CH_2$ plus $\mathit{CH_3}-\overset{\mathit{CH_3}}{\overset{\vert}{CH}}-CH_2-CH_2-CH_2$
8.8 ↓ 8.5 c	8.8 ↓ 8.5 c	$-\mathit{CH_2}-\overset{CH_3}{\overset{\vert}{\mathit{CH}}}-\mathit{CH_2}-\mathit{CH_2}-C$
6.60, 6.53, 6.46 t	6.52, 6.45, 6.38 t	$CH_2-\overset{CH_3}{\overset{\vert}{CH}}-CH_2-\mathit{CH_2}-OH$

[a] d = doublet, c = complex, t = triplet, N.D. = not determined.
[b] ±0.01 τ
[c] In the hexahydropolyprenols these two peaks (9.09 + 9.12τ) sometimes appear coalesced to give one peak.

by the 8.5–9.2 τ region of the spectrum. A doublet close to 9.1 τ corresponds in position and area to a methyl group in the group

$$\begin{array}{c} \quad\;\; CH_3 \\ \quad\;\; | \\ -CH_2-CH-CH_2 \end{array}$$

(Table 3). A complicated pattern of absorption in the region 8.5 to 8.8 τ corresponds in position and intensity to the remaining five protons (two methylenes and one methine) of this same group. The spectrum of citronellol confirmed these assignments.

In fact the relative areas of the peaks in the 8.5–9.2 τ region of the spectrum of the dihydropolyprenols confirm that the saturated isoprene residue is at the hydroxyl end of the chain. Had the saturated residue been internal, then the area of the 8.5–8.8 τ region should correspond to seven protons. Had the saturated residue been at the ω end of the chain then the area of the doublet near 9.1 τ should have been equivalent to six protons. Ozonolytic degradation has confirmed the presence of a saturated OH-terminal residue in both the dihydro- and hexahydropolyprenols (9, 16).

The hexahydropolyprenols contain four hydrogen atoms more than the dihydropolyprenols. The 8.5 to 9.2 τ region of the spectra of these alcohols shows that two of these are present in a saturated ω-terminal isoprene residue and the other two in a saturated internal isoprene residue. Thus the region 9.0–9.2 τ has the appearance of two overlapping doublets. One of the doublets corresponds to that of citronellol and the dihydropolyprenols (9.09 and 9.19 τ in benzene) and the other to that in the spectrum of phytol (9.02 and 9.12 τ in benzene). The total area of the 9.0–9.2 τ region corresponds to twelve protons and the relative intensities of the two doublets make it clear that the former corresponds to one methyl group and the latter to three methyl groups. Since a total of only three saturated isoprene residues is involved, the ω-terminal isoprene residue must be saturated, for this is the only residue containing two methyl groups. The relative area of the 8.5–8.8 τ region of the spectra agrees closely with seventeen protons resonating here, as expected on the basis of one saturated ω-terminal residue, one saturated internal residue, and one saturated "OH-terminal" residue. In fact, mass spectrometry and ozonolytic degradation show the saturated internal residue to be adjacent to the saturated ω-terminal residue (9). Nuclear magnetic resonance does not help in the location of the internal saturated residue.

It was mentioned earlier (Table 2) that in benzene most of the prenols give small peaks at 8.32 and 8.43 τ either side of the internal *trans* peak at 8.38 τ. These two peaks were assigned to the *cis* and *trans* methyl protons, respectively, of a normal ω-terminal isoprene residue. It is relevant that these two peaks are also present in the spectra of the dihydropolyprenols

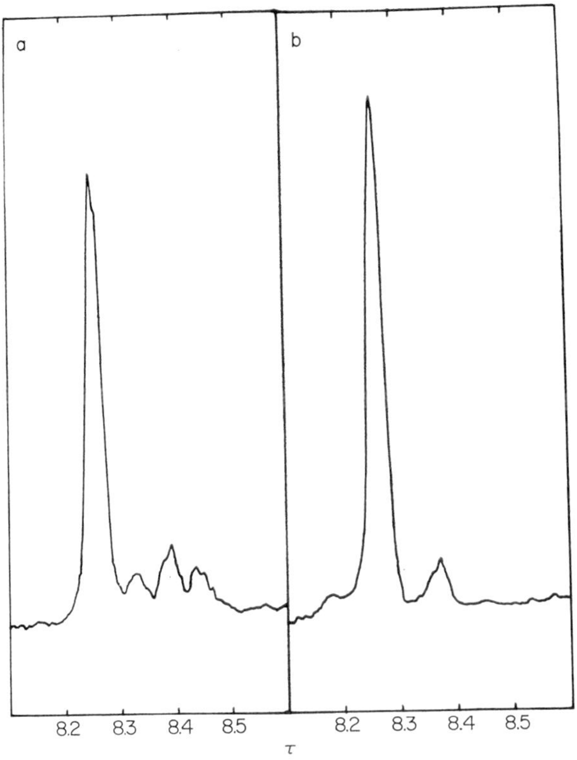

FIG. 5. 8.1–8.6 τ region of the 100 Mc/sec NMR spectrum of benzene solutions of (a) dihydroprenol-19 and (b) hexahydroprenol-21 showing the presence in (a) and absence in (b) of 1 *cis* and 1 *trans* methyl of an unsaturated ω-terminal isoprene residue (see Table 2).

but not in the spectra of the hexahydroprenols (Fig. 5). Also worth noting is the absence of peaks at 8.28 τ (in carbon tetrachloride) and 8.51 τ (in benzene) (Fig. 5) in the spectra of both dihydro- and hexahydropolyprenols. Thus *cis* and *trans* "OH-terminal" residues must be absent—a conclusion in keeping with the assumed saturated nature of the "OH-terminal" residue.

4. *Methylenic Protons of Isoprene Residues*

One of the dominant groups of peaks in the spectra of polyprenols is that close to 8.0 τ (Fig. 1). This is due to the resonance of methylene protons adjacent to a carbon atom on a double bond. In the spectrum of citronellol this resonance occurs as a quadruplet due to splitting by the adjacent methylene and olefinic protons. With benzene as solvent the four peaks are at 7.88, 7.96, 8.04, and 8.12 τ and in carbon tetrachloride there is a slight shift to 7.93, 8.00, 8.08, and 8.16 τ. In the spectrum of phytol this region appears as a rather broad and only partially resolved triplet at 8.01, 8.07, and 8.14 τ when benzene is the solvent or as a broad band at 8.12 τ when carbon tetrachloride is the solvent. As the number of methylene groups involved increased, these individual peaks overlap and in all of the polyprenols a characteristic pattern occurs. When examined as a solution in carbon tetrachloride two overlapping peaks at 7.97 and 8.00 τ with a broad base are present. The more usual pattern when examined in benzene is that of a main peak at 7.83 τ with shoulders at 7.80 and 7.87 τ and a small peak at 7.95 τ. Occasionally, however, the 7.87 τ shoulder disappears and the 7.80 τ shoulder appears as a peak. Polyprenols have been observed to give both patterns when examined on different occasions in benzene. This phenomenon is not yet understood.

5. *Olefinic Protons*

In spectra of citronellol the olefinic proton resonates near 5.0 τ and appears as a triplet at 4.90, 4.97, and 5.04 τ in carbon tetrachloride and at 4.71, 4.78, and 4.84 τ in benzene. This splitting is caused by the protons of the adjacent methylene group. In phytol the triplet occurs at 4.54, 4.62, and 4.70 τ in carbon tetrachloride and at 4.51, 4.57, and 4.63 τ in benzene. Geraniol, nerol, and solanesol showed a broad band corresponding in position to the citronellol triplet and a triplet corresponding to the phytol triplet. It seems likely that in these three spectra the former triplet can be assigned to olefinic protons of ω-terminal and internal residues and the latter triplet to the olefinic proton of the "OH-terminal" residue. The other unsaturated polyprenols gave a similar picture in this region. The dihydro- and hexahydropolyprenols would be expected to lack a triplet corresponding in position to that of phytol. In fact, this was not detected in the spectra, but it has to be admitted that a triplet corresponding in area to one proton could easily be missed in the spectrum of polyprenols containing 20 or more isoprene residues.

6. *Hydroxyl Proton*

It is well known that the position of resonance of hydroxyl protons is very variable. Changes in solvent, in dilution, and in the nature of the compound carrying the group cause large shifts in peak positions. Frequently in the spectra of the polyprenols the resonance peak of the hydroxyl group was not detected. It was usually assumed to have coincided with the methyl or methylene peaks. This was not considered a serious matter, for the increase in these areas by an amount equivalent to one proton was almost negligible. When it has been necessary to demonstrate the presence of a hydroxyl group it has been found convenient to shake the solution of prenol with deuterium oxide. An exchange reaction causes the hydroxyl resonance to be quenched. The decrease in intensity of a peak, or the disappearance of a peak of intensity equivalent to one proton, after treatment with deuterium oxide reveals the former position of the hydroxyl resonance. This method is well known and its use is illustrated in Figure 4. The peak at 9.30 τ (traces A and B) is seen to have disappeared on shaking with deuterium oxide (trace C). The peak is equivalent in size to one proton and is assumed to have been due to the hydroxyl proton.

7. *Quantitative Assessment of the Number of cis and trans Isoprene Residues*

All of the leaf polyprenols studied, except for solanesol, contain both *cis* and *trans* isoprene residues. The number of isoprene residues of each configuration in each molecule can be determined by measuring the ratios of the areas of the resonance peaks for methyl protons in the 8.2–8.5 τ region. Knowing the molecular size of the polyprenol, these ratios can be converted into the absolute number of protons on methyl groups in each configuration and hence to the absolute number of *cis* and *trans* isoprene residues. Mass spectrometry is the most reliable technique for determining molecular size but in a good NMR spectrum comparison of the total area of the 8.2–8.5 τ region with that of the doublet at 6.0 τ or, alternatively, the triplet at 6.5 τ (always equivalent to two protons), will give a fairly accurate assessment of the number of methyl protons in unsaturated isoprene residues per molecule. The relative areas of well-resolved peaks can be measured directly from the integration plotted on the spectrum. In this way, using spectra determined in carbon tetrachloride, it is possible to measure the area of the 8.42 τ peak and the combined areas of the 8.28 and 8.34 τ peaks. Although the 8.28 and 8.34 τ peaks are insufficiently separated to be measured independently, the number of protons resonating at 8.34 τ can be derived, for it is known that the area of the 8.28 τ peak, that due to the methyl protons of the "OH-terminal" residue, must be equivalent to three protons. It is also known that in the fully unsaturated polyprenols the 8.34 τ peak includes the *cis* methyl protons of the ω-terminal isoprene residue, the *trans* methyl protons of this residue resonating at 8.42 τ. Thus, it is possible to arrive at the number of protons of methyl groups in *cis* internal isoprene residues (8. 34 τ) and in *trans* internal isoprene residues (8.42 τ).

Analysis in this way of the spectra, determined both in carbon tetrachloride and benzene, of all of the leaf polyprenols studied shows that each prenol contains 8.6 ($\pm$0.4 S.D.) protons on methyl groups in *trans* internal isoprene residues. It follows that each of these polyprenols contains three *trans* internal isoprene residues. It is also clear that each of these alcohols contains a *cis* "OH terminal" isoprene residue. The polyprenols appear to differ from each other only in the number of *cis* internal isoprene residues. It may well be that the three *trans* internal isoprene residues are adjacent to the ω-terminal residue. This situation would be consistent with each leaf polyprenol having been formed from all *trans*-geranyl-geranyl pyrophosphate. It would also mean that each leaf polyprenol of the same chain length is in fact the same compound. Unfortunately, NMR spectrometry provides no information on the precise position in the molecule of the *cis* or *trans* internal residues.

In a similar manner it can be calculated that each polyprenol from the wood of *Betula verrucosa* contains 5.9 (±0.3 S.D.) protons on methyl groups in *trans* internal isoprene residues per molecule. This is equivalent to two *trans* internal isoprene residues and if these are adjacent to the ω-terminal the situation is consistent with the wood polyprenols having been formed from all *trans*-farnesyl pyrophosphate by addition of *cis* isoprene residues.

Each dolichol spectrum also indicated two *trans* internal isoprene residues per molecule. The dolichols may thus have the same all *trans* precursor as the wood polyprenols of *Betula verrucosa*.

The hexahydropolyprenols from *Aspergillus fumigatus* gave spectra showing 5–7 methyl protons in internal *trans* isoprene residues. This is clearly in close agreement with two internal *trans* residues. However, if we bear in mind a possible slight overlap of this region with that for methylenes and methines of saturated residues, and also the possible error in measuring the area of a peak equivalent to one or two methyls adjacent to a peak equivalent to, for example, 16 or 17 methyl groups, it is just possible that these compounds contain only one *trans* internal isoprene residue. It is known that the ω-isoprene residue and the residue adjacent to this (ψ-isoprene residue) are saturated. It is therefore conceivable that these compounds are also formed from all *trans*-geranyl-geranyl pyrophosphate (just possibly from all *trans*-farnesyl pyrophosphate) by addition of *cis* residues and that the ω- and ψ-*trans* isoprene residues and the "OH-terminal" isoprene residue are then saturated.

Clearly nuclear magnetic resonance spectrometry provides information essential to the understanding of the biochemistry of polyprenols, in particular, and of polyisoprenoid compounds in general.

SUMMARY

Nuclear magnetic resonance can be used to identify the presence in polyprenols of *cis* and *trans* and of saturated isoprene residues. It will also allow recognition that the residues are internal, ω-terminal, or "OH-terminal" in the polyisoprenoid chain. The use of benzene as a solvent, as well as carbon tetrachloride, is shown to offer advantages in these studies.

The application of the technique to obtain quantitative data on the number of residues of different type and configuration is illustrated by reference to naturally occurring polyprenols. The significance of the findings to the biosynthesis of these polyprenols is discussed.

REFERENCES

1. Hemming, F. W., *in* "Terpenoids in Plants." Academic Press, New York-London, 1967.
2. Wellburn, A. R., Stevenson, J., Hemming, F. W., and Morton, R. A., *Biochem. J.* **102,** 313 (1967).
3. Stone, K. J., Wellburn, A. R., Hemming, F. W., and Pennock, J. F., *Biochem. J.* **102,** 325 (1967).
4. Wellburn, A. R., and Hemming, F. W., *Phytochemistry* **5,** 969 (1966).
5. Lindgren, B. O., *Acta Chem. Scand.* **19,** 1317 (1965).
6. Wellburn, A. R., and Hemming, F. W., *Nature* **212,** 1364 (1966).
7. Pennock, J. F., and Hemming, F. W., unpublished work.
8. Hemming, F. W., Pennock, J. F., Gloor, U., and Burgos, J., unpublished work.
9. Stone, K. J., Butterworth, P. H. W., and Hemming, F. W., *Biochem. J.* **102,** 443 (1967).
10. Bates, R. B., and Gale, D. M., *J. Am. Chem. Soc.* **82,** 5749 (1960).
11. Bates, R. B., Carnighan, R. H., Rakutis, R. O., and Schauble, J. H., *Chem. Ind. (London)* **1962,** 1020.
12. Bates, R. B., Gale, D. M., and Gruner, B. J., *J. Org. Chem.* **28,** 1086 (1963).
13. Pennock, J. F., *in* "Biochemistry of Quinones" (R. A. Morton, ed.), p. 67. Academic Press, New York-London, 1965.
14. Chen, H. Y., *Anal. Chem.* **34,** 1793 (1962).
15. Williams, B., and Hemming, F. W., unpublished work, 1966.
16. Burgos, J., Hemming, F. W., Pennock, J. F., and Morton, R. A., *Biochem. J.* **88,** 470 (1963).

ANALYTICAL BIOCHEMISTRY 20, 16–23 (1967)

Spectrophotometrical Method for Determination of Nitrogen in Biological Preparations Based on Thymol-Hypobromite Reaction

L. I. GLEBKO, J. I. ULKINA, AND V. E. VASKOVSKY

Institute of Biologically Active Substances, Siberian Department of the Academy of Sciences, Vladivostok 22, USSR

Received November 17, 1966

The determination of nitrogen is a routinous analyses used in the biochemistry of proteins, lipids, nucleic acids, and certain carbohydrates. Colorimetric procedures involving Nessler's reagent (1–3) are most commonly applied. The major disadvantage of the method is the fact that the colored complex does not form a molecular solution; moreover, the analysis cannot be performed in the presence of cations forming precipitates with alkali. Minute amounts of heavy metals produce a considerable inhibition.

Other colorimetric techniques have been used in a number of recent studies (4–7). Among them, the phenol-hypochlorite procedure (8–10) seems the most advantageous; the sensitivity of this method is of the order of that involving Nessler's reagent.

In 1939, Hansen and Nielsen demonstrated that the thymol-hypobromite reaction is more suitable than the phenol-hypochlorite one, and elaborated a procedure involving distillation of ammonia (11) for the determination of nitrogen in plant materials. This method, now widely used in inorganic analysis (12–14), has not been applied since that time to biochemical analysis.

The present paper is concerned with the study of the effect of experimental conditions on the thymol-hypobromite reaction and of its applicability to the analysis of various biological substances.

REAGENTS

All the reagents were of analytical grade.

Water was twice glass-distilled in the presence of H_2SO_4 (1 ml/liter).

Commercial thymol was purified by vacuum distillation. An alkaline solution of thymol was prepared daily by dissolving 2.265 gm of thymol in 8 ml 2 N NaOH and adjusting with water to 100 ml.

~0.1 N hypobromite was prepared as follows: 12 ml of water was added to 28 ml of 40% NaOH; the solution was cooled, treated dropwise with continuous stirring with 3.8 ml Br_2, and adjusted to 1 liter with water. The concentration of hypobromite was determined as follows: 5 ml of the solution was added to 10 ml water, 0.2 gm KI, and 10 ml 10% H_2SO_4 in a glass-stoppered Erlenmeyer flask, left for 10 min in the dark, and the liberated free iodine titrated with 0.1 N $Na_2S_2O_3$; 7.3–7.4 ml of thiosulfate solution must be consumed. The freshly prepared hypobromite solution was kept in the refrigerator for three days before use; it is stable for about 4 weeks at 4–5°.

Ammonium sulfate was used as a reference substance; it was twice recrystallized from water and dried to a constant weight at 70–80°.

Standard solutions: Solution A, 100 γ N/ml—0.4717 gm $(NH_4)_2SO_4$ in 1 liter of water. Stable for 2 months. Solution B, 20 γ N/ml—5 times diluted solution A; a series of standard solutions were prepared from solution B containing 2.5, 5, 10, 20, 30, and 40 γ of nitrogen in 5 ml. Solution B and the standard solutions used for measuring the calibration curve were used immediately after preparation.

EXPERIMENTAL RESULTS

Absorption Spectrum of Indothymol

The absorption maximum of indothymol dye in the mixture n-butyl alcohol/methanol (24/1) is at about λ 686 mμ (Fig. 1).

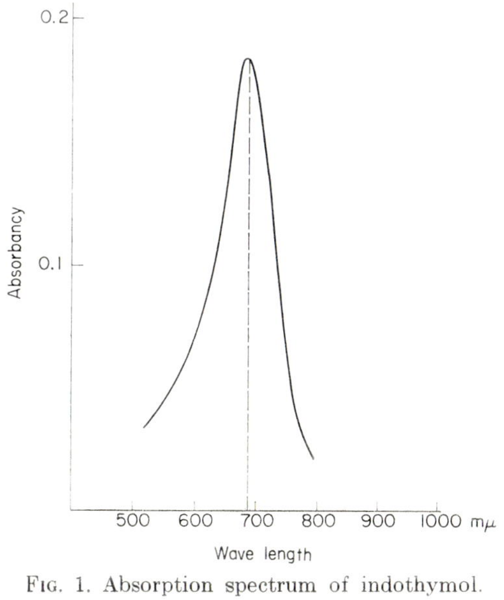

FIG. 1. Absorption spectrum of indothymol.

The molar extinction coefficient (ϵ) at this wavelength is 6.2×10^3. The range of nitrogen concentrations convenient for direct colorimetric measurements is between 1.12 and 56.25 γ N/25 ml; precise measurements performed in the range 2.5–40 γ provided the best reproducibility.

No changes in optical density of indothymol solution in *n*-butanol occurred during at least three days storage.

Reagent Ratio

The optimum conditions for quantitative binding of nitrogen in the form of NH_4^+ in indothymol critically depend on the amounts of thymol and hypobromite, on their ratio, and on the order of addition (Table 1).

TABLE 1
Dependence of Optical Density on Reagent Ratio

Reagent added, ml			Optical density		Ratio of reagents, thymol to hypobromite
Thymol	Hypobromite	Thymol	Control	Test	
0.5	0.5	0.5	0.005	0.068	2:1
0.5	1.0	0.5	0.008	0.118	1:1
0.5	1.5	0.5	0.010	0.149	1:1.5
0.5	2.0	0.5	0.013	0.173	1:2
0.5	2.5	0.5	0.016	0.124	1:2.5
0.5	3.0	0.5	0.017	0.74	1:3
1.0	0.5	1.0	0.005	0.37	4:1
1.0	1.0	1.0	0.007	0.64	2:1
1.0	2.0	1.0	0.007	0.127	1:1
1.0	3.0	1.0	0.010	0.157	1:1.5
1.0	4.0	1.0	0.014	0.171	1:2
1.0	5.0	1.0	0.030	0.050	1:2.5
1.5	6.0	1.5	0.015	0.175	1:2
2.0	4.0	2.0	0.032	0.117	1:1
2.0	8.0	2.0	0.020	0.173	1:2
2.5	10.0	2.5	0.21	0.174	1:2

As can be seen in Table 1, the thymol-hypobromite ratio of 1:2 provides the maximum optical density.

The optimum ratio of reagents was determined by adding thymol twice 0.5 ml (Table 1). Addition of the same amount of thymol (once 1 ml) produces nearly a twofold decrease in optical density. Thus, by adding thymol twice 0.5 ml, the optimum density for 10 γ of nitrogen is 0.173 and, by adding thymol once 1 ml, the optimum density is 0.106; for 40 γ of nitrogen these values are, accordingly, 0.715 and 0.475.

TABLE 2
Comparative Determination of Nitrogen Content by Three Independent Methods

Materials	Nitrogen content, %		
	Dumas method	Kjeldahl method	Thymol-hypobromite reaction
Valine	12.05	12.05	12.03
Glutamic acid	9.52	9.41	9.52
Alanine	15.77	15.75	15.65
Sphingosin	3.80	3.79	3.74
Cerebroside preparations:			
first sample	2.10	1.95	2.07
second sample	1.74	1.67	1.66
third sample	2.08	1.93	2.00
DNA preparation	15.40	15.32	15.26

Amount of Reagents

The amount of reagents is critical for quantitative yield of the reaction (Fig. 2): 1 ml of thymol solution and 2 ml of hypobromite solution are enough for nitrogen amounts up to 30 γ; at 70 γ, this

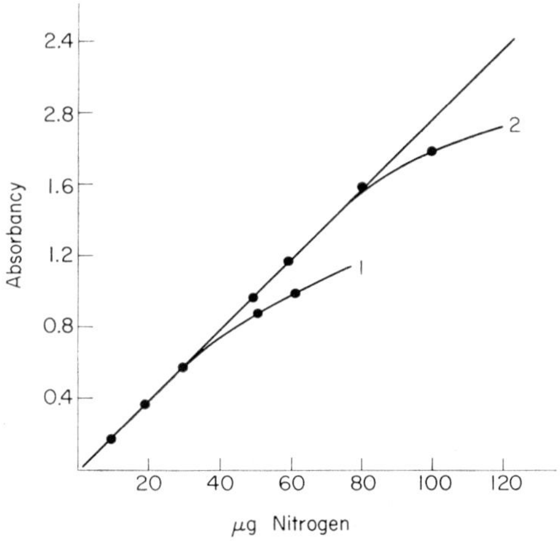

FIG. 2. Amount of reagents needed for different amounts of nitrogen. Standard solutions containing 2.5 to 100 γ nitrogen were prepared (see text). Curve 1 was obtained by addition of 1 ml thymol solution and 2 ml hypobromite solution to standard solutions. Curve 2 was obtained with double the amount of reagents.

amount must be increased twofold. At the optimum ratio specified in the above paragraph, an excess of reagents does not produce an increase of optical density (curves 1 and 2 for amounts from 2.5 to 30 γ N overlap, Fig. 2).

Time Required for Formation of Indothymol

Figure 3 shows that the minimum time for color development is 50 min at room temperature.

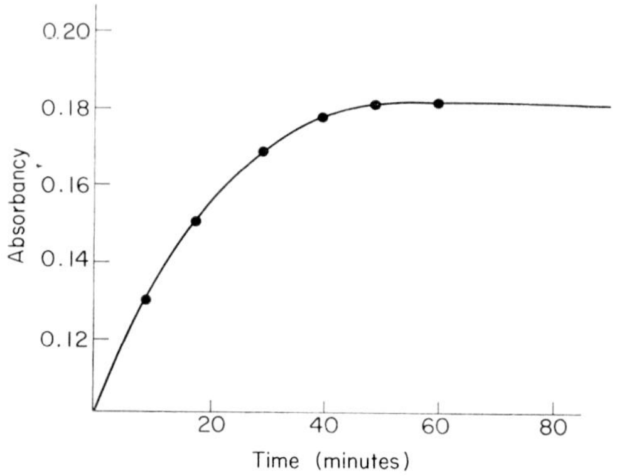

FIG. 3. Time required for formation of indothymol. Optical density of solution containing 10 γ of nitrogen and reagents was measured at time intervals.

Effect of Temperature

An increase of temperature from 30° to 40°C results in both optical density increase and higher rate of formation of indothymol.

It is more convenient, however, to work at room temperature (22–25°C); in this narrow temperature interval, temperature has no effect on the results.

Effect of Methanol

In the process of extraction of indothymol with *n*-butanol, drops of lower phase in the upper one produce a turbidity that interferes with colorimetry. The addition of methanol (1–1.5 ml) results in clarification of the solution. Addition of more than 2 ml of methanol, on the other hand, also results in a turbidity due to insolubility of indothymol; the effect increases with increasing indothymol concentration.

RECOMMENDED PROCEDURE

A solid sample (3–5 mg) is placed in a thick-walled combustion tube (1×12 cm) and 0.5 ml concentrated H_2SO_4 added. If the substance is in solution, an aliquot of this solution is evaporated in the tube and 0.2 ml concentrated H_2SO_4 is added.

Flame-seal the tubes, place in an oven, and heat at 400–410°C for a time required for complete mineralization. Cool with solid carbon dioxide, open the tubes, and heat for 5 min at 80–90°C to remove CO_2, SO_2, and other combustion gases.

Transfer into a flask and adjust to a known volume to a concentration of 2.5–40 γ N/5 ml.

Place 5 ml aliquots into 50 ml extracting funnels and carefully neutralize with 2 *N* NaOH (methyl red as indicator). Add 1 ml of alkaline thymol solution and, immediately thereafter, 4 ml of hypobromite solution dropwise, with agitation. After 5 min add 1 ml of thymol solution and leave for 50 min. Extract indothymol dye repeatedly with 3–4 ml portions of *n*-butanol and transfer extracts into a 25 ml measuring flask containing 1–1.5 ml methanol. Thoroughly mix and adjust to 25 ml with n-butanol.

Measure the optical density at 686 mμ (optical cuvet length 1 cm) with *n*-butanol as reference substance. Under the same conditions, prepare a control blank solution.

DISCUSSION

Lapin and Gein propose the use of thymol and hypobromite for the microanalytical determination of ammonia (15). Later Lapin studied this reaction in detail (16) and demonstrated that it involves three steps. The first step, more specific and typical, gives rise to *p*-aminophenol. The second results in conversion of *p*-aminophenol to a halo derivative of quinonimide. The third step results in indophenol.

The use of thymol instead of phenol permits extraction of the dye formed into an organic solvent. The reaction is highly specific because, except for some primary amines, other compounds, both organic and inorganic, do not interfere with the determination (15, 16).

At present, the thymol-hypobromite reaction is extensively used for the quantitative determination of nitrogen in steels (12, 13), of ammonia in feed water (17), and of nitrogen in titanium carbide and titanium boride as well as in other hard-melting materials (14).

However, the papers mentioned specify different conditions of indothymol formation and various amounts and concentration of reagents. It seems that the relationship between the amount of reagents and nitrogen concentration has not been studied in detail although it is very important in the analysis of biological materials, in which the amount of nitrogen may widely vary. We have also failed to find the molar extinction coefficient in any paper.

Many authors point to the instability of alkaline hypobromite solution. This complicates the work, the calibration curve of every new batch of reagent must be measured.

Hashmi, *et al.* (18, 19) have found that hypobromite solution prepared by mixing bromine and an appropriate amount of NaOH contains negligible amounts of bromites and bromates and is stable at an alkali concentration of 0.4–0.5 N. Our solutions prepared on the basis of this observation were stable for 4 weeks.

The alkaline solution of thymol becomes colored during storage and gives poor results. As the solution is simple to obtain, it is advisable to prepare it daily, immediately before use.

Amines, amino acids, albumin, preparations of sphingosins and cerebrosides, DNA, and RNA have been examined by this procedure. The preparations were of varying grades of purity and contained 3–18% of ash. The amount of nitrogen in the above materials was simultaneously determined by three methods: by combustion according to Dumas, by distillation of ammonia according to the classical Kjeldahl procedure, and by the thymol-hypobromite reaction (Table 2). The results show that the thymol-hypobromite reaction can be applied to the analysis of biological substances contaminated with reagents used during chromatography and does not require preliminary distillation of ammonia.

The method is especially convenient in serial analysis. Due to the stability of indothymol color in n-butanol, the colorimetry may be done the next day.

Statistical treatment of the results shows that the method has the same accuracy as that of Kjeldahl and, like the latter, gives rise to no appreciable systematic errors.

SUMMARY

Optimum conditions have been established of the thymol-hypobromite reaction with ammonium ion and the possibility has been demonstrated of its application to the quantitative determination of nitrogen in biological preparations.

A detailed procedure of the analysis is presented.

The spectrophotometric method of nitrogen estimation based on the thymol-hypobromite reaction provides the same accuracy as the classical Kjeldahl procedure and gives rise to no appreciable systematic errors.

REFERENCES

1. Williams, P. C., *Analyst* **89**, 276 (1964).
2. Rusanov, E., and Balevska, P., *Izv. Inst. po Fiziol. Bulgar. Akad. Nauk* **7**, 199 (1964).
3. Minari, O., and Zilversmit, D. B., *Anal. Biochem.* **6**, 320 (1964).
4. Kruse, J. M., and Mellon, M. G., *Anal. Chem.* **25**, 1188 (1953).
5. Kala, H., *Pharmazie* **18**, 29 (1963).
6. Prochazkova, L., *Anal. Chem.* **36**, 865 (1964).
7. Konnov, V. A., *Tr. Inst. Okeanol. Akad. Nauk SSSR* **79**, 11 (1965).

8. Mann, L. T., *Anal. Chem.* **35,** 2179 (1963).
9. Totlow, J. A., and Wilson, A. L., *Analyst* **89,** 453 (1964).
10. Muftic, M. K., *Nature* **201,** 622 (1964).
11. Hansen, P. A., and Nielsen, V., *J. Biol. Chem.* **137,** 309 (1939).
12. Veinberg, G. Ya., *Zavodsk. Lab.* **7,** 1251 (1938).
13. Veinberg, G. Ya., *Zavodsk. Lab.* **9,** 1073 (1940).
14. Klibus, A. Kh., and Nasarchuk, T. N., *Zh. Analit. Khim.* **16,** 79 (1961).
15. Lapin, L. N., and Gein, V. O., *Z. analyt. Chem.* **98,** 236 (1934).
16. Lapin, L. N., *Tr. Komis. po Analit. Chim., Akad. Nauk SSSR. Inst. Geokhim. i Analyt. Khim.* **5,** (8), **77** (1954).
17. Kulenok, M. I., *Gigiena i Sanit.* **10,** 45 (1950).
18. Hashmi, M. H., Ayaz, A. A., Rashid, A., and Ali, E., *Anal. Chem.* **36,** 1379 (1964).
19. Hashmi, M. H., Ali, E., and Umar, M., *Anal. Chem.* **34,** 988 (1962).

ANALYTICAL BIOCHEMISTRY 20, 24–29 (1967)

Mobility-Molecular Weight Relationships of Small Proteins and Peptides in Acrylamide-Gel Electrophoresis

L. INGRAM, M. P. TOMBS, AND A. HURST[1]

Unilever Research Laboratory, Colworth House, Sharnbrook, Bedford, England

Received November 28, 1966

Previous results have shown that the mobility of proteins and peptides in acrylamide-gel electrophoresis is strongly dependent on the concentration of the gel (1, 2). Generally, the more concentrated the gel, the lower is the mobility. In presenting our earlier results (2) for proteins of molecular weight 10,000 to 700,000 we tried to arrive at a relationship between mobility and molecular weight in this range. A reasonably good empirical relationship was found, though it did not agree with that suggested by a theoretical approach. Calculations of the diameters of peptides of the order of 1000 molecular weight suggested that they were of the same order as the pore sizes in acrylamide gels and could be expected to show some retardation, especially at high gel concentration. This paper presents some data for peptides of molecular weight 1200 upward and derives an empirical relationship similar to that previously described (2).

EXPERIMENTAL

Chemicals: Polymyxin and bacitracin were purchased from Burroughs Wellcome & Co., London. Gramicidin S was a gift from Astra Laboratories, Sweden. Subtilin was a gift from Dr. J. C. Lewis, Western Regional Laboratories. Nisin was a gift from Dr. J. Tramer, United Dairies Central Laboratory, London. Saramycetine was obtained from Hoffmann-La Roche, New Jersey. Insulin was obtained from British Drug Houses Ltd., Poole, England, ribonuclease from L. Light & Co., Colnbrook, England, lysozyme from Armour Pharmaceutical Co. Ltd., Eastbourne, England, and trypsin from Seravac Laboratories (Pty.) Ltd., Maidenhead, England. Other reagents were of A. R. grade.

Methods: Acrylamide gels were made from Cyanogum 41 obtained from British Drug Houses Ltd. A batch to batch variation of this product was observed. Gels were made in distilled water according to Tombs (2) and with the exception of saramycetine all the peptides were run in a pH 2.2

[1] Formerly A. Hirsch.

glycine + HCl buffer (50 ml 1.0 *M* glycine + 44 ml 1.0 *M* HCl made up to 1 liter) in a cold room at 2°. Saramycetine was run in a Tris-citrate/sodium borate discontinuous buffer, pH 8.6 (2). Each substance was run in nine gel concentrations ranging from 5 to 30% (w/v) and the mobility expressed as cm^2/min-V. The potential gradient was separately determined on each gel. Zones were detected with naphthalene black and measurements of mobility made to the center of the zone. Duplicate and in some cases triplicate determinations were made at each gel concentration, and the mean value used for calculation.

Plots of mobility against reciprocal of gel concentration were then made. They always showed a flat part at low gel concentrations and this was used to estimate the mobility at zero gel concentration. Then the gel concen-

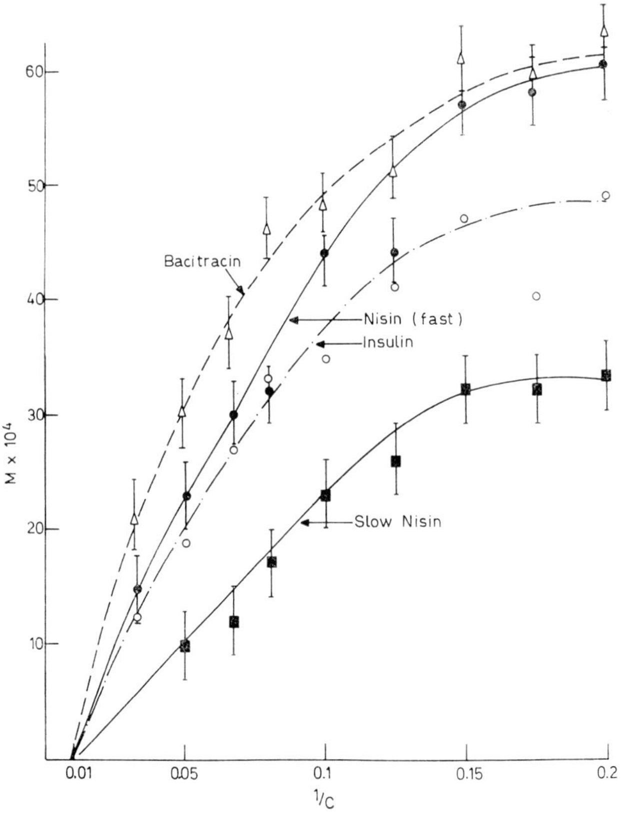

FIG. 1. Variation of mobility with gel concentration (expressed as concentration (w/v) of monomer used to make gel) for bacitracin, two forms of nisin, and insulin. An estimate of error is shown for bacitracin, and the nisin points. They are omitted for the sake of clarity from the insulin curve.

tration (c') required to give half of this mobility was found graphically. Some typical plots are shown in Figure 1, as well as an estimate of the error of individual determinations.

RESULTS AND DISCUSSION

Our previous theories (2) on the relationship between the mobility of a protein and the gel concentration introduced the concept of a limiting pore size in the gel, P_L, which the protein molecule could not quite enter. By assuming:

(i) that there is a normal distribution of pore sizes in the gel, of mean pore size $\bar{p}$ and standard deviation σ,
(ii) that there is a limiting pore size P_L, and
(iii) that the mobility is proportional to the fraction of pores that the molecule can penetrate,

we derived the following equation:

$$\frac{M}{M_{\text{sol}}} = Q\left(\frac{P_L - \bar{p}}{\sigma}\right) \tag{1}$$

where Q is a standard normal probability integral, M is the mobility and M_{sol} the mobility in free solution (i.e., zero gel concentration).

One important consequence of this result is that, when the mobility is half that in free solution, then $P_L = \bar{p}$, where $\bar{p}$ is the average pore size of the gel at the concentration (c') required to produce 50% retardation. In order to make use of this result we also need the relationship between pore size and gel concentration, since the gel concentration is the quantity actually measured. We obtained previously (2) the relation:

$$p + d = \frac{\sqrt{3\pi d}}{4\sqrt{c}} \tag{2}$$

where d is the diameter of the strands making up the gel. It is assumed that the strands are in a regular rectangular array. Clearly if c in the above equation is c', then p becomes P_L.

It is also possible to obtain P_L in another way. Thus, if we assume that the molecules are spherical and of density 1.3, the (unsolvated) diameter of the molecule can be calculated from the molecular weight (2). The approximate molecular diameters are shown in Table 1. Even peptides of quite low molecular weight have diameters of the order of the pore sizes to be expected in the acrylamide gels used in practice. Thus polymyxin has a diameter of about 15 Å while lysozyme with about ten times its molecular weight has a diameter of only 34 Å. This is, of course, a consequence of the dependence of diameter on the cube root of molecular weight and suggests that the filtration effect of polyacrylamide gels should be observable with compounds having a molecular weight of the order of 1000.

The limiting pore size, that is the "diameter" of a pore which the protein cannot quite enter, can be equated with the molecular diameter. Figure 2 shows the relationship between molecular diameters and $1/c'$. A straight

TABLE 1
Calculated Molecular Diameters and Determined Values of $1/c'$ (molecular diameters were calculated as described in reference 2 from the molecular weights given in the references)

Protein	M.W.	Ref.	Approx. molecular diam. Å (equal to limiting pore size P_L)	$1/c'$
Arachin				
Dimer	340,000	10	96	0.170
Monomer	170,000	10	74	0.138
α-Chain	35,000	10	41	0.085
γ-Chain	10,000	10	30	0.056
Glycinin				
15S	700,000	11	100	0.196
11S	350,000	11	96	0.170
7S	175,000	11	76	0.144
Albumin				
Dimer	132,000	12	66	0.220
Monomer	66,000	12	53	0.108
Ovalbumin	44,000	12	44	0.098
β-Lactoglobulin	35,000	12	41	0.113
Trypsin	24,000	12	38	0.084
Lysozyme	15,000	12	34	0.077
Saramycetine	14,000	8	32	0.085
Ribonuclease	13,000	12	30	0.073
Nisin	7,000	7	28	0.068
Insulin	5,700	12	26	0.062
Subtilin	3,200	8	24	0.058
Bacitracin	1,400	8	20	0.053
Gramicidin S	1,350	8	16	0.053
Polymyxin B	1,225	8	15	0.048

line describes it well over the wide molecular weight range tested (1.2×10^3 to 7×10^5). We can also calculate a possible theoretical relationship between molecular diameter and $1/c'$, for example by using equation 2, providing some assumption of the value of d is made. Figure 2 shows two curves, for $d = 10$ Å and $d = 18$ Å. It is clear that these lines are not in agreement with the experimental data. This is the same conclusion as reached previously for a narrower range of molecular weights (2). The

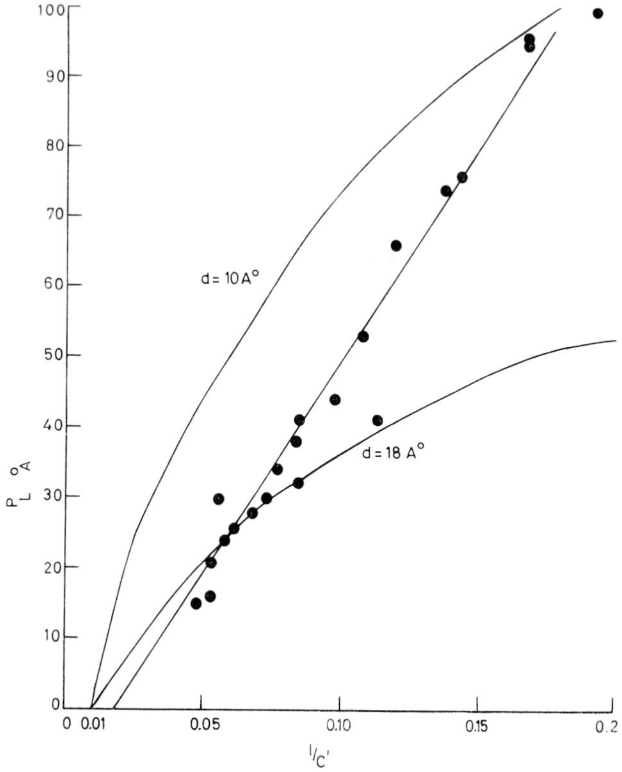

FIG. 2. Plot of P_L (in Å), calculated from molecular weight, against $1/c'$. The two curves are calculated from equation 2 by assuming, for the upper curve $d = 10$ Å and for the lower $d = 18$ Å. The straight line through the points (data from Table 1) was fitted to a regression equation:

$$P_L = -8.84 + 540\ (1/c')$$

where P_L is the calculated molecular diameter, and c' is the gel concentration required to reduce mobility to half its value in free solution.

reasons for the failure of equation 2 to fit the experimental data are not clear. It may be that the assumptions underlying equation 1 are not valid, although some equation of this form must be used to explain the sigmoid M vs. $1/c$ plots. (Equation 1 predicts a sigmoid relationship between mobility and $1/c$. Several examples of this were described previously (2) and the smaller peptides gave very similar results, though higher gel concentrations were needed to produce significant retardation and the full sigmoid shape for the smaller molecules could not be obtained (Fig. 1).)

It seems more likely that the various models used for the gel structure, leading to results such as equation 2, are inadequate. No direct evidence on the structure of acrylamide gels is available: the mechanism of polymerization is complex (3) and it is likely that the gel structure becomes qualitatively different, apart from the simple concentration effect predicted by equation 2, as monomer concentration increases. For example if d is not constant, and varies with gel strength, some approximation to the experimental data could be made.

The empirical relationship shown in Figure 2 permits an approximate estimate of molecular weight, perhaps to about $\pm$ 20%. If we bear in mind the necessary simplifying assumption made, such as that the molecules are spherical, this is as good as can be expected.

Recently, there was much work on the relationship between excluded volume and log molecular weight in gel filtration (4). Theoretical treatments (5) are available based on an approach similar to that used here, and suffering from similar difficulties. For example all protein molecules are certainly not spherical, so that only approximate molecular weights can be determined by either method. Some improvement can be made by using Stokes radii (6) but this involves collecting much extra data from other techniques. Electrophoresis has a greater resolving power than gel filtration and the general approach described here can be used, for example, in assigning molecular weights to the components of a complex mixture, and particularly in studying monomer-polymer systems, both of which can be difficult by gel filtration methods.

The usefulness of the method is illustrated by the estimation of the molecular weight of nisin, which was thought to be about 7000 (7). This figure was challenged by Bodansky and Perlman (8), who suggested that the molecular weight of nisin was one-third of the original value. However, a value of 7000 fits the straight line of Figure 2, supporting this estimate; this nisin corresponds with the "fast nisin" component recently described in a similar preparation (9). The "slow nisin" (Fig. 1) component has an apparent molecular weight of 14,000 and could be a dimer of "fast nisin."

REFERENCES

1. Raymond, S., and Nakamichi, M., *Anal. Biochem.* **3,** 23 (1962).
2. Tombs, M. P., *Anal. Biochem.* **13,** 121 (1965).
3. Davis, B. J., *Ann. N. Y. Acad. Sci.* **121,** 421 (1964).
4. Andrews, P., *Biochem. J.* **96,** 595 (1965).
5. Laurent, T. C., and Killander, J., *J. Chromatog.* **14,** 317 (1965).
6. Siegel, L., and Monty, K., *Biochim. Biophys. Acta* **112,** 346 (1966).
7. Cheeseman, G. C., and Berridge, N. J., *Biochem. J.* **71,** 185 (1959).
8. Bodansky, M., and Perlman, D., *Nature (London)* **204,** 840 (1964).
9. Hurst, A., *J. Gen. Microbiol.* **45,** 503 (1966).
10. Tombs, M. P., *Biochem. J.* **96,** 119 (1965).
11. Wolf, W. J., and Briggs, D. R., *Arch. Biochem. Biophys.* **85,** 186 (1957).
12. "The Proteins" (H. Neurath, ed.). Academic Press, New York-London, 1965.

ANALYTICAL BIOCHEMISTRY 20, 30–36 (1967)

A Coupled Optical Enzyme Assay for 5′-Nucleotidase

P. L. IPATA

Institute of Biological Chemistry, University of Pisa, Pisa, Italy

Received December 2, 1966

The activity of 5′-nucleotidase (5′-ribonucleotide phosphohydrolase, EC 3.1.3.5) is generally measured from the amount of inorganic phosphate liberated from adenosine 5′-monophosphate, or other nucleoside 5′-monophosphates (1–3).

Because of the limits of the sensitivity of the methods for inorganic phosphate (4), the reaction velocities of a 5-mononucleotidase, recently purified from sheep brain (5), could not be measured at low concentration of adenosine monophosphate (AMP), a difficulty which had also been encountered by Bodansky and Schwartz for bone and liver phosphatases (6).

The enzyme activity has therefore been measured from the amount of adenosine released from AMP, by a more sensitive coupled optical enzyme assay. The adenosine formed is determined spectrophotometrically, from the rate of its deamination, after addition of an excess of commercial adenosine deaminase.

METHODS

Adenosine deaminase (10 mg/ml stabilized solution), free of any detectable 5-nucleotidase and adenylic deaminase activity, was obtained from Boehringer & Soehne, Mannheim, Germany, and was diluted 1000-fold with water before use. 5′-Nucleotidase was prepared from sheep brain as described previously (5). The enzyme preparation was free of any detectable adenosine or AMP deaminase activity, and contained 1.1 mg proteins/ml.

The experiments were carried out at room temperature, in 1 ml 1 cm path cuvets, in a final volume of 0.910 ml, and the change in optical density at 265 mμ (ΔE/min) was determined with a recording Zeiss PQM II spectrophotometer.

The detailed standard procedure for the coupled optical enzyme assay was as follows: 0.6 ml of 0.05 M Tris-HCl buffer, pH 7.4, was pipetted into one cuvet, followed by different amounts of aqueous solutions of substrate, contained in a maximal volume of 0.2 ml, 30 μl of diluted adenosine deaminase, and enough water to bring the volume to 0.860 ml; finally 50 μl of the 5′-nucleotidase preparation was added, the mixture was rapidly mixed, and the change in optical density was followed against a reference cuvet, in which AMP was substituted with water. Modifications of the standard conditions are described in the presentation of the experimental data.

Inorganic phosphate was determined according to Fiske and SubbaRow (4).

RESULTS

Figure 1 shows the velocity of adenosine deamination catalyzed by adenosine deaminase, measured during the initial zero-order portion of

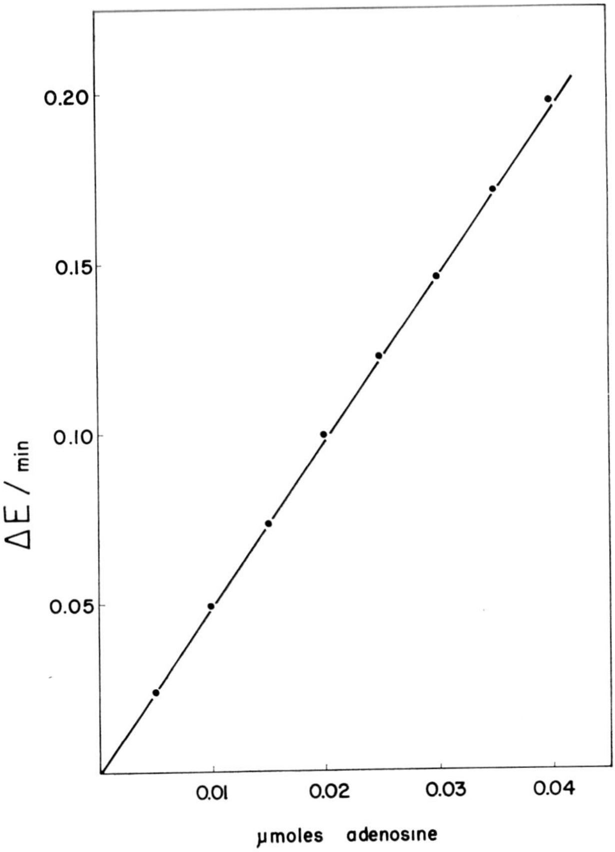

FIG. 1. Effect of adenosine concentration on initial velocity of adenosine deaminase at room temperature. *Reaction mixture:* 0.6 ml 0.05 *M* Tris-HCl buffer, pH 7.4; varying amounts of adenosine, as indicated on abscissa; 0.3 μg commercial adenosine deaminase; final volume 0.910 ml.

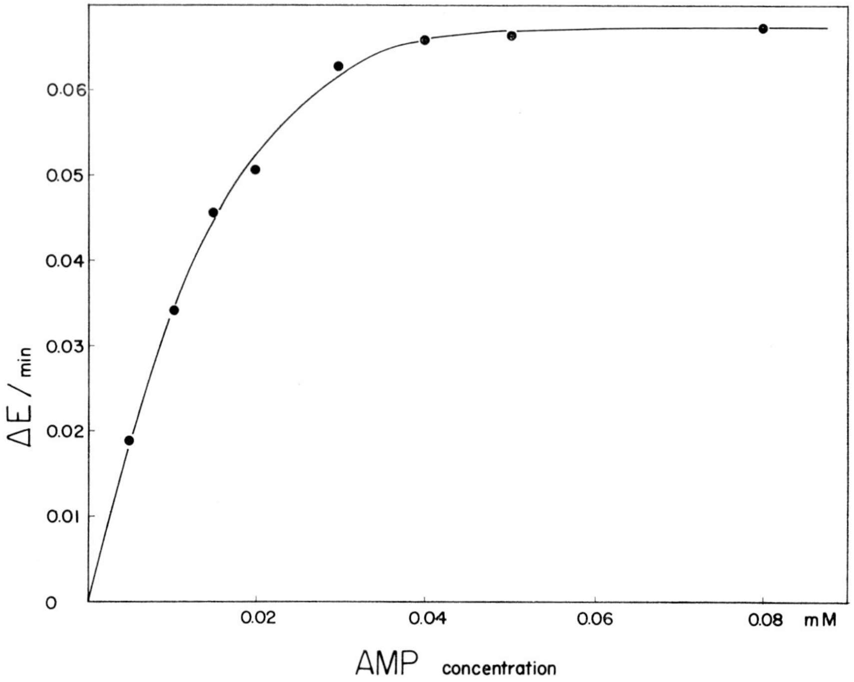

FIG. 2. Effect of AMP concentration on maximal velocity of sheep brain 5′-nucleotidase, with the coupled optical enzyme test, at room temperature. *Reaction mixture:* 0.6 ml 0.05 *M* Tris-HCl buffer, pH 7.4; varying concentrations of AMP, as indicated on abscissa; 0.3 μg commercial adenosine deaminase; 55 μg 5′-nucleotidase; final volume 0.910 ml.

the time curve, as a function of adenosine concentration. The velocity of the enzyme reaction is proportional to adenosine at low concentrations; therefore the nucleoside can be measured from the initial velocity of its deamination.

The optimum level of AMP concentration for 5′-nucleotidase determination under the conditions of the standard procedure is about 0.04 m*M* (Fig. 2).

At concentrations of adenosine deaminase higher than 0.1 μg per reaction mixture no lag period was observed, and the rate of the decrease in optical density at 265 mμ remained constant with increasing concentrations of adenosine deaminase; the velocity of the reaction is therefore determined by the rate at which adenosine is released from AMP (Fig. 3).

The time course of the 5′-nucleotidase reaction in the presence of different levels of the enzyme, recorded during the coupled optical test, is

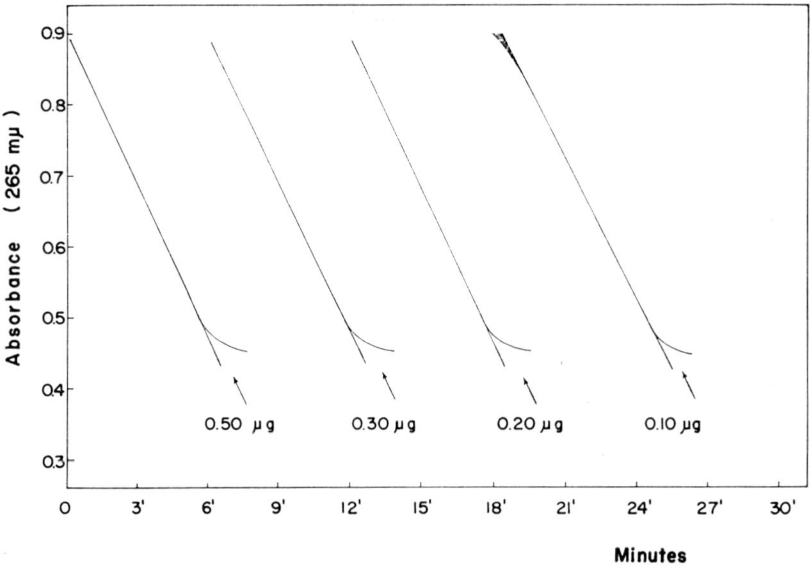

FIG. 3. Time course of change in optical density at 265 mμ during coupled optical test for 5′-nucleotidase at room temperature; effect of different concentrations of adenosine deaminase. *Reaction mixture:* 0.6 ml 0.05 *M* Tris-HCl buffer, pH 7.4; 0.06 μmole AMP; 55 μg 5′-nucleotidase; varying amounts of adenosine deaminase as indicated; final volume 0.910 ml.

TABLE 1
5′-Nucleotidase Activity as Measured by Coupled Optical Enzyme Assay and by Inorganic Phosphate Determination

Δ*E*/min at 265 mμ	5′-Nucleotidase, μg	Adenosine formed, μmoles/min	Phosphate formed, μmoles/min
0.247	220	0.026	0.025
0.220	165	0.023	0.023
0.159	110	0.017	0.016
0.107	82.5	0.011	0.010
0.077	55	0.008	0.008
0.048	33	0.005	Not measurable
0.044	27.5	0.0046	Not measurable
0.032	22	0.0036	Not measurable
0.018	11	0.0019	Not measurable
0.007	5.5	0.00074	Not measurable

Reaction mixture: 0.6 ml 0.05 *M* Tris-HCl buffer, pH 7.4; 0.12 μmole AMP; 0.3 μg adenosine deaminase; varying amounts of 5′-nucleotidase; final volume 0.910 ml. The amount of adenosine formed was determined from the change in optical density/min as described in the text. For the inorganic phosphate determination the reaction was stopped 3 min after addition of 5′-nucleotidase with 1.8 ml 10% trichloroacetic acid; tubes were centrifuged, and inorganic phosphate was determined on 2 ml portions of the supernatant fluid according to Fiske and SubbaRow (4).

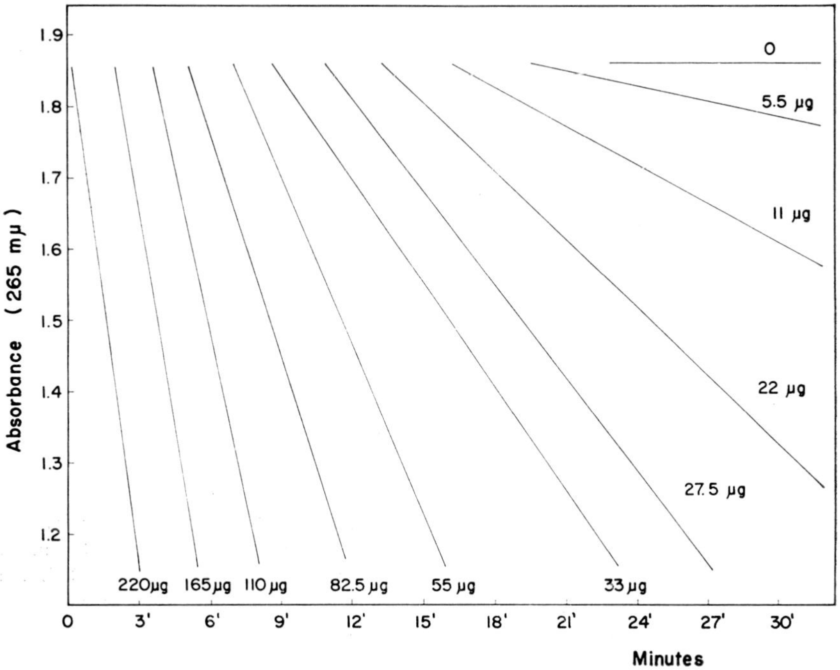

FIG. 4. Effect of varying concentrations of 5′-nucleotidase on time course of change in optical density at 265 mμ during coupled enzyme reaction at room temperature. *Reaction mixture:* 0.6 ml 0.05 *M* Tris-HCl buffer, pH 7.4; 0.3 μg commercial adenosine deaminase; 0.12 μmole AMP; varying amounts of 5′-nucleotidase as indicated; final volume 0.910 ml.

shown in Figure 4. From these curves, representing the rate of deamination of adenosine released from AMP, the change in optical density (ΔE/min) was determined. 5′-Nucleotidase activity can be calculated from the following formula:

$$(\Delta E/\text{min}) \times F = \mu\text{moles adenosine/min}$$

F (= 0.105 in our experimental conditions) is calculated from the absorption coefficient of AMP and inosine at 265 mμ. From the curves of Figure 4 the optical density changes per minute as a function of 5′-nucleotidase concentration have been determined, and are reported in Figure 5.

Table 1 gives the activity of the 5′-nucleotidase determined by the coupled optical assay, and by measuring the inorganic phosphate released from AMP. The agreement between the two methods is good, but the coupled optical enzyme assay is by far more sensitive.

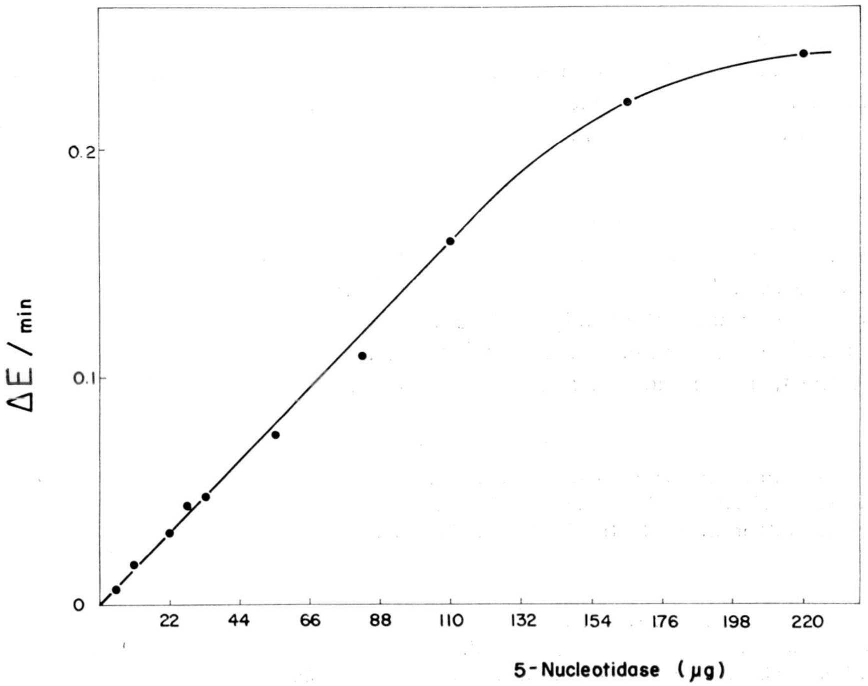

FIG. 5. Rate of optical density change at 265 mμ during coupled optical enzyme test as a function of 5′-nucleotidase concentration. Reaction mixture as in Figure 4.

DISCUSSION

When purified 5′-nucleotidase was used, no change in optical density at 265 mμ was observed in the absence of adenosine deaminase. With crude extracts, however, such as a dialyzed 105,000 *g* supernatant fluid of sheep brain homogenate in 0.9% NaCl, a decrease at 265 mμ was observed, due to endogenous adenosine deaminase; this, however, does not interfere with the determination of 5′-nucleotidase which is carried out in the presence of an excess of adenosine deaminase. The method can therefore be used with crude extracts, without correction for endogenous adenosine deaminase, provided they are sufficiently clear and free of AMP deaminase activity.

The technique is not limited by the pH of the assay because adenosine deaminase is active over a wide range of pH (7) and has a higher sensitivity with respect to the usual methods based on inorganic phosphate determination.

Inorganic phosphate does not interfere with the procedure described, which can therefore be used with crude extracts containing high levels of inorganic phosphate, or other compounds that would release inorganic phosphate during the assay.

By using the technique described it has been possible to show that sheep brain 5′-nucleotidase is not inhibited by inorganic phosphate up to concentrations of 2 m*M*.

SUMMARY

A coupled optical enzyme assay for 5′-nucleotidase is described that is based on the spectrophotometric determination of adenosine released from AMP. The amount of adenosine formed is calculated from the decrease in optical density at 265 mμ, after addition of an excess of adenosine deaminase. The method has a higher sensitivity with respect to the usual methods based on inorganic phosphate determination.

ACKNOWLEDGMENTS

This work was supported by a research grant of Impresa Enzimologia del Consiglio Nazionale delle Ricerche, Roma.

The author wishes to thank Mr. R. Parenti for skilled technical assistance.

REFERENCES

1. Reis, J., *Bull. Soc. Chim. Biol.* **22,** 37 (1940).
2. Heppel, L. H., and Hilmoe, R. J., *J. Biol. Chem.* **188,** 665 (1951).
3. Song, C. S., and Bodansky, O., *Biochem. J.* **101,** 5c (1966).
4. Fiske, C. H., and SubbaRow, Y., *J. Biol. Chem.* **66,** 357 (1925).
5. Ipata, P. L., *Nature* **214,** 618 (1967).
6. Bodansky, O., and Schwartz, M. K., *J. Biol. Chem.* **238,** 3420 (1963).
7. Brady, T. G., and O'Connell, W., *Biochim. Biophys. Acta* **62,** 216 (1962).

ANALYTICAL BIOCHEMISTRY 20, 37–39 (1967)

Simultaneous Analysis of Different Specimens in the Ultracentrifuge

W. F. BON

Department of Protein Research of the Laboratory for Biochemistry, University of Amsterdam, Roetersstraat 1, Amsterdam

Received December 5, 1966

Some years ago I described a method of simultaneous analysis of two samples in the ultracentrifuge by utilizing polarization of the beam of light used for the analysis (1). The same principle holds true for un-

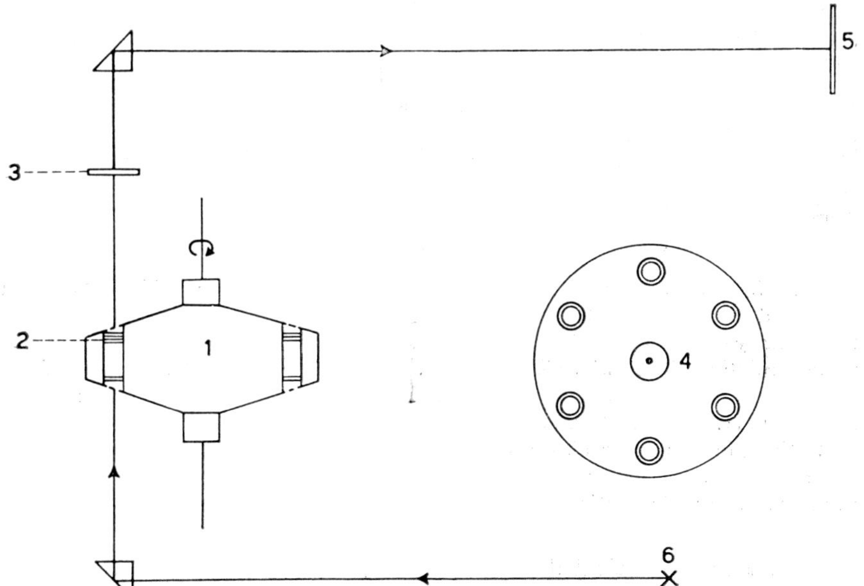

FIG. 1. Analytical ultracentrifuge assembly for six simultaneous samples: (1 and 4) Rotor. (2) Cell with polarizer and color filter mounted. In the following cell the polarizer is mounted at a 90° angle and with the same color filter. The third cell is mounted with polarizer at 0° and another color filter. The fourth is mounted with polarizer at 90° and the same color filter, etc. (3) Analyzer and corresponding color filter. (5) Camera. (6) Light source.

polarized light and suitable sets of color filters which absorb quantitatively each other's transmitted light. In this way three samples can be sedimented in one run (with a rotor which contains three holes) if each cell is provided with one of the color filters ordinarily used for three-color printing and if the transmitted light beam is filtered successively through the corresponding filters. Theoretically this method can be combined with the polarizer-analyzer set which enables photographic exposures to be made in one run consisting of six samples (2). The apparatus is shown schematically in Figure 1.

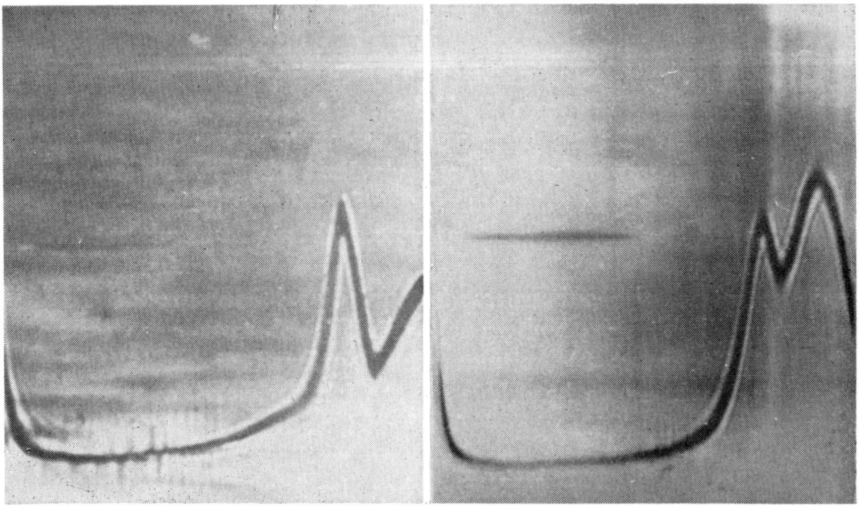

FIG. 2. Simultaneous sedimentation run of two protein extracts: codfish lens extract (left) and cow lens extract (right). The specimen on the left was colored with 0.1% tropaeolin yellow and on the right with 0.0125% methylene blue, dissolved in the protein solutions in 0.1 *M* sodium acetate, pH 8.0. 5–6°C, 29,500 rpm, respectively after 48 and 49 min, attaining full speed. Exposure times were for yellow: 65 sec. and for blue: 30 sec. Corresponding filter solutions in distilled water, same concentrations, in glass Petri dishes with flat bottom, installed in the light beam above the mercury lamp. Depth: yellow color solution 15 mm, blue 12 mm. Photographic plate, Perutz panchromatic.

Some severe practical difficulties stand in the way of introducing this method: up to now it has been impossible to manufacture polarization and color filter discs able to withstand very strong centrifugal forces. The familiar quinine sulfate foils, clipped between glass or quartz discs, and the retailed color filters can be used only at rotor speeds up to 10,000 *g*. Another difficulty is the high loss of light energy by passing through the polarization assembly and the color filters, which necessitates extremely long exposure times.

METHOD

It is, however, possible to use ordinary standard cells without any alteration of the ultracentrifuge equipment; the protein solutions themselves can be colored with suitable solvable dyes such as pararosaniline, naphthol green, and toluidine blue, and analyzed with the corresponding dye solutions or with glass filters such as those manufactured by Scholl (Western Germany), red RG 2, yellow-green VG 12, blue BG 12. These glass filters are simply placed on the mercury lamp holder in the light beam during the exposures.

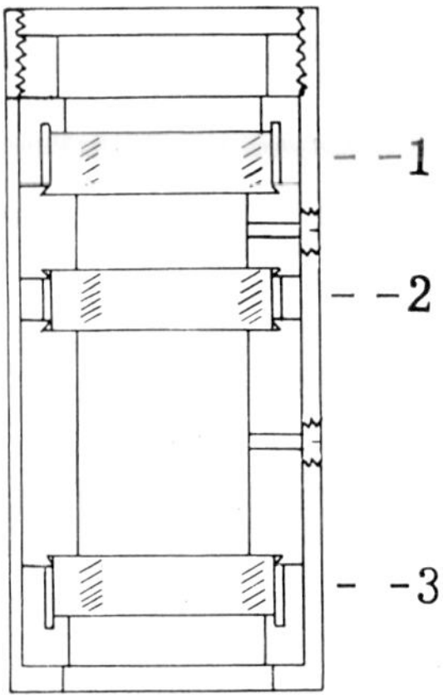

FIG. 3. Schematic section of a double chamber cell suggested for holding the filter solution and the protein sample in series in the light beam. 1, 2, and 3 are quartz windows.

We made a run with the Spinco E analytical ultracentrifuge using standard cells in the an-D rotor. In this way the sediment patterns of two different protein mixtures were made visible. For details see the legend for Figure 2.

It should be possible to construct a double chamber cell for holding the filter solution and the protein sample in series in the light beam (see Fig. 3).

Substitution of the mercury lamp by a more powerful light source (xenon lamp) is advisable for shortening the exposure times.

SUMMARY

A simple experiment is described in which two different protein mixtures could be sedimented and photographed simultaneously with a slightly adapted commercial apparatus.

REFERENCES

1. BON, W. F., *Rec. Trav. Chim. Pays-Bas* **77**, 1135–1137 (1958).
2. BON, W. F., Netherlands Pat. 105,710 (16-6-1963).

ANALYTICAL BIOCHEMISTRY 20, 40–50 (1967)

A Gas-Flow System for Control of the Temperature of an Electron Paramagnetic Resonance Sample at Temperatures Between 80 and 273 Degrees Kelvin

RAYMOND E. HANSEN, THEODORE T. KALAL, AND HELMUT BEINERT

Institute for Enzyme Research, University of Wisconsin, Madison, Wisconsin 53706

Received December 6, 1966

The amplitude of an electron paramagnetic resonance (EPR) signal, in general, is proportional to the reciprocal of the absolute temperature. In the simplest case, a change of 1 to 2°K in the temperature range of interest will produce about 1% change in signal amplitude. However, very different behavior has been observed among some EPR signals. In biological materials, the amplitude of the signal observed at $g = 1.94$ under reducing conditions shows a striking dependence on temperature (1). This signal is attributed to a nonheme iron structure found in a group of enzymes and proteins which are currently of great interest. It has been reported, for instance, that the signal at $g = 1.94$ observed in xanthine oxidase doubles in intensity on passing from 97 to 88°K. Therefore, control of temperature to at least ±0.5°K is desirable for the quantitative study of a material exhibiting the $g = 1.94$ signal. Furthermore, since the intensities of a highly temperature dependent signal such as the $g = 1.94$, is often marginal in biological materials, the lowest temperature which can be conveniently and economically produced and maintained is desirable. In addition, it is sometimes necessary to make intermittent observations of signals at temperatures higher than those at which the $g = 1.94$ signal is studied (98 to 80°K). Therefore, it is desirable to reach a temperature or cycle between temperatures with a minimum of delay if experiments are to be done in an expeditious manner. Finally, biological EPR studies are becoming quite lengthy and complex, involving power saturation studies or improvement of signal-to-noise ratio by an on-line computer, etc. Consequently, a cooling system is required to operate at least 3 to 5 hr and with the minimum amount of attention. To our knowledge there is no commercially available instrument that will satisfy these special needs. This report presents a gas-flow system for controlling the temperature of an EPR sample between 80 and 273°K. This system has adequately satisfied the temperature requirements set forth for the $g = 1.94$ signal.

MATERIALS AND METHODS

The temperature control system has several essential features, any one of which, if missing, would not allow the system to function properly. The gaseous nitrogen used as the heat transferring medium is produced by boiling liquid nitrogen (2). This feature is essential if the system is to provide a temperature that approaches the temperature of liquid nitrogen. The pressure of the gas produced in this manner is also controlled. The leaking of heat through the walls of the transfer tubes and Dewars of the system is responsible for an inverse relationship between the flow of the gas and the temperature of the gas. Therefore, the regulation of the flow of gas acts to preregulate the temperature of the gas. Finally the temperature of the gas is regulated by adding a controlled amount of heat to the flowing gas.

A schematic diagram of the nitrogen gas flow system is shown in Figure 1. Nitrogen gas at a temperature of 100°K and a rate of flow as

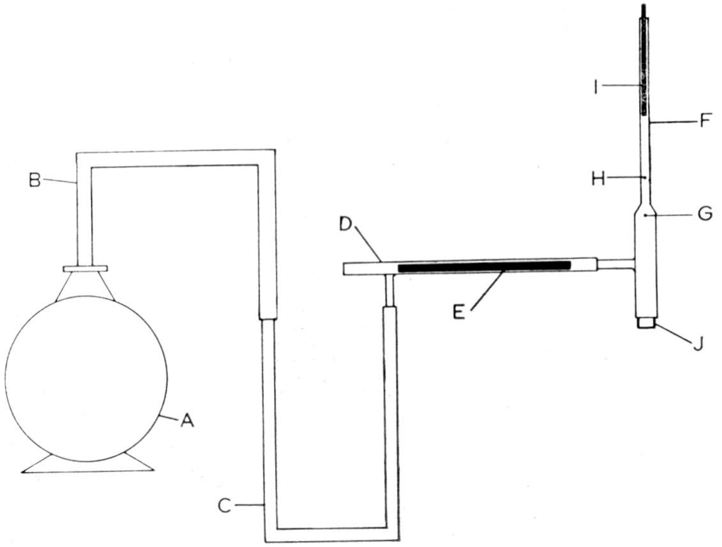

FIG. 1. Schematic diagram of gas-flow system: (A) nitrogen generator, (B) transfer tube, (C) liquid nitrogen heat exchanger, (D) heater tube mantle, (E) heater tube and heater element, (F) sample Dewar, (G) temperature controlling thermocouple, (H) temperature measuring thermocouple, (I) EPR sample tube, (J) thermocouple mount.

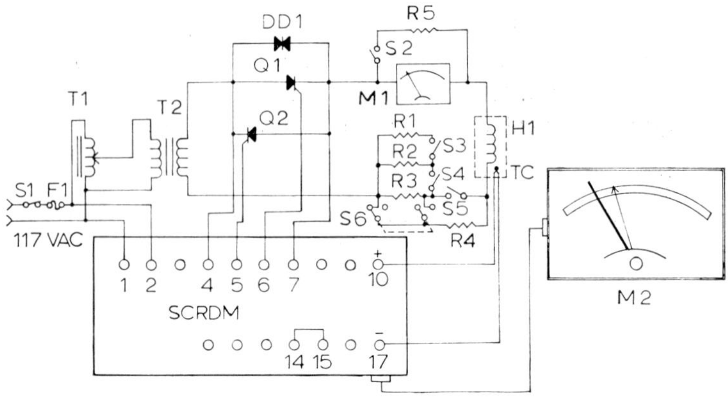

FIG. 2. Schematic of the transfer tube heater control:

R_1, R_2, R_3, R_4	20 ohm, 50 W (for current limiting)
R_5	Shunt resistance for 5 A sensitivity
T_1	Autotransformer, 120 V AC, 165 V A (servo gain)
T_2	Filament transformer, primary 110 V AC, secondary 25.2 V AC at 2 A
Q_1, Q_2	SCR type 2N688
DD1	Int. rect. DD04
S_1, S_2, S_3, S_4, S_5	Toggle switch SPST
S_6	Toggle switch DPDT
F_1	2 A fuse
SCRDM	Assembly Product Instrument Corp., SCR driver module 915B
M_1	1 A AC meter
M_2	Assembly Product Instrument Corp., optical relay meter No. 1602-L, range −210 to −0°C, control pointer to the left, for Cu-Constantan thermocouple
H_1	Transfer tube "E" heater element (see text)
TC	Thermocouple "G" (see text)

high as 4 liters per second is delivered from the nitrogen generator A and transferred to the liquid nitrogen heat exchanger C through the transfer tube B. The gas is cooled to 80°K by the heat exchanger. The gas is then heated to the desired temperature in heater tube E. The gas passes through Dewar F containing the sample. Thermocouples G (controlling) and H (measuring) are supported in the sample Dewar on thermocouple mount J. A 5 liter Dewar, into which liquid nitrogen heat exchanger C is placed, is not shown.

Servo Loop for Temperature Control: The potential developed by thermocouple H is measured with a temperature potentiometer (Leeds & Northrup Company, Cat. No. 8692). Thermocouple G is connected to the driver module of the silicon control rectifiers (SCR) as shown in Figure 2. The output of the SCR circuit is applied to the heater element

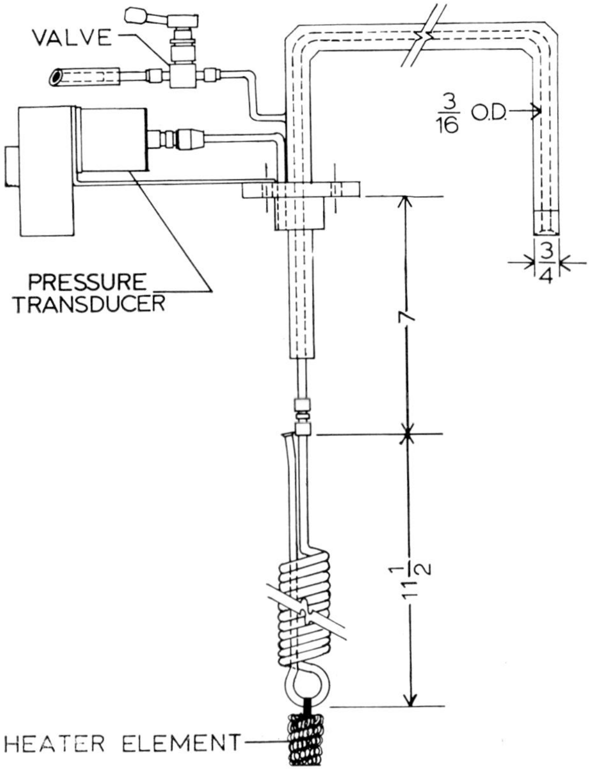

FIG. 3. Transfer tube assembly.

in heater tube E (Fig. 1). Nitrogen gas, flowing over the heater element to the thermocouple G, completes the servo loop.

Servo Loop for Pressure Control: 5 V DC is applied to the pressure transducer, which is part of the transfer tube assembly shown in Figure 3. The output of the pressure transducer is connected to an SCR driver module as shown in Figure 4. The output of this SCR circuit is applied to the heater shown in Figure 3. When gas is generated by the heater, the pressure produced completes the servo loop.

Nitrogen Gas Generator, Gas Heater, and Thermocouples: The nitrogen gas generator consists of a 25 liter Dewar (Linde LD-25) and a transfer tube assembly. The transfer tube assembly consists of a heater, transfer tube, precooling heat exchanger, and pressure transducer (Computer Instrument, Type 4000, 0–25 psi). The assembly is shown in Figure 3. The valve used in sealing the evacuated transfer tube is a stainless-steel Whiting, type 314-1GS4.

The transfer tube is constructed of thin-wall stainless-steel tubing (to

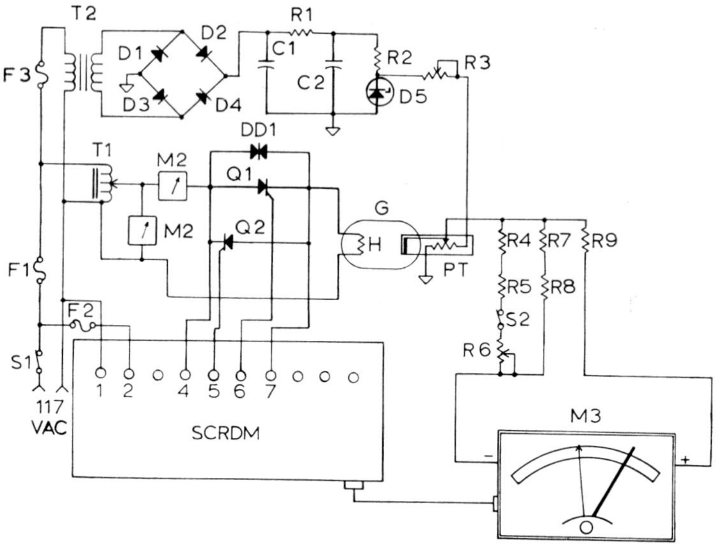

FIG. 4. Schematic for pressure control:

R_1	10 ohm, 10 W
R_2	470 ohm, ½ W
R_3	200 ohm, ½ W, variable (pressure transducer calibration)
R_4	10 ohm, ½ W
R_5, R_7	820 ohm, ½ W
R_6	1 ohm, ½ W, variable (meter calibration)
R_8	390 ohm, ½ W
R_9	51 ohm, ½ W
C_1, C_2	500 μF at 50 V DC
T_1	Autotransformer, 120 V AC, 1 K VA (servo gain)
T_2	Filament transformer, primary 110 V AC, secondary 12.6 V at 2.5 A
Q_1, Q_2	SCR type 2N 688
DD_1	Int. rect. DD04
D_1, D_2, D_3, D_4	Int. rect. 5MA4
D_5	1N 1521
S_1, S_2	Toggle switch SPST
F_1	Fuse, 10 A
F_2	Fuse, 2 A
F_3	Fuse, 1 A
SCRDM	Assembly Product Instrument Corp., SCR driver module 911B.
M_1	AC meter, 50 V
M_2	AC meter, 10 A
M_3	Assembly Product Instrument Corp., optical relay meter No. 502-L, 0–100 μA, single pointer to the right.
PT	Pressure transducer (see text)
H	Nitrogen gas generator heater (see text)
G	Nitrogen gas generator Dewar (see text)

control heat loss); the tube joints are silver soldered. All the other parts are of stainless steel, except the precooling heat exchanger, which is made of copper tubing ¼″ o.d., wound in a tight spiral 1⅛″ o.d. The i.d. of the transfer tube is ⅛″, the o.d. 3/16″; the o.d. of the outer vacuum jacket is ¾″. The output end of the transfer tube is a drilled piece of solid stainless steel ¾″ in diameter and 1″ in length. Two slots (S) are milled into the output end of the transfer tube as shown in Figure 5. The transfer tube is fastened to the ball end of the liquid nitrogen heat exchanger with a pinch clamp (A. H. Thomas 3241, No. 12).

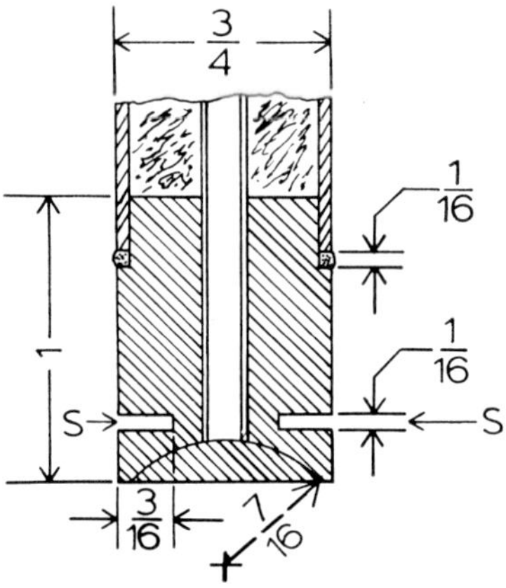

FIG. 5. Detail of output end of the transfer tube assembly.

An adapter collar is clamped around the neck of the Dewar. Four Allen head-cap screws fasten the transfer tube assembly to the adapter collar. An O-ring is used as a seal between the Dewar and the transfer tube assembly.

The heater element, used for boiling the liquid nitrogen, is a coil of No. 24 Nichrome wire, 3/16″ in diameter. It is spirally wound on a Transite form ¾″ in diameter and 1⅛″ in length. The heater's resistance is 5 ohms. Two thermal plastic insulated standard wires, 18 gage (16 × 30), are fed through two holes in the cover plate of the transfer tube assembly. These wires provide power for the heating element.

The liquid nitrogen heat exchanger C, heater tube E (including the heater element), and its mantle D (Fig. 1) are all parts of the Varian 4547 variable-temperature accessory.

The thermocouple mount shown in Figure 6 is made of annealed acrylic plastic. A quartz male 10/30 taper joint is cemented with epoxy into the groove in the base of the mount. The wires of the two thermocouples to be are brought through the four holes in the stem of the mount.

The thermocouples are made in the usual manner. After the thermocouples are tested, their lead wires are cemented with epoxy at the point where base and stem of the mount are joined. Next, the thermocouple wires are made rigid by twisting several times. Both thermocouples are copper-Constantan (Leeds & Northrup, No. 24-55-1-A).

The temperature measuring thermocouple H is 1⅜″ below the sample tube I. Thermocouple G is 1⅝″ above the nitrogen gas entrance port of the sample Dewar and 1⅜″ below thermocouple H (Fig. 1).

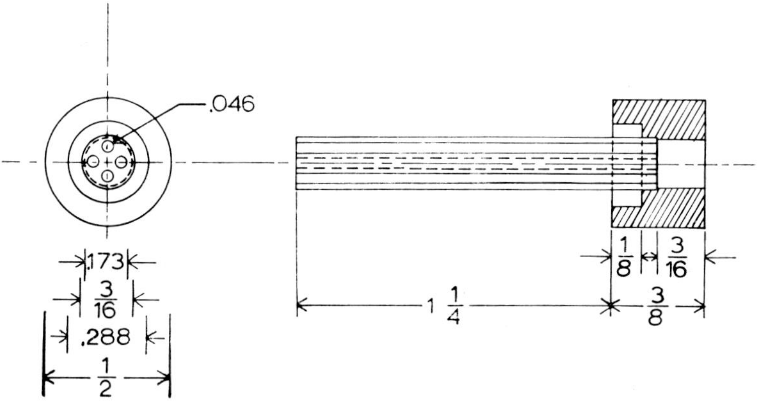

FIG. 6. Annealed acrylic plastic thermocouple mount.

Operation of the System: 20 liters of liquid nitrogen is required to fill the nitrogen generator Dewar to the proper volume. Any excess of liquid nitrogen is expelled when the generator starts to build up pressure. After all parts have been assembled as shown in Figure 1, the nitrogen generator pressure is set for 20 psi to facilitate rapid cooling of the EPR sample. The heat exchanger Dewar is filled with liquid nitrogen. When the desired temperature has been reached, the nitrogen pressure and heater controls are set. Usually by the time this is done the temperature is lower than desired. However, within 5 to 8 min the system stabilizes at the desired temperature.

In Table 1 the power requirements and flow rates are given for some of the temperatures most commonly used in this laboratory. These values were determined for the most efficient use of liquid nitrogen.

It should be emphasized that maximal efficiency can be achieved only when all gas transferring components and their couplings are clean and

TABLE 1

Degrees K	Gas flow, liter/sec	N_2 pressure, psi	Power required for N_2 pressure, W	Heater power required for control, W
80	2.12	12.5	265	—
83	1.68	9.9	194	1.4
88	1.44	8.6	180	1.1
93	0.70	4.1	123	0.4
98	0.43	2.7	112	0.6
103	0.43	2.7	112	1.7
113	0.43	2.7	53	5.3
133	0.25	1.6	53	4.2
173	0.25	1.6	53	13.7
173	0.13	0.8	26	2.5
223	0.13	0.8	26	11.7
273	0.13	0.8	26	19.0

free of moisture. Also, all connections should be fastened securely to prevent gas leaks.

RESULTS

Experiments were designed to demonstrate the effect of a change in rate of flow on the temperature, rapidity with which the temperature could be changed, and length of time that temperature could be maintained.

The first experiment (Fig. 7) demonstrates the effect of a change in

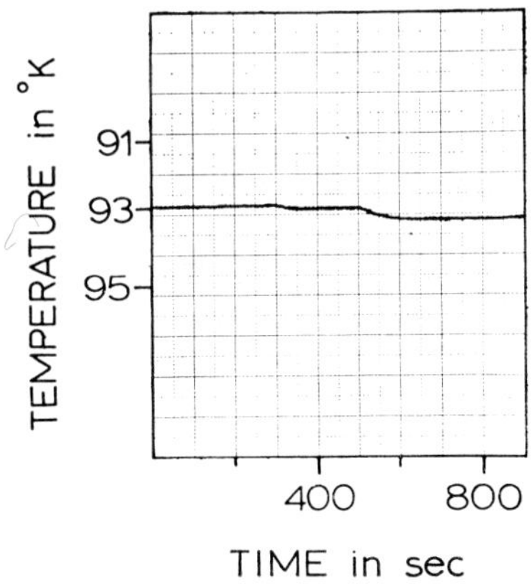

FIG. 7. Curve demonstrating effect on temperature when EPR sample tube was inserted into sample Dewar, thereby restricting gas flow. Experiment was carried out at 93°K, flow rate 0.9 liter per second. Time 0 to time 300 sec, no sample tube in Dewar; time 300 to time 500 sec, 4.0 mm sample tube in Dewar; time 500 to time 900 sec, 5.0 mm sample tube in Dewar.

the rate of flow on the temperature stability. The rate of flow was changed by changing the cross-sectional area of the sample Dewar. The sample Dewar in this experiment had an inner diameter of 6 mm. Its cross-sectional area was 28.3 sq mm. The transfer tube assembly had a cross-sectional area of 7.9 sq mm. Comparisons of these cross-sectional areas reveal the fact that the transfer tube assembly controls the rate of flow. When a 4.0 mm sample tube was inserted into the sample Dewar, the cross-sectional area was reduced from 28.3 to 16.7 sq mm. This decrease in the cross-sectional area limited the rate of flow, since there

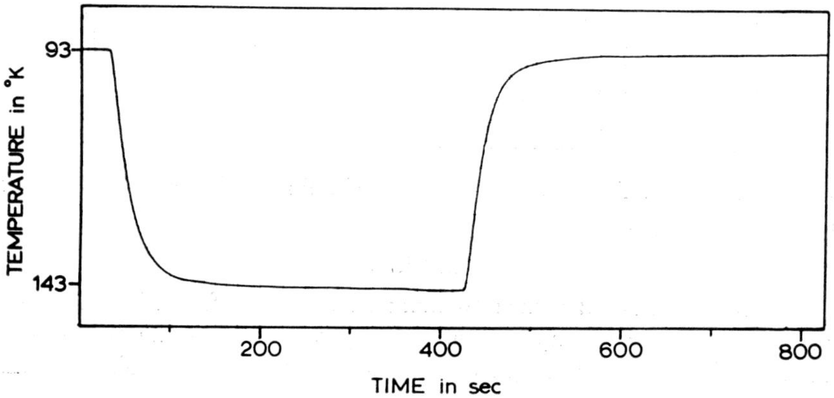

FIG. 8. Curve demonstrating rapidity at which temperature can be cycled from 93 to 143°K and from 143 back to 93°K. Flow rate 0.9 liter per second. One major division on the ordinate represents 5°K.

was an increase in temperature of about 0.25°K. The effect became greater when a 5.0 mm sample tube was inserted into the sample Dewar. The cross-sectional area was reduced to 8.6 sq mm, with an increase in temperature of 0.5°K.

The second experiment demonstrates the rapidity with which the temperature of the sample could be changed. Since the pressure had to be changed, the experiment was divided into two parts. In the first part of the experiment the rate of flow was 0.9 liter per second. The temperature of the sample varied between 93 and 143°K. As shown in Figure 8, the temperature reached 142°K in about 125 sec. The final temperature of 143°K was reached 225 sec later. Then the temperature of the sample was reduced from 143 to 93°K. The time required to reach 94°K was 125 sec; the final temperature, 93°K, required an additional 225 sec. In the second part of the experiment the rate of flow was controlled at 0.25 liter per second. The temperature of the sample was raised from 173 to 273°K. As shown in Figure 9, the temperature of the sample reached 272°K in 200 sec; the final temperature, 273°K, required an additional 150 sec. Return of the sample to its initial temperature required 325 sec. In addition, a similar experiment was performed for the range of temperatures between 80 and 110°K at flow rate of 2 liters per second. This experiment provided results similar to those previously described.

Data were collected during the routine operation of the system to determine temperature drift. Short-term drift (1 sec to 30 min) was

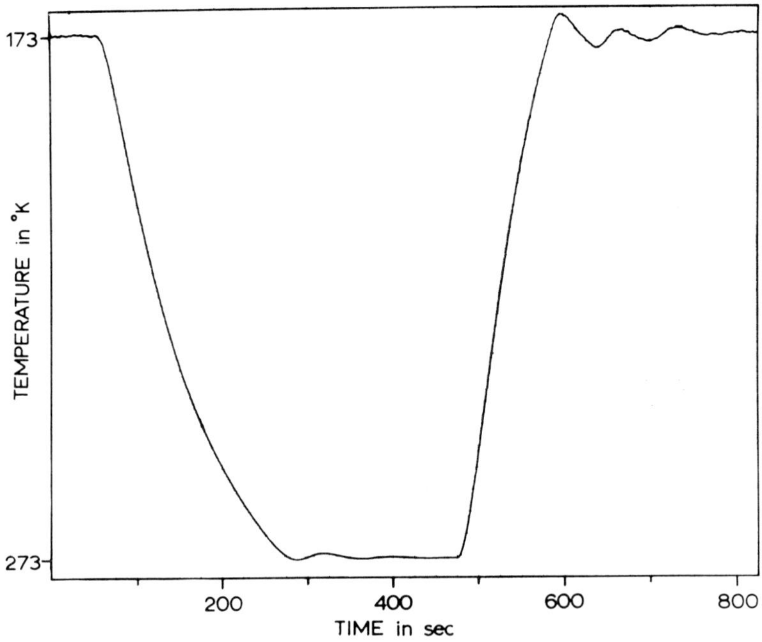

FIG. 9. Curve demonstrating rapidity at which temperature can be cycled from 173 to 273°K and from 273 to 173°K. Flow rate 0.25 liter per second. One major division on the ordinate represents 5°K.

found to be undetectable after the servo had locked on the desired temperature. However, short-term drift did occur when the over-all gain of the servo loop which controls the temperature was set too high. This type of drift is analogous to hunting action observed with a strip-chart recorder. Long-term drift was found to be 1°K in the first hour after the temperature and pressure servos had locked at a specific initial temperature. Thereafter, changes of 0.25°K per hour were observed in the 3 hr period that followed.

Finally, experiments were done to determine the capabilities of the gas generator. It was found that the gas generator could sustain a sufficient flow of gas to maintain a temperature of 80°K for 3 hr and a temperature of 113°K for 8 hr. It was also found that a maximum pressure of 25 psi in the gas generator would produce a flow of 4 liters of gas per second.

DISCUSSION

A system for controlling the temperature of an EPR sample has been described which meets the requirement set forth in the introduction. The data of the first experiment show a change of 0.5°K in the temperature of the gas flow when a sample tube of maximal dimensions, which can be conveniently inserted and removed, is placed into the sample Dewar. The second experiment demonstrates several capabilities of the system: (*1*) the rapidity at which the temperature can vary over a large differential in temperature, the extreme example being 5.4 min for a differential in temperature of 100°K; (*2*) the range of temperatures for which the temperature of the sample can be changed without having to change the rate of flow, the ranges of temperature being 100°K for warm temperatures and 30°K for cold temperatures; (*3*) the reset of the temperature, which is at least 1°K or better.

The experiments also show that the system, because of the use of liquid nitrogen as a source of gas and the application of established cryogenic techniques in construction, can produce sample temperatures which approach the temperature of liquid nitrogen, thereby eliminating the need of a special sample Dewar for performing experiments at the temperature of liquid nitrogen.

SUMMARY

A low-temperature control system for use with an EPR spectrometer is presented. It provides a satisfactory control of the EPR sample temperature when studying such highly temperature-dependent EPR signals as those found in biological materials at $g = 1.94$.

ACKNOWLEDGMENTS

The authors are grateful to Leo M. Skille, who fabricated the electronic portions of this instrument, and John C. Drake, who fabricated the nitrogen gas generator. We are also grateful to Mary V. Buell for her criticism of the manuscript. Supported by grant GM-12394 from the National Institutes of Health and a Research Career Program award (GM-KG-18,442) to H. Beinert.

REFERENCES

1. BEINERT, H., HEINEN, W., AND PALMER, G., "Enzyme Models and Enzyme Structure," *Brookhaven Symp. Biol. No.* **15**, 234 (1962).
2. EHRENBERG, A., *Arkiv Kemi* **19**, 119 (1962).

ANALYTICAL BIOCHEMISTRY 20, 51-57 (1967)

Column Chromatography of Neutral Sugars:

Operating Characteristics and Performance of a Newly Available Anion-Exchange Resin

J. I. OHMS, J. ZEC, J. V. BENSON, JR., AND J. A. PATTERSON[1]

Spinco Division, Beckman Instruments, Inc., Palo Alto, California 94304

Received December 12, 1966

Since the initial reports of Khym and Zill (1, 2) on the chromatographic separation of borate complexes of neutral sugars, a variety of ion-exchange matrices and modifications of the procedure have been reported (3–10). Desired resolution often required exacting selection of resin batches, sizing of resin particles, high column back pressure, and long operating time. Despite limitations of this nature, the separation of 15 sugars in an automated procedure has been reported (8, 10).

This paper reports the operating characteristics and performance of a newly available anion-exchange resin, Beckman Custom Spherical Resin Type 1-S, specifically designed for automated analysis of neutral sugars using methodology similar to that of Green (10). This resin was formulated to achieve the following goals:

1. Reproducibility of cross linking, spherical shape, particle size, and chemical composition by rigid control in manufacture.
2. Improved stability of a quaternary amine, anion-exchange resin.
3. Completion of a chromatographic analysis of neutral sugars within the confines of one working day.
4. Operation at reasonable back pressures ($<$300 psi).
5. Resolution similar to that of Green (10).

MATERIALS AND METHODS

Resins: A strongly basic anion-exchange resin was formulated as described by D'Alelio (11) with a nominal 8% divinylbenzene cross linking. Resin spheres were $17 \pm 6\ \mu$ in diameter. Prior to column packing, the resin was converted sequentially to the chloride form with 1.0 *N* HCl, to the hydroxyl form with 1.0 *N* NaOH, and to the borate form with 0.5 *M*

[1] Consultant to Beckman Instruments, Inc.

H_3BO_3 on a Büchner funnel with a Teflon[2] glass fiber filter.[3] The resin was equilibrated on the Büchner funnel with 10 vol of borate buffer (pH 8.9, 0.215 *M*) containing 0.01% Brij-35[4] and packed as an approximate 1:1 slurry in a 0.9 cm column to a 55 cm bed height with a pump flow rate of 1.15 ml min^{-1} at 50°C. Use of a thick slurry and the addition of Brij-35 improved the reproducibility of column packing. The packed column was equilibrated for approximately 8 hr with 0.042 *M* borate buffer without Brij-35.

Column Operating Conditions: Elution was performed with a linear gradient of borate buffer at a flow rate of 1.15 ml min^{-1} and at a temperature of 50°C. The gradient was formed in a two-chambered device which contained 325 ml of limiting borate buffer (38.9 gm $Na_2B_4O_7 \cdot H_2O$ and 7 gm H_3BO_3 per liter, pH 8.9) in a reservoir and 325 ml of starting buffer (1/5 dilution of limiting buffer, 0.042 *M*) in a mixing chamber. The mixing chamber of the gradient device was jacketed to allow warming to 50°C with circulating water. Buffers were prefiltered through Millipore type GS filter[5] (0.22 μ) and through an instream MSA Micule filter[6] installed ahead of the column. All water used for buffer formulation was deionized on a mixed-bed resin (Amberlite IRA-400 and Dowex 50-X8, both 16–50 mesh, 2:1) to produce an initial specific conductance of 0.5×10^{-6} mho cm^{-1}. Buffers were held preferably in glass containers "seasoned" with borate buffers or in polyethylene containers to reduce the possibility of silica contamination.

Standard Sugar Samples: A synthetic mixture of 14 saccharides at levels of 0.5 μ*M* (sucrose, raffinose, cellobiose, maltose, lactose, and ribose) and 1.0 μ*M* (rhamnose, mannose, fructose, arabinose, galactose, sorbose, xylose, and glucose) in a volume of 110 μl was mixed with 200 μl of the limiting borate buffer and held at 50°C for 15 min to form a sugar-borate complex prior to sample application. This sample was forced into the resin bed with about 15 psi air pressure and followed in like manner by two washes of starting buffer. To maintain the initial gradient definition, the top of the column was fitted with an adapter to eliminate all but 2 mm liquid head space above the resin bed. Elution time of glucose was often reduced by switching to limiting buffer alone following elution of xylose. When glucose had been eluted, the column was reequilibrated for 7 hr with the starting buffer in preparation for the next run.

Automated Analysis: An automatic sugar analyzer similar to that re-

[2] E. I. du Pont de Nemours & Co., Wilmington, Del.

[3] Fiber Film Filter, Pallflex Products Corp., Putnam, Conn.

[4] Atlas Chemical Industries, Inc., Wilmington, Del.

[5] Millipore Filter Corp., Bedford, Mass.

[6] Beckman Part No. 331010.

ported by Green (10) was used for these studies. The eluate was processed continuously with 5% phenol and concentrated sulfuric acid. The absorbance of the resultant stream was monitored by a colorimeter with filters at 480 and 490 mμ in 15 mm light path length cuvets and at 486 mμ in a 5 mm light path length cuvet. The flow rates for the phenol and sulfuric acid added to the eluate stream were 0.6 and 3.05 ml min^{-1}, respectively. The conductivity of the column eluate was continuously monitored by a flow-through conductivity cell and recorded simultaneously with the absorbance by a multichannel recorder.

RESULTS

A typical analysis requiring approximately 7.5 hr is shown in Figure 1. The area of 12 peaks can be calculated. A series of 12 experiments with cellobiose yielded recoveries of 100 ± 3% compared to a 0.2 μM standard over the range 0.05 to 1.0 μM. Sorbose and xylose emerge as a single peak, while raffinose-cellobiose, lactose-ribose-rhamnose, and fructose-arabinose emerged as close doublet or triplet peaks. Peak height-to-valley ratios[7] of 0.50 of the absorbances of these doublet peaks were sought as the necessary criteria of resolution for experimental resin and methodology.

The ionic strength of the developing buffer was the most critical parameter affecting elution in these studies. As the slope of the linear buffer gradient was increased or decreased by varying the starting buffer ionic strength from 0.035 to 0.046 M, the resolution of the closely emerging doublet peaks was affected differently. Therefore, the compromise linear buffer gradient reported herein was established for optimum over-all resolution. Increasing the buffer-gradient slope from this optimum improved the resolution of the raffinose-cellobiose doublet peak, but reduced the resolution of lactose from ribose, ribose from rhamnose, and fructose from arabinose. Decreasing the slope of the buffer gradient markedly diminished the resolution of lactose, ribose, and rhamnose.

Reduction of the eluant pH to 8.45 changed the results only slightly. The elution time of maltose was reduced and the resolution of lactose and ribose slightly improved. Total analysis time was not significantly altered by reduction of eluant pH. Reduction of ionic strength of both pH 8.45 and pH 8.9 eluants gave essentially the same results, indicating an insignificant interaction between ionic strength and pH.

[7] Peak height-to-valley ratio: where two peaks are juxtaposed so that the valley between them does not reach baseline, the peak height-to-valley ratio is a/b, where a is the absorbance read at the minimum of the valley and b is the absorbance at the maximum of the lower of the two peaks. The absorbance values of the peaks and valleys must be corrected to zero baseline on the chromatogram. These ratios are indicative of the resolving power.

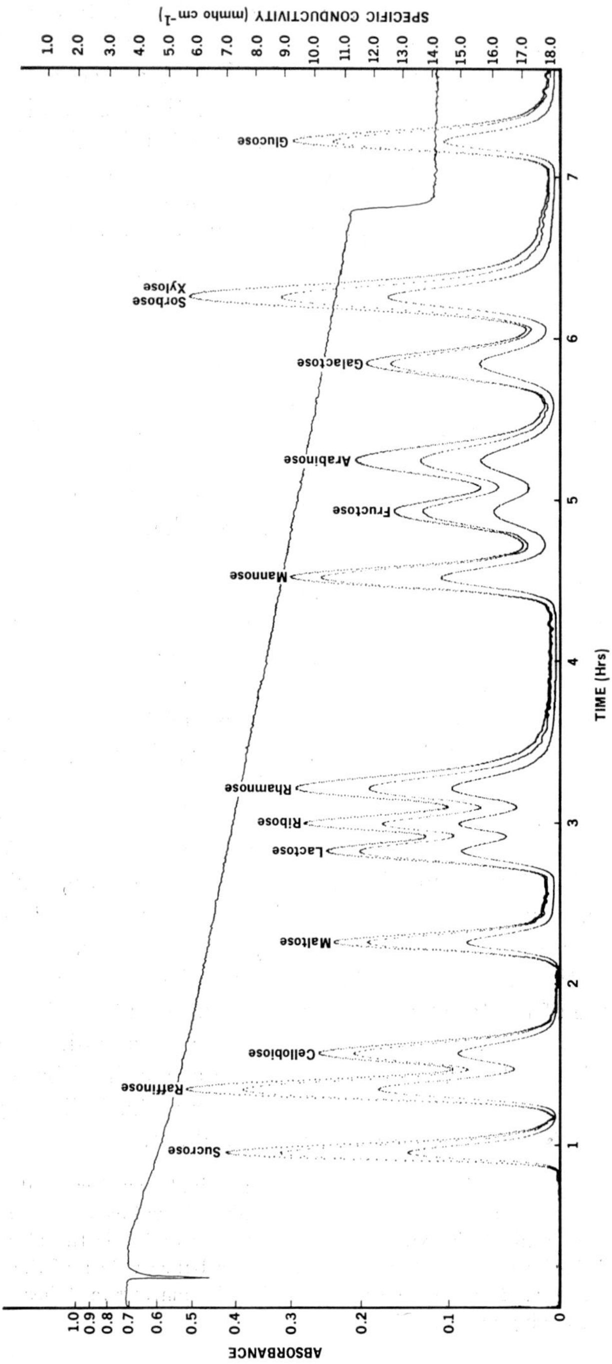

FIG. 1. Chromatogram of synthetic mixture of neutral sugars. Absorbance recorded at: 480 mμ, 15 mm path length (upper trace); 490 mμ, 15 mm path length (middle trace); 486 mμ, 5 mm path length (lower trace).

Experiments on the complexing of sugars and borate prior to application of the sample vs. complexing on the column were inconclusive. The widths of some peaks at the base were slightly reduced when the samples were applied as borate-sugar complexes. Elution times of peaks were unaffected.

DISCUSSION

The methodology required for chromatography of sugars imposes several severe operating conditions on anion-exchange resin: use of borate buffers and alkalinity. As a consequence, avoidance of contamination of the resin and attainment of optimal packing density require close scrutiny. On several occasions in these studies it was noted that loss of resolution and skewing of the peaks could not be corrected by repacking of the column or simple regeneration of the resin.

Anion exchangers, especially the strong base resins with quaternary ammonium groups, are notably inferior to cation exchangers in chemical and thermal stability (13). Breakdown is more marked under alkaline conditions and would be expected to cause progressive loss of resolution under the conditions used for sugar analysis. However, in these studies, contamination or blocking of the resin exchange sites appears to be a more likely cause of loss of resolution than lack of resin stability. A number of possible sources of contaminating ions were encountered in these experiments from sources such as the borate reagents and the glass columns.

Initial research on this problem was directed to a brown ring which formed on the surface of the resin column and enlarged with successive analyses. Similar behavior was noted by Kesler and Dickey (9). When borate buffers were filtered through a 0.22 μ Millipore filter, a brown precipitate collected which caused partial plugging of the filter. Filtration of the buffer reduced the formation of the brown ring, but did little to remedy the resolution problem. Instream installation of a Micule filter further reduced the brown ring but did not eliminate the resolution problem. This filter improved repeatability of back pressure on successive analyses, but it was necessary to regenerate or replace the filter as frequently as every fourth analysis.

The borate buffer reagents are evidently an important source of contamination. Furthermore, the manufacturer's analysis for sodium tetraborate (J. T. Baker lot No. 26034) and boric acid (J. T. Baker lot No. 30663) lists PO_4, SO_4, Ca, Fe, and heavy metals (Pb) which could cause interference with borate-ion exchange. During a single run the contribution from heavy metals alone, calculated as lead, is 10 meq. Since unpacking and regenerating the resin with 3 N HCl and 0.1% EDTA did not conclusively improve resolution, other sources of contamination were sought.

Such evidence led to the suspicion that silicate contamination was involved. Furthermore, loss of resolution was positively correlated with visible etching of the glass column surface on two occasions. Normal regeneration procedures, i.e., conversion through the Cl^-, OH^-, and borate forms, and repacking in a new column failed to improve results, indicating that the resin itself had been affected. It was found that initial performance of the resin could be recovered only by regeneration with 1.0 *N* NaOH at 40°C to remove the suspected silicate contamination. To achieve complete and rapid equilibration of the resin with NaOH, 50 gm batches were packed in 1.9 cm diameter columns held at 40°C. Approximately 500 ml of NaOH was pumped through the packed column at a flow rate of 1.15 ml min^{-1}. The resin was then washed with water, either in the column or on a Büchner funnel, to a phenolphthalein end point and converted to the borate form with 0.5 *M* boric acid in the routine manner. This treatment, although directed primarily toward silicate contamination, probably owes its success in part to the simultaneous removal of carbonate contamination on the resin.

Good resin stability is inferred. Performance has been restored to initial levels following treatment in 1.0 *N* NaOH at 40°C as many as three times on the same batch of resin. Performance is also unchanged after storage in the chloride form at 25° for more than a year. The resin does not, however, withstand freezing. Inadvertent storage of a packed column at —20°, sufficient to rupture the glass column, resulted in irretrievable loss of resolution upon repacking, although neither alteration of normal operating characteristics nor microscopic changes in the resin were detected.

Alfredsson *et al.* (12) noted that when a repacked column was used for the first time, the separation was poorer than it was after a number of analyses. By the fourth analysis the number of theoretical plates had increased nearly threefold over the first analysis. Therefore, these authors recommended that a large volume of eluant be forced through the column at high speed to closely pack the resin bed prior to use of the column in an analysis. This phenomenon was also noticed in our laboratory and was thought to be caused by incomplete conversion of the resin to the borate form in addition to lack of optimum packing density. Treatment of the resin in hydroxyl form with only the customary starting borate buffer (0.042 *M*) gave results similar to that reported by Alfredsson *et al.* (12) but employment of 0.5 *M* boric acid for hydroxyl to borate conversion yielded stabilized separations by the second analysis. Addition of the detergent Brij-35 to the packing buffer and employment of a thicker slurry ratio (1:1) during packing also aided in attainment of early resin bed stability.

SUMMARY

Chromatographic separation of the neutral sugars, sucrose, raffinose, cellobiose, maltose, lactose, ribose, rhamnose, mannose, fructose, arabinose, galactose, and glucose, as a synthetic mixture, was performed in 7.5 hr on a newly available strong base anion-exchange resin, Beckman Type 1-S. Instrumentation and methodology similar to that of Green (10) were employed.

Performance of the resin under various conditions of sample preparation, eluant ionic strength, and pH are reported. Methods are described for reduction of resin contamination and regeneration of the resin following contamination from such sources as borate buffer reagents and glass columns.

REFERENCES

1. Khym, J. X., and Zill, L. P., *J. Am. Chem. Soc.* **73,** 2399 (1951).
2. Khym, J. X., and Zill, L. P., *J. Am. Chem. Soc.* **74,** 2090 (1952).
3. Zill, L. P., Khym, J. X., and Cheniae, G. M., *J. Am. Chem. Soc.* **75,** 1339 (1953).
4. Nakamura, M., and Mori, K., *Biochim. Biophys. Acta* **34,** 546 (1959).
5. Hallén, A., *Acta Chem. Scand.* **14,** 2249 (1960).
6. Syamananda, R., Staples, R. C., and Black, R. J., *Contrib. Boyce Thompson Inst.* **21,** 363 (1962).
7. Walborg, E. F., Jr., Christensson, L., and Gardell, S., *Anal. Biochem.* **13,** 177 (1965).
8. Green, J. G., and Anderson, N. G., *Federation Proc.* **24,** 606 (1965).
9. Kesler, R. B., and Dickey, E. E., Winter Am. Chem. Soc. Meeting, Jan. 1966, D2.
10. Green, J. G., *Natl. Cancer Inst. Monograph No. 21,* 447 (1966).
11. D'Alelio, G. F., U. S. Pat. 2,366,008 (1944).
12. Alfredsson, B., Gedda, L., and Samuelson, O., *Anal. Chim. Acta* **27,** 63 (1962).
13. Helfferich, F., "Ion Exchange," McGraw-Hill, New York, 1962.

ANALYTICAL BIOCHEMISTRY 20, 58–64 (1967)

A Simple Chemical Synthesis of α-D-Glucose 1,6-Diphosphate[1]

W. A. KHAN, T. BALDWIN, U. BRODBECK, AND K. E. EBNER

Department of Biochemistry, Agricultural Experiment Station, Oklahoma State University, Stillwater, Oklahoma 74074

Received January 6, 1967

A requirement for D-glucose 1,6-diphosphate in the phosphoglucomutase reaction (EC 2.7.5.1) was first demonstrated by Leloir *et al.* (1), and recent studies by Ray and Roscelli (2) have suggested that a continuous replenishment of the cofactor is required during the enzymic reaction. Phosphoglucomutase isolated from *Bacillus cereus* and *Micrococcus lysodeikticus* has an absolute requirement for glucose 1,6-diphosphate (3).

Several enzymes that synthesize glucose 1,6-diphosphate have been isolated. Phosphoglucokinase (EC 2.7.1.10) from muscle and yeast catalyzes the ATP dependent phosphorylation of D-glucose (4). Glucose-1-phosphate dismutase (EC 2.7.1.41) from *Escherichia coli* (5) and rabbit muscle (6) catalyzes the dismutation of glucose 1-phosphate or glucose 6-phosphate to form glucose 1,6-diphosphate. D-Glucose 1,6-diphosphate hydrolyzing enzymes are present in guinea pig liver (8).

It is apparent that the biological role of D-glucose 1,6-diphosphate is under active investigation, but the preparation of this compound at present is difficult and time consuming. D-Glucose 1,6-diphosphate may be synthesized chemically (9) by phosphorylating 2,3,4-triacetyl-α-D-glucosylbromide 6-diphenylphosphate with silver diphenyl phosphate or with trisilver phosphate. Both α-D-glucose 1,6-diphosphate and β-D-glucose 1,6-diphosphate are formed and may be separated by fractional crystallization of the brucine salts or they may more readily be separated by ion-exchange chromatography (2). α-D-Glucose 1,6-diphosphate may be isolated from human erythrocytes by ion-exchange column chromatography with yields between 0.19 and 0.24 μmole/ml of blood (10). Glucose 1,6-diphosphate may be isolated from glucose 1-phosphate by ion-exchange chromatography and yields of 20–25 μmoles from 5 gm of glucose 1-phosphate have been reported (3).

The present procedure is an adaptation of the MacDonald synthesis

[1] Supported in part by a grant from the National Science Foundation, GB-3465.

which has been successfully used to prepare various glycosyl 1-phosphates (11, 12). Glucose 6-phosphate was acetylated to yield 1,2,3,4-tetraacetyl-β-D-glucose 6-phosphate, which was phosphorylated by anhydrous phosphoric acid to yield 2,3,4-triacetyl-α-D-glucose 1,6-diphosphate. The acetyl groups were easily removed by hydrolysis with lithium hydroxide. The over-all yield of the cyclohexylammonium salt was between 20 and 25% when based on glucose 6-phosphate.

MATERIALS AND METHODS

Glucose 6-phosphate, glucose 1-phosphate (Type V, free of glucose 1,6-diphosphate), glucose-6-phosphate dehydrogenase (Type V) and crystalline phosphoglucomutase (rabbit muscle) were obtained from Sigma Chemical Co. Anhydrous phosphoric acid was from Fluka. All other chemicals were of reagent grade. Phosphate assays were determined by the Fiske-SubbaRow method (13), and reducing sugars by the method of Somogyi (14). Inorganic phosphate and acid labile phosphate were detected on chromatograms by use of a $HClO_4$-HCl ammonium molybdate spray (15), and reducing sugars were detected by an aniline phthalate spray (16). Elemental analyses were performed by Galbraith Laboratories, Knoxville, Tennessee. α-D-Glucose 1,6-diphosphate, sodium salt, was a gift from Dr. P. Handler, Duke University, and was isolated from glucose 1-phosphate (3). Enzymic rates were measured on a Cary recording spectrophotometer, model 14, at 25°.

RESULTS

Synthesis of α-D-Glucose 1,6-Diphosphate

(1) *1,2,3,4-Tetraacetyl-β-D-glucose 6-Phosphate.* Freshly fused sodium acetate (0.246 gm, 3 mmoles) was mixed with 3.0 ml of acetic anhydride and the mixture was heated to boiling. Portions of glucose 6-phosphate, disodium salt (1.07 gm, 3 mmoles), were added to the acetylation mixture, which was kept boiling by intermittent heating. When the addition of glucose 6-phosphate was complete, the mixture was refluxed for 10 min, after which 15 ml of absolute ethanol was added to destroy the excess acetic anhydride. The solution was evaporated to dryness under vacuum and the slightly colored product was recrystallized from absolute ethanol after treatment with decolorizing carbon. The product was dried *in vacuo* over magnesium perchlorate. The yield of the hygroscopic product was 1.4 gm (quantitative yield as the free acid). The infrared spectrum compared favorably with that of β-D-glucose pentaacetate (17), indicating that the acetate in the one position was of the β configuration (absence of absorption at 8.7 μ).

(2) *Phosphorylation of 1,2,3,4-Tetraacetyl-β-D-glucose 6-Phosphate.* 1,2,3,4-Tetraacetyl-β-D-glucose 6-phosphate (1.4 gm, 3 mmoles) and anhydrous phosphoric acid (4.0 gm, 41 mmoles) were placed separately in two opposite limbs of Thunberg tubes over magnesium perchlorate and dried *in vacuo.* The two limbs were connected and evacuated and the limb containing the anhydrous phosphoric acid was immersed in a water bath at 50°. When the phosphoric acid had melted, 1,2,3,4-tetraacetyl-β-D-glucose 6-phosphate was added in small portions. There was an immediate vigorous bubbling as acetic acid was liberated. The reaction was continued for 2 hr at 50° and by this time the bubbling had virtually ceased.

(3) *α-D-Glucose 1,6-Diphosphate.* The reaction mixture was extracted with 10 ml of dry tetrahydrofuran and then poured into 200 ml of ice-cold 1.0 *N* lithium hydroxide. The mixture was allowed to stand overnight at room temperature. The precipitated lithium phosphate was removed from the alkaline solution by filtration and the clear filtrate was passed through a Dowex 50 (H^+) column (2 × 25 cm) at 4°. The column was washed until the effluent was neutral. The solution was made basic (pH 8.9) with cyclohexylamine and then evaporated to dryness on a rotary evaporator (4°). The residue was washed three times with absolute ethanol, which was removed *in vacuo.* The slightly colored crystalline solid was mixed with 200 ml of dry 2-propanol at room temperature to dissolve the cyclohexylammonium acetate. The mixture was centrifuged and the product was washed four times with 30 ml portions of 2-propanol. Next, the product was washed with dry ether and dried *in vacuo* over magnesium perchlorate. A small amount of inorganic phosphate was present in the product and this was removed as magnesium ammonium phosphate by adding magnesium acetate (0.5 gm) to a solution of the sugar phosphate in 40 ml of 1.5 *N* ammonium hydroxide. Cations were removed on a small column (1 × 10 cm) of Dowex 50 (H^+). The percolate was made basic (pH 8.5) with cyclohexylamine and the solution was evaporated to dryness under vacuum. The residue was washed with absolute ethanol and dried *in vacuo.* No inorganic phosphate was present in the product (0.47 gm, 21%). The ratio of 7 min phosphate to total phosphate was 1:2.3.

The cyclohexylammonium salt (0.284 gm in 150 ml of H_2O) was further purified on a Dowex 1 (Cl) column (2 × 26 cm). The column was washed with 100 ml of water and then eluted with a linear gradient of LiCl (0–500 millimolar with 500 ml in each vessel). The tubes containing 7 min labile phosphate (eluting at 150 millimolar) were pooled and lyophilized.

The resulting syrup was washed three times with 10 ml of absolute ethanol which was removed by evaporation *in vacuo.* The white crystalline solid was washed repeatedly with 1:1 mixture of absolute ethanol and acetone until chloride ion was absent ($AgNO_3$ test). The product was dried over magnesium perchlorate *in vacuo* and a yield of 100 mg (70%) of the lithium salt was obtained. The chemical composition calculated for $C_6H_{12}O_{12}Li_2P_2 \cdot 2H_2O$ in percent was: C 18.6, H 4.12, and P 15.9; observed—C 19.52, H 3.85, and P 15.67. The ratio of 7 min phosphate to total phosphate to reducing sugar was 1:2:1. The sodium salt of α-D-glucose 1,6-diphosphate was prepared readily from the cyclohexylammonium salt. The cyclohexylammonium salt (125 mg) was dissolved in 20 ml of water and passed through a Dowex 50 (H^+) column (1 × 20 cm at 4°). The column was washed with water until the effluent was neutral. The pH of the effluent was adjusted to 8.5 with 0.5 *N* NaOH and the solution was concentrated to a small volume (2–5 ml). Three to five volumes of absolute ethanol was added and upon cooling and rubbing with a glass rod the sticky solid turned into a crystalline solid. The product was washed with dry ether and dried *in vacuo* over magnesium perchlorate (70 mg).

Characterization of α-D-Glucose 1,6-Diphosphate

The product was characterized to determine if any β-D-glucose 1,6-diphosphate was present in the final preparation. The α and β isomers of glucose 1,6-diphosphate have been separated on a Dowex 1 formate column (2) and, accordingly, the product was chromatographed on Dowex 1 formate and eluted with a linear gradient of 0.75 to 1.5 *M* formic acid-pyridine, pH 3.0. Only one peak having 7 min phosphate was observed and the ratio of total phosphate to 7 min phosphate was 2:1 in the peak tubes.

The first-order rate constant for the hydrolysis of glucose 1,6-diphosphate was determined in 2 *N* H_2SO_4 at 30° and was found to be 7.6×10^{-4} min^{-1}. The reported first-order rate constant for α-D-glucose 1,6-diphosphate under these conditions is 7.8×10^{-4} and for β-D-glucose 1,6-diphosphate is 3.15×10^{-3} min^{-1} (18).

A sample of the product was hydrolyzed for 7 min in 1 *N* H_2SO_4 at 100° and assayed for 7 min phosphate, total phosphate, reducing sugar, and, after neutralization to pH 7.0, for glucose 6-phosphate by glucose-6-phosphate dehydrogenase (19). The observed ratios were 1.0:2.0:1.2:1.1. No reducing sugar or glucose 6-phosphate was present in the unhydrolyzed product. The migration of glucose 1,6-diphosphate on electrophoresis (Table 1) and on paper and thin-layer chromatography (Table 2) was compared to authentic α-D-glucose 1,6-diphosphate (sodium salt) isolated from commercial glucose 1-phosphate.

Dephospho-phosphoglucomutase was prepared from rabbit muscle phosphoglucomutase (20) and was used to determine enzymically the concentration of glucose 1,6-diphosphate. The enzymic assay measured glucose 6-phosphate formation with glucose-6-phosphate dehydrogenase (2). The cofactor assay for glucose 1,6-diphosphate depended on the ability of

TABLE 1
Electrophoresis of Sugar Phosphates

Compound	Distance moved, cm	
	pH 3.6[a]	0.05 *M* borate[b]
Glucose 1,6-diphosphate (Na)	23.0	19.6
Glucose 1,6-diphosphate (standard, Na)	23.0	20.0
Glucose 1,6-diphosphate (Li)	22.9	20.2
Glucose-1-P	15.8	13.6
Glucose-6-P	15.8	14.2
P_i	23.2	21.0

[a] Pyridine-acetic acid-H_2O (1:10:89, pH 3.6), 1 hr at 2500 V, Whatman 3 MM.
[b] 0.05 *M* Na borate, 45 min at 2500 V, Whatman 3 MM.

glucose 1,6-diphosphate to stimulate the dephospho-form of phosphoglucomutase and was previously described (7). Calculation of the amount of glucose 1,6-diphosphate (Li salt) was based on the K_m (6×10^{-8} *M*) and measurement of the initial velocity at a concentration equal to $K_m \cdot V_{max}$

TABLE 2
Paper and Thin-Layer Chromatography of Sugar Phosphates

Compound	$R(P_i)$	
	Paper[a]	Thin-Layer[b]
P_i	1.00	1.00
Glucose-1-P	0.57	0.44
Glucose 1,6-diphosphate (Li)	0.72	0.55
Glucose 1,6-diphosphate (Na)	0.68	0.56
Glucose 1,6-diphosphate (standard, Na)	0.67	0.55
Glucose-6-P	0.74	0.55

[a] Solvent: methanol-formic acid-water (80:15:5 v/v) containing 0.2 gm EDTA/100 ml; acid-washed Whatman 3 MM, ascending.
[b] MN 300 (Brinkman) cellulose plates in the same solvent as for paper chromatography.

was determined under standard conditions. Under identical assay conditions, the determined V_{max} was equal to an absorbance change of 0.011/min at 340 mμ, whereas the velocity measured with 6×10^{-8} *M* glucose 1,6-diphosphate was 0.056/min, thus agreeing well with the expected velocity of $\frac{1}{2}V_{max}$ (0.055/min). The sodium salt was also active at comparable concentrations.

DISCUSSION

α-D-Glucose 1,6-diphosphate was synthesized chemically in a simple two-step reaction from readily available starting materials by adapting the MacDonald synthesis which has been used widely for the synthesis of sugar 1-phosphates (11). The present method should also be useful for the synthesis of other hexose 1,6-diphosphates.

Various sugar 1-phosphates have been prepared by the MacDonald procedure: α-*N*-acetylglucosamine 1-phosphate and α-*N*-acetylgalactosamine 1-phosphate (21), *N*-acetyl-α- and *N*-acetyl-β-glucosamine 1-phosphates (22) and *N*-acetylchondrosine α-1-phosphate (23). MacDonald (12) has reported that acetylated sugars with the 1,2-*trans* diequatorial configuration (e.g., the β-pentaacetate of galactose) readily yield the α-1-phosphates whereas in acetylated reducing sugars with the 1,2-*cis* configuration the acetate in the one position is difficult to displace. The phosphorylation of α-D-pentaacetylgalactopyranose gave low yields of α-D-galactopyranose 1-phosphate and no β isomer was reported (12). There appears to be no report of the occurrence of a β-1-phosphate when the corresponding β-pentaacetate was phosphorylated, though lack of this observation may be due in part to the fact that the β isomer is usually more labile than the corresponding α isomer. Even though the mechanism of the MacDonald reaction is not fully delineated, the present evidence indicates that phosphorylation of a β-1-acetylated sugar gives rise to the corresponding α-1-phosphate.

The data presented in this study on the characterization of α-D-glucose 1,6-diphosphate show that the chemically synthesized compound is of the α configuration and no evidence for the presence of the β isomer was found. Chromatography on paper and thin-layer chromatography and electrophoresis showed that the migrations of the synthesized compound were identical to the reference compound. The first-order rate constant for hydrolysis was similar to the reported value. Perhaps the strongest evidence that the product is a α-D-glucose 1,6-diphosphate comes from the enzymic experiments, where the product was required for the activation of dephospho-phosphoglucomutase. Under standard conditions, the product assayed enzymically as the α isomer. The β isomer is unreactive and is inhibitory in the phosphoglucomutase reaction (2).

The over-all yield of α-D-glucose 1,6-diphosphate based on glucose 6-phosphate was between 20 and 25%. Further experiments have shown that purification of the product on Dowex 1 Cl was not necessary since the sodium salt prepared directly from the cyclohexylammonium salt was active in the phosphoglucomutase reaction at low concentrations (6×10^{-8} *M*).

SUMMARY

α-D-Glucose 1,6-diphosphate was synthesized from glucose 6-phosphate by a simple two-step chemical reaction. Glucose 6-phosphate was acetylated with fused sodium acetate and hot acetic anhydride to yield 1,2,3,4-tetraacetyl-β-D-glucose 6-phosphate, which was phosphorylated with anhydrous phosphoric acid to yield 2,3,4-triacetyl-α-D-glucose 1,6-diphosphate. The acetyl groups were removed by hydrolysis with lithium hydroxide. The yield of the cyclohexylammonium salt of α-D-glucose 1,6-diphosphate was between 20 and 25%.

REFERENCES

1. Leloir, L. F., Trucco, R. E., Cardini, C. E., Paladini, A. C., and Caputto, R., *Arch. Biochem. Biophys.* **19,** 339 (1948).
2. Ray, W. J., and Roscelli, G., *J. Biol. Chem.* **239,** 1228 (1964).
3. Hanabusa, K., Dougherty, H. W., Del Rio, C., Hashimoto, T., and Handler, P., *J. Biol. Chem.* **241,** 3930 (1966).
4. Paladini, A. C., Caputto, R., Leloir, L. F., Trucco, R. E., and Cardini, C. E., *Arch. Biochem. Biophys.* **23,** 55 (1949).
5. Leloir, L. F., Trucco, R. E., Cardini, C. E., Paladini, A. C., and Caputto, R., *Arch. Biochem. Biophys.* **24,** 65 (1949).
6. Sidbury, J. B., Jr., Rosenberg, L. L., and Najjar, V. A., *J. Biol. Chem.* **222,** 89 (1956).
7. Levey, G. S., and Alpers, J. B., *J. Biol. Chem.* **240,** 4152 (1965).
8. Hashimoto, T., and Yoshikawa, H., *J. Biochem.* **59,** 427 (1966).
9. Posternak, T., *in* "Methods of Enzymology" (S. P. Colowick and N. O. Kaplan, eds.), Vol. 3, p. 147. Academic Press, New York, 1957.
10. Bartlett, G., *J. Biol. Chem.* **234,** 449 (1959).
11. MacDonald, D. L., *J. Org. Chem.* **27,** 1107 (1962).
12. MacDonald, D. L., *J. Org. Chem.* **31,** 513 (1966).
13. Fiske, C. H., and SubbaRow, Y., *J. Biol. Chem.* **66,** 375 (1925).
14. Somogyi, M., *J. Biol. Chem.* **195,** 19 (1952).
15. Bandurski, R. S., and Axelrod, B., *J. Biol. Chem.* **193,** 405 (1951).
16. Partridge, S. M., *Nature* **164,** 444 (1949).
17. Kuhn, L. P., *Anal. Chem.* **22,** 276 (1959).
18. Posternak, T., *J. Biol. Chem.* **180,** 1269 (1949).
19. Hohorst, H. J., *in* "Methods of Enzymatic Analysis" (H. V. Bergmeyer, ed.), p. 134. Academic Press, New York, 1963.
20. Yankeelov, J. A., and Koshland, D. E., Jr., *J. Biol. Chem.* **240,** 1593 (1965).
21. Kim, T. Y., and Davidson, E. A., *J. Org. Chem.* **28,** 2475 (1963).
22. O'Brien, P. J., *Biochim. Biophys. Acta* **86,** 628 (1964).
23. Olavensen, A. H., and Davidson, E. A., *J. Biol. Chem.* **240,** 992 (1965).

ANALYTICAL BIOCHEMISTRY **20**, 65–76 (1967)

Influence of Buffers on the Phenol Extraction of Liver Microsomal Ribonucleic Acids[1]

JEAN LUST AND VICTOR RICHARDS

Presbyterian Medical Center and Children's Hospital, San Francisco, California 94115

Received October 17, 1966

The widespread use of preparatory ultracentrifuges has led to extensive studies of the rat liver microsomal fraction (1, 2). First prepared by Claude, it was shown to contain most of the cytoplasmic ribonucleic acids and approximately 40% of its dry weight in lipids (3). Combined use of electron microscopy and differential centrifugation techniques revealed that microsomal material is predominantly derived from the endoplasmic reticulum (4, 5) and that its RNA is concentrated in small, round, electron dense particles, called the ribosomes (6).

Exploration of the properties of high polymeric ribonucleic acids was impeded for a long time by the difficulties in obtaining undegraded ribonucleic acids (RNA). Thanks to the use of phenol, RNA with low content in degrading enzymes can be extracted from tissues and subcellular fractions (7–9).

The present report establishes relationships between yields in microsomal RNA and pH and describes attempts to control yields with appropriate buffers at various pH values close to 7.0.

MATERIALS AND METHODS

Preparation of a Microsome Fraction from Rat Liver

Four rats of the Long Evans strain weighing approximately 300 gm were fasted for 22 hr. The livers were removed under ether anesthesia. All subsequent manipulations were carried out at 4°C. The livers were cut in small pieces measuring approximately 1 cm in their greatest dimension with a scalpel. A pulp was made by forcing the pieces of liver through the screen of a tissue press. The meshes of the screen measured 1 mm in diameter.

A 20 gm portion of pulp was homogenized in a Potter-Elvehjem homog-

[1] Supported by Damon Runyon Memorial Fund for Cancer Research and the Arthritis Foundation, Northern California Chapter.

enizer[2] with a Teflon pestle at 400 rpm[3] with 20 ml of 0.25 *M* sucrose. There were 10 strokes of the homogenizer. The homogenate was diluted to 180 ml with 0.25 *M* sucrose. The cellular debris, nuclei, and large granules were sedimented by a centrifugation at 8000 rpm for 10 min in head #856 of the International Centrifuge HRI at 0°C. The pellets were suspended with 40 ml of the solution of 0.25 *M* sucrose and the suspension recentrifuged at 8000 rpm for 10 min.

The supernatants of both centrifugations were combined (Extract), their volume measured, and centrifuged for 120 min at 37,500 rpm in head #40 of the Spinco L2 centrifuge. Its temperature was set at 2°C. The sediments of microsomes (Mc) were resuspended in 0.25 *M* sucrose. The volume of the suspension of microsomes was either 20 or 50 ml. All sediments were resuspended with glass homogenizers fitting the centrifuge tubes. Aliquot volumes of all fractions were taken for nitrogen determinations.

Phenol Extraction of RNA from the Microsome Fraction

Phenol[4] (113.4 gm was dissolved with 15 ml of deionized water and neutralized to pH 6.0–7.0 with NaOH, 1 *N*. In one experiment *o*-quinolinol[5] was added at a concentration of 0.1% (w/v).

All subsequent manipulations were made in the cold room at 4°C and duplicate samples were made of each condition of extraction. Into a Potter-Elvehjem homogenizer[6] were introduced one-tenth of the volume of suspension of microsomes, 15 ml of phenol, and 13 ml of precooled distilled water or one of the following solutions:

1. KH_2PO_4[7]-NaOH buffer, pH 6.5, at a concentration of 0.05 *M* in KH_2PO_4 (Phosphate Buffer, pH 6.5).
2. Hydroxymethylaminopropanediol-HCl buffer, pH 8.0, at a concentration of 0.05 *M* in hydroxymethylpropanediol[8] (Tris Buffer, pH 8.0).
3. Hydroxymethylaminopropanediol, 0.05 *M* (Tris Buffer, pH 10.5).
4. Glycine-NaOH Buffer, pH 10.0, at final concentrations in glycine[8] varying between 0.05 and 1.0 *M*.
5. EDTA[7] solution at a 10^{-4} *M* concentration and pH 8.0.

There were ten strokes of the homogenizer at 400 rpm. The emulsion was transferred to Lusteroid tubes with a capacity of 38.5 ml and shaken for 60

[2] A. H. Thomas, type B.
[3] Eberbach power unit.
[4] "Baker Analyzed" phenol with 0.15 gm % H_3PO_2 as preservative.
[5] *o*-Quinolinol, Eastman Organic Chemicals.
[6] A. H. Thomas, type C.
[7] "Baker Analyzed."
[8] Eastman Organic Chemicals.

min in a reciprocating shaker[9] at 260 strokes per minute. The tubes were then centrifuged in head #30[10] at speeds ranging from 10 min at 10,000 rpm to 15 min at 15,000 rpm.

In early experiments, there was a second extraction of the phenol with water; between 5 and 15 ml of water was added. The mixture was shaken in the reciprocating shaker for 60 min. The phenol and aqueous phases were separated by centrifugations varying between 10,000 rpm for 20 min and 15,000 rpm for 45 min. The aqueous phase was decanted. Its volume and pH[11] were recorded.

Purification of the Phenol Extracts

In the first experiment, the turbidity of the aqueous phase was removed by a centrifugation at 20,000 rpm for 10 min. Most extracts were dialyzed for 48 hr against 4.6 liters of distilled water. There were five changes of distilled water. Some extracts were purified with six to eight extractions with ether and removal of the residual ether by bubbling nitrogen through the aqueous phase.

Ultraviolet Spectrophotometry

All purified extracts were diluted in a known appropriate volume of 0.025 *M* Na diphosphate buffer, pH 6.8, and read in a recording spectrophotometer.[12] The optical densities (OD) at 260 and 230 mμ were recorded. The yield at 260 mμ was expressed in micromoles (μmoles) of nucleotides of the suspension of microsomes of the experiment. A micromolecular extinction coefficient of 7.5 was used to compute the concentration in nucleotides per milliliter of solution.

RESULTS

Orcinol Spectrophotometry

To 5 ml of each purified extract at 4°C, were added 2.5 ml of 0.5 gm % precooled bovine albumin[13] and 2.5 ml of precooled 1 *N* perchloric acid. The precipitate was centrifuged at low speed[14] and resuspended in 5 ml of distilled water. The RNA was then extracted by heating in 0.5 *N* $HClO_4$ at 70°C for 20 min, centrifugation, and decantation.

The color was developed by a procedure similar to the one described by

[9] Eberbach.
[10] Spinco model L_2 ultracentrifuge.
[11] Radiometer pH meter 22.
[12] Perkin-Elmer model 4000.
[13] Fraction V, Nutritional Biochemical Corp.
[14] International centrifuge, clinical model.

Dische (10). A ferric chloride-orcinol reagent was prepared by extemporaneous addition of 7.15 ml of a 1.5 gm (w/v) of orcinol[15] solution in ethanol to 100 ml of a 0.1 gm % (w/v) solution of $FeCl_3 \cdot 6H_2O$ in HCl (Sp.gr. 1.19); 3 ml of the $HClO_4$ extract was added to 7.5 ml of the ferric chloride orcinol reagent, heated for 15 min in a boiling water bath, cooled in tap water, and read at 665 and 565 mμ[16] by spectrophotometry. Adenylic acid[15] was used as a standard. The amount of RNA was computed by using 388 as the molecular weight of adenylic acid. The computed yield of RNA was that of a harvest of microsomes of one experiment.

Nitrogen Determinations

The amount of nitrogen of the subcellular fractions was determined by a micro-Kjeldahl procedure. Selenized granules[17] were used as a catalyst.

Nitrogen Content of Subcellular Fractions

Our scheme of differential centrifugation, with one washing of the sedimented large granules, cellular debris, and nuclei and prolonged centrifugation of the Extract produced a microsome fraction with a nitrogen content amounting to 18, 19, and 21% of the total nitrogen of the homogenate (Table 1). There was good recovery of the nitrogen of the supernatant and microsomal material in the Extract.

TABLE 1
Nitrogen of Subcellular Fractions

Subcellular fraction	Total nitrogen of fraction, mg[a]			
	Expt. 110	Expt. 111	Expt. 112	Expt. 113
Homogenate	786	848	734	819
Extract	402	432	366	430
Microsome	140	160	155	173
Final supernatant	225	199	191	220

[a] Values corrected for aliquot volumes removed.

Extraction of RNA in Distilled Water

The yield was on the average 98.3 μ. The mean yield of successive experiments varied to a great extent. This was not accounted for by the variation in nitrogen content of different microsomal preparations since there was no significant regression when the changes in nitrogen content were compared to those in yields of RNA. One or several other factors were responsible for the variations in yield between the different experiments and this resulted

[15] Nutritional Biochemical Corp.
[16] Hitachi Perkin-Elmer 139.
[17] Hengar Company, Philadelphia, Pa.

in a deviation from regression which was significantly higher than the random error of the experimental material (Table 2).

There was a significant relationship between the yields in RNA of an experiment and the pH of its aqueous phase (Fig. 1) after centrifugation of the emulsion in phenol. When the pH of the extract was high, the yield was high.

TABLE 2
Yields in RNA[a] Extracted by Phenol in Water

Expt. No.	Mean yield of experiments, μmoles	N content of Mc, mg
116	57 (4)[b]	81
117	92 (4)	77
119	80 (2)	66
120	72 (4)	122
122	118 (4)	120
123	112 (4)	109
124	91 (2)	129
127	123 (2)	107
129	132 (2)	120
139	141 (2)	96
141	101 (2)	114
145	109 (2)	107
148	93 (2)	108

[a] Determined by ultraviolet spectrophotometry. From experiment 116 to 129, Mc was resuspended in 50 ml 0.25 *M* sucrose or an equivalent volume for a smaller number of samples. In other experiments, the sediment of Mc was resuspended in 20 ml 0.25 *M* sucrose. In experiments 116, 117, 123, and 119, the aqueous and phenol phases were separated by centrifugation in excess of 10,000 rpm for 10 min.
[b] Number of samples in each experiment are in parentheses.

When the mixture of phenol and microsomes was centrifuged at a speed higher than 10,000 rpm and for a longer time than 10 min, there was no increase in the aqueous phase volume, which varied between 10 and 13 ml. In an attempt to make a concentrated suspension of microsomal material, it was found that they could be resuspended in as small a volume as 20 ml. A centrifugation at 10,000 rpm for 10 min and a final volume of 20 ml of the microsomal suspension were adopted for all the subsequent experiments. A second extraction yielded only a very small fraction of the material obtained during the first extraction.

Extraction of RNA in the Presence of a Phosphate Buffer (pH 6.5) and a Tris Buffer (pH 8.0)

A. *Removal of impurities by dialysis.* The yield in RNA of each experiment was significantly higher (Table 3) in the aqueous extract containing a Tris Buffer, pH 8.0, than in the extract containing a Phosphate Buffer, pH 6.5.

An analysis of variance including all experiments was made after logarithmic transformation of the data to obtain estimates of the multiplicative effects between the two spectrophotometric procedures and between the yields in each of the two buffers. The yield in Tris Buffer, pH 8.0, was consistently higher than the yield in Phosphate Buffer, pH 6.5, in successive experiments. It was estimated to be 1.71 higher in Tris Buffer, pH 8.0, than in Phosphate Buffer, pH 6.5 (1.63, 1.80).[18] The difference in yield between the two buffers was little affected by variations among experiments. There was a moderate but significant interaction between the effects of buffers and spectrophotometric measurements, which indicated a slight variation between buffers in the ratio of the two spectrophotometric procedures. The estimated ratio

$$\frac{\mu\text{Moles in UV}}{\mu\text{Moles in orcinol}}$$

in Tris Buffer, pH 8.0, was 2.067 (1.929, 2.215). The estimated ratio in Phosphate Buffer, pH 6.5, was 1.807 (1.687, 1.936).

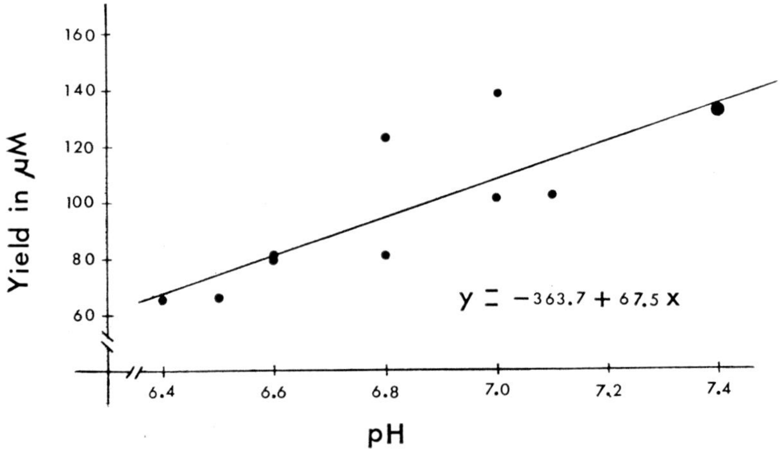

FIG. 1. Regression of yield on pH.

Examination of the ratios $OD_{260\ m\mu}/OD_{230\ m\mu}$ and $OD_{665\ m\mu}/OD_{565\ m\mu}$ revealed no difference between the material prepared in each of the two buffers.

The pH of the aqueous extract varied from 6.4 to 6.6 for the samples separated in Phosphate Buffer, from 7.2 to 7.4 for the samples separated in Tris Buffer. Extraction with phenol lowered the pH in the Tris Buffer.

[18] All confidence intervals will be 95%.

TABLE 3
Yields in RNA in the Presence of a Phosphate Buffer (pH 6.5) and a Tris Buffer (pH 8.0)

Expt. No.	Sample label	Buffer	Removal of impurities[a]	Total yields in RNA, μmoles	
				UV[b]	Orcinol
163	AI	Tris, pH 8.0	D	102	64
	AII			115	62
	BI		E	198	91
	BII			185	92
	CI	Phosphate, pH 6.5	D	58	38
	CII			56	38
	DI		E	112	64
	DII			110	60
165	AI	Tris, pH 8.0	D	157	64
	AII			150	65
	BI		E	165	102
	BII			165	102
	CI	Phosphate, pH 6.5	D	77	38
	CII			80	38
	DI		E	117	72
	DII			127	78
168	AI	Tris, pH 8.0	D	128	58
	AII			121	64
	BI		E	175	108
	BII			195	120
	CI	Phosphate, pH 6.5	D	64	38
	CII			59	33
	DI		E	125	77
	DII			125	77
174	AI	Tris, pH 8.0	D	125	60
	AII			134	68
	CI	Phosphate, pH 6.5		80	41
	CII			77	41
187	AI	Tris, pH 8.0	D	152	67
	AII			149	68
	CI	Phosphate, pH 6.5		85	57
	CII			94	40

[a] D, dialysis; E, ether.
[b] Ultraviolet spectrophotometry.

There were significant regressions of the yields of RNA on the nitrogen content of the microsomal harvests of successive experiments (Fig. 2). The F statistic was 41** in Tris Buffer, pH 8.0, and 19.8** in Phosphate Buffer, pH 6.5. No such regressions were found when the results of orcinol spectrophotometry alone were compared to the nitrogen of the microsomal fraction.

B. *Removal of impurities by ether extraction.* When the data of the samples treated with ether were analyzed as a separate group, there also was a significantly higher yield in Tris Buffer, pH 8.0, than in Phosphate Buffer, pH 6.5. The yield in Tris Buffer, pH 8.0, was estimated to be 1.56 times (1.48, 1.64) the yield in Phosphate Buffer, pH 6.5. As for the samples treated by dialysis, there were smaller interactions between runs and main effects than between procedure and buffer effects, indicating a moderate dependence of the buffer effect on the procedure.

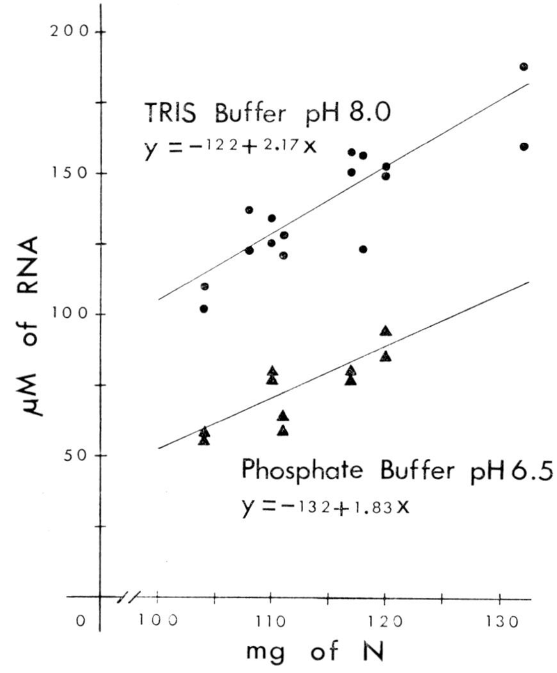

FIG. 2. Regression of yields of RNA on nitrogen of microsomes.

C. *Comparison of both methods of purification.* The total yield was significantly higher in the extracts purified with ether than in the dialyzed extracts. It was estimated to be 1.61-fold higher in the former preparation than in the latter. Thus dialysis removed a large amount of material still present after ether treatment.

The spectra obtained by ultraviolet spectrophotometry were similar in the ether-treated extracts to those obtained by dialysis. No differences in the ratio $OD_{260\ m\mu}/OD_{230\ m\mu}$ were observed between the samples treated by either one of the procedures of purification. However, by orcinol spectrophotometry, there was a marked change in the ratio $OD_{665\ m\mu}/OD_{565\ m\mu}$. It was, on the average, 4.3 for the dialyzed material and 2.5 for the ether-treated material.

Extraction of RNA in the Presence of Chelating Agents

The addition of EDTA to the aqueous phase or *o*-quinolinol to the phenol did not change the yields obtained in two experiments (Table 4). Individual examination of the yields suggested no difference with each of the different solvents used for extraction.

TABLE 4
Yield in RNA in the Presence of Chelating Agents

Expt. No.	Sample label	Buffer	Chelating agent[a]	Yield in RNA,[b] μmoles
148	AI	Tris, pH 8.0	Q	139
	AII			126
	BI		No Q	122
	BII			137
	CI	No buffer	Q	87
	CII			79
	DI		No Q	81
	DII			104
165	AI	Tris, pH 8.0	No EDTA	157
	AII			157
	BI		EDTA, 10^{-4} *M*	147
	BII			147
	CI	Phosphate, pH 6.5	No EDTA	76
	CII			80
	DI		EDTA, 10^{-4} *M*	74
	DII			77

[a] Q, quinolinol.
[b] Determined by ultraviolet spectrophotometry.

Extraction of RNA in the presence of Tris Buffer (pH 10.5) or Glycine-NaOH Buffers (pH 10.0)

Comparison between experiments made with buffers at pH 10.0 with experiments using Tris Buffer, pH 8.0, as a solvent revealed no differences in yield. Raising the pH above 8.0 did not increase further the high yield, which could be obtained by maintaining the pH of the aqueous phase between 8.0 and 7.5 with an appropriate buffer.

DISCUSSION

There is a good over-all agreement between the contents in nitrogen of our homogenates and their subcellular fractions and those reported in the literature (11, 12).

It was previously observed that, during phenol extraction of homogenate, addition of a buffer stabilized the yield in RNA (13). The present work, which establishes a definite linear relationship between the pH of the aqueous phase and its content in microsomal RNA, leads to the two main following conclusions:

(*1*) A high yield of RNA is obtained consistently if the aqueous solvent of the extraction mixture contains a Tris Buffer, pH 8.0, 0.05 *M*. This was repeatedly observed with phenol preserved in hypophosphorous acid and there was no need of a fresh distillation shortly before its use. Other studies have shown that microsomal RNA can be prepared in good yields by adding a sodium dodecylsulfate treatment before the phenol extraction (14).

(*2*) Microsomal RNA is fractionated by the use of buffers at two different pH values. The significant relationship between nitrogen content of microsomes and yield of RNA indicates that the material extracted in the presence of each of the two buffers is representative of the RNA contained in the cytoplasmic fraction.

The large discrepancy in yield between the two pH's investigated and the reproducibility of results in successive experiments suggests that several more discrete fractions of RNA could be isolated by buffers varying very little in pH between each other. The large difference in yield at two pH's close to 7.0, moreover, indicates that the fractions could be made of undegraded RNA since any harsh alkalinity or acidity would be avoided. The significant interaction of our analysis of variance originated from differences in accuracy and specificity between our spectrophotometric procedures. The discrepancy between their measurements can be expected to increase when used with the RNA of small fractions.

The three types of RNA distinguished in tissues (namely, the messenger, ribosomal and transfer RNA) are present in the microsomal fraction of rat liver (15). Each of our fractions is made of ribosomal RNA, since their yield is too large to be made only of messenger RNA or transfer RNA. The fate of the two latter types of RNA in our fractions is unknown.

The effect of the buffers on the yield is observed regardless of the purification procedure employed. There is a larger amount of compounds with a component absorbing primarily at 260 mμ after repeated ether extraction. It is unlikely that it is made only of RNA. Indeed, the dialyzed RNA has a low molecular extinction coefficient and can show only a moderate degree of polydispersity when certrifuged through a sucrose gradient (16). The possibility is thus excluded that the latter RNA would have undergone degradation in small dialyzable fragments that ether would not have removed. In conclusion, a reasonable interpretation is that the microsome fraction contains a sizable proportion of dialyzable material rich in purines and pyrimidines. Since this material is still present after ether extraction, it is difficult to be certain that the buffer effect of those samples is due to RNA only.

o-Quinolinol is known to increase the yield in RNA when the complete homogenate is treated with phenol (17). Our experience indicates that microsomal RNA behaves in a different way in this respect.

It was previously found that increasing the pH above 8.0 does not extract additional RNA from deoxycholate-treated mouse liver microsomal material (18). When nuclei are submitted to phenol treatment, new RNA appear in the aqueous phase when the pH is raised above 8.0 (19, 20). Nuclear preparations appear to react in a different manner from microsomal material in this regard.

SUMMARY

A linear relationship was found between yields of microsomal RNA and the pH of the aqueous phase after phenol extraction. The yield could be controlled by buffers which produced either consistently high yields or reproducible fractions of RNA. The range in pH of these buffers was in the vicinity of 7.0. We therefore avoided submitting RNA to harsh alkalinity or acidity.

ACKNOWLEDGMENTS

The authors are grateful to M. Hamilton and S. Portnoy for their help in the statistical analysis of the data. They also wish to thank J. Castagna and M. Kawahara for their valuable technical assistance.

REFERENCES

1. Petermann, M. L., "The Physical and Chemical Properties of Ribosomes." American Elsevier, New York, 1964.
2. Hoagland, M. B., *in* "The Nucleic Acids" (E. Chargaff and J. N. Davidson, eds.), Vol. III, p. 349. Academic Press, New York, 1960.
3. Claude, A. J., *J. Exptl. Med.* **84,** 1 (1946).
4. Chauveau, J., Gautier, A., Moule, Y., and Rouiller, C., *Compt. Rend.* **241,** 337 (1955).
5. Lust, J., and Drochmans, P., *J. Cell Biol.* **16,** 81 (1963).
6. Palade, G. E., and Siekevitz, P., *J. Biophys. Biochem. Cytol.* **2,** 171 (1956).
7. Kirby, K. S., *Biochem. J.* **66,** 495 (1957).
8. Gierer, A. Z., *Naturforsch.* **13B,** 788 (1958).
9. Kirby, K. S., *in* "Progress in Nucleic Acid Research and Molecular Biology" (J. N. Davidson and W. E. Cohn, eds.), Vol. III, p. 1. Academic Press, New York, 1964.
10. Dische, Z., *in* "The Nucleic Acids" (E. Chargaff and J. N. Davidson, eds.), Vol. I, p. 300. Academic Press, New York, 1955.
11. Hogeboom, G. H., Schneider, W. C., and Palade, G. E., *J. Biol. Chem.* **172,** 619 (1948).
12. de Duve, C., Pressman, B. C., Gianetto, R., Wattiaux, R., and Appelmans, F., *Biochem. J.* **60,** 604 (1955).

13. LUST, J., *Anal. Biochem.* **10,** 1 (1965).
14. DINGMAN, W., AND SPORN, M. B., *Biochim. Biophys. Acta* **61,** 164 (1962).
15. STAEHELIN, T., WETTSTEIN, F. O., OURA, H., AND NOLL, H., *Nature* **201,** 264 (1964).
16. LUST, J., GRIFFITH, O., AND RICHARDS, V., In preparation.
17. KIRBY, K. S., *Biochim. Biophys. Acta* **55,** 545 (1962).
18. BRAWERMAN, G., GOLD, L., AND EISENSTADT, J., *Proc. Natl. Acad. Sci. U. S.* **50,** 630 (1963).
19. GEORGIEV, G. P., AND MANTIEVA, V. L., *Biokhimiya* **27,** 805 (1962).
20. GEORGIEV, G. P., AND MANTIEVA, V. L., *Biochim. Biophys. Acta* **61,** 153 (1962).

ANALYTICAL BIOCHEMISTRY **20**, 77–85 (1967)

Application of Thin-Layer Chromatographic Techniques to the Separation of Δ^{16}-C_{19}-Steroids and Related Compounds

B. P. LISBOA AND R. F. PALMER

The Wenner Gren Institute, University of Stockholm; Hormonlaboratoriet, Karolinska sjukhuset, Stockholm 60, Sweden, and Department of Clinical Endocrinology, Our Lady of Lourdes Hospital, Drogheda, Ireland

Received December 2, 1966

5α-Androst-16-en-3α-ol (5α-A^{16}-3α-ol) has been shown to occur in human urine (1, 2) and to be excreted in increased quantities following stimulation with ACTH (2, 3); the characterization of other Δ^{16}-unsaturated C_{19} steroids in pooled human urine has also been reported (4).

Δ^{16}-Unsaturated C_{19}-steroids have also been detected or isolated during *in vitro* studies, e.g., after incubation of testicular tissue with acetate (5), testosterone (6), and 3β-hydroxypregn-5-en-20-one (7), human liver homogenates with testosterone (8), and adrenocortical tissue with dehydroepiandrosterone (9).

In spite of these studies on the biosynthesis of the androstenol analogs, the chromatographic separation and characterization of these steroids presents serious difficulty if they occur together with their saturated analogs or with other weakly polar steroids. Therefore, for the isolation of the 16-dehydro-C_{19}-steroids, as well as for their specific determination, it was necessary to develop new analytical methods in order to obtain separation from other weakly polar steroids.

By the formation of π-complexes on silver nitrate impregnated silica gel layers, it has been possible to obtain polar derivatives of the Δ^{16}-dehydrosteroids and, therefore, to separate them from their closely related saturated analogs. Also, the resolution of the Δ^{16}-dehydro-C_{19}-steroids has been achieved with both free steroids and as π-complex derivatives.

EXPERIMENTAL

1. *General*

Ascending one-dimensional thin-layer chromatography was performed as previously described using single or multiple developments (10). In

TABLE 1
Systematic Names, Trivial Names, Abbreviations, Sources, and Colors Developed with the Anisaldehyde-Sulfuric Acid Reaction for the Steroids Used in This Investigation

Systematic name	Trivial name	Abbreviation	Source	Color (anisaldehyde-sulfuric acid)
5α-Androstan-3-one	Androstan-3-one	5α-A-3-one	a	Yellow-yellow brown
5α-Androstan-17-one	Androstan-17-one	5α-A-17-one	a	Bright violet-blue violet
5β-Pregnan-3-one	Pregnan-3-one	5β-P-3-one	i	Yellow orange-pink
5α-Androst-2-ene-7,17-dione		5α-A^2-7,17-one	b	Olive
Androst-4-ene-3,17-dione	Androstenedione	A^4-3,17-one	c	Yellow orange-brown
5α-Pregnane-3,20-dione	Allopregnanedione	5α-P-3,20-one	c	Yellow-red brown
5α-Androstan-17β-ol	Androstane-17β-ol	5α-A-17β-ol	d	Blue
5α-Androstan-3α-ol	Androstane-3α-ol	5α-A-3α-ol	a	Lilac-blue
5β-Androstan-3β-ol	Etiocholane-3β-ol	5β-A-3β-ol	a	Lilac-blue
5α-Androstan-3β-ol	Androstane-3β-ol	5α-A-3β-ol	a	Lilac-blue
5β-Androstan-3α-ol	Etiocholane-3α-ol	5β-A-3α-ol	a	Lilac-blue
Androst-5-en-3β-ol	Androst-5-enol	A^5-3β-ol	e	Lilac-blue
5α-Androst-16-en-3α-ol	Δ^{16}-Androstene-3α-ol	5α-A^{16}-3α-ol	f	Bright-violet-blue
5α-Androst-16-en-3β-ol	Δ^{16}-Androstene-3β-ol	5α-A^{16}-3β-ol	f	Bright violet-blue
5β-Androst-16-en-3α-ol	Δ^{16}-Etiocholene-3α-ol	5β-A^{16}-3α-ol	f	Bright violet-blue
Androsta-5,16-dien-3β-ol	Androstadienol	$A^{5,16}$-3β-ol	f	Bright violet-blue
5β-Pregnan-3α-ol	Pregnane-3α-ol	5β-P-3α-ol	i	Bright violet-violet blue
5α-Pregnan-3β-ol	Allopregnane-3β-ol	5α-P-3β-ol	i	Bright violet-violet blue
Pregn-5-en-3β-ol	Pregn-5-enol	P^5-3β-ol	g	Blue
3β-Hydroxyandrost-5-en-17-one	Dehydroepiandrosterone	3β-ol-A^5-17-one	c	Lilac-gray blue
3β-Hydroxyandrost-4-en-17-one	Δ^4-Dehydroepiandrosterone	3β-ol-A^4-17-one	e,h	Lilac-gray blue
3α-Hydroxyandrost-4-en-17-one	Δ^4-Dehydroandrosterone	3α-ol-A-^{4}17-one	h	Lilac-gray blue

Sources: (a) Prof. W. Klyne, M. R. C. Steroid Collection, London, (b) Dr. J. Joska, Academy of Sciences, Prague, Czechoslovakia, (c) Prof. J. Ufer, Berlin, Germany, (d) Dipl. Ing. I. Könyves, Hälsingborg, Sweden, (e) Prof. E. F. Baulieu, Faculté de Médecine, Paris, (f) Dr. D. B. Gower, Guy's Hospital, London, (g) Dr. S. Bernstein, Pearl River, N.Y., (h) Dr. B. Lölan, Department of Experimental Biology, Worcester Foundation, Shrewsbury, Mass., (i) Steraloids Inc., Flushing, N.Y.

these experiments silica gel G (Merck A. G., Darmstadt, Germany) was used as adsorbent. For the separation of Δ^{16}-unsaturated steroids after π-complex formation, chromatoplates were coated with silica gel G impregnated with 25% silver nitrate (w/w). To obtain this level of impregnation the plates were prepared by thoroughly mixing 40 gm of silica gel with 100 ml of a 10% aqueous solution of silver nitrate; the plates were dried in air, stored away from light, and activated only before use by heating for 20 min to 95–100°C.

All the reagents used were of analytical grade and the solvents were distilled before use. Rectangular tanks (21 × 21 × 9 cm, Desaga, Heidelberg) were employed and the chromatoplates were developed singly under saturated conditions. When multiple developments were used the solvent was allowed to move to the top of the plate, i.e., to a distance of 17.5 cm from the starting line. Between two developments the tank was allowed to re-equilibrate for at least 2 hr before being re-used. The sources of the steroids used in this investigation are summarized in Table 1.

2. *Detection of the Spots*

After chromatography the chromatoplates were dried in air and then sprayed with a 1% anisaldehyde solution in sulfuric acid/glacial acetic acid mixture (2/98 v/v), and heated at 95°C for 6–10 min. The colors produced for the different steroids are shown in Table 1.

3. *Solvent Systems*

In this work the following solvent systems were employed for the separation of weakly polar steroids:

Ethyl acetate/cyclohexane/absolute ethanol	45/45/10	(System A)
Ethyl acetate/cyclohexane	50/50	(System C)
Ethyl acetate/*n*-hexane	25/75	(System O)
Ethyl acetate/benzene	50/50	(System Q)
Benzene/absolute ethanol	95/5	(System N)
Benzene/absolute ethanol	98/2	(System P)
Chloroform/absolute ethanol	98/2	

For the separation of π-complexes formed on silver nitrate impregnated plates, two other systems were also employed in addition to systems A, O, C, Q, and N: chloroform/ethanol 95/5 (System L) and ethyl acetate/*n*-hexane 75/25.

RESULTS

In Table 2 are shown the R_f values for 22 weakly polar steroids of the C_{21} and C_{19} series in seven solvent systems; each R_f value is the average of three determinations.

These results show that all the four saturated andostanol isomers as well as the three 16-dehydroandrostanols have been resolved on silica gel G layers; for a complete separation between 5β-androstan-3β-ol and 5β-androstan-3α-ol, multiple one-dimensional chromatography with two or three runs was required, as shown using system O (Table 4).

TABLE 2

R_f Values Obtained for Twenty-Two Weakly Polar Steroids in Seven Solvent Systems with Ascending One-Dimensional Thin-Layer Chromatography on Silica Gel G (R_f value is the mean of at least three experiments. For further particulars, see "Methods.")

	Solvent systems[a]						
Steroid	EtAc 45 Cy 45 EtOH 10	EtAc 50 Cy 50	nHx 75 EtAc 25	EtAc 50 Bz 50	Bz 95 EtOH 5	Bz 98 EtOH 2	Chlr 98 EtOH 2
5α-A-3-one	0.74	0.69	0.53	0.67	0.62	0.53	0.69
5α-A-17-one	0.76	0.72	0.57	0.71	0.65	0.56	0.71
5β-P-3-one	0.76	0.73	0.57	0.66	0.65	0.58	0.69
5α-Δ^2-7,17-one	0.67	0.52	0.27		0.55		
Δ^4-3,17-one	0.53	0.30	0.08	0.40	0.28	0.17	0.52
5α-P-3,20-one		0.52	0.25	0.55	0.48	0.35	0.63
5αA-17β-ol	0.64	0.56	0.31				
5αA-3α-ol	0.69	0.59	0.31	0.50	0.37	0.30	0.48
5βA-3β-ol	0.69	0.57	0.30	0.50	0.35	0.27	0.46
5αA-3β-ol	0.65	0.50	0.21	0.44	0.25	0.20	0.38
5βA-3α-ol	0.68	0.55	0.25	0.50	0.33	0.25	0.43
Δ^5-3β-ol	0.65	0.49	0.23	0.45	0.28	0.20	0.39
5α-Δ^{16}-3α-ol	0.68	0.59	0.29	0.51	0.36	0.28	0.48
5α-Δ^{16}-3β-ol	0.66	0.51	0.20	0.41	0.25	0.18	0.36
5β-Δ^{16}-3α-ol	0.66	0.56	0.24	0.48	0.30	0.23	0.42
$\Delta^{5,16}$-3β-ol	0.66	0.53	0.21	0.45	0.27	0.19	0.38
5β-P-3α-ol	0.69	0.57	0.27	0.49	0.33	0.25	0.45
5α-P-3β-ol	0.66	0.51	0.23	0.45	0.27	0.18	0.38
P^5-3β-ol	0.66	0.50	0.23	0.46	0.29	0.18	0.39
3β-ol-Δ^5-17-one	0.53	0.36	0.08	0.35	0.17	0.14	0.33
3β-ol-Δ^4-17-one	0.53	0.35	0.09	0.38	0.18	0.14	0.36
3α-ol-Δ^4-17-one	0.53	0.32	0.05	0.31	0.15	0.09	0.34

[a] EtAc = ethyl acetate, Cy = cyclohexane, EtOH = absolute ethanol; nHx = *n*-hexane; Bz = benzene, Chlr = chloroform.

The chromatographic mobilities obtained on silica gel G for saturated and 16-dehydroandrostanol pairs differing in the configuration 5α/3β-ol and Δ^5/3β-ol show that these steroid pairs are very difficult to separate; however, in the 16-dehydrosteroid series a complete separation of these two compounds was achieved on silica gel plates impregnated with silver nitrate, in all the solvent systems employed (Table 3).

On silica gel plates it was impossible to separate 16-dehydroandrostanols from the corresponding saturated compounds; separation was achieved, however, on silver nitrate impregnated plates. The Δ^{16}-steroids form a π-complex with silver nitrate which resulted in a large increase in their polarity. This permitted a very great separation from the corresponding saturated compounds, the latter having the same mobility as when chromatographed on untreated silica gel G. The R_f values obtained under these conditions for the unsaturated steroids are summarized in Table 3.

TABLE 3
R_f Values Obtained for Six Unsaturated Steroids in Seven Solvent Systems on Silver Nitrate Impregnated Silica Gel G Layers
(Each R_f value is the mean of three chromatograms.)

	Solvent systems[a]						
Steroid	Chlr 95 EtOH 5	EtAc 45 Cy 45 EtOH 10	EtAc 25 nHx 75	EtAc 75 nHx 25	Cy 50 EtAc 50	Bz 50 EtAc 50	Bz 95 EtOH 5
A^5-3β-ol	0.51	0.67	0.26	0.57	0.50	0.45	0.24
$A^{5,16}$-3β-ol	0.09	0.32	0.04	0.25	0.14	0.12	0.03
5α-A^{16}-3α-ol	0.10	0.37	0.06	0.30	0.21	0.15	0.03
5α-A^{16}-3β-ol	0.14	0.37	0.11	0.31	0.23	0.18	0.04
5β-A^{16}-3α-ol	0.06	0.34	0.06	0.15	0.08	0.07	0.03
P^5-3β-ol			0.26			0.45	0.31

[a] For abbreviations, see footnote to Table 2.

From the results given in Table 3 and in Figure 1 it can be seen that on silica gel-silver nitrate plates the unsaturated steroids can not only be separated from the saturated ones, but can also be resolved from each other.

The two isomeric androstanones investigated here (androstan-3-one and androstan-17-one) could be partially separated on silica gel G, using solvent systems ethyl acetate/benzene 50/50 or systems of the benzene/ethanol type. They are completely resolved after two developments in solvent systems P or O (Table 4). Androstane-3-one and androstane-17-one also develop different colors with the anisaldehyde-sulfuric acid reagents.

For the less polar steroids considered in this study, the following sequence of polarity has been found for the three hydroxyl groups:

$$3\alpha(5\alpha) \leq 3\beta(5\beta) < 3\alpha(5\beta) < 3\beta(\Delta^5) \leq 3\beta(5\alpha).$$

This sequence is slightly different from that found with 17-substituted C^{19}-steroids and from pregnane steroids.

After formation or π-complexes, this sequence changed to the following order of polarity:

$$3\beta(5\alpha) < 3\alpha(5\alpha) < 3\beta(\Delta^5) < 3\alpha(5\beta).$$

The three following steroid pairs could not be resolved: androst-5-en-3β-ol and pregn-5-en-3β-ol, 5β-pregnan-3α-ol and 5β-androstan-3α-ol, and 5α-pregnan-3β-ol and 5α-androstan-3β-ol. Thus, for these steroid groups, the androstane derivative was only slightly more polar than the corresponding pregnane analog (Table 4).

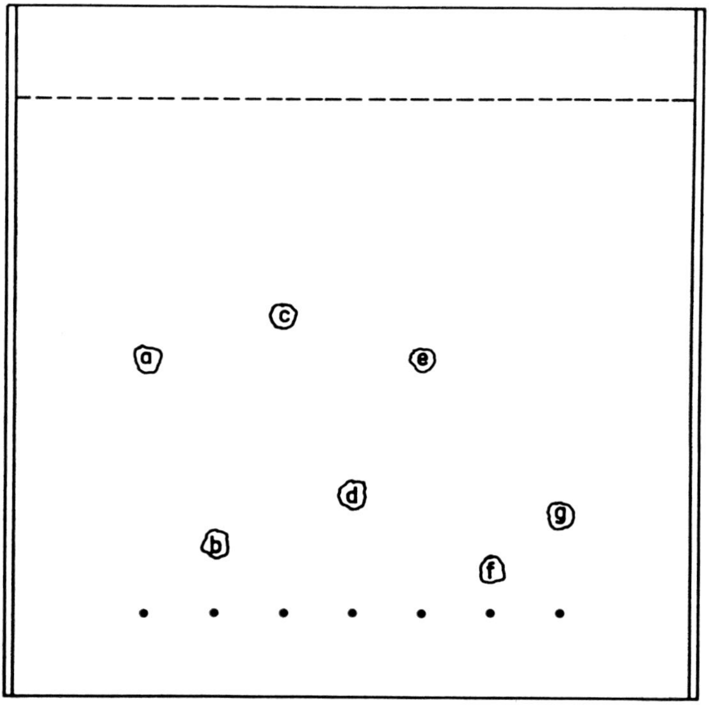

FIG. 1. Ascending one-dimensional thin-layer chromatography on silver nitrate-silica gel G layers of four 16-dehydro-C_{19}-steroids and the corresponding 16-dihydro compounds using solvent system C (ethyl acetate/cyclohexane 50/50). Steroids: (a) androst-5-en-3β-ol, (b) androst-5,16-dien-3β-ol, (c) 5α-androstan-3α-ol, (d) 5α-androst-16-en-3β-ol, (e) 5α-androstan-3β-ol, (f) 5β-androst-16-en-3α-ol, (g) 5α-androst-16-en-3α-ol.

DISCUSSION

In the present investigation thin-layer chromatography has been employed to separate very weakly polar steroids of the C_{19} and C_{21} series. Most of these monohydroxylated, monoketonic, and diketonic steroids are isomers, or differ from each other by the presence of only one isolated bond. Their chromatographic mobilities are greater than those of androstenedione and progesterone in the systems of cyclohexane/ or *n*-hexane/ethyl acetate type (e.g., solvent systems O, C, and A) (10, 11); this permitted a group separation in these systems between the very weakly polar steroids considered here and those of greater polarity such as the monohydroxy-monoketonic steroids.

TABLE 4
Mobility of Twenty Weakly Polar Steroids on Silica Gel G Obtained in Three Solvent Systems Using Ascending One-Dimensional Multiple Thin-Layer Chromatography, Following Two Developments (↑ ↑)
(For the composition of the solvent systems and further particulars, see "Methods.")

Steroid	Mobility (in cm) of solvent systems		
	P↑↑	O↑↑	C↑↑
5α-A-3-one	13.9	13.1	13.8
5α-A-17-one	14.4	13.9	14.0
5β-P-3-one	14.4	13.9	14.1
A^4-3,17-one	6.3	2.8	8.0
5β-A-3β-ol	8.7	9.3	12.1
5α-A-3α-ol	9.6	9.6	12.2
5β-A-3α-ol	8.2	8.2	11.7
5α-A-3β-ol	6.7	7.3	10.8
A^5-3β-ol	7.2	7.3	11.4
5α-A^{16}-3α-ol	9.2	9.0	11.9
$A^{5,16}$-3β-ol	7.1	7.2	10.9
5β-A^{16}-3α-ol	8.1	7.9	11.5
5α-A^{16}-3β-ol	6.9	6.9	10.9
5β-P-3α-ol	8.4	8.6	11.9
5α-P-3β-ol	6.9	7.7	11.0
P^5-3β-ol	7.4	7.6	11.6
3α-ol-A^4-17-one	3.9	2.6	7.4
3β-ol-A^4-17-one	4.9	3.5	8.5
3β-ol-A^5-17-one	4.8	3.5	8.4
3β-ol-P^4-20-one[a]	5.4	4.5	9.4

[a] 3β-Hydroxypregn-4-en-20-one obtained by courtesy of Dr. F. Kincl, Syntex Research Center, Palo Alto, Calif.

In the systems specially developed for the steroids investigated here, separation can normally be achieved after a single development but the use of one-dimensional multiple chromatography permitted a better separation of some steroid pairs; for instance, 5α-androstan-3α-ol and 5β-androstan-3β-ol were completely resolved after two runs in system P on silica gel G.

The separation of Δ^5-3β-hydroxysteroid and its related 3β-hydroxy-5α-compound (e.g., dehydroepiandrosterone and epiandrosterone) has been reported to be difficult on thin-layer chromatography (12) even when multiple chromatography was employed (13, 14). Indeed both 5α-androstan-3β-ol/androst-5-en-3β-ol and 5α-pregnan-3β-ol/pregn-5-en-3β-ol steroid pairs have been completely resolved by multiple one-dimensional chromatography in systems P or C.

Using the conventional techniques of thin-layer chromatography on silica gel G, Gower (15) could not separate androstanedienol and Δ^{16}-androstene-3β-ol as free steroids in any one of the systems employed, and even after four runs their separation was incomplete. Neither was it possible to separate these compounds on silicic acid impregnated paper either as free or as acetylated compounds. Also with gas-liquid chromatography after trimethyl silyl ether formation using T S-1265 as stationary phase (4), only a small degree of separation could be achieved. The separation of these two steroids, partially achieved on silica gel G in solvent system Q, was complete when silver nitrate-silica gel G layers were used.

Thus the data presented in this paper on the chromatographic mobilities of very weakly polar steroids can be used in conjunction with data in previously published papers (10, 11, 13, 16) to allow separation of complex mixtures of weakly polar steroids and those of greater polarity.

SUMMARY

The behavior of weakly polar steroids and their corresponding Δ^{16}-compounds on thin-layer chromatography was studied. A method is presented for the separation of the four androstanol isomers as well as a complete separation of these from Δ^{16}-compounds using π-complex formation on $AgNO_3$ treated chromatoplates. This technique also permitted complete separation of the four Δ^{16}-compounds from each other. The results are compared to those obtained by the use of untreated plates and to both reverse-phase chromatography on paper and gas-liquid chromatography.

ACKNOWLEDGMENTS

For a generous supply of the steroids used in this work, the authors are greatly indebted to Prof. E. E. Baulieu, Faculté de Médecine, Paris, France; Dr. S. Bernstein, American Cyanamid Co., Pearl River, N. Y.; Drs. D. B. Gower and B. W. L. Brooksbank, Guy's Hospital, London, England; Dr. J. Joska, Academy of Sciences, Prague, Czechoslovakia; Prof. W. Klyne, M. R. C. Steroid Collection, London, England; Dipl. Ing. I. Könyves, Leo AB, Hälsingborg, Sweden; Dr. J. Ufer, Schering AG, Berlin, Germany; Dr. F. Kincl, Syntex Research Center, Palo Alto, Calif. For a personal grant in Reproductive Endocrinology, one of us (B.P.L.) is pleased to express his gratitude to Schering AG, Berlin, Germany. Part of the expenses of this investigation were defrayed by Hoffmann-La Roche, Basle, in a grant to one of us (R.F.P.).

REFERENCES

1. Brooksbank, B. W. L., and Haslewood, G. A. D., *Biochem. J.* **80,** 488 (1961).
2. Brooksbank, B. W. L., *J. Endocrinol.* **24,** 435 (1962).
3. Palmer, R. F., Ph.D. Thesis, University of Birmingham, 1963.
4. Brooksbank, B. W. L., and Gower, D. B., *Steroids* **4,** 787 (1964).
5. Gower, D. B., and Haslewood, G. A. D., *J. Endocrinol.* **23,** 253 (1961).
6. Stylianou, M., Forchielli, E., and Dorfman, R. I., *J. Biol. Chem.* **236,** 1318 (1961).
7. Ahmad, N., and Gower, D. B., *Biochem. J.* **98,** 25 (1966).
8. Stylianou, M., Forchielli, E., Tumillo, M., and Dorfman, R. I., *J. Biol. Chem.* **236,** 692 (1961).
9. Gower, D. B., *J. Endocrinol.* **26,** 173 (1963).
10. Lisboa, B. P., *Steroids* **6,** 605 (1965.
11. Lisboa, B. P., *J. Chromatog.* **19,** 81 (1965).
12. Cerny, V., Joska, J. and Lábler, L., *Collection Czech. Chem. Commun.* **26,** 1658 (1961).
13. Lisboa, B. P., *J. Chromatog.* **19,** 333 (1965).
14. Galletti, F., *Research on Steroids,* Vol. 2, p. 189. Il Pensiero Scientifico, Rome, 1965.
15. Gower, D. B., *J. Chromatog.* **14,** 424 (1964).
16. Lisboa, B. P., *Clin. Chim. Acta* **13,** 179 (1966).

ANALYTICAL BIOCHEMISTRY 20, 86–93 (1967)

Automated Determination of Protein in the Presence of Sucrose[1]

HERBERT SCHUEL[2] AND REGINA SCHUEL

Department of Biology, Oakland University, Rochester, Michigan 48063

Received December 8, 1966

The development of the zonal centrifuge (1) has made it possible to achieve extremely high-resolution, large-scale fractionations of subcellular particles from homogenates. Zonal centrifuge systems now commercially available have capacities ranging from 300 to 1700 ml and operate at speeds ranging from 1000 to 40,000 rpm (2, 3). These devices make it possible to isolate particles ranging in size from whole cells and nuclei to viruses, ribosomes, and large protein molecules on the basis of sedimentation velocity and sedimentation to the isopycnic or density equilibrium position in sucrose density gradients (1–3).

One major objective of this line of investigation has been to isolate and characterize chemically and physically all the subcellular components from a given cell type. This has required the utilization of automated procedures (4) whenever possible to handle the large volume of analytical work (5–8). As a part of this program it was necessary to routinely determine the protein concentration in the isolated fractions. Initially this was accomplished by employing an automated (4) modification of the Lowry procedure (9). However, the sucrose concentration of the density gradient was observed to progressively reduce the amount of color developed. The present communication describes an attempt to overcome this sucrose-induced inhibition.

MATERIALS AND METHODS

The concentration of protein was analyzed automatically initially using modules of the Technicon AutoAnalyzer (4)—sampler tray, proportioning pump, transmission lines, mixing coils, colorimeter, and recorder modules—by means of the Standard Lowry procedure (9). A schematic diagram

[1] This work was supported in part by a grant (GB-3388) from the National Science Foundation.

[2] Part of this work was carried out at the Biology Division, Oak Ridge National Laboratory, during the tenure of a Postdoctoral Fellowship from the Division of General Medical Sciences, National Institutes of Health, U. S. Public Health Service.

of the assay system can be seen in Figure 1. The experiments evaluating the effect of sucrose on color development were performed with an almost identical module assembly, except that a standard 8 mm light path Technicon flow cell was used in the colorimeter module in place of the 15 mm tubular flow cell represented in the diagram.

The reagents and flow rates employed were as follows: (I) 0.1% $CuSO_4 \cdot 5H_2O$ in 0.2% sodium and potassium tartrate, or in the absence of the copper reagent 0.1% disodium Versenate (0.6 ml/min); (II) water (1.6 ml/min); (III) bicarbonate buffer—84 gm $NaHCO_3$ and 45 gm NaOH per liter—(1.6 ml/min); (IV) Folin-Ciocalteau reagent, diluted 3× with water (1.2 ml/min); air to segment the fluid stream (1.6 ml/min); tissue sample (0.42 ml/min).

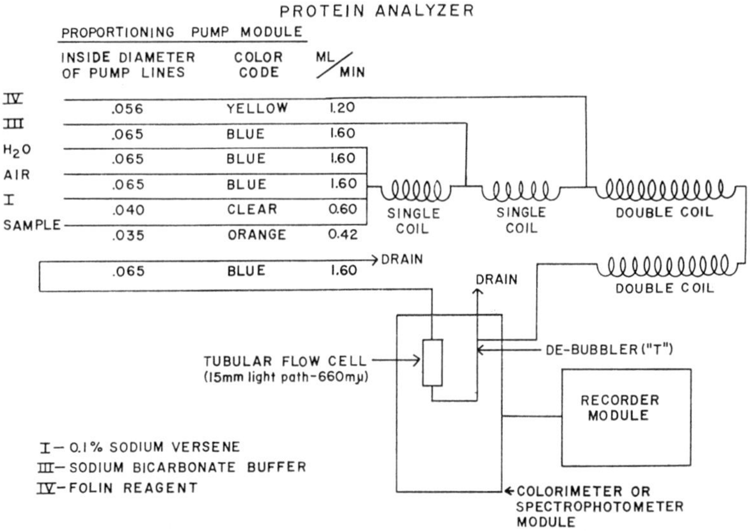

FIG. 1. Schematic diagram for automated assay system for protein utilizing modules of the Technicon AutoAnalyzer. Flow rates based on specifications provided by Technicon Instruments Corp. for the manifold tubing on the proportioning pump of the AutoAnalyzer.

The optical density of the fluid passing through the flow cell in the colorimeter module was monitored at 660 mμ, and the data were displayed on a strip-chart recorder. The original experiments were performed using standard Technicon colorimeter and recorder modules, while at the present time a Beckman DB spectrophotometer equipped with a special 15 mm Technicon tubular flow cell and a Sargent SRL linear-log recorder are employed. Satisfactory results were obtained with either set of components.

The assay system was calibrated using crystalline bovine serum albumin (BSA) obtained from Sigma Chemical Co. as a standard.

The sucrose concentration in the test samples was determined at 20°C with a Bausch & Lomb Abbe-3L refractometer.

EXPERIMENTAL

The effect of sucrose on the amount of color developed in the standard Lowry procedure is illustrated in Figure 2. In this set of experiments, the protein source consisted of an equal amount of rat liver homogenate in

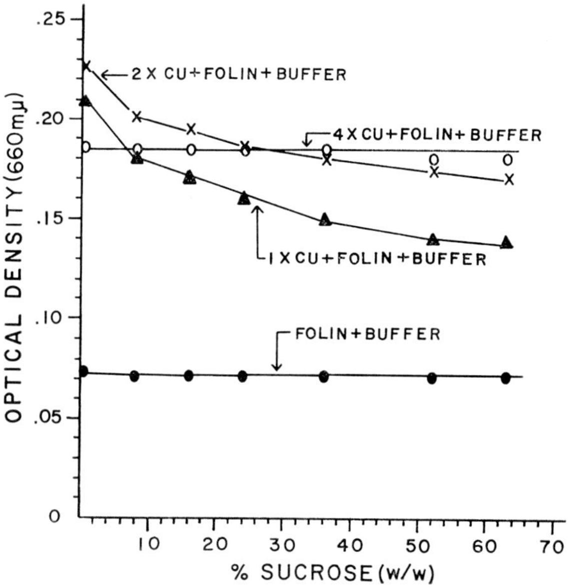

FIG. 2. Effect of sucrose on color development in the standard and modified Lowry procedures for protein. Test solutions contained an equal volume of rat liver homogenate.

the presence of various concentrations of sucrose (8.5 to 66% w/w) similar to those employed to construct the density gradients in the zonal centrifuges. Sucrose clearly produced a large and significant reduction in color development.

A number of procedural modifications were tested in an attempt to overcome the sucrose effect:

(*1*) The concentrated sucrose solutions employed are quite viscous, and it appeared that the adverse effects upon color development might result from an inadequate mixing of the sample with the other reagents in the system. Accordingly a power mixer consisting of a solenoid and magnetic fleas within the lines was added at the junction point of the sample stream and copper reagent. This resulted in an improvement in the symmetry of the peaks (probably the result of a reduction in smearing of the sample along the fluid lines), but failed to improve color development.

(*2*) The amount of copper in the system was increased. This approach appeared to be successful, since with 2× copper reagent the sucrose inhibition was reduced, while with 4× copper reagent the sucrose effect was abolished. The tartrate concentration in the copper reagent was increased proportionally. However, the copper-tartrate reagent was extremely unstable, and the copper rapidly precipitated out of solution, usually to a large extent within the course of an hour. As a result this modification proved to be unreliable as a routine analytical tool.

(*3*) An attempt was made to overcome the instability of the copper-tartrate reagent by dissolving it in the alkaline (bicarbonate) buffer—to essentially prepare a biuret reagent. This reagent proved to be extremely stable, but the sucrose inhibition persisted.

Sucrose did not appear to interfere with color development of the Folin-phenol reaction attributable to tyrosine residues in the protein. The advent of the new Technicon tubular flow cell with a 15 mm light path made it possible to exploit this observation, since a satisfactory level of sensitivity could be obtained. This is illustrated in Figure 3. A linear response of color development to protein concentration (bovine serum albumin) was obtained over a range of 0.05 to 8.00 mg/ml. The sensitivity of this procedure was thus equivalent under these conditions to the complete Lowry method with the old standard 8 mm light path Technicon flow cell.

An illustration of the use of the modified automated protein assay with the Folin reagent in conjunction with tissue fractionation in the zonal centrifuges is presented in Figure 4. In this experiment a rat liver homogenate was fractionated in the type A-XII zonal centrifuge (10). The distribution of subcellular particles in the sucrose density gradient was monitored by the continuous analysis of the gradient for ultraviolet absorbance (254 mμ) as it emerged from the rotor and passed through a quartz flow cell (0.2 cm light path) in a recording Gilson #254 UV meter. The sucrose concentration in the gradient was assayed refractometrically.

DISCUSSION

These observations demonstrate that the Folin reaction can be used for the automated determination of the protein content of subcellular fractions isolated in the zonal centrifuges. The procedure is dependable, and is not affected by the concentrated sucrose solutions used to construct the density gradients. An adequate degree of sensitivity can be obtained by means of the long light path of the new Technicon 15 mm tubular flow cell. Consequently, this automated modification of the Lowry (9) protein assay procedure has been routinely employed as an analytical component of the zonal centrifuge system (5–8, 11–14).

The primary disadvantage of this procedure consists in its dependence essentially upon the presence of a single amino acid tyrosine, and to a minor extent upon tryptophan. Thus spurious results could be obtained if a subcellular fraction contained either an unusual abundance or paucity of these residues.

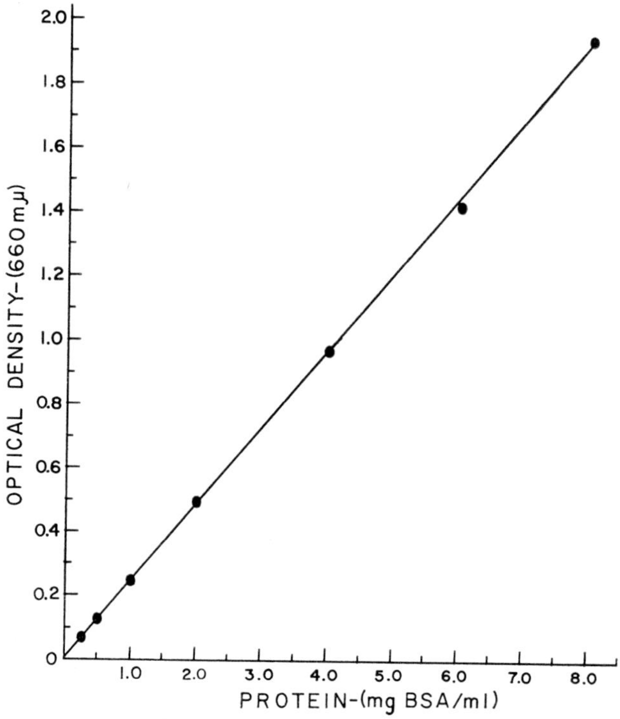

FIG. 3. Relationship between protein concentration (bovine serum albumin) and color development using the Folin-Ciocalteau reagent and 0.1% disodium Versenate in place of the copper-tartrate reagent. Colorimeter module contained Technicon 15 mm light path tubular flow cell.

The data suggest that sucrose interferes with color development in the Lowry reaction because it forms a chemical complex with the copper ions, thus making them unavailable for interaction with the protein. This hypothesis is based on the observation that interference with color development is reduced by increasing the concentration of copper ions. In addition sucrose has been found to produce an intense absorption in the near-ultraviolet upon incubation with the biuret reagent (15). This observation made it impossible to take advantage of the intense absorption in the near-ultraviolet produced by the protein-biuret complex (16) for protein assays of subcellular fractions isolated in sucrose density gradients.

The exact role played by copper ions in color development in the complete Lowry procedure is not clearly understood at the present time. The

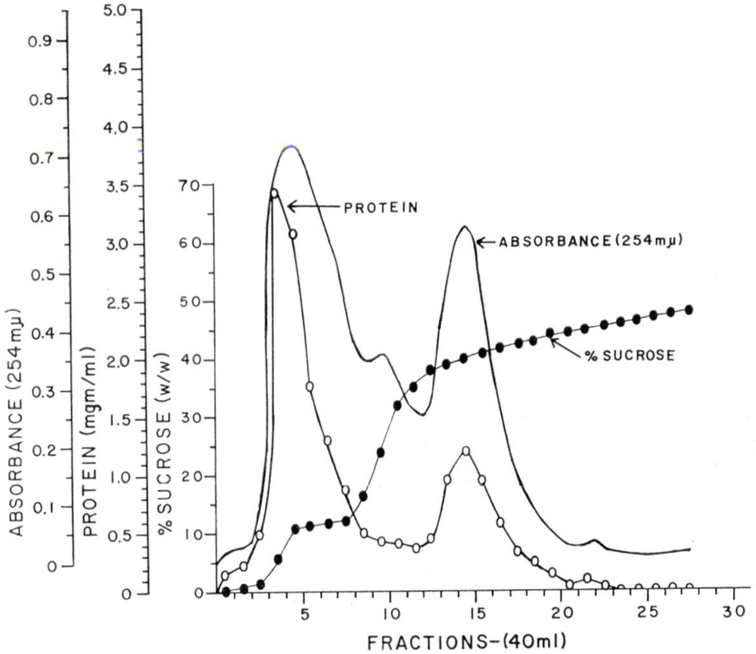

FIG. 4. Fractionation of rat liver homogenate in type A-XII zonal centrifuge at 3500 rpm for 5.5 hr. Data presented show distribution of particles (in terms of absorbance at 254 mμ, 0.2 cm light path) in the gradient, protein concentration, and sucrose concentration in the isolated fractions.

alkaline copper reaction appears to be related to the biuret reaction, although the contribution of copper to the color developed with the Folin reagent was not directly proportional to the amount of biuret color (9). This hypothesis appears to be supported by the sucrose inhibition observed in the present study and by the reaction of sucrose with the biuret reagent detected by absorption spectra in the ultraviolet (15).

However, if one wished to use the complete Lowry (9) reaction, an alternative solution to the problem of progressive sucrose interference with color development could be employed. This would require the preparation of a calibration curve for the sucrose effect (as in Fig. 2), and the subsequent correction of the optical density readings obtained in each of the isolated zonal centrifuge fractions for the amount of sucrose present.

The most satisfactory test for proteins would be one that detects the presence of peptide bonds, and does not depend upon the presence of a limited number of amino acid residues. The biuret reaction meets these requirements. It is hoped that future work will increase the sensitivity of the biuret procedure, and also liberate it from interference by sucrose.

SUMMARY

The advent of the zonal centrifuges utilizing sucrose density gradients has made it necessary to measure routinely the protein content of subcellular fractions containing variable amounts of sucrose with automated procedures. The color development in the Lowry reaction was found to be progressively reduced by increasing concentrations of sucrose. The sucrose inhibition could be overcome by increasing the amount of copper in the system. However, the copper-tartrate reagent was extremely unstable, and the copper quickly precipitated out. The copper-tartrate was stable when dissolved in bicarbonate buffer, but this modification failed to overcome the sucrose effect. Sucrose failed to impair the contribution of the Folin reaction to color development, and sufficient sensitivity could be obtained by using the new Technicon tubular flow cell with a 15 mm light path. Under these conditions a linear response to protein concentration was obtained from 0.05 to 8.00 mg bovine serum albumin per milliliter.

ACKNOWLEDGMENT

We wish to thank Dr. Norman G. Anderson for his advice and encouragement during the course of this investigation.

REFERENCES

1. Anderson, N. G., *J. Phys. Chem.* **66,** 1984 (1962).
2. Anderson, N. G., *Natl. Cancer Inst. Monograph No. 21* (1966).
3. Anderson, N. G., *Science* **154,** 103 (1966).
4. Skeggs, L. T., *Am. J. Clin. Pathol.* **28,** 311 (1957).
5. Schuel, H., and Anderson, N. G., *J. Cell Biol.* **21,** 309 (1964).
6. Schuel, H., Lorand, L., Schuel, R., and Anderson, N. G., *J. Gen. Physiol.* **48,** 737 (1965).
7. Schuel, H., and Schuel, R., *J. Gen. Physiol.* **50,** 1085 (1967).
8. Schuel, H., Tipton, S. R., and Anderson, N. G., *J. Cell Biol.* **22,** 317 (1964).
9. Lowry, O. H., Rosebrough, N. J., Farr, A. L., and Randall, R. J., *J. Biol. Chem.* **193,** 265 (1951).
10. Anderson, N. G., Barringer, H. P., Cho, N., Nunley, C. E., Babelay, E. F., Canning, R. E., and Rankin, C. T., *Natl. Cancer Inst. Monograph No. 21,* 113 (1966).
11. Barber, M. L. S., and Canning, R. E., *Natl. Cancer Inst. Monograph No. 21,* 345 (1966).

12. Barber, A. A., Rankin, C. T., and Anderson, N. G., *Natl. Cancer Inst. Monograph No. 21,* 333 (1966).
13. Fisher, W. D., and Canning, R. E., *Natl. Cancer Inst. Monograph No. 21,* 403 (1966).
14. Hayek, D. H., and Tipton, S. R., *J. Cell Biol.* **29,** 405 (1966).
15. Anderson, N. G., and Anderson, M. L., unpublished data, 1958.
16. Mehl, J. W., *J. Biol. Chem.* **157,** 173 (1945).

ANALYTICAL BIOCHEMISTRY 20, 94–101 (1967)

The Separation of Nucleotides and Their Derivatives by Continuous Free-Flow Electrophoresis[1]

E. SULKOWSKI AND M. LASKOWSKI, SR.

Laboratory of Enzymology, Roswell Park Memorial Institute, Buffalo, New York 14203

Received December 12, 1966

Paper electrophoresis of nucleotides and derivatives was described by Markham and Smith (1) in 1952. It still is a very useful analytical method, and numerous modifications and extensions of this technique have been made, e.g., fingerprinting of enzymic digests (2, 3).

Several years ago an attempt was made to use continuous paper electrophoresis as a semimicro preparative method for mononucleotides (unpublished). The spectra of the obtained products indicated a contamination with substances eluted from the paper curtain. Since formate buffer of pH 3.5 was used for the separation, a significant amount of dephosphorylation occurred during the subsequent lyophilization. The preparations thus obtained were no purer than those obtained from a small column, and the method was discontinued even though sharp separations had been obtained.

The availability of a free-flow continuous electrophoresis apparatus led us to reconsider the method. Since in this apparatus there is no supporting medium, contamination by the paper was eliminated. Partial dephosphorylation occurring during lyophilization was eliminated by carrying out the lyophilization in the presence of triethylamine at pH 9.0.

This paper describes the separation of: (*1*) four deoxymononucleotides, (*2*) adenosine mono-, di-, and triphosphates (AMP, ADP, and ATP), (*3*) some derivatives of deoxyadenylate, (*4*) some pairs of dinucleotides. These methods of separation and subsequent recovery by lyophilization at pH 9 are particularly recommended for the identification and quantitative determination of terminal groups in short oligonucleotides, because the products obtained are of high purity and can be used for further spectral or chromatographic analysis.

[1] Supported by Grants E 157G and PRP-30 of the American Cancer Society, GB-4274 of the National Science Foundation, and DRG-934 of the Damon Runyon Memorial Fund, and contract AT(30-1)3630 from the Atomic Energy Commission.

METHODS AND MATERIALS

The instrument, a continuous-flow electrophoretic separator (model FF), was purchased from Brinkmann Instruments, Inc., Westbury, New York. Tygon tubing (i.d. 1.5 mm) was used throughout. The selection of appropriate values for the buffer velocity and for the suction intervals was chosen from Table I of "Operating Manual 109" supplied by the manufacturer. Nepton ion-exchange membranes were used in both electrode compartments. All separations were performed at 5°. The smallest dosing pump supplied by the manufacturer was used to provide a feeding rate of sample in the range of 0.5 to 1.5 ml/hr.

Adenosine mono-, di-, and triphosphates, and 5′-deoxyribomononucleotides were purchased from P-L biochemicals, Inc., Milwaukee, Wis. The 3′-terminated deoxyribonucleotides (mono- and di-) were isolated in this laboratory from a digest of thymus DNA (4) with micrococcal nuclease (5). Dephosphorylation of d-ApAp was accomplished with prostatic phosphatase (6), and hydrolysis into A and pAp with venom exonuclease (7). Buffers were prepared from reagent-grade chemicals.

RESULTS

Several attempts were made to separate the four mononucleotides by varying the concentration and flow rate of buffer, the voltage, and the rate of sample feeding. The cleanest separation achieved is illustrated in Figure 1. Conditions for the separation are specified in the legend. The

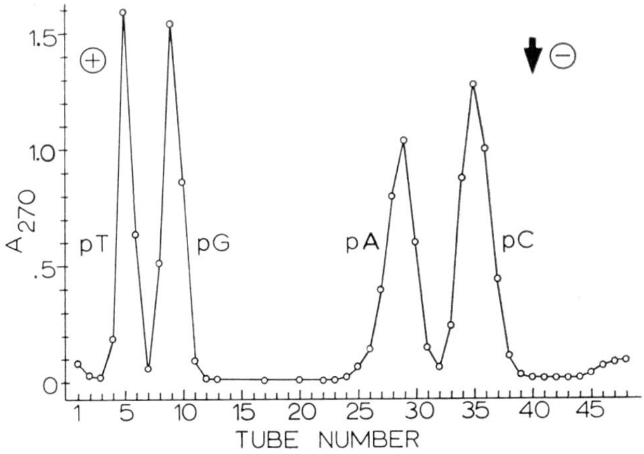

FIG. 1. Separation of deoxyribonucleotides. Buffer, ammonium acetate, pH 3.5. Electrode rinsing buffer, 0.5 M. Buffer in separation chamber, 0.15 M. Buffer flow, 60 ml/hr. Peristaltic pump set at 4 rpm. Rate of sample feeding, 0.5 ml/hr. Substance concentration, 20 A_{260} units/ml. Volts 2500, mA 100. In this and in all subsequent figures the arrow indicates the sample entrance port.

same pattern was obtained with sample feed rates as high as 1.5 ml/hr. As expected, the method is equally successful with 3′-mononucleotides (not shown).

The separation of 5′-AMP, ADP, and ATP was first attempted at a pH around 9 (the optimum of venom exonuclease). AMP was separated completely from the other two, but only a partial separation of di- and triphosphate occurred. At pH 5.0, complete separation of all three nucleotides was obtained, as shown in Figure 2.

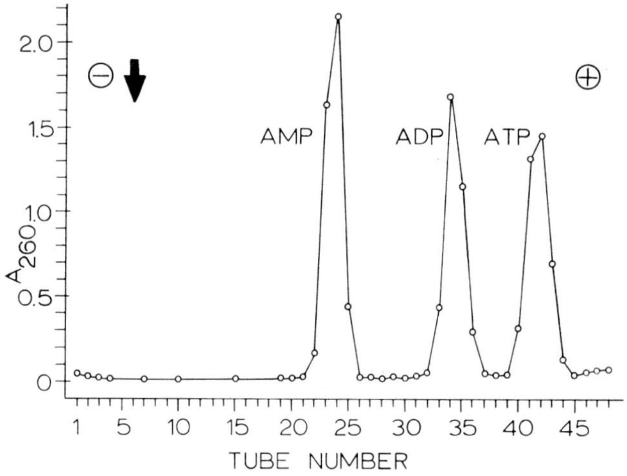

FIG. 2. Separation of AMP, ADP, and ATP. Buffer, ammonium acetate, pH 5.0. Electrode rinsing buffer, 0.15 *M*. Buffer in separation chamber, 0.05 *M*. Buffer flow, 50 ml/hr. Peristaltic pump set at 3.5 rpm. Rate of sample feeding, 0.5 ml/hr. Substance concentration, 35 A_{260} units/ml. Volts 1400, mA 155.

The mononucleotide d-Ap and the dinucleotide d-ApAp were isolated from a sample of thymus DNA digested with micrococcal nuclease. A portion of the dinucleotide was digested with venom exonuclease to form d-A + d-pAp. Another portion was dephosphorylated with prostatic phosphatase to yield d-ApA. The mixture of these five components (deoxyadenosine was supplemented) was resolved under the conditions specified in Figure 3. The separation of all five components was satisfactory.

The experiment illustrated in Figure 4 was selected to show the removal of a colored contaminant acquired during the preceeding chromatography on Dowex 1-X2. This contaminant, which has a high absorbancy at 260 mμ, is quantitatively removed in the first 4 tubes adjacent to the cathode. The experiment (Fig. 4) also illustrates the broadness of the region in which dinucleotides appear, since d-CpCp is the slowest moving dinucleotide whereas d-GpGp is the third fastest. The fastest is d-TpTp.

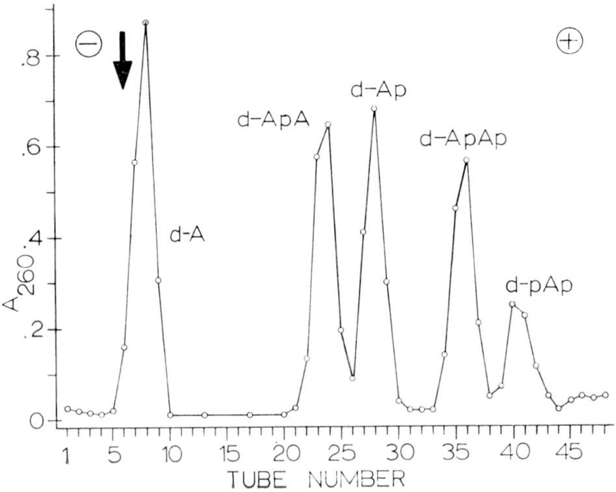

FIG. 3. Separation of d-A, d-Ap, d-ApA, d-ApAp, and d-pAp. Buffer, ammonium acetate, pH 5.0. Electrode rinsing buffer, 0.15 *M*. Buffer in separation chamber, 0.05 *M*. Buffer flow, 50 ml/hr. Peristaltic pump set at 3.5 rpm. Rate of sample feeding, 1.5 ml/hr. Substance concentration, 15 A_{260} units/ml. Volts 1600, mA 180.

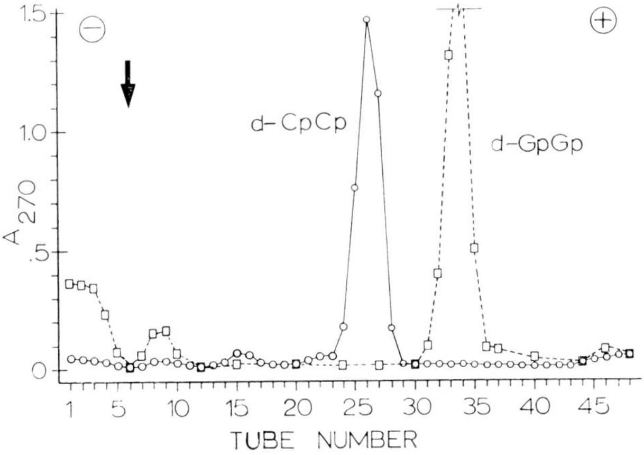

FIG. 4. Separation of dinucleotides from Dowex contaminants. Buffer, ammonium acetate, pH 5.0. Electrode rinsing buffer, 0.15 *M*. Buffer in separation chamber, 0.05 *M*. Buffer flow, 50 ml/hr. Peristaltic pump set at 3.5 rpm. Rate of sample feeding, 1.5 ml/hr. Substance concentration, 15 A_{270} units/ml. Volts 1400, mA 180. Squares and circles indicate separate runs.

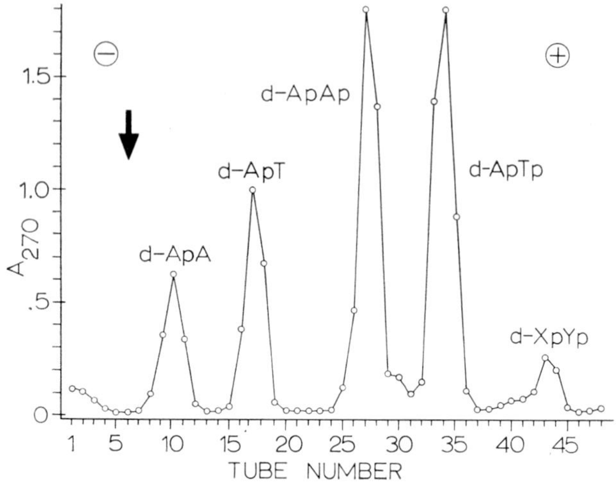

FIG. 5. Separation of d-ApAp, d-ApTp, d-ApA, d-ApT, and d-XpYp. Buffer, ammonium acetate, pH 3.5. Electrode rinsing buffer, 0.5 M. Buffer in separation chamber, 0.15 M. Buffer flow, 82 ml/hr. Peristaltic pump set at 5 rpm. Rate of sample feeding, 1.5 ml/hr. Substance concentration, 15 A_{270} units/ml. Volts 2500, mA 100.

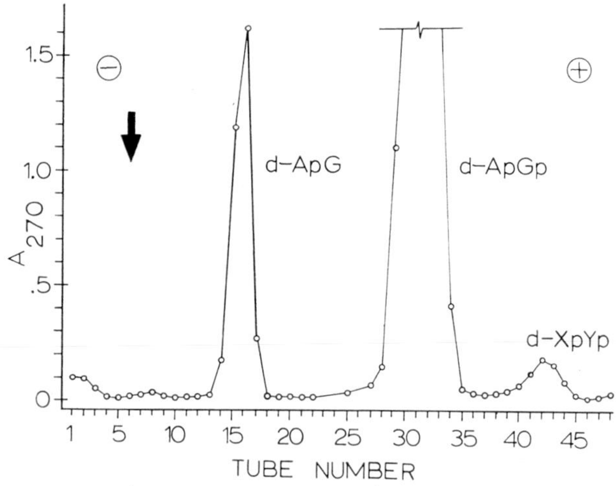

FIG. 6. Purification of d-ApGp. Buffer, ammonium acetate, pH 3.5. Electrode rinsing buffer, 0.5 M. Buffer in separation chamber, 0.15 M. Buffer flow, 82 ml/hr. Peristaltic pump set at 5 rpm. Rate of sample feeding, 1.5 ml/hr. Substance concentration, 30 A_{270} units/ml. Volts 2500, mA 100.

Figure 5 shows the separation of two dinucleotides (d-ApTp and d-ApAp) and their respective dephosphorylation products (d-ApT and d-ApA). The small peak, representing a third dinucleotide, was not identified.

The next three figures indicate the efficiency of purification of a dinucleotide d-ApGp. The experiment shown in Figure 6 was performed with the material obtained from a Dowex 1-X2 column, after preliminary removal of a colored contaminant at pH 5.0 (not illustrated). At pH 3.5 (Fig. 6), dinucleotide is separated from a small amount of an unidentified contaminating dinucleotide, and from a fairly large amount of d-ApG produced by dephosphorylation during lyophilization for several days in the presence of ammonium acetate. Figure 7 illustrates an experiment in which the d-ApGp recovered in the previous experiment was lyophilized for 24 hr directly from ammonium acetate buffer. As expected, significant dephosphorylation occurred again. However, when the peak representing d-ApGp was lyophilized after adjusting the pH to 9.0 with triethylamine, dephosphorylation was prevented, as is shown in Figure 8.

DISCUSSION

Figure 3 should be considered as a simplified case (because only one base is involved) of separation of products expected from the digestion by micrococcal nuclease of a pentanucleotide terminated in a 5′-monophosphate:

$$\text{pApApApApA} \rightarrow \text{pAp} + \text{ApAp} + \text{Ap} + \text{ApA} + \text{A}$$

In the case of a more complex pentanucleotide, where two dinucleotides may be formed, fractionation at pH 5.0 should not be attempted; but in a significant number of possible combinations fractionation at pH 3.5 is likely to succeed.

At pH 5.0 no complete segregation of dinucleotides and mononucleotides into separate groups can be assured. A comparison of Figures 2 and 4 shows that overlapping of fast mononucleotides with slow dinucleotides can occur. However, with the limited number of combinations expected in digests of homogeneous pentanucleotides, the chance of successful group segregation is quite high.

SUMMARY

A semimicro preparative electrophoretic method for the isolation of nucleotides and their derivatives is described. The instrument used is a continuous-flow electrophoretic separator (model FF, Brinkmann). The method is applicable to separation of (*1*) mono-, di-, and triphosphates of a nucleoside, (*2*) individual mononucleotides from their mixtures, (*3*)

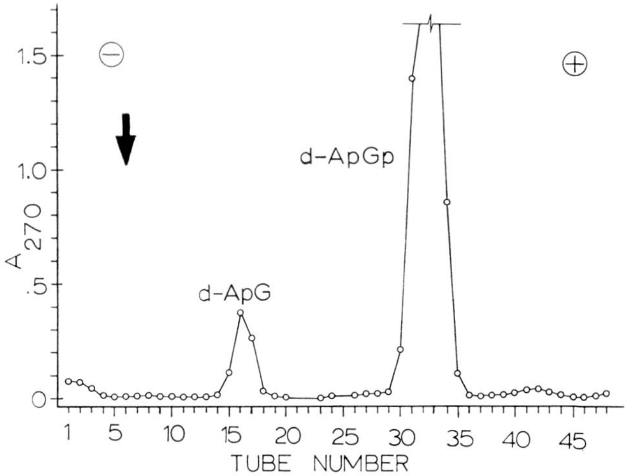

FIG. 7. Purification of d-ApGp. Conditions of separation as shown in Figure 6 except for substance concentration of 15 A_{270} units/ml.

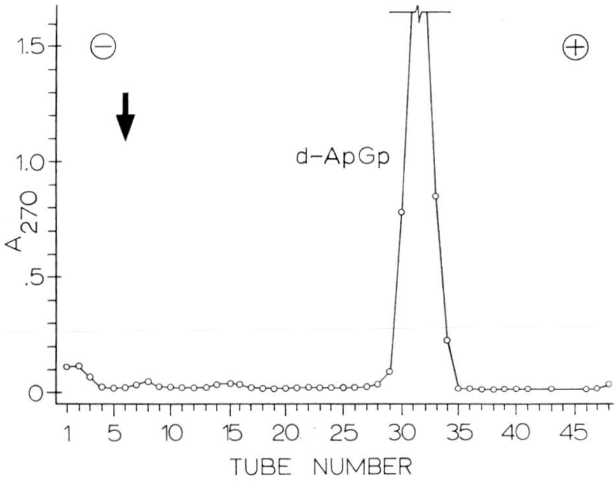

FIG. 8. Purification of d-ApGp. Conditions of separation as shown in Figure 6 except for substance concentration of 15 A_{270} units/ml.

various digestion products of deoxyadenylic pentanucleotide, and (*4*) pairs of some dinucleotides and their dephosphorylation products.

REFERENCES

1. Markham, R., and Smith, J. D., *Biochem. J.* **52**, 558 (1952).
2. Rushizky, G. W., and Knight, C. A., *Virology* **11**, 236 (1960).
3. Peterson, G. B., *Biochim. Biophys. Acta* **51**, 212 (1961).
4. Kay, E. R. M., Simmons, N. S., and Dounce, A. L., *J. Am. Chem. Soc.* **74**, 1724 (1952).
5. Sulkowski, E., and Laskowski, M., Sr., *J. Biol. Chem.* **241**, 4386 (1966).
6. Ostrowski, W., and Tsugita, A., *Arch. Biochem. Biophys.* **94**, 68 (1961).
7. Richards, G. M., Tutas, D., Wechter, W. J., and Laskowski, M., Sr., (unpublished).

ANALYTICAL BIOCHEMISTRY 20, 102–113 (1967)

A Combination Membrane–Gas Detector for Monitoring Concentrations of Dissolved Volatiles[1]

ARTHUR KARMEN

Department of Radiological Science, The Johns Hopkins Medical Institutions, Baltimore, Maryland 21205

Received January 11, 1967

Gas chromatography (GC) is often the method chosen for measuring the concentration of one volatile substance dissolved in another primarily because of the high sensitivity of the GC detector. When it is desired to monitor a concentration that changes rapidly the several minutes usually necessary for analysis by GC may be a limitation. In many of these instances it may be possible to select a detector that is insensitive to the larger component of the mixture, the solvent, and highly sensitive to the smaller component, or solute. Continuous measurement or monitoring of the concentration of solute is then possible, provided that a means can be found to deliver the sample to the detector.

In this paper, a method is described for continuously measuring the concentration of a volatile compound dissolved in an aqueous stream, suitable for use with a variety of sensitive detectors, that is based on the high permeability of thin elastomer membranes to volatile compounds. A thin membrane is mounted so that one surface is in contact with the solution to be sampled. A stream of gas is passed over the other surface, and then is delivered to the detector, carrying with it the volatile material that has permeated the membrane.

MATERIALS AND METHODS

Membrane Mounting

Two kinds of membrane mountings were used. The first was designed for sampling solutions flowing in narrow-bore channels such as blood vessels. In two of the constructions shown in Figure 1, the membrane was mounted by clamping it between two sections of closely fitting, concentric polytetrafluoroethylene tubing. In the third, the rubber sheeting was cemented to itself to form a tightly fitting sleeve over a perfo-

[1] This work was supported by U.S.P.H.S. Grant GM-11535.

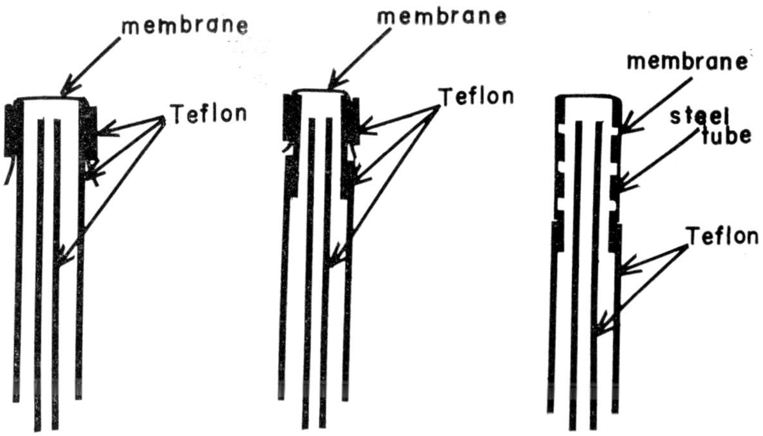

FIG. 1. Membranes mounted at or near the ends of long, narrow bore tubes.

rated stainless steel tube. An example of the second kind of mounting, for use in sampling larger volumes of solution, is shown in Figure 2. The membrane was clamped between the nylon ferrules of a tubing connector provided with a gas inlet and outlet.

Membrane Materials

A number of different kinds of membranes were tested. The silicone rubber was a dimethyl silicone film (Dow Corning Corp.) 0.005 in.

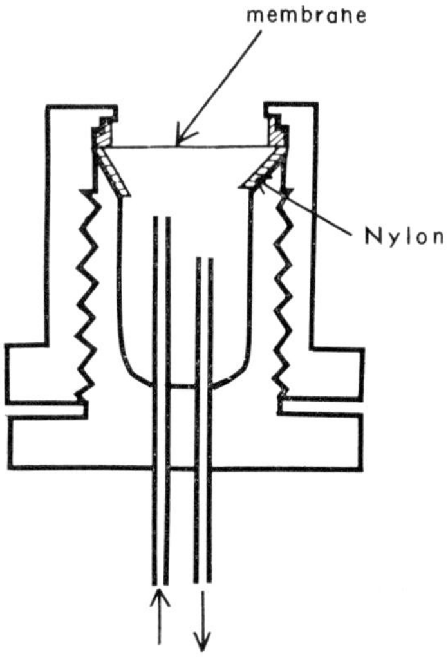

FIG. 2. Membrane clamped between ferrules of modified gas tubing connector provided with gas inlet and an outlet.

thick; the polyethylene film, 0.009 in. thick, was low-density polyethylene; the Teflon film was Du Pont polytetrafluoroethylene, 0.00012 in. thick; dental dam was 0.003 in. thick (Hygienic Dental Manufacturing Co., Akron, Ohio). Saran, 0.001 in. thick, was the commercial wrapping product (Dow Saran Wrap). The "cellophane" was A. H. Thomas Co. dialyzer tubing, 0.001 in. thick.

Detector

The detector chosen for most of the work reported here was a hydrogen flame ionization detector essentially as described for use in gas chromatography by McWilliam and Dewar (1). The detector was constructed as shown in Figure 3. Hydrogen gas and an inert carrier gas (such as nitrogen, or argon) were delivered to the base of the stainless-steel jet, mixed, and burned in air that was supplied through a separate connection at the base of the outer cylinder. The entire detector was electrically grounded except the platinum wire ring electrode suspended above the jet, which was maintained at 90 V above ground. The current flowing through the gas between the ring electrode and the detector body was monitored using a Cary model 31 vibrating reed electrometer and a strip-chart recorder. The response of this detector had been found experimentally in GC analyses to be linearly related to the rate of delivery of organic vapor.

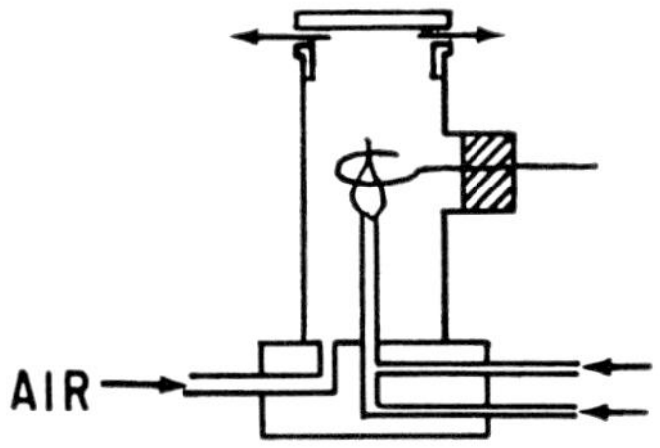

FIG. 3. Schematic diagram of hydrogen flame ionization detector used in most of this work.

Gas Connections

Carrier gas was delivered to a membrane mounted over the end of a tube through a smaller diameter tube threaded through the bore of the tube and returned through the unfilled bore. External gas connections were made with the fitting shown in Figure 4. The diameters of the steel tubes were slightly larger than the inner diameter of the Teflon tubes so that, when the Teflon tubes were pushed over the steel tubes, the resulting connections were gastight.

Test Solutions

Dilute aqueous solutions containing "known" concentrations of diethyl ether and chloroform were prepared by injecting small quantities of these compounds, less than required to saturate the solution, directly into the water. Dilute solutions of ethylene and acetylene were prepared by saturating water at 0°C with these gases and then diluting these solutions. The values for the solubility of these gases quoted in "Handbook of Chemistry and Physics" (2) were used to estimate the final concentrations.

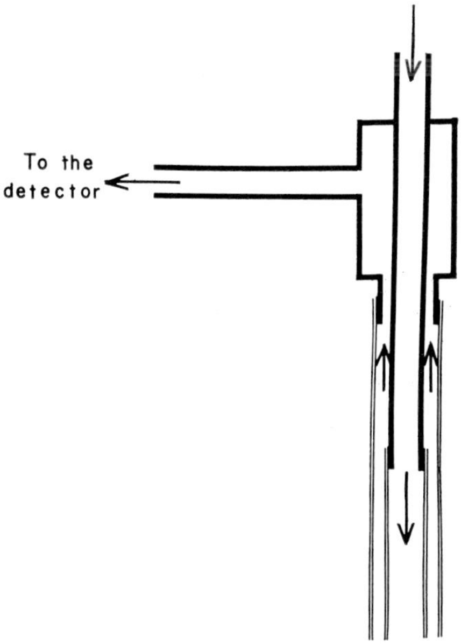

FIG. 4. Device for delivery of carrier gas to inner, narrow-bore tube leading to membrane and for conducting gas returning from membrane in unfilled bore of outer tube to the detector.

Effects of Concentration, Area of Membrane, Temperature, and Pressure on Response of the System

The relationship between the response of the membrane-ionization detector and the concentration of ether or chloroform in the water was determined by immersing a membrane in a continuously stirred volume of water and injecting successive 10 μl aliquots of ether or chloroform into the water.

The relationship between the area of the membrane and the response of the system was tested using membranes 2.8, 78, and 109 mm^2 in area. The first membrane was mounted as shown in the center picture of Figure 1, and the other two as in Figure 2. Two different concentrations of ether in water were tested with each membrane. Also tested were the effect of temperature of the solution, between 5 and 40°C, and the effect of change of external pressure between atmospheric pressure and 10 psi above atmospheric pressure.

Permeability of Membrane to Different Compounds

When a membrane sampling device is placed in a solution of an organic compound, the response of the detector depends on the permeability of the membrane and the sensitivity of the detector to that specific compound, as well as on its concentration in the solution. Since the sensitivity of the flame detector to different compounds is different, the permeability cannot be read directly from the detector response. The permeabilities were measured by determining the clearance of each compound, which may be defined as the volume of solution containing the quantity of compound that is delivered to the detector in a unit time period, the volume which, if completely cleared, would have supplied that quantity to the detector. Clearances were measured as follows: a glass-T filled with glass wool was placed in the gas line between the membrane and the flame detector. The membrane was placed in a water solution of the substance to be tested and the increase in current, the signal current, was measured. Known small amounts of the same solution were then injected into the T, yielding "peaks" of current. The signal current in amperes (coulombs/sec) divided by the area of the peak (coulombs/μl injected) yielded the "clearance" of this substance in microliters of solution per second. The clearance measurements were thus independent of the differences in the sensitivity of the hydrogen flame ionization detector for different substances.

The response time of a catheter tip detector was studied by mounting it in a flowing tap water stream and rapidly injecting 2 ml aliquots of saturated solutions of ether, chloroform, ethylene, and acetylene approximately 2 in. upstream from the detector. The water flow rate was sufficiently high so that the lag between the time of injection and the time of arrival of the solution at the membrane was insignificant. It was assumed that the water in the vicinity of the membrane contained organic material only very briefly and that its concentration as a function of time could be considered a spike of insignificant width and that any width in the observed detector response reflected the response time of the system. The effect of gas-flow rate through the catheter on the speed of response was then determined by varying the flow between 15 and 60 ml/min.

RESULTS

Relationship between Response and Concentration

The response of a silicone rubber–flame ionization detector system to diethyl ether or chloroform in aqueous solution was linearly related to their concentrations in the water (Figures 5A and B).

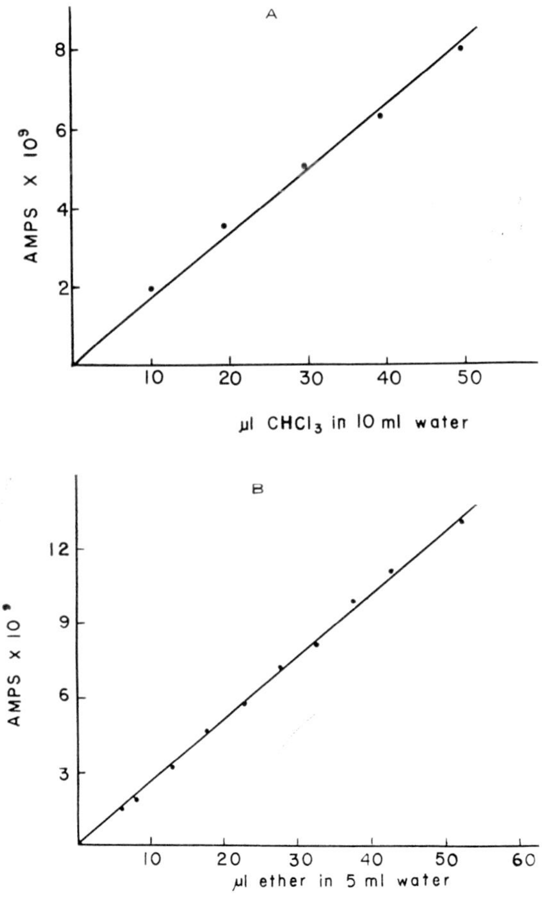

FIG. 5. Relationship between response of silicone rubber membrane (3 mm^2)–flame ionization detector system and concentration of (A) chloroform and (B) ether.

Relationship between Response and Area of Membranes, Temperature and Pressure

The rate of delivery of ether to the detector was directly proportional to the area of the membrane (Table 1) and increased linearly with

TABLE 1
Relationship between Area of Membrane and Quantity of Ether Passing through It in a Given Time

Membrane diameter, mm.	Current, A	Relative area	Relative current
1. 1.9	0.33×10^{-11}	1	1
2. 10.0	10.2×10^{-10}	27.7	30.9
3. 11.8	13.0×10^{-10}	38.6	39.4
Repeated at second concentration of ether in water			
1. 1.9	1.17×10^{-10}	1	1
2. 10.0	3.76×10^{-9}	27.7	32.1
3. 11.8	4.36×10^{-9}	38.6	37.3

temperature over the range tested (Figure 6). Increasing the external pressure on the solution, over the range of 0 to 300 mm Hg, had no effect on the rate of transport of ether.

Clearance of Various Compounds through Silicone Rubber Membrane

The clearances of chloroform and ethylene by the silicone rubber membrane were several times greater than the clearances of acetylene, ether, and ethanol (Table 2).

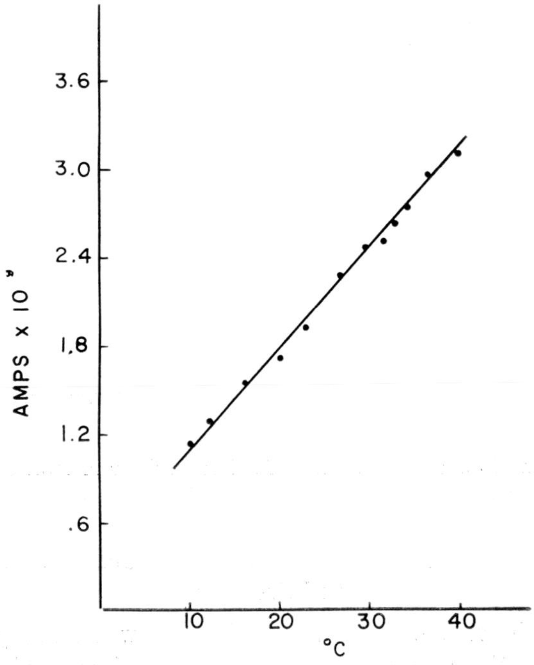

FIG. 6. Relationship between detector response and temperature of solution.

TABLE 2
Clearances through 2 mm Diameter Membranes (in μl/sec)

Membrane	Diethyl ether	Chloroform	Ethanol	Acetylene	Ethylene
Silicone rubber 0.005″	0.1	0.36	10^{-3}	0.16	0.34
0.003″ (stretched)	0.31	0.62	3×10^{-3}	0.17	0.37
Saran 0.001″	—	—	1.3×10^{-5}	—	—
Dental dam 0.003″	5×10^{-2}	0.33	10^{-4}	0.037	0.1
Polyethylene 0.0009″	0.008	2.4×10^{-2}	4×10^{-5}	3.7×10^{-3}	10^{-2}
Teflon 0.00012″	5×10^{-3}	10^{-2}	3×10^{-4}	1.3×10^{-2}	3.7×10^{-2}
Cellophane 0.001″	7×10^{-2}	7×10^{-2}	3×10^{-3}	2.5×10^{-2}	10^{-2}

Speed of Response of Membrane Detector

The responses of the silicone rubber membrane mounted on the end of a long tube detector to the passage of very narrow spikes of concentrations of ether, chloroform, ethylene, and acetylene past the membrane are shown in Figure 7. There were no appreciable differences

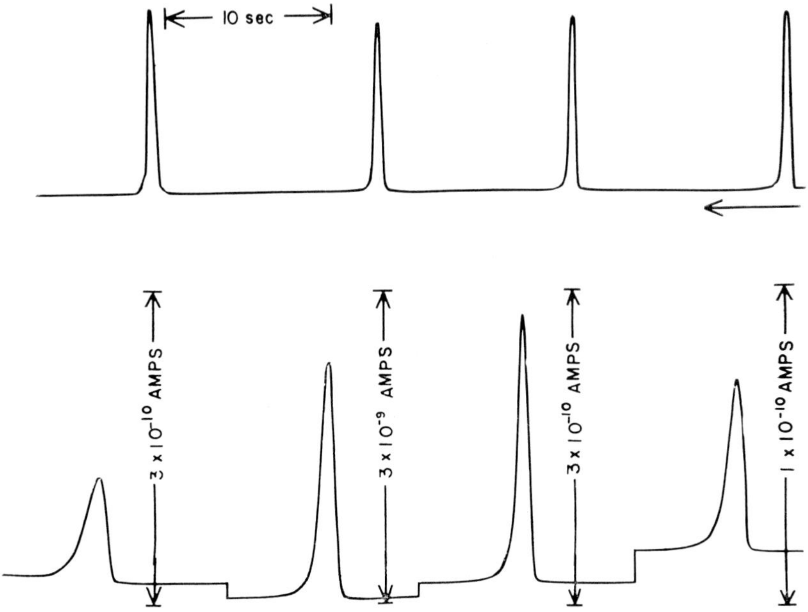

FIG. 7. Responses of silicone rubber membrane to sharp spikes of concentrations of various organic compounds passing the membrane. An electrical impulse was recorded on the upper channel of the 2-channel recorder at the time of the injection; the response of the detector was recorded on the lower channel. The compounds were, right to left: (1) ethylene, (2) acetylene, (3) diethyl ether, and (4) chloroform, injected as 2 ml samples of aqueous solutions.

among the responses to these compounds. There was a lag of approximately 4 sec on the average between the time of injection and the time of arrival of the material at the detector. The lag was reduced by increasing the gas-flow rate up to 60 ml/min. Further increase in flow caused no further reduction.

Effect of Stirring

All the experiments reported above were performed with the solution tested kept stirred briskly, usually through the use of a magnetic stirrer. When the stirring was stopped, the response fell to less than 20% of its previous level, although it remained directly related to the concentration of the organic material in the water.

APPLICATIONS

This method of detecting volatile organic compounds in aqueous solutions was of particular interest because of the possibility of using the membrane as an intravascular detector to monitor materials dissolved in blood. An experiment was performed in which a silicone rubber membrane, 2 mm in diameter, mounted over the end of a long tube that simulated a cardiac catheter, was placed in the pulmonary artery of a dog. Figure 8 shows the response of the hydrogen flame ionization detector when a 2 ml sample of saline saturated with diethyl ether was injected into the femoral vein.

There was no detectable change in the response of the membrane during prolonged immersion in either saline or citrated blood *in vitro*.

DISCUSSION

The hydrogen flame ionization detector is well suited for monitoring organic compounds in aqueous solution, as described here, because of its insensitivity to water vapor and because of its high sensitivity to a variety of compounds. If more than one volatile is present and it is necessary to distinguish among them, more selective responses can be obtained with other detectors. Exploratory experiments with an electron affinity detector showed that much smaller concentrations of chloroform could be detected. Unfortunately, the sensitivity of this detector was decreased when the membrane was immersed in water. It therefore seemed likely that smaller membranes would be required for use with this detector despite their lower permeation rates, to minimize the concentration of water vapor reaching the detector. Fewer difficulties of this type would be expected with other, more specific devices such as halogen detectors and radioactivity detectors.

The combination of silicone rubber membrane and hydrogen flame detector has many possible applications. It could form the basis of a detection system for liquid chromatography, particularly for analyses of volatile organic compounds that can be chromatographed with aqueous solvents. In this application it would offer the advantages of insensitivity to nonvolatile inorganic materials and also to nonvolatile organic compounds as long as they did not change the permeability of the membrane. The same characteristics would be useful if the system were used for continuously following the progress of enzyme reactions that result in the formation of volatile products.

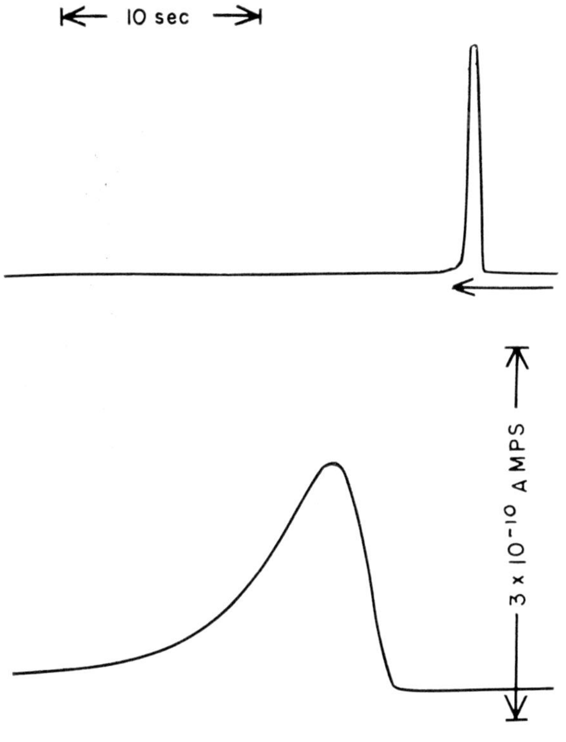

FIG. 8. Concentration, as a function of time, of diethyl ether in pulmonary arterial blood of a dog after injection into a femoral vein of 2 ml normal saline saturated with ether. The concentration was sensed by a silicone rubber membrane inserted within the artery. The pulse on the upper graph was recorded at the time of injection. The response of the hydrogen flame ionization detector is recorded in the lower graph.

A variety of membrane materials can be used. Several offer selectively high permeability to specific compounds. It is also possible to sample the gas above the gas–liquid interface, instead of the gas above the membrane surface. The detector response then depends more directly on the vapor pressure of the organic material in the solution. When an open-end tube was placed open end down in a solution and was supplied with afferent and efferent gas flows, just as though a membrane were present, the detector response was also linearly related to the concentration of organic volatile in the solution. However, since the tube tended to entrap a small volume of liquid near its opening, diffusion of volatiles from the neighboring solution determined the response of the system rather than only the rate of passage of the volatile into the gas phase. A faster response was obtained when the gas pressure in the tube was increased so that a small number of bubbles escaped continuously from the end of the tube.

The membrane–gas detector combination was of particular interest because of the possibility of using the membrane as an intravascular detector. It could be used, for example, for monitoring the blood levels of volatile anesthetic agents or for monitoring the concentration of injected tracer substances at various points in the circulatory system which would be useful in studies of cardiovascular dynamics and in the detection of abnormal circulatory pathways. The solutions of volatile compounds detected as described here could substitute as tracers for solutions of dyes detected by colorimetry and for solutions of easily reduced or oxidized compounds detected by polarographic methods. There should be no significant hazard from gas embolism since only low flow rates are required and it is possible to use carbon dioxide, which is highly soluble in blood, as the inert gas. Several of the experiments reported here were designed to determine which organic compounds would be most suitable as tracers. Several of those tested had limited solubility in water, several were not cleared efficiently, and others were not sensitively detected by the flame detector. Diethyl ether, chloroform, and acetylene seemed most promising.

With appropriate detectors, the same approach can also be used for monitoring the blood levels of radioactive gases and for monitoring the "tensions" of such nonradioactive gases as carbon dioxide and oxygen. The response of the membrane is not quite so rapid as those of some of the polarographic intravascular detectors. The membrane systems would therefore be less useful for following very rapid changes in concentration such as those that accompany individual cardiac contractions. Since many phenomena of biological interest do not occur quite so rapidly, the somewhat slower response time of the membrane system may not represent a serious limitation.

SUMMARY

A method is described for monitoring the concentration of a volatile organic compound dissolved in an aqueous medium. A thin rubber membrane is mounted so that one surface is in contact with the solution to be monitored. A stream of gas passing over the other surface delivers the volatile material that has permeated the membrane to a sensitive gas chromatography detector. The response of the membrane–detector system is proportional to the concentration of organic materials in the water. The permeability of different membranes to different compounds varies offering a degree of selectivity. The membrane–gas detector has been used as an intravascular sampling device for monitoring the changes in the blood concentrations of volatile organic compounds injected as tracers.

ACKNOWLEDGMENT

Much of the experimental work reported here was performed in the Laboratory of Technical Development of the National Heart Institute. The expert assistance of Mrs. Betsy Nagel and the advice and encouragement of Dr. Robert L. Bowman are greatly appreciated.

REFERENCES

1. McWilliam, I. G., and Dewar, R. A., *Nature* **181,** 760 (1958).
2. "Handbook of Chemistry and Physics," (Weast, R. C., ed), 45th ed. Chemical Rubber Co., Cleveland, Ohio, 1964.

ANALYTICAL BIOCHEMISTRY **20**, 114–149 (1967)

Tables for Estimating Sedimentation through Linear Concentration Gradients of Sucrose Solution

C. R. McEWEN

Beckman Instruments, Inc., Spinco Division, 1117 California Avenue, Palo Alto, California 94304

Received July 24, 1966

The separation of particles according to rate of sedimentation through sucrose density gradients has become a widely used technique in biology. This paper presents extensive tables by means of which band velocity (rate-zonal) centrifuge experiments can be designed and interpreted. That is, the time required for a particle of known sedimentation coefficient to move a given distance at a given rate of rotation can be estimated, or the sedimentation coefficient associated with an observed movement of zone can be inferred.

The computation has been made under the assumption that the sucrose concentration varies linearly with distance from the center of rotation.

The computational model is essentially that of an inert, nondiffusing particle sedimenting through an unchanging density gradient, and has been discussed by numerous authors (1–5). In this model the rate of sedimentation varies directly with density difference between particle and solution, and inversely with solution viscosity.

There are experimental situations to which the computational model will not apply, such as:

(*a*) The particle density is affected by the gradient; for example, the state of hydration may be a function of the water activity.

(*b*) The movement of a zone differs from the movement of a single particle as a result of particle concentration; for example, a local density inversion may cause convection if concentrations were to build up (6). When diffusion is important, the concentration maximum may not coincide with the movement predicted from the sedimentation coefficient alone (7).

(*c*) The sucrose concentration distribution changes appreciably during the separation. Thermodynamic treatment of the type outlined by Ifft *et al.* (8) and Trautman (9) shows that commonly used preformed sucrose gradients are more shallow than the equilibrium gradients at rates of rotation higher than about 25,000 rpm, and therefore that sedimentation of sucrose will occur. However, we find that more than 24 hr, even at 65,000 rpm, is required before serious changes in gradient shape appear (10).

(*d*) Pressure-dependent effects become important. In the lower parts of columns being centrifuged at rates of rotation of 50,000 rpm and up, the sucrose solution viscosity and density, as well as the particle density, may be affected. We do not have data at present to account adequately for this. The viscosity data for water (11) indicate that the pressure should not change the viscosity, and hence the instantaneous sedimentation rate, by more than 10%, and probably by much less in the typical situation. The density correction is probably smaller than the viscosity correction.

Outside of these restrictions, there remain many applications for which the computed results should be useful. This includes rate separations for viruses, nucleic acids, proteins, and cell organelles.

MATHEMATICAL STATEMENT OF THE PROBLEM

Symbols and Their Dimensions

G, relative sedimentation velocity, dimensionless

I, sedimentation integral, dimensionless

r, distance in direction of centrifugal force field (L)

t, time (T)

p, subscript referring to sedimenting particle

s, sedimentation coefficient (T)

T, temperature (°C)

w, subscript referring to pure water

z, solute concentration, weight fraction (dimensionless)

z_0, solute concentration corresponding to extrapolation of linear solute concentration distribution to zero radius

ω, angular velocity (T^{-1})

ρ, solution density (ML^{-3})

η, solution viscosity ($ML^{-1}T^{-1}$), where M, L, and T are mass, length, and time)

The instantaneous rate of sedimentation is given by:

$$\frac{dr}{dt} = s(r)\omega^2 r \tag{1}$$

The sedimentation coefficient can be determined for any sucrose concentration and temperature from:

$$s(z, \mathrm{T}) = s_{20,w} \frac{\eta_{20,w}}{\eta(z, \mathrm{T})} \cdot \frac{\rho_p - \rho(z, \mathrm{T})}{\rho_p - \rho_{20,w}} \tag{2}$$

(See reference 12 for example.) In our computation, a particle density and a temperature are assumed.

Define the following function:

$$G(z, \mathrm{T}, \rho_p) = \frac{\eta(z, \mathrm{T})}{\eta_{20,w}} \cdot \frac{\rho_p - \rho_{20,w}}{\rho_p - \rho(z, \mathrm{T})} \tag{3}$$

Using this function in equation 1, we have, upon integration:

$$s_{20,w} \int \omega^2 \, dt = \int \frac{G(z, \mathrm{T}, \rho_p)}{r} \, dr + \text{const.} \tag{4}$$

The left-hand member of equation 4 is a dimensionless grouping which reflects the total sedimentation effect. If acceleration and deceleration times are negligible, it simplifies to $s_{20,w}\omega^2 t$, where t is the total time of centrifugation at angular velocity ω.

The right-hand member can be evaluated for a given temperature and particle density if we express either $G(z, \mathrm{T}, \rho_p)$ as a function of position, through the given linear concentration distribution, or r as a function of concentration. It is more convenient to do the latter because the empirical function G need be evaluated only once. Instead of thinking of a particle as moving through the gradient from one radius to another, we can equally well think of it as moving from one sucrose concentration to another.

We specify that the linear sucrose distribution pass through the points (r_1, z_1) and (r_2, z_2), generally the "top" and "bottom" of the gradient at the meniscus and bottom of the tube, although any two positions in the gradient can be used. Let z_0 be the (extrapolated) value which z would have at $r = 0$. Then we have:

$$\frac{dz}{dr} = \frac{z_2 - z_1}{r_2 - r_1} = \frac{z - z_0}{r} \tag{5}$$

Equation 4 then becomes:

$$s_{20,w} \int \omega^2 \, dt = \int \frac{G(z, \mathrm{T}, \rho_p)}{z - z_0} \, dz + \text{const.} \tag{6}$$

A convenient form for computing z_0 is:

$$z_0 = \frac{z_1 r_2 - z_2 r_1}{r_2 - r_1} \tag{7}$$

Generally z_0 will have a negative value, but in cases of shallow gradients and small radii it can be positive.

SOURCES OF DATA ON SUCROSE SOLUTIONS

Density

0°C: Landolt-Börnstein,"Physikalische-Chemische Tabellen," Table 101 d, p. 463. Springer-Verlag, Berlin, 1923.

5°C: *0–30% concentration,* Table 101 f, p. 465, Landolt-Börnstein (see above). *30–70% concentration,* by interpolation and extrapolation of the data from Landolt-Börnstein. By taking differences in Table 101 f, it was found that the first difference (i.e., slope) in the specific volume-concentration data at 5°C is very nearly a constant proportion of the difference between the differences at 0°C and 10°C. That is, representing differences by Δ and temperature by a subscript:

$$\frac{\Delta_5 - \Delta_0}{\Delta_{10} - \Delta_0} = \text{const.} = 0.567$$

This value was assumed to be valid at higher concentrations, and a table of first differences for the specific volume-concentration data obtained by interpolating between the first differences at 0°C and 10°C:

$$\Delta_5 = \Delta_0 + 0.567(\Delta_{10} - \Delta_0)$$

From the table of first differences at 5°C, the specific volume table was obtained by adding up the differences, starting at 30% concentration.

20°C: Schneider, F., Schliephake, D., and Klimmek, A., Sonderbeilage zur Zeitschrift *Zucker* **16,** 1–19 (1963).

Viscosity

Viscosity data are all based on the publication of Swindells, J. F., Snyder, C. F., Hardy, R. C., and Golden, P. E., "Viscosities of Sucrose Solutions at Various Temperatures: Tables of Recalculated Values," Supplement to *National Bureau of Standards Circular 440 (1958).*

Viscosity-concentration data above 20% concentration are entered directly from Table 132 (revised 1957).

Viscosity data between 0 and 20% concentration are obtained by an interpolation formula suggested in the above publication:

$$\ln \frac{\eta(\mathrm{T}, z)}{\eta(\mathrm{T}, w)} = A(\mathrm{T}) \frac{z}{1 - z} + B(\mathrm{T})z^2$$

Values for the constants A and B were obtained by fitting the above interpolation formula to the viscosity data at 20 and 30% concentration for each temperature desired, with the following results:

T(°C)	*A*	*B*
0	2.7373	1.6371
5	2.6941	1.3697
20	2.5031	0.9366

The ratio of the viscosity of water at a given temperature to its viscosity at 20°C was obtained from the data of Bingham and Jackson, as given in the "Handbook of Chemistry and Physics," 40th ed., pp. 2156, 1958–1959:

T(°C)	$\eta(T, w)/\eta_{20,w}$
0	1.7832
5	1.5113
20	1.0000

USE OF TABLES

The tables contain entries which are the result of carrying out the integration indicated in equation (6) by Simpon's Rule using concentration intervals of 1%. Call the value of the integral $I(z)$. $I(0) = 0$ is the starting point for the integration when $z_0 < 0$. $I(z = 2\%) = 0$ is the starting point when $z_0 = 0$. When $z_0 > 0$, the integration is started at the lowest possible even value of concentration. For example, when $z_0 = 5$, the integration is started at $I(z = 6\%) = 0$.

The appropriate column in the tables is located for temperature, particle density, and gradient orientation (z_0). We then concern ourselves with the sedimentation of the particle from concentration z_1 to concentration z_2. The sedimentation effect is the difference between the two values of the integral in the table, that is:

$$s_{20,w} \int_{t_1}^{t_2} \omega^2 \, dt = I(z_2) - I(z_1) \tag{8}$$

or if constant angular velocity is assumed:

$$s_{20,w} \, \omega^2 (t_2 - t_1) = I(z_2) - I(z_1) \tag{9}$$

Knowledge of any three of the four quantities in equation (9) immediately makes an estimate of the fourth possible. Thus the time for a particle of given sedimentation coefficient to sediment from one position to another in the gradient can be estimated, or conversely the sedimentation coefficient can be inferred from an observed band movement.

Example: How long should we centrifuge a sample in the SW39 rotor to move a 100 S particle having a density of 1.30 to the middle of the tube, which contains a 5 to 20% sucrose gradient? The temperature is 20°C.

1. *Estimate* z_0. $r_1 = 6$ cm, $r_2 = 9$ cm:

$$z_0 = \frac{z_1 r_2 - z_2 r_1}{r_2 - r_1} = \frac{(5 \times 9) - (20 \times 6)}{9 - 6} = -25$$

2. *Determine starting and ending sucrose concentrations.* The starting concentration would be 5%, except that diffusiun would tend to lower it somewhat. Use 4%. The concentration at the middle of the tube would be 12.5%. Suppose we use 12%.

VALUES OF TIME INTEGRAL FOR SUCROSE GRADIENT CENTRIFUGATION
TEMPERATURE 0.0 DEG C PARTICLE DENSITY 1.10

WT.PCT. SUCROSE	ZO= 5	ZO= 0	ZO= -5	ZO= -10	ZO= -15	ZO= -20	ZO= -25	ZO= -30	ZO= -40	ZO= -60	ZO=-100
0	0.0	0.0	0.0	0.0	0.0	0.0	0.0	0.0	0.0	0.0	0.0
2	0.0	0.0	0.6517	0.3538	0.2430	0.1851	0.1495	0.1254	0.0949	0.0638	0.0385
4	0.0	1.5503	1.2161	0.7004	0.4933	0.3810	0.3104	0.2619	0.1996	0.1353	0.0823
6	0.0	2.6175	1.7457	1.0531	0.7578	0.5925	0.4867	0.4130	0.3172	0.2167	0.1327
8	3.4457	3.5221	2.2719	1.4244	1.0447	0.8263	0.6840	0.5837	0.4515	0.3109	0.1917
10	5.3925	4.3763	2.8205	1.8286	1.3647	1.0912	0.9099	0.7806	0.6083	0.4223	0.2622
12	6.9947	5.2471	3.4189	2.2846	1.7330	1.4001	1.1759	1.0142	0.7961	0.5572	0.3485
14	8.5374	6.1955	4.1039	2.8207	2.1734	1.7739	1.5006	1.3011	1.0289	0.7263	0.4577
16	10.1974	7.3020	4.9340	3.4849	2.7271	2.2485	1.9159	1.6704	1.3311	0.9479	0.6023
18	12.1917	8.7105	6.0229	4.3725	3.4762	2.8965	2.4869	2.1807	1.7519	1.2595	0.8075
20	14.9842	10.7703	7.6547	5.7237	4.6291	3.9019	3.3783	2.9813	2.4170	1.7564	1.1375
22	20.5157	14.9947	11.0720	8.5928	7.1017	6.0743	5.3154	4.7292	3.8793	2.8585	1.8758

VALUES OF TIME INTEGRAL FOR SUCROSE GRADIENT CENTRIFUGATION
TEMPERATURE 0.0 DEG C PARTICLE DENSITY 1.20

WT.PCT. SUCROSE	ZO= 5	ZO= 0	ZO= -5	ZO= -10	ZO= -15	ZO= -20	ZO= -25	ZO= -30	ZO= -40	ZO= -60	ZO=-100
0	0.0	0.0	0.0	0.0	0.0	0.0	0.0	0.0	0.0	0.0	0.0
2	0.0	0.0	0.6323	0.3430	0.2356	0.1795	0.1449	0.1216	0.0919	0.0618	0.0374
4	0.0	1.4383	1.1549	0.6638	0.4672	0.3607	0.2938	0.2478	0.1888	0.1280	0.0778
6	0.0	2.3755	1.6195	0.9732	0.6991	0.5462	0.4484	0.3804	0.2919	0.1993	0.1220
8	2.8537	3.1209	2.0528	1.2789	0.9353	0.7386	0.6107	0.5208	0.4024	0.2768	0.1705
10	4.3437	3.7734	2.4716	1.5873	1.1794	0.9407	0.7831	0.6710	0.5220	0.3618	0.2243
12	5.4606	4.3796	2.8880	1.9045	1.4356	1.1555	0.9681	0.8335	0.6526	0.4556	0.2843
14	6.4174	4.9671	3.3121	2.2364	1.7082	1.3868	1.1690	1.0110	0.7967	0.5602	0.3519
16	7.3012	5.5557	3.7535	2.5895	2.0024	1.6390	1.3896	1.2072	0.9572	0.6779	0.4287
18	8.1607	6.1621	4.2220	2.9712	2.3246	1.9176	1.6351	1.4265	1.1380	0.8118	0.5168
20	9.0304	6.8028	4.7292	3.3910	2.6826	2.2298	1.9118	1.6750	1.3444	0.9659	0.6191
22	9.9402	7.4959	5.2891	3.8606	3.0870	2.5848	2.2283	1.9604	1.5831	1.1457	0.7395
24	10.9206	8.2632	5.9194	4.3954	3.5515	2.9953	2.5960	2.2935	1.8633	1.3584	0.8830
26	12.0077	9.1329	6.6442	5.0167	4.0952	3.4787	3.0310	2.6890	2.1980	1.6144	1.0571
28	13.2481	10.1437	7.4971	5.7545	4.7451	4.0595	3.5561	3.1680	2.6055	1.9282	1.2721
30	14.7082	11.3522	8.5280	6.6533	5.5419	4.7750	4.2053	3.7623	3.1137	2.3223	1.5440
32	16.4873	12.8446	9.8133	7.7820	6.5480	5.6825	5.0319	4.5211	3.7657	2.8311	1.8975
34	18.7496	14.7645	11.4808	9.2558	7.8684	6.8785	6.1248	5.5274	4.6342	3.5129	2.3744
36	21.7937	17.3743	13.7648	11.2862	9.6960	8.5401	7.6481	6.9336	5.8531	4.4753	3.0517
38	26.2296	21.2117	17.1461	14.3083	12.4279	11.0327	9.9399	9.0545	7.6988	5.9408	4.0896
40	33.6444	27.6782	22.8794	19.4578	17.1014	15.3108	13.8843	12.7136	10.8953	8.4922	5.9073
42	51.3033	43.1941	36.7161	31.9434	28.4763	25.7565	23.5412	21.6923	18.7685	14.8096	10.4353

VALUES OF TIME INTEGRAL FOR SUCROSE GRADIENT CENTRIFUGATION
TEMPERATURE 0.0 DEG C PARTICLE DENSITY 1.30

WT.PCT. SUCROSE	ZO= 5	ZO= 0	ZO= -5	ZO= -10	ZO= -15	ZO= -20	ZO= -25	ZO= -30	ZO= -40	ZO= -60	ZO=-100
0	0.0	0.0	0.0	0.0	0.0	0.0	0.0	0.0	0.0	0.0	0.0
2	0.0	0.0	0.6252	0.3391	0.2329	0.1774	0.1433	0.1202	0.0909	0.0611	0.0369
4	0.0	1.4023	1.1344	0.6517	0.4585	0.3539	0.2883	0.2432	0.1853	0.1255	0.0763
6	0.0	2.3013	1.5799	0.9483	0.6809	0.5318	0.4365	0.3702	0.2841	0.1939	0.1187
8	2.6939	3.0040	1.9884	1.2364	0.9035	0.7131	0.5895	0.5025	0.3882	0.2670	0.1644
10	4.0728	3.6075	2.3757	1.5217	1.1293	0.9000	0.7489	0.6415	0.4988	0.3455	0.2142
12	5.0848	4.1566	2.7529	1.8089	1.3613	1.0946	0.9164	0.7886	0.6171	0.4305	0.2685
14	5.9318	4.6767	3.1282	2.1027	1.6025	1.2993	1.0942	0.9457	0.7446	0.5231	0.3283
16	6.6943	5.1844	3.5089	2.4072	1.8563	1.5168	1.2845	1.1149	0.8830	0.6246	0.3945
18	7.4147	5.6926	3.9015	2.7271	2.1262	1.7502	1.4901	1.2987	1.0345	0.7367	0.4683
20	8.1201	6.2122	4.3129	3.0675	2.4165	2.0033	1.7145	1.5001	1.2019	0.8617	0.5513
22	8.8311	6.7538	4.7503	3.4343	2.7324	2.2807	1.9618	1.7231	1.3883	1.0022	0.6453
24	9.5649	7.3280	5.2220	3.8346	3.0800	2.5879	2.2370	1.9724	1.5980	1.1613	0.7527
26	10.3388	7.9471	5.7379	4.2768	3.4670	2.9319	2.5465	2.2538	1.8362	1.3435	0.8766
28	11.1709	8.6251	6.3100	4.7716	3.9029	3.3215	2.8987	2.5751	2.1095	1.5539	1.0208
30	12.0827	9.3797	6.9537	5.3328	4.4003	3.7681	3.3040	2.9461	2.4267	1.7999	1.1905
32	13.1001	10.2331	7.6885	5.9781	4.9755	4.2870	3.7765	3.3799	2.7994	2.0907	1.3926
34	14.2569	11.2147	8.5410	6.7315	5.6505	4.8983	4.3351	3.8942	3.2433	2.4392	1.6362
36	15.6001	12.3661	9.5486	7.6271	6.4566	5.6311	5.0070	4.5143	3.7808	2.8636	1.9349
38	17.1917	13.7428	10.7615	8.7111	7.4364	6.5250	5.8288	5.2749	4.4426	3.3890	2.3069
40	19.1212	15.4251	12.2527	10.0502	8.6516	7.6373	6.8542	6.2260	5.2735	4.0520	2.7792
42	21.5265	17.5372	14.1355	11.7485	10.1984	9.0574	8.1668	7.4462	6.3430	4.9099	3.3938
44	24.6114	20.2637	16.5781	13.9609	12.2202	10.9188	9.8914	9.0528	7.7562	6.0488	4.2142
46	28.6879	23.8877	19.8400	16.9265	14.9389	13.4285	12.2220	11.2281	9.6757	7.6028	5.3397
48	34.2623	28.8697	24.3435	21.0353	18.7165	16.9245	15.4754	14.2704	12.3685	9.7926	6.9339
50	42.2094	36.0068	30.8204	26.9639	24.1824	21.9946	20.2032	18.6992	16.3001	13.0032	9.2829
52	54.1483	46.7767	40.6299	35.9702	32.5071	29.7337	27.4336	25.4837	22.3396	17.9552	12.9238
54	73.2918	64.1169	56.4772	50.5614	45.0267	42.3283	39.2217	36.5624	32.2281	26.0948	18.9366
56	107.3615	95.0951	84.8785	76.7815	70.3767	65.0573	60.5320	56.6207	50.1774	40.9255	29.9427
58	179.5187	160.9384	145.4240	132.8183	122.5299	113.8302	106.3363	99.7970	88.9093	73.0449	53.8867
60	433.0125	393.0603	359.4978	331.4482	307.7947	287.4150	269.6265	253.9456	227.5360	188.4339	140.3039

VALUES OF TIME INTEGRAL FOR SUCROSE GRADIENT CENTRIFUGATION
TEMPERATURE 0.0 DEG C PARTICLE DENSITY 1.40

WT.PCT. SUCROSE	ZO= 5	ZO= 0	ZO= -5	ZO= -10	ZO= -15	ZO= -20	ZO= -25	ZO= -30	ZO= -40	ZO= -60	ZO=-100
0	0.0	0.0	0.0	0.0	0.0	0.0	0.0	0.0	0.0	0.0	0.0
2	0.0	0.0	0.6210	0.3368	0.2313	0.1762	0.1423	0.1194	0.0903	0.0607	0.0367
4	0.0	1.3835	1.1233	0.6451	0.4538	0.3503	0.2853	0.2407	0.1833	0.1242	0.0755
6	0.0	2.2635	1.5594	0.9354	0.6715	0.5244	0.4304	0.3650	0.2801	0.1912	0.1170
8	2.6174	2.9458	1.9559	1.2151	0.8876	0.7004	0.5789	0.4935	0.3812	0.2621	0.1614
10	3.9451	3.5269	2.3288	1.4897	1.1049	0.8803	0.7323	0.6272	0.4876	0.3377	0.2093
12	4.9104	4.0506	2.6885	1.7637	1.3262	1.0659	0.8921	0.7675	0.6004	0.4187	0.2611
14	5.7104	4.5417	3.0430	2.0411	1.5540	1.2592	1.0600	0.9159	0.7208	0.5061	0.3175
16	6.4229	5.0161	3.3987	2.3256	1.7911	1.4624	1.2378	1.0739	0.8501	0.6010	0.3794
18	7.0884	5.4855	3.7613	2.6211	2.0404	1.6780	1.4277	1.2437	0.9901	0.7046	0.4476
20	7.7319	5.9595	4.1365	2.9316	2.3052	1.9089	1.6324	1.4274	1.1427	0.8186	0.5233
22	8.3718	6.4469	4.5302	3.2617	2.5895	2.1585	1.8549	1.6281	1.3105	0.9449	0.6079
24	9.0225	6.9561	4.9484	3.6166	2.8977	2.4309	2.0989	1.8491	1.4964	1.0861	0.7031
26	9.6977	7.4962	5.3985	4.0024	3.2353	2.7310	2.3690	2.0946	1.7042	1.2450	0.8112
28	10.4108	8.0773	5.8888	4.4265	3.6089	3.0648	2.6707	2.3699	1.9384	1.4253	0.9347
30	11.1770	8.7113	6.4297	4.8980	4.0268	3.4401	3.0113	2.6817	2.2049	1.6320	1.0773
32	12.0132	9.4128	7.0337	5.4284	4.4996	3.8665	3.3996	3.0382	2.5113	1.8710	1.2434
34	12.9410	10.2000	7.7173	6.0326	5.0409	4.3568	3.8476	3.4506	2.8672	2.1504	1.4388
36	13.9886	11.0980	8.5031	6.7311	5.6696	4.9283	4.3716	3.9343	3.2864	2.4814	1.6717
38	15.1915	12.1383	9.4197	7.5502	6.4099	5.6038	4.9926	4.5090	3.7865	2.8784	1.9528
40	16.5978	13.3645	10.5066	8.5262	7.2957	6.4145	5.7400	5.2022	4.3920	3.3616	2.2970
42	18.2791	14.8408	11.8225	9.7132	8.3767	7.4070	6.6573	6.0550	5.1395	3.9612	2.7265
44	20.3318	16.6550	13.4478	11.1853	9.7220	8.6455	7.8048	7.1239	6.0798	4.7189	3.2724
46	22.8899	18.9291	15.4947	13.0462	11.4278	10.2202	9.2671	8.4888	7.2841	5.6940	3.9785
48	26.1482	21.8411	18.1268	15.4476	13.6357	12.2634	11.1685	10.2668	8.8579	6.9736	4.9101
50	30.4005	25.6597	21.5922	18.6195	16.5600	14.9759	13.6978	12.6361	10.9611	8.6912	6.1667
52	36.1044	30.8049	26.2784	22.9218	20.5366	18.6727	17.1516	15.8768	13.8459	11.0564	7.9056
54	43.9651	37.9247	32.7849	28.9124	26.0871	23.8433	21.9909	20.4248	17.9051	14.3975	10.3735
56	55.2143	48.1524	42.1611	37.5680	34.1249	31.3457	29.0248	27.0453	23.8292	19.2919	14.0054
58	71.9707	63.4405	56.2176	50.5766	45.2309	42.6663	39.6557	37.0656	32.8172	26.7444	19.5600
60	98.0183	87.2834	78.1999	70.9677	65.2457	60.4787	56.4088	52.8784	47.0340	38.5733	28.4146

VALUES OF TIME INTEGRAL FOR SUCROSE GRADIENT CENTRIFUGATION
TEMPERATURE 0.0 DEG C PARTICLE DENSITY 1.50

WT.PCT. SUCROSE	Z0= 5	Z0= 0	Z0= -5	Z0= -10	Z0= -15	Z0= -20	Z0= -25	Z0= -30	Z0= -40	Z0= -60	Z0=-100
0	0.0	0.0	0.0	0.0	0.0	0.0	0.0	0.0	0.0	0.0	0.0
2	0.0	0.0	0.6181	0.3352	0.2302	0.1754	0.1416	0.1188	0.0898	0.0604	0.0365
4	0.0	1.3713	1.1158	0.6407	0.4507	0.3479	0.2833	0.2390	0.1821	0.1233	0.0750
6	0.0	2.2396	1.5461	0.9271	0.6654	0.5196	0.4264	0.3617	0.2775	0.1894	0.1159
8	2.5713	2.9096	1.9355	1.2018	0.8776	0.6925	0.5723	0.4878	0.3768	0.2591	0.1595
10	3.8688	3.4774	2.2998	1.4701	1.0900	0.8682	0.7222	0.6185	0.4808	0.3329	0.2063
12	4.8074	3.9865	2.6495	1.7364	1.3051	1.0486	0.8775	0.7549	0.5904	0.4117	0.2567
14	5.5808	4.4613	2.9922	2.0046	1.5253	1.2355	1.0398	0.8983	0.7068	0.4962	0.3112
16	6.2656	4.9173	3.3340	2.2780	1.7532	1.4308	1.2107	1.0502	0.8311	0.5873	0.3707
18	6.9013	5.3657	3.6805	2.5603	1.9913	1.6368	1.3921	1.2123	0.9648	0.6863	0.4358
20	7.5120	5.8155	4.0365	2.8550	2.2427	1.8559	1.5863	1.3867	1.1096	0.7945	0.5076
22	8.1150	6.2748	4.4075	3.1660	2.5105	2.0911	1.7960	1.5758	1.2677	0.9135	0.5874
24	8.7236	6.7511	4.7987	3.4980	2.7988	2.3458	2.0242	1.7825	1.4416	1.0455	0.6764
26	9.3501	7.2522	5.2163	3.8559	3.1120	2.6242	2.2748	2.0103	1.6344	1.1929	0.7767
28	10.0061	7.7867	5.6673	4.2460	3.4557	2.9313	2.5524	2.2635	1.8498	1.3589	0.8903
30	10.7044	8.3646	6.1602	4.6757	3.8366	3.2734	2.8627	2.5476	2.0927	1.5472	1.0203
32	11.4590	8.9975	6.7052	5.1543	4.2631	3.6581	3.2131	2.8693	2.3691	1.7629	1.1701
34	12.2870	9.7001	7.3154	5.6935	4.7462	4.0957	3.6130	3.2374	2.6868	2.0123	1.3445
36	13.2112	10.4923	8.0086	6.3097	5.3008	4.5999	4.0752	3.6641	3.0566	2.3042	1.5500
38	14.2588	11.3983	8.8068	7.0231	5.9456	5.1881	4.6160	4.1646	3.4921	2.6499	1.7948
40	15.4665	12.4513	9.7402	7.8613	6.7062	5.8843	5.2578	4.7599	4.0121	3.0649	2.0904
42	16.8883	13.6998	10.8531	8.8651	7.6204	6.7236	6.0336	5.4810	4.6442	3.5719	2.4536
44	18.5951	15.2083	12.2044	10.0890	8.7389	7.7534	6.9876	6.3698	5.4260	4.2019	2.9074
46	20.6825	17.0638	13.8746	11.6074	10.1309	9.0383	8.1808	7.4835	6.4087	4.9975	3.4836
48	23.2861	19.3907	15.9778	13.5263	11.8951	10.6709	9.7001	8.9042	7.6661	6.0200	4.2279
50	26.6051	22.3712	18.6826	16.0020	14.1775	12.7880	11.6742	10.7534	9.3077	7.3605	5.2086
52	30.9405	26.2820	22.2444	19.2720	17.2000	15.5978	14.2993	13.2165	11.5003	9.1582	6.5303
54	36.7379	31.5329	27.0430	23.6901	21.2933	19.4110	17.8682	16.5705	14.4938	11.6221	8.3503
56	44.7507	38.8179	33.7214	29.8552	27.0184	24.7547	22.8782	21.2860	18.7132	15.1081	10.9370
58	56.2146	49.2772	43.3380	38.7548	35.3005	32.4994	30.1509	28.1411	24.8621	20.2064	14.7369
60	73.2083	64.8322	57.6791	52.0576	47.7053	44.1197	41.0801	38.4568	34.1365	27.9230	20.5130

VALUES OF TIME INTEGRAL FOR SUCROSE GRADIENT CENTRIFUGATION
TEMPERATURE 0.0 DEG C PARTICLE DENSITY 1.60

WT.PCT. SUCROSE	Z0= 5	Z0= 0	Z0= -5	Z0= -10	Z0= -15	Z0= -20	Z0= -25	Z0= -30	Z0= -40	Z0= -60	Z0=-100
0	0.0	0.0	0.0	0.0	0.0	0.0	0.0	0.0	0.0	0.0	0.0
2	0.0	0.0	0.6157	0.3339	0.2293	0.1747	0.1411	0.1183	0.0895	0.0601	0.0363
4	0.0	1.3623	1.1101	0.6374	0.4483	0.3460	0.2818	0.2377	0.1811	0.1227	0.0746
6	0.0	2.2224	1.5363	0.9211	0.6610	0.5161	0.4236	0.3592	0.2756	0.1881	0.1151
8	2.5396	2.8840	1.9208	1.1923	0.8705	0.6868	0.5676	0.4838	0.3736	0.2569	0.1582
10	3.8169	3.4429	2.2794	1.4564	1.0796	0.8598	0.7151	0.6124	0.4760	0.3296	0.2042
12	4.7377	3.9423	2.6224	1.7176	1.2906	1.0368	0.8675	0.7462	0.5836	0.4069	0.2536
14	5.4938	4.4065	2.9574	1.9798	1.5059	1.2194	1.0261	0.8864	0.6973	0.4894	0.3070
16	6.1608	4.8506	3.2904	2.2461	1.7278	1.4097	1.1926	1.0343	0.8184	0.5782	0.3649
18	6.7776	5.2857	3.6265	2.5199	1.9588	1.6095	1.3686	1.1916	0.9481	0.6742	0.4281
20	7.3678	5.7203	3.9706	2.8047	2.2017	1.8212	1.5563	1.3602	1.0880	0.7788	0.4975
22	7.9479	6.1622	4.3275	3.1040	2.4595	2.0475	1.7580	1.5421	1.2402	0.8933	0.5742
24	8.5309	6.6184	4.7022	3.4219	2.7356	2.2915	1.9766	1.7401	1.4067	1.0198	0.6595
26	9.1281	7.0961	5.1003	3.7631	3.0341	2.5569	2.2154	1.9572	1.5905	1.1603	0.7550
28	9.7503	7.6031	5.5280	4.1331	3.3600	2.8482	2.4787	2.1974	1.7948	1.3176	0.8628
30	10.4090	8.1482	5.9930	4.5385	3.7193	3.1708	2.7715	2.4654	2.0239	1.4953	0.9854
32	11.1167	8.7418	6.5042	4.9873	4.1194	3.5317	3.1001	2.7671	2.2832	1.6976	1.1259
34	11.8887	9.3969	7.0730	5.4901	4.5698	3.9396	3.4729	3.1103	2.5794	1.9301	1.2885
36	12.7447	10.1306	7.7151	6.0608	5.0835	4.4066	3.9010	3.5054	2.9218	2.2005	1.4788
38	13.7083	10.9640	8.4493	6.7169	5.6766	4.9477	4.3984	3.9658	3.3224	2.5185	1.7040
40	14.8110	11.9254	9.3015	7.4822	6.3710	5.5833	4.9844	4.5093	3.7972	2.8973	1.9739
42	16.0987	13.0562	10.3094	8.3914	7.1990	6.3435	5.6870	5.1625	4.3697	3.3565	2.3028
44	17.6314	14.4107	11.5229	9.4904	8.2034	7.2682	6.5437	5.9605	5.0717	3.9222	2.7103
46	19.4885	16.0616	13.0088	10.8413	9.4418	8.4113	7.6053	6.9513	5.9460	4.6301	3.2229
48	21.7818	18.1111	14.8614	12.5315	10.9957	9.8493	8.9435	8.2027	7.0535	5.5307	3.8785
50	24.6735	20.7080	17.2179	14.6884	12.9842	11.6939	10.6634	9.8138	8.4837	6.6986	4.7330
52	28.4064	24.0751	20.2847	17.5040	15.5866	14.1131	12.9236	11.9345	10.3715	8.2463	5.8709
54	33.3338	28.5381	24.3631	21.2590	19.0657	17.3540	15.9569	14.7852	12.9158	10.3405	7.4177
56	40.0478	34.6422	29.9591	26.4248	23.8628	21.8315	20.1547	18.7363	16.4512	13.2614	9.5851
58	49.5043	43.2700	37.8916	33.7659	30.6945	28.2199	26.1539	24.3909	21.5232	17.4668	12.7195
60	63.2808	55.8802	49.5176	44.5501	40.7507	37.6402	35.0138	32.7534	29.0416	23.7223	17.4019

VALUES OF TIME INTEGRAL FOR SUCROSE GRADIENT CENTRIFUGATION
TEMPERATURE 0.0 DEG C PARTICLE DENSITY 1.70

WT.PCT. SUCROSE	ZO= 5	ZO= 0	ZO= -5	ZO= -10	ZO= -15	ZO= -20	ZO= -25	ZO= -30	ZO= -40	ZO= -60	ZO=-100
0	0.0	0.0	0.0	0.0	0.0	0.0	0.0	0.0	0.0	0.0	0.0
2	0.0	0.0	0.6137	0.3328	0.2286	0.1741	0.1406	0.1179	0.0892	0.0599	0.0362
4	0.0	1.3552	1.1055	0.6346	0.4464	0.3445	0.2806	0.2367	0.1803	0.1222	0.0743
6	0.0	2.2089	1.5285	0.9162	0.6575	0.5134	0.4213	0.3573	0.2741	0.1871	0.1145
8	2.5160	2.8643	1.9094	1.1849	0.8650	0.6824	0.5639	0.4806	0.3712	0.2552	0.1571
10	3.7784	3.4166	2.2638	1.4459	1.0716	0.8534	0.7097	0.6078	0.4724	0.3271	0.2026
12	4.6863	3.9091	2.6020	1.7035	1.2796	1.0279	0.8600	0.7397	0.5784	0.4032	0.2513
14	5.4300	4.3656	2.9315	1.9613	1.4914	1.2076	1.0160	0.8776	0.6903	0.4845	0.3038
16	6.0845	4.8014	3.2582	2.2226	1.7092	1.3942	1.1793	1.0227	0.8091	0.5716	0.3606
18	6.6880	5.2271	3.5871	2.4906	1.9353	1.5897	1.3516	1.1767	0.9360	0.6655	0.4225
20	7.2640	5.6513	3.9228	2.7684	2.1722	1.7963	1.5347	1.3411	1.0726	0.7675	0.4902
22	7.8284	6.0813	4.2701	3.0597	2.4230	2.0165	1.7310	1.5181	1.2206	0.8790	0.5648
24	8.3940	6.5238	4.6336	3.3681	2.6909	2.2532	1.9430	1.7102	1.3822	1.0016	0.6476
26	8.9715	6.9857	5.0185	3.6981	2.9796	2.5099	2.1740	1.9202	1.5599	1.1375	0.7400
28	9.5711	7.4743	5.4308	4.0546	3.2937	2.7906	2.4277	2.1516	1.7568	1.2892	0.8439
30	10.2037	7.9979	5.8773	4.4439	3.6388	3.1005	2.7089	2.4090	1.9769	1.4598	0.9616
32	10.8810	8.5659	6.3665	4.8734	4.0216	3.4458	3.0234	2.6977	2.2249	1.6534	1.0961
34	11.6168	9.1902	6.9087	5.3526	4.4509	3.8345	3.3787	3.0248	2.5072	1.8750	1.2510
36	12.4293	9.8867	7.5181	5.8943	4.9384	4.2778	3.7850	3.3999	2.8323	2.1316	1.4316
38	13.3399	10.6743	8.2120	6.5144	5.4989	4.7891	4.2551	3.8349	3.2108	2.4321	1.6444
40	14.3772	11.5787	9.0136	7.2343	6.1522	5.3871	4.8063	4.3462	3.6574	2.7885	1.8983
42	15.5827	12.6372	9.9572	8.0854	6.9273	6.0987	5.4641	4.9576	4.1934	3.2184	2.2062
44	17.0101	13.8987	11.0873	9.1089	7.8627	6.9598	6.2619	5.7009	4.8471	3.7452	2.5857
46	18.7300	15.4276	12.4634	10.3600	9.0095	8.0185	7.2450	6.6185	5.6568	4.4007	3.0605
48	20.8415	17.3146	14.1691	11.9161	10.4402	9.3425	8.4771	7.7706	6.6765	5.2299	3.6641
50	23.4872	19.6906	16.3252	13.8896	12.2596	11.0301	10.0508	9.2447	7.9851	6.2985	4.4459
52	26.8797	22.7507	19.1122	16.4484	14.6247	13.2287	12.1048	11.1720	9.7007	7.7051	5.4800
54	31.3258	26.7776	22.7923	19.8365	17.7638	16.1530	14.8417	13.7441	11.9964	9.5946	6.8757
56	37.3370	32.2428	27.8024	24.4616	22.0588	20.1618	18.6001	17.2816	15.1617	12.2097	8.8161
58	45.7334	39.9034	34.8458	30.9797	28.1246	25.8340	23.9267	22.3023	19.6651	15.9437	11.5991
60	57.8558	50.9995	45.0758	40.4691	36.9734	34.1232	31.7228	29.6607	26.2807	21.4480	15.7193

VALUES OF TIME INTEGRAL FOR SUCROSE GRADIENT CENTRIFUGATION
TEMPERATURE 0.0 DEG C PARTICLE DENSITY 1.80

WT.PCT. SUCROSE	Z0= 5	Z0= 0	Z0= -5	Z0= -10	Z0= -15	Z0= -20	Z0= -25	Z0= -30	Z0= -40	Z0= -60	Z0=-100
0	0.0	0.0	0.0	0.0	0.0	0.0	0.0	0.0	0.0	0.0	0.0
2	0.0	0.0	0.6119	0.3318	0.2279	0.1736	0.1402	0.1176	0.0889	0.0598	0.0361
4	0.0	1.3492	1.1015	0.6323	0.4447	0.3432	0.2795	0.2358	0.1796	0.1217	0.0740
6	0.0	2.1978	1.5219	0.9122	0.6546	0.5111	0.4194	0.3557	0.2729	0.1862	0.1140
8	2.4972	2.8483	1.8999	1.1788	0.8605	0.6789	0.5609	0.4781	0.3692	0.2538	0.1563
10	3.7480	3.3955	2.2510	1.4374	1.0652	0.8482	0.7054	0.6040	0.4695	0.3250	0.2013
12	4.6460	3.8826	2.5855	1.6922	1.2709	1.0208	0.8540	0.7345	0.5744	0.4004	0.2495
14	5.3803	4.3333	2.9109	1.9467	1.4800	1.1982	1.0080	0.8706	0.6848	0.4806	0.3014
16	6.0253	4.7628	3.2328	2.2042	1.6946	1.3821	1.1690	1.0137	0.8019	0.5664	0.3573
18	6.6190	5.1815	3.5563	2.4678	1.9170	1.5745	1.3384	1.1651	0.9267	0.6588	0.4182
20	7.1843	5.5979	3.8859	2.7406	2.1496	1.7773	1.5182	1.3265	1.0608	0.7590	0.4846
22	7.7373	6.0191	4.2261	3.0259	2.3953	1.9930	1.7105	1.5000	1.2058	0.8682	0.5577
24	8.2901	6.4517	4.5814	3.3273	2.6571	2.2243	1.9177	1.6877	1.3637	0.9880	0.6386
26	8.8533	6.9022	4.9568	3.6491	2.9387	2.4746	2.1430	1.8925	1.5370	1.1206	0.7288
28	9.4368	7.3776	5.3580	3.9960	3.2443	2.7478	2.3898	2.1177	1.7286	1.2681	0.8298
30	10.0508	7.8857	5.7913	4.3739	3.5792	3.0485	2.6628	2.3675	1.9422	1.4337	0.9441
32	10.7064	8.4356	6.2649	4.7897	3.9498	3.3828	2.9672	2.6469	2.1823	1.6211	1.0743
34	11.4167	9.0383	6.7883	5.2523	4.3642	3.7581	3.3102	2.9627	2.4548	1.8350	1.2239
36	12.1989	9.7087	7.3750	5.7737	4.8336	4.1848	3.7013	3.3238	2.7678	2.0821	1.3977
38	13.0729	10.4647	8.0409	6.3689	5.3715	4.6756	4.1525	3.7413	3.1311	2.3705	1.6020
40	14.0654	11.3300	8.8079	7.0577	5.9966	5.2477	4.6799	4.2305	3.5584	2.7115	1.8449
42	15.2150	12.3395	9.7077	7.8693	6.7358	5.9263	5.3072	4.8136	4.0695	3.1214	2.1385
44	16.5714	13.5382	10.7817	8.8420	7.6246	6.7446	6.0654	5.5199	4.6907	3.6221	2.4992
46	18.1999	14.9859	12.0847	10.0266	8.7105	7.7470	6.9962	6.3887	5.4574	4.2427	2.9486
48	20.1914	16.7657	13.6934	11.4943	10.0599	8.9958	8.1583	7.4753	6.4192	5.0248	3.5180
50	22.6767	18.9975	15.7187	13.3480	11.7689	10.5810	9.6364	8.8600	7.6483	6.0285	4.2523
52	25.8496	21.8595	18.3254	15.7412	13.9809	12.6373	11.5575	10.6625	9.2529	7.3441	5.2195
54	29.9888	25.6086	21.7514	18.8955	15.9034	15.3598	14.1056	13.0572	11.3902	9.1032	6.5188
56	35.5581	30.6720	26.3932	23.1805	20.8826	19.0738	17.5876	16.3345	14.3227	11.5260	8.3166
58	43.2970	37.7326	32.8850	29.1882	25.4734	24.3018	22.4971	20.9620	18.4734	14.9675	10.8817
60	54.4086	47.9035	42.2620	37.8863	34.5843	31.8997	29.6431	27.7068	24.5374	20.0129	14.6583

VALUES OF TIME INTEGRAL FOR SUCROSE GRADIENT CENTRIFUGATION
TEMPERATURE 0.0 DEG C PARTICLE DENSITY 1.90

WT.PCT. SUCROSE	Z0= 5	Z0= 0	Z0= -5	Z0= -10	Z0= -15	Z0= -20	Z0= -25	Z0= -30	Z0= -40	Z0= -60	Z0=-100
0	0.0	0.0	0.0	0.0	0.0	0.0	0.0	0.0	0.0	0.0	0.0
2	0.0	0.0	0.6102	0.3309	0.2272	0.1731	0.1398	0.1172	0.0887	0.0596	0.0360
4	0.0	1.3440	1.0978	0.6302	0.4433	0.3421	0.2786	0.2350	0.1790	0.1213	0.0737
6	0.0	2.1883	1.5162	0.9087	0.6520	0.5091	0.4177	0.3543	0.2718	0.1855	0.1135
8	2.4816	2.8346	1.8917	1.1736	0.8566	0.6758	0.5584	0.4759	0.3675	0.2527	0.1556
10	3.7230	3.3777	2.2402	1.4302	1.0598	0.8439	0.7017	0.6009	0.4670	0.3233	0.2003
12	4.6130	3.8604	2.5717	1.6827	1.2637	1.0149	0.8490	0.7302	0.5710	0.3980	0.2480
14	5.3398	4.3066	2.8937	1.9346	1.4706	1.1905	1.0015	0.8649	0.6803	0.4774	0.2993
16	5.9773	4.7310	3.2119	2.1892	1.6827	1.3723	1.1606	1.0063	0.7960	0.5622	0.3547
18	6.5632	5.1443	3.5312	2.4493	1.9022	1.5621	1.3278	1.1558	0.9192	0.6534	0.4147
20	7.1203	5.5546	3.8560	2.7181	2.1314	1.7619	1.5049	1.3148	1.0513	0.7521	0.4802
22	7.6644	5.9690	4.1907	2.9988	2.3732	1.9742	1.6941	1.4855	1.1940	0.8595	0.5521
24	8.2075	6.3939	4.5397	3.2949	2.6303	2.2014	1.8977	1.6699	1.3491	0.9773	0.6316
26	8.7597	6.8357	4.9079	3.6105	2.9064	2.4469	2.1186	1.8707	1.5190	1.1072	0.7200
28	9.3309	7.3011	5.3005	3.9501	3.2056	2.7142	2.3602	2.0911	1.7066	1.2517	0.8189
30	9.9308	7.7975	5.7240	4.3192	3.5329	3.0081	2.6269	2.3352	1.9153	1.4135	0.9305
32	10.5702	8.3338	6.1858	4.7247	3.8943	3.3341	2.9238	2.6077	2.1494	1.5962	1.0575
34	11.2615	8.9204	6.6952	5.1749	4.2976	3.6994	3.2576	2.9151	2.4147	1.8044	1.2031
36	12.0212	9.5716	7.2650	5.6814	4.7535	4.1138	3.6375	3.2658	2.7186	2.0444	1.3720
38	12.8682	10.3042	7.9104	6.2582	5.2748	4.5894	4.0748	3.6704	3.0707	2.3239	1.5699
40	13.8279	11.1408	8.6521	6.9242	5.8791	5.1426	4.5847	4.1434	3.4839	2.6536	1.8047
42	14.9368	12.1146	9.5200	7.7071	6.5922	5.7972	5.1898	4.7059	3.9769	3.0490	2.0880
44	16.2420	13.2681	10.5534	8.6430	7.4475	6.5846	5.9193	5.3855	4.5747	3.5308	2.4350
46	17.8049	14.6574	11.8039	9.7799	8.4896	7.5466	6.8127	6.2193	5.3104	4.1264	2.8664
48	19.7110	16.3608	13.3436	11.1846	9.7811	8.7418	7.9249	7.2593	6.2309	4.8749	3.4113
50	22.0827	18.4907	15.2764	12.9537	11.4121	10.2546	9.3355	8.5807	7.4040	5.8328	4.1121
52	25.1016	21.2139	17.7565	15.2307	13.5167	12.2111	11.1633	10.2958	8.9306	7.0845	5.0323
54	29.0276	24.7697	21.0060	18.2225	15.2886	14.7933	13.5801	12.5670	10.9577	8.7529	6.2647
56	34.2920	29.5560	25.3938	22.2729	20.0499	18.3040	16.8716	15.6650	13.7298	11.0431	7.9641
58	41.5818	36.2068	31.5087	27.9319	25.3162	23.2286	21.4960	20.0238	17.6395	14.2849	10.3802
60	52.0095	45.7517	40.3086	36.0947	32.9279	30.3589	28.2022	26.3535	23.3303	19.0197	13.9243

VALUES OF TIME INTEGRAL FOR SUCROSE GRADIENT CENTRIFUGATION
TEMPERATURE 5.0 DEG C PARTICLE DENSITY 1.10

WT.PCT. SUCROSE	ZO= 5	ZO= 0	ZO= -5	ZO= -10	ZO= -15	ZO= -20	ZO= -25	ZO= -30	ZO= -40	ZO= -60	ZO=-100
0	0.0	0.0	0.0	0.0	0.0	0.0	0.0	0.0	0.0	0.0	0.0
2	0.0	0.0	0.5523	0.2998	0.2060	0.1569	0.1267	0.1063	0.0804	0.0541	0.0327
4	0.0	1.3098	1.0291	0.5926	0.4173	0.3223	0.2626	0.2216	0.1689	0.1144	0.0696
6	0.0	2.2080	1.4748	0.8894	0.6399	0.5004	0.4110	0.3488	0.2678	0.1830	0.1120
8	2.8893	2.9663	1.9159	1.2007	0.8804	0.6963	0.5763	0.4918	0.3804	0.2619	0.1615
10	4.5142	3.6792	2.3737	1.5380	1.1475	0.9173	0.7649	0.6562	0.5112	0.3549	0.2203
12	5.8442	4.4020	2.8704	1.9164	1.4532	1.1738	0.9857	0.8501	0.6671	0.4669	0.2920
14	7.1163	5.1840	3.4352	2.3585	1.8163	1.4819	1.2533	1.0866	0.8591	0.6062	0.3820
16	8.4736	6.0887	4.1139	2.9016	2.2690	1.8700	1.5929	1.3885	1.1061	0.7874	0.5002
18	10.0844	7.2263	4.9933	3.6184	2.8739	2.3933	2.0540	1.8006	1.4460	1.0391	0.6659
20	12.2888	8.8521	6.2813	4.6848	3.7839	3.1868	2.7575	2.4324	1.9708	1.4312	0.9263
22	16.3557	11.9569	8.7923	6.7927	5.6002	4.7825	4.1804	3.7162	3.0447	2.2405	1.4684

VALUES OF TIME INTEGRAL FOR SUCROSE GRADIENT CENTRIFUGATION
TEMPERATURE 5.0 DEG C PARTICLE DENSITY 1.20

WT.PCT. SUCROSE	Z0= 5	Z0= 0	Z0= -5	Z0= -10	Z0= -15	Z0= -20	Z0= -25	Z0= -30	Z0= -40	Z0= -60	Z0=-100
0	0.0	0.0	0.0	0.0	0.0	0.0	0.0	0.0	0.0	0.0	0.0
2	0.0	0.0	0.5357	0.2906	0.1996	0.1521	0.1228	0.1030	0.0779	0.0524	0.0317
4	0.0	1.2163	0.9776	0.5619	0.3954	0.3053	0.2487	0.2098	0.1598	0.1083	0.0659
6	0.0	2.0068	1.3695	0.8228	0.5911	0.4618	0.3791	0.3215	0.2468	0.1685	0.1031
8	2.4017	2.6340	1.7341	1.0800	0.7898	0.6236	0.5156	0.4397	0.3398	0.2337	0.1440
10	3.6521	3.1816	2.0856	1.3389	0.9947	0.7932	0.6603	0.5658	0.4401	0.3050	0.1891
12	4.5867	3.6888	2.4340	1.6043	1.2090	0.9730	0.8151	0.7017	0.5494	0.3835	0.2393
14	5.3846	4.1787	2.7876	1.8810	1.4363	1.1659	0.9826	0.8497	0.6695	0.4707	0.2957
16	6.1190	4.6679	3.1544	2.1744	1.6808	1.3754	1.1660	1.0127	0.8029	0.5685	0.3595
18	6.8306	5.1699	3.5423	2.4905	1.9475	1.6061	1.3692	1.1943	0.9526	0.6794	0.4324
20	7.5475	5.6980	3.9603	2.8365	2.2426	1.8634	1.5972	1.3991	1.1227	0.8064	0.5168
22	8.2937	6.2665	4.4195	3.2216	2.5743	2.1546	1.8568	1.6332	1.3185	0.9539	0.6155
24	9.0937	6.8926	4.9339	3.6580	2.9533	2.4896	2.1569	1.9050	1.5471	1.1274	0.7326
26	9.9756	7.5981	5.5218	4.1620	3.3943	2.8816	2.5097	2.2258	1.8186	1.3350	0.8738
28	10.9752	8.4126	6.2092	4.7565	3.9181	3.3497	2.9328	2.6118	2.1470	1.5880	1.0471
30	12.1429	9.3792	7.0336	5.4754	4.5553	3.9219	3.4521	3.0871	2.5534	1.9031	1.2645
32	13.5537	10.5626	8.0528	6.3704	5.3531	4.6415	4.1075	3.6888	3.0704	2.3065	1.5448
34	15.3280	12.0683	9.3606	7.5262	6.3886	5.5794	4.9646	4.4780	3.7516	2.8412	1.9188
36	17.6802	14.0849	11.1254	9.0952	7.8008	6.8634	6.1417	5.5645	4.6934	3.5849	2.4422
38	21.0371	16.9888	13.6842	11.3820	9.8681	8.7495	7.8758	7.1694	6.0900	4.6938	3.2275
40	26.4545	21.7133	17.8728	15.1441	13.2824	11.8749	10.7574	9.8425	8.4251	6.5576	4.5553
42	38.0635	31.9123	26.9672	23.3498	20.7577	18.7392	17.1031	15.7424	13.5982	10.7081	7.5299

VALUES OF TIME INTEGRAL FOR SUCROSE GRADIENT CENTRIFUGATION
TEMPERATURE 5.0 DEG C PARTICLE DENSITY 1.30

WT.PCT. SUCROSE	Z0= 5	Z0= 0	Z0= -5	Z0= -10	Z0= -15	Z0= -20	Z0= -25	Z0= -30	Z0= -40	Z0= -60	Z0=-100
0	0.0	0.0	0.0	0.0	0.0	0.0	0.0	0.0	0.0	0.0	0.0
2	0.0	0.0	0.5297	0.2873	0.1973	0.1503	0.1214	0.1018	0.0770	0.0518	0.0313
4	0.0	1.1861	0.9604	0.5517	0.3881	0.2996	0.2440	0.2059	0.1568	0.1063	0.0646
6	0.0	1.9449	1.3364	0.8020	0.5758	0.4497	0.3691	0.3131	0.2402	0.1640	0.1004
8	2.2693	2.5368	1.6804	1.0447	0.7633	0.6025	0.4980	0.4245	0.3280	0.2255	0.1389
10	3.4281	3.0439	2.0059	1.2844	0.9530	0.7595	0.6319	0.5413	0.4209	0.2915	0.1807
12	4.2762	3.5041	2.3220	1.5251	1.1475	0.9225	0.7723	0.6646	0.5200	0.3627	0.2262
14	4.9841	3.9387	2.6357	1.7706	1.3491	1.0936	0.9209	0.7959	0.6265	0.4401	0.2762
16	5.6194	4.3617	2.9528	2.0243	1.5605	1.2748	1.0794	0.9368	0.7418	0.5246	0.3313
18	6.2176	4.7837	3.2789	2.2899	1.7846	1.4686	1.2502	1.0894	0.8677	0.6178	0.3927
20	6.8012	5.2136	3.6191	2.5715	2.0248	1.6781	1.4358	1.2561	1.0061	0.7212	0.4613
22	7.3869	5.6598	3.9795	2.8738	2.2851	1.9066	1.6395	1.4398	1.1597	0.8369	0.5387
24	7.9890	6.1309	4.3665	3.2021	2.5702	2.1586	1.8653	1.6443	1.3317	0.9675	0.6269
26	8.6209	6.6364	4.7878	3.5632	2.8862	2.4395	2.1181	1.8741	1.5262	1.1162	0.7280
28	9.2970	7.1873	5.2526	3.9653	3.2404	2.7560	2.4042	2.1351	1.7483	1.2872	0.8452
30	10.0339	7.7972	5.7728	4.4188	3.6424	3.1170	2.7317	2.4349	2.0047	1.4860	0.9823
32	10.8516	8.4830	6.3634	4.9374	4.1047	3.5339	3.1115	2.7836	2.3042	1.7197	1.1447
34	11.7754	9.2669	7.0442	5.5391	4.6437	4.0221	3.5576	3.1943	2.6587	1.9980	1.3393
36	12.8399	10.1794	7.8427	6.2489	5.2826	4.6030	4.0900	3.6858	3.0847	2.3343	1.5760
38	14.0911	11.2616	8.7961	7.1009	5.0527	5.3056	4.7360	4.2836	3.6049	2.7473	1.8684
40	15.5948	12.5726	9.9582	8.1446	6.9997	6.1724	5.5352	5.0248	4.2523	3.2640	2.2365
42	17.4484	14.2004	11.4092	9.4534	8.1918	7.2668	6.5467	5.9651	5.0766	3.9251	2.7101
44	19.7954	16.2746	13.2676	11.1365	9.7299	8.6829	7.8587	7.1874	6.1517	4.7915	3.3342
46	22.8514	18.9914	15.7129	13.3597	11.7680	10.5643	9.6058	8.8181	7.5906	5.9565	4.1780
48	26.9650	22.6678	19.0361	16.3916	14.5556	13.1440	12.0065	11.0630	9.5777	7.5723	5.3543
50	32.7251	27.8408	23.7306	20.6887	18.5172	16.8188	15.4332	14.2730	12.4272	9.8993	7.0568
52	41.1957	35.4819	30.6902	27.0785	24.4234	22.3095	20.5630	19.0864	16.7121	13.4126	9.6399
54	54.4584	47.4952	41.6693	37.1872	33.7897	31.0350	28.7297	26.7616	23.5627	19.0516	13.8054
56	77.2105	68.1825	60.6353	54.6965	50.0500	46.2127	42.9600	40.1557	35.5484	28.9546	21.1545
58	122.5723	109.5740	98.6958	89.9221	82.8339	76.8713	71.7522	67.2957	59.8943	49.1436	36.2042
60	253.7656	229.6937	209.4659	192.6932	178.6834	166.6727	156.2236	147.0344	131.5981	108.8210	80.8915

VALUES OF TIME INTEGRAL FOR SUCROSE GRADIENT CENTRIFUGATION
TEMPERATURE 5.0 DEG C PARTICLE DENSITY 1.40

WT.PCT. SUCROSE	ZO= 5	ZO= 0	ZO= -5	ZO= -10	ZO= -15	ZO= -20	ZO= -25	ZO= -30	ZO= -40	ZO= -60	ZO=-100
0	0.0	0.0	0.0	0.0	0.0	0.0	0.0	0.0	0.0	0.0	0.0
2	0.0	0.0	0.5262	0.2854	0.1960	0.1493	0.1206	0.1011	0.0765	0.0514	0.0311
4	0.0	1.1703	0.9510	0.5461	0.3842	0.2965	0.2415	0.2037	0.1552	0.1052	0.0639
6	0.0	1.9134	1.3192	0.7913	0.5680	0.4435	0.3640	0.3087	0.2369	0.1617	0.0989
8	2.2059	2.4883	1.6534	1.0269	0.7500	0.5919	0.4892	0.4170	0.3221	0.2215	0.1364
10	3.3222	2.9769	1.9668	1.2578	0.9328	0.7431	0.6181	0.5294	0.4116	0.2850	0.1766
12	4.1319	3.4161	2.2685	1.4876	1.1183	0.8987	0.7521	0.6471	0.5062	0.3530	0.2201
14	4.8011	3.8269	2.5650	1.7196	1.3089	1.0604	0.8926	0.7712	0.6068	0.4261	0.2673
16	5.3953	4.2225	2.8617	1.9569	1.5066	1.2299	1.0408	0.9030	0.7147	0.5052	0.3189
18	5.9485	4.6128	3.1632	2.2025	1.7139	1.4091	1.1988	1.0441	0.8311	0.5913	0.3756
20	6.4817	5.0055	3.4740	2.4598	1.9333	1.6004	1.3683	1.1963	0.9575	0.6857	0.4383
22	7.0097	5.4077	3.7988	2.7322	2.1679	1.8064	1.5519	1.3619	1.0960	0.7900	0.5081
24	7.5445	5.8262	4.1426	3.0239	2.4212	2.0303	1.7524	1.5436	1.2488	0.9060	0.5864
26	8.0970	6.2681	4.5109	3.3396	2.6974	2.2758	1.9734	1.7445	1.4188	1.0360	0.6748
28	8.6778	6.7414	4.9102	3.6849	3.0017	2.5477	2.2192	1.9687	1.6095	1.1829	0.7754
30	9.2987	7.2552	5.3485	4.0670	3.3404	2.8518	2.4952	2.2213	1.8255	1.3504	0.8910
32	9.9730	7.8208	5.8355	4.4947	3.7215	3.1956	2.8083	2.5087	2.0725	1.5431	1.0248
34	10.7166	8.4518	6.3835	4.9790	4.1554	3.5886	3.1674	2.8393	2.3578	1.7671	1.1815
36	11.5506	9.1666	7.0090	5.5350	4.6559	4.0436	3.5845	3.2244	2.6915	2.0305	1.3669
38	12.5011	9.9887	7.7333	6.1823	5.2409	4.5773	4.0752	3.6785	3.0867	2.3442	1.5890
40	13.6040	10.9503	8.5856	6.9477	5.9355	5.2130	4.6613	4.2221	3.5615	2.7232	1.8589
42	14.9092	12.0964	9.6073	7.8692	6.7748	5.9836	5.3734	4.8841	4.1418	3.1886	2.1924
44	16.4850	13.4891	10.8549	8.9992	7.8074	6.9343	6.2543	5.7047	4.8636	3.7703	2.6114
46	18.4242	15.2129	12.4065	10.4098	9.1005	8.1280	7.3628	6.7393	5.7765	4.5094	3.1466
48	20.8620	17.3916	14.3758	12.2065	10.7524	9.6567	8.7853	8.0695	6.9539	5.4668	3.8436
50	23.9993	20.2090	16.9326	14.5467	12.9099	11.6579	10.6515	9.8176	8.5057	6.7340	4.7707
52	28.1417	23.9457	20.3358	17.6712	15.7979	14.3427	13.1597	12.1711	10.6007	8.4516	6.0335
54	33.7658	29.0396	24.9910	21.9572	19.7690	18.0419	16.6220	15.4249	13.5049	10.8420	7.7992
56	41.6538	36.2112	31.5655	28.0264	25.4050	23.3025	21.5540	20.0670	17.6586	14.2738	10.3457
58	53.1235	46.6758	41.1871	36.9306	33.6914	31.0513	28.8306	26.9258	23.8107	19.3748	14.1476
60	70.5283	62.6074	55.8753	50.5556	45.3966	42.9531	40.0246	37.4914	33.3099	27.2785	20.0639

VALUES OF TIME INTEGRAL FOR SUCROSE GRADIENT CENTRIFUGATION
TEMPERATURE 5.0 DEG C PARTICLE DENSITY 1.50

WT.PCT. SUCROSE	Z0= 5	Z0= 0	Z0= -5	Z0= -10	Z0= -15	Z0= -20	Z0= -25	Z0= -30	Z0= -40	Z0= -60	Z0=-100
0	0.0	0.0	0.0	0.0	0.0	0.0	0.0	0.0	0.0	0.0	0.0
2	0.0	0.0	0.5237	0.2840	0.1951	0.1486	0.1200	0.1006	0.0761	0.0512	0.0309
4	0.0	1.1601	0.9447	0.5424	0.3816	0.2945	0.2398	0.2023	0.1541	0.1044	0.0635
6	0.0	1.8934	1.3080	0.7843	0.5629	0.4395	0.3607	0.3059	0.2347	0.1602	0.0980
8	2.1676	2.4581	1.6363	1.0158	0.7417	0.5852	0.4836	0.4122	0.3184	0.2189	0.1348
10	3.2590	2.9357	1.9427	1.2415	0.9203	0.7330	0.6097	0.5221	0.4059	0.2810	0.1741
12	4.0465	3.3629	2.2361	1.4649	1.1008	0.8844	0.7400	0.6366	0.4979	0.3471	0.2164
14	4.6937	3.7602	2.5228	1.6893	1.2851	1.0408	0.8758	0.7566	0.5952	0.4178	0.2621
16	5.2652	4.1407	2.8081	1.9175	1.4753	1.2038	1.0184	0.8833	0.6990	0.4939	0.3117
18	5.7940	4.5137	3.0963	2.1523	1.6734	1.3751	1.1694	1.0182	0.8102	0.5762	0.3659
20	6.3003	4.8866	3.3915	2.3966	1.8817	1.5567	1.3304	1.1628	0.9302	0.6659	0.4254
22	6.7983	5.2659	3.6978	2.6535	2.1029	1.7510	1.5035	1.3190	1.0608	0.7642	0.4912
24	7.2990	5.6577	4.0196	2.9266	2.3401	1.9605	1.6912	1.4890	1.2039	0.8728	0.5645
26	7.8121	6.0682	4.3617	3.2198	2.5966	2.1886	1.8965	1.6756	1.3617	0.9935	0.6466
28	8.3470	6.5040	4.7294	3.5378	2.8768	2.4390	2.1228	1.8821	1.5374	1.1288	0.7393
30	8.9136	6.9729	5.1294	3.8865	3.1859	2.7165	2.3747	2.1126	1.7345	1.2817	0.8447
32	9.5229	7.4839	5.5694	4.2729	3.5303	3.0272	2.6576	2.3723	1.9577	1.4558	0.9657
34	10.1878	8.0481	6.0594	4.7059	3.9182	3.3785	2.9786	2.6679	2.2128	1.6560	1.1057
36	10.9248	8.6798	6.6122	5.1973	4.3605	3.7806	3.3472	3.0081	2.5077	1.8888	1.2696
38	11.7543	9.3973	7.2443	5.7621	4.8711	4.2464	3.7755	3.4044	2.8525	2.1626	1.4634
40	12.7037	10.2250	7.9779	6.4210	5.4689	4.7936	4.2799	3.8723	3.2612	2.4888	1.6958
42	13.8105	11.1969	8.8442	7.2024	6.1806	5.4469	4.8838	4.4337	3.7533	2.8834	1.9785
44	15.1246	12.3583	9.8847	8.1448	7.0418	6.2398	5.6184	5.1180	4.3552	3.3685	2.3279
46	16.7124	13.7698	11.1551	9.2997	8.1005	7.2172	6.5260	5.9651	5.1027	3.9736	2.7661
48	18.6680	15.5175	12.7349	10.7410	9.4256	8.4434	7.6671	7.0322	6.0472	4.7417	3.3252
50	21.1279	17.7265	14.7395	12.5758	11.1172	10.0125	9.1302	8.4027	7.2638	5.7351	4.0521
52	24.2927	20.5813	17.3396	14.9629	13.3236	12.0636	11.0464	10.2007	8.8643	7.0474	5.0168
54	28.4653	24.3605	20.7933	18.1427	16.2697	14.8080	13.6151	12.6147	11.0188	8.8207	6.3267
56	34.1235	29.5047	25.5091	22.4961	20.3123	18.5813	17.1527	15.9444	13.9982	11.2822	8.1532
58	42.0356	36.7235	32.1463	28.6383	25.0283	23.9264	22.1721	20.6755	18.2419	14.8008	10.7757
60	53.5036	47.2206	41.8241	37.6154	34.3994	31.7681	29.5474	27.6367	24.5004	20.0081	14.6735

VALUES OF TIME INTEGRAL FOR SUCROSE GRADIENT CENTRIFUGATION
TEMPERATURE 5.0 DEG C PARTICLE DENSITY 1.60

WT.PCT. SUCROSE	Z0= 5	Z0= 0	Z0= -5	Z0= -10	Z0= -15	Z0= -20	Z0= -25	Z0= -30	Z0= -40	Z0= -60	Z0=-100
0	0.0	0.0	0.0	0.0	0.0	0.0	0.0	0.0	0.0	0.0	0.0
2	0.0	0.0	0.5216	0.2829	0.1943	0.1480	0.1195	0.1002	0.0758	0.0510	0.0308
4	0.0	1.1526	0.9399	0.5396	0.3796	0.2929	0.2386	0.2013	0.1533	0.1039	0.0632
6	0.0	1.8790	1.2998	0.7792	0.5592	0.4366	0.3583	0.3039	0.2331	0.1591	0.0974
8	2.1413	2.4368	1.6240	1.0078	0.7358	0.5805	0.4797	0.4089	0.3158	0.2171	0.1337
10	3.2158	2.9069	1.9256	1.2300	0.9116	0.7260	0.6038	0.5171	0.4019	0.2783	0.1724
12	3.9886	3.3261	2.2135	1.4493	1.0887	0.8745	0.7317	0.6293	0.4922	0.3431	0.2139
14	4.6216	3.7146	2.4940	1.6687	1.2689	1.0274	0.8645	0.7467	0.5874	0.4122	0.2585
16	5.1784	4.0854	2.7719	1.8910	1.4542	1.1862	1.0034	0.8702	0.6884	0.4863	0.3069
18	5.6917	4.4474	3.0516	2.1189	1.6465	1.3525	1.1499	1.0011	0.7964	0.5662	0.3595
20	6.1812	4.8079	3.3370	2.3551	1.8479	1.5281	1.3056	1.1409	0.9124	0.6529	0.4170
22	6.6605	5.1731	3.6319	2.6024	2.0609	1.7151	1.4722	1.2912	1.0381	0.7476	0.4804
24	7.1404	5.5485	3.9403	2.8641	2.2881	1.9160	1.6522	1.4542	1.1752	0.8517	0.5506
26	7.6298	5.9401	4.2666	3.1437	2.5328	2.1335	1.8479	1.6321	1.3258	0.9668	0.6289
28	8.1375	6.3537	4.6156	3.4456	2.7988	2.3711	2.0627	1.8281	1.4925	1.0952	0.7169
30	8.6724	6.7964	4.9931	3.7747	3.0905	2.6331	2.3005	2.0457	1.6786	1.2395	0.8164
32	9.2443	7.2761	5.4062	4.1375	3.4138	2.9247	2.5660	2.2895	1.8881	1.4029	0.9300
34	9.8647	7.8025	5.8634	4.5415	3.7758	3.2525	2.8656	2.5653	2.1261	1.5898	1.0606
36	10.5481	8.3882	6.3759	4.9971	4.1858	3.6253	3.2073	2.8808	2.3995	1.8056	1.2125
38	11.3119	9.0489	6.9580	5.5172	4.6560	4.0543	3.6017	3.2457	2.7171	2.0577	1.3910
40	12.1798	9.8055	7.6286	6.1195	5.2025	4.5545	4.0628	3.6734	3.0907	2.3559	1.6034
42	13.1836	10.6869	8.4143	6.8282	5.8479	5.1470	4.6105	4.1825	3.5370	2.7138	1.8598
44	14.3655	11.7314	9.3501	7.6757	6.6224	5.8601	5.2712	4.7979	4.0783	3.1500	2.1740
46	15.7805	12.9893	10.4822	8.7050	7.5660	6.7311	6.0800	5.5529	4.7444	3.6893	2.5646
48	17.5062	14.5316	11.8763	9.9768	8.7353	7.8132	7.0869	6.4945	5.5778	4.3670	3.0579
50	19.6538	16.4602	13.6264	11.5787	10.2121	9.1830	8.3643	7.6910	6.6400	5.2344	3.6925
52	22.3850	18.9238	15.8702	13.6387	12.1161	10.9530	10.0179	9.2426	8.0211	6.3668	4.5250
54	25.9403	22.1440	18.8129	16.3481	14.6264	13.2915	12.2065	11.2995	9.8569	7.8778	5.6411
56	30.6948	26.4665	22.7756	20.0061	18.0233	16.4621	15.1791	14.0973	12.3604	9.9460	7.1758
58	37.2420	32.4399	28.2677	25.0886	22.7531	20.8850	19.3325	18.0121	15.8719	12.8576	9.3458
60	46.5717	40.9798	36.1409	32.3918	29.5633	27.2645	25.3325	23.6753	20.9633	17.0938	12.5167

VALUES OF TIME INTEGRAL FOR SUCROSE GRADIENT CENTRIFUGATION
TEMPERATURE 5.0 DEG C PARTICLE DENSITY 1.70

WT.PCT. SUCROSE	ZO= 5	ZO= 0	ZO= -5	ZO= -10	ZO= -15	ZO= -20	ZO= -25	ZO= -30	ZO= -40	ZO= -60	ZO=-100
0	0.0	0.0	0.0	0.0	0.0	0.0	0.0	0.0	0.0	0.0	0.0
2	0.0	0.0	0.5199	0.2820	0.1936	0.1475	0.1191	0.0999	0.0755	0.0508	0.0307
4	0.0	1.1466	0.9360	0.5373	0.3779	0.2917	0.2375	0.2004	0.1527	0.1034	0.0629
6	0.0	1.8677	1.2933	0.7752	0.5562	0.4343	0.3564	0.3022	0.2319	0.1583	0.0968
8	2.1215	2.4203	1.6144	1.0016	0.7312	0.5768	0.4766	0.4062	0.3137	0.2157	0.1328
10	3.1838	2.8850	1.9125	1.2212	0.9050	0.7207	0.5993	0.5132	0.3989	0.2761	0.1711
12	3.9459	3.2984	2.1965	1.4375	1.0796	0.8671	0.7254	0.6239	0.4879	0.3401	0.2120
14	4.5686	3.6806	2.4724	1.6533	1.2569	1.0176	0.8561	0.7394	0.5816	0.4081	0.2559
16	5.1151	4.0445	2.7451	1.8715	1.4387	1.1734	0.9924	0.8606	0.6807	0.4808	0.3033
18	5.6175	4.3988	3.0189	2.0946	1.6269	1.3362	1.1358	0.9887	0.7864	0.5590	0.3548
20	6.0953	4.7507	3.2975	2.3251	1.8236	1.5076	1.2877	1.1251	0.8997	0.6437	0.4110
22	6.5619	5.1062	3.5845	2.5658	2.0309	1.6896	1.4500	1.2715	1.0220	0.7358	0.4727
24	7.0276	5.4705	3.8838	2.8198	2.2514	1.8845	1.6246	1.4296	1.1551	0.8368	0.5408
26	7.5011	5.8493	4.1994	3.0903	2.4881	2.0949	1.8140	1.6018	1.3007	0.9482	0.6166
28	7.9906	6.2481	4.5359	3.3813	2.7445	2.3240	2.0210	1.7907	1.4615	1.0720	0.7014
30	8.5045	6.6735	4.8987	3.6976	3.0249	2.5758	2.2495	1.9998	1.6403	1.2106	0.7970
32	9.0521	7.1327	5.2942	4.0449	3.3344	2.8549	2.5037	2.2332	1.8408	1.3671	0.9057
34	9.6437	7.6347	5.7302	4.4302	3.6795	3.1676	2.7894	2.4962	2.0678	1.5453	1.0303
36	10.2928	8.1911	6.2170	4.8629	4.0690	3.5216	3.1140	2.7958	2.3275	1.7503	1.1746
38	11.0152	8.8159	6.7674	5.3548	4.5136	3.9273	3.4869	3.1409	2.6278	1.9887	1.3434
40	11.8322	9.5282	7.3988	5.9218	5.0281	4.3982	3.9211	3.5436	2.9795	2.2694	1.5434
42	12.7727	10.3540	8.1349	6.5858	5.6329	4.9534	4.4342	4.0206	3.3976	2.6047	1.7836
44	13.8743	11.3276	9.0071	7.3758	6.3548	5.6180	5.0500	4.5943	3.9022	3.0113	2.0765
46	15.1861	12.4937	10.0567	8.3300	7.2295	6.4254	5.7998	5.2941	4.5197	3.5113	2.4386
48	16.7767	13.9152	11.3416	9.5022	8.3072	7.4228	6.7279	6.1620	5.2879	4.1359	2.8933
50	18.7440	15.6819	12.9448	10.9696	9.6600	8.6776	7.8980	7.2580	6.2609	4.9304	3.4745
52	21.2293	17.9237	14.9865	12.8441	11.3926	10.2883	9.4027	8.6699	7.5176	5.9608	4.2321
54	24.4417	20.8333	17.6455	15.2921	13.6608	12.4012	11.3802	10.5284	9.1764	7.3261	5.2405
56	28.7050	24.7093	21.1987	18.5722	16.7067	15.2442	14.0457	13.0371	11.4212	9.1807	6.6166
58	34.5279	30.0219	26.0832	23.0925	20.9133	19.1778	17.7396	16.5188	14.5441	11.7700	8.5465
60	42.7524	37.5500	33.0237	29.5305	26.9166	24.8014	23.0287	21.5110	19.0324	15.5043	11.3418

VALUES OF TIME INTEGRAL FOR SUCROSE GRADIENT CENTRIFUGATION
TEMPERATURE 5.0 DEG C PARTICLE DENSITY 1.80

WT.PCT. SUCROSE	Z0= 5	Z0= 0	Z0= -5	Z0= -10	Z0= -15	Z0= -20	Z0= -25	Z0= -30	Z0= -40	Z0= -60	Z0=-100
0	0.0	0.0	0.0	0.0	0.0	0.0	0.0	0.0	0.0	0.0	0.0
2	0.0	0.0	0.5184	0.2811	0.1931	0.1470	0.1188	0.0996	0.0753	0.0506	0.0306
4	0.0	1.1415	0.9326	0.5353	0.3765	0.2906	0.2367	0.1996	0.1521	0.1030	0.0627
6	0.0	1.8584	1.2877	0.7718	0.5538	0.4324	0.3548	0.3009	0.2308	0.1575	0.0964
8	2.1059	2.4068	1.6064	0.9965	0.7274	0.5738	0.4741	0.4041	0.3121	0.2146	0.1321
10	3.1585	2.8673	1.9019	1.2141	0.8996	0.7163	0.5957	0.5101	0.3964	0.2744	0.1700
12	3.9124	3.2762	2.1827	1.4280	1.0724	0.8612	0.7204	0.6196	0.4845	0.3377	0.2105
14	4.5274	3.6537	2.4552	1.6412	1.2475	1.0098	0.8494	0.7336	0.5770	0.4049	0.2539
16	5.0660	4.0123	2.7240	1.8562	1.4267	1.1634	0.9838	0.8531	0.6747	0.4765	0.3006
18	5.5603	4.3610	2.9934	2.0757	1.6118	1.3235	1.1249	0.9791	0.7787	0.5535	0.3513
20	6.0294	4.7065	3.2669	2.3020	1.8048	1.4918	1.2741	1.1131	0.8899	0.6366	0.4064
22	6.4866	5.0547	3.5481	2.5379	2.0080	1.6701	1.4330	1.2565	1.0098	0.7269	0.4668
24	6.9419	5.4110	3.8408	2.7862	2.2236	1.8607	1.6037	1.4111	1.1399	0.8256	0.5335
26	7.4038	5.7805	4.1487	3.0501	2.4545	2.0660	1.7885	1.5790	1.2820	0.9343	0.6074
28	7.8802	6.1686	4.4762	3.3334	2.7041	2.2890	1.9901	1.7629	1.4384	1.0547	0.6899
30	8.3792	6.5816	4.8284	3.6404	2.9763	2.5334	2.2118	1.9659	1.6120	1.1893	0.7828
32	8.9095	7.0263	5.2114	3.9767	3.2760	2.8037	2.4581	2.1919	1.8062	1.3409	0.8881
34	9.4809	7.5112	5.6324	4.3488	3.6093	3.1056	2.7340	2.4459	2.0254	1.5129	1.0084
36	10.1060	8.0470	6.1013	4.7656	3.9845	3.4467	3.0466	2.7345	2.2755	1.7104	1.1473
38	10.7997	8.6470	6.6299	5.2380	4.4114	3.8362	3.4047	3.0659	2.5639	1.9393	1.3094
40	11.5818	9.3288	7.2343	5.7807	4.9039	4.2870	3.8203	3.4514	2.9006	2.2080	1.5008
42	12.4792	10.1168	7.9366	6.4142	5.4809	4.8167	4.3099	3.9065	3.2995	2.5280	1.7300
44	13.5267	11.0426	8.7660	7.1654	6.1674	5.4487	4.8954	4.4520	3.7793	2.9146	2.0086
46	14.7696	12.1474	9.7604	8.0695	6.9961	6.2137	5.6058	5.1150	4.3644	3.3883	2.3516
48	16.2709	13.4891	10.9732	9.1759	8.0133	7.1551	6.4818	5.9342	5.0894	3.9779	2.7808
50	18.1202	15.1499	12.4802	10.5553	9.2850	8.3347	7.5817	6.9645	6.0041	4.7247	3.3272
52	20.4465	17.2483	14.3914	12.3099	10.9068	9.8423	8.9902	8.2861	7.1805	5.6892	4.0363
54	23.4400	19.9595	16.8690	14.5910	13.0203	11.8111	10.8329	10.0178	8.7261	6.9614	4.9759
56	27.3935	23.5539	20.1642	17.6328	15.8450	14.4476	13.3047	12.3443	10.8078	8.6812	6.2521
58	32.7660	28.4555	24.6707	21.8034	19.7260	18.0768	16.7128	15.5566	13.6891	11.0702	8.0326
60	40.3130	35.3635	31.0395	27.7110	25.2348	23.2372	21.5662	20.1376	17.8076	14.4969	10.5976

VALUES OF TIME INTEGRAL FOR SUCROSE GRADIENT CENTRIFUGATION
TEMPERATURE 5.0 DEG C PARTICLE DENSITY 1.90

WT.PCT. SUCROSE	ZO= 5	ZO= 0	ZO= -5	ZO= -10	ZO= -15	ZO= -20	ZO= -25	ZO= -30	ZO= -40	ZO= -60	ZO=-100
0	0.0	0.0	0.0	0.0	0.0	0.0	0.0	0.0	0.0	0.0	0.0
2	0.0	0.0	0.5169	0.2803	0.1925	0.1466	0.1184	0.0993	0.0751	0.0505	0.0305
4	0.0	1.1371	0.9295	0.5335	0.3753	0.2896	0.2359	0.1990	0.1516	0.1027	0.0624
6	0.0	1.8504	1.2829	0.7688	0.5516	0.4307	0.3534	0.2997	0.2299	0.1569	0.0960
8	2.0929	2.3954	1.5996	0.9921	0.7242	0.5712	0.4720	0.4023	0.3107	0.2136	0.1315
10	3.1376	2.8524	1.8928	1.2081	0.8951	0.7127	0.5926	0.5074	0.3944	0.2730	0.1691
12	3.8849	3.2577	2.1712	1.4201	1.0663	0.8563	0.7163	0.6160	0.4817	0.3357	0.2092
14	4.4937	3.6314	2.4409	1.6311	1.2396	1.0033	0.8440	0.7289	0.5732	0.4022	0.2522
16	5.0261	3.9859	2.7066	1.8437	1.4168	1.1552	0.9768	0.8470	0.6698	0.4730	0.2984
18	5.5140	4.3300	2.9725	2.0603	1.5995	1.3132	1.1161	0.9714	0.7724	0.5490	0.3484
20	5.9764	4.6706	3.2421	2.2834	1.7898	1.4791	1.2631	1.1034	0.8821	0.6309	0.4027
22	6.4263	5.0133	3.5188	2.5155	1.9897	1.6546	1.4195	1.2445	1.0000	0.7197	0.4622
24	6.8736	5.3633	3.8063	2.7594	2.2015	1.8418	1.5872	1.3964	1.1278	0.8167	0.5277
26	7.3267	5.7257	4.1083	3.0183	2.4280	2.0431	1.7684	1.5611	1.2672	0.9233	0.6002
28	7.7931	6.1057	4.4290	3.2956	2.6723	2.2615	1.9658	1.7412	1.4204	1.0413	0.6810
30	8.2808	6.5093	4.7733	3.5958	2.9384	2.5004	2.1826	1.9396	1.5900	1.1728	0.7717
32	8.7981	6.9432	5.1468	3.9238	3.2307	2.7641	2.4227	2.1601	1.7795	1.3206	0.8744
34	9.3544	7.4152	5.5568	4.2861	3.5553	3.0580	2.6913	2.4073	1.9929	1.4882	0.9916
36	9.9617	7.9358	6.0123	4.6910	3.9197	3.3893	2.9950	2.6877	2.2359	1.6800	1.1266
38	10.6342	8.5174	6.5247	5.1489	4.3336	3.7669	3.3422	3.0090	2.5154	1.9019	1.2837
40	11.3907	9.1770	7.1093	5.6739	4.8100	4.2030	3.7442	3.3818	2.8411	2.1618	1.4688
42	12.2567	9.9374	7.7871	6.2853	5.3668	4.7142	4.2167	3.8210	3.2261	2.4706	1.6900
44	13.2651	10.8286	8.5855	7.0084	6.0276	5.3226	4.7803	4.3461	3.6880	2.8428	1.9581
46	14.4585	11.8894	9.5403	7.8764	6.8234	6.0571	5.4624	4.9828	4.2497	3.2976	2.2875
48	15.8961	13.1742	10.7016	8.9359	7.7974	6.9585	6.3013	5.7672	4.9440	3.8621	2.6985
50	17.6619	14.7599	12.1406	10.2530	9.0117	8.0848	7.3515	6.7510	5.8173	4.5753	3.2202
52	19.8766	16.7576	13.9601	11.9234	10.5556	9.5201	8.6924	8.0091	6.9373	5.4935	3.8953
54	22.7174	19.3306	16.3114	14.0883	12.5614	11.3885	10.4412	9.6526	8.4041	6.7008	4.7870
56	26.4571	22.7306	19.4283	16.9655	15.2332	13.8824	12.7792	11.8532	10.3732	8.3276	5.9941
58	31.5212	27.3508	23.6762	20.8966	18.8916	17.3033	15.9917	14.8811	13.0891	10.5795	7.6725
60	38.6089	33.8385	29.6574	26.4448	24.0651	22.1497	20.5498	19.1833	16.9570	13.7976	10.0813

VALUES OF TIME INTEGRAL FOR SUCROSE GRADIENT CENTRIFUGATION
TEMPERATURE 20.0 DEG C PARTICLE DENSITY 1.10

WT.PCT. SUCROSE	ZO= 5	ZO= 0	ZO= -5	ZO= -10	ZO= -15	ZO= -20	ZO= -25	ZO= -30	ZO= -40	ZO= -60	ZO=-100
0	0.0	0.0	0.0	0.0	0.0	0.0	0.0	0.0	0.0	0.0	0.0
2	0.0	0.0	0.3580	0.1943	0.1335	0.1017	0.0821	0.0689	0.0521	0.0350	0.0212
4	0.0	0.8426	0.6646	0.3826	0.2694	0.2080	0.1695	0.1430	0.1090	0.0739	0.0449
6	0.0	1.4150	0.9485	0.5717	0.4112	0.3215	0.2640	0.2241	0.1720	0.1175	0.0720
8	1.8232	1.8930	1.2266	0.7679	0.5628	0.4450	0.3683	0.3142	0.2430	0.1673	0.1031
10	2.8349	2.3368	1.5116	0.9778	0.7290	0.5825	0.4856	0.4165	0.3244	0.2251	0.1397
12	3.6501	2.7797	1.8159	1.2097	0.9163	0.7397	0.6209	0.5353	0.4199	0.2938	0.1836
14	4.4149	3.2497	2.1553	1.4754	1.1345	0.9248	0.7817	0.6774	0.5353	0.3775	0.2378
16	5.2099	3.7796	2.5528	1.7934	1.3996	1.1521	0.9806	0.8542	0.6799	0.4836	0.3070
18	6.1186	4.4212	3.0488	2.1976	1.7407	1.4472	1.2406	1.0866	0.8715	0.6255	0.4004
20	7.2851	5.2813	3.7300	2.7616	2.2219	1.8668	1.6125	1.4206	1.1491	0.8328	0.5380
22	9.1129	6.6757	4.8572	3.7076	3.0369	2.5826	2.2508	1.9964	1.6306	1.1956	0.7810
24	16.5664	12.5413	9.6930	7.8212	6.6161	5.7502	5.0918	4.5719	3.8004	2.8457	1.8967

VALUES OF TIME INTEGRAL FOR SUCROSE GRADIENT CENTRIFUGATION
TEMPERATURE 20.0 DEG C PARTICLE DENSITY 1.20

WT.PCT. SUCROSE	Z0= 5	Z0= 0	Z0= -5	Z0= -10	Z0= -15	Z0= -20	Z0= -25	Z0= -30	Z0= -40	Z0= -60	Z0=-100
0	0.0	0.0	0.0	0.0	0.0	0.0	0.0	0.0	0.0	0.0	0.0
2	0.0	0.0	0.3506	0.1902	0.1306	0.0995	0.0804	0.0674	0.0510	0.0343	0.0207
4	0.0	0.7916	0.6381	0.3667	0.2580	0.1992	0.1622	0.1369	0.1043	0.0707	0.0430
6	0.0	1.3028	0.8915	0.5354	0.3845	0.3004	0.2466	0.2091	0.1605	0.1096	0.0671
8	1.5433	1.7056	1.1257	0.7006	0.5121	0.4043	0.3343	0.2850	0.2202	0.1515	0.0933
10	2.3403	2.0546	1.3496	0.8655	0.6427	0.5124	0.4264	0.3653	0.2842	0.1969	0.1221
12	2.9309	2.3751	1.5698	1.0332	0.7781	0.6260	0.5242	0.4512	0.3532	0.2465	0.1538
14	3.4305	2.6819	1.7912	1.2065	0.9204	0.7467	0.6291	0.5439	0.4284	0.3011	0.1891
16	3.8858	2.9850	2.0185	1.3883	1.0720	0.8766	0.7428	0.6449	0.5111	0.3617	0.2286
18	4.3220	3.2927	2.2563	1.5820	1.2354	1.0180	0.8673	0.7562	0.6028	0.4296	0.2733
20	4.7561	3.6125	2.5094	1.7915	1.4141	1.1737	1.0054	0.8802	0.7058	0.5066	0.3244
22	5.2019	3.9521	2.7837	2.0216	1.6122	1.3477	1.1604	1.0201	0.8228	0.5946	0.3833
24	5.6728	4.3207	3.0864	2.2785	1.8353	1.5449	1.3371	1.1801	0.9573	0.6968	0.4523
26	6.1835	4.7292	3.4269	2.5703	2.0907	1.7719	1.5414	1.3658	1.1145	0.8170	0.5340
28	6.7520	5.1925	3.8178	2.9084	2.3886	2.0381	1.7820	1.5853	1.3013	0.9609	0.6326
30	7.4026	5.7310	4.2771	3.3089	2.7436	2.3569	2.0713	1.8501	1.5277	1.1364	0.7537
32	8.1696	6.3744	4.8312	3.7955	3.1773	2.7481	2.4276	2.1772	1.8088	1.3557	0.9061
34	9.1063	7.1692	5.5216	4.4056	3.7239	3.2432	2.8800	2.5938	2.1683	1.6380	1.1035
36	10.3013	8.1937	6.4182	5.2026	4.4413	3.8954	3.4780	3.1457	2.6467	2.0157	1.3693
38	11.9186	9.5927	7.6508	6.3043	5.4372	4.8040	4.3133	3.9188	3.3195	2.5498	1.7476
40	14.3120	11.6798	9.5011	7.9661	6.9452	6.1844	5.5860	5.0994	4.3508	3.3730	2.3340
42	18.5008	15.3591	12.7815	10.9255	9.6410	8.6596	7.8741	7.2266	6.2157	4.8690	3.4060
44	32.1487	27.4325	23.6060	20.7354	18.6102	16.9209	15.5310	14.3615	12.4946	9.9328	7.0568

VALUES OF TIME INTEGRAL FOR SUCROSE GRADIENT CENTRIFUGATION
TEMPERATURE 20.0 DEG C PARTICLE DENSITY 1.30

WT.PCT. SUCROSE	Z0= 5	Z0= 0	Z0= -5	Z0= -10	Z0= -15	Z0= -20	Z0= -25	Z0= -30	Z0= -40	Z0= -60	Z0=-100
0	0.0	0.0	0.0	0.0	0.0	0.0	0.0	0.0	0.0	0.0	0.0
2	0.0	0.0	0.3477	0.1886	0.1295	0.0987	0.0797	0.0668	0.0505	0.0340	0.0206
4	0.0	0.7748	0.6289	0.3612	0.2541	0.1962	0.1598	0.1348	0.1027	0.0696	0.0423
6	0.0	1.2676	0.8732	0.5238	0.3760	0.2936	0.2410	0.2044	0.1568	0.1071	0.0655
8	1.4653	1.6496	1.0952	0.6804	0.4970	0.3922	0.3242	0.2763	0.2135	0.1468	0.0904
10	2.2082	1.9746	1.3038	0.8340	0.6186	0.4928	0.4100	0.3511	0.2730	0.1891	0.1172
12	2.7478	2.2674	1.5048	0.9872	0.7423	0.5966	0.4993	0.4296	0.3361	0.2344	0.1461
14	3.1945	2.5416	1.7028	1.1421	0.8695	0.7045	0.5930	0.5124	0.4033	0.2832	0.1777
16	3.5919	2.8062	1.9012	1.3007	1.0017	0.8178	0.6922	0.6006	0.4754	0.3361	0.2122
18	3.9626	3.0677	2.1032	1.4653	1.1406	0.9379	0.7980	0.6951	0.5534	0.3938	0.2501
20	4.3205	3.3313	2.3119	1.6380	1.2879	1.0664	0.9118	0.7973	0.6382	0.4572	0.2922
22	4.6758	3.6019	2.5304	1.8213	1.4457	1.2049	1.0354	0.9087	0.7314	0.5273	0.3392
24	5.0366	3.8843	2.7623	2.0181	1.6166	1.3560	1.1707	1.0313	0.8345	0.6056	0.3920
26	5.4106	4.1835	3.0116	2.2318	1.8036	1.5222	1.3203	1.1673	0.9496	0.6936	0.4519
28	5.8055	4.5052	3.2831	2.4666	2.0105	1.7071	1.4874	1.3197	1.0793	0.7935	0.5203
30	6.2298	4.8564	3.5827	2.7278	2.2420	1.9149	1.6760	1.4924	1.2269	0.9079	0.5993
32	6.6933	5.2452	3.9175	3.0217	2.5040	2.1513	1.8912	1.6900	1.3967	1.0404	0.6913
34	7.2083	5.6822	4.2970	3.3571	2.8044	2.4234	2.1399	1.9189	1.5943	1.1955	0.7998
36	7.7904	6.1811	4.7336	3.7453	3.1538	2.7410	2.4310	2.1877	1.8272	1.3794	0.9292
38	8.4604	6.7606	5.2441	4.2015	3.5661	3.1172	2.7769	2.5077	2.1057	1.6005	1.0858
40	9.2462	7.4457	5.8514	4.7468	4.0610	3.5702	3.1945	2.8951	2.4441	1.8705	1.2781
42	10.1873	8.2721	6.5881	5.4113	4.6662	4.1258	3.7081	3.3725	2.8625	2.2062	1.5185
44	11.3410	9.2918	7.5016	6.2387	5.4223	4.8219	4.3530	3.9733	3.3910	2.6321	1.8253
46	12.7907	10.5805	8.6615	7.2933	6.3891	5.7143	5.1817	4.7468	4.0735	3.1846	2.2255
48	14.6645	12.2551	10.1752	8.6743	7.6588	6.8893	6.2752	5.7693	4.9786	3.9206	2.7613
50	17.1696	14.5048	12.2168	10.5430	9.3816	8.4874	7.7653	7.1652	6.2177	4.9325	3.5016
52	20.6586	17.6521	15.0834	13.1748	11.8142	10.7488	9.8781	9.1476	7.9824	6.3794	4.5654
54	25.7750	22.2864	19.3186	17.0742	15.4272	14.1146	13.0283	12.1082	10.6249	8.5545	6.1721
56	33.8222	29.6031	26.0263	23.2666	21.1777	19.4821	18.0607	16.8449	14.8634	12.0564	8.7708
58	47.8996	42.4478	37.8368	34.1971	31.3502	28.9950	26.9943	25.2656	22.4170	18.3199	13.4396
60	77.9747	69.9806	63.2236	57.7483	53.3134	49.5707	46.3475	43.5334	38.8424	31.9883	23.6728

VALUES OF TIME INTEGRAL FOR SUCROSE GRADIENT CENTRIFUGATION
TEMPERATURE 20.0 DEG C PARTICLE DENSITY 1.40

WT.PCT. SUCROSE	Z0= 5	Z0= 0	Z0= -5	Z0= -10	Z0= -15	Z0= -20	Z0= -25	Z0= -30	Z0= -40	Z0= -60	Z0=-100
0	0.0	0.0	0.0	0.0	0.0	0.0	0.0	0.0	0.0	0.0	0.0
2	0.0	0.0	0.3459	0.1876	0.1289	0.0982	0.0793	0.0665	0.0503	0.0338	0.0204
4	0.0	0.7658	0.6238	0.3582	0.2520	0.1945	0.1584	0.1336	0.1018	0.0690	0.0419
6	0.0	1.2494	0.8634	0.5177	0.3715	0.2901	0.2381	0.2019	0.1549	0.1058	0.0647
8	1.4276	1.6213	1.0796	0.6701	0.4893	0.3861	0.3190	0.2719	0.2100	0.1444	0.0889
10	2.1451	1.9352	1.2810	0.8185	0.6067	0.4832	0.4019	0.3442	0.2675	0.1853	0.1148
12	2.6618	2.2155	1.4735	0.9651	0.7251	0.5825	0.4874	0.4193	0.3279	0.2286	0.1425
14	3.0855	2.4756	1.6612	1.1120	0.8458	0.6849	0.5763	0.4978	0.3916	0.2749	0.1724
16	3.4586	2.7240	1.8475	1.2610	0.9699	0.7913	0.6694	0.5806	0.4593	0.3245	0.2048
18	3.8029	2.9668	2.0351	1.4138	1.0989	0.9028	0.7677	0.6684	0.5317	0.3781	0.2401
20	4.1314	3.2088	2.2266	1.5723	1.2341	1.0207	0.8721	0.7622	0.6097	0.4363	0.2787
22	4.4534	3.4540	2.4247	1.7384	1.3771	1.1463	0.9841	0.8632	0.6941	0.4999	0.3213
24	4.7759	3.7064	2.6320	1.9143	1.5299	1.2813	1.1050	0.9727	0.7862	0.5698	0.3685
26	5.1052	3.9698	2.8515	2.1024	1.6945	1.4276	1.2367	1.0924	0.8875	0.6473	0.4211
28	5.4471	4.2484	3.0865	2.3058	1.8736	1.5877	1.3814	1.2244	0.9998	0.7338	0.4804
30	5.8079	4.5470	3.3412	2.5278	2.0704	1.7644	1.5417	1.3712	1.1253	0.8311	0.5475
32	6.1941	4.8709	3.6201	2.7727	2.2887	1.9613	1.7211	1.5358	1.2668	0.9415	0.6242
34	6.6135	5.2268	3.9292	3.0459	2.5334	2.1829	1.9236	1.7223	1.4277	1.0678	0.7125
36	7.0758	5.6231	4.2760	3.3541	2.8108	2.4351	2.1548	1.9357	1.6127	1.2138	0.8153
38	7.5929	6.0703	4.6700	3.7062	3.1291	2.7255	2.4217	2.1827	1.8276	1.3845	0.9361
40	8.1800	6.5822	5.1237	4.1136	3.4988	3.0639	2.7337	2.4721	2.0804	1.5862	1.0798
42	8.8574	7.1770	5.6539	4.5919	3.9344	3.4638	3.1033	2.8157	2.3816	1.8277	1.2529
44	9.6525	7.8796	6.2834	5.1620	4.4554	3.9434	3.5477	3.2296	2.7457	2.1212	1.4642
46	10.6017	8.7235	7.0429	5.8525	5.0884	4.5277	4.0903	3.7361	3.1925	2.4830	1.7262
48	11.7562	9.7552	7.9755	6.7033	5.8706	5.2516	4.7639	4.3660	3.7501	2.9363	2.0563
50	13.1889	11.0418	9.1430	7.7719	6.8558	6.1655	5.6161	5.1642	4.4586	3.5149	2.4796
52	15.0069	12.6817	10.6366	9.1432	8.1232	7.3437	6.7168	6.1970	5.3780	4.2687	3.0338
54	17.3706	14.8226	12.5930	10.9445	9.7921	8.8983	8.1719	7.5645	6.5985	5.2733	3.7758
56	20.5284	17.6935	15.2249	13.3740	12.0482	11.0041	10.1461	9.4227	8.2612	6.6469	4.7951
58	24.8789	21.6627	18.8743	16.7513	15.1911	13.9431	12.9060	12.0241	10.5946	8.5816	6.2370
60	31.0874	27.3456	24.1135	21.6112	19.7229	18.1883	16.8987	15.7926	13.9827	11.4006	8.3471

VALUES OF TIME INTEGRAL FOR SUCROSE GRADIENT CENTRIFUGATION
TEMPERATURE 20.0 DEG C PARTICLE DENSITY 1.50

WT.PCT. SUCROSE	Z0= 5	Z0= 0	Z0= -5	Z0= -10	Z0= -15	Z0= -20	Z0= -25	Z0= -30	Z0= -40	Z0= -60	Z0=-100
0	0.0	0.0	0.0	0.0	0.0	0.0	0.0	0.0	0.0	0.0	0.0
2	0.0	0.0	0.3446	0.1869	0.1284	0.0978	0.0790	0.0662	0.0501	0.0337	0.0204
4	0.0	0.7599	0.6203	0.3561	0.2505	0.1933	0.1574	0.1328	0.1012	0.0686	0.0417
6	0.0	1.2376	0.8570	0.5137	0.3686	0.2878	0.2362	0.2003	0.1537	0.1049	0.0642
8	1.4046	1.6035	1.0696	0.6636	0.4844	0.3822	0.3158	0.2692	0.2079	0.1429	0.0880
10	2.1071	1.9108	1.2668	0.8088	0.5994	0.4773	0.3969	0.3399	0.2642	0.1829	0.1133
12	2.6105	2.1838	1.4543	0.9517	0.7147	0.5740	0.4802	0.4130	0.3230	0.2251	0.1403
14	3.0211	2.4358	1.6362	1.0940	0.8316	0.6732	0.5663	0.4891	0.3847	0.2700	0.1693
16	3.3807	2.6752	1.8157	1.2375	0.9512	0.7757	0.6561	0.5689	0.4500	0.3178	0.2005
18	3.7105	2.9079	1.9954	1.3840	1.0748	0.8826	0.7502	0.6530	0.5193	0.3692	0.2343
20	4.0233	3.1383	2.1778	1.5349	1.2035	0.9948	0.8496	0.7423	0.5935	0.4246	0.2711
22	4.3278	3.3702	2.3651	1.6920	1.3388	1.1136	0.9555	0.8378	0.6733	0.4847	0.3113
24	4.6307	3.6072	2.5598	1.8571	1.4822	1.2403	1.0691	0.9406	0.7599	0.5504	0.3556
26	4.9375	3.8527	2.7643	2.0325	1.6356	1.3767	1.1918	1.0522	0.8543	0.6226	0.4047
28	5.2536	4.1102	2.9816	2.2204	1.8012	1.5247	1.3255	1.1742	0.9581	0.7025	0.4595
30	5.5842	4.3838	3.2150	2.4239	1.9815	1.6866	1.4725	1.3087	1.0731	0.7917	0.5210
32	5.9348	4.6779	3.4682	2.6462	2.1797	1.8653	1.6353	1.4582	1.2015	0.8919	0.5906
34	6.3118	4.9977	3.7460	2.8917	2.3996	2.0645	1.8173	1.6257	1.3461	1.0054	0.6700
36	6.7227	5.3499	4.0542	3.1657	2.6462	2.2887	2.0228	1.8154	1.5105	1.1352	0.7614
38	7.1769	5.7428	4.4002	3.4749	2.9257	2.5437	2.2572	2.0324	1.6993	1.2851	0.8675
40	7.6859	6.1865	4.7936	3.8282	3.2463	2.8371	2.5277	2.2833	1.9184	1.4599	0.9920
42	8.2650	6.6950	5.2468	4.2369	3.6186	3.1789	2.8436	2.5769	2.1759	1.6664	1.1399
44	8.9339	7.2862	5.7765	4.7167	4.0570	3.5825	3.2175	2.9253	2.4822	1.9133	1.3178
46	9.7190	7.9841	6.4046	5.2877	4.5805	4.0658	3.6663	3.3441	2.8518	2.2125	1.5345
48	10.6558	8.8212	7.1613	5.9781	5.2152	4.6531	4.2129	3.8552	3.3042	2.5803	1.8022
50	11.7937	9.8431	8.0886	6.8268	5.9976	5.3789	4.8897	4.4892	3.8670	3.0399	2.1385
52	13.2035	11.1147	9.2468	7.8901	6.9804	6.2925	5.7432	5.2900	4.5798	3.6244	2.5681
54	14.9872	12.7303	10.7232	9.2494	8.2398	7.4657	6.8412	6.3219	5.5008	4.3824	3.1281
56	17.2975	14.8307	12.6486	11.0269	9.8904	9.0063	8.2856	7.6814	6.7172	5.3874	3.8738
58	20.3689	17.6329	15.2250	13.4111	12.1091	11.0810	10.2339	9.5178	8.3644	6.7531	4.8916
60	24.5734	21.4814	18.7730	16.7022	15.1781	13.9559	12.9377	12.0698	10.6588	8.6620	6.3205

VALUES OF TIME INTEGRAL FOR SUCROSE GRADIENT CENTRIFUGATION
TEMPERATURE 20.0 DEG C PARTICLE DENSITY 1.60

WT.PCT. SUCROSE	ZO= 5	ZO= 0	ZO= -5	ZO= -10	ZO= -15	ZO= -20	ZO= -25	ZO= -30	ZO= -40	ZO= -60	ZO=-100
0	0.0	0.0	0.0	0.0	0.0	0.0	0.0	0.0	0.0	0.0	0.0
2	0.0	0.0	0.3435	0.1863	0.1279	0.0974	0.0787	0.0660	0.0499	0.0336	0.0203
4	0.0	0.7555	0.6176	0.3545	0.2493	0.1924	0.1567	0.1322	0.1007	0.0682	0.0415
6	0.0	1.2291	0.8522	0.5107	0.3664	0.2861	0.2348	0.1991	0.1527	0.1043	0.0638
8	1.3888	1.5907	1.0624	0.6589	0.4809	0.3794	0.3135	0.2672	0.2063	0.1418	0.0873
10	2.0811	1.8936	1.2567	0.8020	0.5942	0.4731	0.3934	0.3368	0.2618	0.1812	0.1123
12	2.5756	2.1618	1.4409	0.9423	0.7075	0.5681	0.4752	0.4087	0.3195	0.2227	0.1388
14	2.9776	2.4085	1.6190	1.0816	0.8219	0.6652	0.5595	0.4832	0.3800	0.2666	0.1672
16	3.3284	2.6421	1.7940	1.2217	0.9386	0.7652	0.6471	0.5610	0.4437	0.3133	0.1976
18	3.6490	2.8682	1.9687	1.3640	1.0587	0.8691	0.7386	0.6428	0.5111	0.3632	0.2305
20	3.9518	3.0913	2.1453	1.5101	1.1833	0.9777	0.8349	0.7292	0.5829	0.4168	0.2661
22	4.2455	3.3149	2.3259	1.6616	1.3138	1.0923	0.9369	0.8213	0.6599	0.4748	0.3049
24	4.5363	3.5425	2.5128	1.8202	1.4515	1.2140	1.0460	0.9201	0.7429	0.5379	0.3474
26	4.8296	3.7771	2.7083	1.9878	1.5981	1.3443	1.1633	1.0267	0.8332	0.6069	0.3944
28	5.1303	4.0221	2.9150	2.1665	1.7556	1.4851	1.2905	1.1427	0.9319	0.6829	0.4464
30	5.4431	4.2810	3.1359	2.3591	1.9263	1.6383	1.4295	1.2700	1.0407	0.7673	0.5047
32	5.7731	4.5577	3.3742	2.5683	2.1128	1.8065	1.5828	1.4107	1.1616	0.8616	0.5702
34	6.1259	4.8571	3.6342	2.7981	2.3186	1.9929	1.7531	1.5675	1.2969	0.9678	0.6445
36	6.5081	5.1847	3.9208	3.0529	2.5480	2.2014	1.9442	1.7439	1.4499	1.0886	0.7294
38	6.9278	5.5477	4.2406	3.3387	2.8063	2.4371	2.1609	1.9444	1.6243	1.2270	0.8275
40	7.3948	5.9549	4.6016	3.6628	3.1004	2.7063	2.4091	2.1746	1.8254	1.3875	0.9418
42	7.9222	6.4179	5.0143	4.0351	3.4394	3.0176	2.6968	2.4421	2.0598	1.5755	1.0765
44	8.5265	6.9520	5.4928	4.4684	3.8355	3.3822	3.0346	2.7567	2.3366	1.7986	1.2371
46	9.2297	7.5771	6.0554	4.9799	4.3043	3.8150	3.4365	3.1319	2.6676	2.0665	1.4312
48	10.0608	8.3199	6.7268	5.5924	4.8675	4.3361	3.9214	3.5853	3.0690	2.3929	1.6688
50	11.0603	9.2174	7.5412	6.3379	5.5547	4.9736	4.5158	4.1422	3.5632	2.7965	1.9641
52	12.2849	10.3220	8.5473	7.2616	6.4084	5.7672	5.2573	4.8378	4.1825	3.3042	2.3373
54	13.8160	11.7087	9.8145	8.4282	7.4894	6.7742	6.1997	5.7235	4.9730	3.9549	2.8179
56	15.7730	13.4880	11.4456	9.9339	8.8876	8.0792	7.4232	6.8751	6.0034	4.8061	3.4496
58	18.3374	15.8276	13.5967	11.9246	10.7401	9.8115	9.0499	8.4084	7.3787	5.9464	4.2994
60	21.7925	18.9901	16.5122	14.6291	13.2619	12.1738	11.2717	10.5054	9.2640	7.5151	5.4735

VALUES OF TIME INTEGRAL FOR SUCROSE GRADIENT CENTRIFUGATION
TEMPERATURE 20.0 DEG C PARTICLE DENSITY 1.70

WT.PCT. SUCROSE	ZO= 5	ZO= 0	ZO= -5	ZO= -10	ZO= -15	ZO= -20	ZO= -25	ZO= -30	ZO= -40	ZO= -60	ZO=-100
0	0.0	0.0	0.0	0.0	0.0	0.0	0.0	0.0	0.0	0.0	0.0
2	0.0	0.0	0.3425	0.1857	0.1276	0.0972	0.0785	0.0658	0.0498	0.0335	0.0202
4	0.0	0.7519	0.6153	0.3532	0.2484	0.1917	0.1561	0.1317	0.1003	0.0680	0.0413
6	0.0	1.2224	0.8484	0.5083	0.3647	0.2847	0.2336	0.1981	0.1520	0.1037	0.0635
8	1.3768	1.5808	1.0566	0.6552	0.4782	0.3772	0.3116	0.2656	0.2051	0.1410	0.0868
10	2.0616	1.8804	1.2488	0.7967	0.5902	0.4699	0.3907	0.3345	0.2600	0.1800	0.1115
12	2.5497	2.1451	1.4306	0.9352	0.7020	0.5636	0.4714	0.4054	0.3170	0.2209	0.1377
14	2.9455	2.3880	1.6060	1.0724	0.8147	0.6593	0.5545	0.4788	0.3765	0.2641	0.1656
16	3.2901	2.6174	1.7779	1.2099	0.9293	0.7575	0.6404	0.5552	0.4390	0.3100	0.1955
18	3.6042	2.8390	1.9491	1.3494	1.0470	0.8593	0.7301	0.6353	0.5051	0.3589	0.2277
20	3.9001	3.0569	2.1216	1.4922	1.1687	0.9654	0.8242	0.7198	0.5752	0.4113	0.2625
22	4.1863	3.2749	2.2976	1.6398	1.2959	1.0770	0.9237	0.8095	0.6503	0.4678	0.3003
24	4.4688	3.4960	2.4792	1.7939	1.4297	1.1953	1.0296	0.9055	0.7310	0.5290	0.3416
26	4.7530	3.7233	2.6686	1.9562	1.5717	1.3215	1.1432	1.0088	0.8184	0.5959	0.3871
28	5.0433	3.9598	2.8682	2.1288	1.7238	1.4574	1.2661	1.1208	0.9137	0.6693	0.4374
30	5.3444	4.2090	3.0808	2.3141	1.8880	1.6049	1.3999	1.2433	1.0185	0.7505	0.4934
32	5.6609	4.4744	3.3093	2.5148	2.0669	1.7663	1.5468	1.3782	1.1344	0.8409	0.5562
34	5.9979	4.7604	3.5577	2.7343	2.2635	1.9443	1.7096	1.5280	1.2637	0.9425	0.6272
36	6.3617	5.0722	3.8305	2.9768	2.4818	2.1428	1.8915	1.6960	1.4092	1.0573	0.7081
38	6.7594	5.4162	4.1336	3.2477	2.7266	2.3661	2.0968	1.8860	1.5745	1.1886	0.8010
40	7.2002	5.8005	4.4742	3.5535	3.0042	2.6202	2.3310	2.1032	1.7643	1.3400	0.9089
42	7.6955	6.2354	4.8619	3.9032	3.3226	2.9125	2.6012	2.3544	1.9845	1.5166	1.0354
44	8.2604	6.7346	5.3091	4.3083	3.6928	3.2533	2.9169	2.6485	2.2432	1.7251	1.1855
46	8.9142	7.3158	5.8322	4.7838	4.1287	3.6557	3.2906	2.9973	2.5509	1.9742	1.3660
48	9.6827	8.0026	6.4530	5.3502	4.6494	4.1376	3.7390	3.4166	2.9220	2.2760	1.5857
50	10.6014	8.8276	7.2016	6.0354	5.2812	4.7236	4.2854	3.9284	3.3764	2.6470	1.8571
52	11.7200	9.8366	8.1206	6.8791	6.0609	5.4484	4.9627	4.5639	3.9420	3.1108	2.1980
54	13.1089	11.0946	9.2702	7.9375	7.0416	6.3620	5.8176	5.3674	4.6591	3.7010	2.6340
56	14.8715	12.6971	10.7392	9.2936	8.3008	7.5373	6.9196	6.4045	5.5872	4.4677	3.2029
58	17.1632	14.7879	12.6615	11.0725	9.9563	9.0853	8.3733	7.7747	6.8161	5.4867	3.9623
60	20.2248	17.5902	15.2450	13.4689	12.1909	11.1786	10.3420	9.6329	8.4868	6.8766	5.0027

VALUES OF TIME INTEGRAL FOR SUCROSE GRADIENT CENTRIFUGATION
TEMPERATURE 20.0 DEG C PARTICLE DENSITY 1.80

WT.PCT. SUCROSE	ZO= 5	ZO= 0	ZO= -5	ZO= -10	ZO= -15	ZO= -20	ZO= -25	ZO= -30	ZO= -40	ZO= -60	ZO=-100
0	0.0	0.0	0.0	0.0	0.0	0.0	0.0	0.0	0.0	0.0	0.0
2	0.0	0.0	0.3416	0.1852	0.1272	0.0969	0.0783	0.0656	0.0496	0.0334	0.0202
4	0.0	0.7489	0.6133	0.3520	0.2475	0.1910	0.1556	0.1312	0.1000	0.0677	0.0412
6	0.0	1.2168	0.8450	0.5063	0.3632	0.2836	0.2327	0.1973	0.1514	0.1033	0.0632
8	1.3673	1.5727	1.0518	0.6521	0.4759	0.3753	0.3101	0.2643	0.2041	0.1403	0.0864
10	2.0462	1.8696	1.2424	0.7924	0.5869	0.4673	0.3885	0.3326	0.2585	0.1789	0.1108
12	2.5292	2.1316	1.4223	0.9295	0.6976	0.5601	0.4684	0.4028	0.3149	0.2194	0.1368
14	2.9203	2.3717	1.5955	1.0650	0.8089	0.6545	0.5505	0.4753	0.3737	0.2621	0.1643
16	3.2602	2.5979	1.7652	1.2007	0.9220	0.7514	0.6352	0.5507	0.4354	0.3074	0.1938
18	3.5694	2.8160	1.9337	1.3380	1.0378	0.8516	0.7235	0.6295	0.5004	0.3555	0.2255
20	3.8603	3.0302	2.1032	1.4783	1.1575	0.9559	0.8160	0.7125	0.5694	0.4070	0.2597
22	4.1409	3.2439	2.2758	1.6230	1.2821	1.0654	0.9135	0.8005	0.6429	0.4624	0.2968
24	4.4174	3.4603	2.4535	1.7738	1.4131	1.1811	1.0172	0.8944	0.7219	0.5224	0.3373
26	4.6948	3.6822	2.6385	1.9323	1.5518	1.3044	1.1281	0.9953	0.8073	0.5876	0.3816
28	4.9777	3.9127	2.8329	2.1005	1.6999	1.4368	1.2478	1.1045	0.9002	0.6592	0.4306
30	5.2704	4.1549	3.0395	2.2806	1.8596	1.5801	1.3779	1.2235	1.0020	0.7381	0.4851
32	5.5772	4.4123	3.2611	2.4752	2.0330	1.7366	1.5203	1.3543	1.1143	0.8258	0.5460
34	5.9032	4.6888	3.5013	2.6874	2.2232	1.9088	1.6777	1.4992	1.2394	0.9239	0.6147
36	6.2540	4.9895	3.7644	2.9213	2.4337	2.1002	1.8532	1.6611	1.3797	1.0347	0.6926
38	6.6365	5.3204	4.0559	3.1818	2.6691	2.3149	2.0506	1.8439	1.5387	1.1610	0.7820
40	7.0591	5.6888	4.3825	3.4751	2.9352	2.5585	2.2752	2.0522	1.7206	1.3062	0.8854
42	7.5325	6.1045	4.7530	3.8093	3.2396	2.8380	2.5335	2.2923	1.9311	1.4750	1.0063
44	8.0706	6.5801	5.1790	4.1952	3.5922	3.1626	2.8342	2.5724	2.1775	1.6735	1.1494
46	8.6913	7.1318	5.6756	4.6466	4.0061	3.5446	3.1890	2.9035	2.4697	1.9101	1.3207
48	9.4182	7.7814	6.2628	5.1823	4.4986	4.0004	3.6131	3.3001	2.8207	2.1955	1.5285
50	10.2838	8.5587	6.9681	5.8279	5.0938	4.5525	4.1279	3.7823	3.2488	2.5450	1.7842
52	11.3333	9.5054	7.8304	6.6195	5.8254	5.2326	4.7633	4.3786	3.7795	2.9802	2.1041
54	12.6309	10.6807	8.9044	7.6083	5.7415	6.0860	5.5620	5.1292	4.4495	3.5316	2.5114
56	14.2700	12.1709	10.2704	8.8693	7.9126	7.1790	6.5868	6.0937	5.3124	4.2445	3.0404
58	16.3907	14.1056	12.0493	0.5155	9.4445	8.6115	7.9319	7.3616	6.4497	5.1875	3.7431
60	19.2090	16.6853	14.4276	2.7216	11.5016	10.5385	9.7443	9.0722	7.9876	6.4670	4.7009

VALUES OF TIME INTEGRAL FOR SUCROSE GRADIENT CENTRIFUGATION
TEMPERATURE 20.0 DEG C PARTICLE DENSITY 1.90

WT.PCT. SUCROSE	Z0= 5	Z0= 0	Z0= -5	Z0= -10	Z0= -15	Z0= -20	Z0= -25	Z0= -30	Z0= -40	Z0= -60	Z0=-100
0	0.0	0.0	0.0	0.0	0.0	0.0	0.0	0.0	0.0	0.0	0.0
2	0.0	0.0	0.3407	0.1848	0.1269	0.0967	0.0781	0.0655	0.0495	0.0333	0.0201
4	0.0	0.7462	0.6114	0.3509	0.2468	0.1905	0.1551	0.1308	0.0997	0.0675	0.0411
6	0.0	1.2119	0.8421	0.5044	0.3619	0.2825	0.2318	0.1966	0.1508	0.1029	0.0630
8	1.3593	1.5657	1.0477	0.6494	0.4739	0.3738	0.3088	0.2632	0.2032	0.1397	0.0860
10	2.0334	1.8605	1.2369	0.7888	0.5842	0.4650	0.3866	0.3310	0.2572	0.1781	0.1103
12	2.5124	2.1203	1.4153	0.9246	0.6939	0.5571	0.4659	0.4006	0.3132	0.2182	0.1360
14	2.8997	2.3580	1.5868	1.0589	0.8042	0.6506	0.5471	0.4724	0.3714	0.2605	0.1633
16	3.2359	2.5818	1.7546	1.1931	0.9160	0.7464	0.6310	0.5469	0.4324	0.3052	0.1925
18	3.5413	2.7972	1.9210	1.3286	1.0304	0.8454	0.7181	0.6248	0.4966	0.3528	0.2238
20	3.8281	3.0084	2.0882	1.4670	1.1484	0.9482	0.8093	0.7067	0.5646	0.4036	0.2575
22	4.1044	3.2189	2.2581	1.6095	1.2711	1.0560	0.9054	0.7933	0.6371	0.4581	0.2940
24	4.3762	3.4316	2.4329	1.7578	1.3999	1.1698	1.0073	0.8856	0.7147	0.5171	0.3338
26	4.6486	3.6494	2.6144	1.9134	1.5360	1.2908	1.1162	0.9847	0.7985	0.5811	0.3774
28	4.9257	3.8753	2.8049	2.0782	1.6812	1.4205	1.2335	1.0916	0.8895	0.6512	0.4254
30	5.2120	4.1122	3.0070	2.2543	1.8373	1.5607	1.3607	1.2081	0.9891	0.7284	0.4786
32	5.5116	4.3634	3.2234	2.4443	2.0066	1.7135	1.4998	1.3358	1.0988	0.8140	0.5381
34	5.8292	4.6329	3.4574	2.6511	2.1919	1.8813	1.6532	1.4770	1.2206	0.9097	0.6050
36	6.1704	4.9254	3.7133	2.8786	2.3967	2.0674	1.8238	1.6345	1.3571	1.0175	0.6808
38	6.5416	5.2465	3.9962	3.1314	2.6252	2.2759	2.0154	1.8118	1.5115	1.1400	0.7676
40	6.9509	5.6033	4.3125	3.4154	2.8829	2.5117	2.2329	2.0135	1.6876	1.2806	0.8677
42	7.4083	6.0049	4.6705	3.7383	3.1770	2.7818	2.4824	2.2455	1.8910	1.4436	0.9845
44	7.9270	6.4633	5.0811	4.1103	3.5168	3.0947	2.7723	2.5155	2.1285	1.6351	1.1224
46	8.5238	6.9938	5.5586	4.5443	3.9148	3.4620	3.1134	2.8339	2.4094	1.8625	1.2871
48	9.2209	7.6168	6.1217	5.0580	4.3871	3.8990	3.5201	3.2142	2.7461	2.1362	1.4864
50	10.0487	8.3601	6.7962	5.6755	4.9563	4.4270	4.0125	3.6754	3.1554	2.4705	1.7309
52	11.0495	9.2629	7.6185	6.4303	5.6540	5.0756	4.6184	4.2440	3.6615	2.8854	2.0360
54	12.2832	10.3803	8.6396	7.3704	6.5250	5.8870	5.3778	4.9576	4.2985	3.4097	2.4232
56	13.8365	11.7925	9.9342	8.5655	7.6347	6.9228	6.3489	5.8716	5.1163	4.0853	2.9246
58	15.8395	13.6199	11.6143	10.1203	9.0816	8.2758	7.6194	7.0692	6.1905	4.9759	3.5883
60	18.4921	16.0478	13.8527	12.1966	11.0177	10.0894	9.3252	8.6791	7.6379	6.1802	4.4897

3. *Compute integral.* From the appropriate table $I(12\%) = 0.4993$, $I(4\%) = 0.1597$:

$$I(12\%) - I(4\%) = 0.3396 = s_{20,w}\omega^2 t$$

4. *Compute time.* At 39,000 rpm:

$$\omega \frac{\text{rad}}{\text{sec}} = 4084, \qquad \omega^2 = 16.68 \times 10^6$$

Hence

$$t = \frac{0.3396}{(100 \times 10^{-13})(16.68 \times 10^6)} = 2036 \text{ sec } (34 \text{ min})$$

VERIFICATION OF TABLES

Comparison of present computation with computation of Martin and Ames: Figure 1 shows that the tables presented in this paper give results comparable to the computation of Martin and Ames (2).

Experimental verification, 1% lysozyme: A 13–42.5% sucrose gradient of

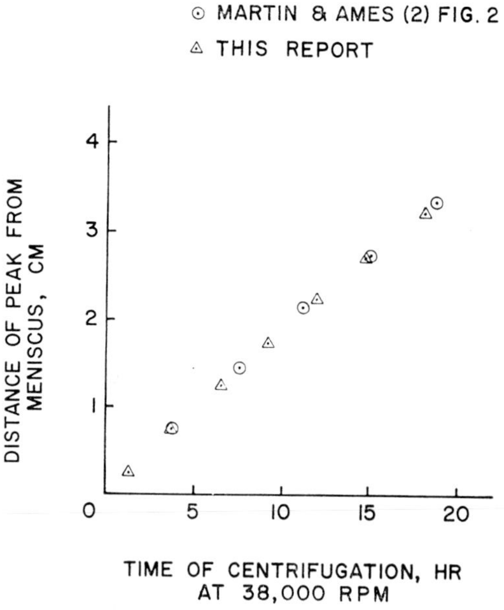

FIG. 1. Computed behavior of a protein of sedimentation coefficient 11.0 S, and partial specific volume, 0.725 cm³ gm⁻¹, sedimenting through a sucrose gradient at 3°C and 38,000 rpm. The limiting concentrations are 4.91 wt % (5% w/v) and 19.39 wt % (20% w/v). Points shown for this report were computed by interpolation from the tables of this report. The value of z_0 computed from the data supplied by Martin and Ames was −19.74, whereas the tabular value of −20 was used.

total volume 5.2 ml was placed in each of the three tubes for the SW65 rotor. Sample layers of 0.2 ml containing 1% egg white lysozyme were applied, and overnight centrifugation for 16 hr at 65,580 rpm and 20°C was carried out. The gradient was displaced through a UV monitor and the positions of the peaks in the three tubes measured to be 0.240, 0.244, and 0.248 of the total distance from top to bottom of the gradient, corresponding to a mean sucrose concentration at zone maximum of 20.2%. The meniscus and tube bottom radii are 4.3 and 8.8 cm, respectively. The computed value of z_0 is -15.2. Using a nominal value of $z_0 = -15$, the value of the integral difference $I(20.2\%)$-$I(13\%)$ was obtained by interpolation in the tables at two different particle densities; 1.3 and 1.4, which covers the range for most proteins. The corresponding estimates of $s_{20,w}$ for this particle are 1.83 and 1.70S. This in acceptably close agreement with the table of Edsall (13), viz. 1.8 to 2.1S.

Experimental verifications, human serum: Normal human serum was diluted to approximately 1% protein concentration and 0.2 ml samples were layered over two 9–28% sucrose gradients and centrifuged overnight for 16 hr at 66,000 rpm and 5°C. The radii of gradient top and bottom were the same as in the lysozyme experiment, giving a value for z_0 of -9.2. Two principal peaks appeared in the gradient, at positions corresponding

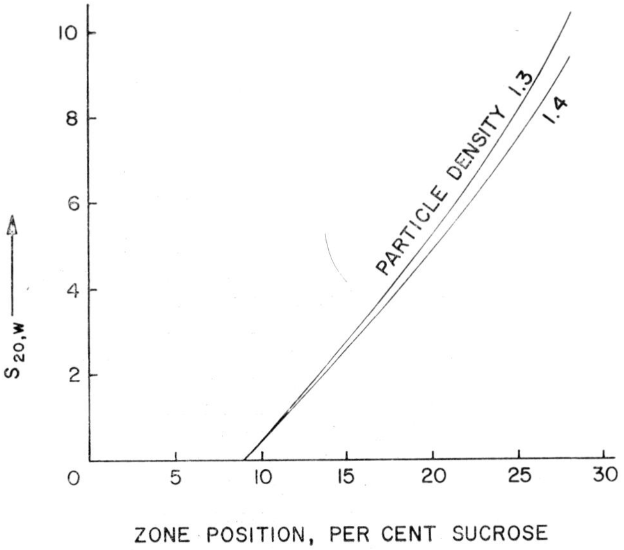

FIG. 2. Computed sedimentation coefficient as a function of position in gradient for $z_0 = -10$, temperature 5°C, rate of rotation 66,000 rpm, duration of centrifugation 16 hr. The two curves correspond to different particle densities, as shown. These curves were used to estimate the sedimentation coefficients of peaks in sedimenting serum.

to 18.0 and 22.2% surose. A cuzve was plotted from the tables giving $s_{20,w}$ as a function of position in the gradient (Fig. 2) for particle densities of 1.3 and 1.4. The peak positions for the two components read from this curve correspond to sedimentation coefficients as follows:

Peak I	4.1 S(ρ_p = 1.3)	and	3.9 S(ρ_p = 1.4)
Peak II	6.3 S(ρ_p = 1.3)	and	5.8 S(ρ_p = 1.4)

These values may be compared to the groups characterized by peak sedimentation coefficients of 4.0 and 6.6 S discussed by Wallenius *et al.* (14).

SUMMARY

A set of tables is presented for use in the design and interpretation of centrifuge experiments involving sedimentation in linear sucrose density gradients. The retarding effect of the sucrose solution is taken into account in such a way that the tables can be used to predict the position of a material of given sedimentation coefficient and density, or alternatively the sedimentation coefficient can be inferred from the measured position of a zone position. The tables compare well with previous theoretical work and with experiments.

ACKNOWLEDGMENT

The data provided by Mr. Owen Griffith on the gradient centrifugation of lysozyme and serum are greatly appreciated.

REFERENCES

1. DeDuve, C., Berthet, J., and Beaufay, H., *in* "Progress in Biophysics and Biophysical Chemistry" (J. A. V. Butler and B. Katz, eds.), Vol. 9, p. 325. Pergamon Press, New York, 1959.
2. Martin, R. G., and Ames, B. N., *J. Biol. Chem.* **236**, 1372 (1961).
3. Nomura, N., Hall, B. D., and Spiegelman, S., *J. Mol. Biol.* **2**, 324 (1960).
4. Kruz, L. E., and Levy, A. H., *J. Bacteriol.* **89**, 462 (1965).
5. Anderson, N. G., et al., Oak Ridge National Laboratory: A numerical solution of the gradient centrifugation problem has been carried out during the course of the Zonal Centrifuge Development Program, jointly sponsored by the National Institutes of Health and the Atomic Energy Commission at the Oak Ridge National Laboratory, and is discussed in the semiannual reports for January 1 to June 30, 1963, and July 1 to December 31, 1963. The problem is also discussed in a monograph (No. 21) from the National Cancer Institute. A study of the fitting of polynomials to density and viscosity data is presented by E. J. Barber in "AEC Research and Development Report K-1635, Calculation of the Density and Viscosity of Sucrose Solutions," June 24, 1965 (Union Carbide Corporation, Nuclear Division, Oak Ridge, Tennessee).
6. Brakke, M. K., *Arch. Biochem. Biophys.* **107**, 388 (1964).
7. Vinograd, J., and Bruner, R., *Biopolymers* **4**, 131 (1966).
8. Ifft, J. B., Voet, D. H., and Vinograd, J., *J. Phys. Chem.* **65**, 11138 (1961).
9. Trautman, R., *in* "Instrumental Methods of Experimental Biology" (D. W. Newman, ed.). Macmillan, New York, 1964.

10. McEwen, C. R., *Anal. Biochem.* **19,** 23 (1967).
11. "International Critical Tables," Vol. 5, p. 10. McGraw-Hill, New York, 1929.
12. Svedberg, T., and Pederson, K. O., "The Ultracentrifuge," p. 35. Oxford University Press, 1940; reprinted by Johnson Reprint Corporation, New York, 1959.
13. Edsall, J. T., *in* "The Proteins" (H. Neurath and K. Bailey, eds.), Vol. I, Part B, p. 634. Academic Press, New York, 1953.
14. Wallenius, G., Trautman, R., Kunkel, H. G., and Franklin, E. C., *J. Biol. Chem.* **225,** 253 (1957).

ANALYTICAL BIOCHEMISTRY 20, 150–154 (1967)

A Procedure for Rapid and Sensitive Staining of Protein Fractionated by Polyacrylamide Gel Electrophoresis

A. CHRAMBACH,[1] R. A. REISFELD,[2] M. WYCKOFF,[1] AND J. ZACCARI[2]

National Institutes of Health, Bethesda, Maryland 20014

Received December 9, 1966

The resolving power of protein fractionations has been spectacularly increased through the introduction of polyacrylamide gel electrophoresis (1, 2) and has been extended to dilute protein solutions through the introduction of "stacking" (2). However, the resolving power of polyacrylamide gel electrophoresis also depends on the degree of fixation of the fractionation product and on the sensitivity with which the protein of interest may be stained. Since fixation and staining are functions of specific chemical properties and of concentration in the fractionation peak (band) their specific conditions have to be determined for each protein system if optimal resolving capacity is to be achieved. It follows that the procedure outlined below should be used as a guideline rather than a "recipe."

Improved sensitivity has been achieved with some proteins by substitution of Coomassie blue in trichloroacetic acid (TCA) for the commonly used fixative-stain, amido black in dilute acetic acid. The dye employed, Coomassie blue, has been described by Fazekas de St. Groth *et al.* (3) as a protein stain of great sensitivity and has been used by Maizel (4) and Meyer *et al.* (5) in polyacrylamide gel electrophoresis. We have extended its usefulness in two directions. First, the sensitivity of detection was increased by fixation of the protein bands in TCA solution prior to staining. Second, the rapid detection of bands was made possible by elimination of a separate destaining step. This may be achieved by the use of solvents of Coomassie blue, such as 12.5% TCA, in which the dye is relatively insoluble and from which it is adsorbed selectively to the protein bands. Alternately, a further increase in sensitivity can be obtained by the use of dye solvents such as 20% TCA.

[1] Endocrinology Branch, National Cancer Institute.

[2] Laboratory of Immunology, National Institute of Allergy and Infectious Diseases.

MATERIALS

(*1*) Coomassie Brilliant Blue R 250: Colab Laboratories, Inc., Chicago Heights, Ill.

(*2*) Trichloroacetic acid: Baker & Adamson, Cat. No. 1208.

(*3*) Ovine prolactin: prepared according to Cole and Li (12).

(*4*) Fc-piece and Fd-piece, light polypeptide chains of rabbit γ_G-immunoglobulins: prepared according to a modification of the procedures of Fleischman *et al.* (13).

(*5*) Heavy polypeptide chain of rabbit γ_G-immunoglobulins: prepared according to Small and Lamm (14).

(*6*) Beef parathyroid hormone: a preparation of Dr. J. Potts, National Heart Institute, Bethesda, Maryland.

(*7*) Pokeweed mitogen and phytohemagglutinin: preparations of Dr. J. Borjeson, National Institute of Allergy and Infectious Diseases, Bethesda, Maryland.

(*8*) Sera from human, rabbit, burro, and calf.

(*9*) Urinary proteins from rabbit.

Preparation 3, 4, 5, 8, and 9 were made by one of the authors (R. A. R.).

METHODS

(*1*) *Polyacrylamide gel electrophoresis* was carried out essentially as described by Davis (6).

(*2*) *Procedure of fixation and staining:* After the electrophoretic fractionation, the polyacrylamide cylinder or slab is suspended in a 10 to 40-fold volume of 12.5% TCA, preferably with agitation. After 30 min it is immersed in staining solution freshly prepared by a 1:20 dilution in 12.5% TCA of a 1% aqueous stock solution of Coomassie blue. After 30 min to 1 hr of staining the gel is transferred into 10% TCA and photographed. The band intensity increases during the succeeding 48 hr of storage.

RESULTS AND DISCUSSION

(*1*) *Protein specificity:* The procedure of staining with Coomassie blue has been applied to the following proteins differing widely from each other with regard to net charge and size: ovine prolactin; Fc-piece and Fd-piece; light polypeptide chains and heavy polypeptide chain of rabbit γ_G-immunoglobulins; beef parathyroid hormone; pokeweed mitogen, phytohemagglutinin; human, rabbit, burro, and calf sera; and rabbit urinary proteins. The Fd-piece of γ-globulin was charged with sodium decylsulfate. In all cases the sensitivity of detection of protein bands has been equal to or better than that obtained with amido black-acetic acid. A representative pattern is that of ovine prolactin depicted in Figure 1.

It is seen that in the case of this protein the sensitivity at the lower load levels is equal for both dyes. However the low relative sensitivity of Coomassie blue at high concentrations of protein has the advantage that the heavy bands remain unblurred; as the minor bands are not overshadowed by major ones they can be detected by use of high loads. Figure 2 illustrates the case of a protein, the light polypeptide chains of rabbit γ_G-immunoglobulins, in which the sensitivity of Coomassie blue is superior to that of amido black.

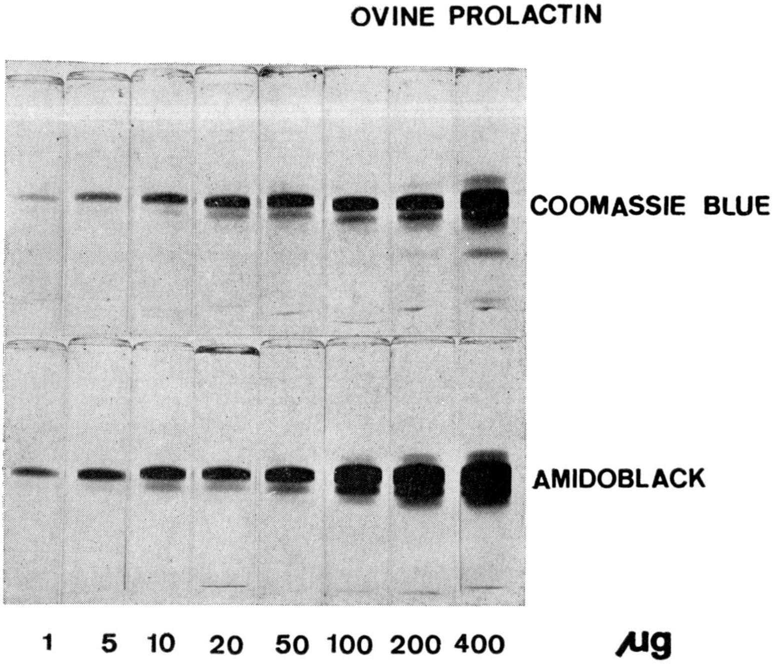

FIG. 1. Comparison between electrophoretic patterns of ovine prolactin obtained by staining with Coomassie blue and amido black. Protein loads range from 1 to 400 µg. Electrophoretic fractionations were carried out in polyacrylamide gels containing 7.5% monomer, in the discontinous Tris system (6) at 25°C. Fixation in 10% TCA for 20 min; staining for 1 hr by 0.025% Coomassie blue in 10% TCA; storage in 10% TCA.

(2) *Polyacrylamide gels:* The procedure has been found applicable equally to acidic (7), neutral (8), and basic (6) multiphasic electrophoretic buffer systems. It has also been applied to longitudinal gel slices (9) without loss of resolution, if one compensates for the decrease in depth of bands by an increased TCA and dye concentration. Gels containing 6–8 M urea have been fixed and stained substituting a (5% TCA, 5% sulfosalicyclic acid) solution (10) for TCA.

(3) *Sensitivity:* The staining procedure is rapid if 10–12.5% TCA is used as fixative and dye solvent in conjunction with Coomassie blue concentrations of 0.025 to 0.05%. The Coomassie blue solutions are roughly saturated with regard to the dye; preferential binding of dye to protein yields a high degree of absorbance contrast between protein zones and background. The sensitivity of this rapid procedure is at least as high as that of staining with amido black.

Maximal sensitivity may be obtained with Coomassie blue under conditions which require a relatively lengthy destaining of the background by diffusion. In this case 12.5–20% TCA is used as fixative and dye

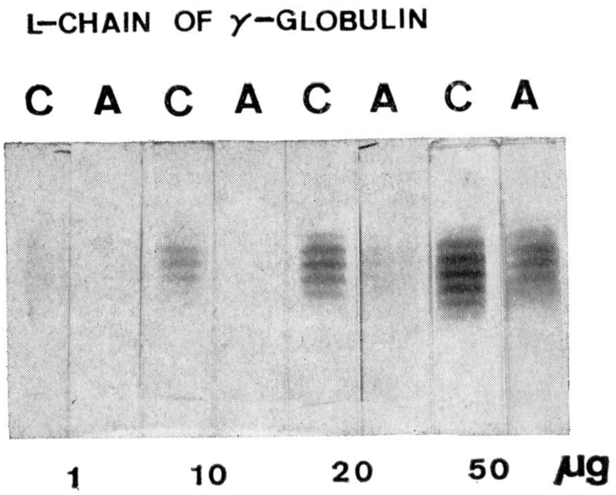

FIG. 2. Comparison between electrophoretic patterns of the light polypeptide chains of rabbit γ_G-immunoglobulins obtained by staining with Coomassie blue (C) and amido black (A). Fractionations were carried out as described in Figure 1. Fixation in 10% TCA for 1 hr; staining for 3 hr by 0.025% Coomassie blue in 10% TCA; storage in 10% TCA.

solvent in conjunction with Coomassie blue concentrations of 0.05 to 0.1%. The fixation and staining times are doubled for the most sensitive detection of prolactin components. Other times may be optimal for other proteins.

It has been found useful to apply on the same gel first a rapid, then a maximally sensitive procedure of staining. Gels stained by the amido black-acetic acid procedure can be stained subsequently by Coomassie blue.

(4) *Storage:* Storage of the gels in 10% TCA usually leads to improved patterns of increased band intensity and decreased background. This is particularly true if sufficient dye remains in the 10% TCA to give it a light blue coloration. Ultimately the gel patterns fade, although the rate

of fading may be reduced by storage in the dark. Faded patterns can be restained.

Photography of the blue bands should employ a red filter (e.g., for use with Polaroid cameras a No. 25 gelatin filter, Eastman Kodak, or an R-2-25A filter).

(*5*) *Quantitation:* The quantitation of proteins by intensity of stain is not possible without availability of identical reference proteins. As the above procedure may involve the use of limiting amounts of dye an additional restriction is imposed on the possibility of quantitation. Determination of stain intensities of bands is feasible by elution of Coomassie blue from thin gel slices (11) by 90% formic acid.

SUMMARY

Protein zones may be stained by Coomassie blue without any destaining of the background and with a sensitivity at least as high as that of amido black. A vastly increased sensitivity may be achieved with Coomassie blue at the price of background destaining.

ACKNOWLEDGMENTS

The authors would like to express their appreciation to Dr. J. Potts for a gift of beef parathyroid hormone and to Dr. J. Borjeson for a gift of pokeweek mitogen and phytohemagglutinin.

REFERENCES

1. Raymond, S., and Wang, Y., *Anal. Biochem,* **1,** 391 (1960).
2. Ornstein, L., *Ann. N. Y. Acad. Sci.* **121,** 321 (1964).
3. Fazekas de St. Groth, S., Webster, R. G., and Datyner, A., *Biochim. Biophys. Acta* **71,** 377 (1963).
4. Maizel, J., *Science* **151,** 988 (1966).
5. Meyer, T. S., and Lamberts, B. L., *Biochim. Biophys. Acta* **107,** 144 (1965).
6. Davis, B. J., *Ann. N. Y. Acad. Sci.* **121,** 404 (1964).
7. Reisfeld, R. A., Lewis, U. J., and Williams, D. E., *Nature* **195,** 281 (1962).
8. Chrambach, A., and Jovin, T., unpublished data.
9. Fairbanks, G., Levinthal, C., and Reeder, R. H., *Biochem. Biophys. Res. Commun.* **20,** 393 (1965).
10. Fazekas de St. Groth, S., personal communication.
11. Chrambach, A., *Anal. Biochem.* **15,** 544 (1966).
12. Cole, R. D., and Li, C. H., *J. Biol. Chem.* **213,** 197 (1955).
13. Fleischman, J. B., Porter, R. R., and Press, E. M., *Biochem. J.* **88,** 220 (1963).
14. Small, P. A., and Lamm, M. E., *Biochemistry* **5,** 259 (1966).

ANALYTICAL BIOCHEMISTRY 20, 155–166 (1967)

A New Method for Determining Micro Quantities of Calcium in Biological Materials

B. C. RAY SARKAR AND U. P. S. CHAUHAN

Institute of Nuclear Medicine and Allied Sciences, Delhi 7, India

Received December 22, 1966

Since the introduction of *o*-cresolphthalein complexone as a common reagent for the detection of calcium, strontium, and barium in traces (1, 2), their quantitative determination using this dye has received considerable attention. The procedure that has been evolved to deal with standard solutions containing Ca^{2+}, Sr^{2+}, or Ba^{2+} ions (3, 4) is not applicable when the ions of these three elements are present together. The separation beforehand of one kind of cation from the other is, however, essential, and on this basis the determination of strontium in some plant materials was recently reported (5, 6). On the other hand, such separation after precipitation as oxalates was not considered necessary in the estimation of serum calcium (7), since traces of strontium and barium would practically be of no consequence. Thus the procedure may be simplified in the case of materials having a wide ratio of calcium to strontium or barium.

Calcium estimation in biological materials being relatively more important, it would be worth while to have a micro method requiring no precipitation of the alkaline earths at any stage, and also capable of yielding quick and reliable results. The possibility is indicated in this paper on the basis of a critical study of the various factors involved.

METHODS

Reagents

All chemicals used were A.R. grade unless otherwise specified.

(i) *Standard solution of calcium chloride,* 10 μg Ca^{2+}/ml, prepared by dissolving the required amount of moisture-free $CaCO_3$ in dilute HCl and making up to a definite volume with water.

(ii) *Standard solution of magnesium sulfate,* 10 μg Mg^{2+}/ml, obtained by dissolving the required amount of $MgSO_4 \cdot 7H_2O$ in a definite volume of water.

(iii) *Ammonia/ammonium chloride buffer,* pH 10.5. A solution of 100 ml was prepared by dissolving 0.24 gm NH_4Cl in 5% NH_4OH solution (v/v), aqueous.

(iv) *o-Cresolphthalein complexone solution,* 0.1%. The dye was obtained from British Drug Houses (Laboratory Reagent); 100 mg was dissolved in 28 ml ammonia/ammonium chloride buffer and diluted to 100 ml with water.

(v) *8-Quinolinol,* a 1% solution in absolute ethanol.

(vi) *Sulfuric acid,* 2/3 N and 1 N, approximately.

(vii) *Ammonium hydroxide,* 2% (v/v), aqueous.

(viii) *Ammonium oxalate,* 4% (w/v), aqueous.

(ix) *Sodium tungstate,* 10% (w/v), aqueous.

(x) *Standard oxalic acid solution,* 0.01 N, aqueous.

(xi) *Standard potassium permanganate solution,* 0.01 N, prepared from stock solution and standardized before use against standard oxalic acid solution.

(xii) *Triethanolamine,* 25% (v/v), aqueous from British Drug Houses (Laboratory Reagent).

(xiii) *Aqueous solutions of inorganic salts (mg %):* NaCl, 50.8; KCl, 38.2; $MgSO_4$, 20.5; $FeCl_3$, 13; $ZnSO_4$, 17.6; $MnCl_2$, 11.6; Na oxalate, 14.6; $CuSO_4$, 15.8; $AlCl_3$, 95.5; and NaH_2PO_4, 19.4.

Instruments

A Bausch & Lomb Spectronic 20 was used for colorimetric readings, a Leeds pH meter for pH adjustment, and a Carl Zeiss flame photometer (employing air-acetylene flame) for flame photometric determinations.

Procedure

(*1*) *Preparation of standard curve:* Different aliquots of the $CaCl_2$ solution with Ca^{2+} content varying from 2 to 10 μg were taken in graduated stoppered tubes and the volume in each case was made up to 5.5 ml with water. Subsequently, 1 ml of 8-quinolinol solution as the masking agent and 2.5 ml ammonia/ammonium chloride buffer were added, and the volume adjusted to 9.0 ml. The contents were finally treated with 1 ml of the *o*-cresolphthalein complexone solution. After addition of each reagent mentioned above, the contents were thoroughly mixed. Water blank in place of $CaCl_2$ solution was simultaneously carried through the entire procedure. Standards were read against the blank in the Spectronic 20, using 1 cm circular cells at 565 mμ.

When inorganic salt solutions were added to the standard solutions, the volume in each case was also made up to 5.5 ml, and then the same procedure was followed.

(*2*) *Serum:* 50 μl of serum was added to each tube directly and made up to 5.5 ml with water. Subsequent steps were the same as described above in the preparation of the standard curve. In addition, two standards containing 4 and 6 μg of Ca^{2+} were run simultaneously to check the dependability of the standard curve already prepared.

In recovery tests, specific volumes of $CaCl_2$ solution were added to the above quantity of serum and made up to 5.5 ml as usual for the rest of the above procedure.

When the analysis was to be conducted after the separation of protein, 0.1 ml of serum was diluted to 2 ml and treated with 0.5 ml of 10% sodium tungstate solution and 0.5 ml of 2/3 *N* H_2SO_4. After thorough mixing the contents were centrifuged and 1.5 ml of the supernatant was diluted to 5.5 ml prior to calcium estimation.

As a standard of reference, the Clark-Collip modification of the Kramer-Tisdall method was followed (8).

(*3*) *Urine, sweat, and water:* The volume taken in each case was 50 μl and the rest of the procedure was similar to that followed in the direct analysis of serum described above. A small quantity of sweat was first collected directly from the skin after washing, and was then centrifuged to get rid of extraneous materials. Insoluble materials in water were removed by filtration. In the case of urine no such step was necessary prior to the analysis.

(*4*) *Milk:* Samples were first diluted 10 times and then an aliquot of 50 μl was taken for direct analysis.

Another procedure was based on prior ashing. In a silica dish, 1 ml of milk was heated to dryness, charred, and then incinerated in a muffle furnace for 2 hr at 550–600°C. The ash was dissolved in 0.1 *N* HCl and the volume made up to 10 ml with water. The analysis was finally performed on a 50 μl aliquot.

When protein-free extract was used, 1.0 ml of milk was diluted to 6 ml and mixed with 2 ml each of the 10% sodium tungstate solution and 2/3 *N* H_2SO_4. The contents were mixed and then centrifuged to give the supernatant from which 50 μl was taken as usual.

(*5*) *Plant materials:* Leafy portions of different green vegetables were first washed with water to remove foreign impurities. After draining off the excess water, 0.1 gm from each was dried at 100–105°C and was incinerated at 550°C for about 2 hr. The ash was dissolved in 0.01 *N* HCl and the filtrate was made up to 10 ml. An aliquot of 0.5 ml was used in each case for the estimation.

(*6*) *Reference method:* The results obtained by the proposed method for urine, sweat, water, milk, and plant materials were compared with those found by published procedures commonly based on oxalate precipitation followed by permanganate titration (9).

RESULTS

In Figure 1 are shown absorbance curves for the (a) dye, (b) excess dye plus Ca-dye complex, and (c) the Ca-dye complex. As would be evident, not only the maximum absorption peaks for the complex as well as for the dye are at 565 mμ, but their difference in absorbance is also maximum at this wavelength. This has, therefore, been the selected wavelength for all measurements.

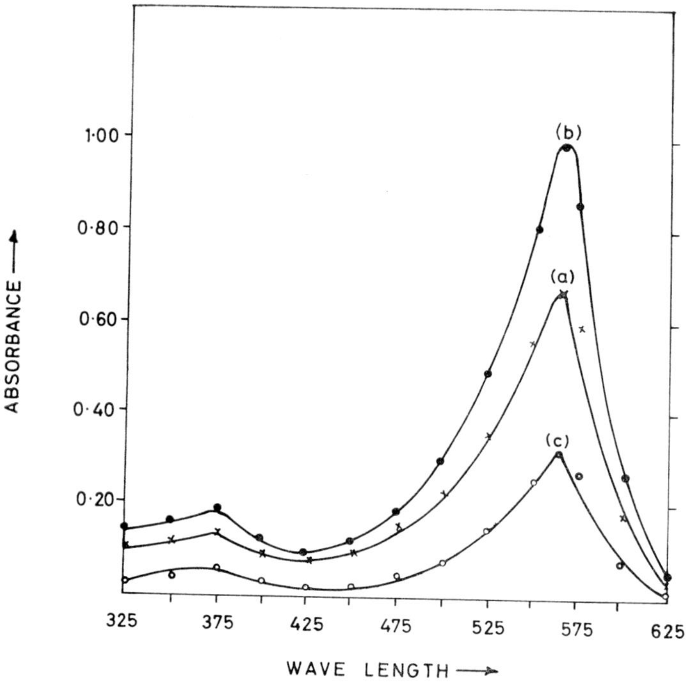

FIG. 1. Absorbance curves: (a) for the dye, obtained by taking absorbance of a solution made up of 1 ml dye solution in 6.5 ml water and 2.5 ml buffer against water; (b) for excess dye and calcium-dye complex, 0.6 ml standard $CaCl_2$ solution added in place of the same volume of water as used for curve (a) and water used as blank; (c) for the calcium-dye complex, obtained by taking absorbance of the solution for curve (b) using the solution for curve (a) as blank.

Regarding the various factors that may influence the formation of the complex, it was observed that the optimum pH required is 10.5; this can be achieved with ammonia/ammonium chloride buffer.

The dye solution should preferably be prepared fresh before use as it remains stable for about 6 hr at the local temperature. Color development due to the complex is complete within 5 min and its absorbance remains constant for about 3 hr.

The standard curve (a) shown in Figure 2 is a linear one within the range of 0–10 μg Ca^{2+}. The sensitivity of the method as indicated by minimum amount of the test substance to give detectable absorbance is about 0.1 μg, and the molar extinction coefficient of Ca^{2+} with the dye is found to be 2.10×10^4.

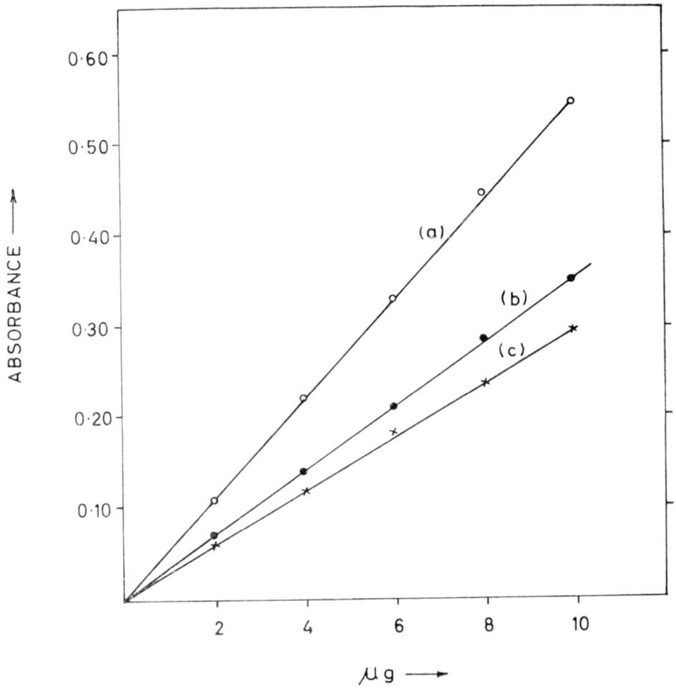

FIG. 2. Standard curves: (a) Ca^{2+} concentration vs. absorbance in absence of masking reagent; (b) Ca^{2+} concentration vs. absorbance in presence of masking reagent; (c) Mg^{2+} concentration vs. absorbance.

In Table 1 are shown data to indicate the effect of various cations and anions on the recovery of calcium from standard $CaCl_2$ solutions. With the lower concentrations of these ions normally expected in biological samples, no significant interference has been observed except in the case of magnesium, which led to calcium values as high as 55 to 111%. Only at higher concentrations of Zn^{2+} and Mn^{2+} not normally expected has there been positive interference. On the other hand, a negative effect has been shown with higher concentration of Al^{3+}. It has been further noted that phosphate does not interfere up to a concentration of about 12 times higher than that of calcium, while its presence causes interference in flame photometric and complexometric methods of calcium estimation.

For simplicity as well as for handling micro quantities of samples, the separation of calcium from magnesium needs to be avoided without sacrificing accuracy. The effect of magnesium was masked with 8-quinolinol, as would be evident from the data in Table 2, though other substances such as triethanolamine and glycine were also tried, with only partial success.

TABLE 1
Degree of Interference Due to Various Ions on Calcium Estimation

Calcium used, μg	Cations and anions added		Calcium found, μg	Apparent recovery of calcium, %
	Ions	Amount, μg		
10	Sodium	10	9.95	99.50
10	Sodium	100	9.90	99.00
10	Sodium	1000	9.90	99.00
8	Potassium	100	8.00	100.00
8	Potassium	500	8.20	102.50
8	Potassium	1000	8.00	100.00
10	Magnesium	10	15.56	155.60
10	Magnesium	20	21.11	211.10
8	Iron	8	8.10	101.25
8	Iron	80	8.10	101.25
8	Copper	8	7.95	99.38
8	Copper	80	7.85	98.12
8	Aluminum	8	8.00	100.00
8	Aluminum	100	7.55	94.40
8	Aluminum	1000	5.80	72.50
8	Zinc	20	10.00	125.00
8	Zinc	80	11.60	145.00
8	Manganese	10	8.10	101.25
8	Manganese	100	14.20	177.50
8	Oxalate	10	8.00	100.00
8	Oxalate	100	7.85	98.12
8	Phosphate	10	8.00	100.00
8	Phosphate	100	7.80	97.50

The effect of the masking agent on the relationship between Ca^{2+} concentration and its absorbance in the presence of Mg^{2+} is indicated by curve (b) in Figure 2. The molar extinction coefficient of Ca^{2+} with the dye has been decreased to 1.40×10^4 and the decrease in sensitivity was about 35%. This curve has been used for measuring calcium content in biological samples tested here. The reduced sensitivity as noted above might have been due to the interaction between the masking agent and *o*-cresolphthalein complexone.

In Table 3 are listed data on the recovery of added calcium in serum, urine, and plant samples; on the average the respective values were 98.75, 98.75, and 100.21%.

TABLE 2
Masking of Interference Due to Mg^{2+} Ions on Calcium Estimation

Calcium used, μg	Magnesium added, μg	8-Quinolinol solution added ml	Calcium found, μg	Recovery of calcium, %
10	—	1	10.00	100.00
10	2	1	10.00	100.00
10	4	1	10.00	100.00
10	6	1	10.00	100.00
10	8	1	9.86	98.60
10	10	1	10.13	101.30
8	10	1	8.11	101.37
6	10	1	6.08	101.33
4	10	1	4.02	100.50
2	10	1	2.00	100.00
—	10	1	Nil	—

Comparative values of calcium in serum, urine, and sweat by the two methods are presented in Table 4. The respective average values were 10.12 ± 0.62 mg/100 ml, 15.09 ± 2.73 mg/100 ml, and 22.85 ± 4.19 mg/100 ml by the present method and 10.19 ± 0.48 mg/100 ml, 13.15 ± 2.08 mg/100 ml, and 23.25 ± 3.32 mg/100 ml by the methed of Clark and Collip. It is evident that the two methods have given more or less concordant results. In these samples protein separation was not found

TABLE 3
Recovery Tests in the Analysis of Some Biological Materials

Sample	Amount taken, μl	Calcium found, μg	Calcium added, μg	Total calcium found, μg	Recovery, %
Human serum	50	5.42	4	9.25	95.75
	50	4.90	4	9.03	103.25
	50	5.64	4	9.51	96.75
	50	5.03	4	9.03	100.00
	50	5.27	4	9.27	100.00
	50	5.67	4	9.54	96.75
Human urine	50	6.75	5	11.50	95.00
	50	5.25	5	10.25	100.00
	50	5.75	5	10.50	95.00
	50	9.00	5	14.25	105.00
Lettuce	500 μl ash soln.	6.83	4	10.98	103.75
Spinach	↓	3.41	4	7.32	97.75
Mustard	↓	7.31	4	11.22	97.75
Radish	↓	9.76	4	13.50	93.50
Fenugreek	↓	9.02	4	13.17	103.70
Cabbage	↓	5.37	4	9.51	103.50

necessary, as the results were found to be identical with and without this step.

Referring to the results of milk analysis as shown in Table 5, it may be noted that the present method applied directly without precipitation of proteins has given values closer to those obtained by the A.O.A.C. method and can obviate the step involving ashing. Deproteinization, however, has led definitely to lower results.

TABLE 4
Comparative Values of Calcium by the Present Method and the Clark-Collip Method

Sample	No. of samples	Present method: Ca range found, mg/100 ml	Present method: Mean value, μ	Present method: S.D., σ	Clark-Collip method: Ca range found, mg/100 ml	Clark-Collip method: Mean value, μ	Clark-Collip method: S.D., σ
Human serum	12	9.15–11.4	10.12	0.62	9.50–11.00	10.19	0.48
Human urine	12	10.50–18.0	15.09	2.73	10.66–18.66	13.15	2.08
Human sweat	4	19.40–30.0	22.85	4.19	20.40–28.90	23.25	3.32

The data in Table 6 add further evidence to the Mg^{2+} effect on calcium estimation by this method in serum, water, and leafy materials. The interference is found to vary with the level of Mg^{2+} content, which was determined separately (10). The significance of a masking agent in giving reliable results is thus more than apparent.

TABLE 5
Calcium in Milk (mg/100 ml)

Present method: Without deproteinization	Present method: After deproteinization	Present method: After ashing	A.O.A.C. method (based on ashing)
131.40	114.00	128.70	130.00
142.80	138.40	138.40	140.40
128.60	117.30	122.60	130.30

As Mg^{2+} also forms a complex with the dye, an additional study was made to utilize this reaction for its determination, the details of which will be reported elsewhere. It may be mentioned only that, for Mg^{2+}, curve (c) in Figure 2 has also been linear, but in this case the absorption peak was at 555 mμ. The molar extinction coefficient for Mg^{2+} is 0.72×10^4 and the sensitivity of the method is 0.167, which is about 60% of that for calcium.

TABLE 6
Magnesium Levels in Biological Samples and Their Effect on Calcium Determination

Sample	Ca found by present method, mg/100 ml*: without 8-quinolinol (a)	Ca found by present method, mg/100 ml*: with 8-quinolinol (b)	Deviation (b − a)/b × 100 (c)	Mg^{2+} found mg/100 ml* (d)	Ca^{2+} by oxalate method mg/100 ml* (e)	Deviation (b − e)/b × 100
Human serum[a]	11.32	10.12	11.85	1.94	10.19	3.13
	±.34	±.40		±.04	±.22	
Lettuce (*Lactuca sativa*)	230.00	136.60	68.40	90.00	143.20	4.83
Mustard leaves (*Brassica compestris*)	188.60	146.40	28.80	49.80	146.00	0.27
Spinach (*Spinacia oleracea*)	112.00	68.20	64.20	61.00	73.00	7.04
Radish leaves (*Raphanus sativus*)	280.00	185.10	51.26	106.80	186.00	0.48
Fenugreek (*Trigonella foenum-graecum*)	208.00	180.50	15.23	45.60	183.40	1.60
Cabbage (*Brassica oleracea capitata*)	126.00	107.40	17.32	39.60	107.40	Nil
Tap water	5.66	3.70	52.90	2.00	3.93	6.21
Jamuna River water	7.64	5.00	52.80	2.52	5.40	8.00
Well water	18.68	14.00	33.43	7.10	14.60	4.30

[a] Twelve samples analyzed.

* Mg/100 g in the case of plant materials.

DISCUSSION

Though various reagents have been employed for the colorimetric estimation of calcium (3, 11–23), the choice has fallen on *o*-cresolphthalein complexone because of its higher sensitivity, as noted here, and by others as well (7, 24). The molecular extinction coefficient of calcium-murexide is reported to be 1.00×10^4 at 506 mμ (25) while that of calcium with the *o*-cresolphthalein complexone is found to be 2.1×10^4. While using eriochrome black T and murexide, the reactions are either too slow or too fast and the Ca complexes formed are not stable for sufficient duration (23, 26). This is not so with the complex formed by *o*-cresolphthalein complexone. Further, the wavelength of maximum absorption of the color complex becomes progressively lower with increasing amounts of Ca^{2+} when murexide is used (27).

Referring to the nature of standard curves, it has been pointed out that the linearity holds good up to 1.2 ppm calcium in the case of reaction with murexide, while in the reaction using *o*-cresolphthalein complexone the linearity is observed up to a concentration of 1.6 ppm calcium (7, 26). The maximum concentration of calcium employed in the present study was 1 ppm and optical density beyond this was too high for reliable measurements by this instrument.

As to the common interference encountered in the various colorimetric estimations of calcium, the effect of magnesium deserves special mention. The murexide reaction is affected by this element at a concentration of 10 ppm or above (24, 26) and the eriochrome black T is equally sensitive for both calcium and magnesium (17). Further, in the case of eriochrome black T, there is serious interference due to Cu, Fe, and K, and calcium values are reported to increase 10% by 50 ppm K (26). Direct application of these reagents to the analysis of biological samples without prior separation of calcium from magnesium evidently leads to erroneous results. The special feature of the present study lies in masking the effect of magnesium without its separation. This has been achieved by the use of 8-quinolinol, which forms a complex with Mg^{2+}. Though the molar extinction coefficient of calcium with *o*-cresolphthalein complexone is thus lowered to 1.4×10^4, this is still higher than that for calcium with murexide. The use of a masking agent has thus facilitated the analysis of biological fluids such as serum, urine, sweat, milk, and water by direct treatment. In the case of plant materials and allied substances, the only additional step required is, however, ashing. The results based on the procedure worked out have favorably compared with those found by the usual standard method. The method is easily adaptable to the analysis of various types of materials on micro scale and will also be useful when it is necessary to dispense with flame photometry, as in the analysis of radio-contaminated samples.

SUMMARY

A procedure has been worked out for the micro estimation of calcium in various types of biological samples with *o*-cresolphthalein complexone as an indicator. This reagent is more sensitive than the other commonly used indicators such as eriochrome black T and murexide. Test solutions containing 2–5 μg calcium can be conveniently dealt with and the method may have a special application in the analysis of radio-contaminated samples.

Though strontium and barium also react selectively with this reagent, their effect is negligible because these two elements normally occur in traces. On the other hand, the most significant effect is due to the presence of magnesium. This interference has been overcome by the use of 8-quinolinol and the method is thereby rendered simple and direct. Results obtained are comparable to those found by the usual standard procedure. In contrast to the method applicable directly to biological fluids such as serum, urine, sweat, milk, and water, an additional step involving prior ashing is required in the case of plant materials. The application of this method may thus be extended further.

ACKNOWLEDGMENT

Thanks are due to Lt. Col. S. K. Mazumdar, A.M.C., Director of the Institute, for his kind interest in this work.

REFERENCES

1. ANDEREGG, G., FLASCHKA, H., SALLMANN, R., AND SCHWARZENBACH, G., *Helv. Chim. Acta* **37**, 113 (1954).
2. SCHWARZENBACH, G., *Analyst* **80**, 713 (1955).
3. POLLARD, F. H., McOMIE, J. F. W., AND MARTIN, J. V., *Analyst* **81**, 348 (1956).
4. RAY SARKAR, B. C., AND CHAUHAN, U. P. S., *Indian J. Chem.* **3**, 542 (1965).
5. RAY SARKAR, B. C., AND CHAUHAN, U. P. S., *Current Sci.* (*India*) **32**, 418 (1963).
6. CHAUHAN, U. P. S., AND RAY SARKAR, B. C., *Indian J. Chem.* **2**, 175 (1964).
7. STERN, J., AND LEWIS, H. P., *Clin. Chim. Acta* **2**, 576 (1957).
8. CLARK, E. P., AND COLLIP, J. B., *J. Biol. Chem.* **63**, 461 (1925).
9. *Methods of Analysis,* 9th ed. p. 75. Association of Official Agricultural Chemists, Washington 4, D. C., 1960.
10. CHAUHAN, U. P. S., AND PANDE, P. C., *Talanta* **14**, 575 (1967).
11. WEYBREW, J. A., MATRONE, G., AND BOXLEY, H. M., *Anal. Chem.* **20**, 759 (1948).
12. KIBRICK, A. C., PALMER, D., AND SKUPP, S., *Proc. Soc. Exptl. Biol. Med.* **76**, 115 (1951).
13. CORNFIELD, A. H., AND POLLARD, A. G., *J. Sci. Food Agr.* **2**, 135 (1951).
14. TSAO, M. U., *J. Biol. Chem.* **199**, 251 (1952).
15. TYNER, E. H., *Anal. Chem.* **27**, 1001 (1955).
16. NATELSON, S., AND PENNIALL, R., *Anal. Chem.* **27**, 434 (1955).

17. YOUNG, A., SWEET, T. R., AND BAKER, B. B., *Anal. Chem.* **27,** 356 (1955).
18. SCHWARZENBACH, G., AND GYSLING, H., *Helv. Chim. Acta* **32,** 1314 (1949).
19. OSTERAG, H., AND RINK, E., *Compt. Rend.* **231,** 1304 (1950).
20. WILLIAMS, N. B., AND MOSER, J. H., *Anal. Chem.* **25,** 1414 (1953).
21. CHILCOTE, M. E., AND WASSON, R. D., *Clin. Chem.* **4,** 200 (1958).
22. HARPER, T. A., *Nature* **183,** 232 (1959).
23. REYNOLDS, S. S., AND LINDE, R. E., *Anal. Biochem.* **5,** 246 (1963).
24. SANDELL, E. B., "Colorimetric Determination of Traces of Metals," 3rd ed., p. 368. Interscience, New York, 1959.
25. CHARLOT, G., "Colorimetric Determination of Elements," p. 207. Elsevier, Amsterdam, 1964.
26. SNELL, F. D., AND SNELL, C. T., "Colorimetric Methods of Analysis," Vol. II A, p. 496. Van Nostrand, Princeton, N. J., 1959.
27. CARLSTROM, G., *Acta Agr. Scand.* **5,** 357 (1955).

ANALYTICAL BIOCHEMISTRY 20, 167–170 (1967)

A Multiple-Wavelength Selector for a Continuous Spectrophotometric Column Monitoring System[1]

K. H. HARAGUCHI, J. C. JANSEN,[2] AND B. V. SIEGEL

Department of Pathology, University of Oregon Medical School, Portland, Oregon 97201

Received January 11, 1967

A versatile, automated analytical system for quantitating proteins, peptides, and nucleic acid derivatives has been described by Anderson (1). In this system, absorbance at one or two wavelengths is continuously monitored and recorded. The two wavelengths in Anderson's dual-beam monitoring system are positioned by an air piston driven mechanical device which may offer some disadvantages. For example, wavelength selection is limited to the stroke length of the air piston, and air lines with pressure gages and regulators are required. Also, the time spent in assembly and disassembly of the modification to the spectrophotometer is lengthy. In the present report, an inexpensive electronic wavelength selector is described which, while performing the same function, eliminates these drawbacks in the Anderson system.

INSTRUMENTATION

The two-point scan system in this study is a modification of the pneumatic system described by Anderson (1). A spectrophotometer with a recording output provision is made to scan between two selected wavelengths which are time-locked to a multipoint recorder. This time sharing of the recorder permits the operator to superimpose the simultaneous records of the absorbance of the two wavelengths.

Figure 1 represents the schematic for the system. Two filament transformers, with their secondaries connected in series, provide AC voltage which is rectified to produce both a positive and a negative DC voltage to power the motor. The positive voltage causes the motor to rotate in one direction while the negative produces the opposite rotation. The volt-

[1] Supported by U. S. Atomic Energy Commission Contract No. RLO-1927-13.

[2] Custom Systems Associates, Inc., 4438 S. W. Corbett Avenue, Portland, Oregon.

ages are connected to the motor through the auxiliary switch deck[3] of Section A in the recorder.

Section A of the added switch is wired so that the motor which drives the wavelength scanner is supplied alternately with a positive and a negative voltage. When the motor reaches the desired limit, one of the selected wavelengths, the micro switch is opened interrupting the current. When the rotary switch moves to the next position, the opposite polarity voltage causes the motor to move to the opposite wavelength limit switch.

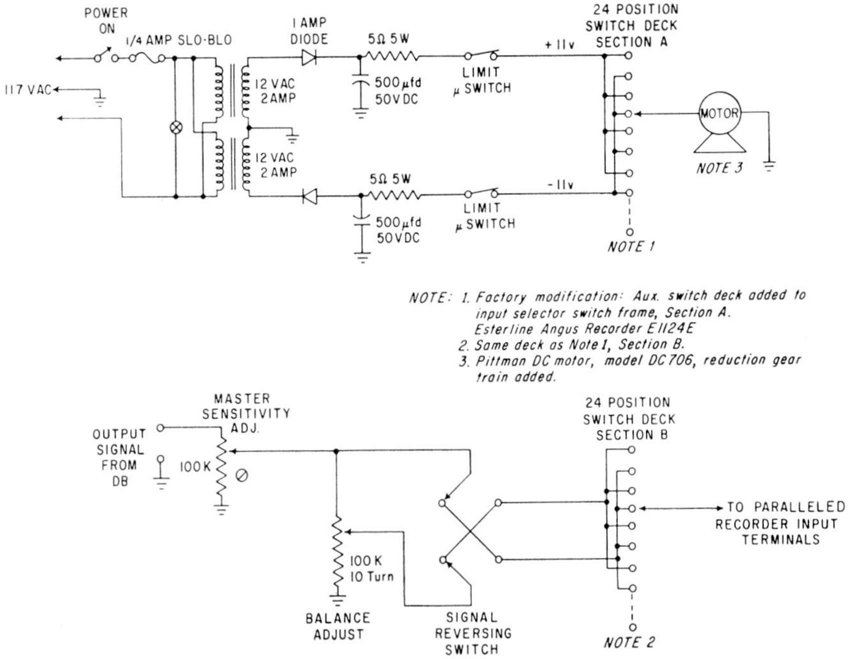

FIG. 1. Circuit diagram of scan control unit and wavelength switching.

The modification of the spectrophotometer[4] has necessitated the removal of the old motor and motor plate. The new motor plate assembly (Fig. 2) includes the two limit micro switches. Two limiter clamps are attached by set screws for the desired wavelengths. If connectors are placed on the wires to the old motor plate assembly, the system can be returned to its original configuration in less than 15 min when unidirectional scan is necessary.

[3] The auxiliary switch deck is a factory modification by the manufacturer of the recorder. It has two poles and twenty-four positions for each pole. Its rotation is coincident with the recorder scanning of each of its twenty-four input points.

[4] Beckman model DB spectrophotometer.

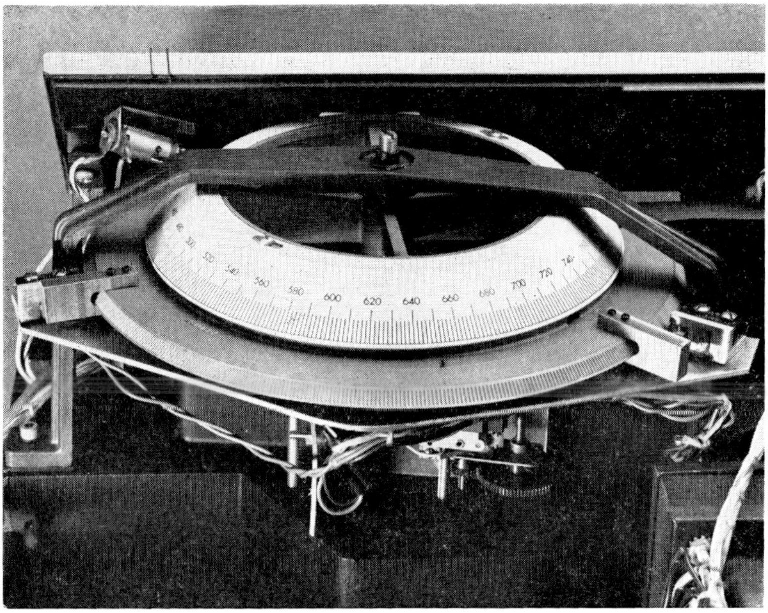

FIG. 2. Photograph of modified motor plate with limit micro switches.

The signal from the spectrophotometer output is connected to the master sensitivity control (Fig. 1). The signal from this adjustment is connected to both the reversing switch and the balance adjustment control. These adjustments allow the operator to set the incoming level and to equalize the output levels. The output from the balance adjust is also connected to the signal reversing switch. The signals are connected to the recorder through Section B of the rotary switch. The recorder is alternately supplied with signals which are produced by the two selected wavelengths. Their amplitudes are equalized by the balance adjustment using a pertinent reference solution. This is accomplished by adjusting the spectrophotometer output and the master sensitivity adjustment. Through the use of these two controls, one sets the lowest reading to equal 100% on the recorder. The greater signal is then adjusted to read 100% on the recorder by using the balance adjustment control. The reversing switch allows the operator to synchronize the selected wavelengths to the point recorder.

This system has a further advantage of lower cost as opposed to the pneumatic system. Also, greater scan widths can be employed, up to 180°, limited by the internal construction of the spectrophotometer, and is readily readjustable for different wavelengths. Presently, a multiwavelength scan system is being developed which will permit any number of points to be scanned with the same over-all scan limits, thereby providing further versatility.

CONCLUSION

A versatile, inexpensive electronic wavelength selector to be used with the Beckman model DB spectrophotometer has been described. This device is ideal for use in the field of continuous spectrophotometeric column monitoring. With this electronic selector, one or two wavelengths may be selected (scan widths up to approximately 180°) and their resultant absorbances continuously monitored and recorded. The selected wavelengths can be set with ease and accuracy. Other devices are available but have their limitations either in cost or complexity of construction.

REFERENCE

1. Anderson, N. G., *Anal. Biochem.* **4**, 269–283 (1962).

ANALYTICAL BIOCHEMISTRY 20, 171–180 (1967)

An Improved Ion-Exchange Procedure for the Chromatography of the Metabolites of Mevalonate

D. N. SKILLETER AND R. G. O. KEKWICK

Department of Biochemistry, The University of Birmingham, Birmingham, England

Received January 12, 1967

A study of the pattern of metabolism of mevalonate and the characterization of the enzymes concerned therewith in the latex serum of *Hevea brasiliensis* necessitated the development of a reliable and reproducible analytical procedure for the detection and estimation of the intermediates concerned, and an efficient method for the isolation of these substances in sufficient amounts, of adequate purity, for use as substrates.

Use of the various paper chromatographic procedures thus far published gave, in our hands, unsatisfactory results. Chromatography of protein-free mixtures derived from incubations of [2-^{14}C] mevalonate with crude enzyme systems from *Hevea* latex or from bakers' yeast revealed the presence of more metabolites than could be accounted for on the basis of the known metabolism of mevalonate, even when the incubations were carried out in the presence of iodoacetamide (5 m*M*) sufficient to inhibit the formation of further metabolites from isopentenyl pyrophosphate. Furthermore, when single spots from these chromatograms were eluted with water and subjected to rechromatography in the original solvent, a separation of further components occurred, suggesting that either the substances were breaking down on chromatography or that the initial resolutions were unsatisfactory. Since further rechromatography produced even more components it seemed that the former explanation was the more likely.

The multiplicity of components found on the initial chromatography of deproteinized incubation mixtures was particularly evident in the chromatography systems containing acid but even the alkaline systems of Henning, Möslein, and Lynen (1) and of Chesterton and Kekwick (2) gave several components when a single spot was rechromatographed in the same solvent.

The procedure for the separation of the products of mevalonate metabolism by ion-exchange chromatography on Dowex 1 columns described by

Bloch, Chaykin, Phillips, and de Waard (3) was also found to have drawbacks. Although the fractions obtained initially from protein-free incubation mixtures could be accounted for on the basis of the known metabolism of mevalonate it was found, on rechromatography of the isolated fractions on the same column, that, whereas mevalonate 5-phosphate showed no evidence of breakdown, mevalonate 5-pyrophosphate was broken down from 25–40%, and isopentenyl pyrophosphate by about 15%, to mevalonate 5-phosphate and isopentenyl monophosphate, respectively.

From this it appeared that more successful separation of the metabolites of mevalonate might be obtained by ion-exchange chromatography not involving the use of extreme conditions of pH.

MATERIALS AND METHODS

Substrates. DL-[2-^{14}C]-mevalonate was obtained as the lactone from Radiochemical Centre, Amersham, England, and was converted into the potassium salt by incubation with slightly more than 1 equiv of KOH before use. ATP[1] (disodium salt) was obtained from Sigma Chemical Co. St. Louis, Mo., and was dissolved in water and adjusted to pH 7.2 with KOH (0.05 N) before use.

Enzyme Preparations. The two types of enzyme preparation used were obtained from freeze-dried *Hevea* latex serum prepared by the procedure of Archer and Sekhar (4), and obtained from Rubber Research Institute of Malaya. The material was reconstituted with water to its original concentration before use. Both enzyme preparations were obtained by the fractionation procedure described by Skilleter, Williamson, and Kekwick (5). Preparation A, which contained the enzymes mevalonate kinase, phosphomevalonate kinase, and mevalonate-5-pyrophosphate decarboxylase, was obtained by concentrating the fractions eluted from the DEAE-Sephadex fractionation, described in that communication, at KCl concentrations below 0.25 M. Preparation B, which contained only mevalonate kinase and phosphomevalonate kinase, was obtained by concentrating the fractions from the same DEAE-Sephadex column eluted at KCl concentrations between 0.1 and 0.25 M.

Ion-Exchange Resins. The DEAE-cellulose used was Whatman grade DE 11 obtained from H. Reeve Angel & Co. Ltd., 14 New Bridge St., London. The resin was subjected to the following washing procedure: (*1*) NaOH (0.5 N) followed by water. (*2*) HCl (0.5 N) followed by

[1] The abbreviations used are: MVA lact. (mevalonate lactone), MVA (mevalonate), MVAP (mevalonate 5-phosphate), MVAPP (mevalonate 5-pyrophosphate), IPP (isopentenyl pyrophosphate), IP (isopentenyl monophosphate), ATP (adenosine triphosphate), ADP (adenosine diphosphate), DEAE (diethylaminoethyl).

water. (*3*) NaOH (0.5 *N*) followed by water. (*4*) NH_4HCO_3 (0.05 *N*). (*5*) NH_4HCO_3 (0.02 *N*). The columns were packed under gravity and were subjected to a head of about 50 cm, the flow rate being adjusted to 1 ml/min.

Dowex 1 (X10 mesh 200–400) obtained from Dow Chemical Co. Midland Mich., was converted to the formate form by the procedure outlined by Hurlbert *et al.* (6). After removing the fine and coarse particles by sedimentation, the resin was washed with sodium formate (3 *M*) until no more chloride was removed, and was then washed with water. The column (8×1.0 cm) was prepared by sedimenting under gravity and was washed with 100 ml sodium formate (1 *M*) in formic acid (6 *M*), followed by 20 ml formic acid (88%), and finally with 500 ml water.

Radioactive Assay. The [^{14}C] content of the column eluates was assayed by use of the Chroma Cell flowthrough scintillation cell assembly made by Nuclear-Chicago Corporation, Des Plaines, Ill. The assembly was placed immediately after the column; the eluate then passed to the fraction collector.

The presence of ATP and ADP was detected by measuring the extinction of the column eluates at 260 mμ in the Unicam SP 500 spectrophotometer.

Paper Chromatography. This was carried out on Whatman No. 1 paper using the following solvent systems:

1. Ethanol/ammonia/water, 7/2/1 by volume, descending (2).

2. 2-Methylbutan-2-ol/acetic acid/water, 4/1/2 by volume, ascending (1).

3. 2-Methylpropan-2-ol/formic acid/water, 20/5/8 by volume, descending (3).

4. Butan-1-ol/formic acid/water, 77/10/13 by volume, ascending (5).

Incubations. All incubations were carried out at 30° in phosphate buffer (0.05 *M*, pH 7.2) and contained *N*-acetylcysteine (2 m*M*). Incubations for the analytical procedure were carried out for 1 hr and those for the preparative procedure for 6 hr.

Protein was removed by addition of an equal volume of ethanol, the mixture being boiled to coagulate the protein and remove the ethanol. The precipitated protein was centrifuged down or filtered off.

RESULTS

The method was based on the technique of Staehelin (8) for the fractionation of oligonucleotides on DEAE-cellulose using an ammonium bicarbonate buffer. From this two procedures were evolved, one for analysis of the metabolites of mevalonate, and the other more specifically for separation of substrate amounts of mevalonate 5-pyrophosphate.

Analytical Procedure. The protein-free incubation mixture (2 ml) was applied to a DEAE-cellulose column (15 × 1.5 cm) previously equilibrated with ammonium bicarbonate (0.02 *M*). A linear gradient of ammonium bicarbonate concentration increasing to 0.2 *M* was then applied to the column using a reservoir and a mixing vessel both of capacity 375 ml. The elution pattern is shown in Figure 1. The material comprising each of the radioactive peaks was pooled, treated with Dowex 50 (H^+) to remove ammonium bicarbonate, and freeze-dried.

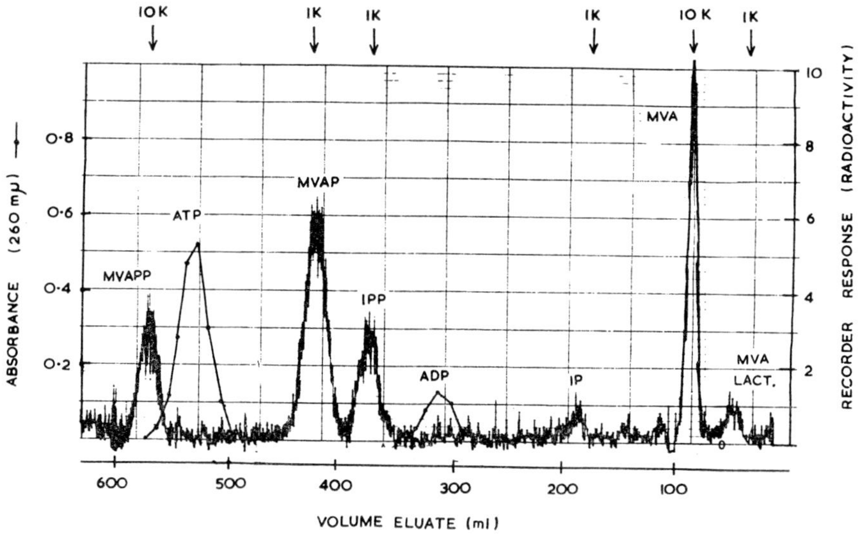

FIG. 1. Chromatography on DEAE-cellulose of [2-^{14}C]-mevalonate derivatives and adenine nucleotides produced from an incubation with enzyme preparation A. Elution with a linear gradient of ammonium bicarbonate 0.02–0.2 *M*, 375 ml in each vessel, column size 1.5 × 15 cm, flow rate 60 ml/hr. Numbers above radioactivity peaks indicate maximum deflection setting of recorder (K = 1000 cpm).

Identification of the Fractions. The nature of the material in each of the fractions from the DEAE-cellulose column was initially ascertained from its behavior on Dowex 1 columns by comparison with the chromatographic characteristics reported by Bloch *et al.* (3) and by Chesterton and Kekwick (2) for the metabolites of mevalonate. The fractions having the chromatographic characteristics of mevalonate 5-phosphate and isopentenyl phosphate appeared to be homogeneous, that corresponding to mevalonate 5-pyrophosphate showed a 2–3% breakdown to mevalonate 5-phosphate, and that corresponding to isopentenyl pyrophosphate showed a 4% breakdown to isopentenyl phosphate. This breakdown appeared to be due to the conditions in which the Dowex 1 column was used, because when the original fractions from the DEAE-cellulose column were subjected to rechromatography on the same column no significant breakdown of any fraction could be detected. Analysis of the fraction chromatographing as 5-phosphomevalonate, prepared using $AT^{32}P$ as a substrate showed one atom of phosphorus per molecule. The material was completely hydrolyzed to mevalonate by incubation with alkaline phosphatase for 15 hr at room temperature. A similar analysis of the fraction corresponding to mevalonate 5-pyrophosphate showed the presence of two atoms of phosphorus per molecule; the material was converted to mevalonate by the action of alkaline phosphatase, and contained one acid-labile phosphate group; incubation of the material at pH 4.0 for 15 min at 60° produced a 10% conversion to mevalonate 5-phosphate. The fraction chromatographing as isopentenyl pyrophosphate contained two atoms of phosphorus per molecule, did not contain the carboxyl carbon of the original mevalonate, and was chromatographically indistinguishable on the DEAE-cellulose column from chemically synthesized [1-^{14}C]-isopentenyl pyrophosphate. The fraction identified as isopentenyl phosphate cochromatographed with a chemically synthesized preparation of isopentenyl phosphate, and contained one atom of phosphorus per molecule; this material also lacked the carboxyl carbon of the original mevalonate.

The results of the analysis of the fractions from the DEAE-cellulose column by paper chromatography in solvents *1* and *2* are shown in Table 1. Chromatography in solvents *3* and *4* gave essentially similar results. Some breakdown of mevalonate 5-pyrophosphate and of isopentenyl pyro-

TABLE 1
Analysis of Fractions from DEAE-Cellulose Column
(provisional identity of fractions deduced from chromatography on Dowex 1)

	MVAP	MVAPP	IP	IPP
		Solvent *1*		
R_f values				
Reported (2)	0.13–0.17	0.08	0.4–0.5	0.2–0.23
Found for major component	0.13–0.18	0.07–0.1	0.4–0.48	0.23–0.32
Found for trace components	None	0.14, 0.17	0.36, 0.25, 0.09	0.45, 0.09
		Solvent *2*		
R_f values				
Reported (1)	0.19	0.09	—	—
Found for major component	0.21–0.31	0.1–0.15	0.6–0.66	0.18–0.24
Found for minor component	None	0.26	0.11, 0.26	0.63, 0.34, 0.10, 0.05

phosphate was evident in all the paper chromatographic solvents used. Isopentenyl phosphate showed some breakdown in all solvents except solvent *3*, and mevalonate 5-phosphate was stable in all solvents except solvent *3*.

Preparative Separation. This procedure was developed for the preparation of substrate amounts of [2-^{14}C]-mevalonate 5-pyrophosphate by enzyme preparation B, which contained mevalonate kinase and phosphomevalonate kinase but which was free from mevalonate-5-pyrophosphate decarboxylase. With an enzyme preparation containing the decarboxylase it should be possible to prepare isopentenyl pyrophosphate by a similar procedure, or mevalonate 5-phosphate with an enzyme preparation containing only mevalonate kinase.

Since the mevalonate 5-pyrophosphate was not well separated from ATP on the DEAE-cellulose column and also in order to apply as much impure mevalonate 5-pyrophosphate to the DEAE-cellulose column as possible, a preliminary separation of the mevalonate 5-pyrophosphate was carried out on a Dowex 1 column essentially according to the procedure of Bloch *et al.* (3).

A preliminary separation of the metabolites of mevalonate, shown in Figure 2 was obtained by applying deproteinized material from an incubation (total volume 40 ml) containing enzyme preparation B (2 mg protein), [2-^{14}C]-mevalonate (0.005 μc/μmole, 200 μmoles), ATP (250 μmoles), *N*-acetylcysteine (80 μmoles), and $MgCl_2$ (275 μmoles), concentrated to 4 ml, to a Dowex 1 column (8 $\times$ 1 cm) and eluting according to a modification of the procedure of Bloch *et al.* (3), details of which are given in the legend to Figure 2. It is seen that the mevalonate 5-pyrophosphate has been satisfactorily separated from ATP. The fractions were placed in ice as they were eluted; the material present in the peak corresponding to mevalonate 5-pyrophosphate was deionized on a Dowex 50 (H^+) column, eluted into ice, and freeze-dried. Care was taken to keep the fractions as cold as possible throughout to minimize breakdown to 5-phosphomevalonate, which could be reduced to 25% by this treatment. The freeze-dried material was dissolved in water and the pH adjusted to 8.0, giving a total volume of 4 ml, which was applied to a DEAE-cellulose column (25 $\times$ 1.5 cm) equilibrated as before. A linear gradient of ammonium bicarbonate from 0.02 to 0.2 *M* was then applied using a reservoir and a mixing vessel, each of 500 ml capacity. The elution profile obtained is shown in Figure 3. The pooled radioactive fractions corresponding to mevalonate 5-pyrophosphate were treated with Dowex 50 (H^+) to remove ammonium bicarbonate, neutralized with a small amount of NaOH (2 *N*), and freeze-dried.

The final yield of [2-^{14}C]-mevalonate 5-pyrophosphate was about 10%

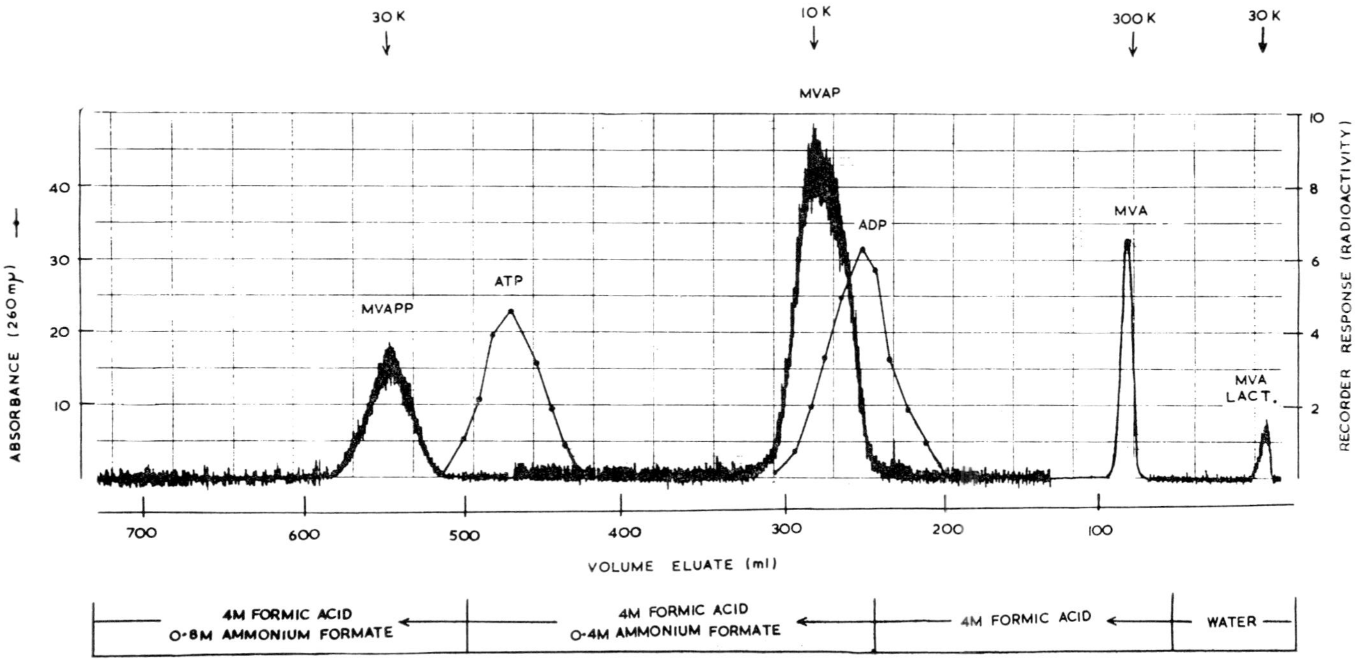

FIG. 2. Preliminary purification of mevalonate 5-pyrophosphate by chromatography on Dowex 1 formate of [2-^{14}C]-mevalonate derivatives and adenine nucleotides produced from an incubation with enzyme preparation B for the preparation of substrate quantities of mevalonate 5-pyrophosphate. Elution with a modification of the gradient according to Bloch *et al.* (3). The mixing vessel contained 210 ml water and after the passage of 60 ml the reservoir was charged with 250 ml quantities of formic acid and ammonium formate as indicated. Column size 1.0 × 8 cm, flow rate 130 ml/hr. Numbers above radioactivity peaks indicate maximum deflection setting of recorder (K = 1000 cpm).

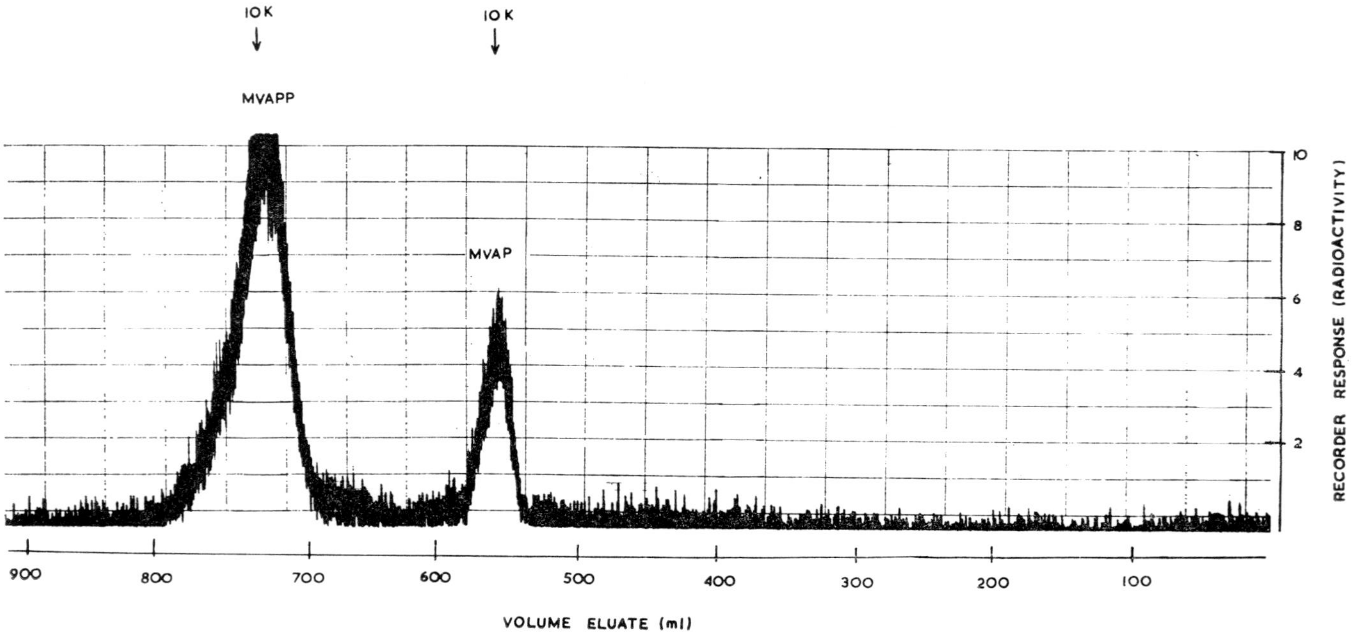

FIG. 3. Purification on DEAE-cellulose of mevalonate 5-pyrophosphate obtained from previous chromatography on Dowex 1 formate. Elution as in Figure 1. Column size 1.5 × 25 cm, 500 ml in each vessel. Numbers above radioactivity peaks indicate maximum deflection setting of recorder (K = 1000 cpm).

of the [2-^{14}C]-mevalonate employed as the initial substrate. This material could be utilized by biochemical systems; it was converted to isopentenyl pyrophosphate by latex serum and incorporated into rubber by whole latex.

DISCUSSION

The preparation procedure for obtaining [2-^{14}C]-mevalonate 5-pyrophosphate from incubations of *Hevea* enzymes with [2-^{14}C]-mevalonate is useful because there appears to be no chemical method published for the synthesis of this substance, but the principle drawback of the method is the necessity for the preliminary fractionation on Dowex 1, during which some breakdown did occur. The need for this stage arose from the necessity to remove as much ATP as possible from the incubation mixture, as this was not well separated from mevalonate 5-pyrophosphate on DEAE-cellulose, and also to effect a preliminary enrichment of the metabolite in order to allow a relatively heavier loading of the DEAE-cellulose column with the required material. Preliminary attempts to remove ATP by means of a specific ATPase did not yield satisfactory results but further experiments might produce a good technique.

An interesting feature observed during the chromatographic studies was the relative stabilities of the compounds involved. The pyrophosphates of mevalonate and isopentenol appeared to be relatively unstable, less stable than ATP or ADP, in acid solvents. The behavior of these substances on successive rechromatography in the same solvent suggested that something more complex than simple hydrolysis of the phosphate group must account for spots of changed R_f value. The phosphates of mevalonate and isopentenol were, on the other hand, found to be relatively more stable but some breakdown of even these substances did occur during chromatography in some acid solvents.

SUMMARY

A method for the analytical separation of the metabolites of mevalonate, and for the purification of mevalonate 5-pyrophosphate by chromatography on DEAE-cellulose, is described which, it is claimed, allows less breakdown of these materials than other methods.

ACKNOWLEDGMENTS

The work described was supported by grants from The Natural Rubber Producers Research Association and The Science Research Council. We are very grateful to Dr. D. Barnard and to Dr. G. P. McSweeney of The Natural Rubber Producers Research Association for gifts of isopentenyl phosphate and isopentenyl pyrophosphate.

REFERENCES

1. Henning, U., Möslein, E. M., and Lynen, F., *Arch. Biochem. Biophys.* **83,** 259 (1959).
2. Chesterton, C. J., and Kekwick, R. G. O., *Biochem. J.* **98,** 26P (1966).
3. Bloch, K., Chaykin, S., Phillips, A. H., and de Waard, A., *J. Biol. Chem.* **234,** 2595 (1959).
4. Archer, B. L., and Sekhar, B. C., *Biochem. J.* **61,** 503 (1955).
5. Skilleter, D. N., Williamson, I. P., and Kekwick, R. G. O., *Biochem. J.* **93,** 27P (1966).
6. Hurlbert, R. E., Schmitz, H., Brum, A. F., and Porter, V. R., *J. Biol. Chem.* **209,** 33 (1954).
7. Tchenn, T. T., *J. Biol. Chem.* **233,** 1100 (1958).
8. Staehelin, M., *Biochim. Biophys. Acta* **49,** 11 (1961).

ANALYTICAL BIOCHEMISTRY 20, 181–191 (1967)

Activation Analysis of Mono- and Oligonucleotides[1]

GEORGE W. RUSHIZKY

Laboratory of Biochemistry, National Cancer Institute, National Institutes of Health, Bethesda, Maryland 20014

AND

WARREN W. MILLER

Department of Chemistry, The Pennsylvania State University, University Park, Pennsylvania 16802

Received February 2, 1967

The determination of limited quantities of nucleic acids is facilitated by incorporation of radioactive tracers. With certain nucleic acids, such as those of many animal viruses, radioactive labeling is not feasible to a degree sufficient for characterization studies. As an alternative, P-containing compounds may be labeled after isolation and fractionation by activation of ^{31}P to ^{32}P with thermal neutrons (1). Separation processing must precede neutron activation since the latter breaks the chemical bonds of the ^{31}P. After separation by paper chromatography, phosphatides containing 0.01–0.05 μg P/cm^2 of filter paper could be thus detected (2).

This report describes an extension of neutron activation to the quantitative determination of mono- and oligonucleotides after separation on filter paper by electrophoresis and chromatography. Application of the procedure to chain length determinations by total vs. terminal phosphate ratios of oligonucleotides is described.

MATERIAL AND METHODS

Enzymes. RNase T_2 was prepared from Japanese takadiastase (Sanzyme) as described (3). Nonspecific phosphodiesterase was isolated from the Marburg strain of *Bacillus subtilis* (4, 5).

Nucleic Acids and Oligonucleotides. RNA of the *Escherichia coli* phage MS 2 was prepared essentially as described by Strauss and Sinsheimer

[1] Abbreviations: kW, kilowatt; MWh, megawatt hours; Ap, Cp, Gp, Up, Tp, nucleoside 3′-phosphates of adenine, cytosine, guanine, uracil, and thymine, respectively.

(6). Calf thymus DNA was isolated by 1 *M* NaCl/phenol extraction (7). Decanucleotides from RNase T_1 digests of MS 2 RNA were obtained by column chromatography on DEAE-Sephadex A-25 in 7 *M* urea at pH 7.5 (8, 9).

Enzymic Digestions and Mapping. For nucleotide composition determinations RNase T_2 was employed in 0.1 *M* NH_4 acetate, pH 4.5 (3). Mononucleotides were separated by paper electrophoresis in 0.1 *M* Tris-acetate, pH 3.6, for 18 hr at 6 V/cm on 46 × 57 cm sheets of Whatman No. 3, Schleicher and Schuell Blue Ribbon 589, or Black Ribbon 589 paper. Pancreatic RNase digests of decanucleotides (see above) were fractionated by electrophoresis in 0.02 *M* NH_4 formate at pH 2.7 followed by chromatography with redistilled *tert*-butanol/0.02 *M* NH_4 formate, pH 4.8 (10). Chain length determinations with alkaline phosphatase (11) from *E. coli* were performed as described in the legend to Table 4. The enzymic digests were fractionated by paper chromatography with *n*-propanol concentrated NH_4OH/H_2O, 55/10/35, v/v (12). Inorganic phosphate was located on the paper with Hanes-Isherwood phosphate spray (13).

The amounts of nucleic acid material were obtained by phosphorus determination (14). Samples were applied to the paper in 0.3–1.0 ml of the buffer used for enzymic digestion. Blank papers received only the buffers. For the determination of nucleotide composition, about 0.5–2 μg P (as mononucleotides) was used. With enzymic digests containing oligonucleotides, about 5–10 μg P, and for marker maps about 25 μg P (as Cp and Up, or as NaH_2PO_4) were applied to each paper.

Irradiation of Samples (2). Prior to irradiation, care was taken to avoid contamination of the maps with fingerprints or metals which would raise the background count. As a check for metal contamination, papers were used directly for electrophoresis and chromatography, or after washing, by chromatography in descent, with about 600 ml of 0.1 *M* $(NH_4)_4$-EDTA pH 8.6 (15) per paper. EDTA was washed out of the paper with H_2O. Irradiation of the papers was performed in low-density polyethylene tubes of i.d. 3.8 cm, length 46 cm, and wall thickness 0.32 cm. Before use, the plasticizer-free tubing was washed extensively with 0.5 *N* HNO_3, then with water, and dried overnight. The papers were rolled up, tied with nylon string, and sealed in the polyethylene tubes.

Because of the geometry of the neutron source, it was desirable to limit the length of the rolls of paper to 23 cm or less. Areas of sample and blank papers to be irradiated were located by superimposition on marker maps containing Cp and Up or NaH_2PO_4. To measure the variation of neutron flux across the papers to be irradiated, 1.0 μg P in a volume of 0.01 ml was spotted with the same micropipet at 2–3 cm intervals along the edges of the paper. Two control experiments were also done. First, decreasing amounts of P (1.00, 0.50, 0.20, and 0.10 μg in 0.01 ml) were applied in three rows on the center area of blank maps together with 1 μg P markers along the edges of the paper. Second, blank maps were spotted, in triplicate, with 0.01 ml volumes containing 1.0 μg of Zn, Na, K, S, Cu, and Ca as $Zn(C_2H_3O_2)_2 \cdot 2H_2O$, $NaHCO_3$, $K_2CO_3 \cdot 1.5\ H_2O$, $(NH_4)_2SO_4$, Cu $(NO_3)_2 \cdot 3H_2O$ and $Ca(C_2H_3O_2)_2 \cdot H_2O$, respectively. Markers of 1 μg P were also applied to the edge of these papers. The sealed polyethylene tubes were irradiated in an air-filled aluminum tube standing alongside the core of the Penn State Triga Reactor for 2 or 5 hr with the reactor operating at a 500 kW power level. The neutron flux to which the samples were exposed was approximately 5×10^{12} cm^{-2} sec^{-1}. Sample temperature during irradiation was about 30°C. The midpoint of the sample tube approximately coincided with the horizontal midplane of the core.

After irradiation, the tubes were left in the reactor pool for 3–7 days to allow for the decay of short-lived isotopes. The polyethylene tubes were then opened with care (2). After this period of cooling, the radiation level of the samples and their container was below 10 mr/hr on contact, with only a minor fraction of that in the papers themselves.

Papers irradiated for 1 MWh were easily unfolded, but those irradiated for 2.5 MWh were fragile and, in order to handle them, they were uniformly covered with cellophane tape on the back. Spots on the papers containing ^{32}P were located and counted as described in the legend for Figure 1.

Variation of Neutron Flux over the Chromatograms. As expected from the geometry of the neutron source, net cpm/μg P differed considerably more along the vertical dimension of papers undergoing irradiation (along the axis of the paper cylinder) than across the horizontal dimension of the paper (around the circumference of the paper cylinder). Therefore, corrections for neutron flux variations were performed only along the vertical dimension of papers. For example, to determine the ^{32}P count of a hypothetical sample at the upper right corner of Figure 1, the average net cpm/μg P along the horizontal dimension of the paper were calculated to be 1521, 1320, and 1139 cpm. The value from the middle of the paper (1320 cpm) was taken as standard. To find the corrected ^{32}P count of the unknown sample at the upper right corner, its net count thus was multiplied by 1320/1521 = 0.87.

RESULTS

The neutron activation of P in the form of NaH_2PO_4 and mono- and oligoribonucleotides was investigated. The samples were fractionated on sheets of filter paper by electrophoresis at pH 2.7 or 3.6 and by chromatography at pH 4.8. The papers in polyethylene tubes were then irradiated for 1–2.5 MWh and cooled as mentioned before. ^{32}P-Labeled material on the papers was located by exposure to x-ray film and the spots cut out with a die together with corresponding areas from irradiated blank papers. Samples were counted in a windowless gas-flow counter. Standards containing 1.00 μg P along the edges of the papers were used to assay the variation of neutron flux across the paper.

	34 cm			Average net cpm/μg P
	$\frac{1510}{458} = 3.3$	$\frac{1595}{515} = 3.1$	$\frac{1460}{444} = 3.3$	1521
19 cm	$\frac{1278}{400} = 3.2$	$\frac{1340}{418} = 3.2$	$\frac{1338}{446} = 3.0$	1320
	$\frac{1152}{361} = 3.2$	$\frac{1170}{366} = 3.2$	$\frac{1095}{365} = 3.0$	1139

FIG. 1. Variation of neutron flux. A 19 × 34 cm sheet of Schleicher and Schuell 589 Black Ribbon paper was washed with 600 ml of 0.1 *M* $(NH_4)_4$-EDTA, pH 8.6, by paper chromatography in descent. The EDTA was washed out of the paper with H_2O. Aliquots of 0.01 ml of a solution containing 100 μg P (in the form of NaH_2PO_4) were then applied to the paper. The paper, together with a blank paper of the same size, was rolled along the 19 cm axis into a cylinder of i.d. 3 cm, and irradiated at 1.5 MWh. After 1 week, ^{32}P-containing areas of the paper were located, by exposure to Kodak Blue Brand Medical x-ray film for about 16 hr, and cut out with a die of diameter 2 cm. Corresponding areas of the blank paper and the samples were placed on Al planchets and counted in a windowless gas-flow counter for at least 10,000 counts. Because the counting rates were below 4000 cpm, no coincidence corrections were applied. The fractions given indicate the net count (sample background)/background for 1 μg ^{31}P irradiated at the corresponding area on the paper. Average values along the horizontal axis are given.

This variation was considerably larger along the axis than across the diameter of the paper cylinder (Fig. 1), as expected from the geometry of the neutron source. Neutron flux corrections were performed as described in the legend to Figure 1 and in the "Methods" section. Furthermore, samples were counted using identical areas of blank paper (irradiated next to the sample paper) as background. Thus, the distance from the neutron source between sample and blank paper differed only by the thickness of one paper. As shown in Table 1, neutron activation of

TABLE 1
Neutron Activation of Decreasing Amounts of P

μg P applied to paper[a]	Net counts, cpm	Average net counts	Average net counts × dilution factor
1.00	1581,1562,1510	1550	1550
0.50	752,810,751	771	1542
0.20	281,292,269	280	1400
0.10	130,89,93	104	1040

[a] P, as NaH_2PO_4, in 0.01 ml, was applied in triplicate to a 9 × 25 cm sheet of SS 589 paper and irradiated at 1.5 MWh. Blanks and ^{32}P-containing areas were counted 7 days after irradiation (see legend to Fig. 1). Neutron flux corrections were not applied.

decreasing amounts of ^{31}P gave linearly decreasing net count rates of ^{32}P down to 0.10 μg P. In other experiments, with likely contaminants of filter paper, 1 μg each of the elements Zn, Na, K, S, Cu, and Ca in a volume of 0.01 ml were irradiated in the same manner as the NaH_2PO_4 samples. Qualitative examination of x-ray prints showed that sulfur caused the most darkening of the film, comparable to that obtained

TABLE 2
Nucleotide Composition of MS 2 RNA and Calf Thymus DNA Determined by Neutron Activation of Separated Mononucleotides

Enzymic digests of RNA or DNA were assayed for P content, and aliquots applied to Whatman No. 3 paper. After electrophoresis at pH 3.8 (see text), the nucleotide-containing areas were cut out. The paper strips (about 8 × 25 cm) were lined with 1.0 μg spots along the edges, folded along the short axis in a roll of i.d. 3 cm and irradiated. ^{32}P areas were located by exposure to x-ray film, cut out with a die of diameter 2 cm, and counted together with corresponding areas of blank paper to 10,000 counts or more. After subtraction of background counts, net cpm were corrected for variation of P content of the mononucleotides, and the % of total cpm due to each nucleotide determined. No neutron flux corrections were applied because the net cpm in the 1 μg P spots did not differ from each other by more than 10%.

MS 2 RNA				Calf thymus DNA			
	by ^{32}P				by ^{32}P		
	% of total net cpm				% of total net cpm		
Base	I	II	by UV[a]	Base	I	II	by UV[b]
Cp	26	24	25	Cp	21	22	21
Ap	24	23	23	Ap	27	27	28
Gp	26	27	27	Gp	22	22	23
Up	24	26	26	Tp	29	29	28
Total μg P used	6	0.55	40–80		1.8	1.1	40–80
Total cpm	6518	1325			1910	1100	
Irradiation level (MWh)	1	2.5			1.5	1.5	
Counted days, after irradiation	11	14			7	7	

[a] These results agree with published values (6).
[b] These results agree with published values (17).

TABLE 3

Neutron Activation of 2 Decamer Fractions from MS 2 RNA after Hydrolysis with Pancreatic RNase and Mapping

Pancreatic RNase digests of two decamer fractions were assayed for P content, and aliquots fractionated in duplicate on Whatman No. 3 paper by electrophoresis and chromatography. Nucleic acid material on the papers was located by comparison with marker maps (see text), cut out, irradiated, and counted as described in the legend to Fig. 1. After correction for background and variations in P content of the compounds, net cpm per oligomer were converted to moles per oligomer by dividing by the chain length. Neutron flux corrections were applied as described in the text. The amount of Gp was arbitrarily set to 100 moles, and the other values multiplied accordingly. The same decamer fractions (9) were analyzed by ^{32}P activation (^{32}P column) and, using larger amounts, by UV spectrophotometry (UV column) after hydrolysis of oligomers to monomers with RNase T_2 (16).

Fraction I			Fraction II		
	Molar ratios			Molar ratios	
Compound	by ^{32}P	by UV	Compound	by ^{32}P	by UV
ApApCp	136	140	ApApApApCp	5	8
ApCp	49	50	ApApApCp	17	15
Cp	470	461	ApApCp	23	20
ApGp	29	31	ApCp	29	28
Gp	100	100	Cp	387	393
Up	134	128	ApApGp	6	4
Ap + Cp + Up/Gp	8.8	8.7	ApApApUp	7	6
Ap + Cp/Gp	7.8	7.7	Gp	100	100
A + Cp/Up	7.5	7.9	ApUp	75	72
Up/Gp	1.0	1.0	Up	137	139
Composition:	$[(Ap + Cp)_8Up]Gp$		Ap + Cp + Up/Gp	8.8	8.7
			Ap + Cp/Up	3.3	3.3
			Ap + Cp/Gp	6.8	6.7
			Up/Gp	2.1	2.1
			Composition:	$[(Ap + Cp)_7Up_2]Gp$	
Total cpm counted:	9385			13251	
μg P fractionated per map:	4.8			7	

when the x-ray film was exposed to irradiated blank paper for 28 days. However, this darkening was considerably less than that due to 1 μg P spots of 2 cm diameter exposed for the same length of time.

It was also observed that the signal-to-noise ratio of Whatman No. 3 paper decreased with time after the first 2 weeks after irradiation. Thus, when the ^{32}P count decreased to 37%, the background only decreased to 48% of the original value. However, the ratio increased when both were counted through a 50 mg/cm^2 absorber of aluminum foil.

As a check on the activation procedure, RNA of the *E. coli* phage MS 2 and DNA of calf thymus were hydrolyzed to mononucleotides. The monomers were separated on filter paper, irradiated, and the base composition obtained by ^{32}P counts and by UV spectrophotometry compared. The results show that base compositions may be determined by neutron activation of samples containing as little as 0.55 μg P (Table 2).

The activation procedure was also applied to the quantitative determination of oligonucleotides. To this end, two decanucleotide fractions (9) from a RNase T_1 (18) hydrolyzate of MS 2 RNA were treated with pancreatic RNase (19). After mapping and irradiation, the amounts of mono- and oligonucleotides were determined by UV spectrophotometry and ^{32}P activity. The results (Table 3) show fair agreement between the two sets of data so obtained.

Chain length determinations of large oligonucleotides were also performed by neutron activation. As shown in Table 4, similar values were obtained by P assay and ^{32}P counts.

TABLE 4

Chain Length Determination of Oligomer Fractions Determined by Ratio of Total to Terminal Phosphate Released by Alkaline Phosphatase

Oligomer fractions were obtained by enzymic hydrolysis (with micrococcal nuclease) of MS 2 RNA adsorbed on DEAE-cellulose (9). Aliquots of the same fractions were digested with alkaline phosphatase (18) and the digests examined for total and terminal phosphate by the procedure of Ames and Dubin (14) and by ^{32}P activation after paper chromatography on SS 589 Black Ribbon paper with *n*-propanol/concentrated NH_4OH/H_2O 55/10/35 (v/v) (12). Neutron flux corrections were applied.

Fraction No.	Chain lengths, determined by P assay	by ^{32}P
1	88,92	78,87
2	178,185	167,170
3	210,214	191,198
4	269,257	241,251
μg P used per detn.	10–150	5–14

DISCUSSION

With nucleic acid derivatives, quantitation by spectrophotometry requires considerably larger amounts of P than 0.01–0.05 μg detected by Benson *et al.* (1) on paper chromatograms of glycerophosphates after neutron activation of ^{31}P to ^{32}P. It was therefore of interest to apply Benson's procedure to the characterization of low concentrations of mono- and oligonucleotides.

Because of the different p*K*'s of the amino groups of Ap, Cp, and Gp at acid pH, a combination of electrophoresis and chromatography on filter paper is preferable, for resolution of mono- and oligonucleotides, to two-dimensional paper chromatography as employed for glycerophosphates (1, 2). A combination of electrophoresis and chromatography on paper was first described by Kickhoefen and Westphal (19) and later proved especially useful for the resolution of peptides derived from different hemoglobins (2). Various combinations of two-dimensional chromatography and/or high-voltage electrophoresis have been reported since (21–24). We prefer the procedure employing Durrum-type electrophoresis, (25) and paper chromatography at pH 2.7 and 3.8 (10) because it (*a*) avoids pH values (pH 1.9) that might lead to depurination of DNA (26, 23); (*b*) minimizes contact (and contamination) of the paper with glass or plastic surfaces during the fractionation procedure; and (*c*) permits, because of low-voltage electrophoresis, the separation of enzymic digests of high ionic strength, such as that due to 0.1 *M* buffers.

As the results indicate, the procedure as described allows quantitation of phosphorus to about 0.10 μg per spot of 2 cm diameter. Lower amounts of phosphorus could be assayed if only qualitative results are sought. Darkening of x-ray film at concentrations of about 0.1 μg P/cm² was obtained by Murray and Offord (27). Since appreciable losses of material occurred in the course of preparation of the samples, the true concentration of P/cm² was considered to be nearer 0.05 μg, while the weaker spots visible on the autoradiographs were estimated to be due to about 0.01 μg P/cm².

To attain higher sensitivity for the activation procedure, the background of the paper may be reduced by extensive washing prior to use. Thus, electrophoresis and chromatography lowers the background of unwashed Whatman No. 3 paper by about 30%. Treatment with 0.1 *M* $(NH_4)_4$-EDTA, pH 8.6, lowers the blank by 50%, and significantly reduces the variation of background across the papers (Fig. 1). With spots of 2 cm diameter, ratios of net cpm per μg P/background cpm of 2–2.3 may be thus obtained with Whatman No. 3 paper, and 3.0–3.3 with SS 589 paper. However, the lower mechanical strength of SS 589 paper also decreases the amount of irradiation the paper can withstand.

Beta absorption and gamma ray spectrum analysis revealed ^{24}Na, ^{35}S, ^{32}P, ^{51}Cr, ^{82}Br, ^{197}Hg, and ^{203}Hg as activated contaminants responsible for the background count of the maps. After the short-lived contaminants had decayed out (2–4 weeks after irradiation), the only identifiable metals were Hg and Cr and possibly Pt. The background could then be reduced to one-fourth through the use of a 50 mg/cm^2 aluminum foil between the paper and the counter, at the expense of decreasing the apparent ^{32}P activity to 60% of the value without the absorber. The soft component of the background was probably mostly ^{35}S, due to ^{34}S(n, γ) ^{35}S and ^{35}Cl(n,p) ^{35}S reactions. Another 40% of the background in the papers was apparently due to ^{32}P derived from ^{32}S(n,p) ^{32}P and ^{35}Cl(n,α) ^{32}P reactions.

An effective means for lowering the background of irradiated papers may be to measure ^{32}P in scintillation, rather than in gas-flow counters. This requires adjustments for different papers and also at different time intervals after irradiation. However, in one experiment, net cpm per μg P/background cpm ratios of 8.1 were obtained with SS 589 paper about 4 weeks after irradiation, when the corresponding ratio measured by gas-flow counter without absorber was 2.8. In this instance, a paper disc of diameter 2 cm was counted in 16 ml of scintillation fluid (4 gm 2,5-diphenyloxazole and 0.1 gm p-bis-2-(5-phenyloxazolyl)benzene in 1 liter toluene).

In order to check out the activation procedure, nucleic acid material was examined which was available in quantities sufficient for analysis by UV spectrophotometry as well as by P determinations. As shown in Tables 3 and 4, analyses of mono- and oligonucleotide content and chain lengths of identical fractions by ^{32}P activity gave similar, but not identical, results. These differences may be due to the activation procedure, especially to the variation in contamination across the irradiated papers (Fig. 1). On the other hand, the chain lengths (Ap + Cp + Up/Gp ratios, Table 3) may vary from theory because the oligomer fractions contained other nucleic acid material to begin with, and/or because the UV spectrophotometry itself does not furnish an absolute standard for comparison.

More ^{32}P activity per spot on the map would be required to test the activation procedure per se rather than to determine the lowest amount of measurable material as well. For example, the spots due to compounds from fraction II, Table 3, contained about 0.18 μg P or more. Better agreement between the ^{32}P and spectrophotometry values might be obtainable with larger quantities of ^{32}P per spot, which, however, would also lower the sensitivity of the activation procedure.

To characterize small amounts of nucleic acid material, by activation analysis, a representative procedure might involve enzymic hydrolyses, fractionation of the digests, and irradiation. One determination of nucleotide composition, mono- and oligonucleotide ratios, and terminal-phosphate chain length would require about 1, 5, and 5 μg P, respectively. For duplicate assays of a sample of average chain length 100, about $2 \times 100 = 22$ μg P or about 0.25 mg of nucleic acid material would be needed. This is about 1/40 of the amount needed for the same determinations by spectrophotometry. The sensitivity of colorimetric P assays on a micro scale is quite comparable to that obtained here by activation analysis. However, the latter procedure also allows for the detection of possible ribonuclease action which would be revealed by paper chromatography of the phosphatase digest prior to irradiation.

SUMMARY

Mono- and oligonucleotides from enzymic digests of RNA and DNA were separated on filter paper and their quantities determined after neutron activation of ^{31}P to ^{32}P. This procedure required about 1/40 of the material needed for the same analyses by UV spectrophotometry.

ACKNOWLEDGMENT

We are grateful to Dr. E. L. Kuff for help and suggestions concerning scintillation counting procedures.

REFERENCES

1. Benson, A. A., Maruo, B., Flipse, R. J., Yurow, H. W., and Miller, W. W., *Proc. U.N. Intern. Conf. Peaceful Uses At. Energy, 2nd, Geneva, 1958* **24,** 289 (1959).
2. Benson, A. A., *in* "Methods in Enzymology" (S. P. Colowick and N. O. Kaplan, eds.), Vol. VI, p. 881. Academic Press, New York, 1963.
3. Rushizky, G. W., and Sober, H. A., *J. Biol. Chem.* **238,** 371 (1963).
4. Nakai, M., Minami, F., Yamazaki, T., and Tsugita, A., *J. Biochem. (Tokyo)* **57,** 96 (1965).
5. Kerr, I. M., Pratt, E. A., and Lehman, I. R., *Biochem. Biophys. Res. Commun.* **20,** 154 (1965).
6. Strauss, J. H., Jr., and Sinsheimer, R. L., *J. Mol. Biol.* **7,** 43 (1963).
7. Colter, J. S., Brown, R. A., and Ellem, K. A. O., *Biochim. Biophys. Acta* **55,** 31 (1962).
8. Tomlinson, R. V., and Tener, G. M., *J. Am. Chem. Soc.* **84,** 2644 (1962).
9. Rushizky, G. W., Skavenski, I. H., and Sober, H. A., *J. Biol. Chem.* **240,** 3984 (1965).
10. Rushizky, G. W., and Knight, C. A., *Virology* **11,** 236 (1960).
11. Sober, H. A., Yaron, A., Schlossman, S. F., Latt, S. A., and Rushizky, G. W., *Biochemistry* **5,** 3608 (1966).
12. Heppel, L. A., Harkness, D. R., and Hilmoe, R. J., *J. Biol. Chem.* **237,** 841 (1962).
13. Hanes, C. S., and Isherwood, F. A., *Nature* **164,** 1107 (1949).
14. Ames, B. N., and Dubin, D. T., *J. Biol. Chem.* **235,** 769 (1960).

15. HIMMELHOCH, S. R., SOBER, H. A., VALLEE, B. L., PETERSON, E. A., AND FUWA, K., *Biochemistry* **5**, 2523 (1966).
16. PRATT, A. W., TOAL, J. N., RUSHIZKY, G. W., AND SOBER, H. A., *Biochemistry* **3**, 1831 (1964).
17. CHARGAFF, E., *in* "Nucleic Acids" (E. Chargaff, and J. N. Davidson, eds.), Vol. I, p. 354. Academic Press, New York, 1955.
18. SATO, K., AND EGAMI, F., *J. Biochem.* (*Tokyo*) **44**, 753 (1957).
19. SCHMIDT, G., CUBILES, R., ZOLLNER, N., HECHT, L., STRICKLER, N., SERAIDARIAN. K., SERAIDARIAN, M., AND THANNHAUSER, S. J., *J. Biol. Chem.* **192**, 715 (1951).
20. KICKHOEFEN, B., AND WESTPHAL, O., *Z. Naturforschung* **7b**, 655, 659 (1952).
21. INGRAM, V. M., *Nature* **178**, 792 (1956).
22. INGRAM, V. M., AND PIERCE, J. G., *Biochemistry* **1**, 580 (1962).
23. ARMSTRONG, A., HAGOPIAN, H., INGRAM, V. M., SJÖQUIST, I., AND SJÖQUIST, J., *Biochemistry* **3**, 1194 (1964).
24. SANGER, F., BROWNLEE, G. G., AND BARRELL, B. G., *J. Mol. Biol.* **13**, 373 (1965).
25. YARON, A., AND SOBER, H. A., *Anal. Biochem.* **12**, 173 (1965).
26. BLOCK, R. J., DURRUM, E. L., AND ZWEIG, G., *in* "A Manual of Paper Chromatography and Paper Electrophoresis." Academic Press, New York, 1955.
27. HUANG, P. C., AND ROSENBERG, E., *Anal. Biochem.* **16**, 107 (1966).
28. MURRAY, K., AND OFFORD, R. E., *Nature* **211**, 376 (1966).

ANALYTICAL BIOCHEMISTRY **20**, 192–194 (1967)

Separation of Adenosine 3′,5′-Phosphate Derivatives on Thin Layers of ECTEOLA Cellulose

MARTIN A. RIZACK

The Rockefeller University, New York, New York 10021

Received February 20, 1967

This method was developed for the isolation of adenosine 3′,5′-phosphate (cyclic-AMP) and its derivatives and determination of their radioactivity by scintillation counting. The separation is performed on thin layers of ECTEOLA cellulose spread on vinyl sheeting in a manner similar to silica gel (1).

EXPERIMENTAL PROCEDURES

Materials. ECTEOLA cellulose for thin-layer chromatography was obtained from Schleicher and Schuell (Selectacel #67, capacity 0.24 meq/gm). Tritiated cyclic-AMP was obtained from Schwarz Bio-Research and other compounds from Nutritional Biochemical. Bakelite (Union Carbide) rigid vinyl calendered sheeting was obtained in 20 × 50 in. sheets, which were cut to 8 × 50 in. on a band saw.

Spreading. A slurry of ECTEOLA was prepared by dispersing 13 gm in 65 ml of distilled water with a semimicro container of a Waring Blendor. The vinyl sheeting was thoroughly washed in detergent and rinsed first in distilled water and then in ethyl alcohol. The ECTEOLA slurry was spread on the dried vinyl sheeting with a variable aperture spreader set at 0.25 mm. The air-dried thin layers were cut into 8 × 8 in. sections with a paper cutter and handled like glass plates.

Chromatography. The chromatograms were run in two directions. First distilled water was allowed to ascend to the edge of the plate separating nucleotides from nucleosides and purine derivatives (2). The chromatogram was then developed in the second direction with citrate buffer, 0.035 *M* at pH 5.5, after the impurities which accumulated at the front had been scraped off.

Counting. Nonradioactive compounds were added to all samples at the origin of the chromatogram to function as both carrier and chromatographic standard. Compounds to be assayed for radioactivity were identified by locating the appropriate absorbing spot under short-wave ultraviolet light. The spots were then cut out with a scissors and placed in a scintillation vial. Sodium hydroxide (0.8 ml of 0.1 N) was added to elute the compounds from the ECTEOLA and 18 ml of scintillation fluid was added directly to this. The scintillation fluid contained 4 gm PPO/liter and 50 mg POPOP/liter in 50% toluene and 50% ethoxyethanol (v/v). It was not found necessary to remove the thin layer and its supporting vinyl sheeting before adding the fluid.

RESULTS

The separation obtained is shown in Figure 1. ATP and ADP are separable from cyclic-AMP in this system since they run ahead of AMP in citrate buffer. ATP and ADP run together with an R_f of 0.61, while the R_f for AMP is 0.56.

The capacity of one of these layers was approximately 6 μg applied to the origin. The application of 2 μg was required to visualize AMP under ultraviolet light, while only 1 μg of the other compounds was

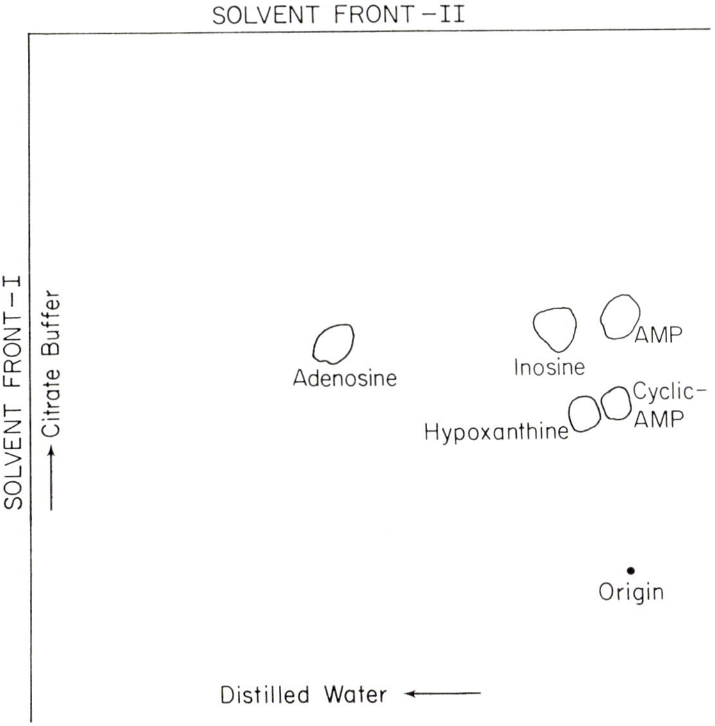

FIG. 1. Tracing of chromatographic separation of cyclic-AMP derivatives on an ECTEOLA cellulose thin layer. Solvent front I (distilled water) was 17.9 cm from the origin and solvent front II (0.035 M citrate buffer at pH 5.5) was 16.2 cm from the origin.

necessary. Overloading caused tailing and incomplete separation of the compounds.

Immersion of chromatograms contaminated the developing solution. Fresh solutions were therefore prepared for each run to prevent impairment of the degree of separation.

The radioactivity recovered was 80–85% of that added to the chromatogram. The ECTEOLA did not cause quenching or self-absorption. The presence of the vinyl sheeting in the scintillation vials reduced the total counts by 2–3%.

DISCUSSION

The method is being used for two purposes: a study of the metabolic products of cyclic-AMP in adipose tissue extracts and an assay for cyclic 3′,5′-nucleotide phosphodiesterase in adrenal, liver, and adipose tissue extracts. The complete separations obtained make it possible to recover any given compound for radioactive assay without contamination by other intermediates. The use of a buffer as a developing solution rather than the acid solutions used previously made it possible to control pH more precisely and thus enhance the degree of separation obtainable. An aqueous system is essential because vinyl sheeting has limited resistance to organic solvents.

SUMMARY

Thin layers of ECTEOLA on vinyl sheeting were used to separate derivatives of cyclic-AMP. The complete separation of the compounds studied (cyclic-AMP, AMP, adenosine, inosine, and hypoxanthine) made it possible simply to cut the area containing any given compound from the chromatogram. With the use of labeled precursors the incorporation of radioactivity into the various compounds could be determined by eluting with alkali in a scintillation vial and adding scintillation fluid without removing the chromatographic medium.

ACKNOWLEDGMENT

The excellent technical assistance of Mrs. Virginia Martin is gratefully acknowledged.

This research was supported by the National Science Foundation Grant GB 1835.

REFERENCES

1. Squibb, R. L., *Nature* **198,** 317 (1963).
2. Randerath, K., *Angew. Chem.* **73,** 674 (1961).
3. Randerath, K., *Angew. Chem.* **74,** 484 (1962).

ANALYTICAL BIOCHEMISTRY 20 (1967)

Short Communications

A Simple Quantitative Assay for *N*-Acetylgalactosaminitol[1]

The presence of alkali-labile glycosidic linkages involving the hydroxyl groups of serine and threonine of mucopolysaccharides and glycoproteins was first demonstrated by Anderson, Hoffman, and Meyer (1). Schiffman, Kabat, and Thompson (2) hydrolyzed blood-group substances in the presence of alkaline borohydride to convert the liberated glycose residue to the corresponding sugar alcohol. Similar hydrolyses of mucins (3, 4) have shown that *N*-acetylgalactosamine is linked to the hydroxy amino acids which results in the formation of *N*-acetylgalactosaminitol and oligosaccharides containing *N*-acetylgalactosaminitol (5).

A simple procedure for the simultaneous quantitation of *N*-acetylgalactosamine and *N*-acetylgalactosaminitol is described in this communication.

Techniques and Results. Compounds were obtained from commercial sources unless otherwise indicated. C^{14}-Acetic anhydride was purchased from New England Nuclear Corporation and was diluted with acetic anhydride (to a final specific activity of 40,000 cpm/μmole). *N*-Acetylgalactosaminitol was prepared by reducing *N*-acetylgalactosamine with sodium borohydride, and crystallized as described by Crimmin (6). Oligosaccharides containing *N*-acetylgalactosaminitol and *N*-acetylgalactosamine were isolated from pig submaxillary mucin (5). High-voltage electrophoresis was performed in a Gilson High Voltage Electrophorator and radioactivity was quantitated with a Packard Tri-Carb liquid scintillation counter in the toluene system described by Wang and Jones (7).

Compounds to be assayed, and standard amounts of galactosamine, were hydrolyzed for 5 hr in 1 ml of 4 *N* HCl at 100° in a sealed tube; a

[1] This investigation was supported in part by Grants AM-10335 and AM-08305 from the National Institutes of Health.

blank was included with each series. The HCl was removed *in vacuo,* in the presence of NaOH, and the samples were dissolved in 0.2 ml of water. *N*-Acetylation was carried out essentially as described by Distler, Merrick, and Roseman (8). The following reagents were added to the samples in an ice bath: 0.025 ml methanol, 0.025 ml 1 *M* $NaHCO_3$, and 0.005 ml C^{14}-acetic anhydride, and the mixtures were kept in ice for 60 min with intermittent mixing. The excess acetic anhydride was destroyed by the addition of approximately 0.1 ml of dry Dowex 50 H^+, 200–400 mesh, X8. Each mixture was then passed through a small column prepared from a disposable pipet, stuffed with a small amount of glass wool, and containing about 0.1 ml of Dowex 50 H^+. The reaction tubes and columns were washed with 1 ml of water (4 aliquots of 0.25 ml) and the eluates were evaporated to dryness on a rotary evaporator. Each sample was dissolved in 0.15 ml of water and 0.10 ml was applied to Whatman 3 MM paper. Electrophoresis was carried out in

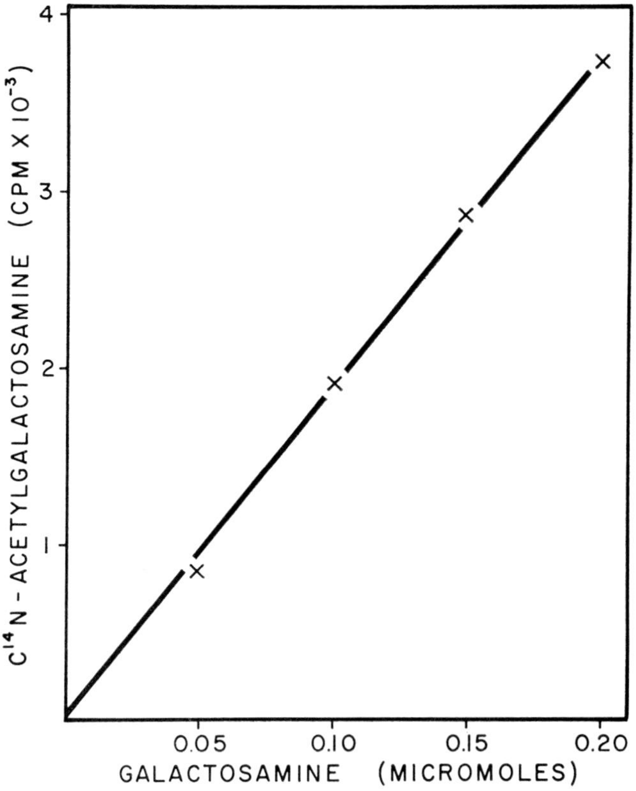

FIG. 1. Galactosamine standard curve.

1% sodium tetraborate buffer at 50 V/cm for 45 min. Under these conditions, *N*-acetylgalactosamine and *N*-acetylgalactosaminitol migrate about 7.5 cm and 20 cm, respectively, toward the anode. *N*-Acetylglucosaminitol and *N*-acetylmannosaminitol, prepared by sodium borohydride reduction of the *N*-acetylamino sugars, were not separable from *N*-acetylgalactosaminitol. One inch segments of the electrophoresis strips were counted in the toluene system.

The increase in radioactivity in *N*-acetylgalactosamine was linear with respect to galactosamine concentration (Fig. 1). Values found for *N*-acetylgalactosaminitol and two oligosaccharides isolated from pig submaxillary mucin (5), based on the galactosamine standard curve (Fig. 1) are presented in Table 1. The sensitivity of the method depends upon the specific activity of the C^{14}-acetic anhydride.

Although this method is adequate for determining the amounts of *N*-acetylgalactosamine and *N*-acetylgalactosaminitol in purified oligosaccharides, caution should be used in applying the method to crude preparations. The *N*-acetylation reaction is not specific and will acetylate other free amino groups.

The quantitative determination of glucosamine, mannosamine, and galactosamine mixtures was possible with this procedure, but electrophoresis for a longer time period (90 min) was necessary for adequate separation. The relative distances of migration (cm) were *N*-acetylglucosamine, 2; *N*-acetylgalactosamine, 9; *N*-acetylmannosamine, 16. If

TABLE 1
Assay of *N*-Acetylgalactosamine and *N*-Acetylgalactosaminitol
(see text for conditions)

	Micromoles[a]			
	N-Acetylgalactosamine		*N*-Acetylgalactosaminitol	
Compound assayed	Theory	Found	Theory	Found
Galactosamine	0.100	0.100	0	<0.001
N-Acetylgalactosaminitol	0	<0.001	0.064[b]	0.058
	0	<0.001	0.032	0.031
Oligosaccharide V[c]	0	<0.001	0.100	0.104
	0	<0.001	0.200	0.210
Oligosaccharide IV[c]	0.080	0.092	0.080	0.086
	0.160	0.181	0.160	0.156

[a] Calculated from galactosamine standard curve (Fig. 1).

[b] Based on nitrogen determination and dry weight.

[c] Oligosaccharide V contains fucose, galactose, and *N*-acetylgalactosaminitol; oligosaccharide IV contains fucose, *N*-acetylgalactosamine, galactose, and *N*-acetylgalactosaminitol. Theoretical concentrations are based on fucose and *N*-acetylgalactosamine values, respectively (5).

samples contain protein, it is necessary to isolate the hexosamine fraction by the method of Boas (9) prior to *N*-acetylation. Treatment of the *N*-acetylated samples with a mixed-bed ion-exchange resin should remove any remaining amino acids.

REFERENCES

1. Anderson, B., Hoffman, P., and Meyer, K., *J. Biol. Chem.* **240,** 156 (1965).
2. Schiffman, G., Kabat, E. A., and Thompson, W., *Biochemistry* **3,** 113 (1964).
3. Tanaka, K., Bertolini, M., and Pigman, W., *Biochem. Biophys. Res. Commun.* **16,** 404 (1964).
4. Best, J. S., Bhavanandan, V. P., and Gottschalk, A., *Biochim. Biophys. Acta* **101,** 141 (1965).
5. Carlson, D. M., *J. Biol. Chem.* **241,** 2984 (1966).
6. Crimmin, W. R. C., *J. Chem. Soc.* **1957,** 2838.
7. Wang, C. H., and Jones, D. E., *Biochem. Biophys. Res. Commun.* **1,** 203 (1959).
8. Distler, J. J., Merrick, J. M., and Roseman, S., *J. Biol. Chem.* **230,** 497 (1958).
9. Boas, N. F., *J. Biol. Chem.* **204,** 553 (1953).

Don M. Carlson

Departments of Biochemistry and Pediatrics
Western Reserve University
Cleveland, Ohio 44106
Received February 21, 1967

Increasing the Sensitivity of Char Sprays for the Detection of Lipids on Thin-Layer Chromatograms by Viewing under Ultraviolet Light

Spots on thin-layer chromatographic (TLC) plates are commonly visualized by spraying with sulfuric acid char reagents and heating, which produces brown or black areas at the specific locations of the various components. We have observed that additional sensitivity can be obtained if the charred TLC plate is viewed under ultraviolet (3600 Å) rather than visible light. The TLC separations can be carried out with any of the usual silica gel absorbents and solvent mixtures, and the spots developed by heating after spraying with sulfuric acid alone or mixed with potassium dichromate followed by heating (at about 185°C for 20–30 min) in a forced draft oven. Very volatile solvents can be removed prior to spraying by air drying while less volatile solvents (acetic acid, butanol) should be removed in a vacuum oven to avoid producing an interfering fluorescent background from residual solvent.

We use routinely silica gel mixed with 10% magnesium silicate for the absorbent (1) and a char spray consisting of 55% sulfuric acid containing 0.6% potassium dichromate (1). After charring, major components appear as black or brown spots with bright green borders under ultraviolet illumination; minor components appear as green spots against the bright blue background. Overspraying with char reagent produces a poorer background which often has a light green mottled appearance. The fluorescent spots are stable for several weeks provided all sulfuric acid is removed during heating.

The sensitivity is increased approximately fivefold using this technique. This was established as follows: 0.1 to 20 μg of neutral lipid standards was applied to a TLC plate as a row of overlapping small spots 1 cm long. The plate was developed one dimensionally with petroleum ether/diethyl ether/acetic acid, 85/15/2. The limits of detectability under visible and ultraviolet light were, respectively: cholesterol, 0.5 and 0.1 μg; cholesterol ester, 2 and 0.5 μg; triolein and oleic acid, 5 and 1 μg.

Neutral lipids, phospholipids, glycolipids, and pigments all yield essentially the same results. Saturated and difficult-to-char compounds show up just as well as unsaturated molecules. Heme pigments which are easily visible on unsprayed, freshly developed TLC plates may vanish completely when the plate is charred; however, they are readily seen as fluorescent spots under ultraviolet illumination.

ACKNOWLEDGMENT

This work was performed under the auspices of the U. S. Atomic Energy Commission.

REFERENCE

1. ROUSER, G., GALLI, C., LIEBER, E., BLANK, M. L., AND PRIVETT, O. S., *J. Am. Oil Chemists' Soc.* **41**, 836–840 (1964).

GARY J. NELSON
ROBERT A. BOOTH

Bio-Medical Research Division,
Lawrence Radiation Laboratory, University of California,
Livermore, California
Received February 20, 1967

Distribution of Rabbit Serum Proteins in Fractionation by the Cold Ethanol Method

Several methods have been developed for the fractionation of the proteins of human plasma with organic solvents at low temperatures. Best known are the techniques using aqueous ether (1) or ethanol systems (2–4). Mackay (5) has described the fractionation of mammalian serum proteins with ether. This communication reports the results of the fractionation of rabbit serum proteins by the ethanol technique.

The method used was based on Methods 6 and 9 of Cohn and his colleagues (2–4), with the following modifications:

(*a*) Since serum was used as the starting material, it was adjusted directly to the conditions for the precipitation of II + III.

(*b*) No filter aid was used at any stage.

(*c*) In the separation of III-2 and III-3, pH was adjusted with sodium bicarbonate solution instead of sodium glycinate buffer.

(*d*) IV-1 was fractionated by the method of Kominz (6) to yield IV-1-1 and IV-1-2; the latter was not washed.

Precipitates obtained from the supernatant liquids of III-0 and IV-6 are designated III-0SP and IV-6SP, respectively.

Serum of female albino rabbits (aged 4–6 months) of mixed laboratory stock was used throughout.

Protein content is expressed as 6.25 $\times$ total nitrogen content, determined by the Kjeldahl or Nessler method. The composition of protein fractions was determined by electrophoresis in 1% agar gel in barbitone buffer, pH 8.6, containing calcium lactate, followed by staining with amido black 10B and scanning in a Chromoscan reflectance densitometer.

Table 1 lists the electrophoretic composition of rabbit serum and its fractions obtained by the ethanol method, as well as the yield of the various fractions; it also includes comparable data for fractions of human plasma (7). The above method can be used to prepare fractions of rabbit serum proteins containing predominantly albumin, α-globulins, or γ-globulins, but it fails to yield reasonably concentrated preparations of β-globulins. The main difference in composition between the rabbit and human protein fractions is in IV-7, which from rabbit serum contains 85% albumin, compared with 79% β-globulins in the case of human plasma.

TABLE 1
Comparative Distribution of Proteins in Rabbit Serum and Fractions of Rabbit Serum and Human Plasma[a] Prepared by the Ethanol Technique

Preparation	Yield, gm/100 gm total proteins		Electrophoretic composition, % of protein							
			Rabbit				Human			
			Albumin	Globulins			Albumin	Globulins		
	Rabbit	Human		α	β	γ		α	β	γ
Serum[b]			69	15	10	6				
Serum[c]			63	14	10	14				
II-1,2	0.8	3.6	—	1	1	98	—	—	2[d]	98
II-3	0.3	4.8	—	—	1	99	—	—	4[d]	96
III-0	6.8	6.1	8	37	32	23	6	5	84[d]	5
III-0SP	2.9		37	37	18	8				
III-1	0.4	3.0		12	21	67	2	18	60[d]	14
III-2	0.4	2.0	2	25	55	18	1	20	77[d]	2
III-3	0.3	0.65	1	17	52	30	3	20	76[d]	2
IV-1		6.					—	89	10	1
IV-1-1	0.4		8	85	7	—				
IV-1-2	5.0		3	90	6	1				
IV-5	4.0	0.9	8	80	12	—	8	87	5	—
IV-6	0.5	1.5	6	90	4	—	6	88	6	—
IV-6SP	0.6		12	67	21	—				
IV-7	25.6	1.0	85	4	11	—	13	8	79	—
IV-8	15.6	1.0	96	3	1	—	91	6	3	—
V	7.3	55.	88	10	2	—	98	2	—	—

[a] Data on human plasma proteins taken from Pennell (7).
[b] Present work.
[c] Data reported by Kozhura (8) for young female rabbits.
[d] Includes fibrinogen.

ACKNOWLEDGMENTS

I am indebted to the United States Public Health Service for a Research Fellowship under grants No. HE 08513-01 and HE 08513-02, and to Miss E. Logounov and Mrs. S. Pajor for technical help.

REFERENCES

1. Kekwick, R. A., and Mackay, M. E., *Med. Res. Council, Spec. Rept. Ser. No. 286,* London, 1954.
2. Cohn, E. J., Strong, L. E., Hughes, W. L., Jr., Mulford, D. J., Ashworth, J. N., Melin, M., and Taylor, H. L., *J. Am. Chem. Soc.* **68,** 459 (1946).
3. Oncley, J. L., Melin, M., Richert, D. A., Cameron, J. W., and Gross, P. M., Jr., *J. Am. Chem. Soc.* **71,** 541 (1949).
4. Surgenor, D. M., Strong, L. E., Taylor, H. L., Gordon, R. S., Jr., and Gibson, D. H., *J. Am. Chem. Soc.* **71,** 1223 (1949).
5. Mackay, M. E., *Biochem. J.* **60,** 475 (1955).

6. Kominz, D., Mimeographed procedure for Department of Biochemistry, Harvard Medical School, 1951, reported by Pennell (**7**).
7. Pennell, R. B., *in* "The Plasma Proteins" (F. W. Putnam, ed.), Vol. I, p. 9. Academic Press, New York, 1960.
8. Kozhura, I. M., *Krovoobrashchenie i Starost, Min. Zdravookhr. Ukr. SSR, Akad. Med. Nauk SSSR, Inst. Gerontologii* **1965,** 135.

I. Salasoo

School of Pathology
University of New South Wales
Kensington, New South Wales, Australia
Received August 29, 1966

Addendum

Vol. **18,** No. 3 (1967), in the Short Communication, "Note on the Disruption of Yeast Cell Walls for the Isolation of Yeast Nucleic Acids," by E. Katona, pp. 587–588:

Table 1 was inadvertently omitted from this article; it is printed below:

TABLE 1

Size of glass beads or Carborundum	Time (sec)	2000 rpm Yield (%)[a]	2000 rpm RNA (%)	2000 rpm Contamination DNA	2000 rpm Contamination Protein	4000 rpm Yield (%)	4000 rpm RNA (%)	4000 rpm Contamination DNA	4000 rpm Contamination Protein
Carborundum 400	10	1.0	49.6	0.5	2.5				
	20	1.0	52.3	0.5	3.0				
	40	1.3	62.1	0.5	3.2				
	60	1.5	56.8	0.7	3.0				
Carborundum 80	10	1.9	58.2	0.7	1.9				
	20	2.7	44.2	1.0	1.6				
	40	2.4	51.9	0.8	3.2				
Glass: 0.17 mm	10	2.5	40.9	0.8	3.9				
	20	3.0	43.4	1.4	2.0	3.3	14.4	3.9	2.6
	40	2.5	37.5	2.7	3.7	3.5	14.9	2.5	3.0
	60	4.5	39.2	0.5	3.0	3.6	16.5	6.5	6.5
Glass: 0.45 mm	20	1.8	29.2	2.6	3.0	6.2	21.2	3.8	3.4
	40	2.0	30.4	3.3	5.7	4.6	14.2	3.8	3.3
	60	6.5	15.4	4.8	4.7	3.3	11.5	3.7	4.2
Glass: 1.0 mm	10	3.4	31.5	1.8	2.1				
	20	3.1	37.0	2.1	2.8	4.8	22.4	2.9	3.3
	40	3.5	27.0	3.7	4.7	4.2	18.4	3.0	4.5
	60	5.8	20.4	3.5	4.4	4.3	13.6	3.0	4.0
Carborundum 80, hand	20 min	2.3	32.0	2.9	5.7				

[a] Yield calculated from dry weight of yeast (about 21% of the wet weight).

ANALYTICAL BIOCHEMISTRY **20**, 205–214 (1967)

A Submicromolar Assay for Nonpolar Acids in Plasma and Depot Fat

HOWARD KO AND MAX E. ROYER

Biochemical Research Division, The Upjohn Company, Kalamazoo, Michigan 49001

Received November 29, 1966

A number of methods have been developed in the past few years to measure nonpolar acids (e.g., fatty acids) in plasma and in tissue (1–7). For small animals (e.g., mice), a method is required which would use only a small portion of the total blood volume during sequential measurements in the same animal. The extraction-titration procedure of the well-known Dole method (1) has been modified (see "Modified Method" below) to improve sensitivity and precision and to reduce interference from polar acids commonly found in plasma. Recoveries of the acids by the modified method were measured by titration or by radioactivity.

MATERIALS AND METHODS

Materials

Nitrogen gas (Ascarite filtered); isopropyl alcohol (redistilled); heptane (Eastman White label).

Indicator solution: 0.01% thymophthalein in spectroscopic-grade acetone.

Extraction Mix: 40/10/1 (v/v/v) isopropyl alcohol/heptane/1.0 *N* H_2SO_4.

TBAH Titrant: About 1.0 *N* tetrabutylammonium hydroxide in methanol diluted with isopropyl alcohol (redistilled) to about 0.01 *N*.

Sodium Palmitate: Sodium palmitate from K & K Laboratories was precipitated from hot absolute ethanol, filtered, and dried.

Krebs-Ringer Albumin Buffer: 1.92% bovine serum albumin (Armour Lot No. W6931201A) in Krebs-Ringer buffer; no glucose was added.

Apparatus: Gilmont ultramicroburet equipped with a 0.25 ml Hamilton gastight syringe.

^{14}C-Labeled Compounds (employed in the recovery studies). Palmitic-1-^{14}C acid, Na pyruvate-1-^{14}C, Na acetate-1-^{14}C, DL-K-β-hydroxy-

butyrate-3-^{14}C, and Na lactate-1-^{14}C were obtained from New England Nuclear Corporation. Radiochromatograms supplied with the materials showed a single peak for each compound. The labeled salts in the dried state and palmitic acid (in NaOH) were refrigerated until just before use.

Modified Method for Extraction and Titration of Nonpolar Acids

Extraction of Nonpolar Acids. S ml (0.1 to 1.0 ml) of sample was added to 3.0 ml of extraction mix, 0.6 ml of heptane, and (3.0 minus S) ml of water in a 15.0 ml glass-stoppered centrifuge tube. Except where noted, the sample volume (S) employed was 0.4 ml.[1] The phases were vigorously mixed on a Vortex rotary shaker. When interfacial fluff or bubbles interfered with recovery of the upper phase, the tube was centrifuged briefly and most of the lower layer was removed by a syringe (Hamilton, gastight) and a long needle. One milliliter of the upper layer was pipetted into a 1 or 2 dram vial for titration.

Titration Procedure. Indicator solution—0.1 ml/ml of upper (heptane) layer—and a 1 ml aliquot of upper (heptane) layer were titrated with the TBAH titrant in the covered vial. Nitrogen gassing mixed the solution and removed CO_2.

Radioactivity Counting Procedure for Recovery Studies. Aliquots of upper or lower phase mixed with Diotol[2] were counted in a Packard EX2 liquid scintillation counter. ^{14}C-Palmitic acid in Diotol was used as internal standard.

RESULTS AND DISCUSSION

Development of the Modified Method. The Dole procedure of extraction and titration of nonesterified fatty acid in plasma (1) is outlined below for later comparison with the modified procedure:

1. Extraction of plasma (1 ml) with extraction mix (5 ml).
2. Addition of heptane (3 ml) and water (2 ml) whereupon two phases are formed: an upper layer, consisting mainly of heptane, and a lower layer of isopropanol and water.
3. Addition of 3 ml of the upper layer to thymol blue indicator in aqueous ethanol (1.0 ml) and titration with NaOH as a two-phase system. The phases are mixed by nitrogen gassing.

[1] In the development of the modified method, steps in which the tube was inserted and allowed to stand 10 min were included at this point. However, since no significant difference ($P > 0.05$, $N = 7$) was found in the average titratable acidity of dog serum with or without the steps, the steps were omitted.

[2] The Herberg (9) counting system, modified by R. C. Thomas (personal communication).

Modification of the Titration End Point

One-Phase versus Two-Phase Titration. In a two-phase titration (e.g., ethanol/water and heptane as in the Dole procedure (1)), time for equilibrium must be provided during titration (possibly because the fatty acid must diffuse out of the heptane phase into the alcoholic eqeous phase) and the extra volume of the aqueous alcohol phase and the turbidity decrease the intensity of the color change. We decided, therefore, to titrate the fatty acids in heptane itself as a single phase.

Titrant. Tetrabutylammonium hydroxide[3] was adopted as titrant since tetrabutylammonium salts of most weak acids are more soluble in organic solvents than are the corresponding sodium or potassium salts and hence difficulties due to precipitation are avoided (8).

Indicator. A variety of indicators were considered and thymolphthalein dissolved in heptane/acetone (10/1, v/v) appeared to be optimal. During potentiometric titration of palmitic acid in heptane and methyl isobutyl ketone, with thymolphthalein as indicator, the end point was reached at a potential when 97% of the palmitic acid had been titrated. Since thymolphthalein turns from colorless to blue at the end point, the color change was found to be easily detected. In contrast, thymol blue turns from yellow to green and finally to blue at the end point (92% titration), which provides some difficulty in deciding when the end point is reached. Thymolphthalein was therefore adopted as the indicator of choice.

Volume Titrated. Minimizing the volume of heptane titrated is desirable for two reasons: (*1*) the increase in volume of solution titrated was found by potentiometric titration to increase the blank value, and (*2*) reducing the volume of heptane titrated sharpens the end point by reducing the amount of indicator required. One milliliter of heptane was chosen as the minimum volume which could be conveniently titrated (the procedure could be modified, however, to use smaller heptane volumes if desired).

Each of the above characteristics (single phase, TBAH titrant, thymolphthalein, and 1-ml volume) was therefore incorporated into a titration procedure.

Modification of the Extraction Conditions

The Dole extraction conditions and the modified (method) extraction conditions are similar in composition of isopropanol (36% by volume) but are different in composition of water and heptane: *modified method,* 46% water and 18% heptane; *Dole conditions,* 28% water and 36%

[3] While this manuscript was in preparation, a fatty acid assay employing tetrabutylammonium hydroxide has appeared (6).

heptane. This difference in the modified method improves recovery of palmitic acid and (as will be described in a later section) reduces interferences from polar acids extracted into the heptane phase. In the modified method, the amount of palmitic acid (as a representative non-polar acid) available for titration was increased to 21% over that obtainable by the Dole conditions by utilizing a greater proportion (about 15%) of the heptane phase and by increasing the efficiency of extraction (Table 1, $P < 0.005$).

The extraction efficiency was improved by reducing the ratio of isopropanol to water. As this ratio was reduced (at constant final percentage of heptane), the concentration of palmitic acid in the heptane phase increased toward maximal values. Separation of the phases, however, became increasingly difficult: these observations confirmed those of Dole and Minertz (1). An isopropanol/water ratio (v/v) of 0.77 which gave near maximal recovery of palmitic acid and adequate phase separation on standing was considered optimal and, therefore, was retained in the modified extraction method.

The effect of sulfuric acid concentration in the extraction mix on the recovery of ^{14}C-palmitate from rat plasma was studied. The extraction conditions of the modified method were employed except that the molarity of sulfuric acid was varied in the extraction mix. Radioactive label was recovered maximally (ca. 95%) when the molarity of sulfuric acid in the aqueous phase was 0.0028 M or more (Fig. 1). The modified

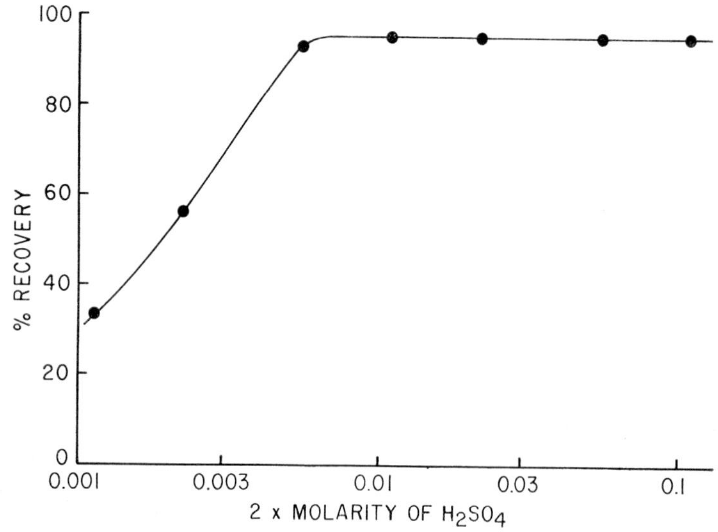

FIG. 1. Effect of H_2SO_4 concentration in the aqueous phase on recovery of ^{14}C-palmitic acid in the heptane phase from rat plasma.

method has sufficient sulfuric acid so that twice this concentration (viz., 0.0056 M) is present in the aqueous phase. If, however, more strongly buffered solutions are extracted, additional acid may be required to achieve good recovery of the nonpolar acids. The recovery of palmitic acid by the extraction conditions of the modified method (two-phase extraction only) was compared with that found when the fatty acid was extracted by a single-phase extraction system and then two phases were formed by adding heptane and water and where the same final volume composition of the phases were obtained. No significant difference ($N = 7$, $P > 0.05$) was detected between the two procedures in extracting palmitic acid from Krebs-Ringer albumin buffer or in extracting ^{14}C-palmitate from rat plasma. If there is a difference, it is less than 0.1% Since the "two-phase" procedure is simpler, it was adopted. In practice, the modified method results in a reduction by ca. one-third of the time required for extraction and titration by the Dole procedure.

TABLE 1
Recovery[a] of Palmitic Acid Added to Krebs-Ringer Albumin Buffer

Method	Amount (X) of titrant employed (arbitrary divisions)		
	Blank	Sample	Sample − blank
(a) Modified Av. ($\bar{X}$)	77.4	480.8	403.4 (N = 7)
S.D. (X)[b]	1.72	3.44	3.8
S.E. ($\bar{X}$)[c]			1.5
Recovery of palmitic acid in the heptane phase: $403.4 \times 1.251 = 504.7$ div[d] or 504.7 div/(872 div/μeq) = 0.5787 μeq.			
Input of palmitic acid = 0.5916 μeq.			
% recovery (±standard error) in the heptane phase: $0.5787/0.5916 = (97.8 \pm 0.36)\%$			
(b) Dole extraction conditions with thymolphthalein indicator			
Av. ($\bar{X}$)	133.5	467.4	333.9 (N = 7)
S.D. (X)	8.9	5.4	10.4
S.E. ($\bar{X}$)			3.9
Recovery of palmitic acid in the heptane phase: $333.9 \times 1.436 = 479.5$ div or 479.5 div/(872 div/μeq) = 0.5499 μeq.			
Input of palmitic acid = 0.5916 μeq.			
% recovery (±standard error) in the heptane phase: $0.5499/0.5916 = (93.0 \pm 1.1)\%$			

[a] Measured by titration.
[b] S.D. (X) ≡ standard deviation of a single reading.
[c] S.E. ($\bar{X}$) ≡ standard error of the average.
[d] div = division(s).

Recovery Studies with the Modified Method

Recovery from various media of the model compound, palmitic acid, by the modified method was studied and the following results were found:

1. The average ($N = 3$) difference of 0.3% between the recoveries of ^{14}C-palmitic acid from 0.1 and 0.4 ml of rat plasma was not statistically significant ($P > 0.05$).

2. The average ($N = 3$) recovery of ^{14}C-palmitic acid from 0.7 or 1.0 ml of rat plasma was only about 0.4 to 1.5% less (statistically significant, $P < 0.05$) than that of the others. In experiments in which greater buffering of solutions extracted may be expected, more sulfuric acid can be added to the extraction mix.

3. The average recovery ($N = 7$, $\pm 95\%$ confidence limits) of ^{14}C-palmitic acid from rat plasma (94.27 ± 0.10)% was not greatly different from the average recovery from water (93.74 ± 0.31)%. The significant 0.53% difference ($P < 0.05$) in the recovery ($\pm 95\%$ confidence limits, $N = 7$) could be due to pipetting errors between different days.

4. The presence or absence of Krebs-Ringer albumin buffer (media used in the epididymal fat pad assay) did not significantly alter ($P > 0.05$) the recovery of palmitic acid from aqueous media.

5. Long-chain fatty acids (C_{14} and higher) are distributed almost completely in favor of the upper phase (Fig. 2) during extraction by the modified method. Thus, nonpolar acids (such as the long-chain fatty acids) usually present in animal plasma and depot fat (epididymal fat pad assay) should be efficiently extracted and titrated by the modified method.

Standard Curve for Palmitic Acid and Variability of the Measurements

A linear standard curve resulted when sodium palmitate, added to a Krebs-Ringer albumin buffer solution, was extracted and titrated by the modified method. The standard deviation of a single determination was equivalent to

$$3.95 \times 10^{-3} \sqrt{1.077 + (P - 0.233)^2/0.6596}$$

microequivalents of acid, where P is the number of microequivalents of acid. We may estimate the lowest amount of blood plasma required for a given error. Since 0.1 ml of blood plasma from fasting rats contains as little as 0.03 μeq of nonpolar acids, titration of plasma by the modified method would involve relative standard deviations for single determination of about 14% for 0.1 ml, and about 7% for 0.2 ml.

Standard deviations of a single determination (or average) for the modified method were found to be significantly less ($P < 0.05$ by the F test) than those when the Dole extraction conditions were used, even though the same indicator, thymolphthalein, was employed. The improved accuracy is probably due to the greater ease in observing the end point, lower blank values, and more efficient removal of CO_2 from the

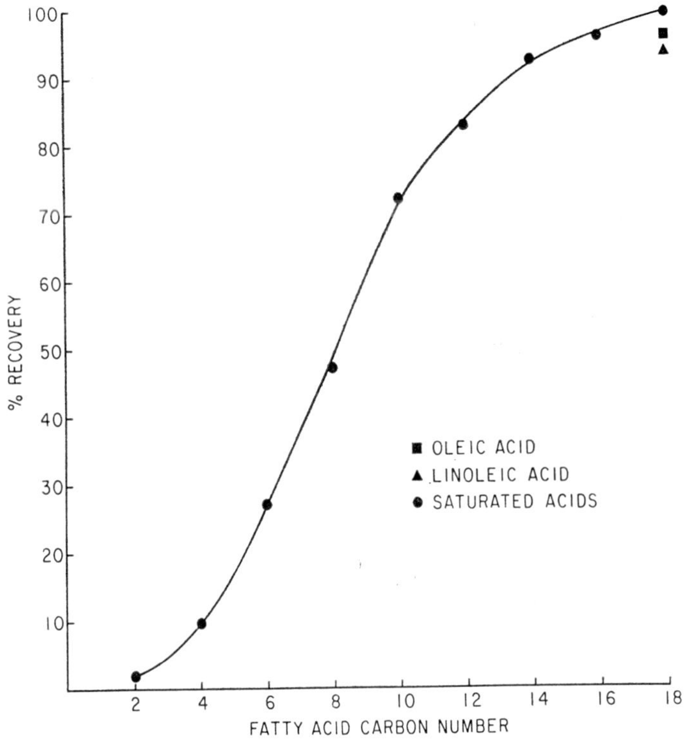

FIG. 2. Recovery of fatty acids in the upper phase ("heptane") by the modified method.

smaller volume by the nitrogen gas. The end point is sharpened since, with the same concentration of indicator and titrant, a given color change is effected by only one-third the titrant in the modified method as compared with that required for the larger volume of heptane (3 ml) used after extraction by the Dole procedure.

Interference by Serum and Buffer Constituents on Nonpolar Acid Determinations

The polar acids, pyruvic acid, β-hydroxybutyric acid, and lactic acid, which are found in plasma (1) can be extracted to some extent by heptane under acid conditions. With the modified method, positive interference (on a molar basis) from these acids is 0.4–0.6% but, with the Dole conditions for extraction, the interference is three to four times higher (Tables 2 and 3). The recovery of acetic acid was about 1.8%.

TABLE 2
Degree of Interference[a] from Pyruvic Acid, β-Hydroxybutyric Acid, and Lactic Acid Using the Two Methods

Substance added	Per cent recovery[a] of added substance in the "heptane" phase when the following constituents are also present in the aqueous phase: 0.9% NaCl	Krebs-Ringer albumin buffer
(a) Modified method:		
Pyruvic acid	0.56	0.49
β-Hydroxybutyric acid	0.55	0.55
Lactic acid	0.39	0.34
(b) Dole extraction method:		
Pyruvic acid	2.02	2.28
β-Hydroxybutyric acid	1.77	2.24
Lactic acid	1.55	1.57

[a] Measured by titration.

If Krebs-Ringer albumin buffer constituents are also present in the sample, recovery of the polar acids by the modified method or the Dole extraction method are not greatly altered.

Since only 1.2 μequiv/ml or less of these polar acids is usually present in plasma, their interference should not be serious. In unusual cases

TABLE 3
Recovery of Various Polar Acids from Plasma by the Modified Method

Spiking substance	Molarity of H_2SO_4 in aqueous phase	Average per cent recovery of label in the "heptane" phase ± standard error
^{14}C-Pyruvic acid	0.005615[a]	0.239 ± 0.005 (N = 4)
^{14}C-β-Hydroxybutyric acid	0.005615	0.356 ± 0.006 (N = 4)
^{14}C-Lactic acid	0.001123	0.00013 ± 0.00003 (N = 2)
	0.005615	0.305 ± 0.002 (N = 4)
	0.01123	0.302 ± 0.004 (N = 2)
	0.05615	0.3305 ± 0.004 (N = 2)
Acetic acid	0.005615	1.770 ± 0.066 (N = 4)

[a] Amount of H_2SO_4 present in the modified method.

where the lactic acid level reaches 20 μeq/ml, the interference would amount to about 10% for a plasma level of 0.6 μeq/ml nonpolar acid. In such cases, the heptane phase can be backwashed with lower phase.

Dole and Minertz (1) has pointed out the seriousness of interference by phospholipids in which the heptane phase must be backwashed to help reduce their interference. Under the extraction conditions of the modified method, the cephalins are recovered to the extent of 27.6% and the lecithins, 5.1%. In titrating these phospholipids, the end point was very broad and hence these recoveries are estimates at best. Since the cephalins are relatively nonpolar, interference from this class of phospholipids would be small only if the levels were sufficiently low in plasma (as had been reported for human plasma by Nelson and Freeman (10); in brain tissue and liver, however, the concentrations of cephalines are sufficiently high (11, 12) that their interference in the measurement of nonpolar acids would be considerable). Since little phospholipid is present in depot fat, this class of lipid should not interfere in the epididymal fat pad assay. Thus, nonpolar acids may be reliably determined only in those tissues whose cephalin content is low relative to nonpolar acid content or, when necessary, a backwash of the heptane phase with lower phase can reduce the interference to an acceptable level.

To test whether too high a concentration of H_2SO_4 in the aqueous phase of the extraction mixture increases the recovery of interfering polar acids to unacceptable levels, up to 10 times as much H_2SO_4 concentration as that of the modified method was employed. Lactic acid still interfered only about 0.3% (Table 3). Since the pK_a values of pyruvic acid, β-hydroxybutyric acid, lactic acid, and acetic acid are similar, their recoveries are not expected to increase substantially by using more acid than that contained in the modified method.

SUMMARY

A simple titrimetric assay, requiring about a third less time than that required for the Dole procedure (2), has been developed for determining submicromolar amounts of nonpolar acids (e.g., long-chain fatty acids) in depot fat and plasma. The method has the following capabilities:

1. 0.03 and 0.06 μeq of added palmitic acid are detected with standard deviations of a single determination of 12–14 and 6–7%, respectively; these amounts of nonpolar acid correspond to those present in 0.1 and 0.2 ml of serum, respectively.

2. About (95–97)% of added palmitic acid is recovered in the heptane phase by the extraction procedure.

3. The common interfering materials in plasma, lactic acid, β-hydroxybutyric acid, and pyruvic acid gave positive interference to the extent of only about 0.3 to 0.5%, values which are about *one-fourth* the interference of the regular Dole extraction method.

4. The presence or absence of Krebs-Ringer buffer or serum components has no significant effect on the recovery of palmitic acid by the

modified method or by Dole's extraction method (1). Thus, standard curves for the esterified fatty acids may be constructed with or without the presence of these substances.

ACKNOWLEDGMENT

We wish to thank Dr. N. B. Marshall, Dr. R. C. Thomas, R. W. Judy, Diana David Schneider, John Schneider, and Dorothy Porten for their willing assistance in supplying information, equipment, and reagents for these experiments. We also wish to thank Ernest Markovich for performing the linear regressions on the IBM 1620 computer.

REFERENCES

1. Dole, V. P., and Meinertz, H., *J. Biol. Chem.* **235**, 2595 (1960).
2. Dole, V. P., *J. Clin. Invest.* **35**, 150 (1956).
3. Duncombe, W. G., *Clin. Chim. Acta* **9**, 122 (1964).
4. Mosinger, F., *J. Lipid Res.* **6**, 157 (1965).
5. Pries, C., and Bottcher, C. J. F., *Anal. Chim. Acta* **31**, 293 (1964).
6. Kelley, T. F., *Anal. Chem.* **37**, 1078 (1965).
7. Novak, M., *J. Lipid Res.* **6**, 431 (1965).
8. Harlow, G. A., Noble, C. M., and Wyld, G. E. A., *Anal. Chem.* **28**, 787 (1956).
9. Herberg, R. J., *Anal. Chem.* **32**, 42 (1960).
10. Nelson, G. J., and Freeman, N. K., *J. Biol. Chem.* **235**, 578 (1960).
11. O'Brien, J. S., *Science* **147**, 1099 (1965).
12. Kaucher, M., Galbraith, H., Button, V., and Williams, H. H., *Anal. Biochem.* **3**, 203 (1943).

ANALYTICAL BIOCHEMISTRY 20, 215-223 (1967)

Influence of Acids on the Determination of Calcium and Magnesium by Atomic Absorption Spectrophotometry[1]

CARL MONDER AND NEWELL SELLS

Research Institute for Skeletomuscular Diseases of the Hospital for Joint Diseases and Medical Center, New York, 10035

Received December 13, 1966

Although blood, urine, and related fluids can be analyzed for calcium and magnesium directly by atomic absorption spectrophotometry after appropriate dilution, other tissues must first be treated to remove organic matter. For most applications, ashing of the sample has been recommended. The ash is dissolved in hydrochloric acid, frequently in the presence of lanthanum or strontium salts added to suppress the effects of interfering substances such as phosphate. There is evidence that lanthanum may enhance and hydrochloric acid diminish the intensity of absorption of calcium in the air-acetylene flame (1, 2), even in the absence of interfering substances. A knowledge of the effects of these components on the measured values for calcium and magnesium would allow us to control these important variables and thus to analyze for the metals with greater precision. The results of a systematic examination of the effects of lanthanum and hydrochloric acid on the measurement of calcium and magnesium by atomic absorption spectrophotometry (AAS) is presented in this communication. Some data on the effects of other acids has also been included.

METHODS

A Perkin-Elmer model 303 spectrophotometer equipped with a standard narrow-slot nebulizer burner with an air-acetylene flame was used in this work. Air pressure, air flow, gas flow, and height above the burner slot were adjusted for maximum absorption (3), starting from the values recommended in the Perkin-Elmer manual on analytical methods (4). Rate of sample uptake by the nebulizer was 5.6 ml/min. Dilutions of metals were made from stock solutions (1000 ppm) of spectral-grade calcium and magnesium salts purchased from Harleco Corporation,

[1] This work was supported by grant P-399 from the American Cancer Society.

Philadelphia, Pa. Polyethylene vessels replaced glass wherever possible. All equipment was kept scrupulously clean according to the recommendations of Thiers (5). Lanthanum oxide (Alfa Inorganic Chemicals, Beverly, Mass.), of purity claimed to be 99.99%, was dissolved in reagent-grade hydrochloric acid. Other salts and reagents were of analytical grade.

RESULTS

The effects of increasing levels of hydrochloric acid on calcium absorption are illustrated in Figure 1. At all levels of calcium, absorbancy increased slightly with low concentration of hydrochloric acid while, at higher levels of acid, a pronounced decrease occurred. This depressing effect of hydrochloric acid was observed even in the presence of lanthanum. Figure 2 compares the response of the calcium standard curve

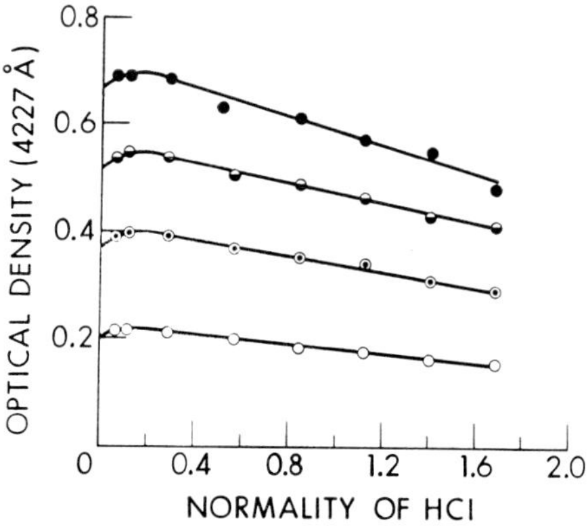

FIG. 1. Effect of hydrochloric acid on calcium absorption: ○, 5 ppm Ca; ⊙, 10 ppm, Ca; ◒, 15 ppm Ca; ●, 20 ppm Ca.

to lanthanum in 0.2 N hydrochloric acid and to lanthanum in 1 N hydrochloric acid. Depression of the standard curve by increasing concentrations of hydrochloric acid is clearly demonstrated. The addition of lanthanum caused a small increase in the absorbance values along the standard curve. In 0.2 N hydrochloric acid the presence of lanthanum resulted in a curve which coincided with the calcium standard curve containing no additions. At higher concentrations of hydrochloric acid the small increase in absorbance caused by lanthanum was insufficient to bring the standard curve back to the unsupplemented values. The compensatory effect of lanthanum was found to be fortuitous since the presence of lanthanum in the blank obliterated the apparent increase in absorbance. The enhancing effect of lanthanum on these curves was due to a positive blank value of the lanthanum, which was superimposed on the observed values obtained in the presence of calcium in hydrochloric acid alone. Figure 3 shows that the blank absorption values for lanthanum were proportional to lanthanum concentration, and that these values were depressed by increasing concentration of hydrochloric acid. The basis for the absorption values observed at this wavelength with lanthanum alone are unclear. They may be due to contamination of the lanthanum by traces of calcium. However, the fact that all curves intersect at the origin makes this possibility unlikely because the presence

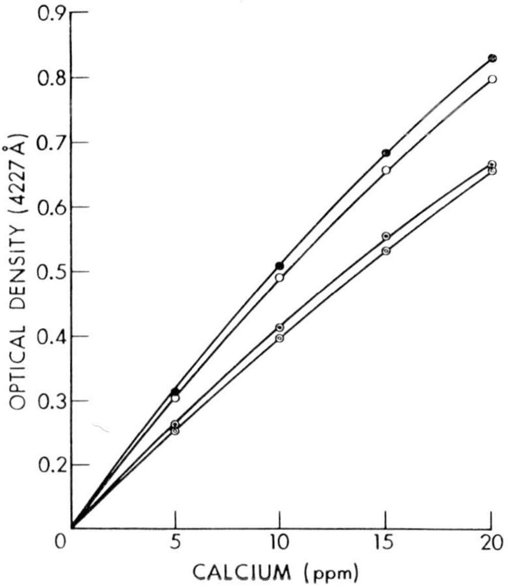

FIG. 2. Effect of lanthanum on calcium absorption: ●, no additions; ●, 1% La in 0.2 *N* HCl; ○, 0.2 *N* HCl; ◎ (lowest curve), 1.0 *N* HCl; ⊙, 1% La in 1.0 *N* HCl.

of calcium in the lanthanum would result in a curve intersecting the ordinate at a value above zero in the absence of added calcium. Other factors, such as light scattering by particles in the flame (6, 7) or molecular absorption by lanthanum chloride or oxide (8), may possibly contribute to the absorption. However, the above explanations would be tenable only if it were assumed that the presence of increasing quantities of calcium in some way caused an enhancement of the anomalous absorption due to these factors. In Figure 4, the effects of varying both lanthanum and hydrochloric acid on calcium measurements are summarized. When the blank values for solutions containing lanthanum and hydrochloric acid alone were subtracted from the values of calcium standards containing lanthanum and hydrochloric acid, the calcium values were essentially superimposable, but still higher than the values for unsupplemented calcium. The slopes of the lines corresponding to acid concentration were the same regardless of whether

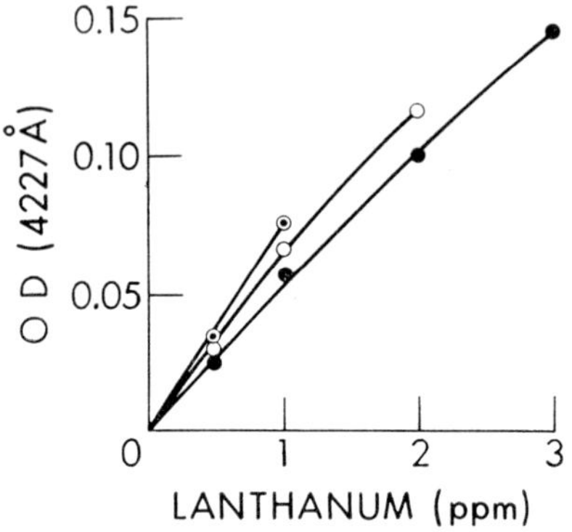

FIG. 3. Lanthanum absorption at wavelength of maximum calcium absorption: ⊙, 0.2 *N* HCl; ○, 0.4 *N* HCl; ●, 1.0 *N* HCl. Identical results were obtained in the presence of 200 ppm phosphorus.

or not lanthanum was present. As shown in Figure 5, a similar relationship prevailed in the presence of phosphate. Thus, under these conditions, the concentration of lanthanum is not an important variable in the measurement of calcium but the concentration of hydrochloric acid

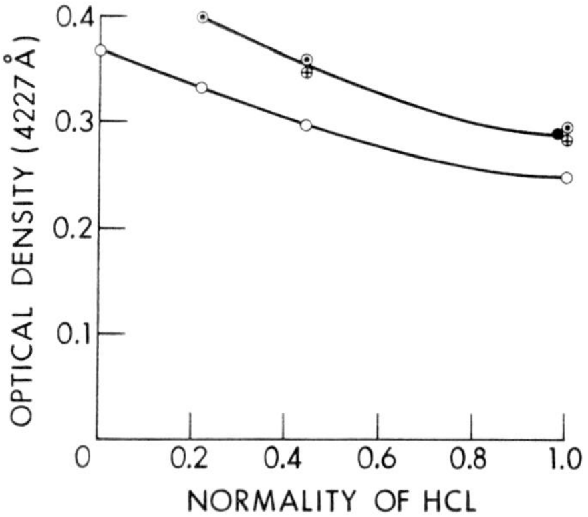

FIG. 4. Effects of lanthanum and hydrochloric acid on calcium absorption: ○, no La; ⊙, 1% La; ⊕, 2% La; ●, 3% La. Calcium concentration, 10 ppm. Blank values of samples containing no Ca were substracted in each determination.

becomes a significant factor. Lanthanum was therefore able to overcome the depression due to phosphate but not that due to hydrochloric acid.

The effects of lanthanum, hydrochloric acid, and phosphate on the absorption values of magnesium were studied in a manner similar to those performed with calcium. Hydrochloric acid depressed magnesium values, but the extent of inhibition was small. Thus 1 ppm Mg with no added acid absorbed 0.342 optical density units, and in the presence of 1 *M* hydrochloric acid absorbed 0.324 unit, a decrease of 5%. Lanthanum had no appreciable effect in overcoming this inhibition. Lanthanum did not influence the magnesium values beyond that due to the acid present, nor did the lanthanum itself show a significant blank value. Phosphate at levels found in biological materials did not depress the absorbance values for magnesium, a finding consistent with previous observations (9). It must thus be concluded that when calcium and, to a lesser extent,

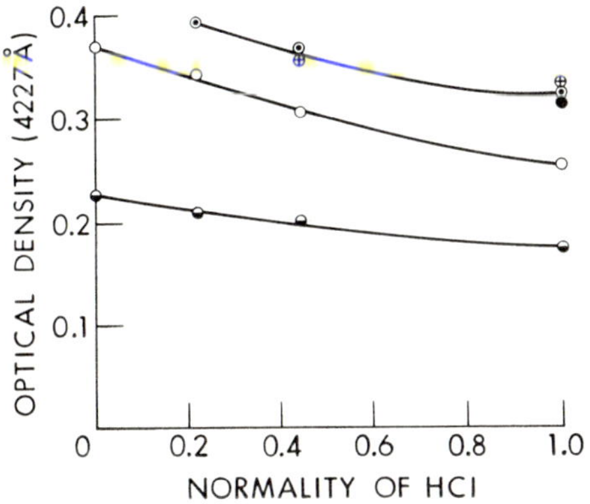

FIG. 5. Effect of lanthanum and hydrochloric acid on phosphate inhibition of calcium absorption: ◒, 100 ppm P; ○, no additions; ⊙, 1% La + 100 ppm P; ⊕, 2% La + 100 ppm P; ●, 3% La + 100 ppm P. Calcium concentration, 10 ppm. Blank values of samples containing no calcium were subtracted in each determination.

magnesium are being determined by atomic absorption spectrophotometry, hydrochloric acid concentration is an important variable which must be carefully controlled. On the other hand, lanthanum concentrations may be varied over fairly wide limits without affecting the results provided that the appropriate blanks are used.

In order to determine if the effects of hydrochloric acid were specific, the influence of other acids on calcium determination was investigated. These results are depicted in Figure 6. Acetic and formic acids had little or no effect on the absorption of calcium while trichloroacetic acid caused a highly significant depression of absorption. Nitric acid and phosphoric acid, as expected, were extremely potent at low concentrations. The results implied that the depression due to hydrochloric acid was not due to protons.

The inhibitory effect of nitric acid was studied in greater detail. Figure 7 shows that lanthanum, in contrast with its ability to overcome

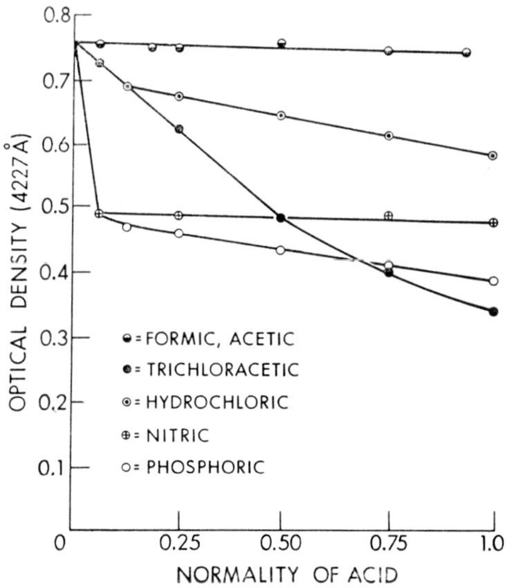

FIG. 6. Effects of various acids on atomic absorption intensity of calcium.

inhibition due to phosphate, appeared to exaggerate the effects of nitric acid. Willis (10) has suggested the use of disodium EDTA as an effective alternative to lanthanum as a suppressor of phosphate inhibition. Although EDTA was completely unsuccessful in our hands in reversing phosphate inhibition, it was found to effectively overcome the inhibitory action of nitrate on calcium. Preliminary investigation revealed that maximum effect was obtained with 0.02 *M* EDTA as the tetramethyl-

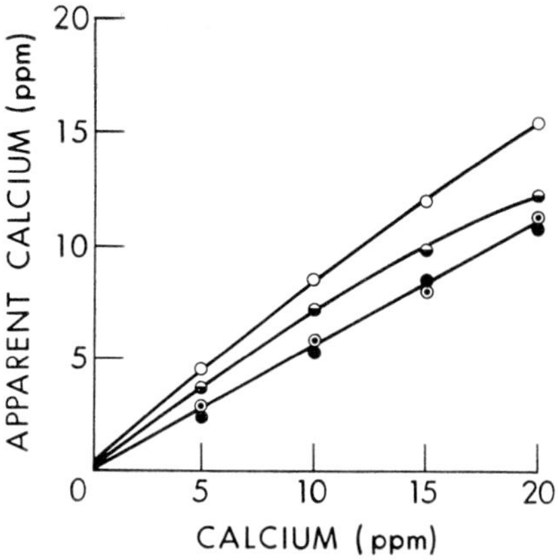

FIG. 7. Effects of lanthanum on inhibition of calcium absorption by nitric acid: ○, no additions; ◒, 1 *M* HNO_3; ⊙. 1% La + 1 *M* HNO_3; ●, 3% La + 1 *M* HNO_3.

ammonium salt. Figure 8 shows that, although EDTA itself suppressed calcium absorption, its presence prevented the profound drop in reading resulting from the relatively high concentration of nitrate. When compared to standard curves of calcium prepared in 0.02 *M* EDTA, concentrations of nitric acid up to 0.5 *M* in 0.02 *M* EDTA did not influence the calcium curve.

Since trichloroacetic acid has been recommended as a precipitating agent for proteins in determination of metals in biological fluids and tissues, a closer examination of the inhibiting effects of trichloroacetic acid on the absorption of calcium was made. A comparison of the effects

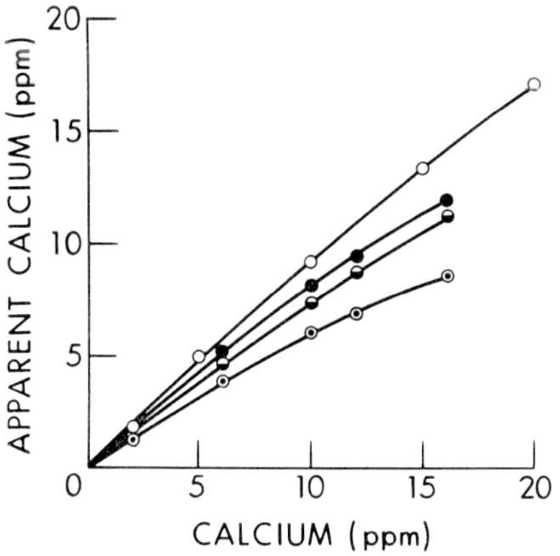

FIG. 8. Effect of EDTA on inhibition of calcium absorption by nitric acid: ○, calcium; ●, calcium + EDTA; ◒, calcium + HNO_3 + EDTA; ⊙, calcium + HNO_3.

of hydrochloric acid and trichloroacetic acid on calcium atomic absorption values indicated that, on an equimolar basis, trichloroacetic acid was three times more effective than hydrochloric acid as a depressant. This may have been due to the presence of three times the equivalents of chlorine in trichloroacetic acid as in hydrochloric acid. The finding that ammonium chloride depressed the absorption of calcium in the same way as an equivalent amount of hydrochloric acid is consistent with this suggestion.

The influence of lanthanum on inhibition of calcium absorption by trichloroacetic acid is shown in Table 1. These data demonstrate that lanthanum had no appreciable effect on the absorbancy values for calcium in the presence of trichloroacetic acid.

Trichloroacetic, acetic, formic, nitric, and phosphoric acids at concentrations up to 1 *N* were without effect on magnesium absorption values. These results conform to published observations, and confirm

TABLE 1
Effect of Lanthanum on Inhibition of Calcium Absorption by Trichoroacetic Acid

Ca, *M*	TCA, *M*	HCl, *M*	La, %	Absorbancy[a]
10	—	—	—	0.640
10	—	1.2	—	0.407
10	—	1.2	1	0.373
10	0.2	—	—	0.458
10	0.2	1.2	—	0.308
10	0.2	1.2	1	0.322
10	—	—	—	0.640
10	—	0.6	—	0.505
10	—	0.6	1	0.470
10	0.2	—	—	0.458
10	0.2	0.6	—	0.375
10	0.2	0.6	1	0.389

[a] Blanks containing no calcium have been substracted.

that the determination of magnesium is relatively insensitive to interferences.

DISCUSSION

Very few studies have been made of the effects of hydrochloric acid on the atomic absorption properties of calcium or magnesium, and the results of these are not in agreement (1, 2, 11). Acid-dependent decreases in absorbancy of other ions have been observed (11), and it has been suggested that these effects are primarily due to changes in viscosity and capillary activity rather than to influences on atomic absorption itself. However, it is possible that processes within the flame are involved (12). It is likely that the ability to observe these effects is a function of the individual instrument, and dependent on nebulizer efficiency, size of droplets, temperature, type, and shape of flame, and on the components of the solution. Although the basis for the inhibition of calcium values in the presence of phosphate may be the formation of compounds which cannot dissociate at the temperature of the air-acetylene flame, inhibition by hydrochloric, trichloroacetic, and nitric acids is harder to understand because the melting points of calcium chloride (772°) and calcium nitrate (561°) are well within the temperature of the air-acetylene flame. In addition, these melting points are not greatly different from that for magnesium chloride (708°), yet chloride does not interfere with magnesium determinations. The depression of calcium absorption by trichloroacetic acid is particularly noteworthy, since this acid has been recommended as a protein precipitant prior to atomic absorption spectrophotometry of calcium (13). The data presented here show that this precipitant can introduce substantial errors into calcium determinations.

The high blank value for lanthanum in the calcium region appears to be dependent on lanthanum concentration. Since lanthanum has no absorption at 4227 Å, salt mist in the flame may scatter calcium light. This is rendered less likely by the observation that there was no blank associated with lanthanum in the region of the magnesium maximum (2852 Å), though an increase in light scatter would be expected with decreasing wavelength (7, 14). However, the possibility remains that a molecular form of lanthanum has a spectrum which overlaps the calcium line at 4227 Å. Part of the blank absorption due to lanthanum in the calcium region may indeed be due to calcium contamination, but this probably represents only a small contribution.

SUMMARY

Calcium and magnesium were determined by atomic absorption spectrophotometry. Hydrochloric acid inhibited calcium absorption, and this inhibition was evident in the presence of lanthanum. Lanthanum itself showed a strong absorption at the calcium line that was partially suppressed by hydrochloric acid. Increasing concentration of lanthanum when added to overcome phosphate interference did not, in contrast with hydrochloric acid, interfere with the determination of calcium. Nitric, phosphoric, and trichloroacetic acids inhibited calcium absorption strongly. Inhibition by nitric acid was partially overcome by EDTA. The effects on magnesium absorption of the factors studied were small.

REFERENCES

1. Zettner, A., and Seligson, D., *Clin. Chem.* **10,** 869 (1964).
2. MacIntyre, I., *Biochem. J.* **67,** 164 (1957).
3. Cellier, K. M., and Tace, H. C. T., *Appl. Spectry.* **20,** 26 (1966).
4. "Analytical Methods for Atomic Absorption Spectrophotometry," Perkin-Elmer Corp., Norwalk, Conn., 1964.
5. Thiers, R., *in* "Methods of Biochemical Analysis" (D. Glick, ed.), Vol. **5,** p. 273. Interscience, New York, 1957.
6. Willis, J. B., *in* "Methods of Biochemical Analysis" (D. Glick, ed.), Vol. **11,** p. 1. Interscience, New York, 1963.
7. Billings, G. K., *Atomic Absorption Newsletter* **4,** 357 (1965).
8. Koirtyohann, S. R., and Pickett, E. E., *Anal. Chem.* **38,** 585 (1966).
9. Allan, J. D., *Analyst* **83,** 466 (1958).
10. Willis, J. B., *Spectrochim. Acta* **16,** 259 (1960).
11. Leithe, W., and Hofer, A., *Mikrochim. Acta* **1961,** 268.
12. Prudnikov, E. D., *Vestn. Leningr. Univ.* **20,** *Ser. Fiz. i Khim.* No. 2, 125 (1965).
13. Willis, J. B., *Clin. Chem.* **11,** 251 (1965).
14. Slavin, W., *Atomic Absorption Newsletter,* No. 24 (Sept. 1964).

ANALYTICAL BIOCHEMISTRY **20**, 224–232 (1967)

Use of a Sensitive New Method for Determination of the Urinary Excretion of Dichlorodiphenylacetic Acid (DDA) by Human Subjects

B. STAVRIĆ, W. J. JOHNSON, AND A. CHARTRAND

Food and Drug Research Laboratories, Department of National Health and Welfare, Ottawa, Canada

Received January 13, 1967

DDA[1] is the principal urinary metabolite of DDT in mammals (1–3). Studies in progress related to the isolation of urinary DDA conjugates (4, 5) necessitated the development of sensitive chromatographic methods of separation. An outcome of this work was the development of a sensitive method for the separation and determination of DDA in urine and other biological fluids.

Hitherto, the most commonly employed method for the isolation of urinary DDA was that of Cueto *et al.* (6), involving the use of an ion-exchange resin and a specially designed flask heater. The need for a more sensitive method was recently expressed by Durham *et al.* (7), who were able to detect DDA in the urine of only 26% of a representative sample of the human population. Other workers failed to detect, in urine (5), liver and kidney (8) of untreated rats, any metabolites of DDT which, however, are known to be present. Attempts to utilize the Davidow column to determine DDA in human fat were unsuccessful due to poor recovery; only 2.2% of a known amount of DDA added to the column was recovered as compared to 101% for DDT and DDE (9). Equally poor recoveries were encountered with gas-liquid chromatography (7). A model system for the isolation of DDA employing a silicic acid column with gradient elution was recently reported (10) but its applicability to DDA present in biological materials was not demonstrated.

The present method depends upon the combined use of a Florisil column and TLC for the separation of DDA from urine. It permits the identification and estimation of DDA in the order of 0.005 ppm and has

[1] The abbreviations used are: DDA, bis(*p*-chlorophenyl)acetic acid, dichlorodiphenylacetic acid; DDT, 1,1,1-trichloro-2,2-bis(*p*-chlorophenyl)ethane; DDE, 1,1-dichloro-2-bis(*p*-chlorophenyl)ethylene; TLC, thin-layer chromatography.

enabled us to detect DDA in the urine of all members of a group of human subjects selected at random from the general population.

MATERIALS AND METHODS

DDA (m.p. 164–166°C) was prepared by the method of Grummitt *et al.* (11), involving oxidation of DDT. All organic solvents used were A. R. grade, freshly distilled from all-glass apparatus. Florisil, 60–100 mesh, was purchased from Fisher Scientific Company, and was used without prior activation.

Extractors with all-glass joints (designed for liquid-liquid extraction with solvents of lower specific gravity than the liquid being extracted) were used for extraction of the urine samples. The bottom end of the inner tube contained a fritted disc of coarse porosity for better dispersion of the solvent. Two extractors of different size, with capacities of 100 and 500 ml, were employed.

Florisil Column. An ordinary 25 ml buret (9 mm) was used for the Florisil column. A small wad of glass wool was placed in the bottom of the column and organic solvent (benzene/glacial acetic acid, 8/2) added. The column was packed in the usual manner by adding Florisil in small portions to the organic solvent and tapping lightly on the outside of the column. When 7.0 gm of Florisil had been added the column was capped with glass wool. The flow rate was adjusted to 1 ml/4 min, and the sample applied after 50–60 ml of organic solvent had passed through the column. All steps were carried out at room temperature.

TLC Separation. Eastman Chromagram sheets, type K-301 R (20 $\times$ 20 cm), coated with silica gel and containing a fluorescent indicator, were used without prior activation for TLC separation. Before use, each TLC plate was prewashed by developing in the solvent system of benzene/glacial acetic acid (8/2), and air-dried. The same solvent system was employed in developing the "spotted" chromatogram. The sample was applied in the form of a strip with the Camac Chromatocharger. In the procedure finally adopted, a sandwich chamber (Distillation Products Industries) was employed for developing the chromatogram. However, an ordinary TLC chamber (21 $\times$ 21 $\times$ 9 cm jar) gave equally good results. The Eastman Chromagram sheets can be replaced by silica gel coating (0.3 mm thickness) on a glass plate (Kieselgel Camag with UV indicator, 20 $\times$ 20 $\times$ 0.5 cm), after activation in the oven at 100°C for 1 hr followed by prewashing in benzene/glacial acetic acid (8/2), as described for Eastman Chromagram sheets.

The DDA standard reference (from stock solution, 100 μg DDA/ml in ether) was usually spotted on the left-hand side of the plate with a 20 μl micropipet. The separate zones on the TLC plate were made visible by a short-wave UV lamp as dark violet-blue quenching or fluorescent spots (zones). Usually 6 or 7 different zones were observed (Fig. 1). Benzene/glacial acetic acid (8/2) was found to be the best solvent system for the separation of DDA from other urinary metabolites. The DDA reference had an R_f of 0.95.

Procedure. Urine (total 24 hr volume), collected from individuals on their normal daily diet, was stored under refrigeration without added

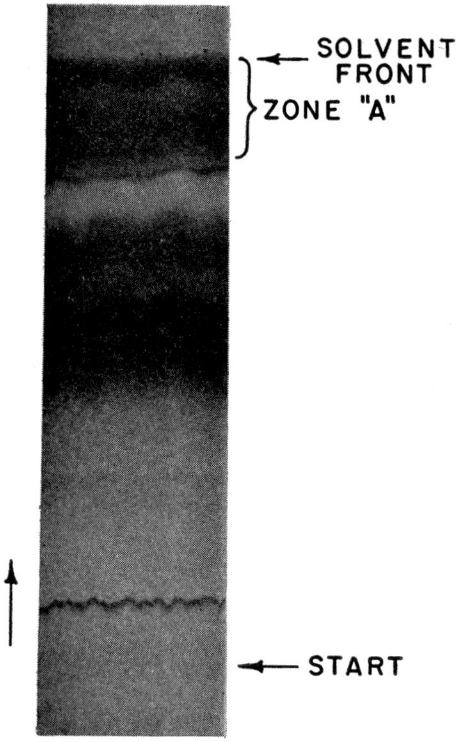

FIG. 1. Thin-layer chromatogram of effluents from the Florisil column in solvent system of benzene/glacial acetic acid (8/2).

preservatives. A known amount of urine, usually 500 ml, was acidified to pH 2 with 6 N H_2SO_4 and extracted in a liquid-liquid extractor with 200 ml of ether for 1 hr. The ether extract was washed in a separatory funnel once with 30 ml of distilled water, and once with 30 ml of saturated NaCl solution. The ethereal supernatant was evaporated on a warm water bath under a stream of air. The dry residue was extracted twice with small amounts (0.5 and 1.0 ml, respectively) of benzene/glacial acetic acid (8/2). The first extract (0.5 ml) was put carefully into the previously prepared Florisil column. Upon descent, the second extract (1.0 ml) was introduced into the col'ımn, followed by additional benzene/ acetic acid solvent. Collection of the effluent was begun as soon as the first extract (0.5 ml) was drawn into the column. The first 5 ml of effluent was discarded. The following 11.0 ml volume, which contained all the DDA, was collected and evaporated to dryness under a jet of air, and the residue extracted with 0.2–0.4 ml of absolute ethanol. The ethanol extract was transferred to a 15 ml conical centrifuge tube and 4–5 vol of ether added. After 5 min of centrifugation at 1000 rpm, the clear supernatant, containing the DDA, was decanted and concentrated in a stream of air to a volume slightly less that 1.0 ml. The concentrated, usually yellowish, ethanol/ether solution was applied to a TLC plate in the form of a strip. Development of the chromatogram in benzene/glacial acetic acid (8/2) required about 1.75 hr (frontal migration of 15 cm). A typical chromatogram with separated zones as seen under a short-wave UV lamp (2540 Å), is shown in Figure 1. Zone A, which contains all the

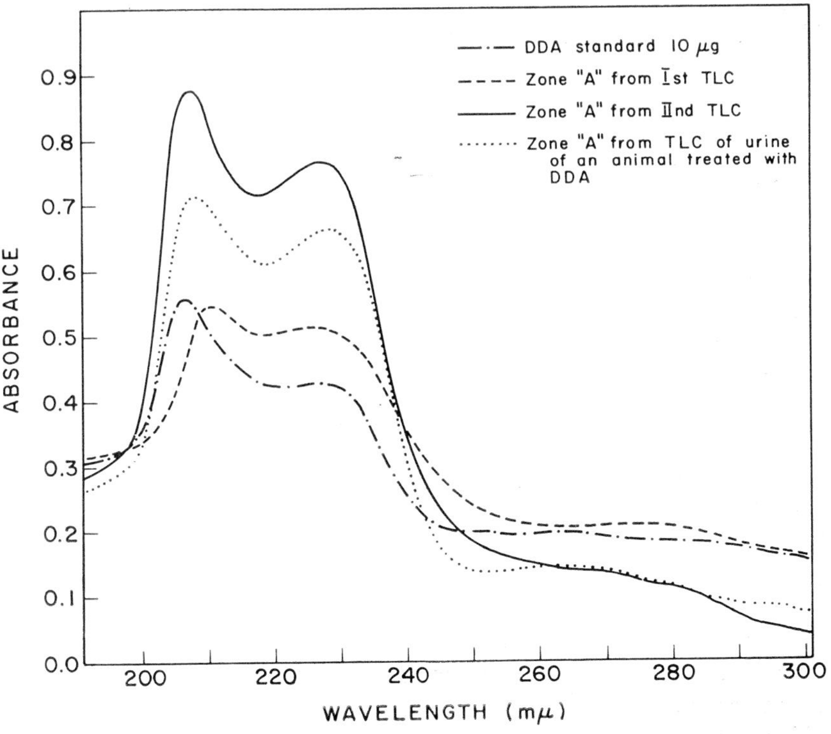

FIG. 2. Ultraviolet absorption spectra (in absolute ethanol) of DDA collected as eluates from the chromatogram shown in Figure 1.

DDA (R_f 0.75–1.00), was removed with a scalpel, transferred to a test tube, and extracted twice with small amounts (4–5 ml) of absolute ethanol. After centrifugation, the pooled supernatant was checked for UV absorption in a Bausch & Lomb Spectronic 502 with 3 ml cuvets of 1 cm light path (Fig. 2, Zone "A" from 1st TLC), and rechromatographed on a TLC plate as described above. In the second TLC separation, the DDA was located in a narrow zone of R_f 0.90–0.95 corresponding to the R_f of the DDA reference standard. The DDA zone was removed from the plate, extracted twice with absolute ethanol, and after centrifugation, the pooled ethanol extract was transferred to a boiling tube for colorimetric determination of DDA by the Schechter-Haller method (12) as modified by Ofner and Calvery (3). Absorption of the pink-colored tetranitro derivative was read at 540 mμ in the Bausch & Lomb Spectronic 20. The absorption spectra from 400–600 mμ was identical with that described by Ofner and Calvery (3). It was further established that only one TLC separation was actually required for accurate determination of DDA since other substances present in Zone A of R_f 0.75–1.00 (Fig. 1) did not interfere appreciably with the colorimetric determination of DDA. Consequently, in all routine urine assays, only one TLC separation was employed.

RESULTS

Standard solutions consisting of known amounts (5–100 μg) of DDA added to 500 ml samples of DDA-free urine were used for sensitivity and recovery tests. Urine free of DDA was obtained by extracting acidified urine with ether for 1 hr in a liquid-liquid extractor. "Cleaned" urine was required because nearly all samples of "normal" urine contained variable amounts of DDA which could influence recovery values. The sensitivity of the method was found to be such that 5 μg of DDA in 500 ml of urine could be readily detected.

Recoveries of different amounts (5, 10, 20, 30, and 50 μg) of DDA added to DDA-free urine in duplicate were 70, 60, 65, 77, and 70%, respectively (mean 68.4%). Figure 3 shows that a nearly linear relationship exists between μg DDA added and μg DDA found, up to additions of 50 μg. Consequently, the method provides a good estimation of urinary DDA when the assay values are multiplied by a mean factor of 100/68.4 to correct for losses. It was established that the latter were distributed to an approximately equal extent among the 4 procedural steps: urine extraction, Florisil column chromatography, TLC, and colorimetric determination.

Absorption curves of the UV spectrum for urinary DDA as compared with the DDA reference standard are shown in Figure 2. DDA isolated

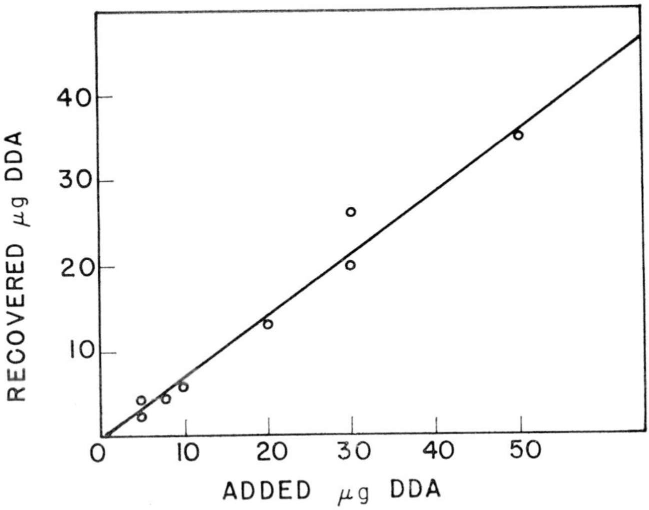

FIG. 3. Recovery of DDA, as determined by the procedure described under "Methods," plotted as a function of known amounts of DDA added to DDA-free urine.

TABLE 1
Determination of DDA in Human Urine

Subject No.	24 hr urine[a]		
	Volume, ml	DDA found, μg	DDA output,[c] μg/24 hr
1	2000	80	117
2	1900	50	73
3	2200	66	96
4	1100	13	19
5	1200	12	18
6	1800	43	63
7	1800	29	42
8	2100	17	25
9	1200	9	13
10	1800	22	32
11[b]	1100	Trace	Trace
12	1115	40	58
13	1100	34	50

Experimental conditions are described under "Methods."
[a] Assays were performed on 500 ml aliquots.
[b] Subject No. 11 was a vegetarian.
[c] DDA found × correction factor 100/68.4 (see text).

from the urine of rabbits and rats treated with DDA (300 mg/kg orally) was found to have identical physical and chemical properties (UV absorption, R_f values, visible absorption of the nitro derivative) as DDA isolated from the urine of untreated humans. It is of some interest that DDA was isolated also from the liver and urine of rabbits and rats untreated with DDA, thus indicating that these animals had obviously ingested DDT present as a contaminant in their normal diet.

The average amount of DDA found in 24 hr urine samples taken from 13 human subjects selected at random from the general population was 0.028 ppm or 46.4 μg/day (Table 1), ranging from 13 to 117 μg/day (0.011 to 0.058 ppm). The average value of 46.4 μg DDA/day, equivalent to 52.7 μg DDT, is in agreement with the published results of Durham *et al.* (13), who found that the average person consumes about 0.038 mg DDT/day in his food. Traces of DDA (less than 3 μg/500 ml) were

TABLE 2
Variability of DDA Excretion during 24 Hours in Two Human Subjects

Subject No.	Urine samples: Collection period	Volume, ml	DDA found, μg
1	7:30 am–11:00 am	140	0
	11:30 am– 4:30 pm	200	10
	4:30 pm–10:00 pm	300	30
	10:00 pm– 7:30 am	475	Trace
2	9:00 am– 5:00 pm	460	8
	5:00 pm–11:30 pm	360	8
	11:30 pm– 9:00 am	280	18

Experimental conditions are desciibed under "Methods."

found in only one 24 hr urine sample (No. 11, Table 1), and it was later ascertained that this sample came from a vegetarian, while all other subjects ate meat once or twice daily. There was some degree of variation in urinary DDA levels from day to day in all individuals, as well as fluctuation in the rate of DDA excretion throughout the day. The latter is well illustrated by the results shown in Table 2. These fluctuations most probably are related to time of consumption of foods containing DDT. Thus, it is apparent that total 24 hr urinary DDA excretion cannot be ascertained by extrapolation from the DDA content of a single arbitrary voiding (14).

DISCUSSION

Several investigators have reported difficulties in the extraction of urine with organic solvents due to the formation of stubborn and heavy emulsions upon shaking (6). To circumvent these difficulties we have used a solvent-extraction method employing an ordinary liquid-liquid extractor in which DDA is removed very easily from urine in almost quantitative yield with ether or ethyl acetate as solvent.

While several investigators have reported the use of Florisil and other adsorbents for cleanup procedures in the analysis of organochlorine metabolites, to our knowledge the literature contains no reference to the use of Florisil for separating DDA from other organic materials. Similarly, the separation of some organochlorine pesticide derivatives on TLC has been described (15, 16) but not that of DDA.

To obtain a more sensitive procedure for the determination of DDA than those presently in use (6), it was clear that a rigorous extraction procedure was required as well as a selective method for separating DDA from other coextracted urinary constituents. The Florisil column gave satisfactory results in our hands, but there were difficulties associated with different lots of Florisil, and has been reported by others (17–19), consisting mainly of variation in retention time during elution of DDA from the column, and the presence of a contaminant with absorption at 208–210 mμ. Consequently, it was found necessary to standardize each lot of Florisil before use.

The lower limit for the determination of DDA by the Ofner and Calvery method (3) was found to be 3 μg. Some authors (3, 6) have noted interference by the yellow color produced upon nitration of extracts of tissue or urine. We have eliminated this undesirable feature of the Ofner and Calvery method by using a cleanup technique with Florisil, followed by TLC separation, which removes almost completely the extraneous yellow color in the DDA-containing urine extract.

The present method permits the isolation and identification of DDA from human urine in the presence of large amounts of drugs and their metabolites. For example, 11–17 μg of DDA was isolated from 500 ml of urine from a tuberculosis patient (No. 6, Table 1) under daily treatment with 300 mg of isoniazid and 12 gm of *p*-aminosalicylic acid.

Recovery values of approximately 70% of the known amount of DDA added to urine prior to the extraction procedure (Fig. 3) indicate that the actual amount of free DDA in urine is about 30% higher than the assay values (Tables 1 and 2). Accordingly, the average value for DDA excretion in man would be about 46 μg/day, corresponding to approximately 52 μg DDT/day. However, the total daily excretion of DDA would be somewhat higher than the values obtained for free urinary DDA due to the fact that DDA is excreted, in part, as conjugates (8), which are present in feces as well as in the urine.

DDA now appears to be a "normal" constituent of human urine, as a consequence of the ubiquitous presence of DDT in the human environment.

SUMMARY

A simple procedure for the isolation and determination of *p*-dichlorodiphenylacetic acid (DDA) in urine and other biological fluids has been presented. The method, utilizing inexpensive laboratory apparatus, commercially available Florisil, and prepared thin-layer chromatography sheets, permits the identification and estimation of DDA in the order of 0.005 ppm. The average recovery of from 5 to 50 μg DDA added to DDA-free urine was 68.4%. Urinary DDA excretion of 13 human subjects picked at random from the general population was found to average 46 μg/day, ranging from 13 to 117 μg/day.

ACKNOWLEDGMENTS

We thank Mr. G. Morris for line drawings and Mr. Benjamin Korda for photographs.

REFERENCES

1. White, W. C., and Sweeney, T. R., *U. S. Public Health Repts.* **60**, 66 (1945).
2. Neal, P. A., Sweeney, T. R., Spicer, S. S., and Von Oettinger, W. F., *U. S. Public Health Repts.* **61**, 403 (1946).
3. Ofner, R. R., and Calvery, H. O., *J. Pharmacol. Exptl. Therap.* **85**, 363 (1945).
4. Johnson, W. J., Weiss, S., and Chartrand, A., *Proc. Can. Fed. Biol. Soc.* **8**, 69 (1965).
5. Pinto, J. D., Camien, M. N., and Dunn, M. S., *J. Biol. Chem.* **240**, 2148 (1965).
6. Cueto, C., Barnes, A. G., and Mattson, A. M., *J. Agr. Food Chem.* **4**, 943 (1956).
7. Durham, W. F., Armstrong, J. F., and Quinby, G. E., *Arch. Environ. Health* **11**, 76 (1965).
8. Peterson, J. E., and Robinson, W. H., *Toxicol. Appl. Pharmacol.* **6**, 321 (1964).
9. Mattson, A. M., Spillane, J. T., Baker, C., and Pearce, G. W., *Anal. Chem.* **25**, 1065 (1953).
10. Schuntner, C. A., and Schnitzerling, H. J., *J. Chromatog.* **21**, 483 (1966).
11. Grummitt, O., Buck, A., and Egan, R., *in* "Organic Synthesis," Coll. vol. 3, p. 270. Wiley, New York, 1955.
12. Schechter, S., and Haller, H. L., *J. Am. Chem. Soc.* **66**, 2129 (1944).
13. Durham, W. F., Armstrong, J. F., and Quinby, G. E., *Arch. Environ. Health* **11**, 641 (1965).
14. Hayes, W. J., Durham, W. F., and Cueto, C., *J. Am. Med. Assoc.* **162**, 890 (1956).
15. Adamovic, V. M., *J. Chromatog.* **23**, 274 (1966).
16. Kovacs, M. F., Jr., *J. Assoc. Offic. Anal. Chemists* **49**, 365 (1966).
17. Tolbert, C. E., *J. Assoc. Offic. Anal. Chemists* **49**, 386 (1966).
18. Wood, B. J., *J. Assoc. Offic. Anal. Chemists* **49**, 472 (1966).
19. Cummings, J. G., Zee, K. T., Turner, V., and Quinn, F., *J. Assoc. Offic. Anal. Chemists* **49**, 357 (1966).

ANALYTICAL BIOCHEMISTRY 20, 233–245 (1967)

A Method for the Determination of Progesterone in Biological Specimens

D. J. WATSON, E. B. ROMANOFF, J. KATO,[1] AND D. B. BARTOSIK[2]

Worcester Foundation for Experimental Biology, Shrewsbury, Massachusetts 01545

Received January 19, 1967

The analysis of progesterone in blood and tissues is at best a tedious process. If many samples must be analyzed at one time, the difficulty increases enormously. By taking advantage of recent developments in thin-layer chromatography (TLC) (1), we have developed a method for the analysis of progesterone in whole blood and tissues which is rapid, sensitive, reliable, and adapted for the routine analyses of between 10 to 40 samples at one time.

The method combines the isolation of pure progesterone (as demonstrated by radiochemical technique) with quantitation based on the formation of progesterone-3,20-bisdinitrophenylhydrazone (prog-DNPH) and consists of the following steps:

1. Extraction of whole blood or tissues with either ethanol/acetone (1/1) or isopropyl acetate.
2. Partition of the extract between 70% methanol and *n*-hexane.
3. Preliminary TLC of the 70% methanolic fraction in the system methanol/methylene chloride (2/98) to yield an eluate of a progesterone area.
4. Acetylation of the above eluate.
5. Rechromatography in the system cyclohexane/ethyl acetate (50/50) to isolate radiochemically pure progesterone.
6. Formation of the prog-DNPH derivative.
7. Chromatography of the prog-DNPH derivative in the system chloroform/cyclohexane (3/1).
8. Quantitation by absorbance density at 380 mμ in chloroform.

[1] Fellow, Training Program in Physiology of Reproduction. Present address: Department of Obstetrics and Gynecology, Faculty of Medicine, University of Tokyo, Tokyo, Japan.

[2] Fellow, Steroid Training Program.

MATERIALS

Solvents: Reagent-grade ethyl acetate, isopropyl acetate, cyclohexane, chloroform, and methylene chloride were redistilled without prior treatment through an 80 cm fractionating column packed with coarse stainless-steel wool (2). Methanol was gently refluxed overnight with reagent-grade 2,4-dinitrophenylhydrazine (1–2 gm/liter) and concentrated H_2SO_4 (5 ml/liter) before distillation. *n*-Hexane was first washed with concentrated H_2SO_4 until no further color could be extracted, then with distilled water until neutral prior to distillation.

Dinitrophenylhydrazine hydrochloride was prepared by recrystallizing the Eastman reagent-grade compound first from ethanol/concentrated HCl, 5/1 (v/v), and then from ethanol/concentrated HCl, 19/1 (v/v). The crystals were stored in a desiccator.

Dinitrophenylhydrazine reagent was prepared by dissolving 100 mg of the above crystals in 30 ml of methanol and 1.5 ml of concentrated HCl. This reagent is stable at room temperature for at least one month.

Benedict's reagent (3) was prepared by dissolving 173 gm sodium citrate (anhydrous) and 100 gm Na_2CO_3 (anhydrous) in 800 ml of distilled water containing 17.3 gm of $CuSO_4 \cdot 5H_2O$. The final volume was made up to 1 liter with water.

Progesterone used for recovery experiments was recrystallized from *n*-hexane and then from methanol (m.p. 128–130°C, uncorr.). It was chromatographically pure in the systems used. Progesterone-4-^{14}C (758,000 dpm/γ) was obtained from New England Nuclear Corp. and used as received after establishing chromatographic purity.

Progesterone-3,20-*bisdinitrophenylhydrazone* (prog-DNPH) was prepared according to the method of Reich *et al.* (4) and was recrystallized first from absolute ethanol, then from methanol/benzene (m.p. 284–286°C, uncorr.). A stock solution of prog-DNPH was prepared by dissolving 10.0 mg of the compound in 10.0 ml of chloroform.

Thin-layer chromatography equipment was obtained from Brinkmann Instruments Inc. Standard 20 $\times$ 20 cm thin-layer plates were coated with a slurry of Brinkmann silica gel GF in water (1/2, w/v) at a thickness of either 250 or 500 μ, dried at 110°C for 2 hr, and stored without special precautions. Rectangular tanks, lined with Whatman 3 MM filter paper, were equilibrated with the respective solvent systems for at least 1 hr before use. Appropriate standards were always run on the same plate as the unknowns. Radioactivity measurements were made by plating aliquots of a sample on aluminum planchets at infinite thinness and counting in an automatic Tracerlab thin-window counter (efficiency 23.6%, ^{14}C).

Absorbance readings were made in a Beckman DK recording spectrophotometer utilizing 1 cm light path silica cells. When minimal solvent volumes were required, Beckman microcells (Cat. #97250) were used.

Solvents in test tubes were evaporated under a fine stream of nitrogen in a water bath at 40–60°C. Large volumes of solvents were removed under reduced pressure in a rotary evaporator under nitrogen at 40–60°C.

METHOD

Whole blood is collected with anticoagulant (citrate, oxalate, or heparin) and chilled immediately to prevent transformation of progesterone (5). If not extracted immediately, the samples should be frozen and stored in a deep freeze.

Extraction. Two extraction methods may be employed: The first, utilizing isopropyl acetate (IPA), is intended primarily for extracting large volumes of blood (greater than 50 ml). The second method, based on the use of ethanol/acetone (1/1, v/v), is especially suitable for small blood volumes and for tissues and homogenates such as are obtained in incubation studies.

1. IPA extraction: The blood sample is diluted with an equal volume of distilled water and 37 gm NaCl/100 ml blood is added. The mixture is extracted 4 times with 4 vol of IPA. The pooled extracts are dried over anhydrous Na_2SO_4, filtered through glass wool, and evaporated to a dry residue. The recovered solvent may be reused after redistillation.

2. Ethanol/acetone extraction: Blood is added slowly to 6 or more volumes of ethanol/acetone with vigorous swirling. Tissues are homogenized in 5–10 vol of the solvent. The mixture is filtered (Whatman 541 or 1), and the precipitate is washed twice with half-volumes of solvent. The combined blood or tissue extracts and washes are concentrated to an aqueous residue, which is then diluted to 25 ml with distilled water and extracted 3 times with 4 vol of methylene chloride. The combined extracts are evaporated to dryness.

Partition of Crude Extract. The residue obtained by either extraction procedure is dissolved in *n*-hexane and is extracted 4 times with 0.5 vol of 70% methanol; 50 ml of *n*-hexane is adequate for blood volumes up to 100 ml. The volumes may be scaled down for more convenient handling of large numbers of small samples: 20 ml *n*-hexane is usually adequate for partitioning the ethanol/acetone extract of as much as 1 gm of luteal tissue or 50 ml of blood. The combined methanolic extract is evaporated to dryness *in vacuo*.

Preliminary TLC. The residue from the 70% methanol fraction is quantitatively transferred to a 13 × 100 mm test tube from which it is applied to the origin of a silica gel GF thin-layer plate (5¾″ disposable

Pasteur pipets are ideal for this purpose). The plate is developed in the system methanol/methylene chloride (2/98, v/v) in which progesterone has an R_f between 0.4 and 0.5. The unknown area parallel to the progesterone standard may usually be detected under UV light (253 mμ). An area of silica gel extending 1 cm above and 1 cm below the area indicated by the progesterone standard is scraped into a centrifuge tube and eluted 4 times with 3 ml of either ethyl acetate or methanol/chloroform (1/1, v/v). The eluates are pooled and evaporated to a dry residue *in vacuo*.

Acetylation. The residue is subjected to acetylation in a mixture of 0.1 ml acetic anhydride and 0.2 ml pyridine. The stoppered test tube is kept either in a 60°C water bath for 1 hr or at room temperature overnight. The reagents are then evaporated in a fume hood.

Rechromatography. The residue obtained above is applied to a thin-layer silica gel GF plate and is developed in the system cyclohexane/ethyl acetate (1/1, v/v), in which the R_f for progesterone is between 0.3 and 0.4. The progesterone eluted from this chromatogram is radiochemically pure, and if present in high concentration may be quantitated by UV spectroscopy. However, if small amounts of progesterone are present, sensitivity is increased by forming the bisdinitrophenylhydrazone derivative as described below.

Formation of Progesterone-3,20-bisdinitrophenylhydrazone (Prog-DNPH). The residue is taken up in 0.2 ml methanol and 0.2 ml of DNPH reagent is then added. The stoppered test tube is allowed to stand for 1 hr at room temperature; 1.0 ml of Benedict's reagent and a boiling stone are then added, and the tube is placed in an 80°C water bath for 10 min. After cooling, 5.0 ml of chloroform is added, the tube is shaken vigorously, and the phases are separated by centrifugation. The upper dark green aqueous layer is aspirated and discarded. The chloroform solution is then washed first with 1 ml of 1 *N* HCl, then with 1 ml of distilled water, and filtered through glass wool. The filtrate is evaporated to dryness.

Chromatography of the Prog-DNPH Derivative. The residue is quantitatively transferred to a silica gel GF thin-layer plate using chloroform as the solvent. The developing system is cyclohexane/chloroform (1/3, v/v), in which the prog-DNPH has an R_f of about 0.25 (6).

The orange-yellow band of prog-DNPH may be seen if more than 0.1 γ of the compound is present. An area absorbing UV light (253 mμ) slightly less polar than the prog-DNPH is usually, but not always, seen, and is derived from the reaction with Benedict's reagent. It should be avoided when eluting the prog-DNPH with chloroform in the manner already described.

Quantitation. The absorbancies at 350, 380, and 410 mμ are determined on a chloroform solution of the prog-DNPH. The "Allen-corrected" (7) absorbance is compared with that of standard prog-DNPH prepared as described above. For quantities of progesterone between 0.5 and 2.0 γ, a 1.0 ml dilution may be used. For amounts below 0.25 γ, the residue should be dissolved in 0.1 ml and scanned in the Beckman microcell. If a blank is carried through the procedure beginning with the formation of the prog-DNPH, 0.04 γ of prog-DNPH dissolved in 0.1 ml of chloroform may be measured. For quantities of prog-DNPH less than 0.25 γ the use of a blank is suggested.

EXPERIMENTAL

To determine the optimal conditions for forming the prog-DNPH derivative, the reaction mixture was allowed to stand at room temperature for either 1 or 24 hr. The average recoveries for quadruplicate samples ranging from 0.2 to 4.0 γ progesterone were 87.1 and 88.5%, respectively. The recovery was less, 83.8%, when the reaction mixtures were heated for 1 hr at 60°C. The conditions for the reaction were therefore standardized at room temperature for 1 hr. Solutions of prog-DNPH at concentrations as low as 0.084 γ/ml in either chloroform or ethanol/HCl (19/1, v/v) were stable for at least 24 hr.

Evidence for Purity of the Isolated Progesterone. The free progesterone obtained after the second thin-layer chromatography (Step 5) may be quantitated by determining the UV absorption at 240 mμ as demonstrated by the following experiment: Bovine ovaries containing corpora lutea (luteal ovaries) were perfused with acetate-1-^{14}C and aliquots of the venous effluent of two separate perfusions were analyzed according to the method presented. In the first experiment, 244.0 γ of progesterone with a specific activity of 1482 dpm/γ and in the second experiment 345.5 γ of progesterone with a specific activity of 1505 dpm/γ were isolated. Aliquots of these two samples were then carried through the DNPH procedure. The resultant specific activities, calculated as free progesterone, were 1432 dpm/γ and 1511 dpm/γ, respectively. Infrared spectra of the free progesterone and the prog-DNPH were identical with those of authentic reference samples. *Radiochemical purity:* Bovine luteal ovaries were perfused with acetate-1-^{14}C. After isopropyl acetate (IPA) extraction of the venous effluent, free progesterone was isolated as described. Carrier progesterone was added, and the mixture was crystallized to constant specific activity using three different solvents. Radiochemical purity is indicated by the constancy of the specific activities of the crystals and mother liquors summarized in Table 1.

TABLE 1

Radiochemical Purity of Progesterone Demonstrated by Recrystallization to Constant Specific Activity (progesterone was isolated from effluent of an ovary perfused with 1-^{14}C-acetate)

Solvent	Weight[a] before crystallization, mg	Weight recovered, mg[b]		Total radioactivity, dpm		Specific activity, dpm/mg	
		Crystals	Mother liquor	Crystals	Mother liquor	Crystals	Mother liquor
n-Hexane	5.65[c]	2.93	2.48	171,600	124,100	58,450	50,800
Methanol	2.93	1.68	1.18	92,900	64,550	55,450	54,800
Acetone/water	1.68	1.11	0.41	64,100	21,100	57,550	51,230

[a] Weight of starting material.

[b] Mass determined by ultraviolet absorption at 240 mμ and applying the Allen correction.

[c] Progesterone sample: 187.0 γ, 313,500 dpm. Carrier progesterone added, 5.46 mg.

Recoveries at Different Stages of the Procedure. Recovery data are expressed as the average per cent ± standard deviation.

(*a*) Extraction and partition of the sample: Progesterone-4-^{14}C, approximately 40,000 dpm, was added with carrier (0.2–2.0 γ) to 20 ml aliquots of citrated bovine blood. Extraction with IPA as described yielded an average 93.3 ± 8.3% recovery of the added radioactivity. When the extracts were subjected to partition between *n*-hexane and 70% methanol, the over-all recovery of added radioactivity was 92.0 ± 8.9% ($n = 6$).

(*b*) Efficiency of elution procedures: Aliquots of progesterone-4-^{14}C with 0.1–2.0 μg of carrier were chromatographed and eluted with methanol/chloroform as described. In three separate experiments the average recoveries were 97.8 ± 2.1% ($n = 8$), 96.8 ± 3.3 ($n = 5$), and 96.8 ± 7.0% ($n = 8$).

(*c*) Recovery of progesterone from biological specimens: Progesterone-4-^{14}C and carrier (0.09–10.3 μg) were added to 20 ml aliquots of bovine blood, which were then extracted with IPA. These data are summarized in Table 2. After the second chromatography, the average recovery of radioactivity was 89.9 ± 8.0% ($n = 22$). After formation of the prog-DNPH, the average recovery of added progesterone was 66.4 ± 10.4% ($n = 22$) based on spectrophotometry, and 64.5 ± 8.4% based on radioactivity.

In another experiment, six groups of serial blood samples were obtained during perfusion of luteal ovaries. Following addition of tracer progesterone-4-^{14}C, each sample was extracted with ethanol/acetone, and the progesterone was quantitated as the prog-DNPH. These data are summarized in Table 3. With the exception of Group IV, in which the progesterone contents of the samples were unusually high, the recovery of radioactivity was consistent between groups, with an over-all recovery of 65.7 ± 6.3% ($n = 49$).

In another experiment, four groups of luteal tissue incubations were quantitated as the prog-DNPH after the addition of tracer progesterone-4-^{14}C. The recovered radioactivity in the four groups were, respectively: 46.3 ± 6.3 ($n = 5$), 63.8 ± 8.3% ($n = 6$), 60.7 ± 10.9% ($n = 5$), and 60.6 ± 9.5% ($n = 5$). The mean recovery was 58.3 ± 10.7% ($n = 21$).

NOTES

1. Extraction of large volumes of blood may result in a 70% methanol residue which is too "dirty" for efficient thin-layer chromatography. Such a residue may be considerably cleaned by column chromatography with neutral alumina. A Pasteur pipet is lightly plugged with glass wool and approximately 1.2 gm of neutral alumina (Woehlm, with no special

TABLE 2
Progesterone Recoveries at Different Stages in Procedure

Progesterone added to whole blood		After acetylation and second TLC		After formation of progesterone-3,20-DNPH			
dpm	Carrier (γ)	dpm	% recovery	dpm	% recovery radioactivity	Mass (γ)[a]	% recovered mass
84,000	10.26	63,350	75.5[b]	59,900	71.2[b]	7.02	68.4[b]
94,400	1.80	89,600	94.8 ± 5.9[c]	64,800	69.7 ± 5.5	1.33	73.9 ± 12.3
94,400	1.03	90,450	95.8 ± 1.5	64,250	68.0 ± 7.4	0.77	75.5 ± 5.9
105,900	0.55	87,600	82.7 ± 5.8	54,000	50.9 ± 1.3	0.29	53.2 ± 4.0
105,900	0.23	93,800	88.6 ± 4.9	67,600	63.7 ± 3.7	0.15	63.1 ± 5.6
42,000	0.094	35,700	84.1 ± 4.8	26,900	63.4 ± 2.9	0.061	64.4
Average:			89.9 ± 8.0		64.5 ± 8.4		66.4 ± 10.4

Recovery of progesterone-4-^{14}C with carrier added to 20 ml aliquots of whole blood (conc. varies from 0.0047 γ to 0.513 γ/ml). Quadruplicate samples except where noted.

[a] Mass of progesterone calculated as free compound.

[b] Two samples only; no standard deviation.

[c] Standard deviation.

TABLE 3

Progesterone in 20 ml Whole Blood Serial Samples of Ovarian Perfusates (recoveries are based on tracer progesterone-4-^{14}C added to each sample)

	Perfusion											
	I		II		III		IV		V		VI	
Sample No.	γ/ml	Per cent recovery	γ/ml	Per cent recovery	γ/ml	Per cent recovery	γ/ml	Per cent recovery	γ/ml	Per cent recovery	γ/ml	Per cent recovery
1	0.227	53.0	1.200	43.6	0.395	49.2	4.784	82.5	0.491	72.5	0.863	61.7
2	0.278	62.1	0.984	50.1	0.533	53.8	5.212	72.4	0.539	66.4	0.821	60.9
3	0.230	69.9	2.075	59.2	0.505	56.8	5.765	78.9	0.734	65.0	0.852	67.8
4	0.250	63.5	2.111	64.0	0.557	54.2	7.986	86.0	0.932	57.6	0.669	68.1
5	0.241	64.5	2.484	68.1	0.991	52.5	6.976	82.4	0.924	73.6	1.024	72.2
6	0.347	59.3	3.203	51.9	0.997	72.2	6.990	89.3	1.183	66.6	0.934	62.2
7	0.520	74.0	2.195	61.6	1.598	65.2	7.199	64.8				
8	0.551	46.4	2.519	78.5	2.026	67.7	8.543	90.6				
9	0.677	48.1	2.202	61.4	3.335	78.0	10.045	74.9				
10					3.672	83.8						
Av. recovery	60.1 ± 9.4%		59.8 ± 10.4%		62.3 ± 10.9%		80.5 ± 7.7%		66.9 ± 5.8%		65.4 ± 4.6%	

treatment) in benzene is added. The 70% methanol residue, dissolved in 2 ml of benzene, is applied to the column. The container is rinsed twice with 1 ml portions of chloroform which in turn are added to the column. These effluents are discarded. The progesterone is then quantitatively eluted with a total of 4 ml of methanol. A dark brown material which is sometimes extracted from whole blood with ethanol/acetone is adsorbed on the alumina.

2. After the second chromatography (Step 5), the radiochemically pure free progesterone may be quantitated by spectroscopy at 240 mμ, if present in amounts greater than 2 μg in the total sample. In order to improve the separation of progesterone from certain contaminants which have an absorption at the far end of the UV spectrum, we have developed the following procedure. The residue in a centrifuge tube is dissolved in 0.3 ml of methanol, and is diluted to 30% by the subsequent addition of 0.7 ml of water. The progesterone is then extracted 3 times with 2 ml portions of acid-washed *n*-hexane. Centrifugation and aspiration of the *n*-hexane is easily accomplished, leaving considerable interfering material in the 30% methanol. This partition is also effective for removing interfering material from eluates of paper chromatograms and can be applied to steroids with polarities equal to or less than 17α-hydroxyprogesterone.

3. During the formation of the prog-DNPH, several yellow and/or ultraviolet absorbing compounds derived from the reaction mixtures are formed. These are effectively separated from the prog-DNPH by TLC in the system cyclohexane/chloroform (1/3). This solvent system is sensitive to changes in room temperature and the proportion of chloroform must be reduced to 1/2 or 1/1 at room temperatures below 25°C. Chromatography tends to become erratic after more than three plates have been developed, and a new tank should therefore be prepared. For a better separation of the prog-DNPH from impurities derived during the reaction, the plate may be rerun in the same system. Occasionally the syn- and anti-forms of the prog-DNPH are separated after two or more developments in this system (6), and this should be taken into account.

4. If excess DNPH reagent is present in the final prog-DNPH residue, its absorption maximum at 360 mμ interferes with that of the prog-DNPH absorption maximum at 380 mμ. This occurs if inadequate amounts of Benedict's reagent had been used to destroy the excess DNPH reagent in the reaction mixture. If this happens, the eluted prog-DNPH must be retreated with fresh Benedict's reagent as described, and rechromatographed. The loss involved is minimal.

5. When maximum sensitivity is required, advantage may be taken of the sharpness of the prog-DNPH absorption peak at 380 mμ. By reading the absorbance at 380 mμ against a blank carried through the procedure beginning with the DNPH reaction, and dispensing with the Allen correction, the "apparent" sensitivity is increased by a factor of at least two. However, it must be realized that this is done at the expense of some certainty as to the validity of the determination. Zero or baseline absorbance for the blank should be adjusted at 550 mμ.

6. The limiting step in the procedure is the evaporation of the crude extracts and the 70% methanolic fractions. With three rotary vacuum evaporators, one person is able to complete 20 to 40 blood analyses in ten working days.

7. When assaying the radioactivity of the prog-DNPH derivative by liquid scintillation counting, we have observed that amounts of prog-DNPH greater than 1 μg cause quenching. Chloroform eluates of thin-layer plates prepared with silica gel GF also cause quenching in scintillation counting. If this counting procedure is used, then the final chromatography should be carried out on thin-layer plates prepared with silica gel G (no fluorescent agent).

DISCUSSION

Earlier methods used for the analysis of progesterone have been reviewed by Short (8) and by Zander (9). These methods have utilized a single paper chromatography of a crude extract to yield a progesterone area which was then quantitated by its UV absorption at 240 mμ. While this is satisfactory in terms of sensitivity and specificity, provided the separation method is good, interference in the far UV range is common (10). Impurities absorbing between 220 and 260 mμ are present not only in blood extracts (11), but also in eluates of filter paper (12) and silica gel GF (13).

The specificity of present methods for the analysis of progesterone (or any other steroid hormone) in biological material depends primarily on the separation of the progesterone from interfering substances. Bush (14) has recommended the use of two chromatograms in systems giving low R_f values and a large ΔR_{ms}, as well as a chemical modification of the compound sought. In the present method these conditions are satisfied both directly and indirectly. Although the R_f (and consequently the R_m) of progesterone is nearly the same in the first two chromatographic systems utilized, the values for possible contaminants are quite different. While acetylation of the sample does not affect progesterone, many impurities are effectively modified and removed in the subsequent chromatogram. We have observed that labeled material present in the venous effluent of perfused placentae (15) and of bovine ovaries perfused *in vitro* with acetate-1-^{14}C (16) could not be separated from progesterone by extensive chromatography unless the mixture was subjected to acetylation. Although the free progesterone obtained after the second TLC (Step 5) is radiochemically pure, quantitation of small amounts of progesterone by UV spectroscopy is still difficult because of the presence of substances absorbing in the far-UV range. In the present method, this interference has been effectively eliminated by the formation of the prog-DNPH derivative which has an absorption maximum in chloroform at 380 mμ. Because the prog-DNPH derivative has a $\lambda_{max}^{CHCl_3}$ 380 mμ, $\epsilon = 49{,}000$, the sensitivity is increased 2.8 times above that of free progesterone λ_{max}^{EtOH} 240 mμ, $\epsilon = 17{,}000$. Moreover, it is quantitatively formed in acid methanol in less than 1 hr and is stable both in the dry state and in solution.

The sensitivity of the method is such that amounts of progesterone as low as 0.04 γ in the final chloroform solution may be measured without the need for special precautions. Thus, this degree of sensitivity compares favorably with that obtained in methods utilizing gas-liquid chromatography (17, 18).

Although the method may be easily used for the relatively rapid analysis of single samples, it has been primarily developed for the routine analyses of a large number of samples at one time. When batches of 10 to 40 samples are processed, the time invested per sample becomes small and compares favorably with other less specific or more costly methods. The use of thin-layer chromatography in the purification technique affords a great saving of both laboratory space and special equipment costs. These advantages coupled with the speed inherent in the technique should make the method useful in routine analytical as well as in research laboratories.

SUMMARY

A method for the analysis of progesterone has been described which combines the isolation of radiochemically pure progesterone with quantitation based on the formation of progesterone-3,20-bisdinitrophenylhydrazone. The method has been developed for the analysis of progesterone in whole blood and tissues.

ACKNOWLEDGMENTS

This work has been supported by U.S.P.H.S. Grants HD-0117 and AM-06294. We wish to thank Dr. Jordanilo Vujosevic, Dr. Vasant Patwardhan, Mr. Ajai Haksar. and Miss Elaine Scricco for contributions to this work.

REFERENCES

1. Stahl, E., *in* "Thin Layer Chromatography" (G. B. Marini-Bettolo, ed.), p. 1. Elsevier, Amsterdam, 1964.
2. Fieser, L. F., "Experiments in Organic Chemistry." Heath, Boston, 1955.
3. Benedict, S. R., *J. Biol. Chem.* **5,** 485 (1908-09).
4. Reich, H., Crane, K. F., and Sanfilippo, S. J., *J. Org. Chem.* **18,** 822 (1953).
5. Coyle, M. G., and Romanoff, E. B., *Federation Proc.* **23,** 462 (1964).
6. Watson, D. J., and Romanoff, E. B., *J. Chromatog.* **22,** 192 (1966).
7. Allen, W. M., *J. Clin. Endocrin.* **10,** 71 (1950).
8. Short, R. V., *in* "Hormones in Blood" (C. H. Gray and A. L. Bacharach, eds.), p. 379. Academic Press, New York-London, 1961.
9. Zander, J., *in* "Methods in Hormone Research" (R. I. Dorfman, ed.), p. 91. Academic Press, New York-London, 1962.
10. Short, R. V., and Eton, B., *J. Endocrin.* **18,** 418 (1959).
11. Short, R. V., *J. Endocrin.* **16,** 415 (1958).
12. Bush, I. E., *Recent Progr. Hormone Res.* **9,** 321 (1954).
13. Bartosik, D. B., unpublished data.
14. Bush, I. E., *in* "The Biosynthesis and Secretion of Adrenocortical Steroids" (F. Clark and J. K. Grant, eds.), p. 19. Cambridge University Press, London, 1960.
15. Hagopian, M., Pincus, G., Carlo, J., and Romanoff, E. B., *Endocrinology* **58,** 387 (1956).
16. Romanoff, E. B., and Watson, D. J., unpublished data.
17. Collins, W. P., and Sommerville, I. F., *Nature* **203,** 836 (1964).
18. Lurie, A. O., Villee, C. A., and Reid, D. E., *J. Clin. Endocrin.* **26,** 742 (1966).

ANALYTICAL BIOCHEMISTRY 20, 246–257 (1967)

Separation and Quantitation of Lactic Dehydrogenase Isoenzymes by Disc Electrophoresis

ALBERT A. DIETZ AND TINA LUBRANO

Research Service, Veterans Administration Hospital, Hines, Illinois 60141

Received January 23, 1967

Several methods of electrophoresis have been applied to the separation and estimation of the lactic dehydrogenase (LDH) isoenzymes of serum. They include the use of paper (1, 2), starch gel (3), agar gel (4–11), and cellulose acetate strips (12–15). The disc electrophoresis method of Davis (16), developed for the separation of serum proteins, has certain advantages. The time for separation is short, the proteins are generally resolved into sharp bands, and the resulting gel is clear permitting the ready quantitation of the bands.

In trying to apply the disc electrophoresis method (16) to the separation of the LDH isoenzymes, we found, as did Matson (17) and Schrauwen (18), that the resolution was incomplete. We have modified the method to obtain consistently excellent separations of the five isoenzymes. We report here the details of the modifications, data to substantiate the conditions selected, and values obtained for normal serums. A preliminary report has been given (19).

MATERIALS

Where possible, the nomenclature of Davis (16) has been retained.

Solution A. Dissolve 48 ml 1 *N* HCl, 36.3 gm Tris, and 0.23 ml *N,N,N′,N′*-tetramethylethylenediamine in water to make 100 ml of solution, pH 8.9.

Solution C. Dissolve 30 gm acrylamide and 0.8 gm *N,N′*-methylenebisacrylamide in water to make 100 ml of solution. Solutions *A* and *C* are stable for many months if stored in a brown bottle at 5°.

Ammonium persulfate. Prepare weekly a solution containing 140 mg $(NH_4)_2S_2O_8$/100 ml aqueous solution.

Prepare a 7.5% *gel solution* by mixing 2 ml solution *A*, 4 ml solution *C*, 2 ml water, and 8 ml ammonium persulfate solution. Dilute 11 ml of this solution with 4 ml of water to prepare a 5.5% gel. This is sufficient for 12 tubes.

Photo Flo 600, Eastman Kodak Company. Prepare a 1:600 dilution with water.

Sucrose. Dissolve 40 gm sucrose/100 ml aqueous solution.

Serum. Dilute normal serum 1:1 with 40% sucrose, and serums with elevated LDH activities according to their total activity.

Electrophoresis buffer. Dissolve 6 gm Tris and 28.8 gm glycine in water to make 1 liter of solution. Store this buffer at 5° and dilute 10 times for use, pH 8.3.

Bromphenol blue. Dissolve 10 mg bromphenol blue in 1 liter water.

Staining solution. The staining solution of van der Helm (20) was modified by substituting NaCl for NaCN. This resulted in less background staining. The stock solutions and the volumes used are (NAD = nicotinamide-adenine dinucleotide):

Stock solution	Amount used, ml
Sodium lactate, *M*	1.0
NAD, 10 mg/ml	1.0
NaCl, 0.1 *M*	1.0
$MgCl_2$, 5 m*M*	1.0
Phosphate buffer, 0.5 *M*, pH 7.4	2.5
Nitroblue tetrazolium, 1 mg/ml	2.5
Phenazine methosulfate, 1 mg/ml	0.25

The stock solutions, with the exception of the NAD, are stable for long periods when stored at 5° in the dark. The NAD solution is prepared weekly.

A Canalco model 12 electrophoresis cell was used for electrophoresis, and their model E densitometer for the quantitation.

METHOD

1. Rinse sections of clean tubing, 63 mm long and with an i.d. of 7 mm, with Photo Flo solution and let them air dry. Fill them to a 42 mm mark with freshly prepared 5.5% gel solution and overlay the solution with water. After the solution has gelled, decant the water and blot with the twisted end of a facial tissue.
2. Mark each tube exactly 35 mm below the surface of the gel.
3. Add 10 μl of diluted serum and 30 μl of 40% sucrose.
4. Overlay the sample-sucrose with freshly prepared 5.5 or 7% gel solution and allow it to gel under a layer of water.
5. Shake off the water and place the tubes in the grommets of the electrophoretic cell. Transfer to a refrigerator at 5° and add cold diluted buffer to the electrode vessels. Add 7 ml bromophenol blue solution to the cathode chamber.
6. Run the electrophoresis at 50 V and 2.5 mA/tube until the albumin has migrated to the 35 mm mark, about 45 min.

7. Rim the gels according to the method of Reisfeld *et al.* (21) and transfer them to 75 × 10 mm culture tubes. Cover the gels with 2.3 ml staining solution and incubate them at 37°.

8. When the gels are adequately stained, 0.75–2 hr, wash them with tap water and place them in 7.5% acetic acid.

9. Quantitate the isoenzyme bands with a Canalco model E or other suitable densitometer. Use a Wratten X-1 filter in the light path.

The band moving farthest toward the anode is designated as LDH-1 and the slowest moving band LDH-5. For some comparative purposes, the total muscle monomer (M-LDH) was calculated. This calculation is based on the tetramer structure of LDH with bands 1 through 5 containing 0, 25, 50, 75, and 100%, respectively, of the M-LDH (22). Total LDH activity was determined by the method of Henry *et al.* (23). The normal serum LDH activity is 206 ± 52 μmoles/min/liter at 37°.

Notes on the method: Commercially obtainable chemicals are satisfactory for the gel preparation. The 5.5% gel takes about 35 min to polymerize. We have prepared gels as long as a week before use and find them satisfactory provided they have not dried.

Even though the same depth of polyacrylamide is gelled, the exact height of the column may vary a few mm. It is, therefore, important to mark the tube accurately 35 mm below the surface of the gel, after the water is blotted off. When the albumin–dye marker reaches the 35 mm mark in a specific tube, the current to that tube is stopped by inserting a plastic rod into the top of the grommet. The current is reduced in proportion to the number of plugs inserted. In this way very reproducible results are obtained.

The sample and the sucrose can be added together or separately, though we have observed slightly better results when they are added separately. By polymerizing a gel over the sample, the procedure up to this point can be done at room temperature. It has the further advantage in that migrations toward the cathode can be detected. However, the upper gel can be omitted, in which case the tubes after Step 2 are inserted into the grommets of the electrode vessel at 5°, the cold buffer added, and the air bubbles removed. The sample–sucrose solution is then injected with a syringe directly onto the upper surface of the separating gel.

The stained gels may be stored up to one week at 5° in 7.5% acetic acid without fading, but will fade after one day at room temperature.

In densitometry, a clear portion of the gel is used for adjusting the meter control so that the integrator rarely clicks when set at 4 mm^2/integration. Both the 4 and 20 mm^2 settings are used, depending on the density of the individual bands. The recorder can be run at the slowest speed.

RESULTS AND DISCUSSION

Stacking Gel and Gel Concentration. In the original method of Davis (16), a stacking gel was used. When this was tried, only 4 bands could be demonstrated in serum. In Figure 1, gels B, D, and F show examples of this. When the stacking gel was omitted as described in this paper, the separations seen in gels A, C, and E result. Five bands are clearly shown in the separating gel. Gels A and B were 7% and the others 5.5%.

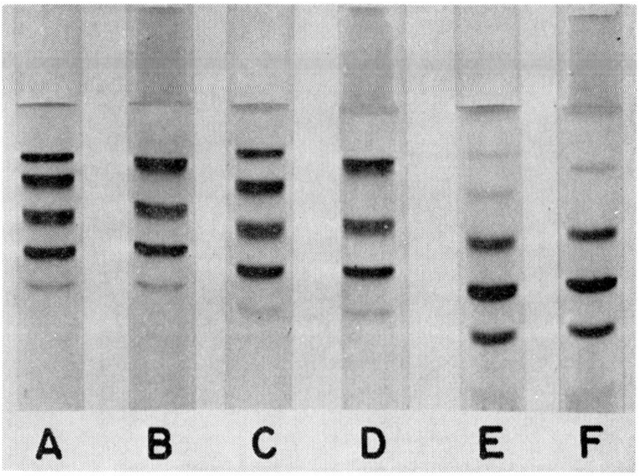

FIG. 1. Effect of gel concentration and stacking gel on the LDH isoenzyme separation in serum. A 7% gel was used in A and B and a 5.5% gel in C–F. Separations in B, D, and F were achieved with the use of a stacking gel (16), and in A, C, and E with the method described in this paper. In gels A–D, 10 μl of a 1:10 dilution of a pathological serum (6750 μmoles/min/liter at 37°) was applied, and in gels E and F, 10 μl of a 1:1 dilution of a normal serum. Because of the dilution of the serum applied, the albumin–dye front could not be seen in gels A–D and so the dye front was used to stop the electrophoresis at the 35 mm mark. For this reason the migrations in C and D are a little shorter than in E and F.

It will be noted that the spacing is less uniform and the total migration shorter in the 7% gel. The 5.5% gel usually had less background than the 7% gel. For these reasons, 5.5% gel was used for the remainder of the work. The bands that appear to be a combination of LDH-4 and -5 when the stacking gel was used were 10, 7, and 1.5% less than the sum of the two bands in the corresponding gels A, C and E.

"Nothing" Dehydrogenase. All the gels in Figure 1 show a band at the top of the separating gel. This has been erroneously called LDH-5 by

some (24). When lactate is omitted from the staining solution, the band still appears, as seen in Figure 2. This band, the "nothing" dehydrogenase, has been considered to be alcohol dehydrogenase (25) or protein sulfhydryl groups (26). Figure 2 also shows diffuse staining throughout the gels stained without lactate which may be due to protein sulfhydryl groups. The background stain is unusually intense in these examples as the staining time was purposely prolonged. Ordinarily in the method outlined the background staining is minimal.

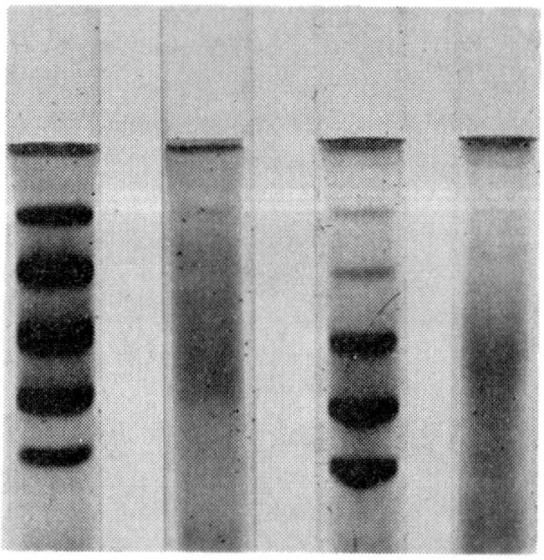

FIG. 2. "Nothing" dehydrogenase. The first and third gels represent a pathological and a normal serum, respectively, separated and stained as described in this paper. In the other 2 gels, the lactate was omitted from the staining solution.

Sucrose Concentration. The use of 40% sucrose solution is a necessary part of the present procedure. Hjertén *et al.* (27) have shown that a solution with a low electrolyte concentration imparts a stacking effect. Narayan *et al.* (28, 29) used both a stacking gel and a sucrose solution and Broome (30) used a sucrose/Sephadex G-200 mixture. To determine the optimum sucrose concentration, a series of gels were run with 0–50 μl of 40% sucrose added to the sample. The results are seen in Figure 3. Volumes of less than 20 μl did not give a proper resolution of LDH-4 and -5. The gels with 20–50 μl have a similar appearance, and densitometry shows the same distribution of the isoenzymes. We have routinely used 30 μl/tube.

Storage of Serum. It is generally agreed that LDH-5 is not stable on storage, but there is disagreement on the best method of storage. Kreutzer and Fennis (31) found storage at room temperature superior to storage at 0° or −10°. Chilson *et al.* (32) have found that, after rapid freezing at −65° and rapid thawing, about 10% of the LDH activity is lost. Rabinowitz (33) has found that leucocyte LDH is stable if the cells are rapidly frozen and stored at −98°. Grieff and Kelly (34) find it advantageous to slowly freeze (1°/min) beef heart LDH.

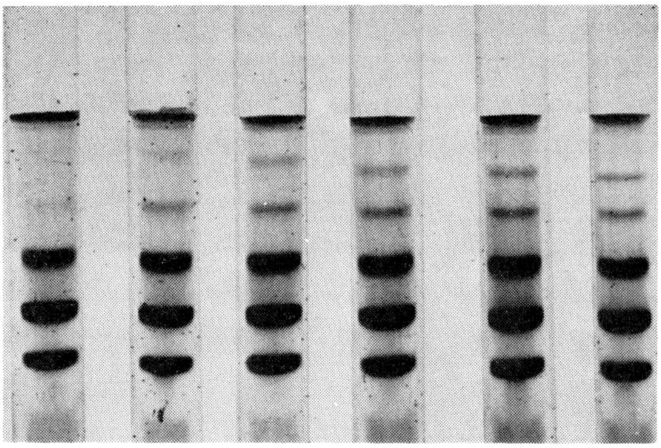

FIG. 3. Effect of sucrose concentration on separation of serum LDH isoenzymes. 10 μl of diluted normal serum was used for each gel. From left to right, 0, 10, 20, 30, 40, and 50 μl of 40% sucrose was applied after the sample.

We have studied the effect of storage at various temperatures on the total activity and isoenzyme pattern of several serums, using room temperature, 5°, —20°, and —65°. The results are given in Figure 4, where the change in the isoenzyme pattern is indicated in the percentage of the M-LDH. We find that there is some loss of activity no matter how the serum is stored. During the first day the loss is least at room temperature. Freezing at —65° led to a 10% loss in agreement with the findings of

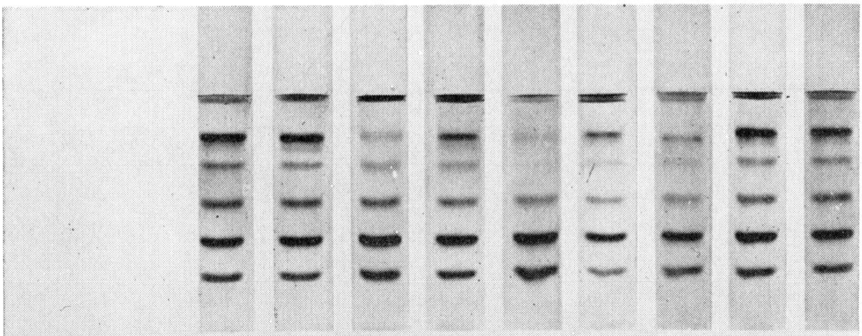

Temperature, °		25	25	5	5	-20	-20	-65	-65
Days	0	1	7	7	35	7	35	7	35
Total LDH	480	458		347	302	362	273	424	383
M-LDH %	55	54	32	28		47	34	54	49

FIG. 4. Effect of storage temperature on LDH activity and isoenzyme distribution of serum. A pathological serum was used as a source of a high LDH-5. The fresh serum assayed 480 μmoles/min/liter at 37°.

Chilson *et al.* (32). The loss appeared to be in all isoenzymes as there was no difference in their distribution. With storage at —65°, a small change in the isoenzyme pattern was noted after 5 weeks. The losses were greatest in the isoenzymes containing the most muscle monomer.

TABLE 1
Effect of Freezing on the Distribution of LDH Isoenzymes of Normal Serum, $N = 6^a$

Serum	% LDH isoenzymes ± S.D. LDH-1	LDH-2	LDH-3	LDH-4	LDH-5	% M-LDH
Fresh	30.1 ± 4.08	46.4 ± 3.92	19.8 ± 2.33	2.9 ± 0.74	0.8 ± 0.32	24.5 ± 1.33
Frozen	31.0 ± 4.11	46.2 ± 3.17	18.8 ± 3.09	3.2 ± 0.37	0.8 ± 0.29	24.2 ± 1.66

The electrophoresis was done the same day the blood was drawn. The remaining serum was frozen at −65° and thawed for electrophoresis 24 hr after. No significant difference was found for any of the fractions when calculated for paired data.
[a] N = Number of serums.

Normal serums stored at —65° for several months and repeatedly frozen and thawed show a 10% loss in total LDH after the first freezing, but no change in the isoenzyme distribution. Table 1 shows that the freezing of 6 normal serums for 1 day at —65° had no effect on the isoenzyme distribution. Some pathological serums could be stored longer than others. This greater stability of some serums may be due to their NAD content since Zondag (35) has shown that the addition of NAD to muscle homogenates preserves LDH-5 at —20°.

TABLE 2
Reproducibility of the Serum LDH Isoenzyme Patterns

No.	% LDH isoenzymes ± S.D. LDH-1	LDH-2	LDH-3	LDH-4	LDH-5	% M-LDH
6	27.6 ± 0.82	45.6 ± 1.01	22.0 ± 0.68	2.9 ± 0.38	1.9 ± 0.37	26.4 ± 0.66
6	19.1 ± 2.02	32.0 ± 2.18	25.3 ± 0.91	11.9 ± 1.53	11.7 ± 1.57	41.1 ± 1.66
7	7.2 ± 0.82	25.7 ± 2.18	35.4 ± 1.40	19.3 ± 1.03	12.4 ± 1.79	51.0 ± 1.09

In each case the replica determinations were done simultaneously. The first row represents a normal serum and the other 2 abnormal samples. See also Table 4.

Reproducibility. Several samples were run repeatedly and the results are given in Table 2. The standard deviations are within acceptable limits.

The precision of the densitometry is indicated in Table 3. For this, a single stained sample was analyzed 8 times, each time with a resetting of the densitometer and with different chart speeds and integrator rates. Again the standard deviations are within acceptable limits.

Sample size and staining time. The effect of varying the sample size is shown in Figure 5 for normal serum and Figure 6 for a pathological serum. In these cases, there was no difference in the distribution of the isoenzymes as determined by densitometry. We generally used 10 μl of a 1:1 dilution of normal serum for routine work and pathological serums were diluted according to their total activity. The staining time can partly correct for misjudgment in sample application.

TABLE 3
Reproducibility of Densitometry on a Single Gel, $N = 8$

	LDH-1	LDH-2	LDH-3	LDH-4	LDH-5
Mean, %	4.58	34.74	38.34	12.40	9.98
S.D., %	0.61	1.69	1.81	1.25	1.61
C.V.,[a] %	13.4	4.9	4.7	10.1	16.1

[a] C.V. = coefficient of variation.

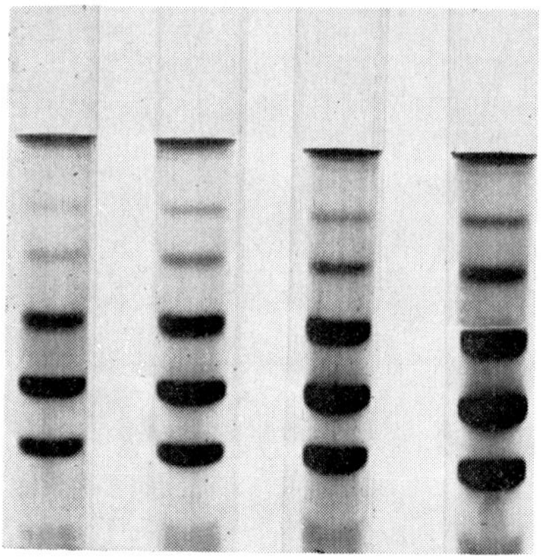

FIG. 5. Effect of sample size on LDH isoenzyme distribution in a normal serum. From left to right, 5, 10, 15, and 20 μl of a 1:1 dilution of serum (186 μmoles/min/liter at 37°) was applied. Staining time was 1.5 hr at 37°.

When the sample size is too great or the staining time too long, experience has shown that the less concentrated bands increase in percentage at the expense of the most concentrated ones. This is perhaps due to an exhaustion of the substrate in the region of the more concentrated isoenzymes and is shown in Table 4. We consider 90 min as the optimum staining time and do not stain for less than 45 min or more than 2 hr.

Comparison with cellulose acetate electrophoresis. For this purpose leucocyte extracts were used (36) as they conveniently gave preparations with variable isoenzyme patterns. Sepraphore III strips were used, and the LDH bands were quantitated either with cleared strips on a Densi-

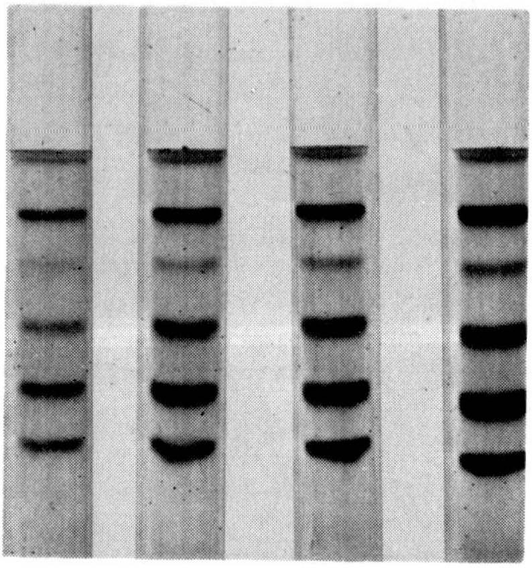

FIG. 6. Effect of sample size on isoenzyme distribution in a pathological serum (1000 μmoles/min/liter at 37°). From left to right, 5, 10, 15, and 20 μl of a 1:5 dilution of serum was applied. Staining time was 1 hr at 37°.

cord instrument fitted with a green filter or by dissolving the bands in a 1:1 mixture of methanol/acetic acid. Results by the former method are given in Table 5. LDH-2 and LDH-3 were higher on disc electrophoresis, and LDH-4 and LDH-5 lower. Part of this difference may result from

TABLE 4
Effect of Prolonging Staining Time on Distribution of the LDH Isoenzymes of a Normal Serum

		% LDH isoenzymes ± S.D.				
Staining time, hr	No.	LDH-1	LDH-2	LDH-3	LDH-4	LDH-5
1.5	8	30.0 ± 1.0	44.2 ± 1.6	22.2 ± 1.3	2.9 ± 0.4	0.7 ± 0.3
2	4	30.5 ± 0.8	39.5 ± 2.8	24.1 ± 2.0	4.4 ± 1.1	1.6 ± 0.5
t		0.95	3.15	1.71	2.77	3.08
p		0.4	0.01	0.2	0.025	0.01

10 μl of a 1:1 dilution of normal serum with a LDH activity of 181 μmoles/min/liter at 37° was used. t = Student's t-distribution. p = probability.

inclusion of the "nothing" dehydrogenase in the LDH-4 and 5 region on the cellulose strips.

Normal values. Average values for the LDH isoenzymes of 20 normal serums are given in Table 6. As expected, the standard deviations of the more active LDH isoenzymes are higher than found in the replicate determinations given in Tables 2 and 3. The values obtained are similar to those reported by others (3, 7, 11–15) using paper, starch, and agar electrophoresis. Other groups (1, 2, 4, 10) have reported higher values for

TABLE 5
Comparison of Disc Electrophoresis with Cellulose Acetate and Densicord Quantitation (differences in %, disc—cellulose acetate, $N = 7$)

	LDH-1	LDH-2	LDH-3	LDH-4	LDH-5
Mean of differences of paired experiments	0	6.26	8.14	−8.63	−4.60
S.D.	7.4	3.18	3.27	2.32	1.26
p	N.S.	<0.01	<0.001	<0.001	<0.01

p = probability. N.S. = not significant.

LDH-4 and LDH-5; perhaps some of these results are due to relative substrate exhaustion, as mentioned earlier.

The densitometry record for a normal serum is shown in Figure 7 and for a pathological serum in Figure 8. For the small peaks 4 squares were

TABLE 6
Distribution of the LDH Isoenzymes in Normal Serums, $N = 20$

	LDH-1	LDH-2	LDH-3	LDH-4	LDH-5	M-LDH
Mean, %	32.7	45.1	18.5	2.9	0.85	24.1
S.D.	4.60	3.53	2.69	0.86	0.55	2.95
C.V., %	14.1	7.8	14.5	29.7	64.7	12.2

The average ratio of LDH-2/LDH-1 is 1.42 ± 0.31.

counted per integration, and for the large peaks, 20 squares. These records are typical and we had no difficulty in obtaining reproducibility, largely due to the care taken in obtaining a uniform distance of migration and in avoiding overstaining of bands.

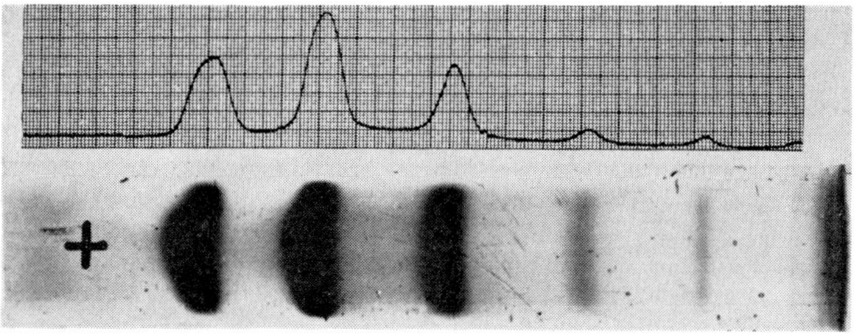

FIG. 7. Densitometry of LDH distribution of a normal serum. The Canalco model E microdensitometer was used in this and the following figure, but the integrations are not shown.

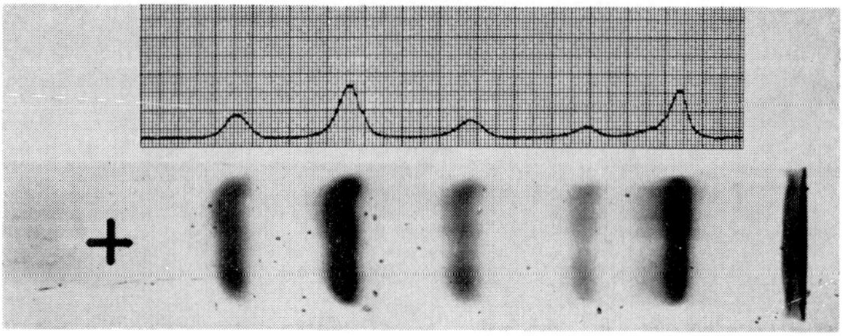

FIG. 8. Densitometry of LDH distribution of a pathological serum. See Figure 7. Same serum as in Figure 4.

SUMMARY

The disc electrophoresis method of Davis (16) does not permit the separation of all 5 isoenzymes of LDH. The method was modified by omitting the stacking and sample gels, and substituting 40% sucrose solution. All 5 isoenzyme fractions then migrate into the separating gel.

The material staining at the surface of the separating gel is shown to be "nothing" dehydrogenase.

By accurately marking the distance the albumin–dye or the dye front is to migrate, excellent reproducibility of the isoenzyme separation can be achieved. The separations are such that there is no doubt as to the identification of the individual bands, and quantitation can readily be achieved.

ACKNOWLEDGMENTS

We wish to acknowledge the aid given by Dr. H. M. Rubinstein of the Medical Service, and to thank Mr. Robert Kostro of the Medical Illustrations Department for the care he took in photographing the gels.

REFERENCES

1. RAABO, E., *Scand. J. Clin. Lab. Invest.* **15,** 405 (1963).
2. MOLLER, C. E., AND RAABO, E., *Acta Med. Scand.* **175,** 31 (1964).
3. WROBLEWSKI, F., ROSS, C., AND GREGORY, K., *N. Engl. J. Med.* **263,** 531 (1960).
4. BERGERMAN, J., *Clin. Chem.* **12,** 797 (1966).
5. BLANCHAER, M. C., *Clin. Chim. Acta* **6,** 272 (1961).
6. COHEN, L., DJORDJEVICH, J., AND ORMISTE, V., *J. Lab. Clin. Med.* **64,** 355 (1964).
7. VAN DER HELM, H. J., *Clin. Chim. Acta* **7,** 124 (1962).
8. KREUTZER, H. H., AND EGGELS, P. H., *Clin. Chim. Acta* **12,** 80 (1965).
9. RESSLER, N., SCHULZ, J., AND JOSEPH, R. R., *J. Lab. Clin. Med.* **62,** 571 (1963).
10. STARKWEATHER, W. H., SPENCER, H. H., SCHWARZ, E. L., AND SCHOCH, H. K., *J. Lab. Clin. Med.* **67,** 329 (1966).
11. WRIGHT, E. J., CAWLEY, L. P., AND EBERHARDT, L., *Am. J. Clin. Pathol.* **45,** 737 (1966).
12. BARNETT, H., *J. Clin. Pathol.* **17,** 567 (1964).

13. Mager, M., Blatt, W. F., and Abelmann, W. H., *Clin. Chim. Acta* **14,** 689 (1966).
14. Opher, A. W., Collier, C. S., and Miller, J. M., *Clin. Chem.* **12,** 308 (1966).
15. Preston, J. A., Briere, R. O., and Batsakis, J. G., *Am. J. Clin. Pathol.* **43,** 256 (1965).
16. Davis, B. J., *Ann. N. Y. Acad. Sci.* **121,** 404 (1964).
17. Matson, C. F., *Abstracts,* American Chemical Society meeting, Sept. 9–13, 1963, p. 86c.
18. Schrauwen, J., *J. Chromatog.* **23,** 177 (1966).
19. Dietz, A. A., and Lubrano, T., N. Y. Academy of Sciences, Meeting on the "Multiple Molecular Forms of Enzymes," Dec. 1–3, 1966.
20. van der Helm, H. J., *Lancet* **2,** 108 (1961).
21. Reisfeld, R. A., Lewis, U. J., and Williams, D. E., *Nature* **195,** 281 (1962).
22. Markert, C. L., *Science* **140,** 1329 (1963).
23. Henry, R. J., Chiamori, N., Golub, O. J., and Berkman, S., *Am. J. Clin. Pathol.* **34,** 381 (1960).
24. Konda, H., "Disc Electrophoresis Information Service," Canal Industrial Corp., Bethesda, 1966, Abstr. No. 382.
25. Shaw, C. R., and Koen, A. L., *J. Histochem. Cytochem.* **13,** 431 (1965).
26. Katz, A. M., and Kalow, W., *Can. J. Biochem.* **43,** 1653 (1965).
27. Hjertén, S., Jerstedt, S., and Tiselius, A., *Anal. Biochem.* **11,** 211 (1965).
28. Narayan, K. A., Narayan, S., and Kummerow, F. A., *J. Chromatog.* **16,** 187 (1964).
29. Narayan, K. A., Narayan, S., and Kummerow, F. A., *Clin. Chim. Acta* **14,** 227 (1966).
30. Broome, J., *Nature* **199,** 179 (1963).
31. Kreutzer, H. H., and Fennis, W. H. S., *Clin. Chim. Acta* **9,** 64 (1964).
32. Chilson, O. P., Costello, L. A., and Kaplan, N. O., *Federation Proc.* **24,** S-55 (1965).
33. Rabinowitz, Y., *Blood* **27,** 470 (1966).
34. Greiff, D., and Kelly, R. T., *Cryobiology* **2,** 335 (1966).
35. Zondag, H. A., *Science* **142,** 965 (1963).
36. Rabinowitz, Y., and Dietz, A. A., *Blood* **29,** 182 (1967).

ANALYTICAL BIOCHEMISTRY 20, 258–274 (1967)

Analysis of Neutral Sugars by Gas-Liquid Chromatography of Alditol Acetates:

Application to Thyrotropic Hormone and Other Glycoproteins[1]

JE H. KIM,[2] BASUDEV SHOME, TA-HSIU LIAO, AND JOHN G. PIERCE

Department of Biological Chemistry, UCLA School of Medicine, Los Angeles, California 90024

Received January 23, 1967

Although gas-liquid chromatography has been successful in the analysis of carbohydrates (1, 2), few descriptions of its application to the analysis of the oligosaccharides of glycoproteins have appeared. The chromatography of the trimethylsilyl ethers (3) of constitutent monosaccharides of glycoproteins has been described (4, 5); this approach, however, has the disadvantage that it may require separation and measurement of as many as four derivatives of each sugar, which result from anomer formation and ring isomerization. An approach which circumvents isomerization is that described recently by Sawardeker, Sloneker, and Jeanes (6), who separated synthetic mixtures of the common monosaccharides after their conversion to alditol acetates. This paper reports application and adaptation of the gas chromatography of alditol acetates to the analysis of the neutral sugars of several glycoproteins with special emphasis on the pituitary thyroid-stimulating hormone (TSH).[3] Because only small amounts of many glycoproteins are obtainable, a procedure was devised to permit hexosamine analysis of the same hydrolyzate by ion-exchange chromatography. To test accuracy and reproducibility, two well-characterized glycoproteins, thyroglobulin and ovalbumin, were analyzed. The results show that analyses equivalent to those in the literature can be easily obtained with only one or two milligrams of glycoprotein.

The carbohydrate composition of bovine TSH has been studied by

[1] Supported in part by a grant (No. C-2290) from the National Cancer Institute of the United States Public Health Service and Cancer Research Funds of the University of California.

[2] Present address: Wilson Laboratories, Chicago, Illinois.

[3] Abbreviations used: TSH, thyroid-stimulating hormone; DEAE-, diethylaminoethyl-; CM-, carboxymethyl-.

conventional methods and it was found to contain fucose, mannose, glucosamine, and galactosamine (7). All sugars appeared to be in a single oligosaccharide moiety covalently linked to the protein. Galactose was not found in significant amounts, but the question of the presence of galactose in the hormone arose recently when enzymic degradation of the glycopeptide from TSH showed galactose as well as fucose and mannose to be released (8).

METHODS AND MATERIALS

Chromatography. The gas chromatograph was a model 1609, F & M Scientific Corporation, Avondale, Pennsylvania, and was equipped with a hydrogen flame detector. Columns were stainless steel (10 ft by 0.125 in. o.d.), and were packed with Gas Chrom Q, 60–80 mesh, precoated with 3% ECNSS-M, an organosilicone polyester phase resulting from the combination of ethylene glycol succinate and a silicone of a cyanoethyl type (6) (prepared by Applied Science Laboratories, State College, Pennsylvania). The chromatography was carried out isothermally at 175° with an injection port temperature of 300° and a detector temperature of 215°. The carrier gas was helium with a flow of 45–50 ml/min. The detector settings were: range 10, attenuation 2×, 4×, or 8×. These permitted measurement of each sugar in amounts of 0.1–2 μg. Peak areas were measured by planimetry.

Glucose and, in some experiments, galactosamine and norleucine, were introduced prior to hydrolysis as internal standards and were obtained from Mann Research Laboratories, New York. To calibrate the detector and calculate results (6), a standard curve was prepared by chromatographing different amounts of fucose, mannose, and galactose with the amount of the internal standard, glucose, held constant, both with and without subjecting the sugars to the hydrolytic conditions before derivative formation.

The ion-exchange chromatography of hexosamines was done on a Spinco model MS amino acid analyzer either with the 15 cm column for basic amino acids (9) or on the 50 cm column (10) with the buffer change made after 125 min.

Preparation of Samples. An outline of the preparation of the sample for both gas-liquid and ion-exchange chromatography is shown in Scheme 1. In most experiments, 2 mg of glycoprotein was hydrolyzed in 1.5 ml of 0.25 N sulfuric acid plus 200 mg of Dowex 50-X12, 200–400 mesh (H^+ form). The internal standards (50 μg of glucose, 50 μg of galactosamine, and 25 μg of norleucine) were added in 0.2 ml of water and the mixture was hydrolyzed at 100° in an evacuated sealed tube. The usual time of hydrolysis was 24 hr and the tubes were rotated in an oven to give con-

SCHEME 1
Preparations of samples for chromatography

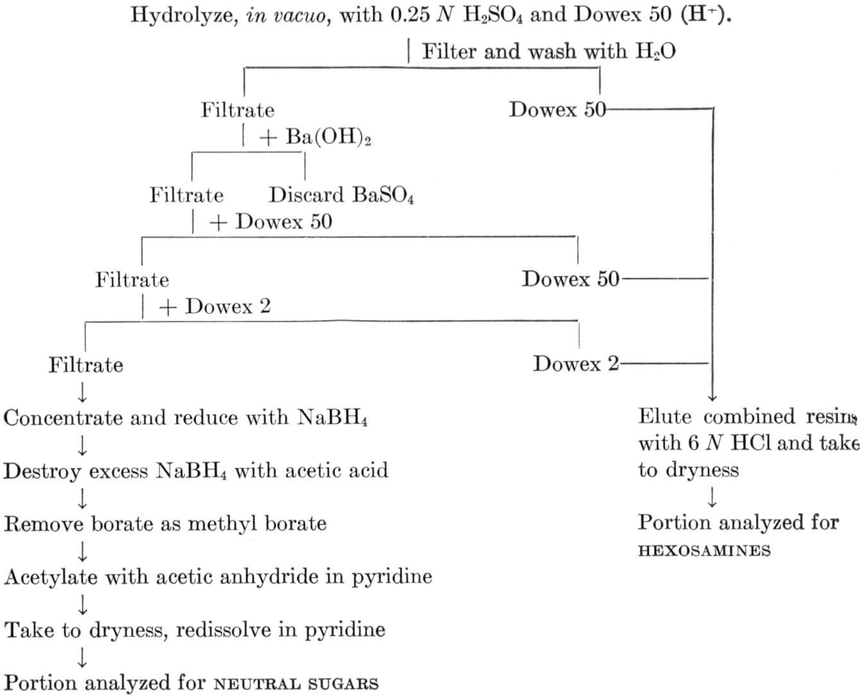

stant stirring. After hydrolysis, the resin was removed by filtration through a small column (0.6 × 10 cm, e.g., a disposable capillary pipet) with a glass wool plug at the tapered end and was washed with glass-distilled water. The filtrate was brought to pH 5.0–5.5 with saturated barium hydroxide solution. The precipitate was removed by centrifugation and washed twice with hot water. The supernatant and washings were then passed through a second column containing about 100 mg of Dowex 50-X12 (H^+) and finally through a small amount (10–20 mg) of Dowex 2 (×8 cross link, 200–400 mesh, formate form) to exchange any remaining anions. These resins were combined with that used for hydrolysis and stored at —20° until the hexosamine analysis.

The solution, which was tested for absence of amino acids by spotting a drop on paper and reacting with ninhydrin, was then freeze-dried and, redissolved in 0.5 ml of water, and sodium borohydride dissolved in 0.1 ml of water was added dropwise at 0°. The amount of borohydride was calculated on the basis of 5 mg/mg of the estimated amount of monosaccharides. The solutions were stored overnight at 4° and then the excess borohydride was destroyed by addition of glacial acetic acid. The solution was passed through a column of about 50 mg of Dowex 50 (H^+) to remove sodium ions. The effluent and washings were taken to dryness on a rotary evaporator; 3 ml of absolute methanol was added; the solution was brought to 50° for 30 sec and then taken to dryness at room temperature. This procedure, which removes the borate as methyl borate, was carried out twice again.

The sugar alcohols were acetylated by refluxing (bath temperature 100°C) for 20 min in the presence of 300 μl of pyridine and 200 μl of acetic anhydride. The reaction products were transferred to a micro centrifuge tube and dried *in vacuo* over NaOH and H_2SO_4. The sample was redissolved in pyridine (10–20 μg of estimated total carbohydrate per microliter of pyridine) and samples of 0.3–0.5 μl injected into the gas chromatograph. One milligram of glycoprotein yielded sufficient material for several replicate injections. When sample size was other than 2 mg, the amounts of sulfuric acid and Dowex 50 were changed proportionately.

For hexosamine analysis, the combined resins were eluted in a small column with 10 ml of 6 *N* HCl; 5 ml was taken to dryness and a suitable aliquot placed on the amino acid analyzer.

Glycoprotein Preparations. The properties of the bovine TSH and thyroglobulin have been described (7, 11–13). The biological potency of the bovine TSH is approximately 20 USP units/mg; samples were also rechromatographed on both DEAE- and CM-cellulose. Porcine TSH (20 USP units/mg) was isolated from whole glands exactly as described for bovine material (7, 11). The porcine hormone showed similar polymorphism on gel electrophoresis to that of bovine TSH (14) and had an almost identical mobility at pH 9.5. Human TSH (15) was prepared from a concentrate of human pituitaries kindly supplied by Dr. Harold Elrick, Veterans Administration, Denver, Colorado. The material analyzed (approximately 10 USP units/mg) was one of two biologically active fractions obtained by chromatography on DEAE-cellulose which was followed by chromatography on CM-cellulose (7). In gel electrophoresis these fractions also showed polymorphism but were more electronegative at pH 9.5 than bovine TSH. Crystalline ovalbumin (recrystallized 5 times) was from Sigma Chemical Co. Rechromatography of ovalbumin was carried out on CM-cellulose as described by Rhodes *et al.* (16). Orosomucoid was a gift of Drs. Henry Weimer and W. A. Krotoski. Heterothyrotropic factor (17) was kindly supplied by Dr. Yves Fontaine. Prolactin was a gift of the Endocrine Study Section, National Institutes of Health.

RESULTS

To investigate loss of sugars during hydrolysis and derivatization, samples of standards were hydrolyzed in both the presence and the absence of prolactin, a protein containing no carbohydrate. Analyses of

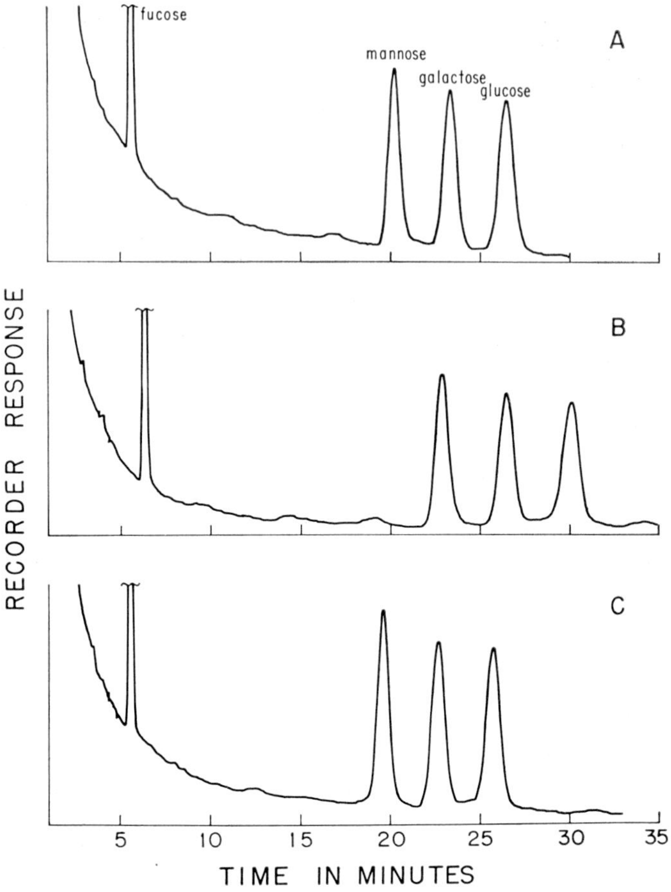

FIG. 1. Gas chromatograms of mixtures of known sugars: (A) 50 μg of each sugar not subjected to the hydrolytic conditions but added to 0.25 N sulfuric acid and carried through the deionization and derivatization. Volume of final pyridine solution, 20 μl; 0.5 μl injected into chromatograph; range, 10; attenuation, 2×. (B) Same as above but subjected to hydrolysis conditions for 24 hr. (C) Same as above but with 2 mg of prolactin added before hydrolysis. The differences in absolute retention times are due to variations in carrier gas flow rate and because all samples were not run on the same column. The peaks emerge in the order: fucose, mannose, galactose, and glucose.

these samples were then compared with those of standards not subjected to the hydrolytic conditions but dissolved in 0.25 M sulfuric acid and carried through deionization and derivative formation. Figure 1 shows clearly that no qualitative differences result from subjecting the mixtures of the sugars to the procedure and that no spurious peaks result from hydrolysis in the presence of protein. Fucose emerges first followed by

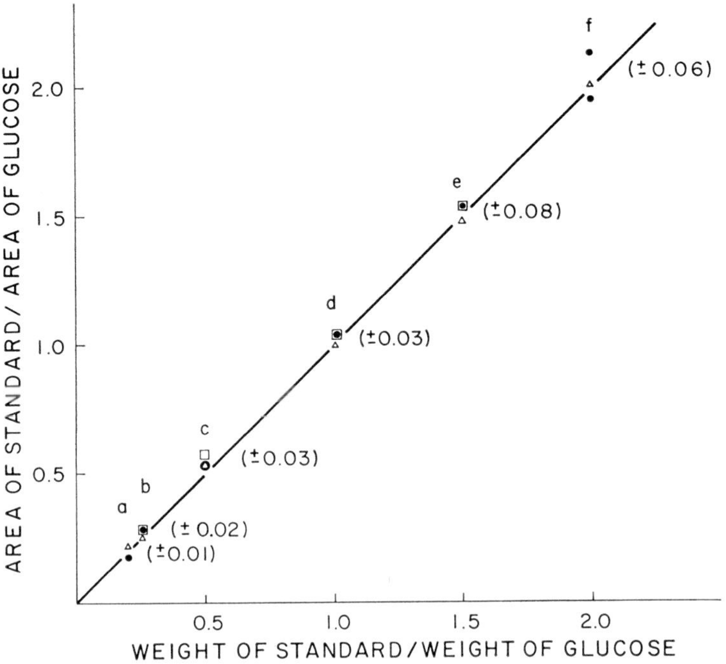

FIG. 2. Calibration curve for fucose (□), mannose (●), and galactose (△) with glucose as an internal standard. Values at *a, b,* and *d* are from analysis of 50 μg of glucose plus the other sugars in the ratios indicated on the abcissa. These samples were subjected to the hydrolysis conditions together with 2 mg of prolactin. Values at *c, e,* and *f* represent 50 μg of glucose plus other sugars not subjected to hydrolysis conditions (except for the lower mannose value at *f*). Each symbol represents the mean of 5–6 injections and the figures in parentheses give the *largest* standard error of the mean for any of the individual sugars at that ratio. Analyses at the same ratios as shown at point *d* but without prolactin did not differ significantly from the data shown. The range setting in these determinations was 10, attenuation 2×.

mannose, galactose and glucose. The data given in Figure 2 show no significant losses of any sugar relative to the internal standard. Runs were included in which quantities of fucose and galactose were low relative to mannose, thus mimicking the proportions of these sugars suspected to be in TSH. Chromatography of a known amount of the crystalline hexaacetate of mannitol (18) showed the over-all recovery of sugars carried through the entire procedure to be in excess of 85%.

Figure 3 shows typical elution profiles of the neutral sugars of human thyroglobulins obtained from a pool of glands from normal subjects and from an individual with a multinodular nonmalignant goiter. The upper curve shows no glucose to be present in hydrolyzates of thyroglobulin when the internal standard was not added, a fact also established for

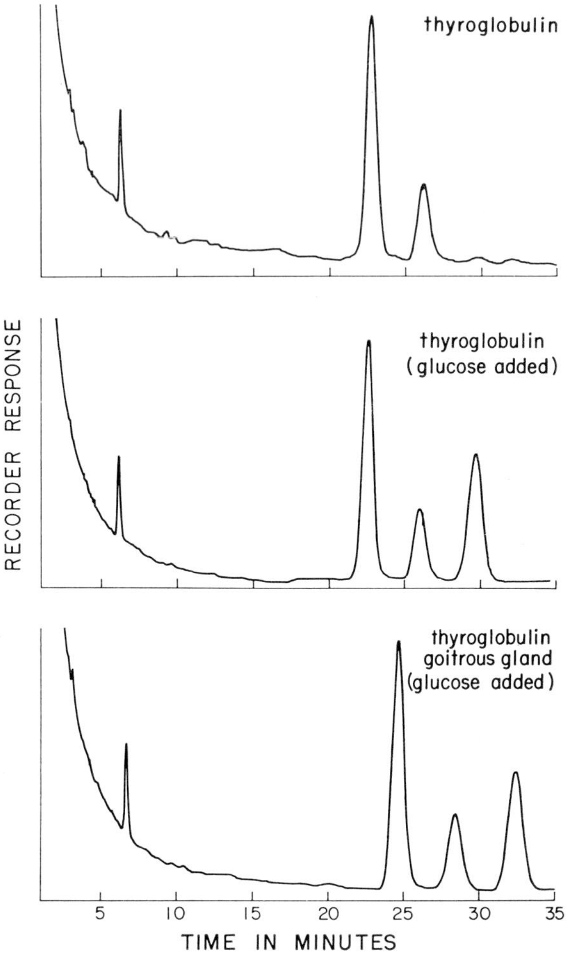

FIG. 3. Elution profiles of the neutral sugars of "normal" and "goitrous" thyroglobulin. The samples are as indicated and the range and attenuation were 10 and 2×, respectively. The total amount of hexose (excluding glucose) injected in a 0.5 μl volume was about 2–2.1 μg. Weight of samples hydrolyzed, 2 mg. Samples were chromatographed at different times and the variation in absolute retention time is due to minor variations in helium flow and/or column packing.

TSH. The absence of any galactose in the glucose standard was also demonstrated by gas chromatography, and analyses in which glucose was added to ribonuclease A, which contains no carbohydrate (19), again showed that the peak at the position of galactose did not originate during the hydrolysis procedure.

The quantitative results of neutral sugar analyses of the thyroglobulins

TABLE 1
Hexose and Hexosamine Content of Human Thyroglobulins

Source of sample[a]	Residues per molecule of protein[a]			
	Fucose	Mannose	Galactose	Glucosamine[c]
Normal subjects[b]	19.9 (0.4)	147 (2)	53 (0.8)	119
	18.2 (0.4)	138 (2)	51 (0.5)	124
	17.2 (0.3)	142 (3)	52 (0.9)	133
	20.5 (0.3)	145 (2)	54 (0.2)	124
Value from literature (13)	21	130	50	127
Goitrous subject	15.7 (0.7)	161 (4)	54 (0.4)	124
	15.7 (0.9)	151 (3)	54 (0.6)	122

[a] The preparation and amino acid composition of these samples has been described (12). Values (expressed to nearest integer with the exception of fucose) are calculated on the basis of a molecular weight of 670,000.

[b] Values from four replicate determinations are shown. For the hexoses they are the mean of three to seven injections for each determination and the figures in parentheses are the standard errors of the means of the series of injections.

[c] Corrected by use of galactosamine as an internal standard. Actual recovery of galactosamine in individual determinations varied from 85–89%.

by gas chromatography together with the analysis for hexosamine content by ion-exchange chromatography are given in Table 1. These values and the chromatograms shown in Figure 3 were determined with range and attenuation near maximum sensitivity (10 and 2×, respectively). Subsequent work showed range and attenuation settings of 10 and 8× or 4× to give more stable baselines with a far superior signal/noise ratio (see Fig. 4) and with considerably less variation of values from separate injections than that shown by the standard errors of the means given in Table 1. At attenuation settings of 8× or 4×, three injections of each sample were made.

The results of analyses of the ovalbumin both before and after its rechromatography on CM-cellulose are shown in Table 2. Included are data which show results of hydrolysis with HCl plus Dowex 50 (with HCl removed by taking the hydrolyzate to dryness at low temperature) and with Dowex 50 alone. Although the original ovalbumin had been recrystallized five times, the hexosamine values are about one-half residue higher than the usual values reported (20). Starch-gel electrophoresis at pH 8.6 showed the preparation to be contaminated with several components other than the A_1, A_2, and A_3 ovalbumins (21). After rechromatography on CM-cellulose, the proteins other than the A_1, A_2, and A_3 components of ovalbumin were no longer detected by gel electrophoresis in the ovalbumin fractions. Analyses of the rechromatographed ovalbumin show an apparent drop in the glucosamine content

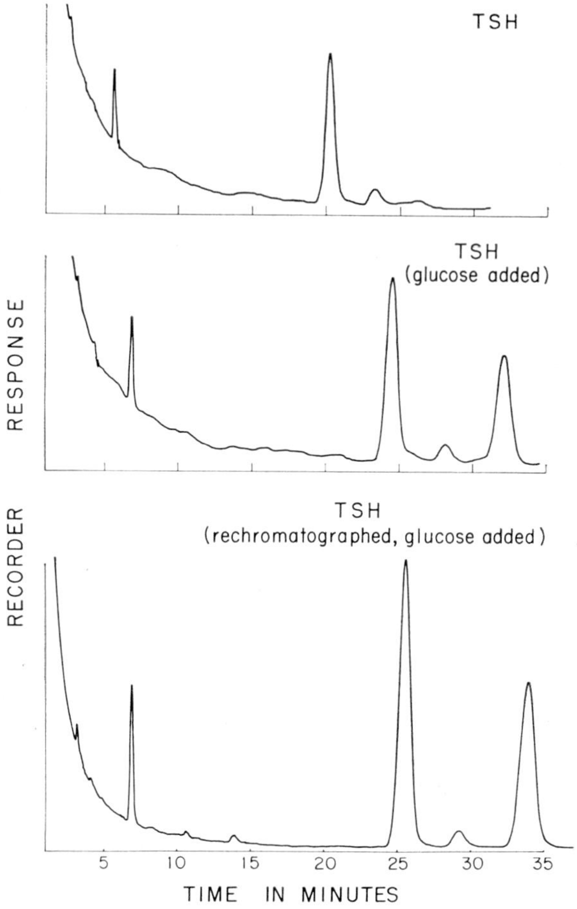

FIG. 4. Gas chromatograms of the neutral sugars of TSH: (top) TSH without internal standard; (middle) same preparation plus 50 μg glucose; (bottom) a TSH preparation following rechromatography on DEAE-cellulose. The total amount of hexose injected in 0.5 μl in the two top chromatograms was 2–25 μg and of glucose 1–1.25 μg. Weight of samples hydrolyzed, 2 mg. Samples were chromatographed at different times and some variation in retention time occurs due to minor variations in helium flow and/or column packing. The bottom chromatogram was run with a less sensitive attenuation setting (i.e., 8$\times$ rather than 2$\times$) which gives a more stable baseline. A correspondingly larger sample was injected. The second small peak emerging after fucose has the retention time of xylose.

(3 of 4 analyses) but not of the material emerging at the position of galactose. It is noteworthy that this component (0.1% of the protein) present in about one-twentieth the amount of mannose was not definitively found in Analysis 1, Table 2, in which the attenuation was at 2$\times$,

TABLE 2
Hexose and Hexosamine Content of Ovalbumin and α_1-Acid Glycoprotein

Sample	Residues per molecule of protein[a]			
	Fucose	Mannose	Galactose	Glucosamine
Ovalbumin (5 × recrystallized)				
Analysis 1		5.0	T.D.	3.4[b]
		5.1	"	3.3
Analysis 2		4.5	"	3.7[c]
		4.6	"	3.6[c]
		4.7	"	N.D.
		4.6	"	"
Analysis 3		4.7	0.24	"
hydrolyzed with 0.25 *N* H_2SO_4 + resin		4.6	0.24	"
hydrolyzed with 0.25 *N* HCl + resin		4.1	0.27	"
hydrolyzed with resin alone		3.4	0.18	"
Ovalbumin (chromatographed on CM-cellulose)		4.5	0.26	2.7
		4.9[d]	0.26	3.2
		4.7[d]	0.28	2.5
		4.7[d]	0.26	3.5
Values from literature (20)		5.4 ± 1.2		3.0 ± 0.8
		4.8 ± 0.7		3.2 ± 0.8
α_1-Acid glycoprotein	3.4	15.5	19.2	28.8

T.D., trace detected. N.D., not determined.

[a] The molecular weight of ovalbumin was taken as 45,000; that of α_1-acid glycoprotein as 44,100. Replicate analyses where performed are shown.

[b] Galactosamine not used as an internal standard. A recovery of 89% was assumed on the basis of recoveries of internal standard in Analysis 2.

[c] Galactosamine used as internal standard. Actual recoveries of 86 and 93% were found.

[d] The samples were hydrolyzed for 36 hr. Galactosamine used as an internal standard in this analysis.

but was clearly detected in the subsequent analyses with attenuation settings of 8×. Identification as galactose was confirmed by paper chromatography of the sugars obtained by hydrolyzing 10 mg of ovalbumin. One of the ovalbumin fractions prepared by rechromatography was shown by gel electrophoresis to contain only component A_1. The fraction had the same mannose to galactose ratio as did the fractions containing A_1, A_2, and A_3.[4] Table 2 also shows an analysis of α_1-acid glycoprotein

[4] Another interesting example of the detection of small amounts of neutral sugars was found with pancreatic ribonuclease B. Commercial samples of this protein, which has been shown to contain mannose and glucosamine (19), were found also to contain about 0.3% galactose. Rechromatography of the protein on IRC-50 (19) yielded a protein with ribonuclease activity and free of galactose, and a second protein of unknown identity which was correspondingly enriched in galactose.

and although considerable variation is found among the analyses reported in the literature (22), our values agree well with other recent determinations.

Figure 4 illustrates typical elution profiles of the neutral sugars of bovine TSH in the absence and presence of added glucose and also after its rechromatography on DEAE-cellulose. Evidence that the material emerging between mannose and glucose is galactose was again shown by

TABLE 3
Hexose and Hexosamine Content of Thyrotropins and Heterothyrotropic Factor

Sample	Residues per molecule of protein[a]				
	Fucose	Mannose	Galactose	Glucosamine[b]	Galactosamine[b]
Bovine TSH					
Prep. 1	0.92	7.2	0.40	—	—
	1.15	7.4	0.49	7.5	3.6
Prep. 2, rechromatographed on DEAE-cellulose	1.12	7.2	0.56	7.5	2.8
	1.10	7.4	0.59	7.6	2.9
	0.99	7.2	0.55	7.5	3.1
Bovine TSH,[c] Prepn. 2, rechromatographed on both DEAE- and CM-cellulose	1.15	7.3	0.49	—	—
Porcine TSH[d]	0.93	4.1	0.44	5.6	1.8
Human TSH[d]	1.02	4.8	1.5	5.3	1.7
Bovine heterothyrotropic factor[d]	1.86	5.4	4.4	5.9	3.6

[a] The molecular weight of bovine TSH was taken as 26,000 on the basis of recent ultracentrifugal studies in this laboratory; for comparative purposes the molecular weights of the other preparations were arbitrarily chosen to be 26,000. Replicate analysis, where performed, are shown.

[b] The values for the hexosamines are uncorrected except in the analyses of Preparation 2, rechromatographed on DEAE-cellulose. Norleucine was used as an internal standard in this experiment and its recovery (93–100%) was used as a basis for correction of losses during manipulation.

[c] Moisture content assumed to be the same as other TSH preparations.

[d] Moisture and ash content not determined because of small amounts of material available; therefore only the molar ratios are significant.

paper chromatography (7) of identical hydrolyzates in which a spot was obtained with the R_f of galactose and approximately the intensity of fucose. Quantitative data on bovine TSH and on the heterothyrotropic factor are given in Table 3 as well as analyses of human and porcine TSH preparations. The latter two contain less mannose and amino sugars relative to fucose than does bovine TSH, and the human preparation is relatively rich in galactose.

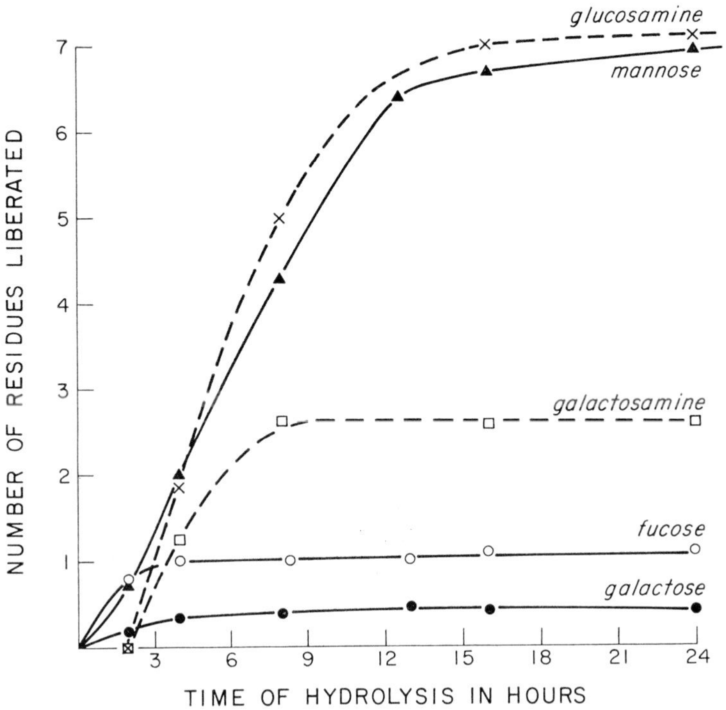

FIG. 5. Release of neutral and amino sugars with time of hydrolysis. Two analyses were carried out at times of 13, 16, and 24 hr. Conditions of hydrolysis are as described in the experimental section with approximately 0.7 mg of TSH hydrolyzed for each point. Moisture was not determined on these samples but was assumed to be 10% (based on the average of previous determinations). The glucosamine and galactosamine values are uncorrected for any destruction during hydrolysis.

To determine possible destruction of galactose and the other sugars during hydrolysis, a study of their release with time from bovine TSH was made (Fig. 5). These data show that galactose and fucose are completely released after 4 hr with no destruction during the subsequent 18 hr. It should also be noted that no hexosamines are released after 2 hr while nearly 1 residue each of mannose and fucose and 0.25 residue of galactose appear.

DISCUSSION

Our data show gas chromatography of alditol acetates to be excellent for analyses of the neutral sugars of glycoproteins. When combined with hexosamine determination by ion-exchange chromatography, a complete analysis of all monosaccharide components other than sialic acids can be obtained with 1 mg of glycoprotein. Good approximations can be made with less material. Other advantages are that only one peak appears for each sugar, which is particularly valuable for determination of trace components such as the galactose in TSH and in the ovalbumin. Separation of an internal standard with similar properties is also easily obtained. Rigid exclusion of moisture is not necessary for derivative formation and problems of the solubility of the sugars do not arise (23). The hexaacetates are stable and analysis of samples stored at 4° for several months were unchanged. These advantages plus the excellent over-all recovery outweigh the fact that more manipulations are needed to form the alditol acetates than, for example, trimethylsilyl derivatives. Two precautions must be observed. First, although no problems of identification will be found with most glycoproteins in which the only neutral sugars are fucose, mannose, and galactose, the fact that two glycoses can yield the same alditol by reduction requires that analysis of unknown materials be accompanied by qualitative identification. Second, if insufficient borohydride is used, spurious peaks arise; many apparently due to pentaacetates of α and β anomers.

The fact that no preferential loss of any neutral sugar is shown by the data in Figure 5, together with the agreement with analyses previously reported, indicates that the method of hydrolysis and chromatographic separation can be generally applied to glycoproteins.[5] The use of sulfonic acid ion exchangers for hydrolysis has been reported by several investigators (5, 25) and the hydrolysis of glycoproteins has recently been reviewed (26). Hydrolysis by resin, which gives high local proton concentrations, apparently circumvents many of the problems concerning the destruction of sugars and the resistance of some glycosidic bonds (e.g., bonds involving *N*-acetylhexosamines). The hexosamine analyses show, however, somewhat greater scatter than those of the neutral sugars, especially with ovalbumin; complete liberation of hexosamines without destruction is notoriously difficult. Particular care to exclude oxygen during hydrolysis is also needed (27). Another problem may be the fortuitous emergence from the amino acid analyzer of a resistant peptide under a hexosamine peak. Thus the 50 cm column of the analyzer is preferable because of greater resolution. This difficulty was found in one analysis of ovalbumin in which the galactosamine peak was asymmetric and the recovery of added galactosamine was about 10% higher than the usual 85–90%. Recoveries of norleucine were usually 100 ± 3%, showing that the lower recoveries of glucosamine and galactosamine (see data in Table 2) are due to destruction. Evidence that 10–15% destruc-

[5] A report of the chromatography of the alditol acetates of the sugars of phytohemagglutinin has recently appeared (24).

tion of both the added and constituent hexosamines was found in an experiment with TSH where galactosamine was added to one of two replicate samples. By using the equations x/y = ratio found of glucosamine/galactosamine (without addition of galactosamine) and $x/(y + a)$ = ratio found of glucosamine/galactosamine (where a = μmoles galactosamine added) and x and y are μmoles of glucosamine and galactosamine in the sample), respective values 14 and 6% higher than those obtained in the absence of internal standard were found. When corrections are made for 10% destruction during hydrolysis, highly purified bovine TSH preparations contain 8–9 residues of glucosamine and 3–4 residues of galactosamine per 26,000 molecular weight.

Because the carbohydrate structure and stoichiometry are not completely defined for any glycoprotein, no absolute standards are available. Our analyses of neutral sugars and glucosamine of human thyroglobulin agree well with those in the careful study of Spiro and Spiro (13) except that our average mannose value is higher (i.e., 145 residues instead of 130). These investigators did, however, obtain higher total hexose values by the anthrone procedure than their total mannose and galactose values reported, which were obtained after hydrolysis, separation by paper chromatography, and measurement of reducing power. With respect to the "goitrous" thyroglobulin, further work is needed to see if the differences in fucose and mannose versus "normal" thyroglobulin are significant. One difficulty was an occasional low value for fucose; this appeared to be remedied by careful exclusion of air during hydrolysis.

The mannose analyses of ovalbumin also agree well with the accepted value of 5 residues. Chromatographic purification did not cause any lowering of the galactose found, and further studies are needed to determine if the possible heterogeneity of the oligosaccharide moiety of ovalbumin (28) includes the presence of galactose. In the initial sample the glucosamine values were high after correction for destruction based on the recovery of the added galactosamine. It is not clear whether rechromatography of the ovalbumin led to a significant drop in glucosamine content. Rechromatography should remove any ovomucoid which is rich in glucosamine (ca. 14%) (29) as it removed the other contaminants which can be detected by starch-gel electrophoresis.

With bovine TSH, the fucose and total hexose values agree well with the data obtained by colorimetric procedures (7). Both the porcine and human TSH preparations differed from the bovine, each yielding higher ratios of fucose to mannose and the human material containing more galactose. The galactose found in bovine TSH persists despite repeated purification and the data in Figure 5 demonstrate the unlikelihood of extensive destruction and thus that one residue was originally present.

Destruction cannot, however, be completely excluded; Jamieson has reported possible preferential losses of galactose during hydrolysis of transferrin and ceruloplasmin (30). Destruction of galactose, under the conditions of hydrolysis previously used, is the probable explanation for failure to detect other than traces of galactose in earlier studies (7). The fractional residue could also exist because the TSH, although extensively purified, is still heterogeneous. Although it is beyond the scope of this paper to discuss fully the problems of TSH purification, there are pituitary glycoproteins which contain much larger amounts of galactose than TSH (7), among them, heterothyrotropic factor. This factor is separated from TSH by chromatography on CM-cellulose. Our purified TSH did not cross-react in precipitin tests with antisera to HTF preparations unless a 100-fold excess of antigen was used. Luteinizing hormone also has been particularly difficult to remove completely from TSH, but rechromatography on DEAE-cellulose has lowered the content of this hormone in our preparations to less than 1% by weight.[6] Other possibilities for the presence of a fractional residue of galactose are that transglycosylation occurs during purification or that there is variation in the carbohydrates of the several hormonally active and immunochemically identical components of the purified preparations (11, 14). The sensitivity of the gas chromatographic analysis will permit investigation of the latter possibility.

The data in Figure 5 showing release of fucose, galactose, and mannose after 2 hr and prior to the appearance of significant amounts of amino hexoses also support the results of enzymic studies which indicated that these three sugars occupy terminal positions in the oligosaccharide (8).

SUMMARY

A method has been developed for the quantitative determination of the neutral sugars of several glycoproteins including thyrotropic hormone, thyroglobulin, and ovalbumin by gas-liquid chromatography of alditol acetates. This approach has the advantage that only one peak for each sugar is present in the chromatograms, which is particularly valuable in the determination of trace components. The same samples are analyzed for hexosamines by ion-exchange chromatography and the combination of methods permits analyses for all sugar components other than sialic acid on one or two milligrams of glycoprotein. In addition to the fucose and mannose previously reported, highly purified bovine thyrotropin contains approximately one-half residue of galactose per molecule with the human hormone purified by similar methods relatively richer in this

[6] B. Shome, V. D. Ramirez, and J. G. Pierce, unpublished work.

sugar. Trace amounts of galactose have also been found in crystalline ovalbumin preparations further purified by chromatography.

ACKNOWLEDGMENTS

The authors are grateful for the capable assistance of Miss Tiiu Reimo during this investigation and to Mr. A. B. Rawitch for the preparations of thyroglobulin. Advice concerning gas chromatographic techniques was generously given by Dr. Om P. Bahl.

REFERENCES

1. Bishop, C. T., *in* "Advances in Carbohydrate Chemistry" (M. L. Wolfrom, ed.), Vol. 19, p. 95. Academic Press, New York, 1964.
2. Yamakawa, T., and Ueta, N., *J. Exptl. Med. (Japan)* **34,** 37 (1964).
3. Sweeley, C. C., Bentley, R., Makita, M., and Wells, W. W., *J. Am. Chem. Soc.* **85,** 2497 (1963).
4. Bolton, C. H., Clamp, J. R., and Hough, L., *Biochem. J.* **96,** 5C (1965).
5. Oates, M. D. G., and Schrager, J., *Biochem. J.* **97,** 697 (1965).
6. Sawardeker, J. S., Sloneker, J. H., and Jeanes, A., *Anal. Chem.* **37,** 1602 (1965).
7. Carsten, M. E., and Pierce, J. G., *J. Biol. Chem.* **238,** 1724 (1963).
8. Pierce, J. G., Goetinck, P. F., and Cady, A. R., "Proceedings of the Sixth Pan American Congress of Endocrinology." Excerpta Medica Foundation, Amsterdam, 1966.
9. Spackman, D. H., Stein, W. H., and Moore, S., *Anal. Chem.* **30,** 1190 (1958).
10. Beckman Technical Bulletin A-TB-008, Beckman Instruments Co., Palo Alto, California, 1964.
11. Goetinck, P. F., and Pierce, J. G., *Arch. Biochem.* **115,** 277 (1966).
12. Pierce, J. G., Rawitch, A. B., Brown, D. M., and Stanley, P. G., *Biochim. Biophys. Acta* **111,** 247 (1965).
13. Spiro, R. G., and Spiro, M. J., *J. Biol. Chem.* **240,** 997 (1965).
14. Carsten, M. E., and Pierce, J. G., *J. Biol. Chem.* **235,** 78 (1960).
15. Condliffe, P. G., *Endocrinology* **72,** 893 (1963).
16. Rhodes, M. B., Azari, P. R., and Feeney, R. E., *J. Biol. Chem.* **230,** 399 (1958).
17. Fontaine, Y. A., and Lebelle, N., *in* "Current Topics in Thyroid Research" (C. Andreoli, ed.), p. 424. Academic Press, New York, 1965.
18. Abdel-Akher, M., Hamilton, J. K., and Smith, F., *J. Am. Chem. Soc.* **73,** 4691 (1951).
19. Plummer, T. H., and Hirs, C. H. W., *J. Biol. Chem.* **238,** 1396 (1963).
20. Clamp, J. R., and Hough, L., *Biochem. J.* **94,** 502 (1965).
21. Lush, E., *Genet. Res. Comb.* **5,** 257 (1964).
22. Gottschalk, A., and Bruce Graham, E. R., *in* "The Proteins" (H. Neurath, ed.), 2nd ed., Vol. 4, p. 95. Academic Press, New York, 1966.
23. Sweeley, C. C., Wells, W. W., and Bentley, R., *in* "Methods in Enzymology" (Neufeld, E. F., and Ginsburg, V., eds.), Vol. VIII, p. 95. Academic Press, New York, 1966.
24. Takahashi, T., Ramachandramurthy, P., and Liener, I. E., *Biochim. Biophys. Acta* **133,** 123 (1967).
25. Haab, W., and Anastassiadis, P. A., *Can. J. Biochem. Physiol.* **39,** 671 (1961).
26. Neuberger, A., and Marshall, R. D., *in* "Glycoproteins" (A. Gottschalk, ed.), p. 190. American Elsevier, New York, 1966.
27. Walborg, E. F., and Ward, D., *Biochim. Biophys. Acta* **78,** 304 (1963).

28. Cunningham, L., Ford, J. D., and Rainey, J. M., *Biochim. Biophys. Acta* **101,** 233 (1965).
29. Melamed, M. D., *in* "Glycoproteins" (A. Gottschalk, ed.), p. 317. American Elsevier, New York, 1966.
30. Jamieson, G. A., *J. Biol. Chem.* **240,** 2019 (1965).

ANALYTICAL BIOCHEMISTRY 20, 275–281 (1967)

Gas-Liquid Chromatography of Derivatives of Several Amino Acids That Occur in the Actinomycins[1]

MARTHA A. WARD, TIMOTHY E. McCARTHY, AND JONATHAN S. NISHIMURA

Department of Biochemistry, Tufts University School of Medicine, Boston, and Department of Chemistry, Boston College, Newton, Massachusetts

Received February 1, 1967

The actinomycins are chromopeptides, each containing a phenoxazinone, actinocin, to which is attached two cyclic pentapeptide chains (1). These compounds possess potent antitumor and antibiotic activity. Recent research on the actinomycins has been largely concerned with their antagonism of ribonucleic acid synthesis (2) and with their biosynthesis in several strains of *Streptomyces* (3). In both areas the structural chemistry of these antibiotics has been of utmost interest. Thus, the ability of an actinomycin to inhibit DNA-directed RNA polymerase may be lost by alterations of the antibiotic molecule which affect its binding to double-stranded DNA. From the viewpoint of their biosynthesis the actinomycins are derived entirely from amino acid precursors; they are different from one another by virtue of the fact that several amino acids in the pentapeptide chains may be replaced by homologs or analogs.

In studies on the biosynthesis of molecules as complex as are the actinomycins, sensitive methods are required to determine the composition of intermediates and products. Amino acid analysis of actinomycin hydrolyzates is made difficult by the great variation in reactivity to ninhydrin displayed by the individual components. For example, *N*-methylvaline may be detected on paper chromatograms by the use of ninhydrin; however, the color produced by this reaction is highly variable in intensity and tends to fade rapidly. Furthermore, the amino acid does not react significantly in solution with ninhydrin (4) and for this reason does not lend itself to analysis by automated ion-exchange chromatography (5).

The present investigation was prompted by the possibility that gas-liquid chromatography of derivatives of the amino acids concerned would

[1] Supported by a grant (AI-06366) from the United States Public Health Service.

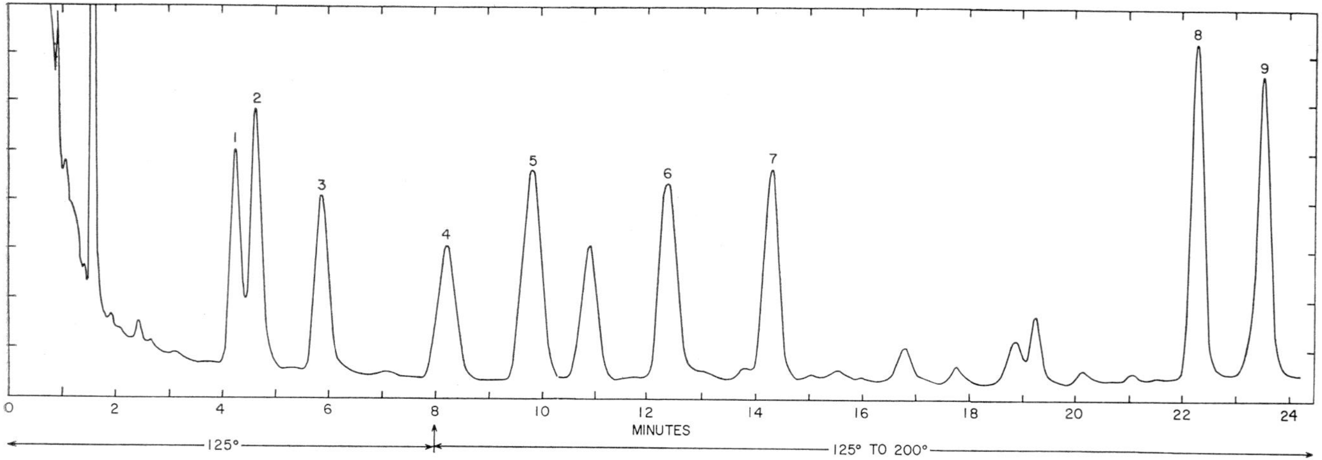

FIG. 1. Gas chromatographic separation of acetylated *n*-amyl esters of (1) sarcosine, (2) *N*-methyl-L-valine, (3) D-valine, (4) D-alloisoleucine, (5) L-leucine (internal standard), (6) L-proline, (7) L-threonine,[3] (8) 4-hydroxy-L-proline,[3] and (9) 4-allohydroxy-D-proline.[3,4] Each peak corresponds to 10^{-8} mole of the amino acid. Experimental details are described in the text.

[3] The compound is diacetylated (6).

[4] The L-enantiomer is actually the species of interest, but there is no difference in the retention time of derivatives of either D or L forms.

not only circumvent problems attending photometric measurements employed in the more commonly used techniques, but would provide a more sensitive method as well.[2] In this study several amino acids known to occur in actinomycins were converted to *n*-amyl *N*-acetyl esters (6) and analyzed as such by gas-liquid chromatography. The procedure was also effectively applied to hydrolyzates of actinomycin IV (also referred to as actinomycin D (7) and to actinomycin IV which had been reduced by exposure to lithium borohydride.

MATERIALS AND METHODS

Sarcosine, D-valine, D-alloisoleucine, L-leucine, L-proline, L-threonine, and 4-hydroxy-L-proline were obtained from Mann Research Laboratories. 4-Allohydroxy-D-proline was purchased from Nutritional Biochemicals. *N*-Methyl-L-valine was synthesized by Mr. Jerald D. Gass, according to the procedure described (9). Lithium borohydride was a product of Metal Hydrides Inc., Beverly, Mass. Actinomycin IV was the generous gift of Dr. David Hendlin of Merck, Sharp & Dohme Research Laboratories. Actinomycin IV was also isolated from culture filtrates of *Streptomyces parvullus* 3677, grown in minimal medium containing D-galactose and L-glutamic acid (10). A culture of the organism was the gift of Dr. Walter J. Nickerson. The antibiotic was purified according to the procedure of Katz and Weissbach (11).

Chromatography. An F & M Scientific Corporation model 400 gas-liquid chromatograph with flame-ionization detector was used in these studies. The apparatus was equipped with a 1.83 meter U-shaped glass column (4 mm diameter) packed with Chromosorb W, which was coated with 0.2% by weight of each of three liquid phases: Versamid, neopentylglycol succinate, and Carbowax 1540 (12). The flash heater was set at 200°. The column temperature was adjusted to 125° and the detector set at 240°. The flow rates of hydrogen, helium, and air were 60, 75, and 420 ml/min, respectively. Amino acids were converted to their *n*-amyl *N*-acetyl esters by a modification of the procedure described (6) and the derivatives were dissolved in acetone. In the modification, HCl was used instead of HBr during the esterification step (13). The sample (1–2 μl)

[2] While this manuscript was in preparation, a paper appeared describing a comparison of the ninhydrin reactivity (as applied in ion-exchange chromatography) of a variety of *N*-methyl amino acids with their detectability as *N*-trifluoroacetyl methyl ester derivatives by the flame-ionization technique (as applied in gas-liquid chromatography) (8). These workers have concluded that greater sensitivity and uniformity in detectability is afforded by the latter technique. The color yield in the reaction of ninhydrin with the *N*-methyl amino acids tested varied from 1.4 to 20% that given by the parent amino acid.

was injected with a Hamilton syringe. Eight minutes after introduction of the sample, the temperature was increased to 200° at the rate of 4°/min.

Reduction of Actinomycin IV with Lithium Borohydride and Acid Hydrolysis of the Antibiotic. Actinomycin IV was subjected to reduction with $LiBH_4$, essentially as described (14). Actinomycin IV (0.25 μmole) isolated from *Streptomyces parvullus* filtrates was dissolved in 1.0 ml tetrahydrofuran containing 0.224 *M* $LiBH_4$. The mixture was shaken at 25° for 1 hr. Water (1.0 ml) was added, followed by addition of 6 *N* HCl until a sample of the mixture gave a blue reaction on Congo red test paper. The tetrahydrofuran was removed from the acidified mixture under a stream of air. The mixture was then extracted several times with equal volumes of ethyl acetate. The combined extracts were reduced to dryness, dissolved in 6 *N* HCl (1.0 ml), and heated for 6 hr at 121° in a sealed glass tube. After hydrolysis the hydrochloric acid was removed by repeated flash evaporation. The residue was then treated to yield the derivatized amino acids. Unreduced actinomycin IV (0.01 to 0.10 μmole) was hydrolyzed and prepared for gas chromatographic analysis in the same way.

RESULTS

A mixture of several amino acids known to occur in the actinomycins was converted to the corresponding *n*-amyl *N*-acetyl esters and subjected to gas-liquid chromatography, as described under "Methods." The results shown in Figure 1 demonstrate that good separation of nine amino acid derivatives was achieved. L-Leucine was used as the internal standard. Chromatography of "blanks" in which the derivatization procedure was carried out without amino acids and the reagent residue analyzed showed that the substance appearing between peaks 5 and 6 did not arise from degradation products of the amino acids or from impurities present in the original amino acid samples. In addition, the small components appearing between peaks 7 and 8 were found in virtually identical amounts in "blank" chromatograms. As shown in the figure, the amounts chromatographed correspond to 10^{-8} mole of each amino acid. Without further attenuation of the instrument it may be demonstrated that at least 10^{-9} mole of each derivative is detectable.

The detector response of each amino acid derivative has been compared with that of the L-leucine derivative. The results are shown in Table 1. The detector response in each case has been demonstrated to be proportional to the amount of derivative chromatographed.

Acid hydrolyzates of actinomycin IV obtained from Merck and actinomycin IV isolated from culture filtrates of *Streptomyces parvullus* were also analyzed in the manner described above. The derivatives of the amino acids *N*-methylvaline, sarcosine, proline, valine, and threonine emerged from the column with the expected retention times. These amino acids are present in equimolar amounts in the intact antibiotic. The amount of threonine derivative actually observed was usually smaller than the others. Analysis of similar hydrolyzates by the method of Katz and Weissbach (15) has shown that the amounts of threonine found are lower than those of proline and valine. This discrepancy can probably be ascribed to incomplete cleavage of threonine from the chromophoric group (16) and to some degradation of threonine during acid hydrolysis.

TABLE 1
Comparison of Detector Responses Produced by Amino Acid Derivatives

Amino acid	Ratio[a] Response of amino acid derivative / Response of leucine derivative
Sarcosine	0.66[b]
N-Methylvaline	0.79[b]
Valine	0.69
Alloisoleucine	0.75
Leucine	1.00
Proline	0.91
Threonine	0.87
4-Hydroxyproline	1.00
4-Allohydroxyproline	0.95

[a] Detector responses were calculated in mm^2. Except where indicated the results were the average of 13 determinations.
[b] Results were the average of 4 determinations.

An application of this method to the determination of the carboxyl terminal amino acids of the actinomycin pentapeptide chains was suggested by the work of Golub *et al.* (14), who have succeeded in reducing amino acid esters to the corresponding amino alcohols in good yield through the use of lithium borohydride. In several actinomycins the carboxyl terminal *N*-methylvaline residue is linked through an ester bond to the hydroxyl group of the *N*-terminal threonine in the corresponding chain. When reduction of actinomycin IV by $LiBH_4$ was carried out, followed by acid hydrolysis and chromatography of the derivatized hydrolyzate, the result shown in Figure 2 was obtained. As expected, practically all of the *N*-methylvaline was eliminated, the remainder represented by a shoulder on the sarcosine peak. Appearing at 2.3 to 2.4 min was a new peak which gave a detector response approximately equal to that which would have been given by the missing *N*-methylvaline derivative. The new peak is probably diacetylated *N*-methylvalinol.

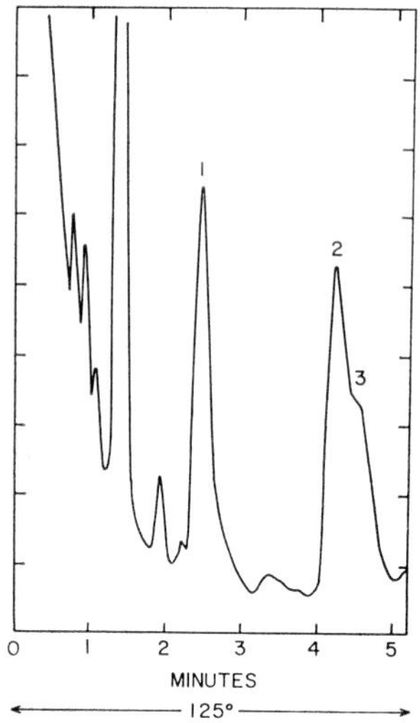

FIG. 2. Gas chromatographic analysis of derivatized hydrolyzate of actinomycin IV reduced by $LiBH_4$: (1) new peak, (2) sarcosine, (3) *N*-methylvaline. Experimental details are described in the text.

Samples of free *N*-methylvaline which have been reduced by $LiAlH_4$ (17) have yielded the same peak on gas-liquid chromatography after acetylation.

DISCUSSION

The results described illustrate that gas-liquid chromatography may be useful in the amino acid analysis of hydrolyzates of actinomycins. The amino acids studied here do not comprise a complete list of those found in all actinomycins. With the exception of alloisoleucine and 4-allohydroxyproline they are, however, amino acids known to occur commonly in the actinomycins elaborated by *S. antibioticus* 3720 (15) and *S. parvullus*. The inclusion of 4-allohydroxyproline in this investigation stems from its value in the determination of the 4-keto-L-proline content of actinomycin V (1). Thus, catalytic reduction of actinomycin V results in the formation from peptide-bound 4-ketoproline of peptide-bound 4-hydroxyproline, 4-allohydroxyproline, or a mixture of the two, depending upon the conditions of catalysis employed (1, 18). Comparison of the 4-hydroxyproline and 4-allohydroxyproline content of the reduced and unreduced antibiotic gives by difference the amount of 4-ketoproline in the unreduced molecule.

SUMMARY

The gas-liquid chromatography of the *n*-amyl *N*-acetyl ester derivatives of a number of amino acids known to occur in the actinomycins is described. Preliminary studies indicate that this procedure may be employed in the analysis of hydrolyzates of these antibiotics with a sensitivity of at least 10^{-9} mole. Application of the procedure to the determination of the carboxyl terminal amino acids in an actinomycin is also described.

ACKNOWLEDGMENTS

The authors wish to thank Dr. Alton Meister for his encouragement during the course of this work. Thanks are also due Mr. Ronald Wagner and Mr. Ellis Golub for valuable assistance in the studies with lithium borohydride.

REFERENCES

1. Brockmann, H., *Ann. N. Y. Acad. Sci.* **89,** 323 (1960).
2. Reich, E., and Goldberg, I. H., *Prog. Nucleic Acid Res. Mol. Biol.* **3,** 183 (1964).
3. Katz, E., and Weissbach, H., *in* "Biosynthesis of Antibiotic Substances" (Z. Vanek and Z. Hostalek, eds.), p. 195. Academic Press, New York, 1965.
4. Plattner, P. A., and Nager, U., *Helv. Chim. Acta* **31,** 665, 2192, 2203 (1948).
5. Ciferri, O., Albertini, A., and Cassani, G., *Biochem. J.* **90,** 82 (1964).
6. Johnson, D. E., Scott, S. J., and Meister, A., *Anal. Chem.* **33,** 669 (1961).
7. Waksman, S. A., Katz, E., and Vining, L. C., *Proc. Natl. Acad. Sci. U. S.* **44,** 602 (1958).
8. Ebata, M., Takahashi, Y., and Otsuka, H., *J. Chromatog.* **25,** 1 (1966).
9. Greenstein, J. P., and Winitz, M., "Chemistry of Amino Acids," p. 2757. Wiley, New York, 1961.
10. Katz, E., Pienta, P., and Sivak, A., *Appl. Microbiol.* **6,** 236 (1958).
11. Katz, E., and Weissbach, H., *Mol. Pharmacol.* **1,** 107 (1965).
12. Polgar, P., and Meister, A., *Anal. Biochem.* **12,** 338 (1965).
13. McCarthy, T. E., and Meister, A., unpublished observations.
14. Golub, E., Marble, S. J., and Meister, A., *Biochim. Biophys. Acta* **103,** 536 (1965).
15. Katz, E., and Weissbach, H., *J. Biol. Chem.* **237,** 882 (1962).
16. Brockmann, H., and Grone, H., *Ber.* **91,** 773 (1958).
17. Fromageot, C., Jutisz, M., Meyer, D., and Penasse, L., *Biochim. Biophys. Acta* **6,** 283 (1950).
18. Brockmann, H., and Manegold, J. H., *Ber.* **93,** 2971 (1960).

ANALYTICAL BIOCHEMISTRY **20**, 282–293 (1967)

Determination of Phosphate in Biological Materials and Reaction Mixtures by Atomic Absorption Spectrophotometry

W. S. ZAUGG AND R. J. KNOX

U. S. Department of the Interior, Bureau of Sport Fisheries and Wildlife, Western Fish Nutrition Laboratory, Cook, Washington 98605

Received February 2, 1967

Numerous spectrophotometric methods have been developed for the determination of inorganic phosphate in biological systems. These methods generally consist of modifications in the original molybdenum blue procedure of Bell and Doisy (1) as modified by Fiske and Subba-Row (2), or of variations in the method of Berenblum and Chain (3) in which phosphate, stoichiometrically complexed to molybdenum, is extracted by an organic solvent. The concentration of the phosphomolybdic acid complex in the organic solvent is then determined by ultraviolet or visible spectrophotometry. Using a modification of the extraction technique, Wadelin and Mellon (4) chose a combination of 20% by volume 1-butanol in chloroform in preference to 1-butyl acetate as a selective extractant. Schaffer *et al.* (5) used 1-octanol because only a small amount of free molybdic acid was extracted by this solvent, thereby giving low blank values. A mixture of isobutanol and benzene (6) has also been used widely as a solvent for this procedure.

Solvent extraction techniques have become important in the determination of many metals by atomic absorption spectrophotometry. Such methods not only concentrate the desired metal in an organic phase, or remove it from corrosive liquids, but often eliminate interfering substances. Molybdenum can be determined in this manner by extraction with ammonium pyrrolidine dithiocarbamate into methyl isobutyl ketone (7, 8).

It was decided to investigate the possibility of developing a procedure whereby phosphate concentrations could be determined indirectly by the atomic absorption spectrophotometric determination of molybdenum extracted into an organic solvent as phosphomolybdic acid. This communication extends preliminary studies (9) and shows the application of these techniques to the determination of phosphate in serum, blood, bone, and other biological tissues, and in reaction mixtures containing enzyme systems.

METHODS

Reagents were prepared as outlined earlier (9). Ammonium molybdate, $(NH_4)_6Mo_7O_{24} \cdot 4H_2O$ (58.4 gms), was dissolved in 200 ml concentrated HCl and diluted to 1 liter with glass distilled water. Citric acid, $C_6H_8O_7 \cdot H_2O$ (143 gm), was dissolved in about 900 ml glass distilled water. This solution was adjusted to pH 2.9 with NaOH (about 14 gm) and the volume brought to 1 liter.

The acid molybdate solution (0.5 ml) and 2-octanol (from 2.0 to 5.0 ml according to need) were added to a test tube containing water and sample having a total volume of 5.0 ml. The tube was capped with a polyethylene cover and shaken manually for 30 sec—all tubes in a series of determinations can be shaken at the same time if held securely in a test tube rack. The cap was then removed, citrate (1.0 ml) added, and the tube recapped and shaken (30 sec). Extraction mixtures were centrifuged briefly at low speeds to facilitate phase separation. The absorption due to molybdenum in the organic phase was determined with a Perkin-Elmer model 303 atomic absorption spectrophotometer. Values were expressed as phosphate concentration by comparison to standard curves constructed from the absorbances obtained by extracting samples of known phosphate concentrations. Wavelengths of 313.3, 379.8, 386.4, or 390.3 mμ were used for analysis, with a slit width of 3 (0.3 mm) and a lamp current of 30 mA (molybdenum lamp). An air–acetylene burner (0.5 $\times$ 110 mm slot) was used with an air supply of 28 psi (flowmeter 7.4) and an acetylene supply of 8 psi (flowmeter 9.0). Higher ratios of acetylene to air resulted in greater sensitivity, but this also caused greater fluctuation of the null meter needle.

Acid-soluble phosphate in serum was determined by adding 0.26 ml cold 13.5% $HClO_4$ to 40 μl serum. After mixing and allowing this mixture to remain in ice for several minutes (5–10), 0.50 ml glass-distilled water was added and mixed, and the precipitated protein was sedimented by centrifugation in the cold (800 g for 15 min). Aliquots of the supernatant liquid (0.50 ml) were carefully withdrawn and assayed as described above using 2.0 ml 2-octanol. For determination of total phosphate 20 μl of serum, 10 μl of heparinized whole blood, or equivalent amounts of diluted samples (serum diluted with water and blood with isotonic NaCl) were digested over a microburner in a test tube containing 0.10 ml of a 2:1 (v/v) mixture of concentrated H_2SO_4 and 70% $HClO_4$ until clear (1–3 min). Water, 2-octanol (3 ml), and acid molybdate were added after cooling, and phosphate was determined as described above. Phosphate in other tissues was determined by digesting an accurately weighed sample of about 0.1 gm in 0.3 ml of the acid mixture mentioned above until clear (2–4 min). After cooling, 1.8 ml water was added and the contents of the tube were thoroughly mixed. Bone samples (0.03 gm) were prepared by the same digesting process but using twice the volumes of acid and water used for other tissues. Aliquots (0.10 ml) of these solutions were withdrawn and assayed for phosphate as described above. Appropriate standards were subjected to the same procedure although experiments indicated that digestion of standards was unnecessary.

RESULTS

Standard Curves and Assay Conditions

Several solvents were tested under the conditions used for extraction with 2-octanol (Table 1). The extraction of free molybdic acid (no phosphate) decreased with increasing length of the carbon chain, showing the

TABLE 1
Comparison of Solvents for Extraction of Phosphomolybdic Acid at pH 1.0–1.1[a]

Solvent	Absorbance at 313.3 mμ		
	No phosphate	Plus phosphate	Difference
1-Butanol	0.879	0.936	0.055
Isobutanol	0.505	0.623	0.118
1-Hexanol	0.094	0.269	0.175
1-Heptanol	0.042	0.210	0.168
1-Octanol	0.023	0.160	0.137
2-Octanol	0.013	0.181	0.168

[a] Samples containing equal phosphate concentrations were assayed as described under "Methods."

lowest value for 2-octanol. Extraction charactetristics of these solvents differ greatly with the pH of the aqueous solution. For example, in the pH range of 3.5–5.5 the extraction of free molybdic acid by 1-butanol or isobutanol was quite low, whereas phosphomolybdic acid was extracted efficiently. 2-Octanol, however, does not extract phosphomolybdic acid above pH 2 (9).

The effect of added acid or base on the extraction of phosphomolybdic acid by 2-octanol is shown in Table 2. Adherence to the described procedure resulted in a final pH of 1.0–1.1 in the aqueous phase of the assay mixture. Because of inherent inaccuracies of pH determinations below 1.0, the actual amounts of acid or base added are presented rather than recording the measured pH. Addition of up to 3.0 ml of 1 *N* HCl did

TABLE 2

Effect of Acid and Base Addition on Extraction of Phosphomolybdic Acid by 2-Octanol[a]

Addition, ml		Absorbance at 379.8 mμ	
1 *N* HCl	1 *N* NaOH	Blank (no phosphate)	Total minus blank
—	—	0.012	0.099
0.5	—	0.015	0.101
1.0	—	0.019	0.097
1.5	—	0.023	0.100
2.0	—	0.027	0.097
2.5	—	0.030	0.096
3.0	—	0.034	0.095
—	0.3	0.009	0.103
—	0.6	0.004	0.103
—	1.0	0.001	0.053

[a] Samples contained 0.1 μmole added phosphate and were assayed as described under "Methods." Values shown are an average of four readings on duplicate samples with a maximum variation of ±3%.

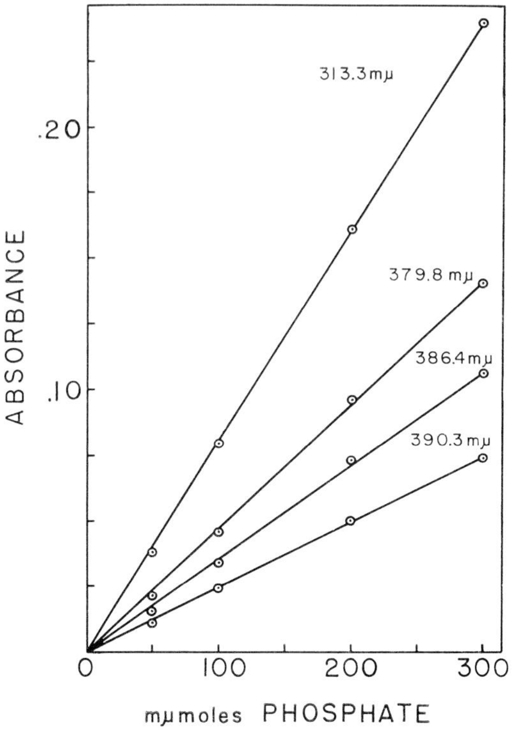

FIG. 1. Standard curves for analysis of inorganic phosphate at four wavelengths. Samples containing known amounts of phosphate were assayed and read at the indicated wavelengths. Values for blanks have been subtracted.

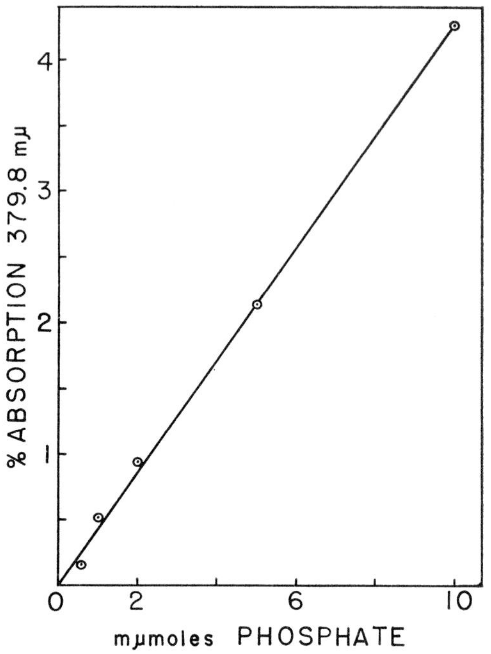

FIG. 2. Standard curve showing lower limits of phosphate determination at 379.8 mμ. Readings were taken on scale 5 and divided by 5 to give per cent absorption values shown in figure. Readings on the ordinate of 1, 2, 3, and 4% absorption correspond to absorbances of 0.0044, 0.0088, 0.0132, and 0.0177, respectively.

not greatly alter the net absorbance observed. Therefore, as long as controls and standards contained the same amount of acid as the sample, reliable determinations could be made with these levels of added acid. Other experiments showed that addition of more than 3.0 ml of 1 N HCl should be avoided. Under these conditions elevation in blank absorption and decrease in net absorption of the sample limited the accuracy of the determination. Addition of more than 0.6 ml of 1 N base greatly reduced the amount of phosphomolybdic acid extracted by 2-octanol, making the determination impractical.

Figure 1 shows standard curves for phosphate analysis (to 300 mμmoles phosphate) by direct determintaion of molybdenum at four wavelengths. Relative sensitivities for wavelengths of 313.3, 379.8, 386.4 and 390.3 mμ were 100, 58, 42, and 30, respectively. Linear response was not obtained above an absorbance of about 0.30, requiring selection of less sensitive wavelengths if linearity was desired at the higher concentrations of phosphate. However, with a working curve, determinations of higher quantities of phosphate can be made in the nonlinear region.

Lower limits of the described procedure are shown by the standard curve in Figure 2. Careful adjustment of the burner, aspirator, and fuel mixture resulted in a greater sensitivity than that seen in Figure 1. Investigators have found that increased sensitivity to molybdenum is achieved by using a three-slot Boling burner (10, 11) or a nitrous oxide–acetylene fuel mixture (12). These modifications might permit determination of even smaller amounts of phosphate.

Interferences

Silicate and arsenate interfered significantly only when present at levels higher than ordinarily encountered in reaction mixtures and tissues. Table 3 shows the increase in absorbance caused by the presence of silicate in the assay mixture. Arsenate had no appreciable effect up to 0.40 μmole. Ferric ion caused the depression observed by others (4). KCl at 0.7 *M* (before citrate addition) did not affect the determination of phosphate but when present at 1.23 *M* caused an 18% depression. No effect was observed when ADP (1 and 5 μmoles) or ATP (0.9 and 4.5

TABLE 3
Effect of Arsenate, Silicate, and Ferric Ions on Phosphate Determination[a]

Addition (μmoles)	Absorbance at 379.8 mμ
None	0.008
Phosphate (0.1)	0.084
+arsenate (0.08)	0.085
+arsenate (0.20)	0.086
+arsenate (0.40)	0.085
+silicate (0.08)	0.085
+silicate (0.20)	0.089
+silicate (0.40)	0.095
+ferric nitrate (1.25)	0.060
+ferric nitrate (2.50)	0.049

[a] See "Methods" for procedure. Arsenate and silicate were added as the sodium salts.

TABLE 4
Overcoming Mannitol Interference by Dilution[a]

Volume[b], ml	Acid molybdate, ml	Citrate, ml	Per cent of control
5.0	0.5	1.0	3
10.0	1.0	2.0	14
20.0	2.0	4.0	91
30.0	3.0	6.0	100

[a] Samples contained 0.5 μmole phosphate and 0.5 mmole mannitol (no mannitol in controls) and were assayed as described under "Methods" using 3.0 ml 2-octanol.

[b] Final volume of added phosphate, mannitol, and glass-distilled water.

μmoles) was present with 0.8 μmole phosphate. Although other levels were not tested, these results indicated that no interference would be expected by ADP or ATP at concentrations normally used in phosphorylation and adenosine triphosphatase studies.

Mannitol interfered with the determination of phosphate by this method, as it did in the colorimetric procedure used by Vreman and Jobsis (13). In the presence of 0.1, 0.2, and 0.3 mmole mannitol, values for the determination of 0.5 μmole phosphate were low by 10, 83, and 96%, respectively. However, this interference could be eliminated by either sample dilution or digestion. Table 4 shows how proper dilution of a sample containing mannitol resulted in complete recovery of phosphate. In these dilutions, the final concentrations of molybdate and citrate remained the same. The recovery of phosphate from a sample containing mannitol depends upon providing sufficient molybdate for the formation of both mannitol and phosphate complexes. Therefore, proper dilution will depend upon the amount of mannitol and phosphate present in the sample. For example, a 4-fold dilution (20 ml volume) was adequate for the determination of 0.5 μmole phosphate in the presence of 0.2 mmole mannitol. An increase in the volume of the aqueous phase of the assay solution does not result in decreased absorbance since phosphomolybdic acid is quantitatively extracted by 2-octanol.

When applicable, acid digestion of a sample containing mannitol offers another means of eliminating interference. Digestion of 0.2 mmole mannitol over a microburner in 0.2 ml of a 2:1 mixture (v/v) of 70% perchloric acid and concentrated sulfuric acid until the solution was clear, and all of the perchloric acid was evaporated, completely eliminated interference in the determination of 0.5 μmole phosphate. If the initial digestion is incomplete, additional aliquots of perchloric acid are permitted if the excess is evaporated before assaying for phosphate. Otherwise, the acid tolerance of the procedure would be exceeded.

Many phosphate assays of biological systems are carried out in the presence of reducing agents such as ascorbate. These reagents reduce the phosphomolybdic acid complex and interfere with its extraction by the organic solvent. Experiments with ATPase activity in trout gill mitochondria showed a 15% depression of determined phosphate levels when ascorbate (0.2 μmole) was present in the assay mixture. Addition of 0.1 ml of 20 m*M* $KMnO_4$ completely eliminated the interference. Permanganate may be added prior to or following acid molybdate addition. If phosphomolybdic acid has been extracted into 2-octanol, and a blue color shows that some reduction has taken place, permanganate can then be added, prior to citrate addition, and the tube shaken again. Complete oxidation and extraction of the complex results.

The presence of protein in the assay mixture caused a severe depression in the determined phosphate concentration. The absorbance of 0.1 μmole phosphate with 91, 181, and 362 μg of bovine serum albumin present in the assay mixture was decreased by 24, 46, and 88% respectively. Prior precipitation of protein in 0.32 *N* $HClO_4$ removed the interference. Likewise, omission of perchloric acid precipitation of serum decreased the determined level of phosphate by 60%. Visual observation of a blue color associated with protein left in the assay mixture and precipitated during the assay procedure indicated that phosphomolybdic acid probably became adsorbed to the denatured protein and could not be extracted by 2-octanol. All protein must therefore be eliminated from samples used for phosphate determination. When this is accomplished by addition of acid, care must be taken not to exceed the acid tolerance of the method.

Application

Table 5 presents data obtained from the measurement of ATPase activity in mitochondria and microsomes isolated from rainbow trout gill homogenates. Absorbance readings decreased after the assay mixture stood for 13 hr, perhaps because a temperature decrease in the samples

TABLE 5
Measurement of ATPase Activity in Mitochondria and Microsomes and Stability of Phosphate Determinations with Time[a]

Preparation	Absorbance: Initial determination	Absorbance: After 13 hr	Phosphate liberated, mμmoles: Initial determination	Phosphate liberated, mμmoles: After 13 hr
I. Blank	0.020	0.015	—	—
Mitochondria	0.383	0.369	413	413
Mitochondria	0.383	0.364	413	410
II. Blank	0.025	0.021	—	—
Microsomes	0.668	0.650	765	769
Microsomes	0.664	0.638	759	751

[a] Mitochondria and microsomes were prepared from trout gill homogenates by differential centrifugation. Reaction mixtures (1.6 ml) contained Tris, pH 8.0 (50 m*M*), $MgCl_2$ (3.3 m*M*), ATP (3 m*M*), and mitochondria (25 μg protein) or microsomes (15 μg protein). After 15 min at 30° the reaction was stopped by addition of 0.1 ml cold 35% $HClO_4$. Determinations were made as outlined under "Methods" on 0.5 ml of the supernatant solution obtained after centrifugation.

resulted in a slower rate of sample uptake. However, the final phosphate determinations remained unchanged. In another experiment, the determined phosphate concentration was unchanged 3 days after the initial determination.

Results from determinations of acid soluble and total phosphate levels

TABLE 6
Determination of Phosphate in Trout Serum, Showing Accuracy, Precision, and Recovery[a]

Phosphate	Serum vol., μl	Phosphate added, μmole	Phosphate determined, μmole	Added phosphate recovered, μmole
Acid-soluble phosphate	20	—	0.067	—
	20	—	0.068	—
	40	—	0.143	—
	40	—	0.142	—
	40	0.05	0.192	0.05
	40	0.05	0.192	0.05
	40	0.10	0.235	0.10
	40	0.10	0.236	0.10
Total serum phosphate	20	—	0.228	—
	20	—	0.227	—
	20	—	0.227	—
	20	—	0.228	—
	20	0.10	0.330	0.10
	20	0.10	0.330	0.10
	20	0.20	0.427	0.20
	20	0.20	0.428	0.20

[a] Assays were peiformed as described under "Methods" on blood serum from one 700 gm rainbow trout.

in trout serum are presented in Table 6. Values obtained for duplicate determinations (quadruplicate for total phosphate) are shown to indicate the degree of reproducibility that can be expected from this method. Table 6 also shows that recovery of added phosphate is complete in both acid-soluble and total phosphate methods.

TABLE 7
Phosphorus Content of Some Trout Tissues[a]

Material	Phosphorus concentration
Serum[b]	
Acid-soluble	10.9 mg/100 ml
Total	36 mg/100 ml
Blood (total)[b]	125 mg/100 ml
+0.1 μmole $Fe(NO_3)_3$	124 mg/100 ml
Muscle (back)[c]	285 mg/100 gm
Liver[c]	440 mg/100 gm
Bone (spine)[d]	2417 mg/100 gm

[a] See "Methods" for a description of the procedure.
[b] From a 700 gm rainbow trout.
[c] From a 10 lb steelhead trout.
[d] Section of the spinal column from a 11.5 gm silver salmon.

Table 7 summarizes values for the phosphate content (expressed as mg phosphorus) of some trout tissues obtained by procedures outlined under "Methods." Iron, added to one sample of blood in an amount approximately equal to that contained in the blood itself, had no effect on the determination. Higher levels of iron are required to cause the depression seen in Table 3. Comparison of samples digested in the presence of added phosphate with others having phosphate added after digestion showed no loss of phosphorus resulting from the digestion process. Repeated determinations on solid tissues resulted in values for phosphate that seldom varied by more than 2%.

DISCUSSION

The procedure described for phosphate determination is rapid, sensitive, and accurate. With this procedure, analysis of large numbers of samples could be accomplished conveniently by methods of automation now employed in atomic absorption spectrophotometry. Other conveniences include the elimination of cuvets required by other spectrophotometric methods and of the associated transfer of the organic solvent to these vessels.

Citrate has been used here, as it was by Marsh (14), to bind excess molybdic acid. Not only does this prevent the molybdenum-catalyzed hydrolysis of labile organic phosphates but prevents further formation of phosphomolybdic acid. Citrate so effectively binds molybdic acid that addition of the amount used in this procedure to an aqueous solution of phosphomolybdic acid apparently caused this complex to dissociate, since none was extracted by the organic solvent. However, citrate did not affect phosphomolybdic acid once it was present in 2-actanol.

Elimination of interference by diluting the interfering substance, as shown here for mannitol, is a method which should work equally well when other molybdate complexing agents (oxalate, citrate, etc.) are present. These dilutions do not affect the sensitivity of the determination since essentially all of the phosphomolybdic acid is extracted by the organic solvent regardless of the volume of the aqueous phase. Vreman and Jobsis (13) used increased concentrations of molybdate and sulfuric acid to overcome mannitol interference, but indicated that one objectional feature was the increased rate of organic phosphate (e.g., ATP) hydrolysis under these conditions. Diluting mannitol by increasing the volume of the assay mixture avoids this problem.

Although 2-octanol was selected for these studies, primarily because of resulting low blank values, it is obvious from Table 2 that other solvents could be used in the described procedure. At pH values from 3.5 to 5.5, 2-octanol failed to extract phosphomolybdic acid whereas isobutanol and 1-butanol were capable of doing so. A mixture of equal parts of 2-octanol and 1-butanol exhibited characteristics of both solvents, extracting phosphomolybdic acid over a pH range from 1 to 5. Ketones and esters offer other possibilities and have been used for phosphomolybdic acid extraction by other investigators (4).

Tissue, blood, and serum digestions were also carried out with combinations of sulfuric acid and 30% hydrogen peroxide or nitric acid. However, when peroxide was used, a preliminary digestion with sulfuric acid was required, followed by a second digestion after the addition of peroxide. Sulfuric acid used with concentrated nitric acid was effective but digestion with this mixture sometimes required more time than the sulfuric acid–perchloric acid mixture described under "Methods."

An important factor to be remembered is that the viscosity of 2-octanol, as well as other rather viscous organic solvents, is affected by temperature. Thus, a change in the temperature of samples being aspirated into the instrument will cause a change in the rate of uptake. As reported earlier (9), a change of 1°C in the range of 17° to 40° resulted in a 2% change in absorption readings, demonstrating the necessity of maintaining a constant-temperature environment for samples during a series of readings.

Should available tissue, blood, or serum samples be in short supply, considerably less than the amounts suggested in the procedures could be used. With care, samples containing as little as 3–4 mμmoles of phosphate can be determined with good precision, especially when using the method of additions or internal standards.

SUMMARY

Extraction of phosphomolybdic acid by 2-octanol, and subsequent determination of the molybdenum concentration by atomic absorption spectrophotometry, provides a rapid, sensitive, indirect method of inorganic phosphate determination. As little as 3–4 mμmoles of phosphate can be determined accurately with a standard air–acetylene burner. Procedures are described for the determination of inorganic phosphate in blood, serum, bone, other biological tissues, and enzyme-containing reaction mixtures.

ACKNOWLEDGMENT

The excellent technical assistance of Mrs. Hazel Jones is gratefully acknowledged. Editorial comments by Dr. C. B. Croston and Mr. C. L. Johnson were greatly appreciated.

REFERENCES

1. Bell, R. D., and Doisy, E. A., *J. Biol. Chem.* **44**, 55 (1920).
2. Fiske, C. H., and SubbaRow, Y., *J. Biol. Chem.* **66**, 375 (1925).

3. BERENBLUM, I., AND CHAIN, E., *Biochem. J.* **32**, 295 (1938).
4. WADELIN, C., AND MELLON, M. G., *Anal. Chem.* **25**, 1668 (1953).
5. SCHAFFER, F. L., FONG, J., AND KIRK, P. L., *Anal. Chem.* **25**, 343 (1953).
6. MARTIN, J. B., AND DOTY, D. M., *Anal. Chem.* **21**, 965 (1949).
7. DELAUGHTER, B., *Atomic Absorption Newsletter* **4** (No. 5), 273 (1965) (Perkin-Elmer Corp., Norwalk, Conn.).
8. MANSELL, R. E., AND EMMEL, H. W,. *ibid.* **4** (No. 10), 365 (1965).
9. ZAUGG, W. S., AND KNOX, R. J., *Anal. Chem.* **38**, 1759 (1966).
10. BOLING, E. A., *Spectrochim. Acta* **22**, 425 (1966).
11. SPRAGUE, S., AND SLAVIN, W., *Atomic Absorption Newsletter* **4** (No. 6), 293 (1965) (Perkin-Elmer Corp., Norwalk, Conn.).
12. WILLIS, J. B., *Nature* **207**, 715 (1965).
13. VREMAN, H. J., AND JOBSIS, F. F., *Anal. Biochem.* **17**, 108 (1966).
14. MARSH, B. B., *Biochim. Biophys. Acta* **32**, 357 (1959).

ANALYTICAL BIOCHEMISTRY 20, 294–298 (1967)

An Automatic Device for Adding Solvents to Chromatography Tanks

CLINTON A. NERENBERG, DINESH C. SHARMA,[1] AND RALPH I. DORFMAN

Institute of Hormone Biology, Syntex Research Center, Stanford Industrial Park, Palo Alto, California 94304

Received February 2, 1967

During the last fifteen years paper chromatographic methods for the separation and purification of micro quantities of steroids and related compounds have proved to be of great value. Most of these methods (systems) are basically related to those described by Burton *et al.* (1951) and Bush (1952). In both types of systems the paper strip loaded with the sample is allowed to equilibrate with the vapors of the solvent system for a certain period of time by allowing it to hang from a glass trough in a sealed glass jar. The atmosphere in the glass tank is kept saturated with the solvent vapors by covering the walls of the tank with filter papers continually soaking with the mobile and stationary phase, and covering the bottom of the tank (about 2 cm deep) with a mixture of these solvents.

After the equilibration period, the chromatogram is developed for a certain period by adding the mobile phase to the trough from which the paper is hanging. The equilibration period as well as the time for developing is as critical as the selection of the systems for separation and purification of compounds. In Bush-type systems (1), an equilibration period of about 4 hr followed by a chromatogram developing period of 4 hr is adequate in general. In Zaffaroni-type systems (1), the equilibration time varies from a few hours to overnight; and the chromatogram developing time may also vary from about 4 hr to several days (3). For effective and reproducible results, it is necessary that the time schedule for equilibration and chromatogram development should be adhered to.

However, to keep these time schedules, it has been the common experience of most research workers that they attend to the chroma-

[1] Correspondence regarding this communication may be addressed to D. C. Sharma.

tography tank at odd hours either to start the development of the chromatogram by adding the mobile phase to the trough or, if they have started it during normal working hours, then to stop it at an odd time. Sometimes, for certain systems this situation can be avoided only by increasing the equilibration time to an overnight period, and then

FIG. 1. Rear view of solvent-adding device with cover panel from the rear removed to show component parts: (A) Stainless-steel reservoirs. (B) Teflon covers for reservoirs. (C) Stainless-steel tubes connecting reservoirs to Teflon valves. (D) Teflon body of valves from Valcor Eng. Corp., Kenilworth, N. J., Part #51-19T34-7; the valve is normally closed (N.C.). (E) Stainless-steel tubes as outlets for solvent from valve; these outlets are connected to the chromatography tanks by Teflon tubing as described in the text. (F) Metal bracket to hold reservoirs. (G) Rear of electric timers (Intermatic clock timer, Model A401-4, 15 A, 1875 W, International Register Co., 2626 W. Washington Blvd., Chicago 12, Ill.). (H) Solenoid portions (metal) of valves (D). (I) Outlet for electric current, 110 V, 60 hz, i.e., cycles.

adding the mobile phase to the trough at the start of the next work day. This practice, while quite justifiable for the obvious convenience, leads not only to a variation in equilibration time but also to the occupation of the equipment needlessly for another work day. It is not possible to do this with a majority of the Zaffaroni-type (1, 3) chromatography systems.

In our laboratory this problem has been resolved by making a simple device which automatically adds the mobile phase to the trough at a preset time at the end of the equilibration period. For the last one year we have been able to start the development of most of our chromatograms during the night at a preset hour so that the chromatogram is ready during the work hours of the following day. The device has helped in keeping reproducible equilibration and developing time without attending the chromatograms at night. Also, due to less traffic in the chromatography room during the night, the temperature was found to be better controlled. Consequently the serious problem of variations in the chromatograms has been virtually eliminated.

Essentially this device consists of four parts:

1. A reservoir to hold the solvent to be added.
2. A Teflon valve actuated by a solenoid; this is normally closed (N.C.) and is attached to the reservoir.
3. An electric timer (24 hr) which has a start and stop switch that can be preset. The timer is connected to the solenoid valve.
4. A Teflon tube attached to the outlet of the valve. The other end goes into the trough through the hole in the lid of the tank. A Teflon

FIG. 2. Front view of device. The levers for setting "on" and "off" time are apparent. The switches turn on the device and the light (red lamp) indicates whether one or both units are in operation.

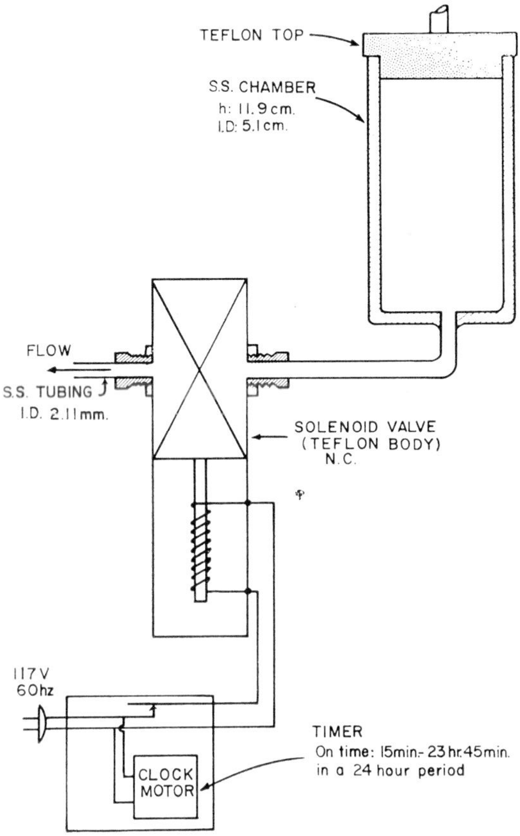

FIG. 3. Schematic diagram for the different components of the device and their dimensions. S.S. chamber—stainless-steel chamber 11.9 cm high, i.d. 5.1 cm. S.S. tubing—stainless-steel tubing, i.d. 2.11 mm. Solenoid valve normally closed (N.C.). Electric current—117 V, 60 hz (or cycles). Timer—at preset hour, the circuit closes for a period of 15 min (on time), actuating the solenoid valve (i.e., opening it) for this period and allowing the mobile phase, stored in the stainless-steel chamber of the unit, to flow by gravity into the trough from which the chromatography paper is hanging. At the end of the 15 min (on time) the circuit is open and the valve is closed (valve is normally closed). The preset hour, and the duration of the on time is set by the worker.

plug in the hole keeps the tube in place and also seals the hole from the outer atmosphere.

Figures 1 and 2 show the device, which has two reservoirs, two timers, and two valves and hence can be used with two tanks simultaneously, although it is not necessary to use both the devices since they are two independent units housed together. If it is necessary to add solvent to more than one trough in the same tank, then a simple glass manifold fitted at the top of the tank serves adequately.

Figure 3 is a diagram of the electrical connections. Further details are given in the legends to the figures.

REFERENCES

1. Burton, R. B., Zaffaroni, A., and Keutmann, E. H., *J. Biol. Chem.* **188,** 763 (1951).
2. Bush, I. E., *Biochem. J.* **50,** 370 (1952).
3. Savard, K., *Rec. Prog. Hormone Res.* **10,** 185 (1954).

ANALYTICAL BIOCHEMISTRY 20, 299–311 (1967)

Rapid Short-Column Chromatography of Amino Acids[1]

A Method for Blood and Urine Specimens in the Diagnosis and Treatment of Metabolic Disease

VIVIAN E. SHIH,[2] MARY L. EFRON,[3] AND GERALD L. MECHANIC[4]

Departments of Neurology and Orthopedic Surgery, Harvard Medical School, and The Joseph P. Kennedy, Jr., Memorial Laboratories at the Massachusetts General Hospital, Boston, Massachusetts 02114

Received February 10, 1967

Recent advances in the methods of ion-exchange chromatography have been directed largely toward accelerated analyses and the use of smaller samples (1–5). While the major impetus for this has been the great interest in protein structure, a parallel growth in knowledge of amino acid metabolism as related to clinical disease has produced an increasing demand for rapid analysis of the amino acids in physiological fluids, especially blood and urine. These fluids differ from protein hydrolyzates in that they may contain 60 or more ninhydrin-positive substances, as opposed to the 20 amino acids in most proteins. For this reason, accelerated analyses are often achieved only at the expense of overlapping peaks and loss of resolution (5).

It is often unnecessary in the course of treatment of a metabolic disease to know the concentration of each amino acid. An investigator or therapist may need to measure only one amino acid, or at most a few amino acids, of interest in the particular clinical situation. He may also need to make repeated measurements of one amino acid, e.g., when following blood or urine levels during dietary treatment, or during loading tests.

For these reasons, we have attempted to achieve a rapid separation on short columns of the relevant amino acids for diagnosis and moni-

[1] Preliminary Report, see also reference 13.

[2] Research Fellow in Neurology, Massachusetts General Hospital, and Harvard Medical School.

[3] Assistant in Neurology and Assistant Biochemist, Massachusetts General Hospital; Assistant Professor in Neurology, Harvard Medical School.

[4] Research Associate in Biological Chemistry, Harvard Medical School; Research Fellow in Orthopedic Surgery, Massachusetts General Hospital.

toring of each presently known clinical disorder of amino acid metabolism in man (6). The separation of tyrosine and phenylalanine in 15 min using the short-column method principle has already been published (7). This report described analogous methods for studying disorders involving other amino acids.

MATERIALS AND METHODS

The short columns may be attached to any amino acid analyzer. The analyses shown in Figures 1–10 were performed by two of us (V.S. and M.E.) on a Technicon amino acid analyzer with a modified ninhydrin system (8, 9). The preparation of the sample and application to the column were as previously described (7–9). All analyses, except for that shown in Figure 11, an accelerated analysis described later, were performed using a 35 cm jacketed column, 0.9 cm i.d., packed with resin (Spherix xx8-60-0, a generous gift from Phoenix Precision Company) to a 20 cm level. The buffer was pumped at a flow rate of 1.0 ml/min.

The compositions of the buffers used were devised as variants of the two buffers (pH 2.875, 0.2 *M* Na citrate, and pH 4.74, 0.8 *M* Na citrate (10) used for the complete amino acid analysis on 50 or 120 cm columns (7, 8, 9). The sodium concentration of the buffers was 0.2 *M* except as noted. Buffers and water jacket temperatures were varied as described below, depending on the separation desired.

BUFFERS AND TEMPERATURE

System 1. *Hydroxyproline*

For separation of hydroxyproline on short columns (Fig. 1), it was necessary to lower the temperature to 33° and the pH of the buffer to 2.45. Hydroxyproline is eluted in 60 min.

System II. *Sarcosine*

Using a buffer of pH 2.65 and a temperature of 65°, sarcosine is eluted as a separate peak between glutamine and glutamic acid (Fig. 2). The temperature is important; at 28–37° the emergence of glutamine is delayed so that it is separated from threonine and serine, and overlaps sarcosine.

The buffer can be made from the standard pH 2.875 buffer by adding two drops of concentrated hydrochloric acid to 100 ml buffer.

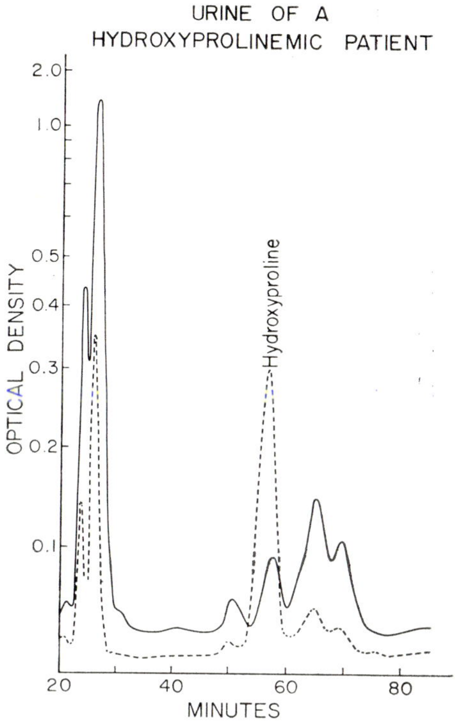

FIG. 1. System I: separation of hydroxyproline.

System III. *Proline through Valine*

When the pH 2.875 is used alone, proline and glycine are readily separated from all other amino acids (Fig. 3). Proline is eluted in 60 min in this system, glycine at 70 min, and alanine at 80 min followed by α-aminobutyric acid and valine. Since valine is not eluted until 105 min, it is more satisfactory to use System VII (see below) for this amino acid.

System IV. *Cystine and Cysteine-Penicillamine Disulfide*

Cystinuric patients on penicillamine therapy excrete both cystine and the mixed disulfide in the urine. Both are resolved in a buffer with a pH of approximately 3.0. This buffer is prepared by adding 2–3 ml of pH 4.74 to 150 ml of pH 2.875 buffer. The absolute pH should be adjusted so that the cystine, which is very sensitive to pH changes, is eluted between valine and methionine. The mixed disulfide is eluted after the cystine and overlaps methionine (Fig. 4). For practical purposes,

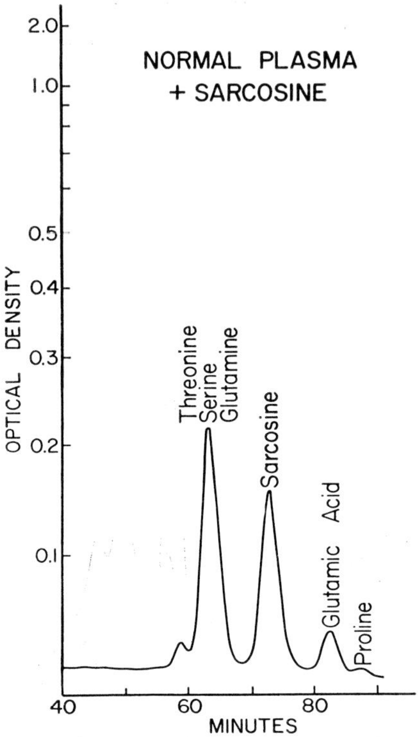

FIG. 2. System II: separation of sarcosine.

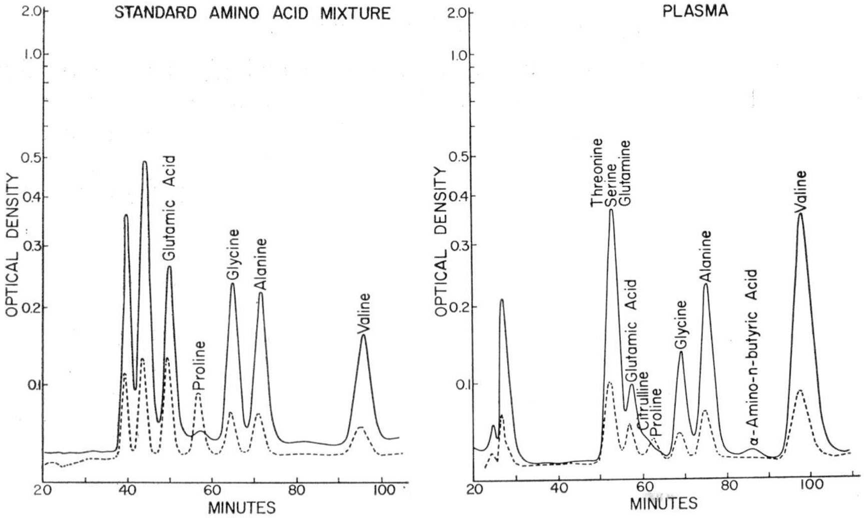

FIG. 3. System III: separation of proline, glycine, alanine, and α-aminobutyric acid.

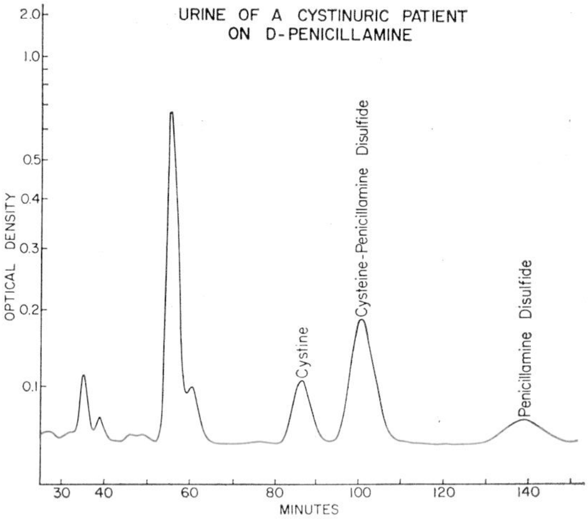

FIG. 4. System IV: separation of amino acids in urine from a cystinuric patient on penicillamine therapy.

this is not important, because cystinurics (and normals) rarely excrete more than 10 mg of methionine per day. Homocitrulline does not interfere in this system, in which it overlaps valine.

System V. *Cystathionine*

A pH 3.25 buffer was made by mixing the 2.875 and 4.74 buffers in the proportion of 175 to 5 ml. Cystathionine was eluted at 85 min following methionine. Cystine emerges at 55 min, just before valine;

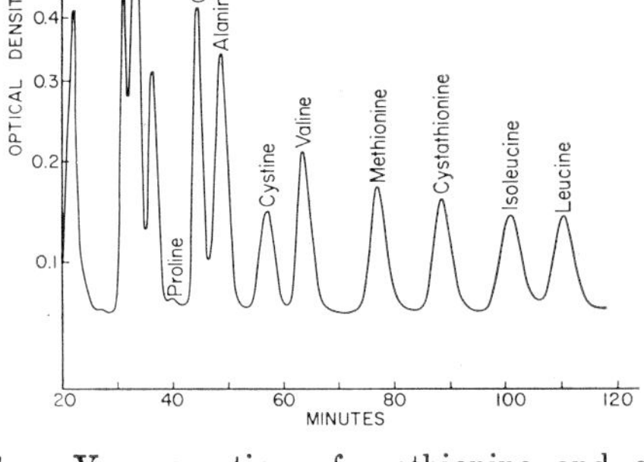

FIG. 5. System V: separation of methionine and cystathionine.

it is not separated from homocitrulline (Fig. 5). When homocitrulline is known not to be present in the sample, this system can also be used to quantitate cystine.

Cystathionine is also sensitive to pH. In the next system (pH 3.50), it overlaps valine.

System VI. *Homocitrulline*

This buffer is a mixture of pH 2.875 and 4.74 buffers in the proportion of 150 to 5 ml. The pH is approximately 3.30 and the sodium

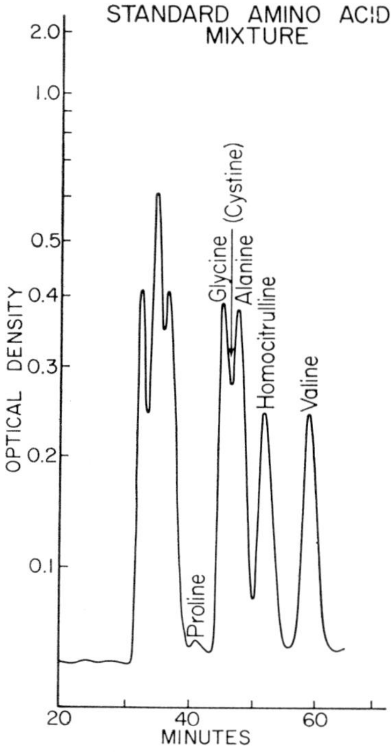

FIG. 6. System VI: separation of homocitrulline.

concentration 0.22 *M*. Homocitrulline is eluted before valine, while cystine overlaps alanine (Fig. 6). The position of homocitrulline is fairly sensitive to pH. At lower pH values, e.g. 3.10, it is moved toward valine.

System VII. *Branched-Chain Amino Acids*

The pH 3.50, 0.24 *M* Na buffer for the separation of the branched-chain amino acids can be made up conveniently by mixing the two standard buffers (pH 2.875 and 4.74) in the proportion 14 to 1. The

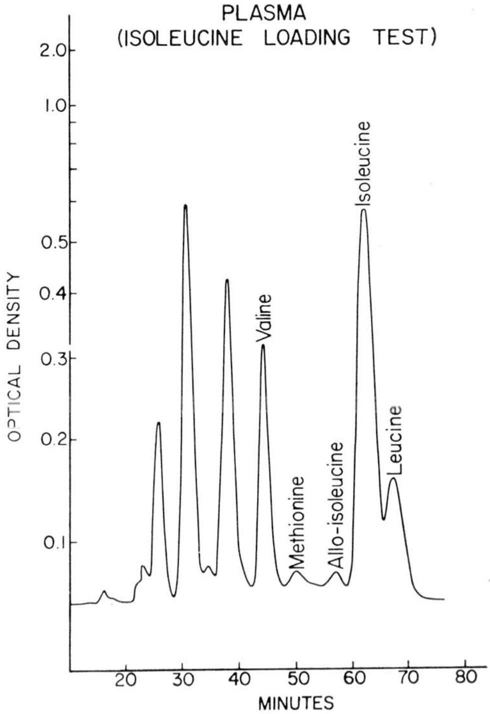

FIG. 7. System VII: separation of branched-chain amino acids suitable for monitoring maple syrup urine disease.

amino acids were eluted in the same sequence as with the 2.875 buffer, except for cystine, which is very sensitive to pH and which emerges before valine, being eluted in a mixed peak with glycine and alanine (Fig. 7). Alloisoleucine is well resolved in this system, making the method quite satisfactory for studies of maple syrup urine disease (11).

System VIII. *Tyrosine–Phenylalanine*

Tyrosine and phenylalanine are resolved using a pH 4.30, 0.4 *M* Na buffer. This is described completely in a previous publication (7). It is noted that buffer with sodium concentration of 0.4 *M* gives the same resolution as that of 0.38 *M*, and that the resolution is satisfactory with any pH between 4.30 and 4.50.

System IX. *Methionine–Homocystine, β-Alanine, γ-Aminobutyric Acid, and Argininosuccinic Acid*

For monitoring homocystinuria, it was necessary to use two buffers. These patients have not only homocystine but also methionine in excess in the blood and urine. In order to resolve the two amino acids in the same analysis, the pH 3.50, 0.24 *M* Na buffer was used until after the emergence of methionine, followed by the same pH 4.30, 0.4 *M* Na buffer which is used for the tyrosine–phenylalanine separation. In our system, there is a 20 min lag before the second buffer reaches the column. The time of buffer change may have to be varied from the 55

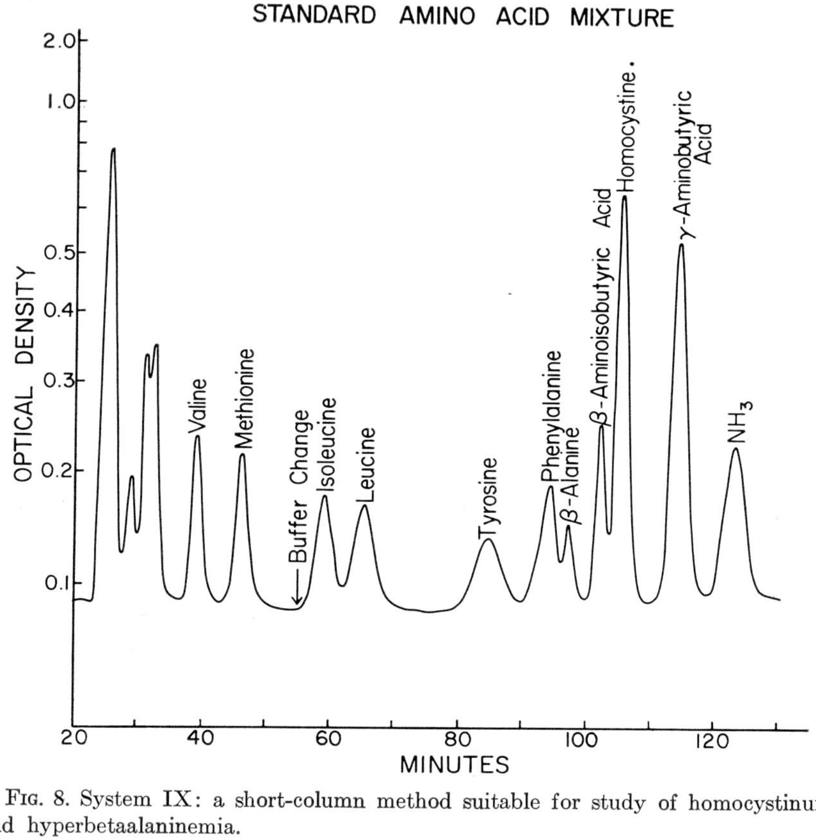

FIG. 8. System IX: a short-column method suitable for study of homocystinuria and hyperbetaalaninemia.

min that has proved satisfactory on our analyzer, if a different system with a different lag time is used (Fig. 8). In the same figure, the positions of β-alanine, β-aminoisobutyric acid, and γ-aminobutyric acid are also shown.

Specimens containing argininosuccinic acid are usually boiled in acid before analysis to convert the unstable free argininosuccinic acid to its anhydrides, B and C of Westall (12). Anhydride B falls between leucine and tyrosine, while anhydride C emerges near homocystine (Fig. 9).

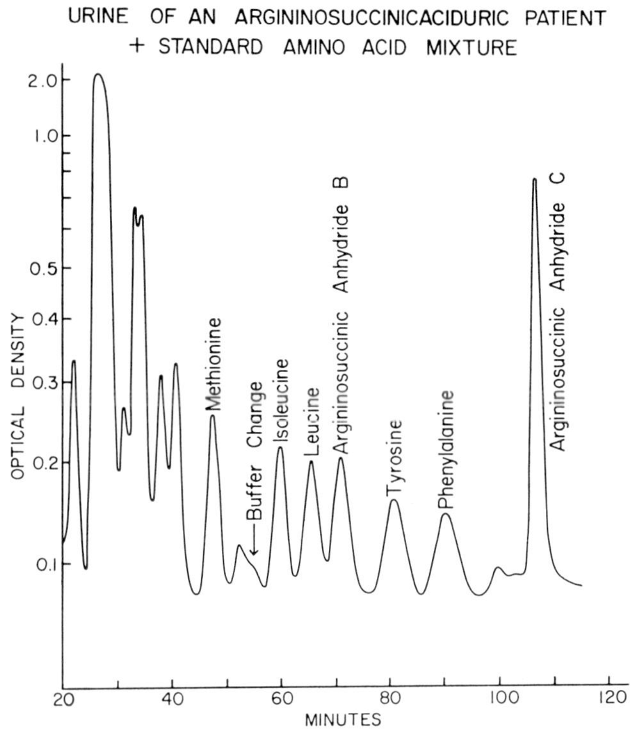

FIG. 9. Separation of argininosuccinic acid and its anhydrides by System IX.

System X. *The Basic Amino Acids*

The pH 4.79, 0.4 M Na buffer can be prepared by diluting the pH 4.74 buffer used in the standard long-column analysis 1:1 with water, and titrating to pH 4.79 with hydrochloric acid. In order to separate histidine and ammonia, the jacket temperature is maintained at 33°. After the emergence of ammonia, the temperature is raised to 65° and the buffer is changed to one of pH 5.8, 0.8 M Na. This is done in order to hasten the emergence of arginine (Fig. 10). It is apparent that there was no marked baseline shift despite the abrupt change in salt concentration.

ACCELERATED ANALYSIS

The analyses described in Figures 1–10 can be further accelerated. Figure 11 is an example; it shows the analysis described in System V but requiring only one-third the time.

This analysis was performed by one of us (G.M.) in a Phoenix model VG8000 amino acid analyzer. For this analysis, a resin which gives bet-

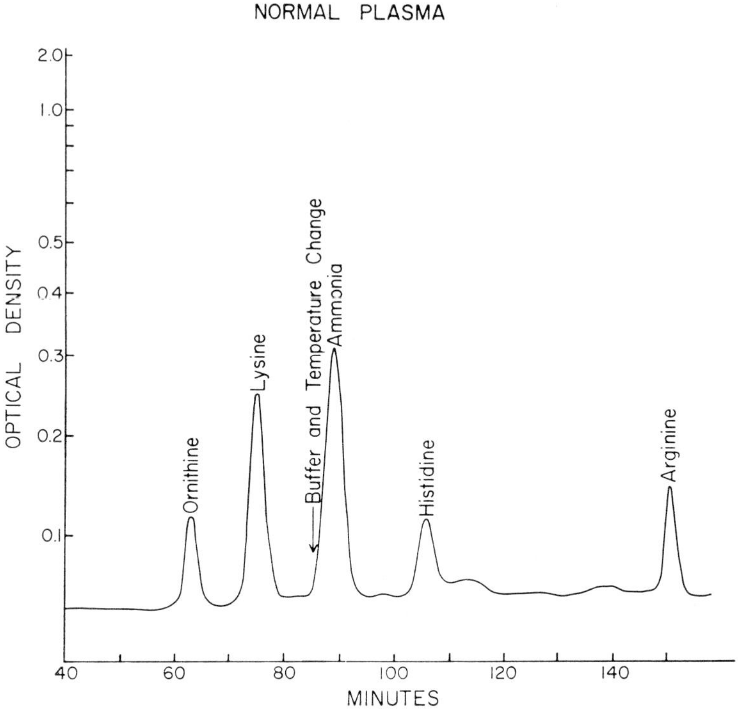

FIG. 10. System X: separation of basic amino acids.

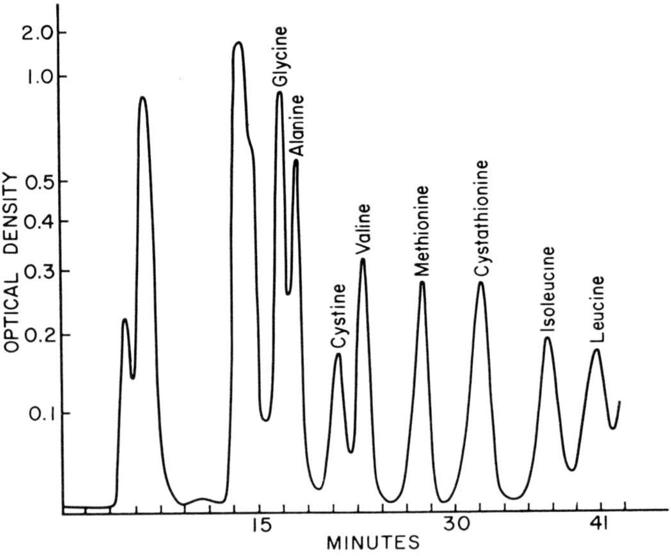

FIG. 11. System V performed at a flow rate of 2.0 ml/min on a 10 cm column of Spherix xx907-10.

ter resolution was used (Spherix xx-907-10, which is now commercially available from Phoenix Precision Company, Philadelphia, Pennsylvania). The resin column was packed in a 0.9 cm column to a height of 10 cm. The flow rate was 2.0 ml/min.

STANDARD SOLUTIONS

Cysteic acid is used as a standard for all analyzers. For each buffer system, the constant for each amino acid (i.e., its color value relative to that of cysteic acid) is determined initially. Thereafter, standardization with cysteic acid is performed each day on each column to be used. One milliliter of a solution containing 0.1 μmole/ml cysteic acid is pumped through the column, using the first buffer to be used for analysis of the unknown. After this peak is recorded, the unknown is placed on the column and analyzed. This daily standardization is necessary on the Technicon amino acid analyzer; such frequent standardization is unnecessary on other analyzers in which the entire effluent enters the recording system.

REGENERATION OF THE COLUMNS

When the run is completed, the buffer is removed from the top of the resin column, and the space filled with 0.4 *M* NaOH containing 0.1% EDTA. The equilibrating buffer line is then attached and the buffer pumped for 20 min, after which the column is both regenerated and equilibrated for the next analysis.

DISCUSSION

The column methods described in this paper can be adapted for use with any amino acid analyzer. With better resins, such as Spherix xx907-10 (11–14 μ), the analyses can be performed with higher flow rates, e.g., 2.0 ml/min on an 0.9×10 cm column. This permits even more rapid analyses with as little as one-third the time required for the analyses described above. With two columns, one can be regenerated and equilibrated while the amino acids are being eluted and quantitated on the other column. Many analyses can, therefore, be performed in one day. The method is ideally suited to automation, and to procedures for accelerated analyses (1, 2).

A gradient system with an Autograd can also be used with the short columns by using the same composition of buffers as for the long columns but proportionately less buffer in each chamber. Obviously, one or two buffer systems are preferable for rapid runs because preparation of the Autograd is time consuming and a gradient elution offers no advantage over single or discontinuous two-buffer systems.

In this laboratory, we routinely perform two 14 hr analyses on two 50 × 0.9 cm columns overnight (9). This is used for measurement of samples in which the entire amino acid content is to be quantitated. During the working day, short-column runs are performed on samples in which only one or a few amino acids are to be measured. Three pumps are used during the day, one for regeneration of the long columns, one for regeneration of one short column, and the third for the amino acid analysis on the other short column. In this way, efficient use can be made of the ninhydrin and recording systems throughout the entire day and night.

It is expected that this system will prove useful for screening and treatment programs which, although concerned almost exclusively with phenylketonuria at present, are now expanding to include other amino acid disorders.

SUMMARY

Methods are described for the rapid analysis of certain individual amino acids (e.g., homocystine) and of groups of amino acids (e.g., the branched-chain amino acids), which are relevant to particular metabolic diseases. All the methods use ion-exchange chromatography on a 20 × 0.9 cm column. These methods were developed especially for clinical application in the diagnosis and therapy of inborn errors of amino acid metabolism. All analyses are completed in less than 2.5 hr.

ACKNOWLEDGMENT

This investigation was supported in part by grants from the U. S. Public Health Service (NB-5260, NB-05096 and AM-06375) and by The Joseph P. Kennedy, Jr., Foundation and The John A. Hartford Fund.

The authors are grateful to Miss Maryellen McCarthy for expert technical assistance.

REFERENCES

1. Hamilton, P. B., *Federation Proc.* **18**, 241 (1959).
2. Hamilton, P. B., *in* "Technicon Symposium on Automation in Analytical Chemistry, New York, N. Y. (1965)," p. 702. Mediad Inc., New York, 1966.
3. Dickenson, J. C., Rosenblum, H., and Hamilton, P. B., *Pediatrics* **36**, 2 (1965).
4. "Spinco DS-248," Beckman Instruments, Inc.
5. Catravas, G. N., *in* "Technicon Symposium on Automation in Analytical Chemistry, New York, N. Y. (1965)," p. 648. Mediad Inc., New York, 1966.
6. Efron, M. L., *New Engl. J. Med.* **272**, 1058, 1107 (1965).
7. Mechanic, G., Efron, M. L., and Shih, V. E., *Anal. Biochem.* **16**, 420 (1966).
8. Efron, M. L., *in* "Technicon Symposium on Automation in Analytical Chemistry, New York, N. Y. (1965)," p. 637. Mediad Inc., New York, 1966.
9. Efron, M. L., Shih, V. E., and Mechanic, G., in preparation.
10. Hamilton, P. B., *Anal. Chem.* **35**, 2055 (1963).

11. NORTON, P. M., ROITMAN, E., SNYDERMAN, S. E., AND HOLT, L. E., *Lancet* **1**, 26 (1962).
12. ARMSTRONG, M. D., YATES, K. N., AND STEMMERMANN, M. G., *Pediatrics* **33**, 280 (1964).
13. MECHANIC, G. L., SHIH, V. E., AND EFRON, M. L., *in* "Technicon Symposium on Automation in Analytical Chemistry, New York, N. Y. (1966)." Mediad Inc., New York, in press.

ANALYTICAL BIOCHEMISTRY 20, 312–320 (1967)

A Gas Chromatographic Method for Analysis of Anomeric Carbohydrates and for Determination of Mutarotation Coefficients

RONALD BENTLEY AND NANCY BOTLOCK

Department of Biochemistry and Nutrition, University of Pittsburgh, Graduate School of Public Health, Pittsburgh, Pennsylvania 15213

Received February 10, 1967

Methods for the assay of mutarotase (EC 5.1.3.3, aldose 1-epimerase) activity fall into two categories:

In the first, changes in optical rotation are measured as the mutarotation of a given sugar anomer proceeds (1–4). The most recent development in this category is the modification introduced by Keston (5); the substrate is a DL sugar and only one enantiomer reacts with the enzyme. This new method is insensitive to nonspecific catalysis, variations in pH, substrate concentration, and temperature. Any inhibitory effect of the enantiomer which is not a substrate is avoided by working with low substrate concentrations.

In the second category, the amount of one anomer, usually β-D-glucose, present in a solution at a given time is determined. In their pioneering work, Keilin and Hartree (1, 2) used glucose oxidase (EC 1.1.3.4, β-D-glucose:oxygen oxidoreductase) for this purpose and followed oxygen consumption manometrically. Keston has similarly used the specificity of glucose oxidase for the β-D-anomer and has assayed the H_2O_2 produced in the reaction by a peroxidase method (6). An automated modification of this latter method has been described by Hill and Cowart (7); this method can measure thirty samples per hour or monitor the effluent from a chromatographic column. Keston and Brandt (8), in a method for analysis of glucose anomers, used glucose oxidase to remove β-D-glucose from mixtures of the α- and β-D-anomers, then assayed the remaining α-D-glucose. Bentley and Bhate (9) had previously determined β-D-glucose by taking advantage of the more rapid oxidation of β- than α-D-glucose by bromine water. In work with the mutarotase from *Escherichia coli,* Wallenfells and Herrmann (10) used α-D-galactose as a substrate; the β-D-galactose formed was oxidized by β-D-galactose dehydrogenase (EC 1.1.1.48, D-galactose:NAD oxidoreductase) from *Pseu-*

domonas saccharophila. The formation of reduced NAD in this second reaction was followed spectrophotometrically in the usual way.

During the development of methods for the gas chromatography of *O*-trimethylsilyl (*O*-TMSi) derivatives of carbohydrates (11, 12) it was observed that the anomeric penta-*O*-TMSi derivatives of hexoses and the anomeric tetra-*O*-TMSi derivatives of pentoses were well separated on a variety of columns. In general, the β anomers had the longer retention times. It was clear, therefore, that gas chromatography could be used to provide a direct measure of the anomeric composition of an aqueous solution if a method could be devised for the preparation of the *O*-TMSi derivatives without change in anomeric composition. The development of such a method and its application to the determination of mutarotase activity is described in this paper. The method takes advantage of the fact that the reagent used to prepare the *O*-TMSi derivatives reacts equally with water. Small volumes of an aqueous solution are diluted with dimethylformamide, frozen at liquid air temperature, and then subject to trimethylsilylation.

METHODS

The α-D-glucose used was a sample of dextrose from the National Bureau of Standards (standard sample 41). The purity of other commercially available carbohydrates was checked by gas chromatography (11, 12). Pyridine was reagent grade and was stored over KOH pellets. Hexamethyldisilazane and trimethylchlorosilane were obtained from Applied Science Laboratories, State College, Pennsylvania, and were used without further purification.

Mutarotase was extracted from hog kidney, essentially as described by Keston (4). The kidney cortex (5.8 gm) was homogenized in a Potter-Elvehjem apparatus with 23.2 ml of 0.025 *M* phosphate buffer, pH 7.1. The homogenate was centrifuged for 30 min at 10,000 g and the supernatant fluid was used in the assays.

EQUIPMENT

For polarimetric measurements, a Rudolph high-precision polarimeter was used. Gas chromatography of *O*-TMSi derivatives was carried out on columns (6′ × 1/8″) of Chromosorb W, 100–120 mesh, containing 3% SE-30. The instrument used was the F & M Scientific Corporation model 402, equipped with a flame detector. The oven temperature was 180° for the TMSi derivatives of glucose, 175° for galactose, 160° for xylose, and 150° for arabinose. Areas under the peaks were assumed to be proportional to the amount of material present. These areas were calculated from the formula: peak height × width of peak at half peak height.

PROCEDURE

Polarimetric Measurements. All measurements were made at 20.0° with a jacketed, 1 dm tube. For the nonenzymic measurements, the sugar was dissolved in 0.001 *N* potassium phthalate buffer, pH 4.7, to give a 2% concentration. For the mutarotase experiments, up to 2.0 ml of the kidney homogenate was diluted to 25 ml with 0.025 *M* phosphate buffer, pH 7.1; 20 ml of this solution was used to dissolve 400 mg of glucose. Control experiments were carried out with 0.025 *M* phosphate buffer, pH 7.1, since it is known that the mutarotation coefficient in phosphate buffer under these conditions is higher than that determined in phthalate buffer at pH 4.7. For the mutarotation reaction

$$\alpha \underset{k_2}{\overset{k_1}{\rightleftharpoons}} \beta$$

the mutarotation coefficient, k, is defined by the following equation: where

$$k = k_1 + k_2 = \frac{1}{t} \log \frac{r_0 - r_\infty}{r_t - r_\infty}$$

r_0 is optical rotation at time zero, r_t the rotation at time t, and r_∞ the rotation of the final equilibrium solution. The slope of the plot of log $r_t - r_\infty$ against t was used to determine the value of k. The mutarotation coefficients are expressed in logarithms to base 10 and reciprocal minutes.

Gas Chromatographic Method. In the nonenzymic experiments, a 40 mg portion of a sugar anomer was dissolved at zero time in 2 ml of 0.001 *N* potassium phthalate buffer, pH 4.7. The buffer solution and solid sugar were kept in the thermostated bath prior to and after solution. If necessary, the solution was shaken until the sugar had dissolved. For mutarotase assay, portions of up to 2.0 ml of kidney homogenate were diluted to 25.0 ml with 0.025 *M* phosphate buffer, pH 7.1; 2 ml of the diluted enzyme solution was then used to dissolve 40 mg of sugar.

Sample Preparation. At appropriate time intervals, 5 μl portions of the mutarotating solution were withdrawn using a glass micropipet. The pipet was kept in a test tube containing the same buffer solution, and held in the same bath between sampling. After each sample was taken, the pipet was rinsed with buffer, then returned to the tube of buffer. The 5 μl sample was blown out into 0.1 ml of dimethylformamide, at room temperature, contained in a 1 dram vial (plastic stoppered). The tip of the pipet was placed in the dimethylformamide and, when the pipet had emptied, the contents of the vial were rapidly mixed by gentle shaking. The vial was quickly placed in liquid nitrogen and was held there for about 30 sec until the vigorous boiling of the nitrogen ceased. A 1 ml portion of silylating reagent was then added to the frozen contents, the plastic stopper was inserted, and the contents were vigorously shaken. The vial was allowed to stand at room temperature, and was shaken intermittently over a 30 min. period.

A sample of the solution of TMSi derivatives (usually 2 μl) was then injected directly into the gas chromatography column. A heavy precipitate formed in the course of the silylation reaction; it was, however, easy to remove the sample from the supernatant fluid above the precipitate. No change in the samples was observed on standing for a period of several hours.

Silylating Reagent. The reagent normally used for anhydrous samples (11, 12) was modified by increasing the proportion of hexamethyldisilazane and trimethylchlorosilane. The mixture contained pyridine, hexamethyldisilazane, trimethylchlorosilane in the proportions 4:1:1 (v/v).

Calculations. The equation for the mutarotation coefficient can also be expressed in the form:

$$k = \frac{1}{t} \log \frac{x_\infty}{x_\infty - x_t}$$

In this equation, x_∞ is the % β anomer in the final equilibrium solution, and x_t the % β anomer at time t. The mutarotation coefficient was, therefore, determined from the slope of the plot of log $x_\infty - x_t$ against t.

RESULTS

The procedure described here gave satisfactory preparation of the *O*-TMSi derivatives of carbohydrates in a volume of water not exceeding 10 μl. Increasing the volume of water beyond 10 μl led to the formation of partially trimethylsilylated derivatives (13) in addition to the penta-*O*-TMSi compounds. That the anomeric composition of the solutions was preserved is shown by the fact that a freshly dissolved sugar anomer gave essentially only a single peak for the correct anomeric form, as well by the fact that the mutarotation coefficients obtained by the method agree with those determined polarimetrically. In a method for the preparation of *O*-TMSi derivatives, Brobst and Lott (14, 15) have used as the catalyst trifluoroacetic acid rather than trimethylchlorosilane, and have stated that this method is operative in the presence of as much as 40 mg of water for a total carbohydrate sample weight of 80–100 mg in a final volume of about 2 ml. The method has the further advantage that no precipitate is formed. In our hands, this method did not lead to solutions containing only the desired completely substituted *O*-TMSi derivatives. Thus, in one experiment, 5 mg of α-D-glucose dissolved in 0.1 ml pyridine

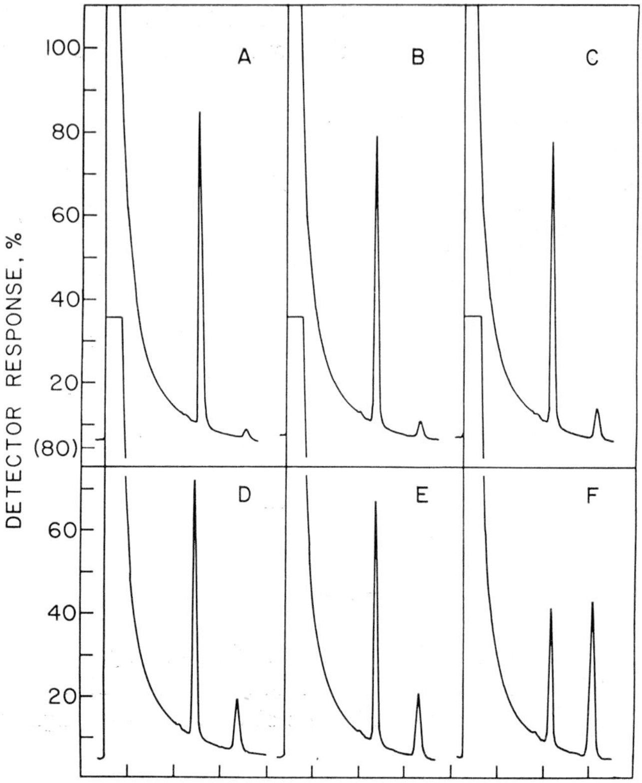

FIG. 1. Mutarotation of α-D-glucose observed by gas chromatography. In these reproductions, the first peak is that for penta-*O*-TMSi-α-D-glucopyranose and the second that for penta-*O*-TMSi-β-D-glucopyranose. The times, in minutes, at which the samples were taken are as follows: (A) 3.0, (B) 7.5, (C) 15.0, (D) 30.0, (E) 40.0, (F) equilibrium. Only a few of the samples analyzed are illustrated here. The calibration points on the abscissa are at intervals of 2 min.

was treated with 0.09 ml hexamethyldisilazane and 0.1 ml trifluoroacetic acid. The solution was vigorously shaken and then was allowed to stand for 15 min at room temperature prior to injection on the gas chromatography column. The chromatogram showed several peaks in addition to that for penta-*O*-TMSi-α derivative. These additional components are, again, most likely to be partial *O*-TMSi derivatives (13).

The course of a typical mutarotation of α-D-glucose at pH 4.7 and 20.0°, is shown in Figure 1. The chromatograms of the various samples show two major peaks for the two anomeric forms. As the mutarotation proceeds, the size of the α peak diminishes and there is a corresponding increase in the size of the β peak. There are occasionally very minor peaks preceding the major peaks in each case. These peaks are probably due to the presence of very small amounts of partial derivatives in the samples; they amounted at most to about 1% of the total TMSi derivatives. The curves shown in Figure 1, and others obtained at different time intervals in the same experiment, were used to calculate values of log $x_\infty - x_t$. The plot of the values of log $x_\infty - x_t$ against t for this mutarotation is shown in Figure 2. The values show a linear relationship as

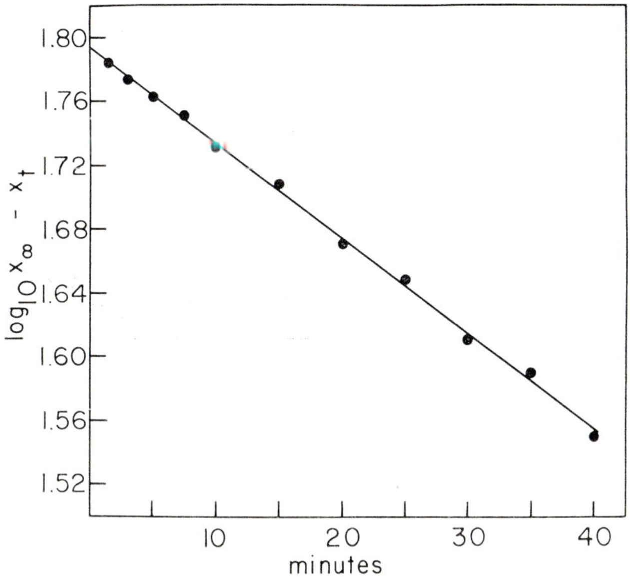

FIG. 2. Determination of mutarotation coefficient from gas chromatographic analysis. The values of log $x_\infty - x_t$ were obtained from all of the measurements made for the run illustrated, in part, in Figure 1. The conditions were α-D-glucose initially, pH 4.7, 20.0°.

required for a reversible first-order reaction. The slope of the line is 0.006, in good agreement with the literature value for the mutarotation coefficient.

Table 1 lists values for the mutarotation coefficients of anomers of arabinose, xylose, galactose, and glucose determined by the gas chromatographic technique. In each case, there is excellent agreement with the literature values for the mutarotation coefficient determined by the polarimetric technique. In the case of galactose, the calculations were based only on the amounts of the α and β anomers present. For this sugar, gas chromatography always shows the presence of a third component, probably a furanose form. The amount of this third component did not change substantially during the mutarotation determinations.

TABLE 1
Mutarotation Coefficients of Various Carbohydrates Determined by the Gas Chromatographic Method

Carbohydrate	Mutarotation coefficient[a]	
	Gas chromatography	Polarimetry
α-D-Glucose	0.00618	0.00629
	0.00629	
	0.00644	
	0.00628	
β-D-Glucose	0.00626	0.00625
	0.00625	
α-D-Galactose	0.00795	0.00803
β-D-Arabinose	0.0301	0.0300
	0.0305	
	0.0291	
α-D-Xylose	0.0192	0.0203
	0.0217	

[a] All the values are for determinations in pH 4.7 phthalate buffer at 20.0°. The polarimetry values are taken from Table 149 by Isbell and Pigman in (16).

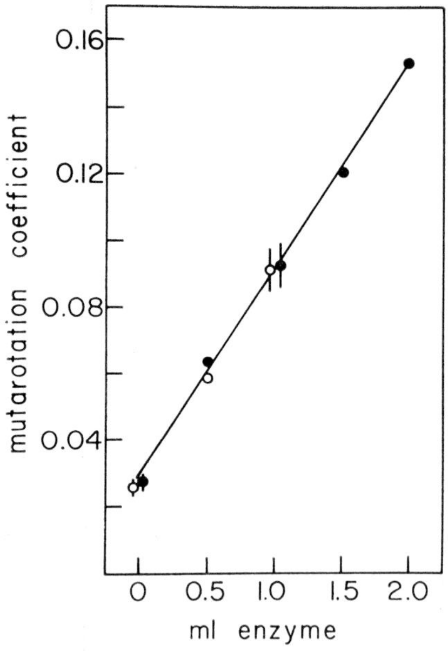

FIG. 3. Assay of mutarotase from hog kidney at 20.0°: (○) values obtained by polarimetry; (●) values by gas chromatography. In some cases, three separate determinations were made by both methods. The bars on the graph represent the upper and lower values which were obtained in these cases and the point plotted is the average of the three determinations. In other cases the points plotted are a single value. The abscissa shows the volume of initial homogenate which was diluted to 25 ml with pH 7.1 phosphate buffer as described in the text.

The application of the gas chromatographic method to the assay of mutarotase activity was studied using enzyme preparations from hog kidney. The mutarotation coefficient at a given enzyme level was determined both by polarimetry and by the new technique. As shown in Figure 3, there was good agreement between the values determined by the two methods. Values for the mutarotation coefficient could be obtained by gas chromatography in solutions that were too turbid for assay by the polarimeter. All values for the mutarotation coefficient showed a linear relationship with the volume of enzyme solution used.

DISCUSSION

The method described here for analysis of carbohydrate anomers in aqueous solution, by freezing in liquid nitrogen and trimethylsilylation, should have many applications. In following a mutarotation reaction of the simple type, $\alpha \rightleftharpoons \beta$, the use of this gas chromatographic procedure has the advantage of providing a direct measurement of the amounts of *both* anomeric forms in solution. In addition, other forms in solution, as, for example, furanoses or possibly the open-chain aldehyde form, should be capable of detection by the method. However, in none of the cases so far examined have we obtained evidence that there are changes in concentration of a third component. In most cases the amounts of a third form in solution are very low. The situation was the same with the mutarotase-catalyzed reaction; no evidence for intermediate forms was apparent in these solutions.

There are several other advantages associated with this method. It can be applied to solutions that are very turbid or highly pigmented, and which, for this reason, present problems in polarimetry. It could, therefore, be very useful in assaying for various mutarotases in biological samples.

The method appears capable of some degree of automation; for example, the area of the two peaks could be determined by automatic integration devices, and from these areas the mutarotation coefficients could be calculated by computer program. The method can be carried out with very small amounts of sugars in small volumes; for example, an accurate mutarotation coefficient for glucose has been repeatedly determined using 2 mg portions of α- or β-D-glucose in a volume of 100 μl. The mutarotation behavior of rare sugars could, therefore, be determined with minimal loss of material.

SUMMARY

A method is described to determine the anomeric composition of aqueous carbohydrate solutions. A small sample (usually 5 μl) is diluted with dimethylformamide, frozen at liquid nitrogen temperature, and then reacted with a mixture of pyridine, hexamethyldisilazane, and trimethylchlorosilane. The proportions of the anomeric forms of the fully trimethylsilylated carbohydrate are determined by gas chromatography. The method gives values for the mutarotation coefficients of glucose, galactose, arabinose, and xylose which are identical to those determined by polarimetry. Application of the method to assay of the enzyme, mutarotase, is described.

ACKNOWLEDGMENTS

We are indebted to Dr. C. C. Sweeley for advice on gas chromatography. This research was supported, in part, by Grant GM 13423 from the United States Public Health Service.

REFERENCES

1. Keilin, D., and Hartree, E. F., *Biochem. J.* **50,** 331 (1952).
2. Keilin, D., and Hartree, E. F., *Biochem. J.* **50,** 341 (1952).
3. Levy, G. B., and Cook, E. S., *Biochem. J.* **57,** 50 (1954).
4. Keston, A. S., *Science* **120,** 355 (1954).
5. Keston, A. S., *Anal. Biochem.* **9,** 228 (1964).
6. Keston, A. S., *Federation Proc.* **17,** 253 (1958).
7. Hill, J. B., and Cowart, D. S., *Anal. Biochem.* **16,** 327 (1966).
8. Keston, A. S., and Brandt, R., *Anal. Biochem.* **6,** 461 (1963).
9. Bentley, R., and Bhate, D. S., *J. Biol. Chem.* **235,** 1219 (1960).
10. Wallenfels, K., and Herrmann, K., *Biochem. Z.* **343,** 294 (1965).
11. Bentley, R., Sweeley, C. C., Makita, M., and Wells, W. W., *Biochem. Biophys. Res. Commun.* **11,** 14 (1963).
12. Sweeley, C. C., Bentley, R., Makita, M., and Wells, W. W., *J. Am. Chem. Soc.* **85,** 2497 (1963).
13. Kim, S. M., Bentley, R., and Sweeley, C. C., unpublished observations.
14. Brobst, K. M., and Lott, C. E., *Cereal Chem.* **43,** 35 (1966).
15. Lott, C. E., and Brobst, K. M., *Anal. Chem.* **38,** 1767 (1966).
16. Bates, F. J., and associates, "Polarimetry, Saccharimetry and the Sugars," U. S. Government Printing Office, Washington, D. C., 1942.

ANALYTICAL BIOCHEMISTRY 20, 321–324 (1967)

Spectrophotofluorometric Determination of Nanogram Amounts of α,ϵ-Diaminopimelic Acid, a Bacterial Cell Wall Constituent

CHARLES J. ROGERS, CECIL W. CHAMBERS, AND NORMAN A. CLARKE

Bacteriological Studies of Germicides, Microbiological Activities, Cincinnati Water Research Laboratory, Cincinnati, Ohio 45226

Received February 13, 1967

Work originally described α,ϵ-diaminopimelic acid (DAP) as a constituent of the bacterial cell wall (1). This acid was separated from cell wall hydrolyzates by paper chromatography and was revealed with ninhydrin. Work and Dewey (2) suggested that the presence or absence of this compound may be of taxonomic importance; this was later confirmed by Cummins and Harris (3). Recently, Shazly and Hungate (4) described a method for estimating bacterial growth in the rumen of cattle by colorimetrically determining DAP.

This report outlines a new procedure for determining DAP in that it utilizes the condensation reaction of DAP with *o*-phthalaldehyde (OPT) to yield a highly fluorescent complex. The method has three important features: it is simple, rapid, and capable of detecting as little as 9 nanograms (ng) of DAP.

METHOD

Apparatus: An Aminco-Bowman spectrophotofluorometer equipped with a 1P21 photomultiplier tube was used to measure activation and fluorescence spectra and fluorometric determinations. Slit arrangement No. 2 was used for all measurements, except a $\frac{3}{16}$-in. photomultiplier slit.

Standard Curve: Aliquots of 0.1 to 1.0 ml of a prepared solution containing 9.25 μg/ml of DAP[1] were added to screw-cap tubes; the volume of each tube was adjusted to 3.0 ml with water. To each tube was added

[1] Purchased from Nutritional Biochemicals Co., Cleveland, Ohio (mention of commercial products does not imply endorsement by the Federal Water Pollution Control Administration).

0.2 ml of a 10% solution of NaOH and 0.2 ml of 1.0% of OPT[1] in absolute methanol. The caps were firmly tightened on the tubes and the tubes placed in an 88°C bath for 4 min. After cooling, the contents of each tube were transferred to 100 ml volumetric flasks and diluted to the mark. Fluorescence was measured using activation and fluorescent wavelengths of 365 and 425 mμ (uncorrected).

RESULTS AND DISCUSSION

Figure 1 shows the activation and fluorescence spectra of DAP. A plot of DAP concentration versus fluorescence is represented in Figure 2. A linear response of fluorescence with increasing DAP concentration was found in the range of 0 to 9.2 μg. The reagent blank value was subtracted from plotted values.

The aliphatic polyamine spermidine (5), amino acid arginine, and

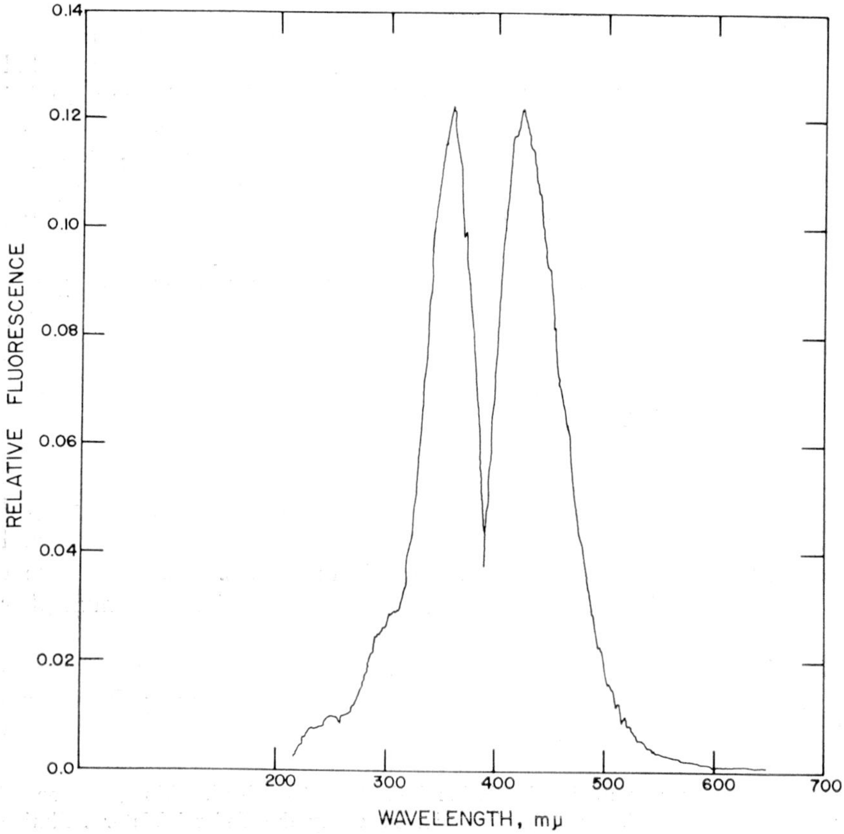

FIG. 1. Activation-fluorescence spectra of DAP (approximately 0.1 μg/ml).

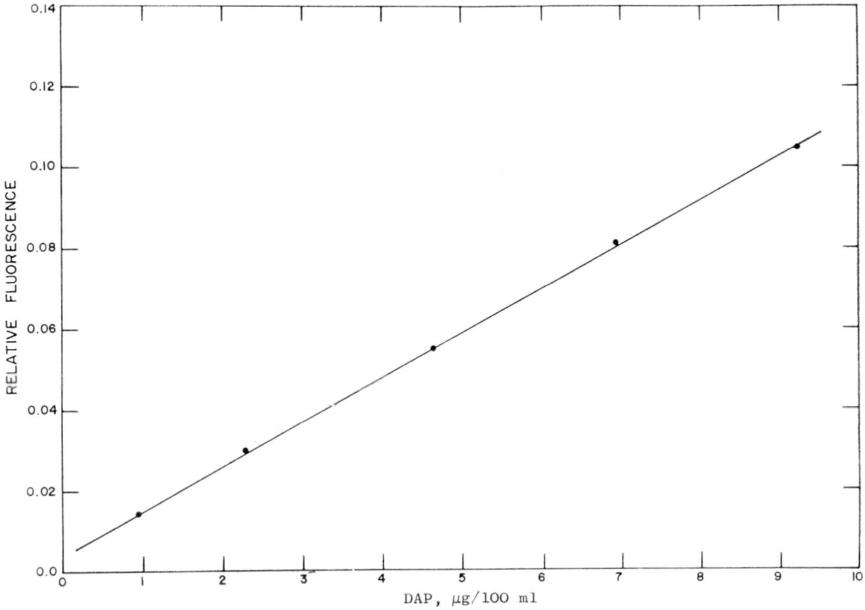

FIG. 2. Standard curve of DAP determined by the procedure described.

amines armatine and histamine (6, 7) are known to condense with OPT to produce fluorescent complexes. DAP, however, may be distinguished from these compounds not only because of the differences in activation and fluorescence wavelengths but because little or no fluorescence is produced until heat is applied to the reaction.

When other aliphatic amino acids in concentrations several times greater than the DAP standard solution were tested, little or no fluorescence was produced. Hexosamines, when tested under described conditions, react with OPT to produce 30% of the fluorescence that results from an equal amount of DAP with activation and fluorescence wavelengths essentially the same as for DAP measurement. Separation of DAP by thin-layer, paper, or column chromatography (described by Shazly and Hungate) would be necessary when hexosamines are present.

Factors affecting development of maximum fluorescence in determining DAP are pH, temperature, and OPT concentration. When DAP was determined at pH 10.0 and at the optimum pH of 11.5, only 20% of the fluorescence was produced at the lower pH. Heating to temperatures of 60 to 95°C will produce fluorescence; however, heating to 88°C for 4 min was found suitable for this study. Longer heating periods greater than 8 min at 88°C caused a gradual decrease in fluorescence.

Results obtained by varying the concentration of OPT indicate that

0.2 ml of a 1% solution gave the best response for the concentrations of DAP investigated. The fluorescence produced is stable for several hours and the precision of reproducibility is ±1% on six replicated determinations of 20 ng/ml of DAP.

When DAP solutions were prepared in dilute hydrochloric acid or in the presence of sodium chloride, a distinct quenching of fluorescence was observed. This quenching effect in the presence of halogens was recently reported by Kremzner (5).

Because most bacteria are among the limited types of living cells that contain DAP (8), this method may be applicable for detection of small numbers of bacteria or to differentiate certain microorganisms.

SUMMARY

A new, rapid, and sensitive method is described for the determination of DAP based on fluorescence development with OPT. Fluorescence versus DAP concentration is linear in the microgram range; consequently, this method is 10,000 times more sensitive than the colorimetric method for determining DAP. Since DAP is a bacterial cell wall constituent, this method may provide a means of detecting small numbers of bacteria, or may provide the possibility of rapidly differentiating certain species of bacteria.

REFERENCES

1. Work, E., *Biochem. J.* **49**, 17–23 (1951).
2. Work, E., and Dewey, D. L., *J. Gen. Microbiol.* **9**, 394 (1953).
3. Cummins, C. S., and Harris, H., *J. Gen. Microbiol.* **14**, 583 (1956).
4. Shazly, K., and Hungate, R. E., *Appl. Microbiol.* **14**, 27–30 (1966).
5. Kremzner, L. T., *Anal. Biochem.* **15**, 270 (1966).
6. Cohn, V. H., Jr., and Shore, P. A., *Anal. Biochem.* **2**, 237 (1961).
7. Shore, P. A., Burkhalter, A., and Cohn, V. H., Jr., *J. Pharmacol. Exptl. Therap.* **127**, 182 (1959).
8. Hoare, D. S., and Work, E., *Biochem. J.* **65**, 441 (1957).

ANALYTICAL BIOCHEMISTRY 20, 325–334 (1967)

Micro Methods for the Quantitative Determination of Iron and Copper in Biological Material[1]

MILDRED VAN DE BOGART[2] AND HELMUT BEINERT

Institute for Enzyme Research, University of Wisconsin, Madison, Wisconsin

Received February 13, 1967

Although many procedures for the quantitative determination of iron and copper have been described, there may still exist a need for relatively simple methods which consume little material and involve a minimum of contamination risks. The procedures described in detail in the following were adapted from methods published by other authors (1–3) and have been used in our laboratory for over 10 years, which has given us the opportunity to recognize and eliminate most difficulties and to develop a procedure suited for routine use.

The following features appeared desirable and were incorporated in the procedures:

(1) Less than 1 μg of element should be required for optimal readout, which generally means, in the case of proteins, approximately 1 mg of total sample.

(2) The samples should be ashed so that all metal is liberated with certainty and any complexing agent (e.g., EDTA) is destroyed, since such compounds are often routinely added to or carried along in preparations containing proteins.

(3) Wet ashing is preferable, and the total volume of liquid to be handled should not exceed ~1 ml.

(4) Neutralization of the acid digest should not require pH measurement with its inherent danger of contamination.

(5) No transfer or volumetric measurement should be necessary.

(6) Spectrophotometry of the colored complex should not be carried out in the original aqueous phase, to avoid, if possible, interference from other solutes.

The essential features of the methods are therefore wet ashing, evap-

[1] This work was supported by the National Institute of General Medical Sciences Grant GM-12394 and a Research Career Program Award (GM-KG-18,442) to H. Beinert.

[2] Present address: Department of Biology, Milton College, Milton, Wisconsin.

oration of excess acid, reduction, neutralization with excess sodium acetate, development of color with a suitable bathophenanthroline, and extraction with a small quantity of organic solvent followed by spectrophotometric determination.

FOR IRON

Reagents

(*1*) Iron standard in dilute H_2SO_4.
(*2*) H_2SO_4, concentrated.
(*3*) HNO_3, concentrated.
(*4*) $HClO_4$, 60%.
(*5*) Mercaptoacetic acid, 1% (w/v) solution.
(*6*) Sodium acetate, saturated solution.
(*7*) 2 *N* HCl.
(*8*) 3-Methyl-1-butanol.
(*9*) 4,7-Diphenyl-1,10-phenanthroline solution in 3-methyl-1-butanol.

Comments to Procurement and Preparation of Reagents

(*1*) A concentrated primary standard, containing approximately 1 mg atom Fe/100 ml is prepared first. From this a working standard of 0.1 μg atom/ml is then derived periodically by dilution with dilute H_2SO_4. The use of HCl is avoided, as iron chloride is volatile. Analytical-grade iron wire (56 mg) is degreased, placed in a 100 ml volumetric flask, and dissolved in a solution containing 2 ml concentrated HCl and 2 ml concentrated HNO_3 in 10–15 ml. When all the iron is dissolved the flask is made to volume with water. This standard is stable indefinitely.

(*2,3,7*) We found that reagent-grade Du Pont acids are satisfactory, since the main contribution to the blank comes from the acetate and isoamyl alcohol; however, these acids can also be obtained as ultrapure reagents from Merck.[3]

(*4*) $HClO_4$, 60%,[4] is satisfactory. Ultrapure $HClO_4$ is also available.[3]

(*5*) Also called thioglycolic acid; the Eastman Kodak white label product, analytical grade, 80% solution in water is satisfactory. The aqueous solution has to be prepared approximately once a month since oxidation destroys it. The original sample, once opened, is also not stable for more than a few months. Low color yield in the reaction with phenanthroline, which curiously may still be proportional to iron concentration, is generally due to deterioration of this reagent.

[3] Ultrapure reagents, under the name Suprapur, are marketed by E. Merck AG, Darmstadt, Germany, and are distributed by Brinkmann Instruments, Westbury, N. Y.

[4] G. Frederick Smith Company, Columbus, Ohio.

(*6*) Sodium acetate may be obtained as ultrapure reagent.[3] However, even this reagent, when used in the quantity needed here, contributes to the blank color. Its use in the required quantities also becomes very costly. Commercial reagent-grade acetate must be purified before use, and it is also advisable to apply the following procedure to the ultrapure reagent. A saturated solution of sodium acetate is prepared. It is advantageous to let this solution sit undisturbed for a few days, as some ferric hydroxide will settle out which does then not have to be removed by the laborious extraction procedure described below. However, extraction has to be carried out in any event, since some iron always remains in solution. After standing, the solution is filtered and collected in an Fe-free bottle. (The filter paper is prepared by washing with one of the Versenes and thereafter with sufficient water to completely remove Versene. The complete removal of Versene is essential or interference with reduction and binding of Fe by the phenanthroline may occur.) To the filtered solution a few milliliters of glacial acetic acid is added (about 6 ml/liter) to lower the pH to about 6, and some undiluted thioglycolic acid (1 ml/liter acetate) is added to reduce the contaminating iron left in solution. Iron is not reduced by thioglycolic acid at a pH higher than 6. Each liter of acetate solution is then shaken out with several 50 ml portions of phenanthroline/isoamyl alcohol reagent. The pink color of the isoamyl alcohol layer increases when the two phases are left standing together for several hours after each extraction. When after several extractions and standing periods only a faint pink color appears in the organic phase, the acetate solution is extracted twice with isoamyl alcohol to remove any phenanthroline from the acetate.

(*8*) Also called isoamyl alcohol, some lots of the reagent-grade alcohol were found satisfactory, while others contained iron. Isoamyl alcohol specially purified for iron analysis can be obtained commercially,[4] or the ordinary reagent can be redistilled.

(*9*) Bathophenanthroline[4] (molecular weight 332), approximately 200 mg dissolved in 250 ml isoamyl alcohol. The reagent dissolves slowly and should preferably be left standing overnight. Warming the suspension in a water bath also speeds dissolution.

Glassware

Conical 12 ml, graduated, centrifuge tubes with ground-joint stoppers (e.g., Pyrex #8144) were found most suitable for ashing and extraction, as the approximate fluid volume can be continuously monitored. Micropipets are used for all additions under 1 ml. In most cases absolute accuracy of these additions is not required, merely repeatability. The pipets are stored in tubes covered by larger tubes and all bottles are covered, since laboratory dust usually contains appreciable amounts of iron or copper. Glassware must be carefully cleaned and water of low metal content must be available. Procedures for achieving this have been published (4). In our laboratory we found it satisfactory to redistill via a Pyrex glass condenser previously deionized or distilled water from a large metal still. Particular attention has to be given to the cleaning of *new* glassware. It should be kept in mind that all glassware that has been used in the analytical procedure, although possibly not "clean" with respect to other uses, is probably still the cleanest for reuse in the same procedure. Thus, the tubes used for ashing are flushed with water, ethanol, and again water and briefly boiled with 2 *N* HCl. After rinsing with water and draining but not necessarily drying, they are ready for reuse. The tubes are touched only at the lower end and care is taken not to contaminate the upper rim since on ashing, through refluxing, as well as during extraction, liquid does wet the upper parts of the tubes. We found it most convenient and safest to store the tubes upside down between analyses, on a rack provided with appropriate clamps (e.g., commercial broom-clips). After the tubes are dry, they are capped with Parafilm. After storage for several weeks the tubes have to be cleaned with acid, and after even longer storage it is advisable to carry them through a blank ashing procedure with the reagents used in the procedure. This is absolutely necessary for new tubes or tubes used for other work. The stoppers are degreased, if necessary, boiled in 2 *N* HCl, flushed with water, and stored in a suitable container. It is recommended that all containers used for storage of stoppers, pipets, or reagents have covers with lids such as Petri dishes which prevent settling out of dust or dirt on the rim, (e.g., a beaker covered with a watch glass is *un*-satisfactory). Pipets are cleaned with chromic or hot nitric acid, flushed, and dried before being used in the analytical procedure. When stored for more than a few days after this treatment they should be flushed before use with 2 *N* HCl, followed with water and then with the reagent to be pipetted. Two samples of reagent are drawn up and expelled into a waste container. After this treatment a pipet is usually used to make additions to a whole series of samples. If the addition of the reagent is made carefully and in order of increasing iron content of the samples, no significant contamination can result. After use, pipets are again flushed with 2 *N* HCl and water. Pipets used for pipetting organic solvents are flushed with ethanol immediately before and after use and otherwise with 2 *N* HCl and water as above. To prevent contamination of the stock reagents it is necessary to have a second set of smaller reagent containers (e.g. glass-stoppered tubes), in which the reagent is frequently renewed. All pipetting is done from this second set of containers.

Apparatus

One adjustable microburner for ashing is sufficient. Occasionally a second burner for expelling condensed water at the upper end of the tube is helpful. The time required to set tubes up properly in a digestion rack and the chance that spattering may occur when the tubes are unattended make it appear more profitable to ash the contents of each tube by hand. With the small quantities of material this requires only 5–10 min/tube. A shaking device is required for extraction. A buzzer according to Bessey *et al.* (4) is satisfactory or a shaker such as the Vortex.[5] Centrifugation is necessary for separating the phases after extraction. The International clinical centrifuge[6] is satisfactory. Spectrophotometry may be performed in any instrument that permits the use of volumes of the order of 0.5 ml. We have used a micro attachment to the Beckman spectrophotometer.

Procedure

See also "Comments to Procedure" below.

(1) Align the tubes in a rack according to increasing iron content and cap with Parafilm. Remove caps only when additions are made, but do not place Parafilm on hot tubes.

(2) Add "blanks," standards, and samples to appropriate tubes.

(3) Add 0.1 ml concentrated H_2SO_4 (reagent *2*).

(4) Add 0.1 ml concentrated HNO_3 (reagent *3*).

(5) Ash over microburner for approximately 6 min.

(6) Add 0.05 ml $HClO_4$ (reagent *4*) to tubes after contents have cooled down.

(7) Ash over microburner an additional 3 min, but avoid boiling.

(8) Add, after cooling, 0.5 ml of water.

(9) Add 0.25 ml 1% thioglycolic acid (reagent *5*).

(10) Add 1.5 ml sodium acetate (reagent *6*).

(11) Add 1.0 ml bathophenanthroline solution (reagent *9*).

(12) Stopper tubes with glass stoppers.

(13) Extract by buzzing or shaking.

(14) Centrifuge to separate layers.

[5] Vortex test tube mixer, Scientific Industries, Inc., Springfield, Mass.
[6] International Equipment Company, Needham Heights, Mass.

(15) Withdraw 0.5 ml of the organic phase and place in dry microcuvet.

(16) Read at 535 mμ against blank containing isoamyl alcohol (reagent *8*).

Comments to Procedure

(to 2) The samples should not contain excessive amounts of interfering ions. Of metals to be expected in biological material, copper should not be present in a more than 5-fold excess over ion. Interference from molybdenum can be controlled by choosing a pH above 5.5 (6, 7). Of anions to be expected in biological material, phosphate, pyrophosphate, and cyanide interfere. When the sample is dissolved in 0.1 *M* phosphate, for instance, the use of a 20 μl sample may be safe, while it is not advisable to use 0.1 to 0.2 ml of a 0.1 *M* phosphate solution. Tris buffers, such as Tris acetate, which decomposes on ashing, are very suitable. It is also advisable to avoid large concentrations of reagents such as sucrose or bile salts, as ashing may become very cumbersome in this case, multiple additions of $HClO_4$ may be necessary, and blanks may rise correspondingly. In general, samples must be prepared in a way suitable to remove contaminating iron. For proteins this may be accomplished by dialysis against chelating agents. After equilibrium has been reached, a sample of the dialyzate, equal to the protein sample, is used as "dialyzate" blank. If such a blank is expected or known to contain not significantly more than the "reagent blank" (containing all reagents only), dialysis fluid may be added to the standards as well, thus eliminating the need for running separate reagent blanks. The samples and standards should contain not more than 25 mμg atoms of iron (~1.5 μg Fe) and 2 mg of organic matter, optimally about 10 mμg atoms of iron and up to 0.5 mg of organic matter. A complete standard curve need not be run, but it is advisable to run standards at two levels, above and below that expected for the sample. If different samples are run with different liquid volumes, it is helpful to run also these same volumes of "dialyzate" blanks. It may be desirable, when a set of carefully calibrated micropipets is not available, to use the same pipet for blanks, standards, and samples, in this order, with appropriate cleaning of the pipets (see above) between sampling.

(to 5) With the conical tubes used, care should be taken never to heat the tip. The tubes are held in a nearly horizontal position so that most of the liquid is in a shallow layer at the place where the tapered and the straight portion of the tube meet. The fumes are driven up the barrel of the tube. Water should not be allowed to condense near the top of the tube, as this may cause spattering should the water run back into the hot tube. A second burner may be used to advantage to expel water condensed in the upper part of the tube. Tubes are capped again with Parafilm as soon as they have cooled down sufficiently.

(to 7) $HClO_4$ usually clears up the digest readily, and only when an excess of organic matter was present is the addition of more $HClO_4$ necessary. The presence of undigested organic matter is generally indicated by the persistance of a yellow-brownish color even after cooling of the digest. Toward the end of the ashing period a bright yellow color may appear, which usually disappears on cooling or further ashing. This color does not stem from organic matter. Ashing may also be effectively accomplished with H_2SO_4 alone by addition of H_2O_2. After heating with the acid and cooling, 20 μl portions of 30% H_2O_2 are added until the digest is clear and colorless; the effect of H_2O_2 is similar to that of $HClO_4$.

(to 10) This amount of acetate was found to buffer the amount of acid, which could maximally be left over, to a pH of about 4.2. The pH should be within the range of 4 to 6 as otherwise reduction and color formation are not optimal. The reductant (reagent *5*) should always be added before the buffer (reagent *6*) in order to ensure rapid and complete reduction of iron.

(to 11) This solution is viscous and drains slowly. It should be slowly and uniformly delivered into all tubes, even if a quantitative delivery is not possible. Only the relative amount delivered to each individual tube is of importance, not the absolute quantity.

(to 13) Vigorous shaking is necessary to extract all the iron into the organic phase. The tubes are buzzed or shaken for 2 min, then centrifuged to clear the walls, buzzed or shaken for 1 more minute, and centrifuged again. The stoppers may be lubricated very slightly with silicone grease.

(to 15) The same transfer pipet and cuvet are used for all samples. The samples are again processed in the order of increasing iron content. Between readings in the spectrophotometer the pipet and cuvet are flushed 3 times with ethanol and dried in a stream of filtered air. If 0.5 ml of reagent is used (see below) it may become difficult to withdraw a sufficient amount of organic phase uncontaminated by aqueous phase. It may be helpful in this case to tilt the tube slightly so that the organic phase breaks from the wall on one side and contracts on the other side, thus providing a thicker layer to draw from.

(to 16) The reagent blank should give an absorbance reading not in excess of about 0.03 (1 cm light path). This blank value is mainly determined by the success in the removal of Fe from the acetate solution. Five mμg atoms of Fe gives a net absorbance value of 0.095 to 0.100 under the conditions described. If only small quantities of iron are present, the extraction may be carried out with 0.5 ml of reagent *9* (Step 11 of procedure). This will of course also increase the absorbance of the blank. If smaller tubes (e.g., Pyrex #8081) are used and a spectrophotometer and cuvets are available suitable for very small volumes, the scale of the whole procedure may be decreased further without significant loss of accuracy and precision. It should be kept in mind that the small quantity of reagent soluble in isoamyl alcohol can extract only a limited amount of Fe. It is stated by Peterson (2) that 1 ml of the reagent can extract 2 μg of Fe. The absorbance should therefore never exceed a value of 0.6. Absorbance and iron content are proportional below this absorbance value. If the amount of iron present in a sample has been underestimated, so that the absorbance is too high, the quantity of reagent *9* added in Step 11 may be increased. It is not sufficient to dilute with solvent after extraction. The amount of reagent should of course then also be increased in all other samples of the series including standards and blanks.

Possible Reasons for Difficulties in Procedure

(*a*) Erratic results with samples, blanks, and standards: contaminated glassware or random contamination during improper handling.

(*b*) Erratic results in samples only: insufficient ashing, not liberating all the iron or leaving organic iron chelators behind; presence of iron complexing salts such as phosphate or pyrophosphate.

(*c*) Low values for standards: deteriorated mercaptoacetic acid.

(*d*) High but reproducible values for blanks and standards: contaminated bathophenanthroline reagent either from contaminated isoamyl alcohol or reagent itself; contaminated acetate or other reagents. The phenanthroline reagent and the acetate are the most likely sources.

(*e*) High values of standards only, not blanks: dilution of secondary working standard is either incorrect or this standard has increased in strength by contamination or evaporation. It is advisable to replace the secondary standard frequently. Significant contamination of the primary standard of high iron content is less likely.

FOR COPPER

The method for the determination of copper is in many ways similar or identical to that used for iron. Details will therefore be given only when differences exist; otherwise reference is made to the iron method by "(See Fe)."

Reagents

(*1*) Copper standard in dilute H_2SO_4.
(*2–4*) (See Fe).
(*5*) Hydroxylamine hydrochloride, 1% (w/v) aqueous solution.
(*6*) Sodium acetate, saturated solution.
(*7*) 2 *N* HCl.
(*8*) 1-Hexanol.
(*9*) 2,9-Dimethyl-4,7-diphenyl-1,10-phenanthroline solution in 1-hexanol.

Comments to Procurement and Preparation of Reagents

(*1*) Since the water content of most copper salts is not well defined, it is advisable to prepare the standard solution from metallic copper, e.g., copper shot of sufficient purity. A concentrated primary standard is prepared by dissolving 63.5 mg metal in a 100 ml volumetric flask (See Fe). The resulting standard contains 10 μg atoms/ml. A secondary working standard is prepared by diluting 1 ml of this standard to 100 ml with dilute H_2SO_4, so that 1 ml contains 0.1 μg atom or 6.35 μg Cu.

(*2,3,7*) (See Fe).

(*5*) Reagent-grade hydroxylamine hydrochloride is satisfactory. This solution should be prepared fresh every two to three months.

(*6*) The acetate solution is prepared similarly to that described for Fe but the solution is shaken with approximately 1/15 its volume of a 0.01% solution of dithizone (diphenylthiocarbazone) in chloroform. The acetate solution is extracted until the purple color of the copper–dithizone complex is no longer visible in the chloroform layer. The chloroform is then shaken out with *n*-hexanol (reagent *8*). Remaining *n*-hexanol, dissolved in the aqueous phase, does not interfere. In order to avoid the formation of stable emulsions, shaking has to be done judiciously. Centrifugation in copper-free tubes may help in breaking emulsions when formed.

(*8*) *n*-Hexanol; it is advisable to redistill the commercial products. *n*-Hexanol purified for copper determination is commercially available.[4]

(*9*) Bathocuproine[4] (molecular weight 360); approximately 25 mg is dissolved in 250 ml *n*-hexanol (See Fe).

Glassware

Similar considerations apply here as for the iron method. After cleaning with acid, glassware may be treated with dithizone in chloroform (0.01%) and then rinsed with chloroform. The acid-cleaned glassware need not be dried before dithizone treatment, if an acetone rinse is included.

Apparatus

(See Fe).

Procedure

(1–8) (See Fe).

(9) Add 0.25 ml hydroxylamine hydrochloride solution (reagent *5*).

(10) Add 1.5 ml acetate solution (reagent *6*).

(11) Add 0.5 ml bathocuproine solution (reagent *9*).

(12–14) (See Fe).

(15) Withdraw 0.3 ml of the organic phase and place in dry microcuvet.

(16) Read at 479 mμ against blank containing *n*-hexanol (reagent *8*).

Comments to Procedure

(to 2) Similar considerations apply here as for the iron procedure and only a few comments specific for the copper procedure will be made. Heavy metals in amounts expected in biological materials do not interfere. The amount of phosphate present should be kept at a minimum. If the ashing is carried out properly, copper-binding anions such as EDTA will be eliminated. The samples and standards should not contain more than 15 mμg atoms of copper (∼1 μg Cu) and 2 mg of organic matter.

(to 16) The reagent blank should give an absorbance reading not in excess of 0.02 (1 cm light path). Five mμg atoms of Cu gives a net absorbance value of 0.105 to 0.115 under the conditions described. Since the solubility of the reagent is limited and therefore the quantity that can be extracted, the total absorbance should not exceed 0.4. Absorbance and copper content are proportional below this value.

Difficulties likely to arise in the procedure for copper and their possible sources are analogous to those discussed above for iron.

REFERENCES

1. Smith, G. F., McCurdy, W. H., and Diehl, H., *Analyst* **77,** 418 (1952).
2. Peterson, R. E., *Anal. Chem.* **25,** 1227 (1953).
3. Borchardt, L. G., and Butler, Z. P., *Anal. Chem.* **29,** 414 (1957).
4. Thiers, R. E., *Methods Biochem. Anal.* **5,** 301 (1957).
5. Bessey, O. A., Lowry, O. H., Brock, M. J., and Lopez, J. A., *J. Biol. Chem.* **166,** 177 (1946).
6. Fortune, W. B., and Mellon, M. G., *Ind. Eng. Chem., Anal. Ed.* **10,** 60 (1938).
7. Sandell, E. B., "Colorimetric Determination of Traces of Metals," Interscience, New York, 1944.

ANALYTICAL BIOCHEMISTRY 20, 335–338 (1967)

Rapid Separation of Some Common Intermediates of Microbial Metabolism by Thin-Layer Chromatography[1]

ARNOLD S. BLEIWEIS,[2] HENRY C. REEVES,[3] AND SAMUEL J. AJL

Department of Biochemistry, Albert Einstein Medical Center, Philadelphia, Pennsylvania 19141

Received February 23, 1967

Glyoxylic acid metabolism in bacteria has been the subject of extensive research in recent years and has been reviewed by Rabin *et al.* (1). Although glyoxylate can react enzymically with various compounds to form several important metabolic products (2–10), our laboratory has been concerned mainly with: (*a*) the condensation with acetyl-CoA to form malic acid (2); (*b*) the condensation with propionyl-CoA to form α-hydroxyglutaric acid (3); and (*c*) the reduction to glycolic acid (10). Although the fate of glycolic acid is unknown in bacteria (10), malic acid can be dissimilated by means of the tricarboxylic acid (TCA) cycle, and α-hydroxyglutaric acid is further metabolized either via citramalic (α-methylmalic) acid or succinic acid (11).

Studies have been initiated to determine the fate of glyoxylic acid in bacteria and fungi using the technique of pulse labeling with C^{14}-sodium glyoxylate. It was necessary, therefore, to develop a chromatographic technique that achieves a rapid and complete separation of glyoxylate from glycolate, malate, succinate, fumarate, α-ketoglutarate, α-hydroxyglutarate, and citramalate. Since α-hydroxyglutarate can lactonize under anhydrous conditions (12), this compound must also be separated. The method presented here permits the resolution of these nine intermediates associated with glyoxylic acid metabolism.

MATERIALS AND METHODS

Gelman ITLC, type SG chromatography medium (Gelman Instrument Co., Ann Arbor, Michigan) was used for the thin-layer chromatographic

[1] This research was supported in part by Public Health Service Grant AI-03866-06 of the National Institute of Allergy and Infectious Diseases and by Grant GB-4680 of the National Science Foundation.

[2] United States Public Health Service Fellow (1 F2 AI-31, 566-01).

[3] Research Career Development Awardee of the National Institutes of Health (5-K3-AI-6928).

separation of the acids. The medium consists of glass microfiber support sheets which are impregnated with silica gel as the adsorbent. The sheets (20 × 20 cm) were loaded with 2.5 μl of each compound (0.3% w/v aqueous solutions) or with 20 μl of a standard mixture of these acids. α-Hydroxyglutaryl lactone was applied from a benzene solution.

Development was two-dimensional using the following solvent mixtures: (I) petroleum ether (b.p. 30–60°C), anhydrous diethyl ether, and formic acid (28/12/1), and (II) chloroform, methanol, and formic acid (80/1/1). All were Mallinckrodt products. The development chamber was rectangular with the following dimensions: 26 × 26 × 7 cm. The solvent fronts were allowed to ascend 15 cm, the sheets air-dried in a hood for 5 min, and the spots visualized by spraying with 0.04% bromphenol blue (ethanolic).

Samples to be measured for radioactivity were placed in 10 ml of 0.04% 2,5-bis-[2-(5-*tert*-butylbenzoxazolyl)]-thiophene (Packard Instrument Co.) made up in toluene absolute ethanol (2/1). These were counted in a Packard Tri-Carb liquid scintillation spectrometer.

RESULTS AND DISCUSSION

Table 1 lists the R_f values obtained for each compound in the two solvent systems. Figure 1 demonstrates the resolution obtained by two-dimensional chromatography employing, first, solvent mixture I, followed by solvent mixture II. It is apparent that complete resolution of the nine acids is achieved.

Of further interest is the rapidity of the entire procedure. Each dimension required only 20–25 min for development and a sample can be resolved, as in Figure 1, in less than 1 hr. Several samples, therefore, can

TABLE 1
Separation of Intermediates Related to Glyoxylate Metabolism

Compound	$R_f \times 100$	
	Solvent I[a]	Solvent II[b]
Glyoxylate	17	55
Glycolate	59	50
α-Hydroxyglutarate	25	17
α-Hydroxyglutaryl lactone	33	73
Citramalate	41	21
Malate	17	11
α-Ketoglutarate	45	35
Succinate	80	65
Fumarate	97	70

[a] Petroleum ether (b.p. 30–60°C), anhydrous diethyl ether, and formic acid (28/12/1).
[b] Chloroform, methanol, and formic acid (80/1/1).

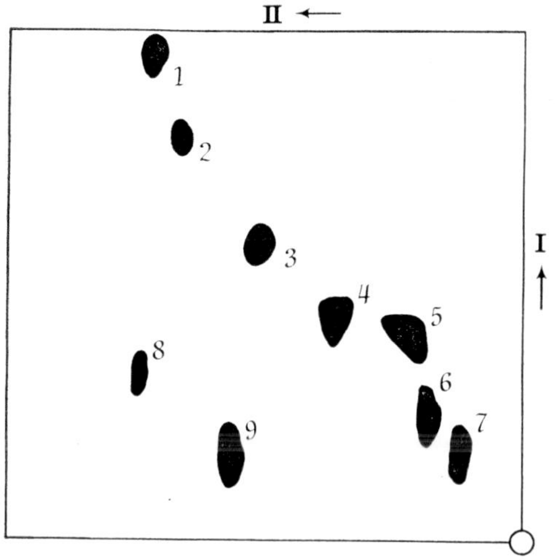

FIG. 1. Thin-layer chromatogram of intermediates associated with glyoxylic acid metabolism. The acids are numbered as follows: (1) fumarate, (2) succinate, (3) glycolate, (4) α-ketoglutarate, (5) citramalate, (6) α-hydroxyglutarate, (7), malate, (8) α-hydroxyglutaryl lactone, and (9) glyoxylate. The origin is indicated by the circle at the baseline. The solvent systems employed were: (I) petroleum ether (b.p. 30–60°C), anhydrous ether, and formic acid (28/12/1) and (II) chloroform, methanol, and formic acid (80/1/1).

be run in a short time. Myers and Huang (13) reported a total elapsed time of 7 hr for the two-dimensional separation of TCA cycle intermediates using conventional thin-layer chromatography with a cellulose adsorbent on glass plates.

In addition to excellent resolution and speed, there is another advantage to the method described here. The sheets, once developed and sprayed to visualize the spots, can be cut quite easily and the spots measured directly for radioactivity. This technique has been applied with success to prove the quantitative conversion of 5-C^{14}-α-hydroxyglutaric acid to its lactone (12). Background emission is negligible and accurate estimates of radioactivity can be obtained after correcting for quenching caused by the spray reagent. The radioactive spots are easily handled without damaging the surface layer.

SUMMARY

A method is presented which permits the complete and rapid chromatographic resolution of nine biologically important carboxylic acids. The technique utilizes two-dimensional thin-layer chromatography and separates glyoxylate, glycolate, α-ketoglutarate, malate, succinate, fumarate, citramalate, α-hydroxyglutarate, and α-hydroxyglutaryl lactone. Some of these acids are intermediates of the TCA cycle and can also be resolved by the TLC procedure recently presented by Myers and Huang (13). We feel, however, that the speed, convenience, and reproducibility of the procedure described here offers many advantages over previously described methods.

REFERENCES

1. RABIN, R., REEVES, H. C., WEGENER, W. S., MEGRAW, R. E., AND AJL, S. J., *Science* **150**, 1548 (1965).
2. WONG, D. T. O., AND AJL, S. J., *J. Am. Chem. Soc.* **78**, 3230 (1956).
3. REEVES, H. C., AND AJL, S. J., *J. Bacteriol.* **84**, 186 (1962).
4. RABIN, R., REEVES, H. C., AND AJL, S. J., *J. Bacteriol.* **86**, 937 (1963).
5. IMAI, K., REEVES, H. C., AND AJL, S. J., *J. Biol. Chem.* **238**, 3193 (1963).
6. GOLDSTONE, A., AND ADAMS, E., *J. Biol. Chem.* **237**, 3476 (1962).
7. KRAKOW, G., AND BARKULIS, S. S., *Biochim. Biophys. Acta* **21**, 593 (1956).
8. OKUYAMA, M., TSUIKI, S., AND KIKUCHI, G., *Biochim. Biophys. Acta* **110**, 66 (1965).
9. KURATOMI, K., AND FUKUNAGA, K., *Biochim. Biophys. Acta* **43**, 562 (1960).
10. BAILEY, E., AND HULLIN, R. P., *Biochem. J.* **101**, 755 (1966).
11. REEVES, H. C., URBANO, C., AND AJL, S. J., Presented at the 65th Annual Meeting of the American Society for Microbiology; Atlantic City, N. J.; (1965).
12. BLEIWEIS, A. S., REEVES, H. C., AND AJL, S. J., in preparation.
13. MYERS, W. F., AND HUANG, K., *Anal. Biochem.* **17**, 210 (1966).

ANALYTICAL BIOCHEMISTRY **20**, 339–357 (1967)

Practical Aspects of the Calibration and Use of the Aminco-Bowman Spectrophotofluorometer

RAYMOND F. CHEN

Laboratory of Technical Development,
National Heart Institute, Bethesda, Maryland 20014

Received February 27, 1967

Although the Aminco-Bowman spectrophotofluorometer is widely employed as an analytical tool, relatively few users of the instrument seem to be familiar with its basic optical features. As a result, optimal performance of the apparatus is frequently not obtained, although it can be adapted to a wide range of fluorescence measurements including corrected excitation and emission spectra, quantum yields, polarization of fluorescence, as well as simple measurements of fluorescence intensity. Increasing interest in emission spectroscopy in recent years has generated a demand for more sophistication in the use of instruments for measuring fluorescence. Fortunately, coincident with these requirements, there have been marked improvements in the stability of lamp sources and in the quality of optical components. It does not seem unreasonable, therefore, that commercially available fluorescence spectrometers may be used for purposes other than the simple measurements for which they were originally intended. The present paper discusses some practical aspects of the use of the Aminco-Bowman spectrophotofluorometer for accurate measurement of spectra in the hope that such a communication will be helpful to those who wish to extend the usefulness of the instrument.

INTRODUCTION

Nowadays, fluorescence spectrophotometers are so common that one tends to forget how "primitive" the commercially available instrumentation was prior to about 1955. Fluorometers at that time often used mercury arc lamps to excite fluorescence, and filters were used to isolate the few suitable lines. Emission was assayed by visual comparators or simple phototube photometers; measurement of ultraviolet fluorescence was both tedious and uncertain with such instrumentation. Any sophisticated fluorescence work required that the operator construct his own apparatus.

An extensive coverage of this period in the development of fluorometry is given by Udenfriend (1).

In 1955, Bowman, Caulfield, and Udenfriend (2) first described a spectrophotofluorometer, i.e., a fluorometer equipped with a light source having an energy continuum over a wide spectral range, monochromators for both excitation and emitted rays, and a fast photomultiplier tube. That report was the first to describe the use of the xenon arc for activation of fluorescence, and this particular innovation was largely responsible for the success of subsequent commercial versions of the instrument. Bowman (3) has reviewed the development of the spectrophotofluorometer.

Several descriptions of the Aminco-Bowman spectrophotofluorometer are available (1, 4, 5). The instrument differs from the original apparatus of Bowman *et al.* (2) in numerous details. For instance, the Aminco-Bowman machine has no lenses and uses grating monochromators, whereas the original instrument (2) employed lenses to focus the xenon arc and used a prism spectrograph to analyze the emission. The original aim of that instrument was said to be to facilitate excitation and emission analysis in the ultraviolet as well as the visible regions (2), and indeed the commercial versions have been quite convenient in analytical procedures since the excitation and emission maxima are easily found. The sensitivity of instruments having two monochromators was surprisingly high, and rivaled that of filter fluorometers fitted with sharp cutoff filters. The sensitivity derived from the fact that the band width of the monochromators could be made very large, and also the finding that spectrophotofluorometers frequently give lower blank readings (higher signal-to-noise ratio) than those obtained with filter fluorometers due to more efficient separation of excitation from emission. Although chemical analysis is still an important use of spectrofluorometers, improvements in their construction and in that of xenon arc lamps and photomultiplier tubes make possible the use of these fluorescence instruments for accurate spectral analysis as well.

The excitation and emission spectra recorded directly from the Aminco-Bowman spectrophotofluorometer are not corrected for the variation with wavelength of either the photon output of the light source or the detector response. Methods have been described for making the necessary corrections for this specific instrument (6–9), but the relative merits of the methods are not clear, and the descriptions of the methods themselves have been too abbreviated to be of use. It is perhaps for these reasons that few laboratories seem to have adopted the practice of calibrating their spectrophotofluorometers and reporting corrected spectra. The calibrations are actually simpler to perform than generally realized, and so a further discussion of the practical aspects involved seems to be justified.

EQUIPMENT

Two Aminco-Bowman spectrophotofluorometers (American Instrument Company, Silver Spring, Maryland) were used and will be referred to as SPF 1 and SPF 2. The optical arrangement of SPF 1 is shown in Figure 1A. The Osram high-pressure 150 W DC xenon lamp was operated by a Sola power supply, and the photomultiplier current was amplified with an Aminco microphotometer and recorded on an Electro Instruments Model 101 X-Y recorder. SPF 2 was fitted with an ellipsoidal off-axis focusing accessory for the arc; its optical diagram is given in Figure 1B. SPF 2 had a Hanovia xenon lamp and a Sorensen power supply, and the spectra were recorded on an Aminco X-Y recorder.

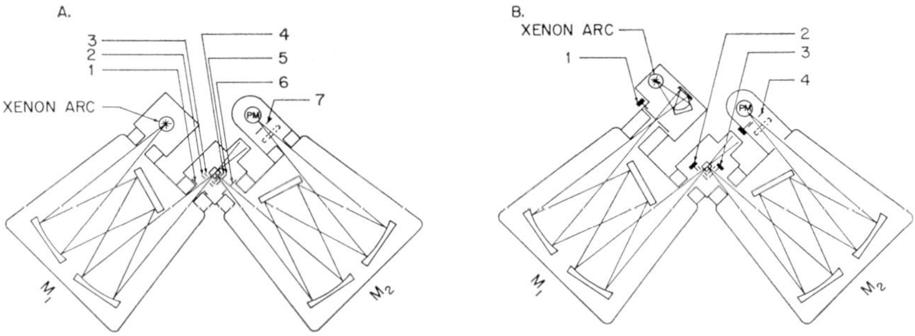

FIG. 1. Optical diagrams for Aminco-Bowman spectrophotofluorometers. M_1 and M_2 are excitation and emission monochromators; PM is the photomultiplier. (A) Standard instrument. The slit positions are numbered. (B) Modified instrument having ellipsoidal condensing system assembly and variable slits in the numbered positions.

A mercury pen light for calibration of the monochromators, and a solid sample accessory to allow fluorescence to be observed from the front surface of a cuvet, were purchased from American Instrument Co. A standard tungsten lamp (G.E. type 100T8½) was purchased from the U. S. National Bureau of Standards.

MATERIALS

Rhodamine B (National Aniline) was purified by crystallization from ether/benzene or chromatography on a column of silicic acid (Mallinckrodt, 100 mesh) developed with chloroform/methanol/acetic acid (100/15/2). 1-Dimethylaminonaphthalene 5-sulfonate was synthesized by Laurance's method (10). Ludox, type LS, a light-scattering colloidal silica preparation, was a product of Du Pont.

DEFINITIONS

A few terms used in the following discussion may be unfamiliar to chemists. *Stray light* is light of unwanted wavelengths emerging from a monochromator. The amount of stray light at any given setting of the monochromator is dependent on such factors as internal reflections and optical design, as well as slit width. Some "stray light figure" is often specified for given monochromators. However, there is no generally accepted method of measuring stray light which, in some applications, may be less bothersome than in others. An example of stray light is the visible radiation which emerges from the excitation monochromator of a spectrophotofluorometer set at wavelengths less than 350 mμ. *Scattered light,* on the other hand, refers to light which is of the same wavelength as that of the exciting beam and which emerges from the fluorescence cuvet. In obtaining a fluorescence spectrum in the Aminco-Bowman instrument, if the sample (e.g., a protein solution) is excited at 280 mμ, scatter peaks will be observed in the emission scan at 280 mμ and also at 560 mμ, the latter being a *second-order scatter* peak. This second scatter peak is due to the fact that diffraction gratings (as opposed to prisms) pass harmonics of the wavelength of interest, so that a grating monochromator set for wavelength λ also passes $\lambda/2$, $\lambda/4$, etc. The "560 mμ" peak is thus due to 280 mμ light which is passed by the emission monochromator.

In the Aminco-Bowman spectrophotofluorometer, only $\lambda/2$ radiation is observed, since the range of observation is only from 200–800 mμ. In fact, such *second-order radiation* cannot be observed from the first monochromator if it is set below 450 mμ because the amount of energy emitted by the xenon arc at wavelengths below 225 mμ is relatively small. Examples of second-order scatter peaks were given by Price *et al.* (5). The *blaze* of a diffraction grating is related to the type of cut used in ruling the grating. The cross section of a groove would approximately describe a V, whose depth, angle, and relation to the plane of the grating all contribute to the transmission efficiency. Gratings are not equally efficient for all wavelengths, but they can be cut (or "blazed") so as to be maximally efficient for a given spectral region. The term "blaze" arises from the fact that, as one turns a grating and observes the dispersed light reflected from it, the color reflected with the highest efficiency appears with particular brilliance. Gratings having highest efficiency at 500 and 750 mμ will therefore appear to "blaze" in the green and red.

A *standard lamp* is one whose spectral distribution is known. When such a lamp is operated at a known *color temperature,* its output can be read from published tables. Definitions of photometric terms such as color temperature are beyond the scope of this paper, but a clear discussion of the subject and of how the emissivity of standard lamps are calculated is given by Seliger and McElroy (11).

SLITS AND RESOLUTION

The standard optical arrangement of the Aminco-Bowman instrument is that of SPF 1 shown in Figure 1A. No mirrors or lenses are used to focus the xenon arc into the first monochromator; instead, the arc is placed at the focal point of the first concave mirror of the excitation monochromator (M_1). The light, after being rendered parallel by the first concave mirror, is dispersed by the grating and falls onto a second concave mirror, which focuses an image of the arc in the center of the cell compartment.

The resolution is determined by the width of the slits, and the most critical slit in the path of the exciting beam appears to be at position 2 (Fig. 1A). In this author's experience, the slit at position 1 may be left out entirely in most applications, although its presence may reduce stray light somewhat. The slit at position 3 limits the size of the beam entering the cuvet; a 1 or 2 mm slit should be used so that, even when a microcuvet is employed, exciting light does not strike the edges of the cell. With the standard 600 groove/mm grating, the nominal band width at half-maximum transmission is found to be 12 mμ/mm slit width at position 2. Two series of slits are available, one calibrated in multiples of 0.5 mm and the other calibrated in fractional inches. The two slits most often used in this laboratory in position 2 have widths of $\frac{1}{32}''$ and $\frac{1}{64}''$, yielding band widths of approximately 10 and 5 mμ.

Slit positions 4–7 occur on the emission side of the instrument (Fig. 1A). Empirically, little is gained by including slits at positions 5 and 6, and satisfactory resolution is obtained by using slits only at 4 and 7. The band width obtained when slits 4 and 7 are made equal, and when the monochromator is fitted with a standard 600 groove/mm grating, is again 12 mμ/mm slit width. The instrument is equipped with sliding filter holders (not shown in Fig. 1) near positions 1 and 6; these can be fitted with polarizers as described elsewhere (12), filters, opaque plates serving as shutters, or kept open.

The optical arrangement of SPF 2 (Fig. 1B) differs from the standard system in that continuously variable slits are present in the numbered positions, and the light is focused onto an entrance slit by an off-axis ellipsoidal mirror assembly. The presence of an entrance slit results in less stray light reaching the sample than in the system of Figure 1A, where light not only from the arc but from other parts of the housing and lamp can gain entrance to the monochromator. Further reference to Figure 1 will be made below.

ALIGNMENT OF MONOCHROMATORS

The instruction manual indicates that the monochromator dial settings can be assumed accurate to only ± 5 mμ. However, they can be aligned more accurately (± 1–2 mμ) by comparison with the known lines of a mercury arc.

The procedure for aligning the emission monochromator is as follows: A mercury pen lamp is placed in the cuvet holder and the smallest available slits are placed in positions 4 through 7. Several sheets of lens paper are inserted between positions 5 and 6 to attenuate the light of the mercury arc. With the detector and mercury arc turned on, a monochromator setting of 546 mμ should coincide with the strong mercury line as indicated by a maximum reading on the microphotometer. If such is not the case, the dial is left at 546 mμ, and the monochromator is adjusted as follows. The cover is removed and the two screws which secure the second concave mirror are loosened. The mirror is then repositioned with the room darkened until the microphotometer gives a maximum response.

Alignment of the excitation monochromator of standard Aminco-Bowman instrument (as exemplified by SPF 1, Fig. 1A): 0.5 mm slits are placed in positions 2, 4, and 7 (Fig. 1A) and a cuvet holding a light-scattering solution (Ludox, diluted 1:10 with distilled water), is placed in the holder. When the emission monochromator M_2 is set at 400 mμ, maximum scatter signal should occur when M_1 is also at 400 mμ. If this is not the case, alignment can usually be done by repositioning the xenon arc. To understand why arc position influences the excitation wavelength, consider the following. In Figure 1A, a ray of light is shown leaving the excitation monochromator grating and being focused on the sample cell. What reaches the sample is actually an arc image of a certain color, whose spectral purity is determined by the exit slit width; since the other colors are lateral to the slit, they are excluded. Therefore, when the arc is moved laterally, the spectrum of arc images also moves across the slit and a new wavelength is admitted. To reposition the arc, the four screws holding the lamp housing cover with the fitting for the upper electrode of the lamp are slightly loosened. It is then found that the cover can be moved several millimeters since the screw holds have extra clearance. With the lamp on, one can find a position of the cover which will result in a maximum scatter signal. (There is some danger involved in manipulating the lamp while it is turned on; one must be careful not to dislodge the electrode connections. A factory technician can perform the alignment if the operator lacks the necessary dexerity.) If the misalignment is severe, it may be necessary to reposition the second concave mirror of M_1, as in the calibration of M_2. In the calibration of SPF 2, the position of the entrance slit to M_1 is fixed, so that alignment must be done by mirror repositioning.

The use of 546 and 400 mμ as the wavelengths for calibrating the monochromators is, to some extent, arbitrary. In the calibration of M_1, 400 mμ was chosen in order to avoid a region of the xenon arc spectrum

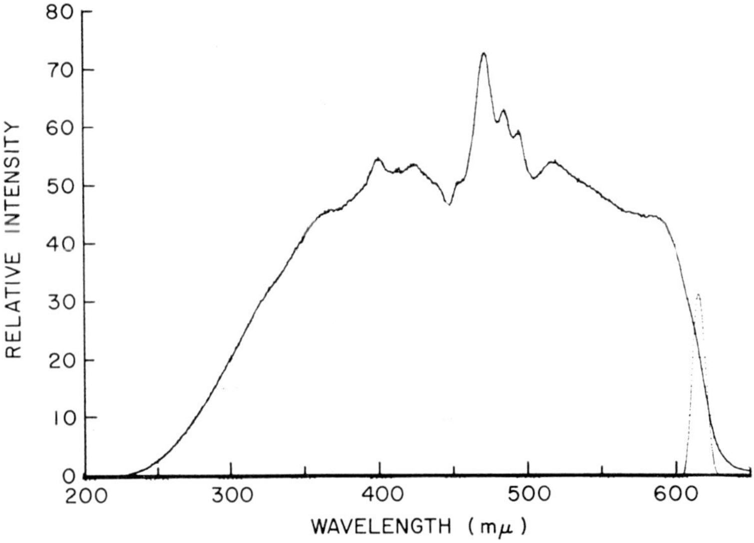

FIG. 2. Excitation system calibration curve (direct tracing). The curve represents the fluorescence observed from the front surface of a cell containing a rhodamine B solution (3 gm/liter in ethylene glycol). A solid sample accessory was used, and the excitation monochromator was scanned with the emission wavelength set at 615 mμ. The scatter peak shown at 615 mμ was obtained by replacing the ethylene glycol solution with water. Instrument, SPF 2 (Fig. 1B) with both variable excitation system slits set at 1.0 mm for approximately 12 mμ bandwidth.

having sharp emission lines since the finite band width of the monochromators may result in some bias toward those lines (see Fig. 2). Also, at 400 mμ, most detector response curves are not changing rapidly, so that bias due to the detector is minimal.

CALIBRATION OF THE LIGHT SOURCE (ARC-MONOCHROMATOR COMBINATION)

Melhuish's method (7) for calibrating the light source is both convenient and accurate. The method uses a concentrated solution of rhodamine B (3 gm/liter in ethylene glycol) as a fluorescent screen. An attachment (available from the American Instrument Co. as a "solid sample accessory") is used instead of the usual cuvet holder to contain the cell with the rhodamine B, and the fluorescence is observed from the front surface at an angle of about 25° to the incident beam. The method relies on the assumptions that the rhodamine B solution has such high absorbancy at wavelengths up to 600 mμ that essentially all excitation energy is absorbed in a thin layer at the surface of the cell, that the quantum yield of rhodamine B is independent of excitation wavelength, and that the fluorescence is therefore proportional only to the number of quanta incident on the fluorescent screen. These assumptions appear to be correct, since Melhuish found that calibrations carried out with his method agreed with those obtained using the thermopile method (6). The emission of rhodamine B is observed at a constant setting of 615 mμ of the emission monochromator through a Wratten 2A filter, which eliminates second-order scattered light. When the excitation monochromator is scanned, the recorded fluorescence signal gives directly a curve showing the output of the lamp-monochromator combination. A typical tracing is shown in Figure 2, which also gives the scatter signal observed by replacing the rhodamine B solution with water.

Possible artifacts in this system could arise from the second-order radiation which is passed by the first monochromator. Thus, when set at 550 mμ, the excitation monochromator also passes light at $\lambda/2$ or 275 mμ. One would expect the amount of second-order radiation from the excitation monochromator to be small, since the grating is blazed at 300 mμ for maximum transmission. In fact, when a tracing such as Figure 2 is made with a glass plate (such as an ordinary microscope slide) in the exciting beam, no significant amount of excitation below 300 mμ can reach the rhodamine B, yet the curve above 400 mμ matches tracings done without the glass plate. Therefore, error from second-order radiation is negligible. The ordinate of Figure 2 is labeled "relative intensity," but from the above arguments it is seen that the actual recorded intensity can be considered to be directly proportional to the relative photon output of the light source. The ordinate of Figure 2 could also be labeled "relative quanta" for this reason.

In the calibration of the light source, stray light could conceivably be a source of error. A fluorescent screen solution with a more restricted absorption region than that of rhodamine B should minimize the effect of stray light. For calibration of the lamp in the ultraviolet, such a fluorescent screen solution is 1-dimethylaminonaphthalene 5-sulfonate, 0.02 *M* in dilute NaOH (13). This solution is practically opaque to radiation below 350 mμ, but has little absorption above 450 mμ. The absorbancy in a 1 cm path length cell was 92 at 312 mμ, 1.0 at 395 mμ, and 0.01 at 438 mμ. Comparison of the calibration curves using rhodamine B and 1-dimethylaminonaphthalene 5-sulfonate show agreement within 2%, a fact which indicates that stray light is negligible in the instrument used.

However, stray light may not always be negligible, since there are individual variations among Aminco-Bowman instruments. Calibration of the ultraviolet emission with 1-dimethylaminonaphthalene 5-sulfonate should be considered more reliable than calibration performed with rhodamine B, if there is a difference between the calibrations.

Figure 2 shows that there are some sharp peaks in the photon output curve due to the emission lines of xenon, especially in the 470 mμ region.

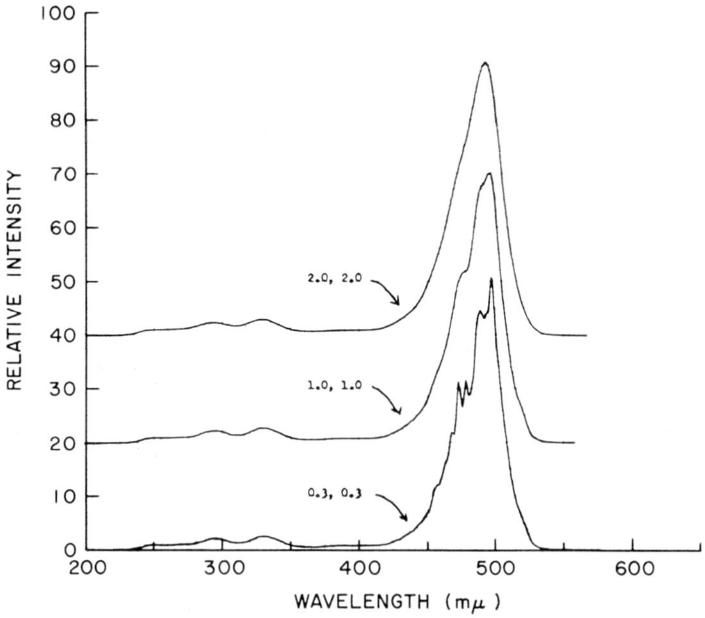

FIG. 3. Apparent excitation spectra of 10^{-6} *M* fluorescein in 0.01 *M* KOH. The three curves were obtained with the indicated slit widths (in mm) in positions 1 and 2 (Fig. 1B) of SPF 2. Each curve was scanned twice (direct recordings).

The sensitivity of the calibration method is such as to allow output curves such as Figure 2 to be obtained with various slit combinations in the excitation side; a convenient signal strength is obtained by variation of the emission slits. With different band widths, the xenon arc lines become more or less resolved. When applying the calibration curve to convert apparent spectra to corrected spectra, it is necessary to use the same slits for the calibration curve as are used in the excitation spectrum scan. Figure 3 shows the apparent excitation spectra of fluorescein obtained with different slits. The superimposed xenon lines become quite prominent at high resolution, and it would obviously be wrong to correct such spectra by using calibration curves obtained with low resolution. In practice, most excitation spectra of organic compounds in aqueous solution near 300°K show little structure, so that low resolution is adequate and also makes manual correction of the spectra much more convenient by reducing the number of points needed to define the curve. When one sees multiple sharp peaks in the excitation spectrum, such as those shown in Figure 3, he should be alert to the possibility that these may be artifacts due to xenon lines rather than true peaks in the spectrum. Such artifacts occur mainly near 470 mμ. For examples of corrected excitation spectra obtained with the Aminco-Bowman spectrophotofluorometer, see references 14 and 15.

CALIBRATION OF THE DETECTOR SYSTEM

Parker and Rees (16) state that probably the easiest way to calibrate detector response is by comparison with the known output of a standard lamp; White *et al.* (6) described such calibrations for the Aminco-Bowman instrument. The detailed procedure followed in this laboratory is as follows:

A U. S. National Bureau of Standards calibrated tungsten-filament lamp is operated at the specified voltage, by means of a Variac, to yield a color temperature of 2854°K. (The voltage required to yield a given color temperature varies from lamp to lamp and is the information supplied by the National Bureau of Standards with the standard lamp. For our particular tungsten lamp, a color temperature of 2854°K is given with an applied voltage of 102.8 V AC.) To obtain a manageably low light signal, the lamp is placed 16 ft from the spectrophotofluorometer, and a blackened cardboard tube is used to direct the light onto the instrument. It is convenient to use 1.0 mm slits at positions 6 and 7 of Figure 1A for these calibrations. In order for the light to fall directly on the entrance of the emission monochromator, it is necessary to remove the lamp housing and one baffle of the sample chamber. Alternatively, a front surface aluminized mirror may be positioned between the lamp housing and the opened sample chamber and the tungsten lamp beam reflected into the monochromator. Selective spectral attenuation by such a mirror in the visible region appears to be negligible. The signal produced by the tungsten lamp is recorded as a function of wavelength and is compared with the known output of the lamp as given by Barbrow (17). His data are in terms of microwatts per wavelength interval and must first be multiplied by λ to give output in terms of quanta per wavelength interval (16). Following Parker and Rees (16), the sensitivity factor, $S(\lambda)$, is obtained by dividing the observed signal into the known lamp output at 10 mμ intervals. $S(\lambda)$ is therefore the factor by which the fluorescence signal must be multiplied when one is correcting emission spectra; the factor is inversely proportional to the sensitivity of the detector.

The standard tungsten lamp method cannot be employed below 400 mμ, so the method of Melhuish (7) was used for calibrating the detector system in the ultraviolet region. This method is essentially also a standard lamp method, but it employs the xenon arc lamp previously calibrated as described above. The output of the lamp is directed into the emission monochromator by one of several possible methods. Melhuish (7) placed a mirror in the cuvet position of the solid sample accessory, and light was reflected off that mirror into a second mirror and thence into the monochromator. A more convenient method seems to be to place either a front-surface mirror or a quartz plate at 45° to the incident beam in the standard cuvet holder. In all cases, the intensity of the reflected light is far too great to be handled by the detector system without attenuation. In SPF 2 (Fig. 1B), attenuation of the xenon arc is accomplished simply by stopping down variable slit #1. However, in the standard Aminco-Bowman spectrophotofluorometer (Fig. 1A), there is no entrance slit; and a convenient method of attenuating the light is to place one or two blackened 30 mesh (30 lines per inch) copper screens just ahead of the second concave mirror in the excitation monochromator. The screens act as neutral density filters: recalibration of the excitation system with the screens in place shows that the relative spectral output is unchanged. (It should be noted that truly neutral *optical* filters do not exist.) To measure the detector response to the xenon arc output, the excitation monochromator is varied in steps of 10 mμ and the emission monochromator is adjusted manually to give the maximum reading at each step. The peak readings, divided by the previously determined relative photon outputs, again give $S(\lambda)$. The maximum reading should be obtained when the two monochromators are set for the same wavelength, but in practice there may be some difference due to irreducible errors in monochromator alignment and bias imposed by the finite band widths in combination with rapidly changing spectral emission and detector response in some regions.

Examples of detector response calibrations are shown in Figure 4. The curves indicate that the tungsten and xenon standard lamp methods together permit calibration of the detector from at least 300 mμ to over 650 mμ, and that, where both methods are used, in the region 400–450 mμ reasonable agreement occurs. The use of the xenon arc to calibrate the detector is inconvenient in the region near 470 mμ because of the sharp xenon lines (see Fig. 2) which will cause large errors in $S(\lambda)$ for small errors in monochromator dial settings. The curves of Figure 4 show also that the calibration curves depend not only on the type of phototube used but also on the type of diffraction grating[1] present in the

[1] Different gratings are available from the manufacturer and should be installed by a factory technician.

emission monochromator. The standard Aminco-Bowman instrument is equipped with an emission grating blazed at 500 mμ and an RCA 1P28 photomultiplier tube (3); the calibration curve for this combination is shown in Figure 4*C*. (Individual gratings and phototubes vary even where they are nominally identical; therefore, as pointed out by White *et al.* (6), it is not valid to assume that the calibrations for any two instruments will be identical.) Another significant feature of Figure 4

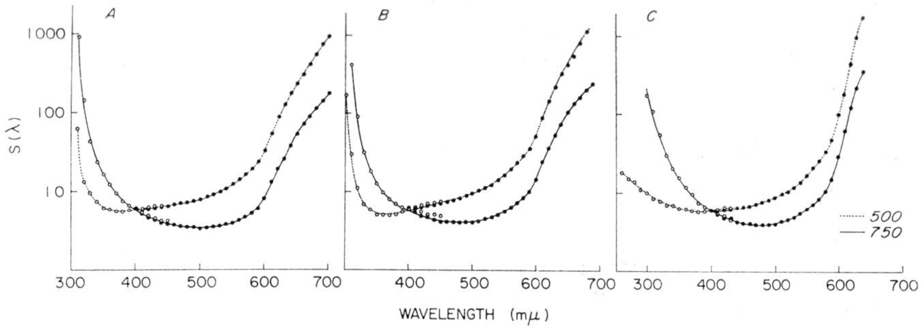

FIG. 4. Detector calibration curves for different phototube-emission grating combinations. (*A*) RCA 4472. (*B*) RCA 1P21. (*C*) RCA 1P28. Filled circles are points obtained by the tungsten lamp method; open circles are points obtained by using the calibrated xenon arc source. The maxima of the grating blazes (in mμ) for the curves are indicated in *C*.

may be indicated. While it is frequently assumed that uncorrected emission spectra obtained on the Aminco-Bowman spectrophotofluorometer are distorted by the detector response characteristics, in certain spectral regions the detector response curves are nearly flat. In Figure 4*C*, for instance, for the combination of RCA 1P28 phototube + 500 mμ blaze grating, $S(\lambda)$ is within 10% of 6.4 over the whole range of 330–460 mμ. Similarly, $S(\lambda)$ for the combination of 4472 phototube + 750 mμ grating is 3.7 ± 10% in the range 440–550 mμ. Each curve in Figure 4, as well as Figure 5, shows a region where detector response is quite constant; these spectral regions are listed in Table 1. Figure 5 is the calibration curve for the combination of 1P28 phototube and 300 mμ blaze emission grating and is of particular interest because it shows that such a detector system has a very linear photon response in the ultraviolet. $S(\lambda)$ is 4.5 ± 8% in the region 260–400 mμ. This important part of the spectrum encompasses the fluorescence of the three aromatic amino acids, tryptophan, tyrosine, and phenylalanine, in addition to the native fluorescence of proteins. This detector combination results in recorded emission spectra which are, without applied corrections, essentially linear in terms of quanta per wavelength interval. This linearity is illustrated in Figure 6, which shows

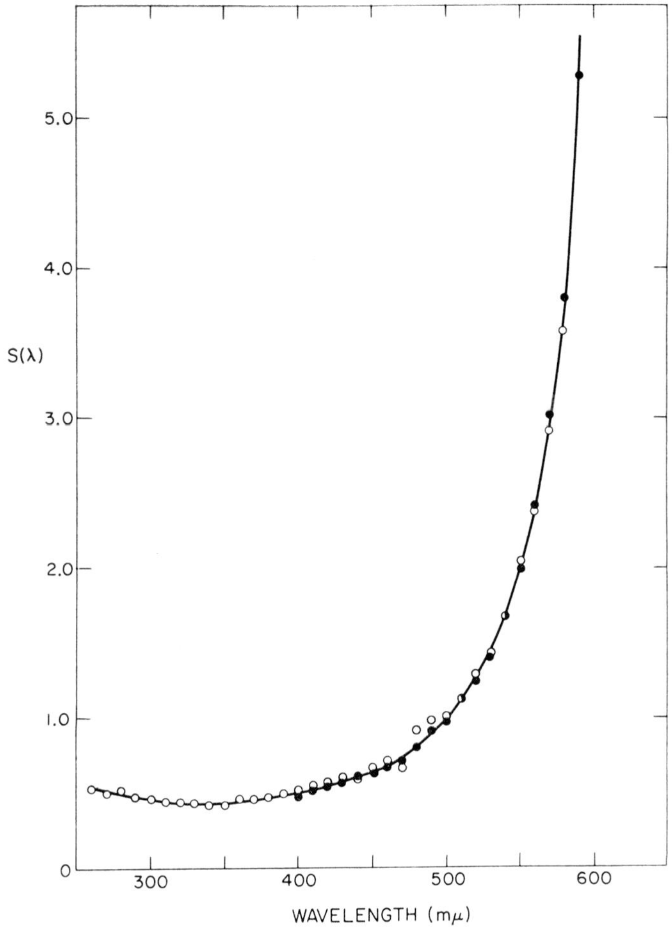

FIG. 5. Detector calibration curve for RCA 1P28 and emission monochromator with grating having a 300 mμ blaze.

TABLE 1
Regions of Linear (±10%) Photon Response of Detectors
(from data of Figures 4 and 5)

Phototube	Grating blaze		
	300 mμ	500 mμ	750 mμ
RCA 4472	—	350–440 mμ	440–550 mμ
RCA 1P21	—	340–410 mμ	430–530 mμ
RCA 1P28	260–400 mμ	330–460 mμ	430–520 mμ

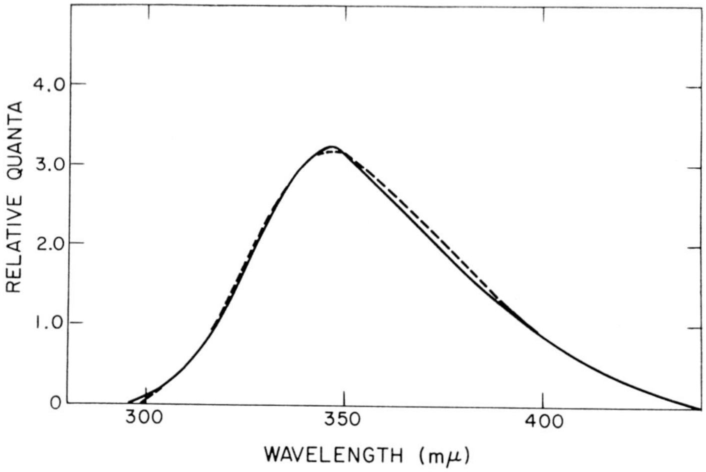

FIG. 6. Comparison of emission spectra of dilute aqueous tryptophan solutions (—) corrected spectrum from Teale and Weber (18); (- - -) uncorrected spectrum obtained with detector system of Figure 5.

that the uncorrected fluorescence spectrum of tryptophan matches almost exactly the corrected spectrum published by Teale and Weber (18). Examples of protein emission spectra obtained with this detector are given in references 19–21.

ACCURACY OF THE CALIBRATIONS

There is no obvious direct method for assessing the accuracy of the calibration of detector response. An error of 3% in the value of the output of the standard lamp at any wavelength may be expected (16). Another 1–2% error may be expected due to uncertainties in achieving the recommended lamp voltage, in the monochromator alignment, and in measuring and recording the photomultiplier current. The over-all accuracy of the detector response at any given point is thus perhaps 5%.

Melhuish (7) has discussed the accuracy of the light source calibration, which appears to be quite high. The chief sources of error would seem to be in the purity of the fluorescent screen materials, but this can be checked by using different screens, as discussed above.

Reasonably accurate detector response calibration employing the calibrated xenon arc can be expected up to about 450 mμ. However, it is necessary that the monochromators be carefully aligned before using this method. Since the monochromator dials can be read to only 1–2 mμ, there will be some unavoidable error in isolating the desired wavelength to be reflected into the emission monochromator. This error is likely to be small, because the xenon arc output does not change abruptly below 400 mμ.

In the determination of quantum yields, the areas beneath the corrected emission curves are employed (22). Even though the error in obtaining the detector response at any wavelength relative to that at another is 5%, the error in determining the areas should be smaller, since it is unlikely that the calibration curve is 5% too high or too low at every point of the spectrum.

QUESTION OF INSTRUMENTAL STABILITY

Several factors are involved in the variation of observed fluorescence intensity with time.

1. *Arc instability.* Variation in the position of the arc passing between the electrodes of the xenon lamp is known as "arc wander." Arc stability has improved considerably in recent years due to better lamp construction and greater stability of the DC power supplies. In the standard Aminco-Bowman spectrophotofluorometer (Fig. 1A), the lateral motion of the arc will cause an apparent shift in the excitation wavelength. In practice, arc wander in SPF 1 has not been a problem. It has not been observed, for instance, that the excitation spectrum shifts with time due to arc wander, although such a shift would be expected. In SPF 2, the ellipsoidal condensing system focuses an enlarged image of the arc onto the entrance slit. This system is much more sensitive to arc instability, but the excitation wavelength stays constant. The effect of arc motion is mitigated to some extent by the fact that the arc image is rotated 90° by the condensing optics, so that arc wander is along, rather than across, the slits. The lamp should of course be replaced if arc wander becomes excessive.[2]

Although the stability of SPF 2 over the long term (over 30 min) seems less than that of SPF 1, the short-term stability of both instruments is such that repeated spectral tracings superimpose. For instance, the curves of Figures 2 and 3 were each traced twice with SPF 2 and the variation is less than the width of the recorder pen line.

2. *Temperature.* Fluorescence efficiency is extremely sensitive to temperature variations. In the case of tryptophan and protein fluorescence, for instance, the quantum yields vary by about 2% per degree near room temperature (23). For accurate work, temperature regulation is necessary; and temperature-regulated cell holders are available from the

[2] Replacements obtained from the American Instrument Co. are tested for stability and may, on the average, be more suitable for use in the spectrophotofluorometer than those obtained directly from the lamp manufacturer (Mr. H. K. Howerton, personal communication).

manufacturer. Also in the standard Aminco-Bowman instrument (see Fig. 1A), the lamp is near the phototube housing, which may heat up with time; this is manifested by an increased dark current and noise. For this reason, it is unwise to leave the instrument on for more than an hour or two at a time. Note that in SPF 2 (Fig. 1B) the lamp is placed at a greater distance from the phototube in order to avoid such heat transfer.

3. *Photodegradation.* This term covers any photo-induced process causing a change in fluorescence signal. The Aminco-Bowman spectrophotofluorometer has high output in the ultraviolet because lenses, with their inherent optical absorption, are not used. However, the intense ultraviolet radiation is accompanied by photodecomposition in many solutions, especially substances like proteins (24). Attenuation of the exciting beam becomes a necessity in such instances. Methods for reducing the intensity of the lamp are discussed above, under the section dealing with detector response calibration.

DISCUSSION

While it is essential that the monochromators be accurately aligned, the calibrations, as such, of both the excitation and emission systems are actually quite simple. One cannot overemphasize the fact that the small amount of work needed to calibrate the Aminco-Bowman SPF results in large dividends, some of which are as follows:

(*1*) With corrected spectra, results from one laboratory can be compared with those of another.

(*2*) Corrected excitation spectra in simple systems may be taken as equivalent to absorption spectra. In more complex systems, comparison of excitation and absorption spectra can reveal the presence of energy transfer or light-absorbing groups which do not fluoresce.

(*3*) Corrected emission spectra can be used to determine quantum yields (which then often are used to calculate fluorescence decay times), to estimate the energy of Stokes' shifts, and to determine the dipole moment of the excited state using Lippert's theory (25). Furthermore, once one has done the calibrations, he may discover that a particular combination of phototube and grating gives a flat response in the spectral region of interest, and that corrections do not need to be applied to the emission spectra.

The following accessories are needed for the calibrations: (*1*) A standard tungsten lamp. (*2*) A solid sample accessory to allow observation of fluorescence from the front surface. (*3*) A front-surface aluminized mirror or a piece of quartz to direct the excitation beam into the second monochromator. (*4*) Attenuating screens to reduce the intensity of the exciting light. These can be made simply by spraying flat black paint over 3 × 3 in. sections of copper screen. (*5*) A mercury pen light.

The procedures described here have certain advantages over other calibration methods described for the Aminco-Bowman instrument: The excitation system can also be calibrated by the use of a thermopile, but Melhuish (7) pointed out that the sensitivity of that method in the ultraviolet was low. Light output can also be measured by chemical actinometry (26), but this is time consuming and not convenient when one wishes to make the calibrations with small slits in place. Calibration can also be made by comparing apparent excitation spectra with absorption spectra (8, 27). Again, the disadvantage here is that calibration cannot easily be performed using different bandwidths. Also, since a discrete number of points are employed for the comparisons, the calibration does not result in a continuous calibration curve as given by Melhuish's method (7). Comparison of apparent fluorescence spectra and "standard" fluorescence spectra of reference compounds has been advocated as a method for calibrating detector response in the Aminco-Bowman spectrophotofluorometer (8). Whether such well-established curves exist for a wide spectral range, however, is still open to considerable question. Quinine in sulfuric acid has been suggested as such a standard (28), but there is still disagreement as to what the corrected emission spectrum is (29). Recently, this laboratory showed that quinine has some anomalous fluorescence characteristics, one of which is that the fluorescence spectrum shifts in position depending on the exciting wavelength (14).

The tungsten lamp calibration used here is fairly rapid and suffers only from the fact that, since the calibration cannot be carried out in the ultraviolet, a separate method is required for the region below 400 mμ. Recently, however, standard quartz–iodine lamps said to be usable in the ultraviolet have been described (30) and are available (31). Such lamps should provide all the necessary information for detector reponse calibration in a single scan of the emission monochromator.

For some time there have been instruments and attachments available commercially which apply corrections to the excitation and emission spectra automatically (32). These instruments would seem to offer great advantages in convenience especially when applied to low temperature work, or compounds having highly structured spectra. Manual correction of spectra obviously takes some time, and may be very difficult where sharp peaks occur within small wavelength intervals. Nevertheless, in most biochemical studies, aqueous solutions are employed, and the spectra obtained are usually broad and structureless. Such curves can therefore be corrected at 10 mμ intervals, and therefore almost all emission spectra can be corrected with 15 points or less. Some of the automatically corrected instruments present spectra which are displayed in terms of energy, rather than quanta. Such spectra would have to be converted to the corresponding quantum-corrected curves for most of the practical applications listed above. To do this, one takes individual points on the energy-corrected curve, divides by the wavelength, and replots the spectrum. Such manual interconversion of spectra forfeits time saved in using an automatic instrument.

Certain of the procedures described in this paper (e.g., moving the monochromator mirrors, moving the lamp housing with the xenon arc turned on) are not without hazard to the apparatus and/or to the operator, so that proper judgement and care must be exercised.

The detector response curves shown in this work suggest that it may be possible to obtain absolute emission spectra without corrections, by selecting the correct detector. This finding raises the question as to whether future development of fluorescence instrumentation should be directed toward better electromechanical methods of correcting nonlinear detector response, or toward development of more linear detectors. The latter alternative would seem to be preferable. Not only are there increasing numbers of photodetectors from which to choose, but also it would seem that gratings could be made so as to compensate for low detector sensitivity in a given spectral region, thus yielding a linear response over a wide range.

SUMMARY

This paper discusses in detail some aspects of the use of the Aminco-Bowman spectrophotofluorometer for obtaining accurate excitation and emission spectra. In particular, these topics are covered: (*1*) Methods for aligning the monochromators. (*2*) Calibration of the light source and detector systems. (*3*) Effect of the type of grating as well as the type of phototube on detector response. (*4*) Resolution and slits. (*5*) Factors affecting "instrumental stability." (*6*) Methods for attenuating the exciting light.

It is shown that different combinations of phototube and grating in the emission monochromator give linear photon response curves in different spectral regions, and in certain instances the uncorrected and corrected emission spectra are nearly identical.

ACKNOWLEDGMENTS

Numerous helpful discussions with the following persons are gratefully acknowledged: Drs. R. L. Bowman and J. E. Hayes, Jr., and Mr. H. K. Howerton of American Instrument Co.

REFERENCES

1. Udenfriend, S., *Fluorescence Assay in Biology and Medicine*. Academic Press, New York, 1960.
2. Bowman, R. L., Caulfield, P. A., Udenfriend, S., *Science* **122,** 32 (1955).
3. Bowman, R. L., *Pharmacol. Rev.* **11,** 256 (1959).
4. Howerton, H. K., *Instr. Soc. Am. J.* **6,** 50 (1959).
5. Price, J. M., Kaihara, M., and Howerton, H. K., *Appl. Opt.* **1,** 521 (1962).
6. White, C. E., Ho, H., and Weimer, E. Q., *Anal. Chem.* **32,** 438, (1960).
7. Melhuish, H., *J. Opt. Soc. Am.* **52,** 1256 (1962).
8. Argauer, R. J., and White, C. E., *Anal. Chem.* **36,** 368 (1964).
9. Drushel, H. V., Sommers, A. L., and Cox, R. C., *Anal. Chem.* **35,** 2166 (1963).
10. Laurance, D. J. R., *in* "Methods in Enzymology" (Colowick, S. P., and Kaplan, N. Q., eds.), p. 174. Academic Press, New York, 1957.
11. Seliger, H. H., and McElroy, W. D., "Light: Physical and Biological Action." Academic Press, New York, 1965.
12. Chen, R. F., and Bowman, R. L., *Science* **147,** 729 (1965).
13. Weber, G., and Teale, F. W. J., *Trans. Faraday Soc.* **53,** 646 (1957).
14. Chen, R. F., and Hayes, J. E., Jr., *Anal. Biochem.* **13,** 523 (1965).
15. Chen, R. F., *Anal. Biochem.* **19,** 374 (1967).
16. Parker, C. A., and Rees, W. T., *Analyst* **85,** 587 (1960).
17. Barbrow, L. E., *J. Opt. Soc. Am.* **49,** 1122 (1959).
18. Teale, F. W. J., and Weber, G., *Biochem. J.* **65,** 476 (1957).
19. Chen, R. F., *Biochim. Biophys. Acta* **120,** 169 (1966).
20. Chen, R. F., *J. Biol. Chem.* **242,** 173 (1967).
21. Chen, R. F., and Cohen, P. F., *Arch. Biochem. Biophys.* **114,** 514 (1966).
22. Chen, R. F., *Science* **150,** 1593 (1965).
23. Gally, J. A., and Edelman, G. M., *Biopolymers Symp.* **1,** 367 (1964).
24. Chen, R. F., *Biochem. Biophys. Res. Commun.* **17,** 141 (1964).
25. Lippert, E., *Z. Elektrochem.* **61,** 962 (1957).
26. Hatchard, C. G., and Parker, C. A., *Proc. Roy. Soc.* (*London*) **A235,** 518 (1956).
27. Lippert, E., Nagele, W., Seibold-Blankenstein, I., Staiger, U., and Voss, W., *Z. Anal. Chem.* **170,** 1 (1959).
28. Melhuish, W. H., *J. Phys. Chem.* **64,** 762 (1960).
29. Borresen, H. C., *Acta Chem. Scand.* **19,** 2089 (1965).
30. Stair, R., Schneider, W. E., and Jackson, J. K., *Appl. Opt.* **2,** 1151 (1963).
31. Electro Optics Associates, Palo Alto, Calif.
32. The Perkin-Elmer Corp. linear energy spectrophotofluorometer was described by Slavin, W., Mooney, R. W., and Palumbo, D. T., *J. Opt. Soc. Am.* **51,** 93 (1961). A newer version is listed as the Model 236. The G. K. Turner Associates Spectro 210 was described by Turner, G. K., *Science* **146,** 183 (1964). A "corrected spectrum attachment" has recently been introduced by American Instrument Co. for the Aminco-Bowman spectrophotofluorometer.

ANALYTICAL BIOCHEMISTRY 20, 358–360 (1967)

Rapid Separation of Thymine Dimer and Pyrimidines on Ion-Exchange Paper

RONALD D. BROWN AND CHARLES E. HOLT

Massachusetts Institute of Technology, Department of Biology, Cambridge, Massachusetts 02139

Received March 6, 1967

During a study of the effect of ultraviolet irradiation on DNA, we found it necessary to separate thymine dimer from cytosine. Several conventional paper chromatographic systems[1] were found to give inadequate separation. An ion-exchange paper system was devised which provides a wide separation of thymine dimer and cytosine. The system has the additional advantages of speed and separation of a number of other nucleic acid derivatives.

Paper loaded with IRC-50 resin (grade WA-2, Reeve Angel, Clifton, N. J.) was used in descending chromatography at room temperature. The solvent was 0.1 *M* acetic acid, which was adjusted with NH_4OH to pH 4.8 except where mentioned. Separations were carried out for 2 hr (about 20 cm between origin and solvent front) or 3 hr (about 30 cm). Spots were located either with an ultraviolet light (maximum output at 254 mμ) or with a Vanguard strip counter. Thymine dimer was prepared from thymine-2-^{14}C (New England Nuclear Corp., Boston) by the method of Beukers and Berends (3). Thymine dimer was identified by the method of Boyce and Howard-Flanders (2), which involves cleavage of alleged dimer by irradiation with ultraviolet light at room temperature; 92% of the thymine dimer was converted to thymine by this treatment.

In 2 hr, thymine dimer, thymine, and cytosine separate as shown in Figure 1. Uracil runs about half-way between thymine dimer and thymine and more time is required for an equivalent separation. The R_f values for a number of additional nucleic acid derivatives are given in Table 1. The values range in an even fashion from 0.05 to 0.98, providing separation of a number of compounds. The components of a mixture of cytosine, uracil, and thymine gave the same R_f values as the corresponding compounds chromatographed alone. Hydrolyzates of DNA derived from a crude sample of *Physarum polycephalum* containing about 1.0 mg of protein,

[1] Systems a, b, f, and j of reference (1) and the system in reference (2).

50 μg of RNA; and 5 μg of DNA were applied directly in the 98% formic acid used for hydrolysis without influence on the R_f values of added thymine, cytosine, or thymine dimer. The compounds can be eluted from the paper (Table 1) with acid, although the recovery is not complete.

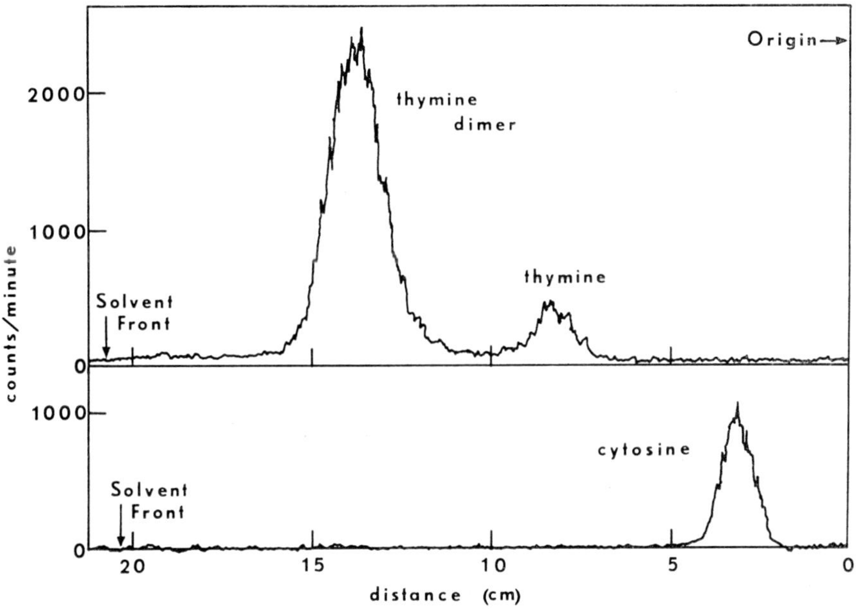

FIG. 1. Separation of ^{14}C-thymine dimer, ^{14}C-thymine, and ^{3}H-cytosine in 2 hr. The thymine dimer and thymine peaks (total of 10 μg) arose from the thymine dimer preparation. The cytosine (100 μg) was run separately. The difference in baseline between the upper and lower tracings is not significant.

Cytosine is particularly difficult to elute which is consistent with its low R_f value. A disadvantage of the system is the difficulty in locating spots with ultraviolet light. About 100 μg of a compound is required for detection by this method.

In Table 1, the tested compounds have been ordered according to decreasing R_f. For a given base, the nucleotide, nucleoside, and free base separate from one another in that order, with the nucleotide moving most rapidly. Within the nucleotides or nucleosides, the derivatives of uracil, thymine, guanine, cytosine, and adenine separate in that order. The same order is found for the free bases except the positions of guanine and cytosine are reversed. The rapid movement of the nucleotides may be caused by repulsion of the negatively charged phosphoryl group from the partial negative charge on the carboxyl groups of the resin. The slower moving bases (adenine, guanine, and cytosine) carry a primary amino

TABLE 1
R_f Values and Recovery Data

Compound	R_f[a]	Recovery from paper,[c] %
5′-UMP	0.98	
5′-TMP	0.88	
5′-GMP	0.81	
5′-CMP	0.77	
Uridine	0.73	
Thymine dimer	0.63–0.70[b]	91[e]
Uracil	0.56–0.59	79[f]
Thymidine	0.53	
Thymine	0.40–0.48	59[f]
5′-AMP	0.37	
Guanosine	0.36	
Cytidine	0.33	
Cytosine	0.15–0.17	48[e]
Guanine	0.15	
Adenosine	0.10	
Adenine	0.05[d]	

[a] Thymine dimer was located only by radioactivity. Cytosine, uracil, and thymine were located by both radioactivity and ultraviolet light, and the remaining compounds by ultraviolet light only.

[b] When a range of R_f is given, it represents the extremes of several experiments. Reproducibility on samples chromatographed simultaneously is much better.

[c] Recoveries were determined on the basis of radioactivity measured in a liquid scintillation counter and represent the fraction of the applied material which was recovered in soluble form.

[d] Adenine forms a streak.

[e] Spot soaked in 2 ml 1.0 *N* HCl.

[f] Spot soaked in 2 ml 0.1 *N* HCl.

group. However, a simple model based on ionic binding between the resin and base does not appear possible, because we observed no change in R_f of cytosine, uracil, and thymine when the pH of the eluting solvent was varied in the range 3.5–6.0.

REFERENCES

1. Wyatt, G. R., *in* "The Nucleic Acids" (E. Chargaff and J. N. Davidson, eds.), Vol. I, p. 252. Academic Press, New York, 1955.
2. Boyce, R. P., and Howard-Flanders, P., *Proc. Natl. Acad. Sci. U. S.* **51,** 293 (1964).
3. Beukers, R., and Berends, W., *Biochim. Biophys. Acta* **41,** 550 (1960).

ANALYTICAL BIOCHEMISTRY **20** (1967)

SHORT COMMUNICATIONS

Zone Sedimentation Analysis of RNA in Angle-Head Rotors

Brakke (1) was the first to point out the advantages of density gradient ultracentrifugation for the separation of molecules. Martin and Ames (2) established the use of density gradient centrifugation for sedimentation coefficient determination, using the swinging-bucket type of rotor (SW 39). The use of conventional rotors (angle-headed) has already been described for proteins (3) and for DNA (4). In the present report, angle-head rotors were employed for zone sedimentation analysis of RNA.

Ribosomal RNA, OD (1 cm, 260 mμ) = 10.0, prepared according to Kirby's method modified by the addition of 0.2 mg/ml purified bentonite (5, 6), was layered on top of a 5–20% sucrose radient (8 ml total volume) prepared in a Britten and Roberts type of chamber (7) and centrifuged in a Spinco model L 50 rotor at 40,000 rpm for 90 min. The tube bottoms were pierced, 15-drop fractions collected, 1 ml water added to each, and optical density determined at 260 mμ.

In order to verify the linearity of the gradient after centrifugation in the angle-head rotor, a 5% sucrose solution containing adenylic acid, OD (1 cm, 260 mμ) = 2.0, was prepared and a gradient run without RNA addition. Fractions were collected in the same way and the optical density determined.

Figure 1 shows both the profile of the gradient before and after centrifugation and the comparison of ribosomal RNA profiles obtained in the SW 39 and the 50 angle-head rotor (approximate sedimentation coefficients 28S for the heavier peak and 18S for the lighter).

Sedimentation coefficients can have only an approximate value, since "wall effects" have not been studied, although it is possible to assume that molecules will back-diffuse to isopionic regions of the gradient after the centrifuge is stopped.

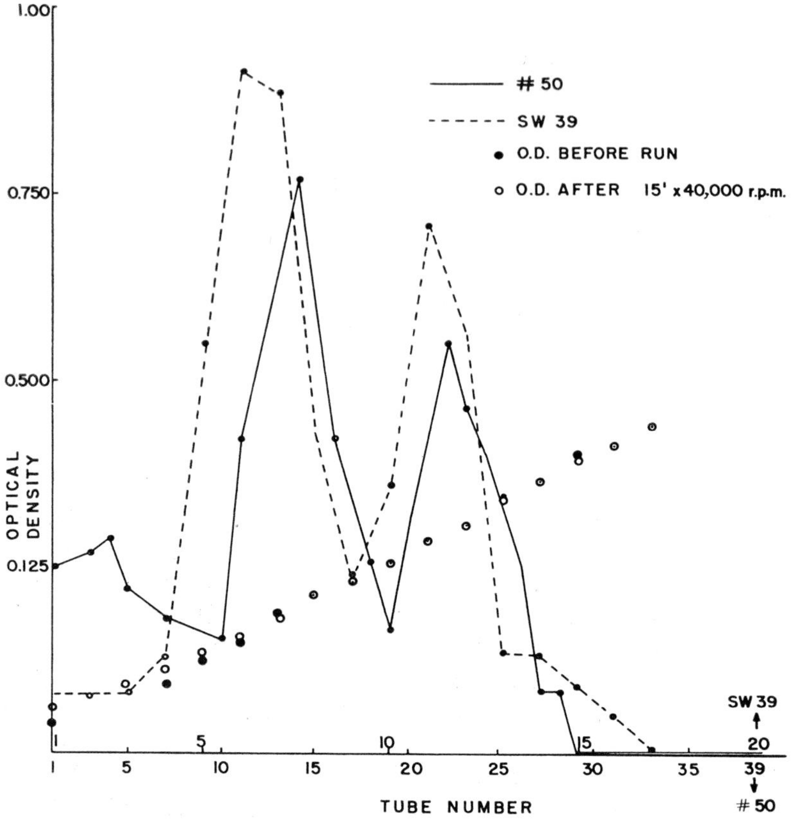

FIG. 1. Gradient profiles.

It has been pointed out (8) that gradients prepared in the 40 rotor are linear in relation to radius but not in relation to volume, so that in the bottom of the tube the gradient will be convex. This could explain the peak found in fractions 1–5 of the gradient run in this rotor.

The use of angle-head rotors offers, over the swinging-bucket variety, the advantage of having an increased capacity at reduced operation time.

REFERENCES

1. BRAKKE, M. K., *J. Am. Chem. Soc.* **73,** 1847 (1951).
2. MARTIN, R. G., AND AMES, B. N., *J. Biol. Chem.* **236,** 1372 (1961).
3. CHARLWOOD, P. A., *Anal. Biochem.* **5,** 226 (1963).
4. FISHER, W. D., CLINE, G. B., AND ANDERSON, N. G., *Anal. Biochem.* **9,** 477 (1964).
5. KIRBY, K. S., *Biochem. J.* **96,** 266 (1965).
6. FRAENKEL-CONRAT, H., AND TSUGITA, A., *Virology* **14,** 54 (1961).
7. BRITTEN, R. J., AND ROBERTS, R. B., *Science* **131,** 32 (1960).

8. FLAMM, W. G., BOND, H. E., AND BURR, H. E., *Biochim. Biophys. Acta* **129,** 310 (1966).

R. BRENTANI
M. BRENTANI
I. RAW

Department of Physiological Chemistry
Faculty of Medicine
University of São Paulo, Brazil
Received February 8, 1967

Ultrafilter for the Concentration of High Molecular Weight Solutes

Various modifications of the dialysis membrane ultrafilter described by Sober, Gutter, Wyckoff, and Peterson (1) have been used extensively in this and other laboratories for the concentration of solutions of high molecular weight substances. They are, however, discouragingly slow when it becomes necessary to concentrate large volumes. The high-capacity modification described here has been in use for some time and has proved quite satisfactory. The principal feature of this ultrafilter is the addition of a Dacron[1] sleeve to support large dialysis tubing so that full vacuum can be used without stretching or breaking the membrane.

Figure 1 shows the assembled ultrafilter. The sizes of the components are given in the legend. These sizes were chosen to accommodate available sizes of dialysis tubing and of Dacron tubing. To assemble, a piece of dialysis tubing a few inches longer than the final length required is wet and knotted at one end. To ensure against leakage through the knot, the end of the dialysis tubing is folded back over the knot and tightly wound with a rubber band. The tube is tested for leaks in the usual manner, then slipped over the inner glass joint far enough so that the length below the joint is equal to or somewhat greater than the length of Dacron sleeve to be used. The Dacron sleeve, knotted at one end, is slipped over the dialysis tube so that the open end is halfway onto the ground portion of the inner glass joint. A wet glass rod may be required

[1] Reference to a company or product name does not imply approval or recommendation of the product by the U. S. Department of Agriculture to the exclusion of others that may be suitable.

for this operation. The closed end of the dialysis tubing must be in close contact with the bottom of the Dacron sleeve to prevent bursting of the membrane when vacuum is applied. The larger O-ring is then placed on the inner joint just below the end of the Dacron sleeve and the smaller O-ring just started onto the joint. The assembly is then slipped into the outer glass joint and the two parts pressed together with considerable

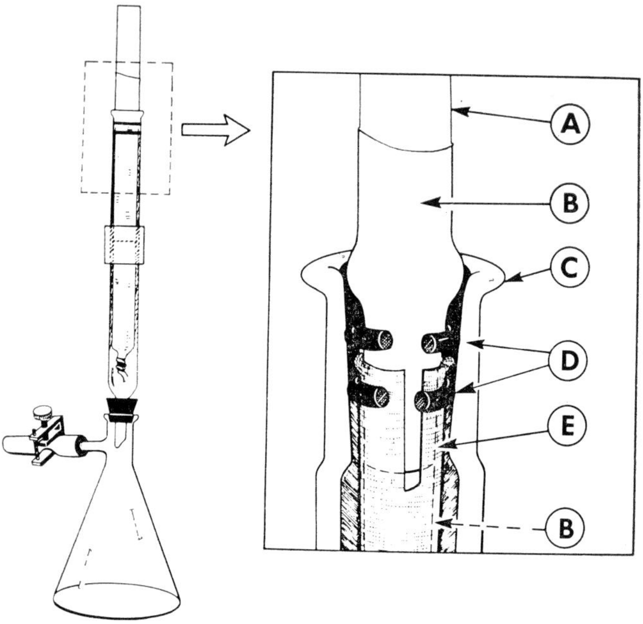

FIG. 1. (A) ₮ 29/42 inner ground-glass joint. (B) Dialysis membrane (size 36, 1.734″ flat width, Visking Division, Union Carbide Corp., 6733 W. 65th St., Chicago, Ill. 60638). (C) ₮ 34/45 outer ground-glass joint. (D) Neoprene O-rings: upper 1¹⁄₁₆″ i.d. × ⅛″; lower 1″ i.d. × ⅛″. (E) Dacron sleeve (woven Dacron tubing, style 9063, 1.76″ flat width, The Lamports Company, 1401 West 6th St., Cleveland, Ohio 44113).

force. The O-rings should roll into their final positions as shown in Figure 1. This assembly is then butt-joined to the lower glass part with a 2″ length of 1¼″ i.d. polyvinyl tubing and the completed assembly placed on a filter flask as shown, or on a vacuum manifold.

To use, the ultrafilter is first filled with water. The filter flask is then evacuated with a water aspirator to check for membrane leaks or vacuum leaks, and to flush the membrane. When the filtrate is the fraction of interest, considerable flushing may be required to remove UV-absorbing materials from the membrane and sleeve. A membrane of the size illustrated (30–35 cm long) should pass 8–10 ml of water per hour. After testing, the water is poured out and the apparatus filled to near the top of the inner glass joint with the solution to be concentrated. If needed, a siphon tube or reservoir may be added to bring solution continuously into the membrane. Since the membrane has very low permeability to air, it is not necessary to keep it full of solution. The filtration rate decreases, of course, as the solution level falls. It also decreases as the solution concentration increases to the point at which osmotic pressure reduces the effective pressure differential across the membrane. With protein solutions, a film will occasionally form on the membrane and reduce the flow. However, in most cases, this is prevented by a decantation effect whereby the concentrated solution adjacent to the membrane drains down and collects at the bottom. The Dacron sleeves may be reused indefinitely if the cut edge at the open end is coated with nail polish or similar binder to prevent unraveling.

REFERENCE

1. Sober, H. A., Gutter, F. J., Wyckoff, W. M., and Peterson, F. A., *J. Am. Chem. Soc.* **78**, 756 (1956).

John Gorton Davis
Mary B. Wiele

Western Regional Research Laboratory
Agricultural Research Service
U. S. Department of Agriculture
Albany, California 94710
Received March 17, 1967

Chemiluminescence of Liquid Scintillation Mixture Components[1]

This report describes a new chemiluminescent reaction that occurs between liquid scintillation mixture components. It has interfered with measurements of radioactivity in biological samples. The reaction occurs between the tissue dissolving quaternary amine preparations, Nuclear-Chicago Solubilizer (NCS), and Hyamine 10X, and the bleaching agent benzoyl peroxide. The latter has been recommended for decolorization of whole tissue preparations to reduce fluor quenching (1,2). Some characteristics of the reaction have been studied and factors involved in the reduction of its magnitude have been determined.

Count rates of greater than 1,000,000 cpm were observed in liquid scintillation preparations that contained no radioactivity. These consisted of 1.0 ml NCS containing 0.2 gm of various dissolved tissues, 1.0 ml of a saturated solution of benzoyl peroxide in toluene, the fluors 1,4-di-2-(5-phenyloxazolyl)benzene (POPOP) and 2,5-diphenyloxazole

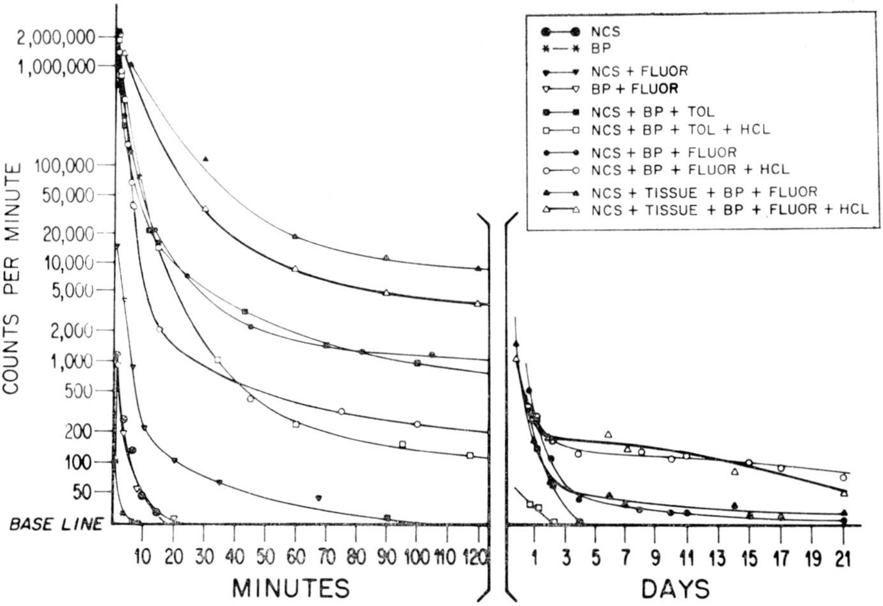

FIG. 1. Chemiluminescence decay curves of liquid scintillation mixture components. Count rates obtained on Nuclear-Chicago Mark I liquid scintillation counter at −4°C. Settings were for H^3 counting. Reagents were all scintillation grade. Vials used only once. All were made to a final volume of 20 ml with toluene. The reagents are: NCS, 1.0 ml; BP (saturated solution of benzoyl peroxide in toluene) 1.0 ml; fluor, PPO and POPOP; HCl, 3 drops; NCS plus tissue, 0.2 gm rat liver in 1.0 ml NCS, prepared by shaking at 25°C for 12 hr.

(PPO), and toluene to a final volume of 20.0 ml. Figure 1 shows the chemiluminescence decay curves of different combinations of the components of this liquid scintillation mixture. The simplest system that gave the initial very high count rates characteristic of the reaction was NCS and benzoyl peroxide in toluene. NCS alone, and benzoyl peroxide alone, in toluene gave very small counts that dropped to baseline values in 20 min. The addition of fluor increased these rates only slightly. The count rate attributable to the reaction between NCS and benzoyl peroxide, with or without other components, falls exponentially over several orders of magnitude within the first 30 min. Several factors influenced the slope of the initial decay. When there is dissolved tissue in the NCS the decrease in count rate is slowest. The addition of fluor to NCS and benzoyl peroxide produced no significant change in the initial count rate, but the preparation with fluor remained elevated over the baseline for more than 3 weeks, while that without fluor reached the baseline in 5 days. The effect of acidification with HCl is complex. Early in the reaction it caused marked reduction in the count rate. This developed instantaneously in preparations acidified at various times up to 24 hr. However, the count rates remained at significantly high levels long after unacidified preparations had reached the baseline. This can be seen in Figure 1 for mixtures with and without dissolved tissue.

The chemiluminescent reaction between NCS and benzoyl peroxide was not affected by heating to 100°C for 10 min, cooling to —12°C, storage in the dark, or exposure to radiant or fluorescent light. The relative amounts of each reagent determine the chemiluminescent output. Count rates for 2.0 ml mixtures of NCS and saturated solutions of benzoyl peroxide, in the indicated ratios (by volume), diluted to 20.0 ml and counted at 10 min, were as follows: NCS/benzoyl peroxide 1/7, 754 cpm; 1/3, 1640 cpm; 1/1, 417,490 cpm; 3/1, 88,070 cpm; and 7/1, 36,240 cpm. The reaction is greatest when the volume of benzoyl peroxide is equal to that of the NCS. This ratio has been suggested for decolorization of NCS tissue preparations (2).

Hyamine-10X, but not tetramethyl of tetraethylammonium hydroxide, caused chemiluminescence when mixed with benzoyl peroxide. The reaction with Hyamine-10X was always less than with NCS. Since NCS and Hyamine 10X are incompletely defined mixtures of organic bases, the specific constituent(s) that enter into the reaction cannot be determined. NCS is a mixture of bases in the molecular weight range of 250–600, produced from a commerical mixture of chlorides of the type formula $R_2R'_2NCl$, where R is methyl and R′ is a straight chain varying from C_6 to C_{20}, with an average of about 12 carbon atoms. It is supplied at a 0.6 *N* base strength in toluene (1). Hyamine 10X, which is p-diisobutylcresoxethoxyethyl)dimethylbenzylammonium chloride, is prepared as the hydroxide (3) and supplied as a 1.0 M solution in methanol (4). When hydrogen peroxide was substituted for benzoyl peroxide, a much smaller and rapidly exhausted chemiluminescent reaction occurred. Oxalyl chloride produced no reaction when substituted for benzoyl peroxide.

Herberg (5, 6) described the occurrence of elevated count rates from preparations of Hyamine 10X in which protein or tissue is dissolved, which he termed "phosphorescence." The "phosphorescence" was dependent upon conditions of light and temperature. Acidification with HCl eliminated the effect and was recommended to enable radioisotope counting in those preparations. We have encountered that effect, although with lower count rates, in systems consisting only of tissue and NCS or Hyamine 10X in toluene. The chemiluminescent reaction we have described is superimposed upon the much lower count rate of the "phosphorescence" phenomenon when benzoyl peroxide is added to the above mixtures. The chemiluminescent reaction was independent of conditions of light and temperature. Acidification does not reduce nonradioactive background counts to levels satisfactory for many C^{14} and H^3 assay requirements.

It has been our experience that the reduction of color quenching by bleaching with benzoyl peroxide increases the counting efficiency only very slightly. In preparations with large amounts of whole tissue dissolved in quaternary amine, the chemical quenching is usually much greater than color quenching. Therefore, it is rarely worthwhile to use benzoyl peroxide or even hydrogen peroxide with such preparations. In general, counting may be performed in 1–2 day old preparations after acidification if the radioactivity in the sample is high. If sample counts are only several times background, it is better not to add acid and count after 2 weeks, or to not use the bleaching agent at all if the improvement in counting efficiency gained by reduction of color quenching is marginal.

REFERENCES

1. Hansen, D. L., and Bush, E. T., *Anal. Biochem.* **18**, 320 (1967).
2. Nuclear-Chicago Radiochemical Bulletin 25 (1966).
3. Passmann, J. M., Radin, N. S., and Cooper, J. A. D., *Anal. Chem* **28**, 484 (1956).
4. Rapkin, E., Packard Technical Bulletin 3 (1961).
5. Herberg, R. J. *Science* **128**, 199 (1958).
6. Herberg, R. J. *Anal. Chem.* **32**, 42 (1960).

James Winkelman[2]
Gary Slater

Department of Pathology
New York University School of Medicine
New York, New York

Received March 23, 1967

[1] This work was supported by USPHS grant CA-08310 from the National Cancer Institute.

[2] New York City Health Research Council Career Scientist, I-409.

The Fluorometric Determination of Brain Serotonin

An improved, simplified, and more sensitive method for the extraction and fluorometric determination of brain serotonin was recently described in this journal (1). Low concentrations of serotonin could be detected by placing a single polarizer[1] (which removed the second-order scatter) in the path of the fluorescent beam (1) and measuring the fluorescence of serotonin (in 3 N HCl) between 500 and 600 mμ (2). The extraction procedure (which, in principle, is similar to the acid-alkaline procedure of Bogdanski *et al.* (2)), also contributed toward greater sensitivity and had the following features: it gave 100%transfer of the serotonin into the final acid phase (0.1 *N* HCl); it produced low fluorescence in the blank; and it greatly facilitated the method and reduced the time required for the determinations.

We have made some minor but important modifications in the use of the sodium phosphate buffer (saturated with NaCl, pH 10.0) employed in the extraction procedure, and investigated in considerably more detail the properties affecting the transfer of serotonin from the initial acid phase to the butanol phase and then into the final acid phase.

In the original experiments, very little trouble was encountered in the preparation of the sodium phosphate buffer; however, more recently, some problems have arisen. In preparing the sodium phosphate buffer, sometimes a supersaturated solution was produced which, upon standing, mechanical manipulation, or slight changes in pH, caused the precipitation of the salts and these, in turn, caused changes in the pH of the buffer. These problems have been completely eliminated by using the more soluble potassium phosphate (2 *M*, saturated with KCl, pH 10.0) in place of the sodium phosphate. The potassium buffer was prepared as follows: 174 gm of potassium phosphate dibasic (anhydrous) was placed in a beaker and water was added up to a volume of 420 to 430 ml. After the phosphate was dissolved, the pH was adjusted to 10.0 with concentrated KOH solution. The resulting solution was saturated with KCl and the volume adjusted to 500 ml (the small amount of excess KCl was left at the bottom of the solution during the storage of the buffer at room

[1] A 9 × 33 mm piece is cut from the Kodak Pola-Screen and placed in the No. 4 slit. The Pola-Screen, which is about 8 in. in diameter and can be purchased separately (Eastman Kodak, Rochester, New York), is part of Kodak's Polar-Light assembly.

temperature). No changes in pH occurred during the saturation step, and the procedure did not produce a supersaturated solution; thus, there was no salt precipitation, and no pH change ocurred upon storage.

Since the potassium buffer had a somewhat lower buffering capacity than the sodium buffer, it was necessary to use 0.02 *N* HCl (saturated with KCl) in the initial extraction step. The modified procedure has been tested wth standard solutions of serotonin and has been found to give 102% ($\pm$7.0% S.D., $N = 10$) transfer of serotonin into the final acid phase. With rat brain, the serotonin content was 429 ng/g ($\pm$26 S.D., $N = 5$) which is similar to other literature values of 440 and 450 (3).

With standard solutions of serotonin (dissolved in dilute HCl), we have investigated the different steps in the transfer of serotonin by the modified extraction procedure as well as some of the factors affecting these steps. On the average, 102% transfer of the amine was found when the following method was used: 3 ml of the standard serotonin solution (100 ng in 0.02 *N* HCl, saturated with KCl) was shaken with 16 ml butanol for 30 sec followed by the addition of 3 ml of the salt-buffer, and the resulting mixture was immediately shaken for 60 sec. The butanol phase was washed with buffer and then the serotonin was transferred into the final acid phase as described before (1). The important aspect of this procedure (which is the same when extracting tissue, see (1)) is that the serotonin is not exposed to the alkaline buffer for any significant period of time. It was found that, when the serotonin standard solution was first mixed with the buffer and then the butanol added and the mixture shaken, 100% transfer did not occur, presumably due to the alteration of the serotonin by exposure to the alkaline pH. This is an important consideration in view of the fact that the widely used method of Bogdanski *et al.* (2) treats the initial serotonin acid extract with sodium carbonate to adjust the pH to 10.0, followed by the addition of the borate buffer (pH 10.0), and last of all the butanol is added in order to extract the serotonin. This type of sequence may account, at least in part, for the over-all 15% loss of serotonin in their extraction procedure. Internal standards can correct for this loss, but only if all of the samples are treated in the same way, especially with respect to the length of time of the exposure of the serotonin to the alkaline pH. This is somewhat difficult to do when a time sequence is involved in a titration step. Thus, the present method which does not require a titration step and which involves a minimum exposure to alkaline pH gives complete transfer of serotonin, and hence does not require an internal standard. However, as the above $\pm$7.0% standard deviation would indicate, a word of caution is needed. The greatest care must be taken in using most fluorometric procedures due to the high sensitivity of these methods and also to the large obscuring effects of small amounts of contaminants, such as those caused by the improper washing of glassware, etc.

Another important consideration is the need to measure the second butanol extract volume and final acid extract volume (i.e., the volume of acid extract after the third extraction) under the conditions in which the method is used, especially since it was found that different amounts of tissue will affect the final butanol volume used in the calculation of the total amount of serotonin. For example, when testing the transfer of serotonin (using standard solutions) and using 16 ml butanol in the initial extraction step, 16.5 ml of butanol (range 16.4–16.6, $N = 5$) was found in the final butanol volume. However, when 1 gm of tissue was extracted with 3 ml of 0.02 N HCl (salt saturated) and with 16 ml butanol (followed by the addition of 3 ml of buffer), 15.76 ml (range 15.6–15.9, $N = 5$) was found in the final butanol volume. Thus, if an aliquot of the final butanol phase is used for the extraction of the serotonin into the 0.1 N HCl, it would be necessary to either directly determine this volume or else prepare a standard curve by determining the effects of different amounts of tissue on the final butanol volume. Another alternative would be to extract the total final butanol phase with the appropriate amount of 0.1 N HCl (2 vol acid per 10 vol butanol phase, see (1). By the same token, the volume of the final acid extract was found to be 2.31 ml (range 2.30–2.35, $N = 5$) when standard serotonin solutions were extracted and 2.27 ml (range 2.25–2.30, $N = 5$) when 1 gm of tissue was extracted.

The foregoing modifications and suggestions should substantially improve our original method (1).

ACKNOWLEDGMENT

The author wishes to acknowledge the skilled technical assistance of Patricia Michalski.

REFERENCES

1. Wise, C. D., *Anal. Biochem.* **18,** 94 (1967).
2. Bogdanski, D. F., Pletscher, A., Brodie, B. B., and Udenfriend, S., *J. Pharmacol. Exptl. Therap.* **117,** 82 (1956).
3. Snyder, S. H., Axelrod, J., and Zweig, M., *Biochem. Pharmacol.* **14,** 831 (1965).

C. David Wise

Research Division
Wyeth Laboratories
Radnor, Pennsylvania 19087
Received March 23, 1967

Erratum

Vol. **18**, No. 2 (**1967**), in the article, "Rapid Nucleotide Separation by Chromatography on Cation-Exchange Columns," by Frederick R. Blattner and Harold P. Erickson, pp. **220–227**:

There is an error in the identification of the last two peaks in the B system for separating **2′-3′**-nucleotides. The correct order of elution is UGAC, not UGCA as stated in the paper. The identification of the 5′ nucleotide peaks in the A system is correct as stated.

ANALYTICAL BIOCHEMISTRY 20, 373–386 (1967)

Measurement of Nucleotide, Amino Acid, and DNA Contents of Tissues after Whole-Body X-Irradiation

CHARLES L. BURGER

State University of New York, Upstate Medical Center, Department of Radiology, Syracuse, New York 13210

Received August 8, 1966

An automated method for the separation of artificial mixtures of nucleotides (1, 2) has been applied to the more difficult problem of obtaining quantitative and qualitative measurements on biologically occurring nucleotides in complex tissues. These data may be correlated with changes in amino acid and DNA contents following whole-body x-ray exposure to intense doses of 2000 roentgens (R). Results indicate that the techniques utilized may be useful in determining the early effects of absorbed energy in tissues.

Liver, gut, and thymus from rats have been used to compare radiation-resistant with radiation-sensitive tissues.

MATERIAL

Sprague-Dawley male rats of the same birth date were used. Irradiation was performed using a GE Maxitron, 300 Kvp, 20 MA. Doses of kV . . . mA 2000 R were given using inherent filtration plus 3 mm Al at 93.7 cm. Irradiation time was 20 ± 1 min. Irradiated animals were sacrificed 1 hr following irradiation. Control and experimental animals were fed and watered ad libitum.

METHODS AND TISSUE PREPARATION

Two experiments were performed (Table 1). Animals differed in age in the two experiments, in order to determine the effects of irradiation

TABLE 1
Animals Used in Experiments

Description	Experiment I		Experiment II	
	Controls	Irradiated	Controls	Irradiated
Number	12	12	12	6
Age, days	36	37	55	80
Average weight, gm	100	104	233	297

TABLE 2
Amount of tissue (in grams)

Tissue source	Experiment I						Experiment II					
	Controls			Irradiated			Controls			Irradiated		
	DNA	Nucleo.	AA	DNA	Nucleo.	AA	DNA	Nucleo.	AA	DNA	Nucleo.	AA
Liver	3.40	5.80	11.10	3.35	12.95	9.60	4.40	15.40	19.18	6.30	24.50	10.00
Gut	1.60	2.85	2.52	1.05	3.25	2.50	—	5.10	5.20	1.40	3.32	4.10
Thymus	2.79	2.44	—	2.45	2.60	—	—	4.60	4.65	1.20	2.55	3.40

or of irradiation and aging on the levels of nucleotides, amino acids, and DNA.

Tissue Preparations—General

Pooled samples of liver, gut, and thymus obtained by animal sacrifice 1 hr following irradiation were used for the analyses shown in Table 2. Tissues were not perfused. Sections of duodenum were cooled on ice and subsequently flushed with water using a polyethylene squeeze bottle. The gut preparations were finally cut with a razor blade on a precooled steel disc. Other tissues were minced with scissors. Samples for DNA and amino acid (AA) analyses were placed in tared beakers of ice-cold 8.5% sucrose for weighing before homogenizing. Tissues for nucleotide analyses were dropped into liquid nitrogen. Time from death to removal of tissues was less than 1 min.

DNA Analysis

Ten per cent homogenates in 8.5% sucrose were prepared from each tissue. Five cc aliquots (0.5 gm tissue) were pipetted to 10 cc centrifuge tubes and extracted twice with 5% trichloroacetic acid (TCA). The mixtures were centrifuged at 4°C for 10 min in an International PR-2 at 2600 *g*. The supernatants were decanted and the pellets frozen until analyzed.

DNA analyses were performed using a modified Webb and Levy technique (3). Changes involved the use of 3 ml of hydrolyzed extract, 3 ml of TCA, and 0.3 ml of reagent.

Herring sperm DNA (Calbiochem grade C) was used for standard preparations. Standards and samples were hydrolyzed 30 min in boiling water using 5% TCA. A 0.5% solution of *p*-nitrophenylhydrazine in ethanol was the reagent. The aqueous phase was read at 560 mμ after extraction with *n*-butyl acetate and addition of NaOH. The method is reproducible, reads 10% lower than the diphenylamine method, but agrees more closely with the P determinations. Advantages of the method are that tissues do not require fat extraction before analysis, proteins or their degradation products do not interfere to the extent they do when using diphenylamine, and ribose at a concentration of 1 mg/ml does not interfere.

Amino Acid Analysis

Tissues extracted for amino acid analyses were prepared according to the Beckman Spinco manual for the model 120 amino acid analyzer. Cold tissues were weighed and immediately blended (MSE Blendor) with 1% picric acid for 2–5 min at 4°C. The suspension was centrifuged and the supernatant placed in ice. The solution was decolorized by passage through a 2–10 cm column of Bio-Rad AG 2-X10 ion-exchange resin prepared in 1 *N* HCl and washed with distilled water until neutral. The resin was washed after sample addition with five 4-ml portions of 0.02 *N* HCl. The combined effluents were adjusted to pH 7.2–7.5 with 1 *N* NaOH. The volume was adjusted by flash evaporation (35°C) to one less than ½ the tissue weight in grams. This material was divided and ½ was treated with 0.2 cc of 0.5 *N* Na_2SO_3 for each 2.5 gm of tissue and allowed to remain open to the air for 4 hr at room temperature.

Both treated and untreated samples were adjusted to pH 2.2 with 1 *N* HCl and made up to a volume such that each ml represented 0.5 gm of original wet weight of tissue.

Samples were frozen until required for analyses. When sufficient material was not available for both sulfite and nonsulfite treatment, the former was chosen.

Samples and standards were run according to the specifications for the analyzer (Spinco 120).

Nucleotide Analysis

Pooled samples were used as for amino acid and DNA analyses. Tissues were dropped into liquid nitrogen as they were removed from the animals. The frozen samples were weighed and then blended 10 min in an MSE blendor at 4°C using 4 vol of cold 0.5 *N* perchloric acid. The suspension was immediately centrifuged at 2600*g* for 10 min (International PR-2 855 head) in the cold and the supernatant placed in ice until neutralized with saturated KOH. Excess $KClO_4$ was removed by centrifugation. Optical density readings at 260 mμ were taken and the sample volume was adjusted by flash evaporation at 35°C to a volume compatible with that required for a column analysis. The prepared samples were frozen until analyzed.

For these experiments, the following parameters were used for the nucleotide analyses: a 160 × 0.9 cm water-jacketed column, packed with a Bio-Rad 1-X8 resin, sized by hydraulic fractionation. The bead size was 36–72 mμ. Samples of 1–2 ml having a total optical density of 190–200 units at 260 mμ were placed on the resin and forced into the bed with compressed air. The column was then filled with 0.15 *M* sodium acetate (starting buffer). Flow rates were 0.75 ml/min for the first 3.25 hr followed by 1.2 ml/min for the remainder of the run. Gradients were linear varying from 0.15 to 3.0 *M* sodium acetate, pH 4.4 (700 ml each), ending with 3.0 *M* acetate (ca. 500 ml). The temperature was maintained at 40°C. The eluent was read in a DB spectrophotometer alternately at 260 and 280 mμ and recorded on a Brown (Honeywell) multipoint Electronik running at 2″/hr.

The column may be regenerated after a run by passing the starting buffer through the resin bed until a stable baseline is reached. Between runs of different tissues the column was routinely repacked after treating the resin sequentially with 0.1 *N* HCl; 0.1 *N* NaOH; 3.0 *M* acetic acid; and 3.0 and 0.15 *M* sodium acetate (these two at pH 4.4).

RESULTS

DNA

DNA analyses are given in Table 3. Gut and thymus control, Experiment II, were omitted due to lack of material.

TABLE 3
Amount of DNA (mg/100 gm tissue)

	Experiment I		Experiment II	
Tissue source	Control	Irradiated	Control	Irradiated
Age (days)	(36)	(37)	(55)	(80)
Liver	247	229	212	213
Gut	296	225	—	273
Thymus	2786	3398	—	2680

Amino Acid

The amino acid data for the control and irradiated groups are given in Tables 4, 5, and 6. Comparisons should be made with regard to both

TABLE 4
Tissues Prepared for Amino Acid Analyses[a]

	Controls				Irradiated			
	Sulfite		Nonsulfite		Sulfite		Nonsulfite	
Tissue source	I	II	I	II	I	II	I	II
Age (days)	(36)	(55)	(36)	(55)	(37)	(80)	(37)	(80)
Liver	3	3	4	4	9	9	10	10
Gut	1	1		2	7	7		
Thymus		5				11		

[a] Not all categories were run due to lack of available tissue. Numbers for reference to Tables 5 and 6.

age and irradiation; Table 7 compares these parameters. The striking feature in the "with age" group is that the amino acids increase with age in the case of gut and decrease with age in the case of liver. Thymus could not be compared in this fashion.

In the "with irradiation" category (same age), gut levels decrease with the exception of ammonia and ethanolamine. Similar data are

TABLE 5
Amino Acid Concentrations[a]
(μmoles/gm in control tissues from various aged rats)

Amino acid	I-3 Liver (36) S	I-4 Liver (36) NS	II-3 Liver (55) S	II-4 Liver (55) NS	I-1 Gut (36) S	II-1 Gut (55) S	II-2 Gut (55) NS	II-5 Thymus (55) S
Phosphoserine	2.15	0.20	0.08	0.05	0.74	0.07	0.11	0.05
Phosphoethanolamine	9.35	9.50	1.22		2.36	4.95	8.07	3.27
Taurine	0.37	2.80	1.52	1.59	4.76	17.23	10.50	6.54
Urea	7.94	6.94	3.26	4.51	1.47	5.06	7.12	3.84
Aspartic acid	0.76	0.73	0.68	0.61	0.42	1.51	1.07	0.92
Threonine	0.49	0.47	0.40	0.36	0.30	0.64	0.48	0.76
Serine	1.48	1.44	1.25	0.80	0.45	0.96	0.77	0.37
Asparagine	4.33	4.20	4.97	4.05	0.47	0.95	1.10	2.24
Proline	0.20	0.15	0.13	0.15	0.43	0.75	0.41	0.46
Glutamic acid	1.54	0.64	2.39	1.88	1.51	3.45	2.34	
Glycine	2.33	2.09	2.85	1.98	0.88	2.14	1.53	2.80
Alanine	2.46	2.49	2.54	1.79	1.58	2.89	2.12	1.71
Valine	0.19	0.20	0.23	0.17	0.17	0.32	0.26	0.19
Methionine	0.06	0.06	0.05	0.05	0.06	0.12	0.07	0.06
Isoleucine	0.11	0.12	0.11	0.10	0.12	0.20	0.14	0.07
Leucine	0.20	0.21	0.20	0.19	0.26	0.23	0.28	0.13
Tyrosine	0.06	0.06	0.05	0.06	0.15		0.13	0.07
Phenylalanine	0.06	0.06	0.05	0.07	0.13	0.17	0.11	0.04
β-Alanine	0.09	0.09	0.04	0.04		0.04		
β-Aminoisobutyric acid	0.06	0.06						
β-Amino-*N*-butyric acid		0.03	0.02		0.14	0.08	0.12	
Ornithine	0.27	0.36	0.16	0.18	0.14	0.04	0.09	
Ethanolamine		0.08	0.09	0.10	0.25	0.12	0.12	0.06
Ammonia	0.42	0.76	0.63	0.63	0.74	0.80	0.59	0.50
Lysine	0.23	0.26	0.13	0.15	0.51	0.20	0.19	0.08
Histidine	0.23	0.28	0.19	0.17				

[a] Age (days) in parentheses. S = sulfite treated; NS = nonsulfite treated.

obtained in the case of irradiated liver at the same age. These data are based on equal weights of tissue.

In examining the effects of "age and irradiation" (liver, sulfite treated at both 37 and 80 and at 55 and 80 days) a general decrease in the amounts of amino acids occurs except for phosphoserine, taurine, β-alanine, ornithine, ammonia, and lysine. The decrease is greater when comparing "age and irradiation" than when comparing "with age" or "with irradiation" separately.

Nucleotides

The chromatograms presented in Figure 1 and 2 are complete except for gut control #1, omitted due to space limitation. Inspection shows

TABLE 6
Amino Acid Concentrations (μmoles/gm) in Irradiated Tissues from Various Aged Rats[a]

Amino acid	I-9 Liver (37) S	I-10 Liver (37) NS	II-9 Liver (80) S	II-10 Liver (80) NS	I-7 Gut (37) S	II-7 Gut (80) S	II-11 Thymus (80) S
Phosphoserine	1.06	0.05	3.38	0.16	0.29		
Phosphoethanolamine	3.05	2.74	0.15	15.16	0.33		
Taurine	0.99	1.00	4.55	16.21	0.08		
Urea	1.04	3.78	0.74	41.18	0.85	7.35	
Aspartic acid	0.66	1.30	0.06	0.64	0.20	1.02	1.27
Threonine	0.32	0.65	0.21	0.28	0.08	0.36	0.33
Serine	1.52	3.08	0.07	0.71	0.13	0.41	0.12
Asparagine	5.24	7.23		8.61	0.19		
Proline	0.15	0.18		0.12	0.24	0.24	
Glutamic acid	1.23	2.45	2.97	2.34	0.59	2.76	4.28
Glycine	1.71	2.86	0.74	1.88	0.30	1.07	0.86
Alanine	0.97	1.58	0.60	2.39	0.56	1.21	0.56
α-Aminoadipic acid	0.06	0.06					
α-Amino-*N*-butyric acid	0.04	0.04					
Valine	0.22			0.30	0.07	0.20	0.20
Methionine	0.04	0.06	0.02	0.05	0.04	0.06	0.04
Isoleucine	0.12	0.16	0.04	0.15	0.08	0.11	0.07
Leucine	0.21	0.26	0.08	0.27	0.19	0.22	0.12
Tyrosine	0.05	0.06	0.03	0.06	0.08	0.08	0.06
Phenylalanine	0.06	0.08	0.03	0.08	0.08	0.07	0.03
β-Alanine	0.09	0.10	0.02	0.06			
β-Aminoisobutyric acid							
β-Amino-*N*-butyric acid							
Ornithine	0.26	0.23	0.10	0.20	0.03	0.08	0.04
Ethanolamine		0.12		0.06	0.31	0.20	
Ammonia	1.04	0.88	4.28	0.73	0.84	2.29	3.56
Lysine	0.39	0.30	0.21	0.29	0.19	0.01	
Histidine	0.33	0.26	0.07	0.21	0.04		

[a] Age (days) in parentheses. S = sulfite treated. NS = nonsulfite treated.

that tissues contain more compounds than were incorporated into the standards.

Reference to Table 8 will show that irradiated tissues of Experiment I compared with the control I group present increases in OD/gm (at 260 mμ) of 3% for thymus, 10% for liver, and 28% for gut. Extracts of control thymus, liver, and gut in Experiment II show increases in OD at 260 mμ with increasing age (55 day old controls compared with those of 37 days) of 15, 34, and 14%, respectively. Irradiation of 80 day old animals drops the levels of 260 mμ absorbing material to values essentially identical to those of the 37 day old animals.

TABLE 7

Percentage Increase or Decrease in Amino Acids (A) with Age, (B) with Irradiation, and (C) with Age and Irradiation[a]
Figures at column tops indicate age of first group and age of group used for comparison, respectively. Changes are given for group two compared with group one.

Amino acid	(A) With age (controls only)		(B) With irradiation (irradiated compared with control)			(C) With age and irradiation (irradiated compared with control)			
	Gut (36–55)	Liver (36–37)	Gut (36–37)	Liver (36–37)		Liver (55–80)		Liver (36–80)	
	S	S	S	S	NS	S	NS	S	NS
Phosphoserine	D- 90	D- 95	D- 60	D- 50	D- 75	I-410	I-220	I- 55	D- 20
Phosphoethanolamine	I-110	D- 90	D- 85	D- 65	D- 70	D- 90		D- 100	I- 60
Taurine	I-260	I-310	D- 95	I-170	D- 65	I-200	I-920	I-1130	I-480
Urea	I-240	D- 60	D- 40	D- 90	D- 45	D- 75	I-815	D- 90	I-490
Aspartic acid	I-260	D- 10	D- 50	D- 15	I- 80	D- 90	I- 5	D- 90	D- 10
Threonine	I-110	D- 20	D- 75	D- 35	I- 40	D- 50	D- 20	D- 60	D- 40
Serine	I-110	D- 15	D- 70	I- 5	I-115	D- 95	D- 10	D- 95	D- 50
Asparagine	I-100	I- 15	D- 60	I- 20	I- 70		I-115		I-105
Proline	I- 70	D- 35	D- 45	D- 25	I- 20		D- 20		D- 20
Glutamic acid	I-130	I- 55	D- 60	D- 20	I-285		I- 25		I-265
Glycine	I-140	I- 29	D- 65	D- 30	I- 40	D- 75	D- 5	D- 70	D- 10
Alanine	I- 80	I- 5	D- 65	D- 60	D- 35	D- 75	I- 35	D- 75	D- 5
α-Aminoadipic acid									
α-Amino-*N*-butyric acid									
Valine	I- 90	I- 20	D- 60	I- 15			I- 75		I- 50
Methionine	I-100	D- 15	D- 35	D- 35	NC	D- 60	NC	D- 70	D- 20
Isoleucine	I- 70	NC	D- 35	I- 10	I- 35	D- 75	I- 50	D- 65	I- 25
Leucine	D- 10	NC	D- 30	I- 5	I- 25	D- 60	I- 40	D- 60	I- 30
Tyrosine		D- 15	D- 50	D- 20	NC	D- 40	NC	D- 50	NC
Phenylalanine	I- 30	D- 15	D- 40	NC	I- 35	D- 40	I- 15	D- 50	I- 35
β-Alanine		D- 55		NC	I- 10	I- 50	I- 50	D- 80	D- 35

β-Aminoisobutyric acid									
γ-Amino-N-butyric acid									
Ornithine	D- 70	D- 40	D- 80	D- 5	D- 35	D- 35	I- 10	D- 65	D- 45
Ethanolamine	D- 50		I- 25	NC	I- 50		D- 40		D- 25
Ammonia	I- 10	I- 50	I- 15	I-150	I- 15	I-580	I- 15	I- 920	D- 5
Lysine	D- 60	D- 45	D- 65	I- 70	I- 15	I- 60	I-100	D- 10	I- 10
Histidine		D- 15		I- 40	D- 30	D- 65	I- 25	D- 70	D- 25

[a] Abbreviations: S = sulfite treated, NS = nonsulfite treated, NC = no change, D = decrease, I = increase. Age (days) in parentheses.

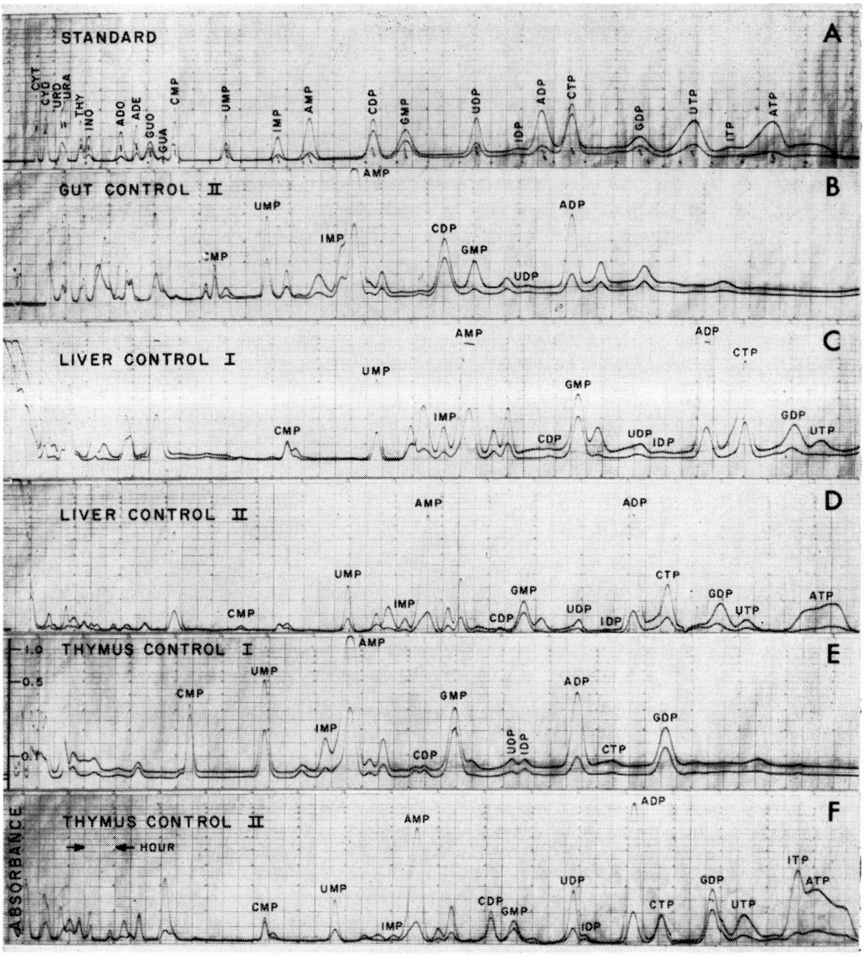

FIG. 1. Chromatograms of standard and control series of tissues. Standards are 2 mM except guanine, which is 0.2 mM. Absorbancy along vertical axis is on a log-scale ranging from 0 to 1.5. Each major division longitudinally represents ½ hr (chart speed 2″/hr). See text for details of flow rates.

Columns 160 × 0.9 cm glass, water-jacketed; 40°C; resin Bio-Rad 1-X8 (Control No. 4764-30 B597); 1 cm quartz flow cell; absorbancy recorded at 260 and 280 mμ; linear gradient of 700 ml of 0.15 M sodium acetate grading into 3.0 M sodium acetate at pH 4.4 for each analysis. See text for further details. *Abbreviations:*

Bases: Cyt, Ura, Thy, Ade, Gua
Nucleosides: Cyd, Urd, Ino, Ado, Guo
Nucleotide monophosphates: (all 5′) CMP, UMP, IMP, AMP, GMP
Nucleotide diphosphates: CDP, UDP, IDP, ADP, GDP
Nucleotide triphosphates: CTP, UTP, ITP, ATP, GTP

(con't)

TABLE 8

Total Acid-Soluble Nucleotides as Measured by OD at 260 mμ

	Irradiated				Control			
	Experiment I (37 days)		Experiment II (80 days)		Experiment I (36 days)		Experiment II (55 days)	
Tissue	OD/gm	gm used	OD/gm	gm used	OD/gm	gm used	OD/gm	gm used
Gut	86.	2.4	89.	2.2	67.	2.8	77.	2.5
Liver	123.	1.6	124.	0.96	112.	1.7	149.	0.79
Thymus	80.	2.6	80.	2.4	78.	2.4	92.	2.1

Comparison of Figure 1-E and Figure 2-E (same age, comparable OD used in analysis and tissue weight represented) shows that CMP, UMP, CDP, GMP, UDP, IDP, ADP, and GDP are noticeably reduced in the irradiated series. Similar data are observed for liver control I and irradiated liver I, except that CTP is also reduced.

Absolute levels of compounds may be determined by integrating the areas beneath the peaks of the chromatograms. The method has been described (1).

DISCUSSION

Amino Acids

Due to the complexity of the tissues analyzed and the standards required, the amino acid data are considered provisional.

Changes in amino acid concentrations are the result of both irradiation and aging and are related to synthetic processes. It is of interest that changes due to age alone or to age plus irradiation may be recognized.

Nucleotides

The techniques described and the results reported suggest that such methods may be used to determine absolute levels of nucleotides, nucleosides, and bases in normal tissues, to compare such levels in various

FIG. 1 *(continued)*

Grams tissue and OD at 260 mμ of acid-soluble extracts used for analysis:

Sample	OD	Tissue, gm	Age, days
B. Gut control II	196	2.5	55
C. Liver control I	193	1.7	36
D. Liver control II	119	.79	55
E. Thymus control I	189	2.4	36
F. Thymus control II	189	2.1	55

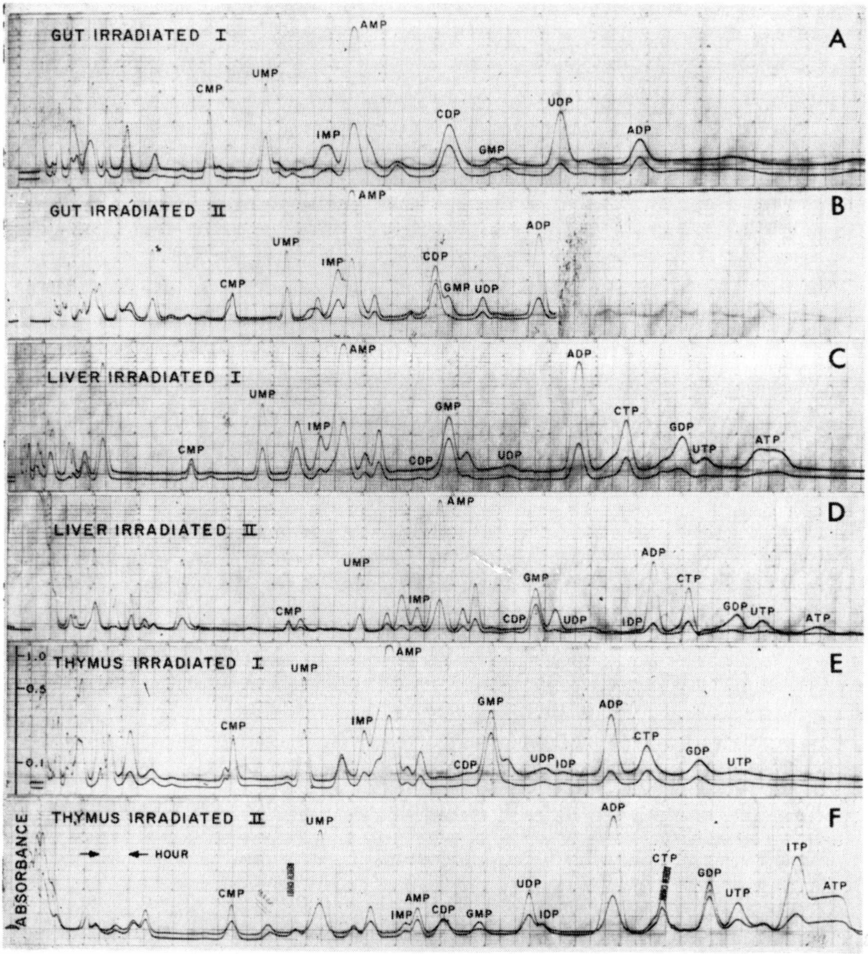

FIG. 2. Irradiated tissue chromatograms run as those in Figure 1. Grams tissue and OD at 260 mμ of acid-soluble extracts used for analysis:

Sample	OD	Tissue, gm	Age, days
A. Gut irradiated I	206	2.4	37
B. Gut irradiated II	196	2.2	80
C. Liver irradiated I	191	1.6	37
D. Liver irradiated II	120	.96	80
E. Thymus irradiated I	209	2.6	37
F. Thymus irradiated II	198	2.4	80

species, and to determine sequential changes in a given tissue after various treatments, e.g., irradiation, trauma of various origins, etc. With the intent of applying similar techniques to the study of growth processes, temperature-synchronized populations of the nongreen flagellate *Astasia longa* in pre- and post-division stages were analyzed. Though these experiments are not reported here, they indicate that quantitative and qualitative changes occur in specific compounds during division. Post-division cells show increases in guanine, CMP, and UMP while decreases are noted in IMP, AMP, UDP, IDP, ADP, and GDP. The nucleotide analyzer unquestionably may be used in exploring the relation of these compounds to growth. The use of synchronized cell populations obviates the difficulties associated with nonhomogeneous populations generally found in tissues.

The fact that changes occur in specific compounds during growth is not new. However, the methods outlined permit quantitative and qualitative analyses in short periods of time of many of the physiologically important precursors involved in synthetic processes of cell population in various states of cell growth. One could spend his career determining such levels. For the investigator wishing to pursue those interests, the technique will prove invaluable.

The methods may be applied to pathological tissues and fluids as well, thereby extending the usefulness of the equipment to the clinical investigator. For those interested in base ratio analyses of nucleic acids, a change in the gradient will permit rapid analysis of small quantities of hydrolyzed materials. This is no longer a tedious process.

In a series of runs (not presented) on normal livers, 33 peaks were observed, 27 of these being reproducible. The standards contain 24 compounds. No attempt has been made to identify the other compounds.

For long-column analysis, the system described appears suitable for liver and thymus. With gut, however, it appears useful only through ADP. The suggestion that triphosphates are not present seems unlikely. The triphosphates may be picked up in a short-column analysis. In general, the triphosphate curves are more Gaussian when shorter columns are used.

The greatest single problem with the nucleotide system described was that of obtaining suitable resins. The original system employed a Bio-Rad AG 1-X8 resin manufactured in 1957. When a similar type but different lot was used, the resolution of the system decreased noticeably. After testing each new batch of AG 1-X8 resin manufactured by Dow Chemical (Midland, Michigan) during a 6 month period, the parameters of the best resin were determined. The problem of resolution is related to the water content of the resin, the higher end of the specification range giving the better separation of those nucleosides and bases which tend to be eluted from the column early.

The technical problems associated with the analysis of complex tissues by this technique are many and varied. Altering the gradient, temperature, flow rate, and/or pressure all change the time of elution or even the order of elution from the column of various constituents. It is apparent that various tissues by virtue of their complexity present specific problems in identification.

The present system employs a reference cell in the DB spectrophotometer through which the buffer passes before going to the column, producing a stable baseline over the entire 30 hr period of the run.

The compounds eluted early in the course of a tissue run by the technique described are difficult to separate. These may be collected and analyzed separately or the gradient and/or resin changed to elute them at different time intervals.

The results indicate that the analyzer is a useful tool in the determination of irradiation damage to cells. In order to make value judgments regarding alterations in biosynthetic pathways, a series of experiments on animals of the same age exposed to varying doses of irradiation is required. These experiments are in progress.

ACKNOWLEDGMENTS

We wish to thank N. G. Anderson, Oak Ridge National Laboratory, for useful discussions; R. E. Lybarger, ORNL, for technical assistance with the amino acid analyzer and calculations of the data in Tables 5 and 6; T. W. James, UCLA, Department of Zoology, for supplying the *Astasia longa;* and P. B. Dewey, Dow Chemical Company, Midland, Michigan, for kindly providing test batches of resin.

REFERENCES

1. Anderson, N. G., *Anal. Biochem.* **4**, 269–283 (1962).
2. Anderson, N. G., Green, J. G., Barber, M. L., and Ladd, Sr., F. C., *Anal. Biochem.* **6**, 153–169 (1963).
3. Webb, J. M., and Levy, H. B., *J. Biol. Chem.* **213**, 107–117 (1955).

ANALYTICAL BIOCHEMISTRY 20, 387–393 (1967)

Determination of Intracellular 2-Deoxy-D-glucose 6-Phosphate and Uridine Diphosphate-2-deoxy-D-glucose

P. BIELY AND Š. BAUER

Institute of Chemistry, Slovak Academy of Sciences, Bratislava, Czechoslovakia

Received January 11, 1967

The inhibitory effects of 2-deoxy-D-glucose (DG) on the metabolism and growth of cells have been postulated to be due to the intracellular accumulation of phosphorylated esters of DG (1–4). The fermentation (2) and respiration (5) of yeast in the presence of DG has been shown to depend on the intracellular concentration of 2-deoxy-D-glucose 6-phosphate (DG-6-P). Heredia *et al.* (2) have concluded that the inhibition of the yeast cell growth might be effected by a trapping of uridine nucleotides involved in the biosynthesis of structural polysaccharides by the phosphorylated DG. The incorporation of DG into UDP-DG in baker's yeast was recently confirmed and along with the latter DG-6-P, DG-1-P, and DG-1,6-di-P have been identified (6).

The intracellular DG-6-P was usually determined in a trichloroacetic acid (TCA) cell-free extract as the difference between 2-deoxy sugars determinations before and after precipitation with $Ba(OH)_2$ and $ZnSO_4$ (1, 7, 8). In some cases, a Ba-alcohol-insoluble fraction of the supernatant obtained after treating the cells with TCA was used for DG-6-P assay (2, 9) by specific reactions according to Cramer and Neville (10) or Waravdekar and Saslaw (11). Letnansky (12) determined DG-6-P using a sample of the neutralized perchloric acid extract of cells after chromatography on a Dowex 2 column in the fraction of phosphorylated sugars.

Since 1-phosphates and uridine nucleotides of 2-deoxy sugars were shown to be extremely acid-labile (6, 13), it may be suggested that, during the above-mentioned preparation of the cell-free extract, hydrolysis of DG-1-P and mainly UDP-DG occurred. Augustin and Hofmann (14) have found in the TCA extract of baker's yeast incubated under aerobic conditions with DG at 19°C a relatively high concentration of free DG which has represented approximately one-half the DG-6-P concentration. However, by a similar incubation of baker's yeast performed at 30°C in the intracellular liquid obtained after freezing the cells with liquid nitrogen, only traces of free DG were detected. After incubation (1 hr) of the yeast with DG in a stream of oxygen, the molar ratio of intracellular DG-6-P:DG-1-P:UDP-DG was found to be approximately 9:1:3 (15).

To obtain the above-mentioned results it was necessary to develop a new method for a simultaneous determination of intracellular DG-6-P and UDP-DG. The method, which is presented in this communication, is based on direct scanning of the chromatograms of the intracellular liquid detected with the reagent specific for 2-deoxy sugars.

MATERIALS AND METHODS

Reagents

DG was synthesized by the glycal method (16).

DG-6-P was prepared enzymically (6).

Intracellular liquid: Yeast was washed thoroughly with cold (0–5°C) 0.05 M KH_2PO_4 solution and centrifuged in plastic tubes. Traces of the buffer were removed from the tubes by strips of filter paper. The tubes were closed and the cells were frozen 3 times with liquid nitrogen. After thawing, the mixture was transferred into glass vessels and centrifuged at 4000 g. An aliquot of the supernatant was, without any treatment, subjected to paper chromatography.

Procedure

The intracellular liquid and reference solutions of DG and DG-6-P were applied on Schleicher and Schuell 2043 B paper on 2 cm lines at distances of no less than 2 cm. Chromatography of the intracellular liquid was carried out using n-propanol/NH_3 25% 3/2 (v/v) as a mobile phase. The development was repeated 4–5 times within 6 days at 15–22°C. In the meantime, of the two subsequent developments, the chromatograms were dried as quickly as possible in a stream of cold air. The chromatogram with the known amounts of *DG-6-P* was developed in the same system for 48 hr and once only. The chromatogram with the known amounts of *DG* was developed in the system n-propanol/H_2O 3/2 (v/v) for 24 hr. When the system containing NH_3 was used, unsuitable shapes of DG spots were obtained after detection.

2-Deoxy sugars were detected on the dry chromatograms in the following way. After immersion in a solution of 1.5 ml 63% $HClO_4$ in 20 ml acetone (17), the paper was dried for 5 min at 20–22°C and placed in an oven at 90°C for 2.5 min. Parts of the chromatogram with the spots of DG metabolites were cut out into pieces (15 × 4 cm) and stored in the dark; 30 min after detection the strips were directly scanned with an ERI-10 densitometer (Zeiss, Jena, Germany) using reflection densitometry with a slit of 36 mm. The areas under the peaks corresponding to the spot densities of DG and its metabolites were calculated as follows: the height of a peak was multiplied by the width at half height. Chromatograms with known amounts of DG or DG-6-P were detected simultaneously and assayed in the same way.

RESULTS

Figure 1 shows the results of the direct scanning of the chromatogram of the intracellular liquid (achieved after freezing the yeast cells incubated with DG in a stream of oxygen). The conditions of incubation and identification of DG metabolites have been described (6). As seen from Figure 1, the separation of UDP-DG and DG-6-P seems to be sufficient,

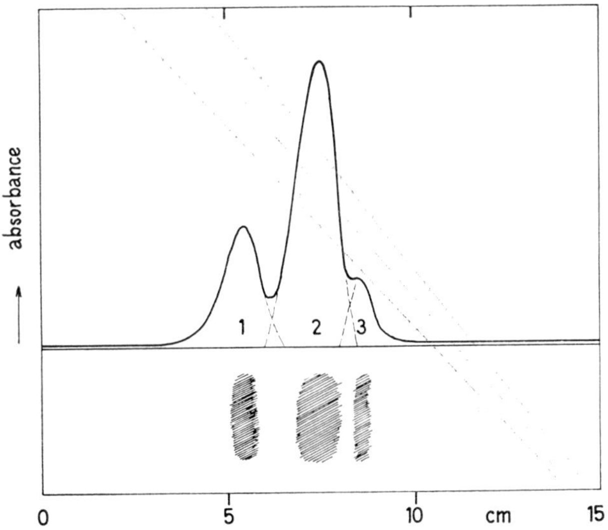

FIG. 1. Diagram of paper chromatogram of intracellular liquid of yeast incubated with DG, and typical curves produced from scanning spots: (1) UDP-DG, (2) DG-6-P, (3) DG-1-P.

and symmetrical peaks were obtained. DG-6-P and DG-1-P were less separated.

The calibration curve (Figure 2) was prepared using DG and DG-6-P solutions of concentration 1×10^{-2} μmole/μl. The single points of the calibration curve were obtained from several experiments in which the spots of 2-deoxy sugars were scanned from 30–60 min after detection. The sensitivity of the detection reagent was found to be the same for both DG and DG-6-P. The influence of the intracellular liquid on the sensi-

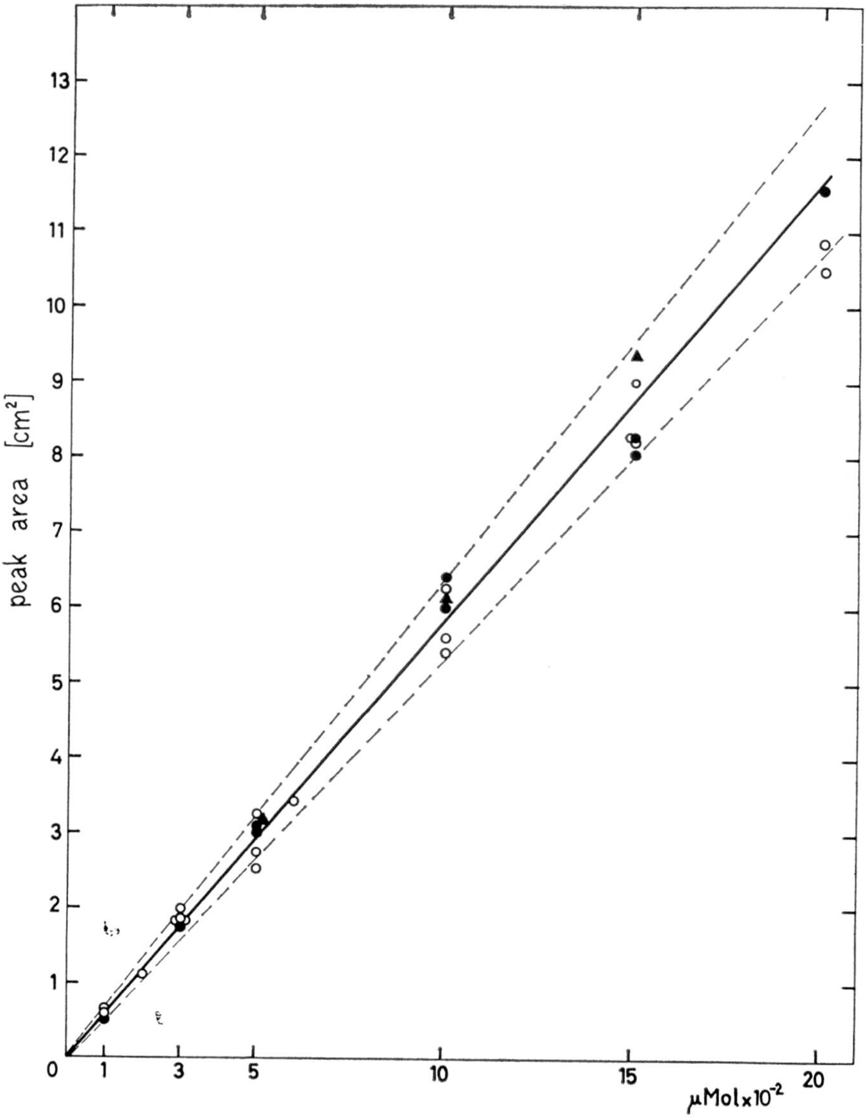

FIG. 2. Calibration curve: (○) DG, (●) DG-6-P, (▲) DG-6-P chromatographed with 30 μl intracellular liquid of yeast not incubated with DG. The dashes represent the upper and lower deviation of the calibration curve values obtained in several experiments.

tivity of the determination was followed by addition of 30 μl of the intracellular liquid from yeast not incubated with DG to a known amount of DG-6-P. As shown in Figure 2, the spot density of DG-6-P was not influenced by the addition of intracellular liquid.

Linearity between the areas under the peaks produced by the scan and the amount of sugar applied existed between 0 and 20×10^{-2} μmole.

The relative standard deviation

$$\%S = \frac{\sqrt{\frac{\Sigma(x_n - x_t)^2}{n-1}}}{x_t} \times 100$$

where n = number of measurements,
x_n = peak area determined at the nth measurement,
x_t = theoretical value of the peak area corresponding to a definite amount of DG or DG-6-P,

on the average for amounts between 1 and 20×10^{-2} μmole was ±9.3%.

The graphic demonstration of the upper relative deviation was represented ±10% (Fig. 2, dashed lines).

The minimal concentration of DG-6-P or UDP-DG in the intracellular liquid necessary for a determination with an accuracy of ±10% is 0.25 m*M* (1×10^{-2} μmole/40 μl). An acceptable separation of the DG metabolites could be obtained when the maximum of 40 μl intracellular liquid was applied.

DISCUSSION

Chromatograms of the intracellular liquid of the yeast incubated with DG were detected for 2-deoxy sugars with the vanillin/$HClO_4$ reagent (18) and tiobarbituric acid after periodate oxidation (19). No satisfactory results were obtained with these reagents as no colorless background was achieved. The only reagent that gave a colorless background was $HClO_4$ in acetone (17). The most intensive spot densities of DG and its metabolites using the latter reagent was obtained after 2.25 min heating of the chromatogram in an oven at 90°C. Insignificant changes of spot densities were observed after longer heating, to 3 min. After further extension of the heating, the paper background became dark and the paper very fragile. UDP-DG (from which free DG is formed upon hydrolysis), DG-6-P, and DG gave the same color. Spots of different shades were observed with DG-1-P and DG-1,6-diP. The DG-1,6-diP concentration, being in the intracellular liquid, was below the limit of the determination by the method described. A calibration curve for DG-1-P was not constructed because no sufficient amount of this ester was available.

The system *n*-propanol/NH_3 25% 3/2 (v/v) was not used for the chromatography of DG standards as no symmetrical peaks were obtained. Scanning of the chromatograms of DG developed in the NH_3-free solvent system gave symmetrical peaks but the peak areas in both cases were the same.

Deviation of the values in addition to usual errors was also caused by the color instability of the spots. As shown in Figure 3, the spot densities (enumerated as areas under peaks) decreased with time, and from 30–90 min after detection the decrease represented 8–10% (double-headed arrows). The chromatograms were therefore scanned within 30–60 min after detection since approximately 20–30 min was necessary for preparing the chromatograms to be measured. In the experiments in which a higher accuracy than ±10% was required or in the case of chromatograms scanned out of the range of 30–60 min after detection the areas obtained under peaks had to be corrected in accordance with the established dependence of spot density on time (Fig. 3).

Deviation of the calibration curve values in a single test represented less than ±10%. The slope of such a standard curve varied slightly in different experiments. It was evident that the most important factor which influenced the reproducibility of the result was observance of con-

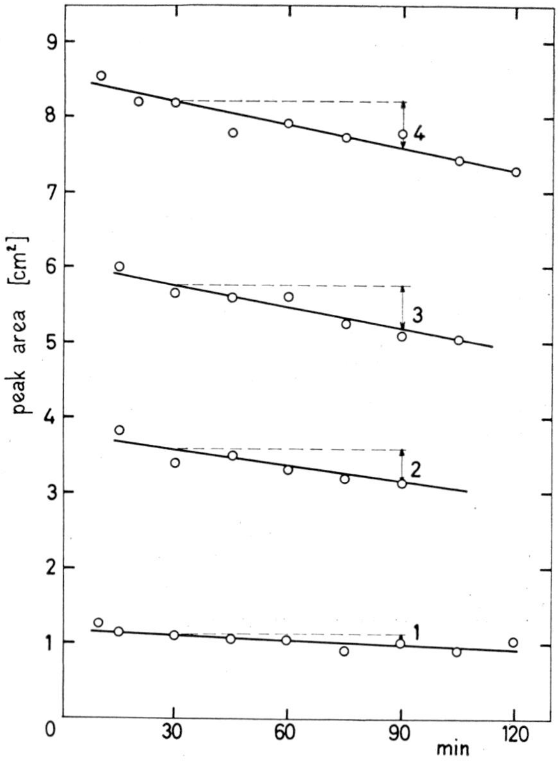

Fig. 3. Spot densities of DG as a function of time after detection of chromatogram: (1) 2×10^{-2} μmole, (2) 6×10^{-2} μmole, (3) 10×10^{-2} μmole, (4) 15×10^{-2} μmole. At time 0 the chromatogram was taken out of the oven.

stant detection conditions. It was therefore necessary in every assay to carry out simultaneously the detection of chromatograms of the intracellular liquid and that of the standards.

In spite of some limitations, the elaborated method was successfully used in studies of the metabolism of DG and the mechanism of cell growth inhibition effected by this sugar.

SUMMARY

A new method for the simultaneous determination of the intracellular DG-6-P and UDP-DG is described. It is based on the direct scanning of the chromatograms of intracellular liquid which were detected by the specific reagent for 2-deoxy sugars according to Weidemann and Fischer. A linear relationship between the amount of sugar and the area under the peak exists between 0 and 20×10^{-2} μmole. The method permits determination of these substances with an accuracy of ±10% at a concentration higher than 0.25 m*M* in the intracellular liquid obtained after freezing the cells with liquid nitrogen.

REFERENCES

1. Barban, S., *J. Biol. Chem.* **237,** 291 (1962).
2. Heredia, C. F., de la Fuente, G., and Sols, A., *Biochim. Biophys. Acta* **86,** 216 (1964).
3. Heredia, C. F., and Sols, A., *Biochim. Biophys. Acta* **86,** 224 (1964).
4. Megnet, R., *J. Bacteriol,* **90,** 1032 (1965).
5. Feldheim, M. E., Augustin, H. W., and Hofmann, E., *Biochem. Z.* **344,** 238 (1965).
6. Biely, P., and Bauer, Š., *Coll. Czech. Chem. Commun.* **32,** 1588 (1967).
7. Kipnis, D. M., and Cori, C. F., *J. Biol. Chem.* **234,** 171 (1959).
8. Fomina, M. P., and Titova, G. V., *Biokhimiya* **26,** 662 (1961).
9. Kiesow, L., *Z, Naturforsch.* **14b,** 492 (1959).
10. Cramer, F. B., and Neville, C. A., *J. Franklin Inst.* **256,** 379 (1953).
11. Waravdekar, V. S., and Saslaw, L. D., *J. Biol. Chem.* **234,** 1945 (1959).
12. Letnansky, K., *Biochem. Z.* **341,** 74 (1964).
13. Fischer, W., and Weidemann, G., *Z. Physiol. Chem.* **336,** 206 (1964).
14. Augustin, H. W., and Hofmann, E., *Acta Biol. Med. Ger.* **11,** 628, (1963).
15. Bauer, Š., and Biely, P., unpublished results.
16. Roth, W., and Pigman, W., *in* "Method in Carbohydrate Chemistry" (R. L. Whistler and M. L. Wolfrom, eds.), Vol. II, p. 405. Academic Press, New York, 1957.
17. Weidemann, G., and Fischer, W., *Z. Physiol. Chem.* **336,** 192 (1964).
18. Mc Lennan, A. P., Randall, H. M., and Smith, D. W., *Anal. Chem.* **31,** 2020 (1959).
19. Anderson, P. J., *J. Chromatog.* **21,** 163 (1966).

ANALYTICAL BIOCHEMISTRY 20, 394–410 (1967)

Determination of Free Estrone in Blood Plasma by Gas-Phase Chromatography with Electron Capture Detection[1]

J. ATTAL,[2] S. M. HENDELES,[3] AND K. B. EIK-NES

Department of Biological Chemistry, University of Utah College of Medicine, Salt Lake City, Utah 84112

Received January 16, 1967

Few adequate chemical assays for estrone[4] in human plasma have been published. This is inevitably coupled with the fact that the circulating level of the hormone in blood from normal subjects is extremely low. The colorimetric techniques (1–5) based on the Kober reaction may give inflated plasma values for estrone unless the plasma sample has been exposed to rigorous purification, and the fluorometric techniques used for the estimation of plasma estrone (6–8) are often difficult to handle due to the problem of quenching and nonspecific fluorescence. The double isotope derivative dilution technique developed by Svendsen (9) for the estimation of estrone in human plasma is sensitive and specific; however, it is a somewhat time-consuming method and is difficult to apply to the measurement of estrone when the hormone has been produced from labeled precursors.

Gas-phase chromatography with ionization detection has been employed for determination of plasma estrogens (10–12). These methods,

[1] This work was supported in part by U. S. Public Health Training Grant No. T01 CA 5000.

[2] Population Council Fellowship Program, The Rockefeller Institute, New York, N. Y. Present address: Laboratoire de Physiologie de la Reproduction, CRVZ, L'Orfrasiere 37, Nouzilly, France.

[3] NATO Postdoctoral Fellowship. Present address: Laboratoire de Gynecologie Experimentale, Hôpital Universitaire Saint-Pierre, Brussels, Belgium.

[4] Trivial names and abbreviations used: estrone = $\Delta^{1,3,5(10)}$-estratriene-3-ol-17-one. Estrone 3-methyl ether = $\Delta^{1,3,5(10)}$-estratriene-3-methyl ether-17-one. Estrone 3-methyl ether 17-pentafluorophenylhydrazone = $\Delta^{1,3,5(10)}$-estratriene 3-methyl ether-17-pentafluorophenylhydrazone. Estradiol = $\Delta^{1,3,5(10)}$-estratriene-3,17β-diol. Androstenedione = Δ_4-androstene-3,17-dione. Testosterone = Δ_4-androsten-17β-ol-3-one. Progesterone = Δ_4-pregnene-3, 20-dione. 17 α-Hydroxyprogesterone = Δ_4-pregnen-17 α-ol-3, 20-dione. DHEA, dehydroepiandrosterone = Δ_5-androsten-3β-ol-17-one. Cholesterol = Δ_5-cholesten-3β-ol. DOCA, deoxycorticosterone acetate = Δ_4-pregnen-21-acetoxy-3,20-dione. HCG, human chorionic gonadotrophin.

however, lack sensitivity for application to the problem of levels of free estrone in normal blood. Landowne and Lipsky (13) showed that the chloroacetate of pure cholesterol could be estimated at low concentrations by an electron capture detector following gas-phase chromatography. Our laboratory observed that submicrogram amounts of pure steroid chloroacetates, testosterone, and 20-reduced progesterone could be detected by electron capture (14). This observation was used in the development of techniques for the estimation of plasma testosterone (14) and estradiol (15). Moreover, plasma progesterone (16), aldosterone, and deoxycorticosterone (17) can be quantitated by electron capture following gas-phase chromatography. Finally, a preliminary note has been published on estimation of plasma estrogens by electron capture (18).

In this communication, a method will be reported for the assay of free estrone in plasma using gas-phase chromatography and electron capture detection of the 3-methyl ether 17-pentafluorophenylhydrazone of purified plasma estrone.

MATERIAL

Solvents and Reagents

Diethyl ether (reagent grade, A.R., Mallinckrodt) was fractionally distilled, washed with 20% (w/v) ferrous sulfate in 0.7 *N* sulfuric acid (50 ml/liter), then washed with water (100 ml/liter) to neutrality, and redistilled before use.

Methanol (anhydrous, analytical reagent, A.R., Mallinckrodt) was distilled from 2,4-dinitrophenylhydrazine.

Ethyl acetate (analytical reagent, A.R., Mallinckrodt) was distilled through a fractionating column, refluxed 4 hr with a mixture of acetic anhydride (100 ml/liter) and concentrated sulfuric acid (5 ml/liter), and then fractionally distilled.

Hexane (analytical reagent, A.R., Mallinckrodt), was washed in sequence with concentrated sulfuric acid (3 times with 100 ml/liter), with water (3 times with 180 ml/liter), with 1.3% (w/v) potassium permanganate in 4 *N* sulfuric acid (3 times with 100 ml/liter), then with water (150 ml/liter) to neutrality, dried over sodium sulfate, and fractionally distilled.

Chloroform (analytical reagent, A.R., Mallinckrodt) was fractionally distilled.

Benzene (nanograde reagent, A.R., Mallinckrodt).

Toluene (analytical reagent, A.R., Mallinckrodt).

Sulfuric acid (ACS, Du Pont).

Acetic acid (glacial, ACS, Allied Chemical).

Pentafluorophenylhydrazine (Pierce Chemical Company, Box 117, Rockford, Ill.) was stored in a desiccator in the cold.

Dimethyl sulfate (Matheson Coleman & Bell) was fractionally distilled.

Silica gel G (Merck, acc. to Stahl, for thin-layer chromatography), was washed 3 times with boiling water and 3 times with boiling methanol, and dried for 24 hr at 100°C.

Phosphor (Du Pont Luminescent Chemicals, Index 609) was washed 4 times with boiling methanol and dried for 24 hr at 100°C.

2,5-Diphenyloxazole (PPO) and 1,4-bis-2-(5-phenyloxazolyl)benzene (POPOP) were obtained from Packard Instrument Company, Inc.

Steroids

Estrone-6,7-H^3 (specific activity 0.25 mc/0.0013 mg) was purchased from New England Nuclear Corporation and purified by paper chromatography in the solvent system benzene/formamide (19). A solution of 3000 cpm purified estrone-6-7-H^3/ml methanol was stored at 5°C.

Estrone (Steraloids, Inc.) was purified by recrystallization in methanol. The corrected melting point for the purified product was 261–262°C.

Estrone 3-methyl ether (Steraloids, Inc.) was recrystallized from a mixture of *n*-hexane/ethyl acetate. The corrected melting point of the crystalline material was 172°C.

Estrone-3-methyl ether 17-pentafluorophenylhydrazone was prepared in the following way: 100 mg of estrone 3-methyl ether, dissolved in 15 ml hot methanol, was mixed with a solution of 100 mg pentafluorophenylhydrazine in 2.5 ml methanol containing 1 ml acetic acid. After standing overnight at room temperature, yellow crystals were formed and the precipitation was completed by leaving the mixture in the cold for 24 hr. The supernatant was then discarded and the precipitate crystallized 3 times from methanol and once from chloroform/hexane. The corrected melting point for the final product was 189–190°C.

Desoxycorticosterone acetate (DOCA) (Steraloids, Inc.). After crystallization from *n*-hexane/ethyl acetate, the crystals showed a corrected melting point of 158–159°C.

METHODS

Thin-Layer Chromatography. Thin-layer chromatography was done on glass plates coated with silica gel G; 45 ml water was added to 15 gm silica gel G mixed with luminescent phosphor (50 mg phosphor/15 gm silica gel), and the slurry spread on glass plates (20 $\times$ 20 cm) at a thickness of 0.2 mm. The plates were heated 1 hr at 100°C before use. Elution of steroids from silica gel after thin-layer chromatography was done as described by Attal *et al.* (20).

Gas-Phase Chromatography. Gas-phase chromatography was performed with a Barber-Colman model 10 gas chromatograph equipped with an Aerograph electron capture cell (Varian Aerograph—formerly Wilkens Instrument & Research, Inc.) and a model 214A pulse generator (Hewlett-Packard Company). Details on this equipment can be found in previous publications (14, 15, 17). A U-shaped glass column, 2 ft long with inside diameter of 0.4 cm, was packed with 1% XE-60 on 80–100 mesh Gas Chrom Q (Applied Science Laboratories). The column was operated at 205°C with inlet pressure of high-purity nitrogen of 30 psi. The electron capture cell was kept at 220° and the flash heater at 225°. A 10 μl calibrated Hamilton syringe was used to apply the sample onto the column and all samples were dissolved in toluene. The areas of the peaks on the gas chromatograms were measured by triangulation.

Spectral Analysis. UV spectra were recorded on a Beckman Instruments, Inc., DK-2 spectrophotometer and radioactivity was measured with a Packard Tri-Carb liquid scintillation spectrophotometer after dissolving dried samples in 10 ml scintillation fluid (4 gm PPO and 40 mg POPOP per liter toluene). The samples were counted 3 times for 10 min each time.

Detection of Steroid Standards Following Thin-Layer Chromatography. Estrone 3-methyl ether was detected by iodine vapor and estrone 3-methyl ether 17-pentafluorophenylhydrazone was visualized on thin-layer plates with a Haines fluorescent scanner.

METHOD FOR ESTIMATION OF FREE ESTRONE IN PERIPHERAL HUMAN PLASMA

Preparation of Plasma Sample. Blood was drawn into heparinized tubes and centrifuged immediately (45 min at 1500 rpm) and the plasma was stored at —15°C until extracted.

Extraction. A solution of estrone-6,7-H^3 (3000 cpm) was dried in a glass tube, 10 ml of plasma added, and the mixture extracted 3 times with 20 ml diethyl ether each time. The pooled extract was washed in sequence with 1/10 vol aqueous (8%) ammonium carbonate and with 1/10 vol water. The washed ether was then evaporated to dryness under nitrogen at 40°. The residue was dissolved in 5 ml toluene and extracted 3 times with 2 ml 1 *N* sodium hydroxide each time.

Methylation of Plasma Estrone. To the sodium hydroxide extract was added 1.5 ml 1 *N* sodium hydroxide and 5 ml 4.5% (w/v) boric acid in water. This mixture was kept at 40° for 5 min; 0.5 ml dimethyl sulfate was then added and the mixture shaken vigorously and left overnight at 40°. The next morning, after addition of 2.5 ml 20% (w/v) sodium hydroxide in water, the mixture was extracted with 12 ml *n*-hexane; the hexane extract was washed with 2 ml distilled water until neutral and then evaporated to dryness in nitrogen. The residue was applied to a thin-layer plate and ascending chromatography was performed in the solvent system benzene/methanol 99/1 (v/v). The tanks used for chromatography were prepared 1 hr before use. Two standards of estrone 3-methyl ether were chromatographed on separate lanes with each chromatogram of plasma samples. The silica gel from the plasma lanes was scraped off 1 cm below and 1 cm above the area corresponding in chromatographic behavior to authentic estrone 3-methyl ether. The removed silica gel was extracted with 6 ml ethyl acetate.

Formation of Estrone 3-Methyl Ether 17-Pentafluorophenylhydrazone. The ethyl acetate extract was evaporated to dryness under nitrogen. The residue was dissolved in 0.2 ml methanol, and 0.2 ml of a pentafluorophenylhydrazine solution (10 mg pentafluorophenylhydrazine in 9 ml methanol and 1 ml acetic acid) was added. The mixture was left overnight at room temperature; 1 ml water was added the next morning and the mixture extracted with 2 ml hexane 3 times. The extract was washed with 2 ml 1 *N* sulfuric acid, then with water to neutrality, and the washed hexane evaporated to dryness under nitrogen. Thin-layer chromatography of the residue was carried out in benzene. Two samples of authentic estrone 3-methyl ether 17-pentafluorophenylhydrazone were chromatographed on separate lanes. Material in the plasma extract chromatographing like authentic steroid was scraped off the plate and the removed silica gel eluted with 6 ml of a mixture of ethyl acetate/benzene 5/95 (v/v) (20). This eluate was washed with 0.5 ml distilled water and carefully centrifuged and the organic solvent layer removed and evaporated to dryness under nitrogen.

Counting of Radioactivity and Gas-Phase Chromatography. The residue was dissolved in 1 ml benzene and 1/10 aliquot was assayed for radioactivity. Depending on the steroid level expected, a variable portion of the remaining benzene was transferred to a 2 ml conical microcentrifuge tube. Then 10 μl of a methanolic solution of deoxycorticosterone acetate (3 μg/ml) was added to this tube as an internal standard. After proper mixing, the solution was evaporated to dryness and the residue dissolved in 15 μl of toluene; 10 μl of this solution was applied onto the gas chromatography column.

Calculations. The amount (E) of estrone in the plasma sample was calculated by the following formula:

$$E\ (\mu g) = \left(\frac{R_p}{10R_s} \times \frac{D_i}{D_s} \times \frac{A_s}{A_i} \times 0.582 \times 0.01\right) - E_1$$

where R_p = cpm of estrone-6,7-H^3 initially added to the plasma,
R_s = cpm of H^3 in the aliquot removed prior to gas-phase chromatography,
D_i = area (cm^2) of 0.03 μg DOCA,
D_s = area (cm^2) of DOCA in sample,
A_s = area (cm^2) of estrone 3-methyl ether 17-pentafluorophenylhydrazone in sample,
A_i = area (cm^2) of 0.01 μg estrone 3-methyl ether 17-pentafluorophenylhydrazone, and
E_1 = μg of estrone-6,7-H^3 initially added to the plasma sample

$$0.582 = \frac{\text{MW estrone}}{\text{MW estrone 3-methyl ether 17-pentafluorophenylhydrazone}}.$$

RESULTS

Characterization of Estrone 3-Methyl Ether 17-Pentafluorophenylhydrazone. This compound, prepared as described, showed a corrected melting point of 189–190°C. Thin-layer chromatography in benzene gave a single UV-absorbing spot with an R(estrone 3-methyl ether) of 3.5. Gas-phase chromatography using an electron capture detector gave a single peak on the following columns: 1% XE-60, 1% SE-30, and 1% EPON 1001. A fluorine analysis, performed by Galbraith Laboratories, Inc., gave a value of 20.70% ± 0.4; the calculated value is 20.45. The ultraviolet spectrum of this estrone derivative showed maximum absorption in methanol at 255 mμ. Compared to published infrared spectra of estrone and estrone 3-methyl ether (21), it is evident from Figure 1 that the absorption band characteristic for a 17-keto group (1740 cm^{-1}) is no longer present in the estrone 3-methyl ether 17-pentafluorophenylhydrazone prepared by our method. A strong absorption at 1560 cm^{-1} is typical for aromatic compounds (Fig. 1 and ref. 21), and the absorption bands at 1015 and 1060 cm^{-1} indicate the presence of an aromatic methyl ether (Fig. 1 and ref. 21). Moreover, the absorption at 1655 cm^{-1} and the sharp stretching band at 3360 cm^{-1} are probably caused by C=N and NH, respectively.

Response of the Electron Capture Detector. The electron capture cell was calibrated for known concentrations of estrone 3-methyl ether 17-pentafluorophenylhydrazone. When amounts of this steroid ranging from 0.00024 to 0.01 μg were plotted against the area of the peak on the gas chromatographic tracings, a straight line was obtained (Fig. 2). The response of the electron capture cell to graded concentrations of the internal standard, deoxycorticosterone acetate, is shown in Figure 3 (17).

Correction by Internal Standardization. DOCA was used as an internal

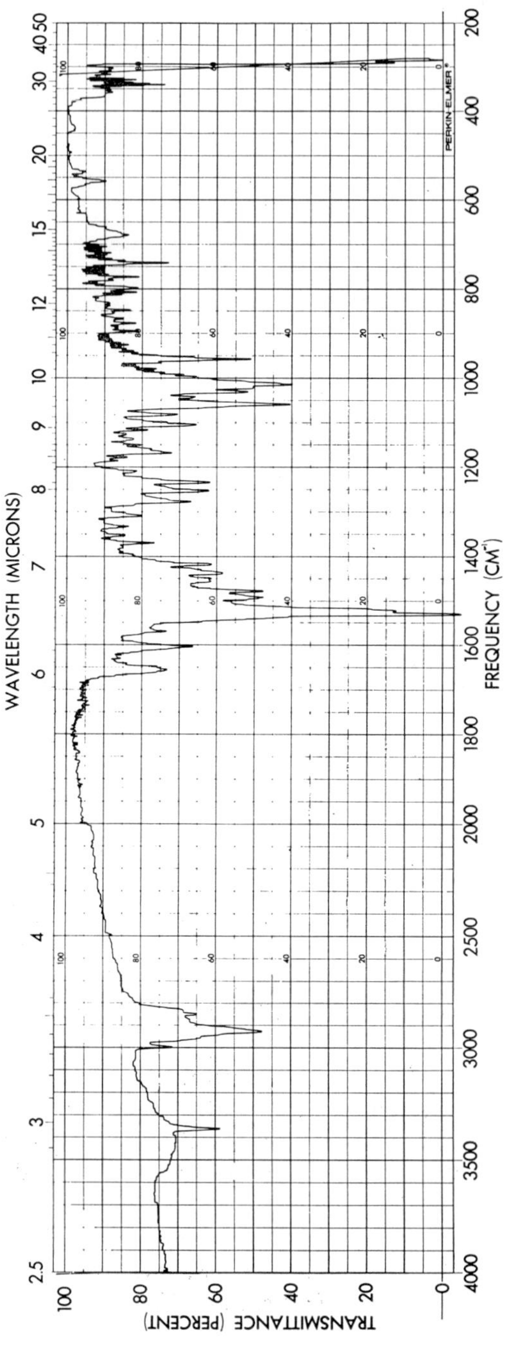

FIG. 1. Infrared spectrum of estrone 3-methyl ether 17-pentafluorophenylhydrazone recorded with a Perkin-Elmer model 621 infrared spectrophotometer. Perkin-Elmer potassium bromide die was used to produce the micropellet. The work was kindly performed by Perkin-Elmer Corporation. For reference spectra of estrone and estrone 3-methyl ether, see reference 21.

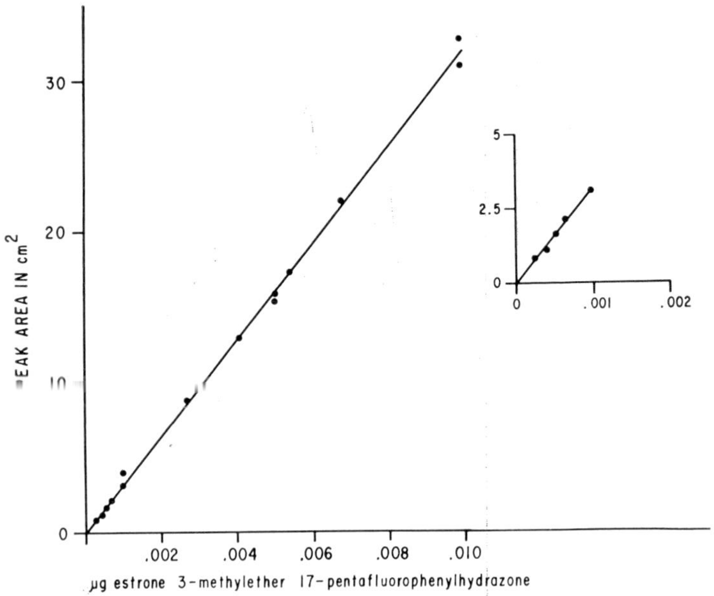

FIG. 2. Response curve for pure estrone 3-methyl ether 17-pentafluorophenylhydrazone following gas-phase chromatography with electron capture detection. The coefficient of linear regression is 0.999.

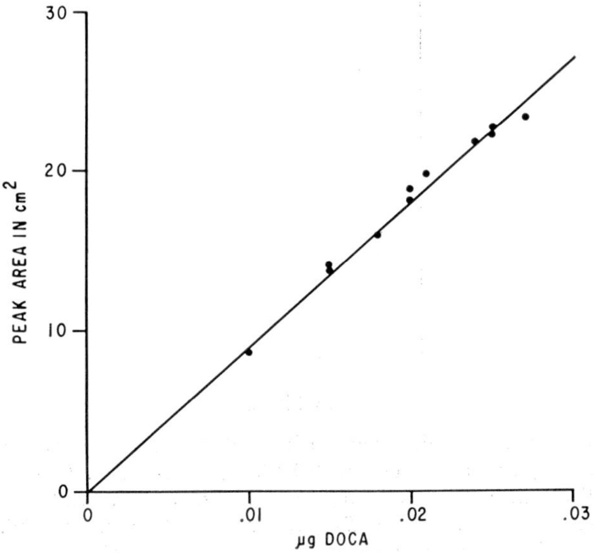

FIG. 3. Response curve for pure DOCA following gas-phase chromatography with electron capture detection. The coefficient of linear regression is 0.995.

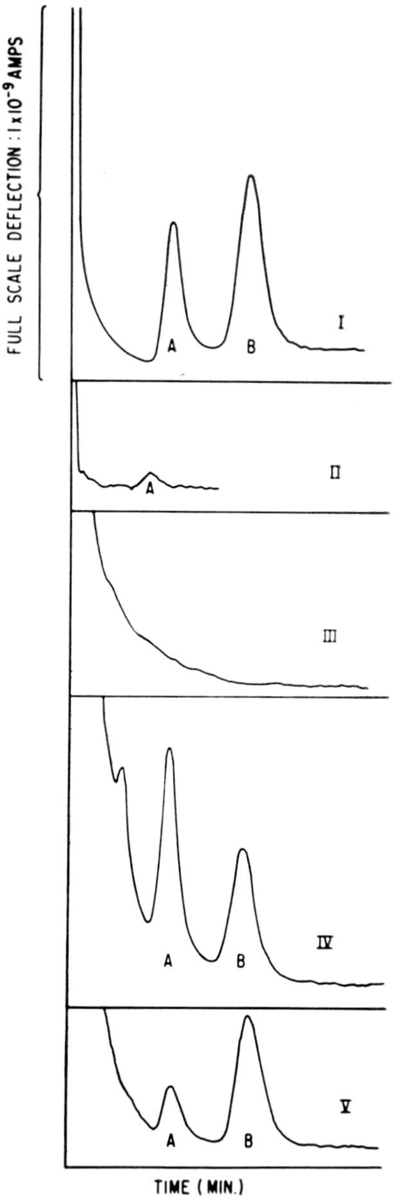

FIG. 4. Gas chromatographic tracings of: (I) 0.003 μg pure estrone 3-methyl ether 17-pentafluorophenylhydrazone (A) and 0.018 μg DOCA (B). (II) 0.00024 μg pure estrone 3-methyl ether 17-pentafluorophenylhydrazone (A). (III) Sample of 10 ml water containing 3000 cpm estrone-6,7-H^3 and processed by our method. (IV) Sample of 10 ml plasma from a pregnant woman; the equivalent of 1 ml plasma was chromatographed. (V) Ovarian venous blood plasma from a dog; the equivalent of 1 ml plasma was chromatographed.

standard to correct for losses during transfer of the sample to the gas chromatograph and to correct for variations in the sensitivity of the electron capture detector. The retention times of estrone 3-methyl ether 17-pentafluorophenylhydrazone and DOCA were 7 and 12.3 min, respectively (Fig. 4). In order to determine if the internal standard interfered with quantitation of estrone 3-methyl ether 17-pentafluorophenylhydrazone, increasing amounts of this steroid derivative were injected with the same quantity of DOCA (0.03 μg). The data of Table 1 indicate that

TABLE 1
Quantitation by Electron Capture Detection of Different Amounts of Pure Estrone 3-Methyl Ether 17-Pentafluorophenylhydrazone in the Presence of a Standard Amount (0.03 μg) of DOCA

Estrone 3-methyl ether 17-pentafluorophenylhydrazone injected, μg	Estrone 3-methyl ether 17-pentafluorophenylhydrazone found, μg
0.010	0.011
0.010	0.011
0.005	0.005
0.005	0.006
0.002	0.002
0.002	0.002
0.001	0.001
0.001	0.001

there was no interference from the internal standard when from 0.001 to 0.010 μg of estrone 3-methyl ether 17-pentafluorophenylhydrazone was chromatographed.

For routine work, different amounts of estrone 3-methyl ether 17-pentafluorophenylhydrazone (0.001 and 0.01 μg) and of DOCA (0.01 and 0.03 μg) were chromatographed every day before and after chromatographing unknown plasma samples on the same column.

Recovery. The recovery at various steps of the method was determined on 10 samples of pooled blood plasma obtained from a pregnant woman; 6000 cpm of estrone-6,7-H^3 was added per 10 ml of this plasma pool and the samples processed through the method.

The recovery of estrone-6,7-H^3 after ether extraction was relatively poor (mean recovery 86%), but this solvent was chosen because of its low emulsion frequency when extracting blood plasma. The recovery after methylation was also low (mean recovery 48%), but improvement in this recovery was achieved by using freshly distilled dimethyl sulfate. Up to the step of gas-phase chromatography, the mean recovery of estrone in these samples was 34%.

Precision and Accuracy. Known amounts of pure estrone (0.005, 0.010,

TABLE 2
Determination of Different Amounts of Pure Estrone Added to Water and Processed through the Method

	Estrone found (μg) for μg estrone added			
	0.005	0.010	0.020	0.040
	0.008	0.010	0.016	0.038
	0.006	0.007	0.021	0.040
	0.006	0.015	0.029	0.041
	0.004	0.007	0.022	0.042
		0.009	0.017	0.039
Mean value	0.006	0.010	0.021	0.040
S.D.[a]	0.002	0.003	0.005	0.002
Precision of assay[b]	33%	30%	24%	5%

[a] One standard deviation.
[b] Standard deviation/mean value.

0.020, and 0.040 μg) were dissolved in 10 ml of water and assayed by our method (Table 2). The precision of assay appears adequate and, as expected, decreased with decreasing amounts of the hormone. Ten replicate determinations were also done on a pool of peripheral blood plasma obtained from pregnant women. A mean value of 0.072 μg free estrone/10 ml plasma was found in this pool with one standard deviation of 0.005. Thus, at a concentration of 7 μg free estrone per liter of plasma,

TABLE 3
Determination of Free Estrone in Different Amounts of Pooled Plasma from a Pregnant Woman

Sample size, ml	Estrone	
	μg/sample	μg/liter
2	0.011	5.5
4	0.026	6.5
8	0.042	5.3
16	0.094	5.9
32	0.179	5.6

the precision of assay is about 7%. Moreover, increasing the amount of pooled blood plasma per estrone assay (Table 3) gave the expected increases in estrone per sample. Finally, little variation was seen in the concentrations of plasma estrone when samples containing from 0.37 to 6.8 μg/liter of plasma were determined by repeated assays on the same purified sample (Table 4).

From the above results it appears that the precision of assay decreases when the amount of estrone in the sample is low. This is mainly due to precision of quantitation by the electron capture cell. The reproducibility

TABLE 4
Quantitation of Free Estrone in Human Plasma following Repeated Application of the Same Purified Sample to Gas-Phase Chromatography
(all data in μg/liter of plasma)

Application	Male plasma	Female plasma (menstrual cycle)	Plasma from pregnant women	
			Subject 1	Subject 2
1st	0.37	0.38	2.8	6.6
2nd	0.42	0.45	2.7	6.9
3rd	0.46	0.48	3.4	6.8

of quantitation of pure estrone 3-methyl ether 17-pentafluorophenylhydrazone was tested and a precision of assay of 2% for 0.010 μg of steroid increasing to 13% for 0.0005 μg steroid was found.

Sensitivity. Gas-phase chromatography of 0.00024 μg of pure estrone 3-methyl ether 17-pentafluorophenylhydrazone (about 0.00014 μg estrone) gave a response from the electron capture cell clearly distinguishable from that of a sample of 10 ml water containing 3000 cpm estrone-6,7-H^3 and assayed by our method (Fig. 4). Since the recovery of known

TABLE 5
Radiochemical Purity of Free Estrone Isolated from Ovarian Vein Blood of a Dog Infused with Tritiated Δ^4-Androstenedione via the Ovarian Artery

Crystallization	Solvent system	Disintegrations/min/mg	
		Crystals	Mother liquor
1st	Chloroform/hexane	1390	1410
2nd	Ethyl acetate/hexane	1390	1430
3rd	Chloroform/methanol	1390	1410

The original sample before crystallization had 1490 disintegrations/min/mg.

amounts of estrone assayed by the method is in the order of 34%, since $1/10$ of the sample is used for calculation of sample recovery, and since transfer of the sample to the column is not complete, only 20% of the original concentration of free estrone in the blood plasma sample is available for electron capture detection. Thus levels of estrone below 0.001 μg per sample cannot be detected with any degree of precision.

Specificity. A normal female dog was given 2000 I.U. HCG intramuscularly every second day for 20 consecutive days. The animal was operated the 21st day and the ovary infused with H^3-Δ^4-androstenedione via the ovarian artery and venous blood collected from the infused tissue. The ovarian venous plasma was assayed for estrone as described except that no radioactive estrone was added and, after the last thin-layer chromatogram, plasma material corresponding in chromatographic mobil-

TABLE 6
Concentrations of Free Estrone in Peripheral Plasma of Pregnant Women

Subject	Duration of gestation, weeks	Estrone, μg/liter
A.A	9	2.2
C.A.	10	3.4
C.C.	12	0.5
P.A.	15	7.4
P.A.	16	6.6
R.S.	19	1.6
R.S.	22	1.1
E.S.	22	1.9
E.E.	23	7.6
E.A.K.	23	1.1
P.C.	24	5.9
D.A.	24	3.5
D.D.	26	7.7
D.T.	30	3.4
D.T.	32	5.7
F.A.	32	7.8
G.H.	34	9.3
J.L.	36	2.8
K.A.	40	9.8

ity to authentic estrone 3-methyl ether 17-pentafluorophenylhydrazone was scraped off the thin-layer plate. The removed silica gel was extracted with ethyl acetate, which was evaporated to dryness. To the residue was added authentic estrone 3-methyl ether 17-pentafluorophenylhydrazone and the mixture crystallized from different solvent mixtures. Specific radioactivity of the crystals and of the mother liquors were calculated.

TABLE 7
Concentrations of Free Estrone in Peripheral Plasma of Women during Midpoint of the Menstrual Cycle

Subject	Length of cycle, days	Day of cycle	Estrone, μg/liter
		13th	0.30
M.C.	28	14th	0.33
		15th	0.25
G.L.B.	32	15th	0.39
		16th	0.27
		10th	1.25
I.P.	22	11th	0.69
		12th	1.20
		14th	0.28
J.J.	30	15th	0.18
		16th	0.19

It is evident from the data of Table 5 that our method isolates free plasma estrone in a high state of radiochemical purity.

Concentrations of Free Estrone in Plasma from Normal Men and Women. The method was applied to estrone determination in peripheral plasma obtained from 10 normal male subjects. The concentration of the hormone varied from non-detectable to 0.84 μg/liter of plasma. The plasma levels of free estrone in normal, pregnant women and in normal women during midpoint of the menstrual cycle are recorded in Tables 6 and 7.

DISCUSSION

The aim of this work was to develop a method for estimation of free estrone in blood plasma less elaborate than double-isotope derivative dilution techniques. The specificity of the present method is as great as that of double-isotope techniques (Table 5); moreover, it is a simple method requiring only 2 thin-layer chromatograms for compound purification. It involves, however, the formation of an estrone derivative via methylation of the phenolic hydroxy group and formation of pentafluorophenylhydrazone at carbon 17. This latter group is responsible for the electron capture ability of the derivative.

It is possible to detect as little as 0.00024 μg of pure estrone 3-methyl ether 17-pentafluorophenylhydrazone (Fig. 4), but at least 0.001 μg of estrone is needed in the original sample for adequate quantitation. With the development of electron capture cells of higher sensitivity than the one used in the current investigation, it is possible that the lower operational limit of our method could be decreased provided that plasma estrone could be purified to an extreme degree *prior to gas-phase chromatography.* In its present form, our method for the quantitation of free estrone in blood plasma appears as sensitive as methods using double-isotope dilution (22). Less than 1 nanogram estrone in the sample cannot be determined by either method (22). At low levels of the hormone, imprecise quantitation of small peaks on the gas chromatographic tracings may give rise to rather poor precision of assay (13% for 0.0005 μg estrone). Since we have not measured the concentration of estrone in pooled plasma samples by our method and by methods based on the principle of double-isotope dilution, strict comparison between these two methods with regard to accuracy and precision cannot be made. Our blank values are, however, not detectable (Fig. 4) and the somewhat thorny problem of positive blank values in methods using double-isotope dilution has not been adequately solved. Finally, as discussed previously in this journal (17), gas-phase chromatography with electron capture detection can be used for the estimation of specific radioactivity of steroids formed from labeled steroid precursors. Such investigations are difficult to perform with methods based on the principle of double-isotope dilution.

As many as 20 plasma samples may be processed by this technique in 3 days, application to the gas chromatograph not included. Only 16 min is needed for elution of estrone 3-methyl ether 17-pentafluorophenylhydrazone and DOCA from the column used; thus a great number of samples can be chromatographed in an 8 hr day. Compared with estrone assay by double-isotope derivative dilution technique, the cost per sample by our method is very low. It should, however, be remembered that our method involves purchase of a rather expensive gas chromatograph in addition to the equipment needed in the isotope derivative dilution techniques.

The method has been used for the determination of free estrone in human peripheral plasma. The results obtained on pregancy plasma (9th to 40th week of gestation, Table 6) are in good agreement with those found by authors using double-isotope technique (23), fluorometry (8), or gas-phase chromatography (12). Levels of free estrone in blood plasma from normal women during the menstrual cycle (Table 7) are in the same range as those published by Svendsen and Sörensen (24) using double-isotope technique, but the concentrations of this hormone in the blood plasma of normal men are lower than those found using fluorometry as end point for assay (7).

Unsuccessful attempts were made in the current investigation to fix pentachlorophenylhydrazine or trichlorophenylhydrazine to keto groups on the steroid skeleton, thus confirming previous observations (25). When keto steroids were reacted with *p*-bromophenylhydrazine, 2,5-dichlorophenylhydrazine, or 2,4,5-trichlorophenylhydrazine, the yield of hydrazone formation was good except for formation of *p*-bromophenylhydrazone. All these hydrazones, however, were unstable and had to be kept in particular solvents (pyridine, tetrahydrofurane, toluene) in a desiccator, in the dark and in the cold room. The derivative formed with pentafluorophenylhydrazine may be kept in any solvent without any particular precautions. Also, the steroid pentafluorophenylhydrazones are easy to handle in thin-layer chromatography. The pentafluorophenylhydrazones were, moreover, formed of different steroids (testosterone, androstenedione, progesterone, 17α-hydroxyprogesterone, DHEA). The monoketosteroids gave with this hydrazine good electron-capturing derivatives when exposed to gas-phase chromatography under the conditions described in this communication. The bishydrazones of androstenedione, progesterone, and 17α-hydroxyprogesterone could not, however, be detected under these conditions. The 3-monohydrazones of some of the above steroids showed considerable ability to capture electrons, but the yield of the 3-monohydrazone formation was disappointingly low.

SUMMARY

A method for the estimation of free estrone in plasma has been developed using gas-phase chromatography with electron capture detection. As little as 0.00014 μg pure estrone can be measured, but at least 0.001 μg of the hormone is needed in the original sample for adequate quantitation. Prior to gas-phase chromatography, plasma estrone is purified by thin-layer chromatography and converted to its 3-methyl ether 17-pentafluorophenylhydrazone. Plasma estrone values in pregnant women (9th to 40th week) ranged from 0.5 to 9.8 μg/liter and in normal women during midpoint of the menstrual cycle from 0.18 to 1.25 μg/liter. These data are in good agreement with estrone concentrations found by other, more time-consuming, methods. The sensitivity, specificity, accuracy, and precision of the method have been discussed.

ACKNOWLEDGMENTS

The authors acknowledge excellent technical assistance with gas-phase chromatography by Mrs. M. Woodward. They are indebted to Dr. I. H. Kaiser, Department of Obstetrics and Gynecology, University of Utah, and Mr. C. Barrett, Holy Cross Hospital, Salt Lake City, for supplying blood plasma. Finally, we would like to express our gratitude to Dr. P. Gardner, Department of Chemistry, University of Utah, for all his help.

REFERENCES

1. Brown, J. B., *Biochem. J.* **60**, 185 (1955).
2. Roy, E. J., and Brown, J. B., *J. Endocrinol.* **21**, 9 (1960).
3. Bauld, W. S., *Mem. Soc. Endocrinol.* **3**, 11 (1955).
4. Ittrich, G., *Physiol. Chem.* **320**, 103 (1960).
5. Smith, O. W., and Arai, K., *J. Clin. Endocrinol. Metab.* **23**, 1141 (1963).
6. Preedy, J. R. K., and Aitken, E. H., *J. Biol. Chem.* **236**, 1300 (1961).
7. Ichii, S., Forchielli, E., Perloff, W. H., and Dorfman, R. I., *Anal. Biochem.* **5**, 422 (1963).
8. Schrepfer, R., and Nicholas, H. J., *Amer. J. Obst. Gynec.* **92**, 755 (1965).
9. Svendsen, R., *Acta Endocrinol.* **35**, 161 (1960).
10. Kroman, H. S., Bender, S. R., and Capizzi, R. L., *Clin. Chim. Acta* **9**, 73 (1964).
11. Panicucci, F., and Taponeco, G., *Boll. Soc. Ital. Biol. Sper.* **41**, 1459 (1965).
12. Touchstone, J. C., and Murawec, T., *Biochemistry* **4**, 1612 (1965).
13. Landowne, R. A., and Lipsky, S. R., *Anal. Chem.* **35**, 532 (1963).
14. Brownie, A. C., van der Molen, H. J., Nishizawa, E. E., and Eik-Nes, K. B., *J. Clin. Endocrinol. Metab.* **24**, 1091 (1964).
15. Eik-Nes, K. B., Aakvaag, A., and Grota, L. J., *in* "Gas Chromatography of Steroids in Biological Fluids" (M. B. Lipsett, ed.), p. 247, Plenum Press, New York, 1965.
16. van der Molen, H. J., and Groen, D., *in* "Gas Chromatography of Steroids in Biological Fluids" (M. B. Lipsett, ed.), p. 153. Plenum Press, New York, 1965.
17. Rapp, J. P., and Eik-Nes, K. B., *Anal. Biochem.* **15**, 386 (1966).
18. Charransol, G., and Wotiz, H. H., *Excerpta Med. Intern. Congr. Ser. No. 111*, p. 117 (1966).

19. Burton, R. B., Zaffaroni, A., and Keutmann, E. H., *J. Biol. Chem.* **188**, 763 (1951).
20. Attal, J., Hendeles, S. M., Engels, J. A., and Eik-Nes, K. B., *J. Chromatog.* In press.
21. Neudert, W., and Röpke, H., "Steroide-Spektrenatlas." Springer-Verlag, Berlin, 1965.
22. Bojesen, E., Svendsen, R., and Thuneberg, L., *Excerpta Med. Intern. Congr. Ser. No. 111*, p. 131 (1966).
23. Svendsen, R., and Sörensen, B., *Acta Endocrinol.* **47**, 237 (1964).
24. Svendsen, R., and Sörensen, B., *Acta Endocrinol.* **47**, 245 (1964).
25. van der Molen, H. J., Groen, D., and van der Maas, J. H., *Steroids* **6**, 195 (1965).

ANALYTICAL BIOCHEMISTRY 20, 411–418 (1967)

Rapid Automated Analysis Involving Liquid-Liquid Extraction:

Atropine by a Prudhomme Method

VOLNEY WALLACE

Chemical Division, Test Operations Directorate, Dugway Proving Ground, Dugway, Utah 84022

Received January 19, 1967

Liquid-liquid extraction has been adapted to the continuous-flow system of automated analysis by Technicon Corporation; a description of the technique is given in their publication on the analysis of alkylbenzene sulfonates (ABS) (1). The method is feasible but is slow and troublesome. The method described here was developed to overcome the marked tendency for colorimeter fouling and to permit operation at the maximal rate of the AutoAnalyzer. This was accomplished by eliminating bubble segmentation and mixing coils and by redesigning the extraction coil, phase separator, and colorimeter hookup.

From experience with Prudhomme-like reactions it is anticipated that the setup described here is applicable to the determination of a wide variety of ionic and ionizable materials. This is discussed under the heading, "The Prudhomme Method." The method described is specifically for atropine. The reaction is a metathetical reaction between atropine sulfate and sodium narceinate with the reaction being forced by extraction of the product—atropine narceinate—by chloroform. The atropine concentration is estimated from the color or narceinate concentration of the extract.

AUTOANALYZER SETUP

The AutoAnalyzer setup for this method is shown in Figure 1; details of the phase separator and colorimeter hookup are in Figures 2 and 3.

The input flow rates given in Figure 1 are not critical. There is a large excess of dye and the sensitivity can be adjusted by changing the sample-to-chloroform ratio.

The small-bore T junctions were used as a precautionary measure, in the expectation that oscillation can occur in the confluence, resulting in

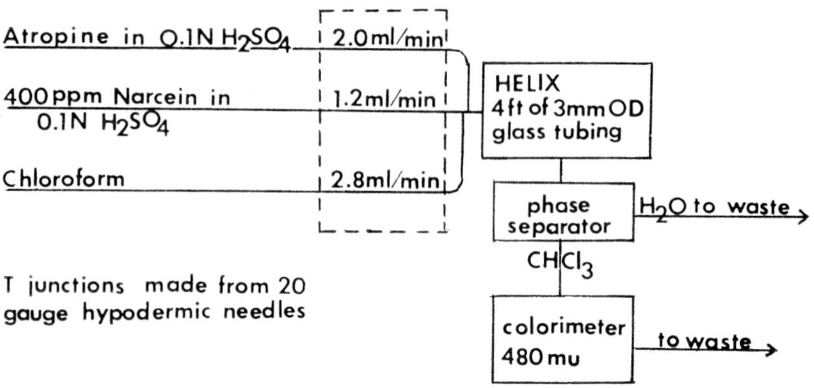

FIG. 1. AutoAnalyzer hookup.

alternating output of the two input streams. A small confluence would limit the magnitude of these oscillations.

The remaining elements of the setup are described separately because their unique design made possible the high rate of analysis which was achieved, and because these elements may be used to advantage in other continuous-flow methods of analysis.

EXTRACTION COIL

The ABS method uses as extraction coil a helix of glass tubing packed with coarse glass beads. Passage of water, chloroform, and air through the bed of beads emulsifies the mixture, effecting thorough extraction. The emulsion may not break and herein lies the objection to this device.

The extraction coil used in this method is less prone to produce troublesome and intractable emulsions but is not entirely free of this problem. Setups with this extraction coil are free, however, of the problem of progressive fouling of the colorimeter flow cell. This fouling is likely to be due to deposition of an unstable dispersion of aqueous droplets in the chloroform phase.

The extraction coil, as indicated in Figure 1, is a 4 ft length of moderately small bore tubing. A 2 ft length was almost as efficient and a shorter length could probably be used if one were willing to compromise yield or if the chloroform phase were introduced axially into the aqueous stream to achieve uniformly small aqueous segments. The basis for this expectation and the observed and deduced characteristics of the extraction coil follow.

It is observed that on entering the extraction coil the chloroform and aqueous phase distribute as an aqueous continuum containing chloroform globules. The chloroform globules are sufficiently large that the tube

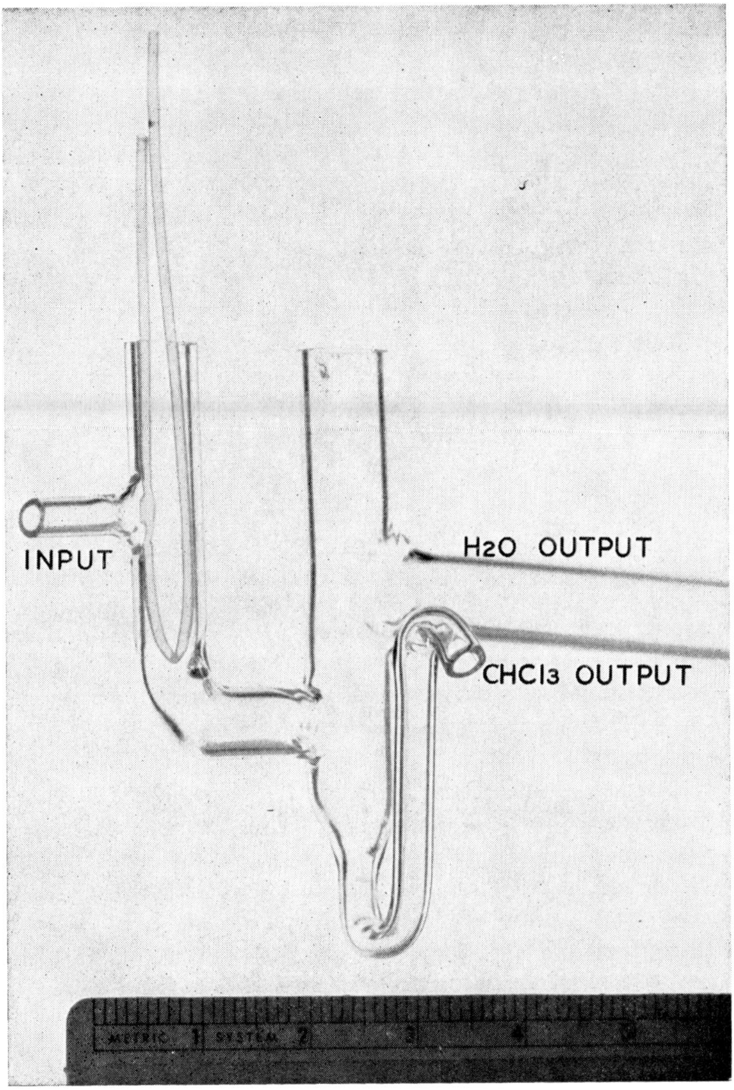

FIG. 2. Phase separator with polyethylene tube in entrance chamber.

forces them into an elongated shape. These globules do not wet the walls of the tube but are separated from it by a thin layer of water. As the segmented stream moves, there is tailing of the aqueous phase from one aqueous segment to the next and there is a convection within both the aqueous and the chloroform phases. The convection current is forward in the axial region and rearward in the outer region, and probably results

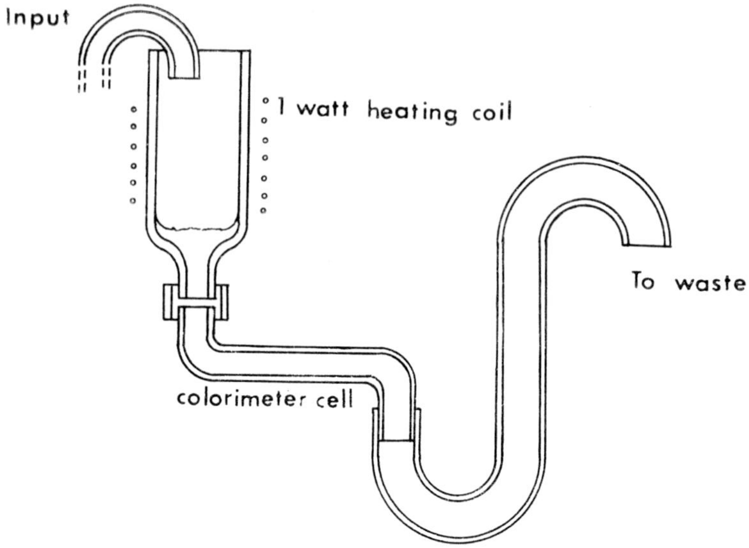

FIG. 3. Colorimeter hookup.

from viscous drag and the finite length of the globules and aqueous segments.

Some extraction probably occurs from the ends of the aqueous segments where the segment meets the chloroform globule but it is believed—and the design of the coil is based on this—that the extraction occurs primarily from the thin aqueous layer that separates the chloroform globule from the wall of the glass tube. This layer is characterized by a high surface-to-volume ratio, a short diffusion distance for ions not already absorbed on the liquid-liquid interface, and a rapid turnover. If the convection currents effect rapid and thorough mixing, as they appear to do, then one can expect that the original contents of an aqueous segment will be depleted by tailing, following first-order kinetics. From this analysis it is expected that extraction in this coil approximates first-order kinetics, with tube length being equivalent to time and the rate constant being a function of the ratio of the tailing rate to the volume of an aqueous segment.

It has been observed that small and even bubble segmentation is obtained in an AutoAnalyzer stream when air and water are merged at a funnel-shaped bottom exit of a chamber. This is essentially introduction of air into the aqueous stream axially; substitution of chloroform for air with the same result appears possible. Though considered, it was not tried as it is difficult to effect and the simple T junction suffices. Where carry-over must be reduced to a bare minimum it may be justified.

Tailing of water past air bubbles is slower than past chloroform globules, probably because the air bubble, having the higher internal pressure (from the higher interfacial tension), exerts a more efficient squeegee action. When there is a bubble in the same aqueous stream as chloroform, the chloroform globules queue up behind the bubble and merge. In the open-tube extraction coil this would inhibit tailing after extraction and would inhibit extraction of an aqueous segment immediately preceding a bubble. Bubble segmentation is not used in this setup, not because of these considerations, however, but simply because it is not needed. In other setups this behavior will have to be evaluated and bubble segmentation used or avoided according to the evaluation.

PHASE SEPARATOR

The conventional debubbler is a simple, but troublesome, device for separating chloroform from an AutoAnalyzer stream. When it malfunctions the line must be broken, the colorimeter flow cell cleaned out, and the debubbler reprimed. This is inevitable when the chloroform supply is allowed to run out and when there is a moderate to severe emulsion in the input stream. It tends also to occur when the recovery of extract is set high, for a variety of reasons. The debubbler is objectionable also because it has a bubble-agitated reservoir of sample, a condition which causes fore and aft spreading of sample in the line.

The phase separator designed to overcome these failings is shown in Figure 2. Once it is primed, only inept handling or a heavy emulsion will cause it to fail. It recovers all of the extract and when there is an interruption in chloroform input it simply holds.

The phase separator consists essentially of an entrance chamber and a U tube with chloroform exiting from one arm of the U and spent reagent from the other. The $CHCl_3/H_2O$ interface in the U tube is near the bottom, just below the connection to the entrance chamber. Because of hydrostatic relationships the vertical distance from the interface to the chloroform exit is two-thirds that from the interface to the reagent exit.

Chloroform on entering the entrance chamber wets the polyethylene tubing and flows down its surface, dripping as medium-size globules from the fold in this tubing near the bottom of the entrance chamber. These globules progress into the U section and merge immediately with the chloroform pool. The extract and spent reagent flow out under force of gravity from the respective arms of the U tube.

The polyethylene tubing inhibits (*1*) formation of a pendant drop of chloroform at the meniscus of the input chamber and (*2*) dwelling of small droplets of chloroform on the chloroform pool. It is essential to the good performance of the phase separator.

It is possible—preferred if carryover must be minimized—to lead the chloroform from the pool directly through the colorimeter flow cell and thence through a low resistance path to an elevation hydrostatically equal to the spent reagent exit. This setup was abandoned in favor of the one described here for reasons of convenience in setting up and of cleaning up after a case of troublesome emulsion.

In this phase separator, the separator is exposed to the atmosphere at three points. This may be an enclosed atmosphere with the extract, spent reagent, and air remerging after the extract has passed through the colorimeter. The remerged stream can then be led to a distant drain or waste crock.

COLORIMETER HOOKUP

The colorimeter hookup shown in Figure 3 is essentially a simple U tube with the entrance arm extending above the exit arm and the colorimeter flow cell part of the U. The input meniscus is relatively stable in position and the input reservoir accordingly can be quite small, a desirable feature. The heater is optional, being used if there is haze in the extract resulting from chilling.

The colorimeter hookup shown can be used without change with bubble-segmented reagent streams. The bubbles break on entering the entrance funnel and the liquid flows through the same as in this method. It is simple and convenient, and requires one less pump line than the conventional debubbler.

PERFORMANCE

This setup permits analysis of atropine at 100 samples per hour with negligible carryover from one sample to the next. At 120/hr there is a 3.7% carryover. Data obtained at 120/hr are given in Table 1, as is, and with correction for carryover. The subject of carryover is treated in another paper (2).

TABLE 1
Absorbance of Atropine Standard Samples
(average and standard deviation of six samples)

Atropine concn., γ/ml	Raw data	After correction for 3.7% carryover
0	0.013 ± 0.009	0.004 ± 0.002
2	0.063 ± 0.011	0.053 ± 0.003
5	0.128 ± 0.010	0.118 ± 0.002
10	0.260 ± 0.011	0.250 ± 0.004
20	0.491 ± 0.013	0.480 ± 0.007
30	0.699 ± 0.010	0.689 ± 0.004

THE PRUDHOMME METHOD

The AutoAnalyzer method described here is applicable or adaptable to a particular class of analytical methods derived from Prudhomme's method for quinine (3). The possible scope of application of this method is therefore best understood from a description of the character and scope of the Prudhomme method.

In the original Prudhomme method, an aqueous solution of quinine sulfate and the dye sodium eosinate was extracted with chloroform. Quinine eosinate was extracted, the excess reagent remaining in the aqueous phase. The quinine concentration was estimated by colorimetric measurement of the extract. This is actually estimation of the eosinate concentration with conversion to quinine concentration on the basis of a constant ratio of the two ions in the extract.

The following changes can be made in this method, provided of course that the reagent salt of the test ion can be selectively extracted:

1. Other colored or otherwise directly measurable ions can be substituted for eosinate ion.
2. Other ions, cationic or anionic, monovalent or polyvalent, can be substituted for the quinine ion.
3. Other solvents may be used.
4. Other spectator ions can be used (e.g., methylene blue sulfate may be used in place of methylene blue chloride as reagent dye, when chloride interferes).

Out of these changes have arisen methods for other alkaloids, fatty amines, cationic and anionic detergents, and a few inorganic ions such as perchlorate. Examples of these are given in references 4 through 9.

The writer is not aware of readout other than colorimetric being used but fluorometric readout could be used in Prudhomme's original method. As to solvent substitution, it is usually found that a particular solvent does not extract the product or that it extracts the reagent dye. It should be pointed out that this categorization is a function of both solvent and dye and that extraction of the reagent dye may be regarded as use of the wrong dye or companion ion for the reagent dye (cf. point 4 above). Extraction of a reagent dye salt may alternatively be regarded as a basis for analyzing for the inorganic ion involved.

Variations in the Prudhomme method are numerous and the AutoAnalyzer setup described here is a convenient method for screening these variations. It is hoped that it will help develop and extend the utility of the Prudhomme method.

SUMMARY

An improved AutoAnalyzer method for liquid-liquid extraction is described with specific application to the analysis of atropine by a modification of the Prudhomme method for quinine.

REFERENCES

1. *Bulletin A10a,* Technicon Controls, Inc.
2. Wallace, V., *Anal. Biochem.* **20,** 517 (1967).
3. Prudhomme, R. O., *Bull. Soc. Pathol. Exotique* **31,** 929 (1938).
4. Auerbach, M. E., *Anal. Chem.* **15,** 592 (1943).
5. Golosnitskayd, V. A., Petrashen, V. I., *Zh. Anal. Khim.* **17,** 878 (1862) (English translation by Ingeborg V. Baker available from Translation Branch, Redstone Scientific Information Center, Redstone Arsenal, Alabama).
6. Divatia, G. J., and Biles, J. A., *J. Pharm. Sci.* **50,** 916 (1961).
7. Hedvick, C. E., and Berger, B. A., *Anal. Chem.* **38,** 791 (1966).
8. Larrick, R. A., *Anal. Chem.* **36,** 1760 (1963).
9. Mukerjee, P., *Anal. Chem.* **28,** 870 (1956).

ANALYTICAL BIOCHEMISTRY 20, 419–422 (1967)

Detection and Differentiation of Sugars on Paper by the p-Anisidine/Periodate Reaction[1]

L. A. VEIGA AND E. L. CHANDELIER

Instituto de Bioquimica da Universidade Federal do Paraná and Instituto de Biologia e Pesquisas Tecnológicas, P. O. Box 939, Curitiba, Pr., Brazil

Received January 23, 1967

During the past few years a considerable amount of work has been reported on the identification and detection of sugars and their derivatives by paper chromatography and thin-layer chromatography (1–12). The periodate/benzidine reagent has been used to differentiate polyols from other sugars (13–15) and Bean and Porter (14) observed that *p*-anisidine could replace benzidine for the same purpose. *p*-Anisidine-phosphoric acid has been found to be a satisfactory reagent for differentiating several classes of sugars, and also for serving as a color reagent for sialic acid compounds on paper chromatograms (15, 16). *p*-Anisidine-phosphate in ethanol has been used as spray reagent for sugars (17, 18). Certain deoxy sugars and aldehydes can be detected by using periodate oxidation followed by thiobarbituric acid (19–21).

This report describes a method for the detection and differentiation of many sugars and sugar derivatives by paper chromatography, based on their reaction with *p*-anisidine and sodium periodate.

MATERIALS AND METHODS

Most of the chemicals used in this work were analytical reagents purchased from commerical sources.

D-Talono-γ-lactone, glucoheptonolactone, mannonolactone, glucuronolactone, and galactonolactone were gifts from Dr. D. Amaral, University of Paraná, Brazil. All the ascending chromatograms were carried out on Whatman No. 1 chromatographic paper, using *n*-butanol/pyridine/water (45/25/40) (22) or acetone/water (85/15) as the solvent mixtures. The purity of some preparations of sugars and sugar derivatives was confirmed by ascending paper chromatography using a two-dimmensional solvent system (water-saturated phenol and *n*-butanol/pyridine/water). The chromatographic papers were cut to form 15 × 15 cm rectangles

[1] Supported by Grant GM 11888 from the National Institutes of Health.

and a baseline was drawn 2 cm from the bottom. The spots were made on the line with lambda pipetes and the papers were stapled together to form a small cylinder. Each paper cylinder was developed by ascending chromatography in a wide-mouth, plastic-stoppered 1 liter bottle which contained 35 ml of solvent.

The chromatograms were allowed to develop until the solvent reached the top of the paper, dried, and the procedure repeated two times. This required 3 hr each time when *n*-butanol/pyridine/water was the solvent, and 1 hr with acetone/water.

The sugars and sugar derivatives were detected first by spraying with *p*-anisidine/ethanol reagent (1 gm *p*-anisidine in 100 ml 70% ethanol), heated 5–10 min at 100–105°C, and then dipped in a 0.1 *M* sodium periodate solution (10 ml 0.1 *M* Na periodate in 100 ml acetone). The chromatograms appeared as spots of different colors on a brownish background.

RESULTS AND DISCUSSION

It is often rather difficult to identify sugars and sugar derivatives on a single chromatogram if they are present as mixtures. Table 1 lists the results obtained with a variety of these compounds after reactions on paper with the *p*-anisidine and sodium periodate reagents. This method was applied to thin-layer chromatography by spraying instead of dipping the reagents over the TLC plates.

Apparently the solvent mixtures employed in paper chromatography cause differences in the colors which develop (Table 1). The uronic acids are readily distinguished from aldonic acids by the color of spots. Aldonic acids are not detected by *p*-anisidine but uronic acids give a brick-red or brown color. After dipping in periodate solution uronic acids keep their brick-red or brown color, which contrasts with the white spots of aldonic acids. It can be used as a method for distinguishing these classes of compounds in paper chromatography, paper electrophoresis, or thin-layer chromatography. Glucosamine and galactosamine can be differentiated from their acetyl derivatives in the same way.

2-Deoxy sugars are very well distinguished from the other carbohydrates tested by their bright yellow spots, which show yellow fluorescence when submited to UV light. Polyols do not react with *p*-anisidine but present white spots on a brownish background after dipping in periodate solution. For reason they can be easily differentiated from all the other carbohydrates tested except certain aldonic acids. This confirms the results of Bean and Porter (14).

Hexoses and pentoses present spots of different colors; the latter show red fluorescence in UV light which provides a convenient way to disting-

TABLE 1

Detection of Sugars and Sugar Derivatives with p-Anisidine and Periodate

Substances	Spot Tests			n-Butanol-Pyridine-Water			Acetone-Water		
	p-Anisidine	Periodate	Sensitivity (µg)	p-Anisidine	Periodate	U V	p-Anisidine	Periodate	U V
Gluconic acid	-	white	1	-	white		-	white	
Glucuronic acid	brick red	brown	1	brick red	brick red		brown	brown	
Galactonic acid	-	white	2	-	white		-	white	
Galacturonic acid	brick red	brown	2	brick red	brick red		brown	brown	
Glucosaminic acid	yellowish	white	1	-	yellowish		-	yellowish	
Glucosamine	light brown	brown	5	brown	brown		yellowish	yellowish	
Galactosamine	light brown	brown	5	brown	brown		yellowish	yellowish	
N-Acetylglucosamine	-	light grey	20	-	greyish		-	yellowish	
N-Acetylgalactosamine	-	light grey	20	-	greyish		-	yellowish	
Glycerol	-	white	2	-	white		-	white	
Erythritol	-	white	2	-	white		-	white	
Arabitol	-	white	1	-	white		-	white	
Xylitol	-	white	1	-	white		-	white	
Ribitol	-	white	1	-	white		-	white	
Fucitol	-	white	1	-	white		-	white	
Dulcitol	-	white	1	-	white		-	white	
Mannitol	-	white	1	-	white		-	white	
Sorbitol	-	white	1	-	white		-	white	
2-Deoxy sorbitol	-	white	5	-	white		-	white	
Inositol	-	grey	20	-	greyish		-	greyish	
Xylose	Yellowish	brown	1	light brown	greenish	red	brick red	yellowish	red
Ribose	Yellowish	yellow	1	light brown	greenish	red	brick red	yellowish	red
Lyxose	yellowish	pale yellow	1	light brown	greenish	red	yellowish	yellow	
Rhamnose	yellowish	brown	2	yellowish	greenish		yellowish	yellowish	
Fucose	yellowish	pale yellow	2	yellowish	yellowish		yellowish	yellowish	
Glucose	yellowish	brown	5	yellowish	yellowish		yellowish	brown	
Galactose	yellowish	brown	1	yellowish	yellowish		yellowish	brown	
Mannose	yellowish	brown	1	yellowish	yellowish		yellowish	brown	
Sorbose	yellowish	brown	1	yellowish	brown		yellowish	brown	
Fructose	yellowish	brown	1	yellowish	pale brown		yellowish	brown	
2-Deoxy-D-glucose	pale yellow	strong yellow	2	yellow	yellow		yellow	yellow	yellow
2-Deoxy-D-galactose	pale yellow	strong yellow	2	yellow	yellow		yellow	yellow	yellow
2-Deoxy-D-ribose	yellow	strong yellow	2	yellow	yellow		yellow	yellow	yellow
Deoxy-1-galactose	pale yellow	yellow	5	yellowish	yellow		yellowish	yellow	
Glucuronolactone	brick red	brown	2	brown	dark brown		brick red	brown	
δ-Gluconolactone	-	yellowish	2	-	white		-	yellowish	
γ-Galactonolactone	-	grey	2	-	white		-	yellowish	
γ-Mannonolactone	-	grey	2	-	white		-	brown	
α-Glucoheptonolactone	-	grey	2	-	white		-	yellowish	

uish them. The method exhibited very high sensitivity to the compounds assayed (1–5 μg) except for *N*-acetylhexosamines and inositol (20 μg).

SUMMARY

A two-reagent system, *p*-anisidine/ethanol followed by sodium periodate/acetone solution, is described for the detection and differentiation of sugars and sugar derivatives by their color reactions. The sensitivity of the method ranges from 1 to 20 μg, depending on the substances assayed. Polyols, sugar acids, 2-deoxy sugars, amino sugars and their acetyl derivatives, pentoses, and hexoses can be identified and characterized by this method.

REFERENCES

1. Heftmann, E. *in* "Chromatography," pp. 506–508. Reinhold, New York, **1961**.
2. Partridge, S. M., and Westall, R. G., *Biochem. J.* **42**, 238 (1948).
3. Hough, L., *Nature* **165**, 400 (1950).
4. Ballou, C., and Anderson, A. B., *J. Am. Chem. Soc.* **75**, 648 (1953).
5. Hirst, E. L., Hough, L., and Jones, J. K. N., *J. Chem. Soc.* **1949**, 928.
6. Jaenicke, L., *Naturwiss.* **39**, 86 (1952).
7. Norris, F. C., and Campbell, J. J. R., *Can. J. Res.* **27C**, 253 (1948).
8. Hough, L., Jones, J. K. N., and Wadman, W. H., *J. Chem. Soc.* **1950**, 1702.
9. Lemieux, R. U., and Bauer, H. F., *Anal. Chem.* **26**, 920 (1954).
10. Wolfrom, M. L., and Miller, J. B., *Anal. Chem.* **28**, 1037 (1956).
11. Gordon, H. T., Thornburg, W., and Werun, L. N., *Anal. Chem.* **28**, 843 (1956).
12. Wanszkiewicz, E. J., *Anal. Chem.* **33**, 252 (1961).
13. Cifonelli, J. A., and Smith, F., *Anal. Chem.* **26**, 1132 (1954).
14. Bean, R. C., and Porter, G. G., *Anal. Chem.* **31**, 1929 (1959).
15. Cerbulis, J., *Anal. Chem.* **27**, 1400 (1955).
16. Cerbulis, J., and Zittle, C. A., *Anal. Chem.* **33**, 1131 (1961).
17. Feingold, D. S., Neufeld, E. F., and Hassid, W. Z., *J. Biol. Chem.* **233**, 783 (1958).
18. Mukherjee, S., and Srivastava, H. C., *Nature* **169**, 330 (1952).
19. Saslaw, L. D., and Waravdekar, V. S., *Arch. Biochem. Biophys.* **90**, 245 (1952).
20. Waravdekar, V. S., *J. Biol. Chem.* **234**, 1945 (1959).
21. Warren, L., *Nature* **186**, 237 (1960).
22. Glegg, R. E., and Eidinger, D., *Anal. Chem.* **26**, 1365 (1954).

ANALYTICAL BIOCHEMISTRY 20, 423–431 (1967)

Direct Spectrophotometric Quantitation of Steroid Chromatograms[1]

1. The Measurement of Corticosteroids

BETTE L. HAMMAN AND MALCOLM M. MARTIN

Department of Pediatrics, The Georgetown University School of Medicine, Washington, D. C. 20007

Received January 26, 1967

In recent years, thin-layer chromatography (TLC) has become recognized as a valuable method for the separation and identification of closely related compounds. The development of a versatile spectrophotometric scanning device (1) has led us to evaluate the many factors involved in direct spectrophotometric quantitation of thin-layer chromatograms. In the past, direct spectrophotometric quantitation of paper chromatograms has been regarded, generally, as inferior to elution methods (2–6). However, the data to be presented suggest that, with the scanning arrangement to be described and careful planimetry, accurate, sensitive, and reproducible direct spectrophotometric measurements can be obtained.

MATERIALS AND METHODS

1. *Instrumentation*

Spectrophotometric measurements were made with the plate scanning attachment to the Aminco-Bowman spectrophotofluorometer developed from the prototype previously published (1). The improved scanner (Fig. 1), situated directly above the spectrophotofluorometer, uses as its light source the beam from the excitation monochromator transmitted via a system of quartz lenses and first surface mirrors. After passing through the TLC plate, the light beam is carried by a flexible fiber optic to the emission monochromator. The stage which holds the chromatographic plate can be positioned manually by means of two calibrated control knobs, which permit lateral adjustment of the plate in two directions at right angles to one another. The instrument scans automatically.

[1] This investigation was supported in part by USPHS Research Grant AM 10910 from the Institute of Arthritis and Metabolic Diseases, National Institutes of Health.

FIG. 1. Photograph of plate scanner mounted above Aminco-Bowman spectrophotofluorometer and connected to X-Y recorder.

In the present studies, the signals generated by the photomultiplier-microphotometer pack were recorded with an Aminco X-Y recorder having a variable time base (full-scale deflection time 1 sec). For absorption-transmission studies, both monochromators of the spectrophotofluorometer were set at the same wavelength.

2. *Preparation of TLC Plates*

The aluminum oxide G and silica gel G used in these studies were obtained from Merck & Co. Slurries prepared in the usual manner were spread with a Warner-Chilcott variable thickness spreader, adjusted to 350 μ. Plates with obviously flawed surfaces were discarded; the others were scanned prior to chromatography to assure a regular film. A variation in transmission over the usable surface of the plate of no more than 10% was considered acceptable.

3. *Chromatography*

A mixture of seven corticosteroid standards (B, E, F, S, THE, THF, THS)[2] was separated on silica gel G by sequential chromatography in a

[2] The following abbreviations and trivial names are used: S = 11-deoxycortisol = 4-pregnen-17α,21-diol-3,20-dione. B = corticosterone = 4-pregnen-11β,21-diol-3,20-

solvent system of chloroform containing 10% ethanol. Three consecutive runs resolved adequately six of the seven compounds; only cortisone and corticosterone failed to separate completely. The plate was air-dried for 15 min before application of the color reagent.

4. *Colorimetric Spray Reagent*

The spray reagent consisted of equal volumes of 1% aqueous blue tetrazolium (BT) and 3 *N* sodium hydroxide in methanol prepared freshly prior to application. Each plate was sprayed twice in a grid fashion until the film became translucent. The chromatogram was then dried thoroughly with a stream of cold air. With this technique and color reagent there was little change in the size of the spots in contrast to the spread encountered with an entirely aqueous BT reagent. Chromatograms were scanned within 5 min of thorough drying, and no later than 30 min after application of the spray reagent.

5. *Scanning*

For quantitation of blue tetrazolium pigments, both monochromators of the Aminco-Bowman were set at 560 mμ. A 0.5 mm slit was used between the light source and the TLC plate. The plate was positioned in the holder and the microphotometer was adjusted to give a reading of 95% transmission on a blank area of the film. The density of the blank area adjacent to the chromatogram was next scanned automatically to establish a baseline. The chromatogram was then carefully aligned manually to ensure that the beam of light would pass through the exact center of each spot before the density of the chromatogram was recorded automatically over that of the baseline. This was necessary when the chromatogram was scanned in the direction of solvent flow. When scanning across the direction of chromatographic development, a blank recording was not required because the area between the spots served as the baseline. A single 17 cm chromatogram required approximately 45 sec to scan. One TLC plate containing eight chromatograms was scanned in both directions in less than 45 min.

6. *Planimetry*

Planimetry was carried out with a Keuffel & Esser planimeter model 4236M. The error of repeated measurements of an area was generally

---

dione. E = cortisone = 4-pregnen-17α,21-diol-3,11,20-trione. THS = tetrahydro-11-deoxycortisol = 5β-pregnan-3α,17α,21-triol-20-one. F = cortisol = 4-pregnen-11β,17α,21-triol-3,20-dione. THE = tetrahydrocortisone = 5β-pregnan-3α,17α,21-triol-11,20-dione. THF = tetrahydrocortisol = 5β-pregnan-3α,11β,21-tetrol-20-one.

less than 3% whether carried out by the same investigator or different investigators.

RESULTS

1. *Transmission of Blank Films*

The variability in transmission of blank silica gel plates prepared in this laboratory was assessed by scrutinizing ten plates selected at random from those acceptable for chromatography. Scanning the central area (approximately four-fifths of the plate's surface excluding a 1.5 cm border at the sides and bottom of the plate and a 5 cm section at the top of the plate) cm by cm showed an average variation in transmission of 1.6% with a maximum variation of 4%, independent of whether the film was scanned in the direction of spread of the adsorbent or at right angles to it. In general, commercially prepared films showed a similar degree of variability when scanned in one direction but a considerably greater variation—up to 15%—when scanned in the other direction. In addition, small pinholes in the surface produced sharp, easily recognizable peaks on the scanning record. Thinner commercial films such as those on plastic or foil backs showed much greater variations in transmission than the 250–350 μ films deposited on glass plates.

2. *Transmission of Sprayed Films*

Single application of the blue tetrazolium reagent to blank silica gel plates, when scanned at 560 mμ, decreased transmission by an average of only 2.5%. Spraying the plate twice in a grid fashion reduced transmission by about 3%. When a sprayed plate was scanned cm by cm and the record compared with that from the unsprayed plate, the difference rarely exceeded 1% and never 1.5%.

3. *Direct Spectrophotometric Quantitation of Steroid Standards*

The accuracy and precision of the instrumental arrangement are illustrated in Figure 2. Five tracings are shown of the chromatogram of a single mixed standard recorded in the direction of chromatographic separation with the pen of the recorder lowered by 1% for each scan to permit comparison. The tracings also reflect the sensitivity of the instrument. Despite the apparent resolution as judged visually, the separation achieved in the solvent system described was nevertheless incomplete between B and E, and THS, F, and THE.

Proportionality in direct spectrophotometric scanning is illustrated by the cross-scan of five standards of compound S ranging in quantity from 0.14 to 1.40 μg (Fig. 3). The same relationship of amount chromato-

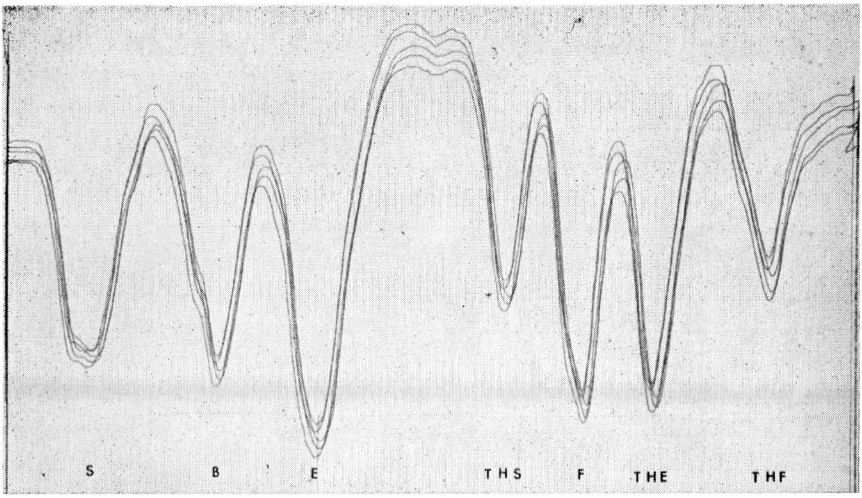

FIG. 2. Multiple scans of chromatogram of a single mixed steroid standard recorded in direction of chromatographic separation. The mixed standard contained 1.4 μg each of S, B, E, THS, F, THE, and THF. In the chromatogram reproduced here, B and E showed better than usual resolution.

graphed to area under each scanning curve applies also to all the other steroid standards examined (Fig. 4).

To test the reproducibility of the direct spectrophotometric scanning procedure, six TLC plates were prepared with six or seven spots of mixed steroid standard per plate in three sets containing 0.7, 1.4, and 3.5 μg respectively of F, E, B, S, THE, THF, and THS per spot. The chromatograms were developed as described, and scanned both in the direction of solvent flow as well as across it. Since, in the particular solvent system

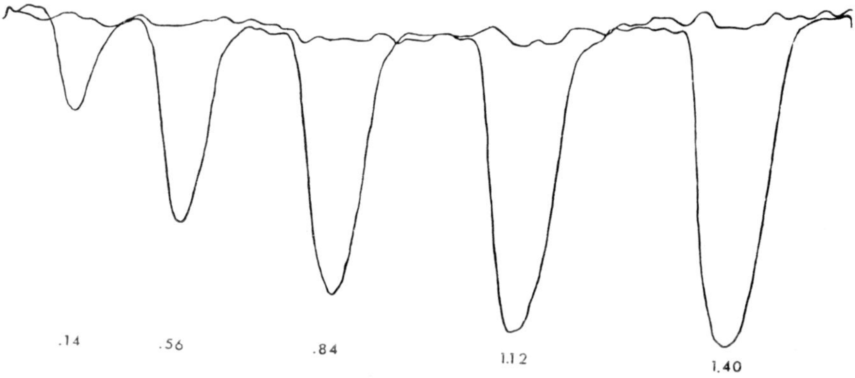

FIG. 3. Cross-scan of compound S in amounts of 0.14 to 1.4 μg, chromatographed out of mixed steroid standards.

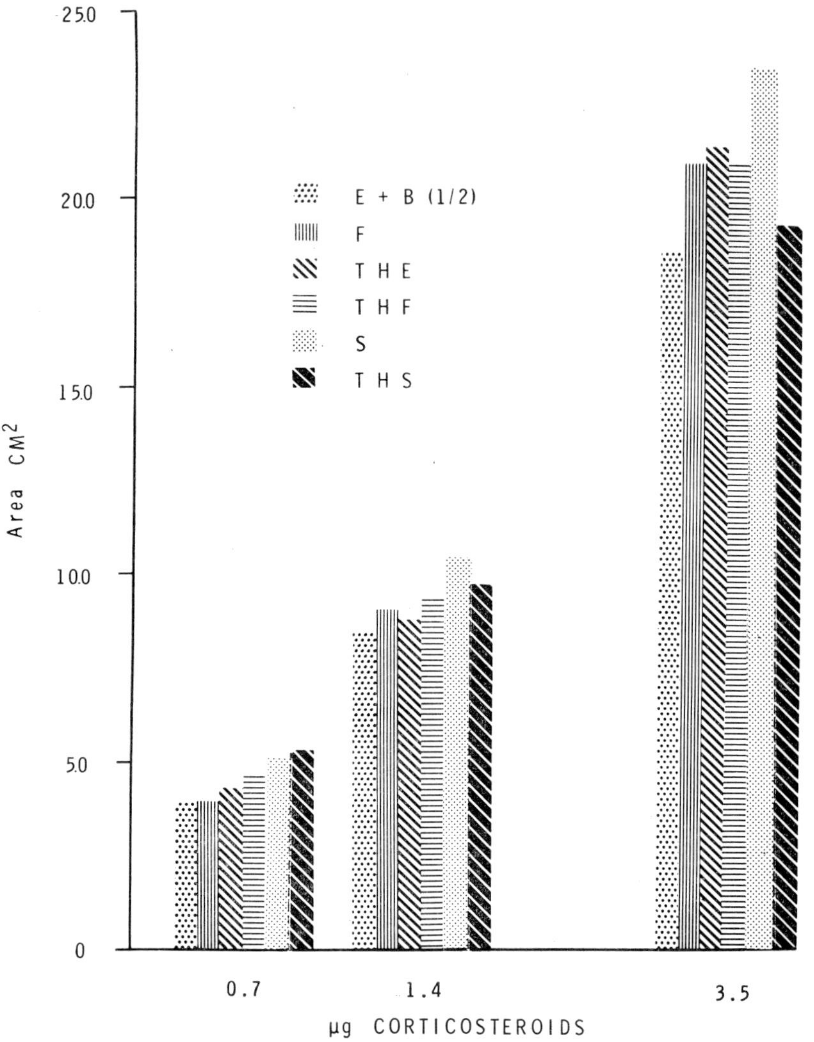

FIG. 4. Histogram illustrating the relationship of area under curve to concentration for six mixed steroid standards chromatographed in three different concentrations.

used the spots were oval, cross-scanning measured the spots along their long axis, which resulted in larger peaks than were recorded in the tracings obtained in the direction of solvent flow. The data presented here are the areas under the peaks of the records obtained by cross-scanning.

The error of direct spectrophotometric quantitation of cortisol chromatographed out of the steroid mixture is of the same order and magnitude for 0.7 μg as for 1.4 and 3.5 μg cortisol independent of whether

TABLE 1
Variation in Quantitation of Identical Cortisol Standards Chromatographed Out of a Mixture of Seven Steroid Compounds

Six plates with six standards each of 0.7, 1.4, and 3.5 μg were developed at different times and scanned across the chromatogram.

	Cortisol		
	0.7 μg	1.4 μg	3.5 μg
Plates	Area of individual peaks in cm² ± S.D.		
1	4.5 ± 0.4	9.1 ± 0.6	20.0 ± 1.3
2	5.7 ± 0.5	8.8 ± 0.5	19.9 ± 1.2
3	4.7 ± 0.5	9.1 ± 1.0	19.8 ± 1.7
4	4.4 ± 0.3	11.6 ± 0.8	20.9 ± 0.7
5	4.6 ± 0.5	9.3 ± 0.9	20.0 ± 1.4
6	4.5 ± 0.5	8.9 ± 0.6	17.7 ± 1.0
Mean ± S.D.	4.7 ± 0.63	9.4 ± 1.37	19.7 ± 1.51

developed on the same or on different plates (Table 1). The reproducibility of quantitation of the various steroid compounds contained in the mixed standard at three different dose levels is shown in Table 2. No attempt was made in this study to completely resolve E and B which were measured together.

TABLE 2
Variability of Direct Spectrophotometric Determination of Six Mixed Steroid Standards Chromatographed in Three Concentrations

		Concentration		
		0.7 μg	1.4 μg	3.5 μg
Compound	No. of obs.	Mean area of peaks in cm² ± S.D.		
S	36	5.1 ± 0.31	10.5 ± 0.65	23.5 ± 0.75
E + B	36	7.9 ± 0.36	17.1 ± 1.65	37.4 ± 2.15
F	36	4.7 ± 0.39	9.4 ± 0.58	20.0 ± 1.33
THS	42	5.2 ± 0.33	9.7 ± 1.12	18.7 ± 1.65
THE	36	4.2 ± 0.11	8.8 ± 0.88	21.3 ± 1.10
THF	42	4.0 ± 0.22	9.1 ± 0.70	21.0 ± 1.65

DISCUSSION

A description of the prototype of the spectrophotometric scanning device for thin-layer chromatograms developed in this laboratory as an accessory to the Aminco-Bowman spectrophotofluorometer has been published (1). Since our original report, American Instrument Company has produced an improved commercial model incorporating quartz lenses which has increased the versatility of the instrument by enabling direct excitation of thin-layer chromatograms in the ultraviolet region of the spectrum. A xenon lamp with DC power supply may not compare with a tungsten lamp and AC power source for densitometric measurements as far as zero drift is concerned; however, thin-layer chromatograms are scanned so rapidly that zero drift amounts to less than 1% per scanning record. It seems justified, therefore, to sacrifice a little baseline stability in densitometric scanning in favor of having one system capable of densitometric as well as fluorescence quantitation.

The regularity of a film of aluminum oxide or silica gel is of the greatest importance in any densitometric study. Uniform thickness is more readily achieved with silica gel than with alumina. In lieu of perfect films, blank values for densitometric studies can best be obtained by scanning an area adjacent to the chromatogram, or else by cross-scanning when a plate blank is provided between the spots. Cross-scanning has the additional advantage of scanning the long axis of an elliptical area, since in most solvent systems spots have an oval shape, which results in larger peaks and greater accuracy in planimetry. Furthermore, this approach permits compounds which are not completely resolved to be quantitated accurately, since the point of maximum density of each individual spot is representative of the pure compound. Minor displacements occur frequently in the development of TLC chromatograms, so that proper alignment prior to automatic scanning is imperative. This applies equally to cross-scanning since considerable variability is encountered also in the distance traveled by identical compounds even on the same plate. The importance of careful alignment for automatic scanning cannot be overemphasized.

Reagents suitable for test tube determinations are seldom concentrated enough to achieve stoichiometric reaction on TLC plates. The surface of the adsorbent film must be thoroughly moistened to assure complete penetration by the reagent, without endangering the integrity of the chromatographic resolution. With aqueous reagents, individual spots had the tendency to spread, which was not the case with concentrated spray reagents in alcoholic solution.

The results suggest that direct spectrophotometric quantitation of BT positive steroids on thin-layer chromatograms is not only feasible but accurate, reproducible, and precise. Compared to standard spectrophotometric methods our technique is approximately ten times more sensitive because of the high concentration of the material to be measured in a small area on the surface of the plate. Quantities as low as 0.1 μg can be identified with considerable accuracy. The limitation is the adequacy of resolution of multicomponent systems on TLC films.

The availability of a sensitive and precise spectrophotometric technique for quantitation of TLC chromatograms will greatly aid studies in many fields. In favor of this approach are its productivity and economy of time and effort. Planimetry was the greatest single source of error as well as the most tedious and time-consuming part of the procedure. Automation of this step by way of integration and printed readout circuits would both reduce error and increase the speed of quantitation.

REFERENCES

1. Hamman, B. L., and Martin, M. M., *Anal. Biochem.* **15,** 305 (1966).
2. Rockland, L. B., and Underwood, J. C., *Anal. Chem.* **28,** 1679 (1956).
3. Bull, H. B., Hahn, J. W., and Baptist, V. H., *J. Am. Chem. Soc.* **71,** 550 (1949).
4. Sendroy, J., and Cecenini, L. P., *Proc. Soc. Exptl. Biol. Med.* **81,** 478 (1952).
5. Block, R. J., *Anal. Chem.* **22,** 1327 (1950).
6. Ingle, R. B., and Minshall, E., *J. Chromatog.* **8,** 369 (1962).

ANALYTICAL BIOCHEMISTRY **20**, 432–438 (1967)

A New Colorimetric Method for Determination of Formiminoglutamic Acid in Urine

U HLA-PE AND AUNG-THAN-BATU

Department of Hematology, Burma Medical Research Institute, 5, Zafar Shah Road, Rangoon, Burma

Received February 8, 1967

Formimino-L-glutamic acid (FIGLU) is an intermediary metabolite in the catabolism of histidine (1–3). The enzymic reaction that converts FIGLU to glutamic acid is tetrahydrofolic acid dependent (4, 5). Excessive FIGLU excretion after oral histidine has been found in folic acid deficiency, and has been used as a useful test for this deficiency in human subjects (6–8).

Several methods have been used to estimate FIGLU in urine, including a microbiological method (9–11), an enzymic method (12–14), high-voltage electrophoresis (15), and ion-exchange chromatography using the Beckman amino acid analyzer (16), but application has been limited to specialized laboratories because of the complexities involved and the elaborate equipment required. Paper chromatography (6, 17) and conventional electrophoresis on cellulose acetate (18) have been introduced as simpler methods, but these are at best semiquantitative. Recently, a colorimetric method employing the alkaline ferricyanide nitroprusside reaction of Tabor and Wyngarden (13) but involving colorimetric readings at different time intervals was reported (19); it seems applicable only to estimation of large quantities of FIGLU in urine. This communication describes a new method using acid activated aluminum oxide adsorption column and the same alkaline ferricyanide nitroprusside color reaction (13).

MATERIALS AND METHODS

Apparatus: Hennessey semimicro adsorption columns[1] with long (5 in.) stems were used for chromatography, and a Coleman Jr. spectrophotometer for absorbancy measurements.

Materials: α-Formimino-L-glutamic acid hemi-barium salt was ob-

[1] Exchange tube, American Association of Analytical Chemists, 6th ed., p. 609 (1945).

tained from Sigma Chemical Co. and aluminum oxide from E. Merck. Urocanic acid, L-histidine monohydrochloride monohydrate, L-ascorbic acid, adenine sulfate, L-arginine, and reduced glutathione were purchased from Nutritional Biochemical Corp. Glass-distilled water and reagent-grade chemicals were used.

Activation of aluminum oxide: Add 1 liter of 1 N HCl to 500 gm of aluminum oxide and shake for 10 min. Decant HCl and wash with 1 liter of distilled water 12 times. Dry at 120°C and store in a stoppered bottle. Chromatographic alumina (acid) type WA-1 (Sigma) and aluminum oxide active (acidic) from Merck were found to be equally good.

Alkaline ferricyanide nitroprusside (AFN) reagent: Dissolve 2 gm each of NaOH, potassium ferricyanide, and sodium nitroprusside in 60 ml of distilled water. Store at 4°C and filter before use. Prepare a fresh solution every week.

Standard FIGLU solutions: 1000 μg/ml (stock)—prepare a solution of sodium salt in 0.6 N HCl after removing barium with sodium sulfite; divide the solution into 2 ml portions and store at —20°C. *Standard FIGLU solution* 200 μg/ml (working)—mix 1 ml of the stock FIGLU solution, 3 ml of water, and 1 ml of 0.5 N NaOH. The solution is stable for at least a week at —20°C.

Histidine administration and collection of urine: Administer L-histidine monohydrochloride monohydrate orally, 0.12 gm/lb of body weight, to the fasting patient and withhold food until 3 hr after the administration of the dose. Collect all the urine passed over 8 hr in a bottle to which has been added 2 ml of 10 N HCl and a few thymol crystals. Measure the urine volume and store an aliquot at —20°C. Urine samples preserved as mentioned above can be stored at room temperature (28°C) for a week or at —20°C for a month without loss of FIGLU content.

Chromatography: Place a piece of glass wool in the tip of the adsorption column and fill the column with activated aluminum oxide to 6 cm depth. A uniformly packed column is easily obtained by tapping the stem of the column. Pipet 2.5 ml of filtered urine (pH 7.5) containing 50–500 μg of FIGLU into the column and allow to drain by gravity into a waste pan. The optimum urine pH for chromatography is between 7 and 8. Wash with 10 ml of distilled water 4 times under low suction at a flow rate of 1–2 ml/min. Elute with 10 ml of saturated sodium tetraborate solution. Discard the first 1 ml of effluent and collect the subsequent 3.5 ml for color development. The first milliliter of the effluent must be discarded in order not only to concentrate the effluent but also to eliminate substances which interfere with the color reaction (Fig. 1).

Development of color: Distribute 1.5 ml of effluent each into two 10 × 75 mm cuvets designated "sample" and "control." Add to the "sample"

0.25 ml each of 2.5 N HCl and NaOH, 0.5 ml distilled water, and 0.5 ml AFN reagent. Read after 60 min on a Coleman spectrophotometer at 485 mμ. Add to the "control" 0.25 ml of 2.5 N NaOH and incubate at room temperature for 60 min to hydrolyze FIGLU. At the end of this time, neutralize by adding 0.25 ml of 2.5 N HCl and proceed as for "sample." Run a separate reagent blank each for the "sample" and "control" using 1.5 ml of saturated sodium tetraborate solution in place of the effluent. Read the tubes containing "samples" and "controls" against their respective blanks. A FIGLU standard of 100 μg in 0.5 ml of water is included in each batch of determinations and processed in the same way as the "sample" urine. The color-developing step should not be delayed, since FIGLU is not stable at alkaline pH. However, it was found that no detectable deterioration of FIGLU in saturated sodium tetraborate solution occurred within 2 hr.

Calculations: Use the following equations when 2.5 ml of urine is employed according to the standard procedure described:

$$\frac{\text{sample OD} - \text{control OD}}{\text{standard OD}} \times 100 \left(\frac{3.5}{2.5 \times 1.5}\right) = \text{FIGLU, } \mu\text{g/ml}$$

$$\text{FIGLU/ml} \times 10^{-3} \times 8 \text{ hr urine volume (ml)} = \text{FIGLU, mg/8 hr}$$

RESULTS AND DISCUSSION

Specificity

Typical elution curves for FIGLU and urinary FIGLU are shown in Figure 1.

It will be seen from Table 1 that, after application of 5 mg each of histidine and urocanic acid to the column, no histidine is present in the effluent. Urocanic acid is present only in small amounts of up to 10% of the quantity applied.

FIGLU, unlike other histidine metabolites, is easily hydrolyzed into glutamic acid by heat (9, 13) or by alkali (9, 13, 18). Histidine and urocanic acid, the two major metabolites appearing in urine after histidine administration (20, 21), are not so hydrolyzed. Therefore, inclusion of an alkali-hydrolyzed urine control in addition to chromatography will eliminate these two metabolites from quantitation by the present method.

It was found that the OD of the alkali-hydrolyzed urine ("control") was a little higher than that of the reagent blank. This showed that the effluent contains a small amount of substances, other than FIGLU, which give the alkaline ferricyanide nitroprusside color reaction. This, then, is another reason for including alkali-hydrolyzed urine control.

It is known that certain reducing substances (22), guanidines, imid-

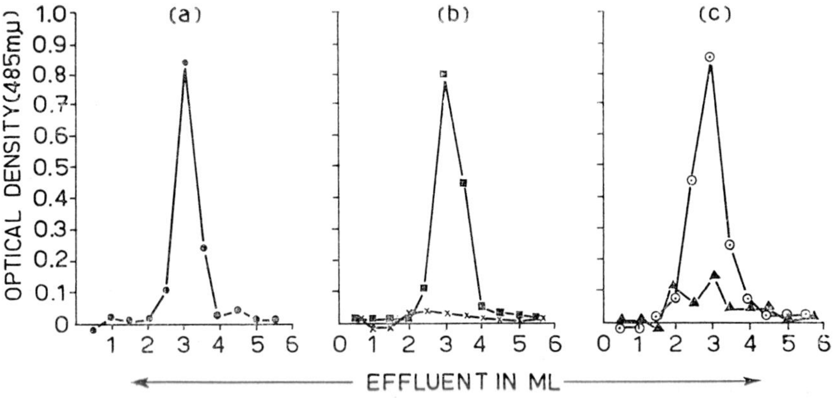

FIG. 1. Elution of FIGLU and urinary FIGLU from an aluminum oxide column: (a) 500 μg FIGLU placed on column (●); (b) 5 ml normal urine placed on column (×) and 5 ml same normal urine plus added 500 μg of FIGLU (■); (c) 5 ml patient's urine placed on column (⊙) and 5 ml same patient's urine after autoclaving for 30 min at 15 lb and pH 8 (▲). Materials applied on column were washed and eluted as described under *Chromatography;* 0.5 ml fractions were collected; 2 ml saturated sodium tetraborate solution and 0.5 ml of AFN reagent were added to each fraction and colorimetric measurements were made after 60 min. Patient's urine was obtained from a folate-deficient megaloblastic patient after oral histidine.

TABLE 1
Test for Interference by Various Substances Known to React with Alkaline Ferricyanide Nitroprusside Reagent

Compound	Amount mg	Compound in urine[a] (OD at 485 mμ)		Compound in water[b]
		Before hydrolysis	After hydrolysis	
α-Formimino-L-glutamic acid	0.75	0.73	0	0.92
L-Histidine·HCl·H_2O	5.0	0	0	2.0
Urocanic acid	5.0	0.23	0.21	1.8
L-Ascorbic acid	2.5	0.005	0	0
L-Arginine	1.0	0	0	1.1
Adenine·SO_4	1.5	0	0	1.1
L-Cystine	10.0	0.08	0.07	0.4
Glutathione (reduced)	5.0	0	0	0
Urine alone		0.28	0.28	

[a] The substances were dissolved in the amount indicated in 5 ml aliquots of normal urine and treated as described under *Chromatography* and *Development of color.* Results have already been corrected for urine OD.

[b] 0.5 ml of the substances in water, in the same concentrations, were directly color developed and the OD values were read. These were then multiplied by four to make them comparable with the values obtained from 1.5 ml of the effluent (the amount of relevant substances present in 1.5 ml of effluent being equivalent to that in 2.1 ml of the original urine before chromatography).

azoles and formimino compounds (19) will react with AFN reagent. Ascorbic acid, reduced glutathione, cysteine, arginine, adenine, urocanic acid, and histidine were added to urine and tested to see whether they produced any interference in the determination of FIGLU by the method being described (Table 1). It may be seen that the combination of chromatography and the alkali-hydrolyzed control almost totally eliminated interference with the test by the above substances.

It was found that urine effluent was colored, especially when 5 ml of urine was used for analysis, but it did not interfere with the determination because a urine control was included; 2 ml only or less need be used in most of the folate deficient cases. An attempt was made to decolorize the urine by charcoal at pH 2 (10). It was found that as much as 20% of FIGLU might be lost due to the procedure.

Recovery

The recovery of FIGLU when 100 μg is added to 5 ml of urine is 85 ± 7.8% S.D. and is 88 ± 10% S.D. on addition of 250 μg. A urine sample obtained after histidine load and containing 19 μg of FIGLU/ml was used for this recovery experiment.

Reproducibility and Sensitivity

In order to test the reproducibility of the method 6 to 11 replicate determinations each were performed on 6 urine samples containing from 18 to 898 μg of FIGLU/ml. The coefficient of variation of the 5 samples with FIGLU concentrations of 28, 37, 72, 182, and 898 μg/ml range from 2.1 to 5.5%. The coefficient of variation of the sample containing 18 μg of FIGLU/ml is 15.5%.

In another experiment 23 to 460 μg of FIGLU was added to 2.5 ml of a urine sample containing no detectable FIGLU and analyzed according to the procedure described above under *Chromatography* and *Development of color*. After chromatography, 1.5 ml aliquots of the effluent contain proportionately 10 to 200 μg of FIGLU. It may be seen from Figure 2 that the absorbancy is proportional to the concentration of FIGLU throughout the range tested. Therefore, FIGLU concentration down to 10 μg/ml may be detected by this method, but the reproducibility at such a low level was not tested. The 15% coefficient of variation obtained at the urinary FIGLU concentration of 18 μg/ml indicates that at this level FIGLU may be detected with a reasonable degree of reliability.

The FIGLU concentration in the urine of 11 healthy males ranged from 0 to 8.7 μg/ml before histidine load. After histidine loading as described under "Materials and Methods" the urinary excretion of FIGLU in 17 healthy males was found to be 24.9 ± 15.1 S.D. μg/ml of urine or 10.2 ±

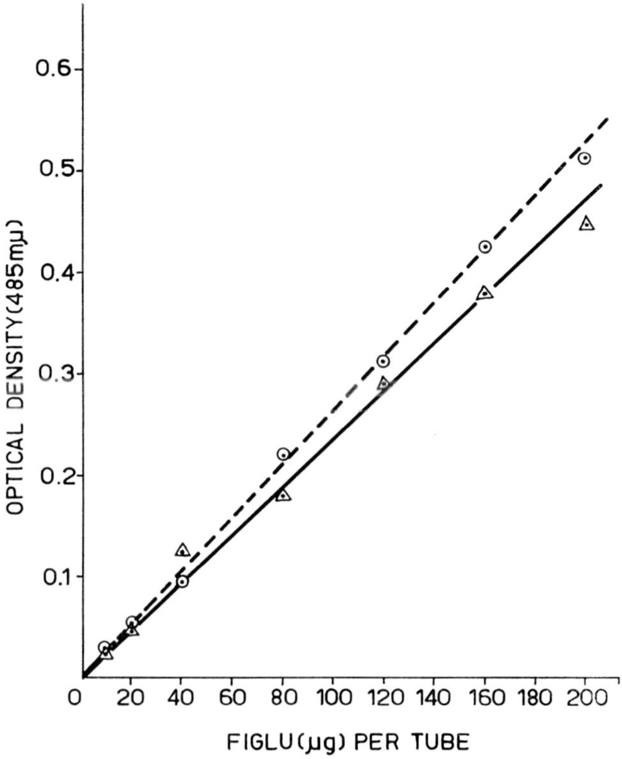

FIG. 2. Optical density obtained for different amounts of FIGLU with AFN reagent: (△) values for FIGLU (23 to 460 μg) added to 2.5 ml urine and after submitting to chromatography; (⊙) values for untreated FIGLU (see text).

8.0 S.D. mg in 8 hr, whereas in 3 megaloblastic patients the FIGLU excretions were 178, 216, and 445 μg/ml or 82, 116, and 156 mg in 8 hr.

SUMMARY

A new method is described for the determination of FIGLU in urine by using an aluminum oxide adsorption column and the alkaline ferricyanide nitroprusside color reaction. The method is simple and has a considerable degree of specificity. It is sensitive enough to measure FIGLU in urine not only of folate-deficient patients but also of normal subjects after histidine administration.

REFERENCES

1. BOREK, B. A., AND WAELSCH, H., *J. Biol. Chem.* **205,** 459 (1953).
2. TABOR, H., AND MEHLER, A. H., *J. Biol. Chem.* **210,** 559 (1954).
3. TABOR, H., SILVERMAN, M., MEHLER, A. H., DAFT, F. S., AND BAUER, H., *J. Am. Chem. Soc.* **75,** 756 (1963).

4. Miller, A., and Waelsch, H. J., *J. Biol. Chem.* **228**, 397 (1957).
5. Tabor, H., and Rabinowitz, J., *J. Am. Chem. Soc.* **78**, 5705 (1956).
6. Luhby, A. L., Cooperman, J. M., and Teller, D. N., *Am. J. Clin. Nutr.* **7**, 397 (1959).
7. Luhby, A. L., Cooperman, J. M., and Teller, D. N., *Proc. Soc. Exptl. Biol.* **101**, 350 (1959).
8. Spray, G. H., and Witts, L. J., *Lancet* **2**, 702 (1959).
9. Silverman, M., Gardiner, R., and Bakerman, H., *J. Biol. Chem.* **194**, 815 (1952).
10. Broquist, H. P., and Luhby, A. L., *Proc. Soc. Exptl. Biol.* **100**, 347 (1959).
11. Davis, R. E., and Onesti, P., *Australian J. Exptl. Biol. Med. Sci.* **38**, 239 (1960).
12. Silverman, M., Gardiner, R. C., and Condit, P. T., *J. Natl. Cancer Inst.* **20**, 71 (1958).
13. Tabor, H., and Wyngarden, L., *J. Clin. Invest.* **37**, 824 (1958).
14. Chanarin, I., and Bennett, M. C., *Brit. Med. J.* **1**, 27 (1962).
15. Knowles, J. P., Prankerd, T. A. J., and Westall, R. G., *Lancet* **2**, 347 (1960).
16. Edozien, J. C., and Modie, J. A., *Lancet* **2**, 1149 (1964).
17. Broquist, H. P., *J. Am. Chem. Soc.* **78**, 6205 (1956).
18. Kohn, J., Mollin, D. L., and Rosenbach, L. M., *J. Clin. Path.* **14**, 345 (1961).
19. Johnstone, J. M., Kemp, J. H., and Hibbard, E. D., *Clin. Chim. Acta* **12**, 440 (1965).
20. Chanarin, I., Rotman, D., and Watson-Williams, E. J., *Lancet* **2**, 1068 (1963).
21. Allen, D. M., and Whitehead, R. G., *Blood* **25**, 283 (1965).
22. Luhby, A. L., and Cooperman, J. M., *in* "Advances in Metabolic Disorders" (R. Levine and R. Luft, eds.), Vol. I, p. 294. Academic Press, New York-London, 1964.
23. Rabinowitz, J. C., and Pricer, W. E., *J. Biol. Chem.* **222**, 537 (1956).

ANALYTICAL BIOCHEMISTRY 20, 439–462 (1967)

A Computer Program for the Calculation of Amino Acid Analysis Data[1]

WESLEY C. STARBUCK, CHARLES M. MAURITZEN,[2] CAROLYN McCLIMANS, AND HARRIS BUSCH

Department of Pharmacology and Biomathematics Research Facility, Baylor University College of Medicine, Houston, Texas 77025

Received February 9, 1967

The automation of amino acid analysis (1) has been one of the more important advances in protein chemistry in the past decade. Within recent years, automatic amino acid analysis has been accelerated (e.g., ref. 2) so that on a properly equipped automatic amino acid analyzer up to 4 complete analyses can be carried out in a working day. Although instrumentation is now available to compute, automatically, the area under the peak as it emerges from the analyzer,[3] the handling of the data to calculate the results can be quite time consuming, especially if the maximum amount of information is to be obtained.

A number of programs have been written for computer computation of amino acid analysis (3–6) but most are either limited in their application and the information that they yield or written for specially designed machines. The present paper describes a program which can be utilized with the hand calculation method (HW[4] method) or an integrator. In addition, the program is written in a common language and can be used on a number of different computers for analysis of amino acids and peptides.

MATERIALS AND METHODS

The computers used were the IBM 7094, 1410, and 360. The program as presented here is written in FORTRAN for the 7094 and 1410, and

[1] This work was supported in part by grants from the U. S. Public Health Service Grants CA 08182, 9589, FR0025902, and FR00254 (Texas Medical Center Common Research Computor Facility), American Cancer Society (P-369), and the Jane Coffin Childs Fund.

[2] Present address: Russell Grimwade School of Biochemistry, University of Melbourne, Parkville, N. 2, Victoria, Australia.

[3] Online integrators for amino acid analyzers are presently available from Infotronics, Inc., Houston, Texas, and Beckman/Spinco, Inc., Palo Alto, California.

can be simply converted to the FORTRAN for the 360. This has been done in the authors' laboratory, but the program presented in this manuscript is for the first two.

Amino Acid Analysis. Amino acid analysis was carried out by a Beckman/Spinco amino acid analyzer accelerated so as to allow one complete analysis every 2.5 hr. The system used for accelerating the amino acid analysis was as follows: the acidic and neutral amino acids were eluted from a column of Biorad Aminex-H beaded resin (batch No. 2719); the buffer used to elute the acidic amino acids was pH 3.25 (1) containing 5% ethanol; standard pH 4.25 buffer (1) was used for the neutral amino acids; the basic amino acids were eluted from a 0.55 × 10 cm column containing Beckman type AA-27 resin (assay number 122084), using the standard pH 5.28 buffer (1). The flow rate of the buffer through these columns was 80 ml/hr.

Proteins were hydrolyzed in constant-boiling hydrochloric acid at 110°C in sealed tubes. Prior to sealing, the tubes were flushed with prepurified nitrogen at least 3 times and then sealed *in vacuo*.

Programs. The programs used are included at the end of the manuscript in an appendix.

USE AND EXPLANATION

Part I. *Computation of Amino Acid Analysis*

These programs, as well as the other programs in this series, accept either integrator or height-width (HW) values. The program provides information on amino acid analyses in several forms and corrects for destruction of amino acids when desired.

Calculation of the Standard Values. The program has been written to average and evaluate one or more standard runs. The computer utilizes the values thus obtained in subsequent runs with protein or peptide hydrolysates.

Table 1 shows the data entry sheet for key punch transmittal for the computation of the standard values. The program for the calculation of this input is Program 1 in the appendix. In the upper left-hand section of Table 1 are the data entry spaces for card A (parameter card) with which the user controls the calculation.

The user has the option of averaging in his previous standard runs or using the current standard only. Spaces 10–12 should indicate this number (right justified).[4] If no previous standard runs are to be averaged with

[4] The following abbreviations are used in this paper: HW, height times width method for calculation of the area under the peaks obtained from the amino acid analyzer (1); "right justified," the term used to indicate that a series of numbers should terminate in the space farthest to the right; ENML, ε-*N*-methyllysine.

the current one, enter zero in space 12. In addition, enter 00 in spaces 22–23 if previous standards are to be averaged or 01 for no previous standard. The number of runs to be averaged refers to the number of standard runs entered in the bottom of Table 1. Any number of standard runs from 1 to 7 can be averaged. Spaces 24–25 are used to indicate whether integrator or manually determined height (H) and width (W) are used.

In the upper right-hand corner of Table 1 are the data entry spaces for card B. Standards run at different concentrations may be averaged in this program. The reference concentration in this program is 10 nmoles (0.01 μmole) of each amino acid. For example, if 50 or 100 nmoles (0.05 or 0.1 μmole) of amino acid standard mixture is analyzed, the user would enter 5 or 10 in the proper spaces (Table 1).

The bottom half of Table 1 shows the key punch transmittal form for the data for integrator values. Table 2 shows the form for HW values. For simplicity, no spaces are used in the program for decimal points. The position of the decimal point is constant and can be indicated by a heavy line between the two columns of figures as in Table 2. For integrators with no 440 printout, proline must be manually calculated and the HW entered. In this case, the decimal point may be treated as with HW input (Table 2).

Table 3 shows the output from the standard program. Column 1 is the average C value for 10 nmoles of each amino acid. Column 2 is the standard deviation for each C value. The values which the computer uses for calculation (column 3) are punched out on cards for use with the other programs. This is the reciprocal of the C value, and also can include previous runs. Column 4 represents the per cent that each standard for each amino acid composes of the total standard amino acids, exclusive of proline and ammonia. Table 4 shows the card order for the program for the computer.

Computation of Amino Acid Composition. The data entry form for computation of amino acid composition is shown in Table 5 and the format for the output from a typical experiment is shown in Table 6. The space in the upper right (Table 5) can be used by the investigator.

In Table 5, spaces 1–10 are for identification, which is printed out at the top of each output page. Enter in spaces 17–22 the known or estimated molecular weight of the protein (do not leave blank). The appropriate number of residues of each amino acid in the protein can be calculated using this value (see Table 6). An amino acid composition can be the average of one or two analyses on a given hydrolysis as indicated in space 25.

When hydrolyzates are made up to a final volume of 1 mg/ml with pH 2.2 buffer, the program calculates per cent of hydrolyzate which is protein. The aliquot corresponding to the number of μl applied to the column of the amino acid analyzer is entered in spaces 37–40.

Although normally 19 amino acids are determined in most proteins, the program allows for the determination of any number above 19 desired, i.e., ϵ-*N*-methyllysine (ENML[4]) in histones. Enter the number of amino acids in spaces 43–44. When more than 19 are determined, a card must be made for each additional one according to the form shown at the bottom of Table 5. The standard value must be in the same form as given in the standard program (Table 3). In the case shown, the value for lysine has been used. In addition, the molecular weight and number of nitrogens must be given or approximated.

The right-hand column in the center of Table 5 is % Off. The program in the example corrected for 7% destruction of threonine, 10% of serine, and 2% of tyrosine, determined the amount of ammonia released, and subtracted this from the ammonia value.

In Table 6 one column in the output is corrected nanomoles of each amino acid obtained by multiplying the standard values times the unknown C value and correcting for destruction. The adjacent columns give the uncorrected molar per cent (number of moles of each amino acid/total moles recovered exclusive of ammonia) corrected molar per cent, weight[5] per cent, the number of amino acid residues in the protein (based on the given molecular weight), nitrogen per cent and C values or average C values entered.

Cards representing the values for corrected molar per cent for each amino acid are programmed to be punched out during the running of the above program. These can be saved and utilized to allow the computer to make tables or histograms to compare various sets of proteins or to average the values obtained. With the use of accelerated systems for amino acid analysis and the computerized computation, the amount of data can become quite large. The use of computer-made tables to compare various sets of proteins is a convenient way of reviewing the data.

Part II. *Calculation of Empirical Composition of Peptides*

This program is designed to calculate the empirical composition of peptides derived from proteolytic digestion of proteins. The program provides information on the corrected nanomoles of each amino acid obtained in

[5] The older forms of expressing results (per cent nitrogen and weight) allow comparison with earlier papers which used these ways of expressing their data. In a similar manner, uncorrected molar per cent allows comparison with data where corrections have not been made for destruction.

the peptide, the ratios of the amino acids to a given amino acid or amino acids, and the per cent yield of the peptides as well as their purity.

The data entry sheet for the peptide program is seen in Table 7 and a typical computer output is seen in Tables 8 and 9. The program for peptides is in the appendix.

The data entry sheet (Table 7) is similar to that described above for amino acid analysis. Hence, only those parts where differences occur for peptides will be discussed. The first is the dilution factor, which is entered in spaces 37–40. The proper use of this factor allows the program to calculate the per cent yield of the peptide (Table 8). The dilution factor is the product of the aliquot of the peptide taken for hydrolysis times the aliquot applied to the amino acid analyzer. In the example shown, 0.2 ml was taken from 1 ml of peptide solution containing in theory 1.8 μmoles of peptide. After hydrolysis, the 0.2 ml aliquot was diluted to 1 ml with pH 2.2 buffer. A 250 μl (0.25 ml) aliquot was applied to the amino acid analyzer. Therefore, the dilution factor would be 20, which represents the dilution of the original sample [5(0.2 ml of 1 ml taken for analysis) × 4(0.25 ml from 1 put on column)]. The computer uses this number in conjunction with the theoretical micromoles of peptide (spaces 49–52) to calculate the theoretical per cent yield of the peptide. The theoretical μmoles of peptide should normally correspond to the number of μmoles of protein hydrolyzed.

The number of peptides allows the program to compute the amount of contamination in a major peptide. In the example given this is a tryptic peptide. Hence, the *C*-terminal amino acids should be either arginine or lysine. The example in Table 7 is a lysine containing peptide with a small amount of an arginine containing peptide, which may be an indication of contamination. The number for the amino acid for the major peptide from the table is entered in spaces 45–46 (in this case it is lysine). Since a small amount of arginine is present, the number for arginine is entered in spaces 47–48. The program calculated the amount of contamination of the lysine peptide by the other peptide(s). 01 entered in columns 43–44 indicates two or more peptides are present.

Table 8 shows the output for this program. The computer gives the ratios of the moles of each amino acid to that of the amino acids named for the major peptide and minor peptide in columns 2 and 3. All amino acids with a ratio of 0.5 or greater to the major amino acid are printed in the part called amino acid one. The rest of the amino acids are compared in a similar manner with amino acid two. The computer determines the molar per cent and the weight per cent that each peptide is of the total peptides as well as the number of mg and μmoles of the peptides.

If there is no contaminating peptide, enter 00 in columns 43–44, Table 7. The calculation will proceed in a similar manner except that only one peptide will be considered (Table 9).

DISCUSSION

The present program has been in use in this laboratory for over one year on machines with both expanded and normal scale recorders, using both integrators and the HW method. It has the advantage that human errors in calculation are very largely avoided, the calculations are accelerated, and added information can be obtained. Analyses of protein hydrolyzates calculated with the computer have been compared with analyses of hydrolyzates of the same proteins calculated by the manual method. The results were virtually identical.

The requirements of many investigators would be different from those of this laboratory. However, the present series of programs may be of general use, since they have been written so that conversion to machines other than the 1410, 7094, or 360 would not be difficult. Further small changes could be made if other investigators should wish to add or subtract different components from a program.

In addition to the programs outlined here, programs have been written and used in this laboratory which can make tables, average amino acid analyses, and calculate the per cent destruction of amino acids from hydrolysis kinetics at 20 to 120 hr. The programs have also been modified to work from cards taken directly from a card punch activated by the integrator of the amino acid analyzer and to work on the Remote Access Systems (RACS) for the IBM 360.

SUMMARY

A program has been written for the computation of the data from amino acid analysis. This program will accept data both from integrators and from the hand calculation method. The program is written in a common language and is divided into two parts so as to convert the analytical data from the amino acid analyzer into several useful forms as desired. The first part calculates amino acid analysis of protein hydrolyzates and the second part calculates the composition of peptides.

REFERENCES

1. Spackman, D. H., Stein, W. H., and Moore, S., *Anal. Chem.* **30,** 1190 (1958).
2. Hubbard, R. W., and Kremen, D. M., *Anal. Biochem.* **12,** 593 (1965).
3. Krichevsky, M. I., Schwartz, J., and Mage, M., *Anal. Biochem.* **12,** 94 (1965).
4. Yonda, A., Filmer, D. L., Pate, H., Alonzo, N., and Hirs, C. H. W., *Anal. Biochem.* **10,** 53 (1965).
5. Graham, G. N., and Scheldrick, D., *Biochem. J.* **96,** 517 (1965).
6. Porter, W. L., and Talley, E. A., *Anal. Chem.* **36,** 1692 (1964).

Appendix

```
                                                                01/20/67
      ACID         -  EFN    SOURCE STATEMENT   -   IFN(S)   -

      DIMENSION  V(19,8), CON(8), OSTAN(19), C(19), SS(19), SD(19),
     1TSTAN(19), STAN(19), NAME(19), PC6(19),DATE(2), H1(19,8), W1(19,8)
    1 FORMAT(6X, A3, I3, I1, A6, A2, 2I2)
    2 FORMAT(F10.6)
      IREAD = 5
      ITAPE = 4
      IPRIN = 6
      READ(IREAD,1) STANO, M, N, DATE, ICODE, NPP                         4
      IF (ICODE) 800,800,900
  800 READ(IREAD,2) (OSTAN(I), I=1,19)                                    11
  900 REWIND ITAPE                                                        18
      WRITE(ITAPE,3)                                                      19
    3 FORMAT(  76HLYS HIS ARG ASP THR SER GLU PRO GLY ALA CY/2CYSAVAL ME
     1T ILEULEU TYR PHE AM   )
      REWIND ITAPE                                                        20
      READ(ITAPE,4) (NAME(I), I=1,19)                                     21
    4 FORMAT (19A4)
      X = N
      IF(NPP)69,80,69
   80 READ(IREAD,81) ((H1(I,J), W1(I,J), J=1,N), I=1,19)                  29
   81 FORMAT(8(F4.0,F3.0))
      DO 82 I = 1,19
      DO 82 J = 1,N
   82 V(I,J) = H1(I,J)*W1(I,J)
      GO TO 72
   69 DO 71 I = 1,19
   71 READ (IREAD,5) (V(I,J), J=1,N)                                      57
    5 FORMAT (8F6.0)
   72 READ(IREAD,6) (CON(J), J=1,N)                                       64
    6 FORMAT (8F2.0)
      WRITE (IPRIN,622)                                                   71
  622 FORMAT (1H1)
      DO 12 J=1,N
      IF (CON(J)- 1.)12,12,13
   13 DO 40 I=1,19
   40 V(I,J) = V(I,J)/CON(J)
   12 CONTINUE
      DO 16 I=1,19
      C(I)= 0.0
      DO 11 J=1,N
   11 C(I) = C(I) + V(I,J)
   16 C(I) = C(I)/X
      Y= M
      DO 21 I= 1,19
      SS(I) =0.0
      DO 20 J=1,N
   20 SS(I)=  SS(I)+ V(I,J)*V(I,J)
      SD(I) =   SQRT((SS(I)- X * C(I)*C(I))/(X-1.))                       119
      TSTAN(I) =10./C(I)
      IF(ICODE)29,29,30
   30 STAN(I) = TSTAN(I)
      GO TO 21
   29 STAN(I) = (Y* OSTAN(I)+ TSTAN(I))/(Y+1.)
   21 CONTINUE
      SUM=0.0
      DO 22 I=1,18
   22 SUM=SUM + STAN(I)
      SUM=SUM-STAN(8)
      DO 23 I=1,19
   23 PC6(I) =(STAN(I)/SUM)* 100.
      WRITE (IPRIN,10) STANO, DATE                                        149
   10 FORMAT (1H ,12HSTANDARD NO., 2X, A3, 6X, 4HDATE, 2X, A6, A2)
      WRITE(IPRIN,7)                                                      151
    7 FORMAT(// ,30X,5HSTAN./5X,4HNAME, 5X, 11HAV. C VALUE, 5X, 4HDEV.,
     17X, 9HNEW STAN., 5X, 7HPERCENT)
      WRITE(IPRIN,8) (NAME(I), C(I), SD(I), STAN(I), PC6(I), I=1,19)      152
    8 FORMAT(1H0, 4X, A4, 6X, F9.2, 5X, F6.2, 4X, F10.6,5X, F6.2)
      WRITE(IPRIN,9) STAN                                                 163
    9 FORMAT(1H$,F10.6)
      WRITE (IPRIN,622)                                                   165
      STOP
      END
```

PROGRAM 1

The program is for the computation of standard value, and as shown is for the 7094 or 1410 computers.

```
      BKBJOB                                                              12/23/67
          MAINP      -  EFN   SOURCE STATEMENT  -  IFN(S)  -

          A BLANK CARD MUST BE INSERTED AT THE END OF THE DATA CARDS
          DIMENSION ANAN(30), PC1(30),PC2(30),GM(30),AMW(30),PC3(30),CTWO(30
         1),PNIT(30),ANIT(30),PC4(30), RE(30),R(9),PCO(30),STAN(30),CONE(30)
         2, C(30), NAME(30), EXNO(2),DATE(2), H1(30), H2(30), W1(30), W2(30)
        1 FORMAT (    A6, A4, 6X, F6.0, A2, I1,A6,A2,1X,A2,F4.0,2I2)
      711 FORMAT(A4, F4.0, F3.0, F4.0, F3.0, F4.3, F10.6, F5.1, F3.0)
      712 FORMAT(A4, 2F6.0, F4.3, F10.6, F5.1, F3.0)
      650 FORMAT ( // 3X, 13HPERCENT YIELD, 11X, F7.2 / 3X, 18HPROTEIN MOLEC
         1. WT., 3X, F8.0)
      100 FORMAT(76HLYS HIS ARG ASP THR SER GLU PRO GLY ALA CY/2CYSAVAL MET
         1ILEULEU TYR PHE AM  )
      101 FORMAT(19A4)
        2 FORMAT(2F6.0, F4.3)
        3 FORMAT(F10.6)
      105 FORMAT(//,24X, 11HUNCORRECTED, 2X, 9HCORRECTED/12X, 9HCORRECTED,
         15X, 8HPERCENTS, 4X, 8HPERCENTS, 2X, 8HPERCENTS, 16X, 7HPERCENT/
         23X, 4HNAME, 5X, 9HNANOMOLES, 6X, 7H(MOLES), 4X, 7H(MOLES),
         34X, 6H(WTS.), 6X,8HRESIDUES, 3X, 8HNITROGEN,6X, 7HC VALUE//)
      106 FORMAT (     3X, A4, 4X, F10.2, 6X, F6.2, 6X, F6.2, 3X, F6.2, 4X,
         1F10.2, 5X, F6.2,4X, F10.2, 4X)
      107 FORMAT( /,  10X, 6HRATIOS/)
      108 FORMAT(1H , 9(/2X, A4, 1H/, A4, 5X,  F8.2)//)
      109 FORMAT(1H , 5X,        19HSUMS(MOLE PERCENTS)//)
      110 FORMAT(1H , 2X, 2(A4,1H,), A4, 7X, F10.2/ 3X, 3(A4, 1H,), A4, 2X,
         1F10.2/ 3X, A4, 1H,, A4, 12X, F10.2/3X, A4, 1H,, A4, 1H-, A4, 7X,
         2F10.2/ 3X, 3(A4, 1H,), A4/ 6X, 2H-(,
         3A4, 1H,,A4,1H),6X,F10.2/ 3X, 2(A4, 1H,), A4/ 6X,2H-(, A4, 1H,, A4,
         41H), 6X, F10.2, 4(/3X, A4, 1H,, A4, 12X, F10.2))
      111 FORMAT(//,  3X, 15HTOTAL NANOGRAMS,  6X,F10.2/3X, 13HRESIDUE TOTAL
         1, 8X, F10.2/)
      112 FORMAT(1H , 2X, 14HEXPERIMENT NO., 2X,A6, A4, 8X, 15HEXPERIMENT DA
         1TE, 2X, A6,A2, 8X, 12HSTANDARD NO., 2X, A2)
      113 FORMAT(1H1)
          AMW(1) = 128.2
          AMW(2) = 137.2
          AMW(3) = 156.2
          AMW(4) = 115.1
          AMW(5) = 101.1
          AMW(6) =  87.1
          AMW(7) = 129.1
          AMW(8) =  97.1
          AMW(9) =  57.1
          AMW(10)=  71.1
          AMW(11)= 102.3
          AMW(12)= 151.2
          AMW(13)=  99.1
          AMW(14)= 131.2
          AMW(15)= 113.2
          AMW(16)= 113.2
          AMW(17)= 163.2
          AMW(18)= 147.2
 4        AMW(19)=  17.0
 5        PNIT(1) = 2.
 6        PNIT(2) = 3.
 7        PNIT(3) = 4.
14        DO 213 I=4,19
      213 PNIT(I)=1.
21        IREAD = 5
          ITAPE = 4
          IPRIN = 6
33        WRITE (IPRIN,113)                                                 11
          REWIND ITAPE                                                      12
          WRITE (ITAPE,100)                                                 13
          REWIND ITAPE                                                      14
          READ(ITAPE,101) (NAME(I),I=1,19)                                  15
          READ (IREAD,3) (STAN(I),I=1,19)                                   22
57    200 READ(IREAD,1) EXNO,PMW,NSTAN,NR,DATE , NS, AL , NPP,N             29
          IF(PMW)500,300,500
65    500 IF(NPP) 201,600,201
72    600 READ (IREAD, 71) (H1(I), W1(I), H2(I), W2(I), PCO(I), I=1,19)     40
       71 FORMAT(F4.0, F3.0, F4.0, F3.0, F4.3     )
          IF(N-19) 507,508,507
```

PROGRAM 2

The program is for computation of data from the amino acid analysis of protein hydrolyzates, and as shown is for the 7094 and 1410 computers.

```
      PKRJOB                                                        12/23/67
         MAINP      -  EFN   SOURCE STATEMENT  -  IFN(S)  -
507 READ(IREAD, 711) (NAME(I), H1(I), W1(I), H2(I), W2(I), PCO(I),
   1STAN(I), AMW(I), PNIT(I), I = 20,N)                                       52
508 DO 68 I = 1,N
    CONE(I) = H1(I) * W1(I)
 68 CTWO(I) = H2(I) * W2(I)
    GO TO 701
201 READ(IREAD,2) (CONE(I), CTWO(I), PCO(I), I=1,19)                          81
    IF(N-19) 506,701,506
506 READ(IREAD,712) (NAME(I), CONE(I), CTWO(I), PCO(I), STAN(I), AMW(I
   1), PNIT(I), I = 20,N)                                                     91
701 IF (NR-1)205,204,205
205 DO 10 I=1,N
 10 C(I) =(CONE(I)+CTWO(I))*.5
    GO TO 206
204 DO 11 I=1,N
 11 C(I)=CONE(I)
206 DO 50 I=1,N
 50 ANAN(I)= C(I)* STAN(I)
    SUM1=0.0
    DO 12 I=1,18
 12 SUM1 =SUM1+ANAN(I)
    IF(N-19)509,510,509
509 DO 511 I=20,N
511 SUM1 = SUM1 + ANAN(I)
510 DO 13 I=1,N
 13 PC1(I)= (ANAN(I)/SUM1)* 100.
    ADD1 = 0.0
    ADD2 = 0.0
    DO 514 I = 1,N
    IF(PCO(I))513,514,513
513 ADD1 = ADD1 + ANAN(I)
    ANAN(I) = ANAN(I)/(1.000-PCO(I))
    ADD2 = ADD2 + ANAN(I)
514 CONTINUE
    ANAN(19) = ANAN(19) - (ADD2-ADD1)
    SUM2=0.0
    DO 14 I=1,18
 14 SUM2 =SUM2 + ANAN(I)
    IF (N-19) 515,516,515
515 DO 517 I = 20,N
517 SUM2 = SUM2 + ANAN(I)
516 DO 15 I=1,N
 15 PC2(I)=(ANAN(I)/SUM2)* 100.
    SUM3=0.0
    DO 20 I=1,18
    GM(I) =ANAN(I)* AMW(I)
 20 SUM3 = SUM3 + GM(I)
    GM(19) = ANAN(19)*AMW(19)
    IF(N-19)999,288,999
999 DO 998 I=20,N
    GM(I) = ANAN(I)*AMW(I)
998 SUM3 = SUM3 + GM(I)
288 DO 28 I=1,N
 28 PC3(I)=(GM(I)/SUM3)* 100.
    TMW = PMW/SUM3
    SUM4 =0.0
    DO 29 I=1,18
    ANIT(I) = ANAN(I)* PNIT(I)
 29 SUM4 = SUM4 + ANIT(I)
    ANIT(19) = ANAN(19)*PNIT(19)
    IF(N-19)997,299,997
997 DO 996 I=20,N
    ANIT(I) = ANAN(I)*PNIT(I)
996 SUM4 = SUM4 + ANIT(I)
299 DO 31 I=1,N
    PC4(I)=(ANIT(I)/SUM4)*100.
 31 RE(I) =  TMW* ANAN(I)
    SUM5= 0.0
    DO 33 I =1,18
 33 SUM5 = SUM5 + RE(I)
    IF(N-19) 518,519,518
518 DO 520 I = 20,N
520 SUM5 = SUM5 + RE(I)
519 R(1) = ANAN(1) / ANAN(3)
    R(2) = ANAN(1) / ANAN(2)
    R(3) = ANAN(1) / ANAN(10)
    R(4) = ANAN(1) / ANAN(4)
    R(5) = ANAN(7) / ANAN(4)
    R(6) = ANAN(6) / ANAN(8)
    R(7) = ANAN(10)/ ANAN(9)
    R(8) = ANAN(17)/ ANAN(18)
```

```
 BKBJOB                                                                  12/23/67
     MAINP      -  EFN   SOURCE STATEMENT  -  IFN(S)  -

     R(9) = ANAN(16)/ ANAN(15)
     SUMB = PC2(1) + PC2(2) + PC2(3)
     SUMC = SUMB +PC2(19)
     SUMA = PC2(7) + PC2(4)
     SUMA1=PC2(7)-PC2(19)  +PC2(4)
     SUMD = SUMC - SUMA
     SUME = SUMB - SUMA
     SUMF = PC2(10) + PC2(9)
     SUMG = PC2(17) + PC2(18)
     SUMH = PC2(16) + PC2(15)
     SUMI = PC2(6) + PC2(8)
     PCY=(SUM3/AL)/10.
     DO 1000 NT=1,2
     WRITE(IPRIN,112) EXNO, DATE, NS                                            283
     WRITE (IPRIN,105)                                                          286
     WRITE (IPRIN,106) (NAME (I), ANAN(I), PC1(I), PC2(I), PC3(I), RE(I
    1), PC4(I),C(I),          I=1,N)                                            287
     WRITE(IPRIN,107)                                                           299
     WRITE (IPRIN,108) NAME(1),NAME(3),R(1), NAME(1), NAME(2), R(2),
    1NAME(1), NAME (10), R(3), NAME(1), NAME(4), R(4),NAME(7),NAME(4),
    2R(5), NAME(6), NAME(8), R(6), NAME(10), NAME(9), R(7), NAME(17),
    3NAME(18), R(8), NAME(16),NAME(15), R(9)                                    300
     WRITE(IPRIN,109)                                                           301
     WRITE(IPRIN,110) NAME(1), NAME(2), NAME(3), SUMB, NAME(1), NAME(2)
    1, NAME(3), NAME(19), SUMC, NAME(7), NAME(4), SUMA, NAME(7), NAME(4
    2), NAME(19), SUMA1, NAME(1), NAME(2
    3), NAME(3), NAME(19), NAME(7), NAME(4), SUMD, NAME(1), NAME(2),
    4NAME(3), NAME(7), NAME(4), SUME, NAME(10), NAME(9), SUMF, NAME(17)
    5, NAME(18), SUMG, NAME(16), NAME(15), SUMH, NAME(6), NAME(8), SUMI         302
     WRITE(IPRIN,111) SUM3, SUM5                                                303
     WRITE (IPRIN, 650) PCY, PMW                                                304
1000 WRITE (IPRIN,113)                                                          305
     WRITE (IPRIN, 675) EXNO, DATE                                              307
 675 FORMAT  ( 1H$, A6, A4, 6X, A6, A2)
     WRITE(IPRIN,676) (PC2(I), I=1,N)                                           310
 676 FORMAT (1H$, F6.2)
     GO TO 200
 300 STOP
     END
```

```
                                                                  01/12/67
      PEP          -  EFN   SOURCE STATEMENT  -  IFN(S)  -

      A BLANK CARD MUST BE INSERTED AT THE END OF THE DATA CARDS
      DIMENSION  RA1(19), RA2(19),IX(19), IY(19), RAONE(19), RATWO(19),
     1GMONE(19),GMTWO(19), ANAN(19), AMW(19), CONE(19), CTWO(19), C(19),
     2RE1(19), RE2(19), STAN(19), NAME(19), EXNO(2), DATE(2), H1(19),
     3H2(19), W1(19), W2(19) ,GM(19), PCO(19),NACID1(19),NACID2(19)
    1 FORMAT (A6,A4,6X, F6.0, 2X, I1,A6,A2,1X,A2, F4.0,4I2, F4.1)
  100 FORMAT(76HLYS HIS ARG ASP THR SER GLU PRO GLY ALA CY/2CYSAVAL MET
     1ILELLEU TYR PHE AM  )
  101 FORMAT(19A4)
  112 FORMAT(1H , 2X, 14HEXPERIMENT NO., 2X,A6, A4, 8X, 15HEXPERIMENT DA
     1TE, 2X, A6,A2, 8X, 12HSTANDARD NO., 2X, A2///)
    2 FORMAT(6X, F6.0)
    3 FORMAT(F10.6)
  113 FORMAT(1H1)
  105 FORMAT(12X,9HCORRECTED, 7X,6HRATIOS,6X,6HRATIOS/ 3X,4HNAME,5X,9HNA
     1NOMOLES,5X, 10H(ACID ONE),2X, 10H(ACID TWO),4X, 7HC VALUE//)
  106 FORMAT(3X,A4,5X,F8.2,6X, F8.3, 4X, F8.3, 3X,F10.2)
  107 FORMAT(///, 18X, 14HAMINO ACID ONE//9X,15HRATIOS ABOVE .5, 9X,
     18HRESIDUES//)
  109 FORMAT(///, 18X, 14HAMINO ACID TWO//9X,15HRATIOS ABOVE .5, 9X,
     18HRESIDUES//)
  110 FORMAT(3X, A4, 5X, F7.2, 15X, F7.0)
  108 FORMAT(///,19X, 10HMICROMOLES,2X, 13HPERCENT YIELD, 2X, 13HMOLAR P
     1ERCENT,2X,11HPERCENT WT.,2X,13HMGMS. PEPTIDE//(3X,A4,1X,7HPEPTIDE,
     22X,F9.2, 7X,F7.2,9X, F7.2, 6X,F7.2,5X, F11.4))
   96 FORMAT(12X, 9HCORRECTED, 7X, 6HRATIOS/3X, 4HNAME, 5X, 9HNANOMOLES,
     15X, 10H(ACID ONE), 4X, 7HC VALUE//)
   97 FORMAT(3X, A4, 5X, F8.2, 6X, F8.3, 3X, F10.2)
   99 FORMAT(///, 19X, 10HMICROMOLES, 2X, 13HPERCENT YIELD, 4X, 11HPERCE
     1NT WT., 6X, 13HMGMS. PEPTIDE//3X, A4,1X, 7HPEPTIDE, 2X, F9.2, 7X,
     2F7.2, 9X, F7.2, 6X, F11.2)
      AMW(1) = 128.2
      AMW(2) = 137.2
      AMW(3) = 156.2
      AMW(4) = 115.1
      AMW(5) = 101.1
      AMW(6) =  87.1
      AMW(7) = 129.1
      AMW(8) =  97.1
      AMW(9) =  57.1
      AMW(10)=  71.1
      AMW(11)= 102.3
      AMW(12)= 151.2
      AMW(13)=  99.1
      AMW(14)= 131.2
      AMW(15)= 113.2
      AMW(16)= 113.2
      AMW(17)= 163.2
      AMW(18)= 147.2
      AMW(19)=  17.0
      IREAD = 5
      ITAPE = 4
      IPRIN = 6
      REWIND ITAPE
      WRITE (ITAPE,100)
      REWIND ITAPE
      READ(ITAPE,101) (NAME(I).I=1,19)
      READ(IREAD,3) (STAN(I), I=1,19)
  200 READ(IREAD,1)EXNO, PMW, NR, DATE, NS, AL, NPP, ICODE, ISUB1, ISUB2
     1, FCON
      IF(AL)500,300,500
  500 IF(NPP) 201,600,201
  600 READ (IREAD, 71) (H1(I), W1(I), H2(I), W2(I), PCO(I), I=1,19)
   71 FORMAT(F4.0, F3.0, F4.0, F3.0, F4.3     )
      DO 68 I = 1, 19
      CONE(I) = H1(I) * W1(I)
   68 CTWO(I) = H2(I) * W2(I)
      GO TO 701
  201 READ(IREAD,2) (CONE(I), I=1,19)
      IF(NR-1)444,333,444
  444 READ(IREAD,2) (CTWO(I), I=1,19)
  333 READ(IREAD,222) (PCO(I), I=1,19)
  222 FORMAT(19F4.3)
```

PROGRAM 3

The program is for computation of data from the amino acid analysis of peptide hydrolyzates, and as shown is for the 7094 and 1410 computers.

```
 7C1 IF (NR-1)205,2C4,205
 205 DC 10 I=1,19
  10 C(I) =(CCNE(I)+CTWO(I))*.5
     GC TO 206
 204 DO 11 I=1,19
  11 C(I)=CCNE(I)
 206 DC 50 I=1,19
  50 ANAN(I)= C(I)* STAN(I)
     ADD1= ANAN(5) + ANAN(6) + ANAN(17)
     ANAN(5) = ANAN(5)/ (1.000 - PCO(5))
     ANAN(6) = ANAN(6)/ (1.000 - PCO(6))
     ANAN(17)= ANAN(17)/(1.000 - PCO(17))
     ADD2 = ANAN(5) + ANAN(6) + ANAN(17)
     ANAN(19) = ANAN(19) -(ADD2 - ADD1)
     SUMX=C.0
     SUM1=0.0
     SUM2=0.0
     SUM3 = 0.0
     SUM4 = 0.0
     K=C.0
     J=C.0
     IF(ICCDE)400,4C1,400
 400 FMIC1 = (ANAN(ISUB1)*AL)/1000.
     FMIC2 = (ANAN(ISUB2)*AL)/1000.
     PCYP1 = (FMIC1/FCON)*10C.
     PCYP2 = (FMIC2/FCON)*100.
     DC 402 I=1,19
     RA1(I)=ANAN(I)/ANAN(ISUB1)
     RA2(I)=ANAN(I)/ANAN(ISUB2)
     IF(RA1(I)-.5)1000,1000,2000
2000 IF(NAME(I) - NAME(ISUB2))3000,1000,3000
3000 J=J+1
     IX(J)=I
     RACNE(J)=RA1(I)
     RE1(J) =RACNE(J)
     NACID1(J) = NAME(I)
     GMCNE(J)= ANAN(I)*AMW(I)
     SUM1= SUM1+ GMONE(J)
     SUM3 = SUM3 + ANAN(I)
     GO TO 402
1000 IF(RA2(I)-.5)4C2,4C2,2001
2001 K=K+1
     IY(K)=I
     RATWO(K) = RA2(I)
     RE2(K) =RATWO(K)
     NACID2(K) = NAME(I)
     GMTWO(K) =ANAN(I)*AMW(I)
     SUM2= SUM2 + GMTWO(K)
     SUM4 = SUM4 + ANAN(I)
 402 CCNTINUE
     SUM=SUM1 +SUM2
     PMG1=SUM1 * AL /1000000.
     PMG2=SUM2 * AL /1000000.
     PCM1= SUM1/SUM
     PCM2= SUM2/SUM
     TPGM= PMG1+PMG2
     PER1=(PMG1/ TPGM) * 100.
     PER2=(PMG2/ TPGM) * 100.
     SUMM = ANAN(ISUB1) + ANAN(ISUB2)
     PCMG1=(ANAN(ISUB1)/SUMM) * 100.
     PCMG2=(ANAN(ISUB2)/SUMM) * 100.
     GC TO 406
 401 FMIC1=(ANAN(ISUB1)*AL)/1000.
     PCYP1=(FMIC1/FCON)*100.
     DC 404 I=1,19
     RA1(I)= ANAN(I)/ANAN(ISUB1)
     GM(I)= ANAN(I)*AMW(I)
     SUMX=SUMX+GM(I)
     IF(RA1(I)-.5)4C4,404,2010
2010 J=J+1
     IX(J)=I
     RACNE(J)=RA1(I)
     RE1(J) =RACNE(J)
     NACID1(J) = NAME(I)
     GMCNE(J)=GM(I)
     SUM1=SUM1+GMONE(J)
 404 CCNTINUE
     PMG1=SUM1*AL   / 1000000.
     SUMX = SUMX * AL / 1000000.
     PER1 = (PMG1/SUMX) * 100.
     GC TO  906
 4C6 WRITE(IPRIN,113)                                                              202
     WRITE(IPRIN,112) EXNO, DATE, NS                                               203
     WRITE(IPRIN,105)                                                              206
     WRITE(IPRIN,106) (NAME(I), ANAN(I), RA1(I),RA2(I),C(I),I=1,19)                207
     WRITE(IPRIN,107)                                                              218
     WRITE(IPRIN, 110)(NACID1(I), RACNE(I), RE1(I), I=1,J)                         219
     WRITE(IPRIN,109)                                                              228
```

```
      WRITE(IPRIN, 110)(NACID2(I), RATWO(I), RE2(I), I=1,K)             229
      WRITE(IPRIN,108)NAME(ISUB1), FMIC1, PCYP1, PCMO1, PEP1, PMG1,
     1NAME(ISUB2), FMIC2, PCYP2, PCMO2, PER2, PMG2                     238
      WRITE(IPRIN,113)                                                  241
      GC TO 200
  906 WRITE(IPRIN,113)                                                  243
      WRITE(IPRIN,112) EXNO, DATE, NS                                   244
      WRITE(IPRIN,96)                                                   247
      WRITE(IPRIN,97) (NAME(I), ANAN(I), RA1(I), C(I), I=1,19)          248
      WRITE(IPRIN,107)                                                  258
      WRITE(IPRIN, 110)(NACID1(I), RAONE(I), RE1(I), I=1,J)             259
      WRITE(IPRIN,99)NAME(ISUB1), FMIC1,PCYP1,       PER1, PMG1         268
      WRITE(IPRIN,113)                                                  270
      GC TO 200
  300 STCP
      ENC
```

TABLE 1

Data Entry Form for Keypunch Transmittal for Calculating Standard Values

The form shown will take integrator data. The computer output of this data is shown in Table 3. For a similar form for utilizing HW data, See Table 2. In this and all subsequent forms, the data have been printed for clarity. However, in actual practice, the data are written in directly from the tape.

CARD A

IDENTIFICATION # B - 2 (7-9)
NO. OF PREVIOUS STANDARDS 0 (10-12)
NO. OF RUNS BELOW TO BE AVERAGED 7 (13)
DATE 8 - 9 - 6 6 (14-21)

AVE. PREV. STANDARDS 0 1 (22-23)
PREPRGM. FOR HW. 0 1 (24-25)
00 Yes 01 No

CARD B

Amount of standard/run No. µl/10

Run #	I		II		III		IV		V		VI		VII	
(columns)	1	2	3	4	5	6	7	8	9	10	11	12	13	14
		5		5		5		5		5		5	1	0

*PLEASE PUNCH THE DATE IN COLUMNS 60-65 OF EACH CARD.
*PLEASE PUNCH CARD SEQUENCE NUMBER IN COLUMNS 69-70 OF EACH CARD.

Amino Acid	Run # I (1–6)	II (7–12)	III (13–18)	IV (19–24)	V (25–30)	VI (31–36)	VII (37–42)
1 LYS	8 3 3 0	8 2 2 5	8 2 6 1	8 3 5 9	8 2 2 9	8 1 7 4	1 6 1 8 3
2 HIS	7 0 0 0	7 1 2 6	7 3 2 0	7 4 0 4	7 1 9 3	7 2 8 9	1 5 2 5 7
3 ARG	7 3 0 0	7 4 6 4	7 5 9 9	7 3 9 0	7 2 7 0	7 5 9 9	1 4 4 7 8
4 ASP	6 3 4 3	6 2 3 8	6 2 9 7	6 1 4 9	6 2 3 2	6 2 3 1	1 2 9 1 8
5 THR	6 7 5 4	6 8 3 6	6 9 2 9	6 8 0 4	6 6 2 7	6 7 6 0	1 3 7 5 9
6 SER	6 3 7 3	6 3 2 7	6 3 9 2	6 3 0 0	6 1 4 1	6 2 2 2	1 2 9 5 7
7 GLU	6 6 4 2	6 8 9 6	6 7 8 5	6 7 8 7	6 7 8 8	6 5 7 4	1 3 1 3 0
8 PRO	4 3 6	4 4 0	4 2 0	4 0 0	4 2 2	4 0 3	7 5 5
9 GLY	6 9 6 8	6 8 8 3	6 9 0 3	6 7 6 0	6 7 0 2	6 9 0 3	1 3 8 7 0
10 ALA	6 5 8 8	6 6 9 3	6 6 6 3	6 5 3 8	6 7 6 0	6 7 3 0	1 3 8 7 3
11 CY/2	3 1 3 1	3 4 9 1	3 2 9 2	3 2 9 1	3 1 7 7	3 1 7 3	6 0 0 0
12 CYSA	6 7 8 9	6 7 7 5	6 7 8 3	6 5 4 0	6 8 0 6	7 0 3 0	1 3 7 5 2
13 VAL	7 0 8 2	7 0 0 1	6 8 1 0	6 7 2 5	6 6 4 3	6 9 5 6	1 3 6 6 6
14 MET	7 0 9 8	7 3 5 7	7 2 1 7	6 9 5 5	6 8 0 5	6 9 5 6	1 3 7 8 1
15 ILEU	7 0 5 9	6 8 2 9	6 8 7 5	6 6 1 6	6 8 5 1	6 7 7 6	1 3 7 7 1
16 LEU	6 7 8 9	6 7 7 5	6 7 8 3	6 5 8 0	6 7 4 3	6 7 1 5	1 3 7 4 6
17 TYR	6 7 2 8	6 5 9 6	6 7 5 7	6 6 9 8	6 5 4 3	6 7 9 2	1 3 7 3 2
18 PHE	6 4 3 8	6 3 7 0	6 6 6 0	6 4 7 1	6 5 4 3	6 4 7 6	1 3 1 7 0

TABLE 2
Data Entry Form for Keypunch Transmittal for Calculating Standard Values from HW Values

CARD A

IDENTIFICATION # H - 1 (7-9)
NO. OF PREVIOUS STANDARDS 3 (10-12)
NO. OF RUNS BELOW TO BE AVERAGED 2 (13)
DATE 1 0 - 1 0 - 6 6 (14-21)

AVE. PREV. STANDARDS 0 0 (22-23)
PREPRGM. FOR HW 0 0 (24-25)
00 Yes 01 No

CARD B

Amount of standard/run No. µl/10

Run #	I		II		III		IV		V		VI		VII	
(columns)	1	2	3	4	5	6	7	8	9	10	11	12	13	14
	2	5	2	5										

*PLEASE PUNCH THE DATE IN COLUMNS 60-65 OF EACH CARD.
*PLEASE PUNCH CARD SEQUENCE NUMBER IN COLUMNS 69-70 OF EACH CARD.

RUN #

AMINO ACID	I H (1-4)	I W (5-7)	II H (8-11)	II W (12-14)	III H (15-18)	III W (19-21)	IV H (22-25)	IV W (26-28)	V H (29-32)	V W (33-35)	VI H (36-39)	VI W (40-42)	VII H (43-46)	VII W (47-49)
1 LYS	550	310	546	325										
2 HIS	368	354	365	350										
3 ARG	241	642	235	663										
4 ASP	532	201	531	200										
5 THR	475	223	470	235										
6 SER	508	220	510	220										
7 GLU	359	320	363	321										
8 PRO	140	322	138	325										
9 GLY	398	348	395	342										
10 ALA	377	365	380	360										
11 CY/2	121	485	120	490										
12 CYSA	303	400	300	415										
13 VAL	512	263	505	270										
14 MET	387	310	391	305										
15 ILEU	330	343	331	340										
16 LEU	303	400	299	411										
17 TYR	208	615	205	610										
18 PHE	198	595	200	595										
19 AM	221	440	212	415										

TABLE 3
A Typical Output from the Computer Showing Computation of Standard Values from the Data in Table 1

STANDARD NO. B-2 DATE 8-9-66

NAME	AV. C VALUE	STAN. DEV.	NEW STAN.	PERCENT
LYS	1648	18	0.00607	4.6
HIS	1456	41	0.00687	5.2
ARG	1482	30	0.00675	5.1
ASP	1256	20	0.00796	6.0
THR	1360	20	0.00736	5.6
SER	1264	22	0.00791	6.0
GLU	1344	25	0.00744	5.6
PRO	83	4	0.12075	91.3
GLY	1373	19	0.00728	5.5
ALA	1340	26	0.00746	5.6
CY/2	644	31	0.01552	11.7
CYSA	1360	29	0.00735	5.6
VAL	1373	31	0.00728	5.5
MET	1408	39	0.00710	5.4
ILEU	1368	27	0.00730	5.5
LEU	1350	18	0.00740	5.6
TYR	1342	22	0.00745	5.6
PHE	1301	19	0.00769	5.8
AM	1201	41	0.00833	6.3

TABLE 4
Card Order for the Programs Described

Program	Standard	Protein	Peptide
1	Job Cards	Job Cards	Job Cards
2	Program	Program	Program
3	Parameter Card (Card A)	Standard Values (19 cards)	Standard Values (19 cards)
4	Previous standard values, if used (19 cards)	Parameter card	Parameter card
5	Data cards (19 cards)	Data cards (19 cards)	Data cards (19 cards)
6	Concentration card (card B)	Card(s) for m extra amino acids (m card(s))	Bland card
7	Blank card	Blank card	End
8	End	End	

TABLE 5

Data Entry Form for Keypunch Transmittal for Calculation of the Amino Acid Analysis of Protein Hydrolyzate

For the computer output of this data see Table 6. Forms for HW data would be identical except for the data portion, which would be like columns 1–14 of Table 2.

EXPERIMENT NO. 2 2 7 F T P 4 3 - 1 (1-10)
EST. MOLECULAR WT. 1 0 0 0 0 0 (17-22)
NUMBER OF ANALYSES 2 (25)
DATE 9 - 6 - 6 6 (26-33)
STANDARD NO. B 5 (35-36)
ALIQUOT (µl) 1 0 0 (37-40)
PREPROGRAM FOR HW. 0 1 (41-42) 00 Yes 01 No
NO. OF AMINO ACIDS 2 0 (43-44)
PLEASE PUNCH EXPERIMENT DATE IN COLUMNS 60-65 OF EACH CARD AND CARD SEQUENCE NUMBER IN COLUMNS 69-70 OF EACH CARD.

For Investigator Only:
Hyd. Tube # 227
Sample Fetal Protein 43-1
Weight 5.89 mg HCl 0.24 ml
Date wgd 9-1-66 Hyd Same
In 4:30 PM Out 12:30 M Temp 110°C
Time 20 H Date opened 9-3
Buffer 5.65 ml pH 2.0
An. #1 Run #1113 AAA# 310
Aliquot 100 µl Date 9-6-66
An. #2 Run #1114 Date ✓
Aliquot 100 µl Checked O.K.

	ANALYSIS #1						ANALYSIS #2						% OFF			
	1	2	3	4	5	6	7	8	9	10	11	12	13	14	15	16
1 LYS			7	7	3	9			7	7	1	2				
2 HIS				6	2	5				6	0	1				
3 ARG			6	3	4	7			6	3	0	1				
4 ASP			2	8	9	7			2	9	6	9				
5 THR			3	6	6	7			3	6	8	0		0	7	0
6 SER			2	4	8	3			2	4	1	9		1	0	0
7 GLU			6	4	8	3			6	4	6	2				
8 PRO				2	1	4				2	0	8				
9 GLY			5	2	2	3			5	2	8	2				
10 ALA			7	2	6	5			7	3	0	3				
11 CY/2					2	0					4	0				
12 CYSA						0						0				
13 VAL			3	1	1	2			3	0	8	8				
14 MET			1	0	3	8			1	1	1	8				
15 ILEU			3	0	9	8			3	1	0	2				
16 LEU			5	4	2	9			5	5	7	0				
17 TYR				5	4	4				5	9	9		0	2	0
18 PHE			1	5	0	3			1	6	0	5				
19 AM			2	3	1	7			2	5	3	4				

EXTRA AMINO ACIDS

Name				An. #1						An. #2						% Off				Stand.										M.W.					# N		
1	2	3	4	5	6	7	8	9	10	11	12	13	14	15	16	17	18	19	20	21	22	23	24	25	26	27	28	29	30	31	32	33	34	35	36	37	38
E	N	M	L				6	4	0				6	2	5				0			0	.	0	0	6	0	6	9	1	6	0	.	2			2

Typical Output from Computer Showing Computation of an Amino Acid Analysis from the Data in Table 5

EXPERIMENT NO. 227FTP43-1 EXPERIMENT DATE 9-6-66 STANDARD NO. B5

NAME	CORRECTED NANOMOLES	UNCORRECTED PERCENTS (MOLES)	CORRECTED PERCENTS (MOLES)	PERCENTS (WTS.)	RESIDUES	PERCENT NITROGEN	C VALUE
LYS	46.89	10.56	10.46	12.26	95.60	14.76	7726
HIS	4.21	0.95	0.94	1.18	8.58	1.99	613
ARG	42.68	9.61	9.52	13.59	87.02	26.87	6324
ASP	23.36	5.26	5.21	5.48	47.63	3.68	2933
THR	29.05	6.09	6.48	5.99	59.24	4.57	3674
SER	21.55	4.37	4.81	3.83	43.94	3.39	2451
GLU	48.16	10.85	10.75	12.68	98.20	7.58	6473
PRO	25.48	5.74	5.68	5.04	51.95	4.01	211
GLY	38.25	8.62	8.54	4.45	78.00	6.02	5253
ALA	54.35	12.24	12.13	7.88	110.81	8.55	7284
CY/2	0.47	0.10	0.10	0.10	0.95	0.07	30
CYSA	0.	0.	0.	0.	0.	0.	0
VAL	22.58	5.09	5.04	4.56	46.04	3.55	3100
MET	7.66	1.72	1.71	2.05	15.61	1.20	1078
ILEU	22.65	5.10	5.05	5.23	46.19	3.57	3100
LEU	40.73	9.18	9.09	9.40	83.05	6.41	5500
TYR	4.34	0.96	0.97	1.45	8.86	0.68	572
PHE	11.94	2.69	2.66	3.58	24.35	1.88	1554
AM	15.92	4.55	3.55	0.55	32.45	2.51	2426
ENML	3.84	0.86	0.86	1.25	7.83	1.21	633

RATIOS

LYS/ARG	1.10
LYS/HIS	11.14
LYS/ALA	0.86
LYS/ASP	2.01
GLU/ASP	2.06
SER/PRO	0.85
ALA/GLY	1.42
TYR/PHE	0.36
LEU/ILEU	1.80

SUMS (MOLE PERCENTS)

LYS,HIS,ARG	20.92	
LYS,HIS,ARG,AM	24.47	
GLU,ASP	15.96	
GLU,ASP -AM	12.41	
LYS,HIS,ARG,AM -(GLU,ASP)	8.52	
LYS,HIS,ARG -(GLU,ASP)	4.97	
ALA,GLY	20.66	
TYR,PHE	3.63	
LEU,ILEU	14.14	
SER,PRO	10.49	
TOTAL NANOGRAMS		49044
RESIDUE TOTAL		914
PERCENT YIELD		49
PROTEIN MOLEC. WT.		100000

TABLE 7

Data Entry Form for Keypunch Transmittal for the Amino Acid Analysis of Peptides

The computer output for this data is shown in Table 8. Forms for HW data would be identical except for the data portion, which would be like columns 1–14 of Table 2.

EXPERIMENT NO. 0 8 - T - G A R (1-10)
NUMBER OF ANALYSIS 1 (25)
DATE 1 2 - 2 7 - 6 6 (26-33)
STANDARD NO. D 3 (35-36)
DILUTION FACTOR 2 0 (37-40)
PREPROGRAM FOR HW. 0 1 (41-42)
00 Yes 01 No
NO. OF PEPTIDES 0 1 (43-44) 00 One 01 Two
AMINO ACID FOR MAJOR PEPTIDE 1 (45-46)
AMINO ACID FOR MINOR PEPTIDE 3 (47-48)
THEORETICAL μMOLES 1 8 (49-52)

Peptide Program:
Hyd. Tube # 8 Protein GAR
Sample TH GAR
*Vlm. 0.2 ml from 1 ml-HCl 0.2
Date msrd Date Hyd 12.15.66
In 4:36 P.M. Out 1:36 P.M. Temp 107.3°
Time 21 h. Date opened 12.19.66
Dried X Titrtd
*Buffer 1.0 ml - pH
C #1 Run No. 1358 AAA No. 371
*Aliquot 0.25 ml from 1 ml
Date Run 12.27.66
C #2 Run No.
*Dilution factor 5 x 4 = 20
Date Run
Checked

		ANALYSIS #1						ANALYSIS #2						% OFF		
	1	2	3	4	5	6	7	8	9	10	11	12	13	14	15	16
1 LYS			9	5	0	0										
2 HIS					1	0										
3 ARG				8	3	0										
4 ASP			5	3	3	0										
5 THR			1	6	6	2								0	7	0
6 SER				8	3	5								1	0	0
7 GLU			2	1	2	6										
8 PRO						0										
9 GLY		1	9	2	5	3										
10 ALA			2	3	7	4										
11 CY/2						0										
12 CYSA						0										
13 VAL		1	5	1	6	7										
14 MET				3	3	5										
15 ILEU			1	5	8	6										
16 LEU			6	3	3	9										
17 TYR						0								0	2	0
18 PHE						0										
19 AM			7	8	3	0										

PLEASE PUNCH EXPERIMENT DATE IN COLUMNS 60-65 OF EACH CARD.
PLEASE PUNCH CARD SEQUENCE NUMBER IN COLUMNS 69-70 OF EACH CARD.

TABLE 8

Typical Output for Computation of an Amino Acid Analysis of a Peptide Hydrolyzate Utilizing the Data Shown in Table 7

EXPERIMENT NO. TR-8-GAR EXPERIMENT DATE 12-27-66 STANDARD NO. D3

NAME	CORRECTED NANOMOLES	RATIOS (ACID ONE)	RATIOS (ACID TWO)	C VALUE
LYS	67.31	1.00	9.87	9500
HIS	0.08	0.00	0.01	10
ARG	6.82	0.10	1.00	830
ASP	68.62	1.02	10.06	5330
THR	21.57	0.32	3.16	1662
SER	11.52	0.17	1.69	835
GLU	26.26	0.39	3.85	2126
PRO	0.	0.	0.	0
GLY	209.20	3.11	30.67	19253
ALA	27.42	0.41	4.02	2374
CY/2	0.	0.	0.	0
CYSA	0.	0.	0.	0
VAL	155.80	2.31	22.84	15167
MET	3.76	0.06	0.55	335
ILEU	18.61	0.28	2.73	1586
LEU	69.37	1.03	10.17	6339
TYR	0.	0.	0.	0
PHE	0.	0.	0.	0
AM	85.17	1.26	12.48	7830

AMINO ACID ONE

	RATIOS ABOVE .5	RESIDUES
LYS	1.00	1.
ASP	1.02	1.
GLY	3.11	3.
VAL	2.31	2.
LEU	1.03	1.
AM	1.27	1.

AMINO ACID TWO

	RATIOS ABOVE .5	RESIDUES
ARG	1.00	1.
THR	3.16	3.
SER	1.69	2.
GLU	3.85	4,
ALA	4.02	4.
MET	0.55	1,
ILEU	2.73	3.

	MICROMOLES	PERCENT YIELD	MOLAR PERCENT	PERCENT WT.	MGMS. PEPTIDE
LYS PEPTIDE	1.35	74.79	90.80	81.36	1.06
ARG PEPTIDE	0.14	7.58	9.20	18.64	0.24

TABLE 9

Typical Output for Computation of an Amino Acid Analysis of a Peptide Hydrolyzate Where Only One Amino Acid Was Named

EXPERIMENT NO. 10-T-GAR EXPERIMENT DATE 12-23-66 STANDARD NO. D3

NAME	CORRECTED NANOMOLES	RATIOS (ACID ONE)	C VALUE
LYS	20.21	1.00	2853
HIS	0.	0.	0
ARG	0.	0.09	225
ASP	3.44	0.17	267
THR	3.12	0.15	240
SER	1.48	0.07	107
GLU	1.85	0.09	150
PRO	0.	0.	0
GLY	22.60	1.11	2080
ALA	0.15	0.01	13
CY/2	0.	0.	0
CYSA	0.	0.	0
VAL	27.14	1.34	2642
MET	0.	0.	0
ILEU	0.	0.	0
LEU	22.87	1.13	2090
TYR	1.56	0.08	145
PHE	0.	0.	0
AM	41.47	2.05	3732

AMINO ACID ONE

	RATIOS ABOVE .5	RESIDUES
LYS	1.00	1.
GLY	1.12	1.
VAL	1.34	1.
LEU	1.13	1.
AM	2.05	2.

	MICROMOLES	PERCENT YIELD	PERCENT WT.	MGMS. PEPTIDE
LYS PEPTIDE	0.30	16.84	85.80	0.15

ANALYTICAL BIOCHEMISTRY 20, 463–465 (1967)

Use of Carbon Disulfide as a Solvent for the Silylation of Submicrogram Amounts of Carboxylic Acids

M. ROWLAND AND S. RIEGELMAN

Department of Pharmaceutical Chemistry, University of California, San Francisco Medical Center, San Francisco, California 94122

Received February 13, 1967

The preparation of the trimethylsilyl (TMS) derivative of carboxylic acids has proved to be a powerful tool in the analysis of these compounds by gas-liquid chromatography. These include aliphatic, aromatic, hydroxy, and phenolic acids (1–6). Normally pyridine is the solvent, while dimethylformamide, dimethylsulfoxide, tetrahydrofuran, dioxane, acetone, chloroform, and the silylation reagent itself have been used. Generally these solvents are acceptable. However, the response of the flame ionization detector (F.I.D.) to these solvents is sufficiently large that, at high instrument sensitivities, 1 μl may result in a full-scale deflection on the recorder lasting for 10 min, and the pen may not return to the baseline for another 10 min. On the other hand, these high sensitivities are necessary when determining submicrogram quantities of acid in biological fluids. Therefore, when determining these small amounts of acid and trying to keep the analysis time within 10 min, the above solvents may not be acceptable. The use of carbon disulfide, to which the response of the F.I.D. is very low, does not appear to have been investigated and is the subject of this paper.

The standard procedure involved the addition of a small amount of the acid to distilled carbon disulfide containing 2% hexamethylidisilazane and 0.1% trimethylchlorosilane. After standing for 30 min, with occasional shaking, 1 μl of the resulting mixture was injected into the chromatograph. A DC-QF 1 column was used and operated isothermally.

It is seen from Figures 1 and 2 that the TMS derivatives of hydroxy, aromatic, and phenolic acids can readily be formed in carbon disulfide and that symmetrical peaks are obtained with the QF-1 column. Also these derivatives appeared to be stable overnight in this solvent. In the case of the steric hindered *o*-phenolic acids (2-hydroxybenzoic acid and

2,5-dihydroxybenzoic acid), two derivative peaks were initially formed (cf. references 1 and 5) which gave one peak on standing overnight. Clear separation from the solvent peak was also achieved even in the measurement of 10–100 nanogram sample injections for which high instrument sensitivity was required. These amounts injected were calculated by preparing stock solutions of some of the acids in carbon disulfide.

We have now successfully applied the formation of the TMS derivative in carbon disulfide to the determination of acetylsalicylic acid in plasma (7). Essentially, the method involves ether extraction of acidified plasma,

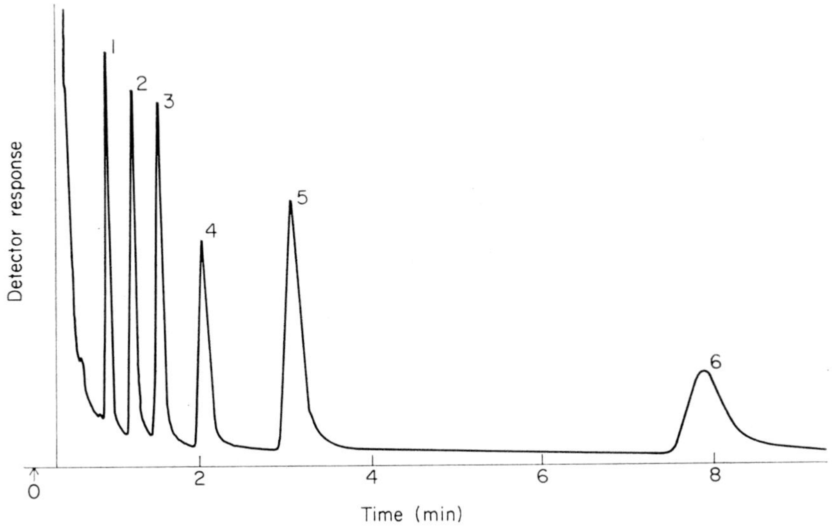

FIG. 1. Chromatogram of the trimethylsilyl derivative of aliphatic and hydroxy acids: (1) malonic acid, (2) fumaric acid, (3) maleic acid, (4) malic acid, (5) tartaric acid, (6) citric acid. F & M 700 gas chromatograph. 7 ft ⅛ in. o.d. stainless-steel column containing 3% DC-QF 1 on Gas-Chrom Q 100/120 mesh. Nitrogen, 40 psi; hydrogen, 16 psi; air, 20 psi. Column temperature 125°. Injection block and detector 200° and 180°, respectively. Range ×1. Attenuation ×32.

concentration of the ether extract, and addition of the TMS reagent in carbon disulfide. On concentrating the carbon disulfide on a water bath at 60°, the remaining small amount of ether is removed. This method allows the determination of less than 1 μg acetylsalicylic acid/ml plasma. At this concentration, although only 5–10 nanograms of the TMS derivative of acetylsalicylic acid is injected into the chromatograph, good separation from the solvent peak is still obtained within a 7 min analysis time.

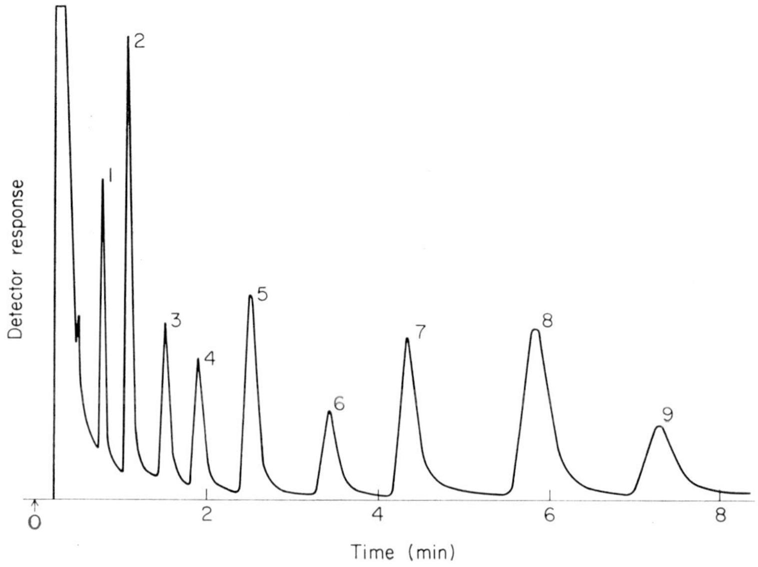

FIG. 2. Chromatogram of the trimethylsilyl derivative of aromatic and phenolic acids: (1) benzoic acid, (2) *m*-toluic acid, (3) mandelic acid, (4) 2-hydroxybenzoic acid, (5) 3-hydroxybenzoic acid; (6) 4-hydroxybenzoic acid, (7) acetylsalicylic acid, (8) 2,5-dihydroxybenzoic acid, (9) isophthalic acid. Column and operating conditions as given for Figure 1. Range ×1. Attenuation ×32.

The application of this general procedure to the determination of other acids in biological fluids is being investigated.

REFERENCES

1. BURKHARD, C. A., *J. Org. Chem.* **22,** 592 (1957).
2. MEHROTRA, R. C., AND PANT, B. C., *J. Indian Chem. Soc.* **40,** 623 (1963).
3. HORII, Z., MAKITA, M., TAKEDA, I., TAMURA, Y., AND OHNISHI, Y., *Chem. Pharm. Bull.* (*Tokyo*) **13,** 636 (1965).
4 HORII, Z., MAKITA, M., AND TAMURA, Y., *Chem. Ind.* (*London*) **1965,** 1494.
5. BLAKLEY, E. R., *Anal. Biochem.* **15,** 355 (1966).
6. DALGLIESH, C. E., HORNING, E. C., HORNING, M. G., KNOX, K. L., AND YARGER, K., *Biochem. J.* **101,** 792 (1966).
7. ROWLAND, M., AND RIEGELMAN, S., *J. Pharm. Sci.* In press.

ANALYTICAL BIOCHEMISTRY 20, 466–476 (1967)

A Method for Semiautomatic Differential Analysis of Urinary Catecholamines[1]

PAUL W. HATHAWAY, LASZLO JAKOI, WILLIAM G. TROYER, JR., AND MORTON D. BOGDONOFF

Department of Medicine, Duke University Medical Center, Durham, North Carolina 27706

Received March 2, 1967

The trihydroxyindole reaction for estimating catecholamines has been applied in a variety of modifications, all of which utilize the oxidation and rearrangement described by Ehrlen (1), Lund (2), Fischer (3), and Harley-Mason (4). The large number of modifications that have been published is evidence that the assay has many variables and unidentified sources of interference (5, 6).

Epinephrine and norepinephrine are isolated by adsorption onto alumina and elution with acid. The eluate is treated with an oxidant to form adrenochrome and noradrenochrome. In the presence of an alkali and a stabilizing agent, rearrangement takes place to form the fluorescent trihydroxyindoles. Ascorbic acid stabilizes both trihydroxyindoles, adrenolutine and noradrenolutine, while thioglycolic acid stabilizes only noradrenolutine, allowing direct measurement of norepinephrine (7, 8). Epinephrine is determined by using ascorbic acid as the stabilizing agent and subtracting the amount of norepinephrine measured in thioglycolic acid. This obviates the need to use a simultaneous equation involving fluorescence values obtained by changing filters or oxidizing twice at a different pH to differentiate norepinephrine from epinephrine.

Merrills, in England, adapted the AutoAnalyzer[2] and a modified Locarte fluorometer[3] to determine norepinephrine and epinephrine of the acid eluate of plasma and tissue. Robinson and Watts (9) established a similar procedure utilizing the AutoAnalyzer and a Turner fluorometer modified by Technicon Instrument Corporation for plasma, tissue, and urine.

[1] This investigation was supported in part by Public Health Service research grants, HE-08571, GM-01238, and in part by the Duke University Center for the Study of Aging (HD00668-09).

[2] Technicon Instruments Corp., Chauncy, New York.

[3] The Locarte Co., Ltd., London, England.

In this paper a method for differential analysis of urinary catecholamines using an AutoAnalyzer with modifications providing increased sensitivity, improved reliability, and greater ease of operation is described in detail. It involves separation of the catecholamines by adsorption onto alumina, adjustment of the alumina eluate to pH 6, and then autoanalysis in which dialysis and oxidation takes place simultaneously. Alkali and a stabilizing agent are automatically added and the resulting fluorescence is measured and recorded.

MATERIALS

Apparatus

An AutoAnalyzer with a Turner fluorometer adapted for use with the AutoAnalyzer by Technicon is used. The lamp in the fluorometer is replaced with a GE F4T5B[4] blue lamp. Two sets of filters are used. With ascorbic acid as the stabilizing agent, the primary is a Wratten 47B,[4] peaking at 436 mμ. The secondary set consists of a Wratten 2A-12[4] sharp cut filter, passing wavelengths longer than 510 mμ in conjunction with a Corning 3-70.[5] With thioglycolic acid as the stabilizing agent the primary filter is an interference narrow band RDUV No. 1,[6] peaking at 400 mμ; the secondary filter is a Corning 3-70, passing wavelengths longer than 490 mμ.

Reagents

Deionized water is used throughout. All chemicals used are of the highest grade available and are not further purified with the exception of Woelm's alumina.

1. *Aluminum oxide* (Woelm Neutral Activity Grade I): Add 100 gm alumina to 500 ml 2 *N* HCl in a 1000 ml Erlenmeyer flask. The mixture is heated at 90–100°C for 45 min with continuous stirring by a mechanical stirrer. After allowing to settle for 5–10 min, the supernate and fines are decanted. The alumina is again suspended in 500 ml 2 *N* HCl, at 70° for 15 min, allowed to settle, and the upper portion decanted as before. The preceding step is repeated once more. The precipitate is washed repeatedly (15–20 times) with water by covering the top of the flask with Parafilm and shaking, allowing to settle, and decanting. When the pH of the supernate is about 4, the precipitate is washed a last time with water. It is slurried into a large evaporation dish, allowed to settle,

[4] Available from Technicon Instruments Corp.
[5] Available from Farrand Optical Co., Inc., Mount Vernon, New York.
[6] Available from Baird Atomic Corp., Cambridge, Massachusetts.

and the water decanted, and then heated for several hours at 250–300°. It is stored in a warm oven to keep dry.

2. *Phosphate buffer:* Add 360 ml 3 *N* NaOH to 600 ml 1 *M* NaH_2PO_4.

3. *Sodium acetate buffer, 0.05 M, pH 6:* Prepared in 20 liter lots and stored in a polyethelene jar. Adjust pH with acetic acid.

4. *Sodium acetate buffer, 0.1 M, pH 6:* Adjust pH with acetic acid.

5. *Potassium ferricyanide, 0.005%* in sodium acetate buffer, 0.05 *M*, pH 6.

6. *Brij 35:*[4] Add 0.75 ml to each liter of sodium acetate buffer, 0.005 *M*, pH 6, working standards, and potassium ferricyanide in sodium acetate buffer. Add 5 ml to each liter of phosphate buffer.

Other reagents include 6 *N* hydrochloric acid, 60% perchloric acid, 0.4 *M* perchloric acid, 2.5 *N* sodium hydroxide, 20% disodium ethylenediaminetetraacetate, 0.5 *M* tris(hydroxymethyl)aminomethane buffer, 0.3 *M* acetic acid, 0.30% ascorbic acid (Sigma), and thioglycolic acid (mercaptoacetic acid, Eastman) 0.95% v/v.

Standards

1. *Epinephrine stock standard, 100 μg free base/ml:* Dissolve 18.2 mg 1-epinephrine bitartrate (Winthrop) in 100 ml 0.01 *N* HCl.

2. *Norepinephrine stock standard, 100 μg free base/ml:* Dissolve 19.9 mg 1-norepinephrine bitartrate monohydrate in 100 ml 0.01 *N* HCl. Both stock standards are stored at 4°C and made fresh every four weeks.

Epinephrine working standard, 0.03 μg/ml, and norepinephrine working standard, 0.07 μg/ml, are made by diluting stock standards with sodium acetate buffer, 0.1 *M*, pH 6.

METHODS

Collection and Preparation of Samples

A 24 hr urine specimen is collected in a glass jug containing 15 ml 6 *N* HCl and kept on ice during the collection period. The total volume is noted and an aliquot is retained for analysis. Care is used in keeping the urine from coming into contact with metal or rubber. If frozen, an acid aliquot is stable for years (10).

After thawing and shaking the aliquot bottle for 3–5 min with a mechanical shaker, 15 ml of urine is pipetted into a 50 ml polypropylene centrifuge tube and 0.6 ml 60% perchloric acid is added. The top is covered with parafilm and the tube shaken for 5 min with a mechanical shaker. It is then spun at 30,000*g* for 10 min at 10°C in a refrigerated centrifuge.

Alumina Adsorption and Elution

Ten ml of the protein free supernate, which contains 9.6 ml urine, is transferred to a 50 ml beaker containing 13 ml 0.4 *M* perchloric acid, 1.0 ml 0.5 *M* tris buffer, and 1.0 ml 20% EDTA. With mechanical stirring the pH is brought near to 8.5 with 2.5 *N* sodium hydorxide, and final adjustment to pH 8.5 with 0.5 *N* sodium hydroxide. Alumina (400 mg) is added and stirring continued for 5 min. The pH is maintained at 8.5 by addition of 0.5 *N* sodium hydroxide. The supernate is poured into a chromatography tube (i.d. 10 mm, length 300 mm, with coarse-porosity fritted disc) into which 400 mg alumina has been previously added. After the supernate has drained, the alumina from the beaker is added as a slurry. The column is washed with at least 100 ml of water, the last drops being forced through with pressure applied at the top of the column.

Elution is carried out by the addition of 0.3 *M* acetic acid; 4 ml is allowed to drain through, followed by two 2 ml aliquots. Ten minutes is allowed for each aliquot added. The last drops are forced through with pressure applied at the top of the column. The eluate is collected in a 12 ml graduated glass centrifuge tube. The eluate is frozen until it is to be assayed with the AutoAnalyzer.

Analysis with the AutoAnalyzer

Using the magnetic stirrer and pH meter the eluate is brought to pH 6 with phosphate buffer, and the final volume recorded. The eluate is centrifuged at 1500 rpm for 10 min to remove the aluminum phosphate. The clear supernate is transferred to an 8.5 ml sample cup.

The schematic of the AutoAnalyzer is shown in Figure 1. The manifold is a modification of the one described by Robinson and Watts (9). The Sampler II is used with a special cam (prepared by removing 2 opposing arms of a 40/hr 2:1 cam) that operates the sampler at 20 samples per hour with a ratio of 1 min in the sample to 2 min in the wash.

The sample is pumped to the upper surface of the type C membrane, while the oxidant is pumped to the lower surface. About 25% of the catecholamines pass through the membrane and are converted into the corresponding chromagens (8). The sodium hydroxide and stabilizing agent are mixed and added to the stream of chromagens. The resulting trihydroxyindoles are delivered to the flow cell of the fluorometer, where fluorescence is recorded.

We have found it necessary to add Brij 35 (a wetting agent which has a low fluorescence) to standards, samples, acetate buffer, and potassium ferricyanide in order to maintain a discrete and consistent bubble pattern, and to prevent surging. By having the concentration equal in all solutions

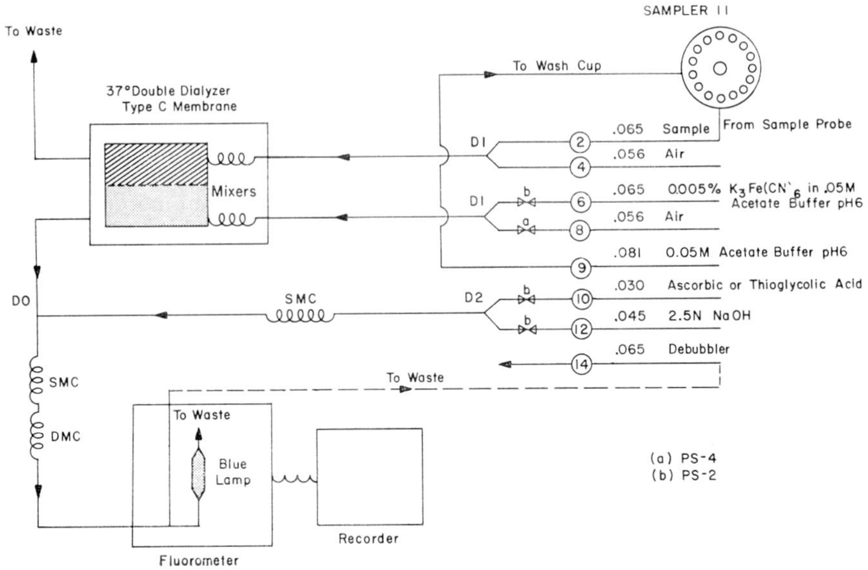

FIG. 1. Schematic for catecholamine AutoAnalyzer showing tubing sizes, reagents, special fittings, and glass fittings. Double dialysis is carried out through a type C membrane.

and samples, the fluorescence of Brij 35 does not measurably interfere with accuracy. It permits a cleaner baseline and consistent reproducible results.

Differentiation of Epinephrine and Norepinephrine

Using the filter combination for ascorbic acid, slit 4, and sensitivity set at full scale, 0.03 μg epinephrine/ml has a net fluorescence of 75 units and 0.07 μg norepinephrine/ml has a net fluorescence of 70 units. Using the filter combination listed for thioglycolic acid, full width slit, and sensitivity set full scale, 0.03 μg epinephrine/ml has a net fluorescence of 0 unit and 0.07 μg norepinephrine/ml has a net fluorescence of 90 units. Epinephrine, 0.03 μg/ml has a fluorescence of 3 units when thioglycolic acid is the stabilizing agent and the first set of filters is used.

The sample is first assayed using slit 4, the sensitivity set at full scale, the appropriate filters, and ascorbic acid as the stabilizing agent. The operation is repeated using full slit, the sensitivity set at full scale, the appropriate filters, and thioglycolic acid as the stabilizing agent. A blank is ascertained as described below.

Standards in duplicate are run at the beginning and at the end of the samples for calibration of fluorescence and to ascertain if sensitivity changes. With the fluorometer turned on 2 hr in advance we have noted no change in sensitivity.

Blanks

In our laboratory we find it necessary to determine blanks, as they vary from urine to urine and when elevated are a clue to the presence of interfering substances. Estimation of catecholamines in urine with a high blank can only be semiquantitative.

A faded blank is determined by replacing the stabilizing agent with water and recording the fluorescence. This is done with full slit and sensitivity set full scale. This blank corresponds to the blank for the thioglycolic acid run. To determine the blank for the ascorbic acid operation multiply the above value by 0.75. Blanks may be obtained by replacing the potassium ferricyanide with 0.1% thioglycolic acid. The values obtained are comparable.

Calculations

Norepinephrine is estimated from the fluorescence with thioglycolic acid from the following formula:

$$\frac{T}{B/N} = \mu\text{g norepinephrine/ml eluate}$$

where T is the fluorescence with thioglycolic acid, corrected for baseline and blank, B is the corrected fluorescence of the norepinephrine standard with thioglycolic acid, and N is the concentration of the norepinephrine standard.

Epinephrine concentration of the eluate is determined from the following equation:

$$\frac{A - N_E(C/N)}{D/E} = \mu\text{g epinephrine/ml eluate}$$

where A is the fluorescence of the eluate with ascorbic acid, corrected for baseline and blank, N_E is norepinephrine in μg/ml eluate, C is the corrected fluorescence of the norepinephrine standard with ascorbic acid, N is the concentration of the norepinephrine standard, D is the corrected fluorescence of the epinephrine standard, and E is the concentration of the epinephrine standard.

The values obtained are multiplied by the recorded volume of the eluate for total epinephrine and norepinephrine per aliquot.

RESULTS

Linearity

Figure 2 illustrates that fluorescence is linear for epinephrine with ascorbic acid as the stabilizing agent and for norepinephrine with ascorbic acid and with thioglycolic acid as the stabilizing agent.

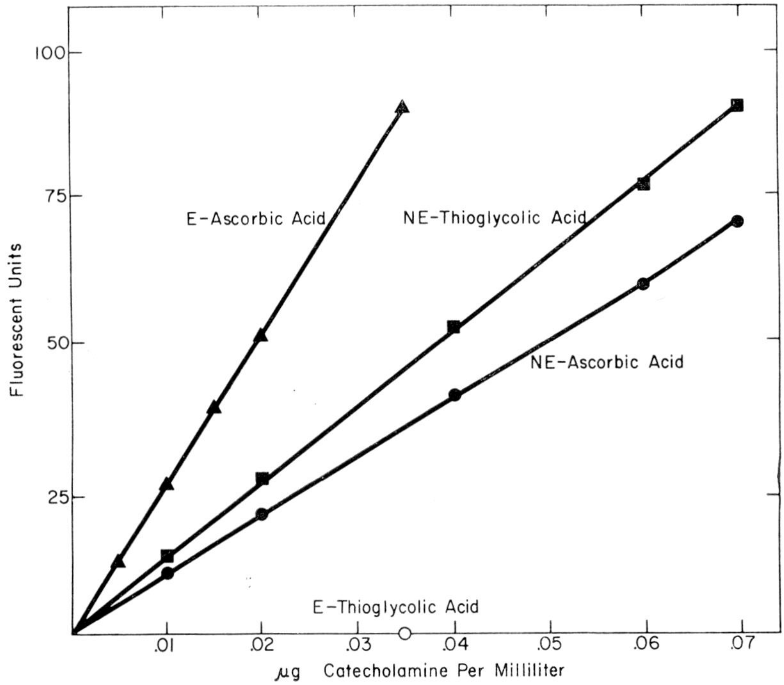

FIG. 2. Linearity of epinephrine (E) and norepinephrine (NE) standards with ascorbic acid and thioglycolic acid as stabilizing agents.

Recovery from Eluate

Recovery of 0.3 μg norepinephrine and 0.15 μg epinephrine added to 10 ml of the alumina eluate ($N = 8$) was 100% for norepinephrine with a range of 98 to 102%, and 96% for epinephrine with a range of 92 to 100%.

Recovery from Urine

Recovery of 0.3 μg norepinephrine and 0.15 μg epinephrine added to 10 ml of urine ($N = 18$) was 89% with a S.D. of 8.9% for norepinephrine with a range of 70 to 103%, and 76% with a S.D. of 6.8% for epinephrine with a range from 63 to 88%.

TABLE 1
Results of Analysis of 24 Hour Urines from 9 Healthy Ambulatory Subjects Analyzed on 3 Successive Days
(expressed as μg/24 hr)

Sex	Day 1		Day 2		Day 3		Mean	
	NE	E	NE	E	NE	E	NE	E
M	17.7	6.4	18.9	5.9	18.6	5.9	18.4	6.1
M	51.8	11.2	49.7	10.5	48.0	9.8	49.8	10.5
M	28.7	8.2	28.8	6.8	23.1	8.5	26.9	7.8
M	32.1	10.2	26.7	11.2	26.0	10.3	28.3	10.6
M	34.0	8.7	30.7	8.4	29.7	8.6	31.5	8.6
F	20.8	7.0	19.2	7.4	18.5	6.9	19.5	7.1
F	26.9	7.5	23.9	7.6	24.2	6.7	25.0	7.3
F	21.4	6.8	25.3	3.6	24.7	3.9	23.8	4.8
F	25.4	4.8	24.9	4.1	22.6	4.7	24.3	4.5
Mean	28.8 ± 10.2	7.9 ± 2.0	27.6 ± 9.2	7.3 ± 2.6	26.2 ± 8.9	7.3 ± 2.2	27.5 ± 9.3	7.5 ± 2.2

Reproducibility

A single urine was divided into 10 equal aliquots and each was carried through the entire procedure. The mean was 23.0 μg/24 hr with a S.D. of 0.66 μg for norepinephrine with a range of 23.3 to 24.8 μg. The mean was 10.7 μg/24 hr with a S.D. of 0.49 μg for epinephrine with a range of 9.8 to 11.3 μg.

Normal Values and Day-to-Day Repeatability

Table 1 shows the results of analysis, uncorrected for recovery, of 9 different 24 hr urine collections from healthy ambulatory subjects, the mean age being 30.6 years (22–43 years). There were 5 men and 4 women. The urines were divided into three equal aliquots and carried through the entire procedure on three different days. The table shows the day-to-day repeatability of this method.

Total creatinine was determined for all urines. If catecholamines are expressed as μg/24 hr, men have a higher mean than women: 31.0 μg norepinephrine and 8.7 μg epinephrine per 24 hr for men compared to 23.2 μg norepinephrine and 5.9 μg epinephrine per 24 hr for women. When expressed as μg/mg creatinine there is little difference: 0.021 μg norepinephrine and 0.0059 μg epinephrine per mg creatinine for men and 0.023 μg norepinephrine and 0.0058 μg epinephrine per mg creatinine for women.

The normal values reported here are comparable to those of other workers. Crout (10) reported an excretion of 30.0 ± 13 μg norepinephrine per 24 hr and 5.6 ± 3.1 μg epinephrine per 24 hr for hospitalized ambulatory patients. Robinson and Watts (9) reported 24.9 ± 4.6 μg norepinephrine per 24 hr and 6.7 ± 1.0 μg epinephrine per 24 hr as normal values.

DISCUSSION

Using available equipment we have been able to measure urinary catecholamines with a high degree of accuracy and facility. The advantages of the AutoAnalyzer and the significance of the use of thioglycolic acid have been discussed elsewhere (7–9).

We have found that an increase in sensitivity is possible by not diluting the sample stream. Precision is improved when Brij 35 is present in equal concentration in the sample, oxidant, acetate buffer wash, and working standards.

Determining blanks leads to greater accuracy and serves as a warning for urines that can be assayed only semiquantitatively. It should be pointed out that certain fluorescent drugs such as tetracyclines, quinine, and quinidine may interfere with catecholamine assay in urine. Such interferences are, however, detectable by high sample blanks, but in other samples no obvious cause for elevated blanks has been found. Urines with high blanks have shown markedly reduced recoveries as low as 0% for norepinephrine when thioglycolic acid is used as the stabilizing agent. These urines have blanks in the range of 30 to 40 fluorescent units and are higher than the fluorescence of the sample when thioglycolic acid is used as the stabilizing agent. With ascorbic acid as the stabilizing agent the recovery of known amounts of epinephrine and norepinephrine in urines with these very high blanks is 40–50%. In diagnosis of pheochromocytoma, a high reading with ascorbic acid would be suggestive, although no specific values could be given due to the blank being higher than the sample when run with thioglycolic acid as the stabilizing agent. We have not attempted further purification to reduce blanks in these urines.

Precision is enhanced by the use of two sets of filters, one of which abolishes the fluorescence of epinephrine when thioglycolic acid is the stabilizing agent.

The use of the modified cam on the Sampler II and the use of 8.5 ml sampler cups simplifies the operation by obviating the need for cups with water between samples and the need to refill the cups for each step of the determination.

Frequent changing of the dialyzing membrane is necessary. With continued use of the same membrane we have noted an increasing disparity between fluorescence of standards and samples, the standards maintaining their usual fluorescence while the fluorescence of the samples gradually decreases. This is demonstrated by Table 1, which shows a gradual decline of the means of days 1, 2, and 3 during which time the membrane was not changed. A change of the membrane is found to correct this disparity.

Two laboratory technicians who also carry out other duties are able to assay about 100 or more urines per week. In one day's operation 32 eluates can be processed easily.

This method is well suited for clinical research demanding numerous determinations and a high degree of precision.

SUMMARY

A semiautomatic method for analysis of urinary catecholamines by the trihydroxyindole reaction utilizing an AutoAnalyzer is described in detail with modifications providing precision and ease of operation. Recovery of norepinephrine is $89 \pm 8.9\%$; of epinephrine $76 \pm 6.8\%$. Values for healthy ambulatory subjects are 27.5 ± 9.3 μg norepinephrine and 7.5 ± 2.2 μg epinephrine per 24 hr. Data regarding linearity, reproducibility, and repeatability are given.

ACKNOWLEDGMENTS

The positive criticism of Dr. Norman Kirshner during preliminary experiments and during the preparation of the manuscript is gratefully acknowledged. We wish to thank Miss Suzan Ferguson and Mrs. Janice Patterson for typing this manuscript.

ADDENDUM

Since preparation of this manuscript it has come to our attention that the Type B-3(A) filter (primary filter for the thioglycolic acid operation) is made several ways, most of which are not suitable. Baird-Atomic, Inc. is now aware of the specific requirements for the filter and will provide the proper filter if the author's name and procedure is specified. Manufacturer's specifications: Type B-3(A), Peak center of 395–410 mμ, Min. transmission at 455 mμ, Block to 690 mμ, Make to provide maximum transmission, Size 2 × 2 in.

REFERENCES

1. Ehrlen, I., ii, *Farm. Revy* **47,** 242 (1948).
2. Lund, A., *Acta Pharmacol. Toxicol.* **5,** 75, 121 (1949).
3. Fischer, P., *Bull. Soc. Chim. Belges* **58,** 205 (1949).
4. Harley-Mason, J., *J. Chem. Soc.* **1950,** 1276.
5. Udenfriend, S., *in* "Fluorescence Assay in Biology and Medicine," p. 141 Academic Press, New York, 1962.
6. Anton, A., and Sayre, D., *J. Pharmacol. Exptl. Ther.* **138,** 360 (1962).
7. Merrills, R., *Nature* **193,** 988 (1962).
8. Merrills, R., *Anal. Biochem.* **6,** 272 (1963).
9. Robinson, R., and Watts, D., *Clin. Chem.* **11,** 986 (1965).
10. Crout, J., *in* "Standard Methods of Clinical Chemistry" (D. Seligson, ed.), Vol. III, p. 62. Academic Press, New York, 1961.

ANALYTICAL BIOCHEMISTRY 20, 477–483 (1967)

Ligand-Exchange Chromatography of Nucleotides, Nucleosides, and Nucleic Acid Bases[1]

GERALD GOLDSTEIN

Analytical Chemistry Division, Oak Ridge National Laboratory, Oak Ridge, Tennessee 37830

Received March 6, 1967

Ligand exchange is a process, first described by Helfferich (1, 2), in which a cation-exchange resin is loaded with a metal ion, usually a transition metal ion, that is capable of forming complexes. Even when attached to the resin, the metal ion retains its ability to coordinate ligands so that complexing agents can be sorbed on the column and then eluted by displacement with another ligand. Separations occur because of differences in the stabilities of the metal-ligand complexes. Previous work in ligand-exchange chromatography has dealt mainly with separations of amines by elution with ammonia. Helfferich (3) employed a nickel-loaded carboxylic acid resin, and Walton and co-workers (4–7) have studied the properties of nickel-loaded resins of various types. A copper-loaded chelating resin has recently been used to collect free amino acids from sea water (8).

The chelating resin is a styrene-divinylbenzene copolymer to which iminodiacetate functional groups are attached. This resin is extremely selective for divalent metal ions, particularly transition metal ions, which are much more strongly bound to the chelating resin than to monofunctional cation exchangers. Consequently there is little tendency for copper to be displaced from the resin.

We show here that ligand-exchange chromatography on a copper-loaded chelating resin is an extremely useful technique for the rapid separation of nucleic acid components.

MATERIALS AND METHODS

Chemicals. Most chemicals were purchased from P-L Biochemicals, Inc., and Sigma Chemical Company. Chelex 100 resin, 200-400 mesh, came from Bio-Rad Laboratories.

[1] Research sponsored by the U. S. Atomic Energy Commission under contract with the National Institutes of Health and Union Carbide Corporation.

Column Preparation. The Chelex 100 resin was treated with 1*M* $CuCl_2$ overnight to convert it into the copper form. Excess $CuCl_2$ was removed by repeated washing with water, and the resin allowed to swell in 1*N* ammonia overnight. A small amount ($\sim$ 1 cm) of uncomplexed resin was poured into the bottom of the column to remove any copper that might bleed from the complexed resin; then a column, usually 35 to 45×0.9 cm, was poured from a slurry of the copper-loaded resin without any special precautions. A circle of glass-fiber paper was placed on top of the column. The column was equilibrated with the eluting agent for several hours.

Column Operation. Samples were placed on the column with micropipets. The eluting agent was pumped (Beckman Accu-Flo Pump) at about 0.75 ml/min (1.2 ml/cm^2/min) at room temperature. The ultraviolet absorption of the effluent was monitored with a Beckman model DB-G spectrophotometer with a 1 cm Oak Ridge Flow Cell (Pyrocell Manufacturing Company), and recorded with a Leeds and Northrup Speedomax W multipoint recorder. A log-to-linear converter was constructed so that absorbance could be recorded linearly.

RESULTS

Nucleotides. Both the 5′- and 2′(3′)-nucleotides are di- or trivalent anions under the conditions normally employed and are not retained on the column. They are washed from the column with water and appear in a sharp band at breakthrough volume.

Nucleosides. Ligand-exchange chromatography appears to be most useful for nucleoside separations. In general, weakly basic nucleosides

TABLE 1
Retention Volumes of Weakly Basic Nucleosides[a]

Nucleoside	Peak		Corrected retention volume[b]
	Time, min	Vol., ml	V'_R, ml
Nucleotides	20.0	15.4	—
Xanthosine	22.5	17.3	1.9
5-Bromouridine	27.5	21.2	5.8
5-Iodouridine	30.5	23.5	8.1
Uridine	31.0	23.9	8.5
Pseudouridine	31.5	24.2	8.8
5-Methyluridine	36.0	27.7	12.3
Thymidine	37.0	28.5	13.1
Dihydrouridine	39.5	30.4	15.0

[a] 43×0.9 cm column; flow rate, 0.77 ml/min; elution with water.
[b] Corrected retention volume = total retention volume minus void volume.

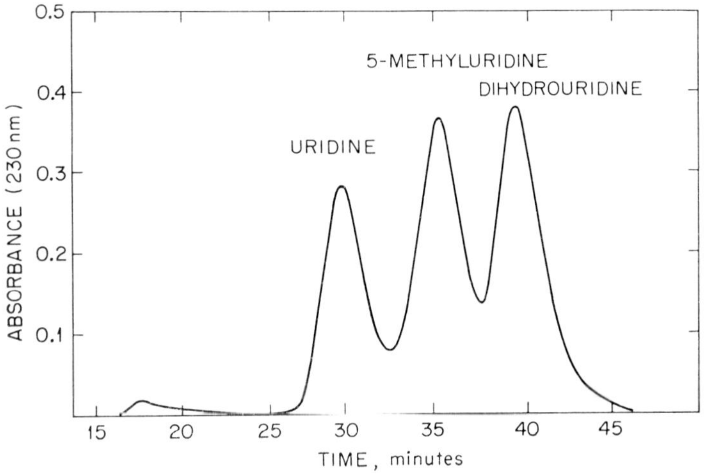

FIG. 1. Separation of three uridine derivatives on a copper-loaded Chelex 100 column. Conditions same as in Table 1.

such as uridine, xanthosine, and their derivatives are only weakly retained by the column, but can be separated by elution with water. Retention volumes are listed in Table 1 and a typical chromatogram showing the separation of three uridine derivatives is shown in Figure 1.

The more basic nucleosides are retained more strongly on the column and cannot be eluted with water but can be displaced by ammonia; 1

TABLE 2
Retention Volumes of More Strongly Basic Nucleosides[a]

Nucleoside	Peak: Time, min	Peak: Vol., ml	Corrected retention volume V'_R, ml
Nucleotides	13.0	10.0	—
7-Methylguanosine[b]	14.0	10.8	0.8
Inosine	15.5	11.9	1.9
Guanosine	16.5	12.6	2.6
1-Methylguanosine	23.0	17.7	7.7
1-Methylinosine	26.5	20.4	10.4
Cytidine	32.0	24.6	14.6
3-Methylcytidine	33.0	25.4	15.4
1-Methyladenosine	41.0	31.6	21.6
Adenosine	46.0	35.4	25.4
N_6-Methyladenosine	52.5	40.4	30.4
N_6-Dimethyladenosine	76.5	58.9	48.9

[a] 33 × 0.9 cm column; flow rate, 0.77 ml/min; 1 N NH_4OH elution.
[b] Decomposition product.

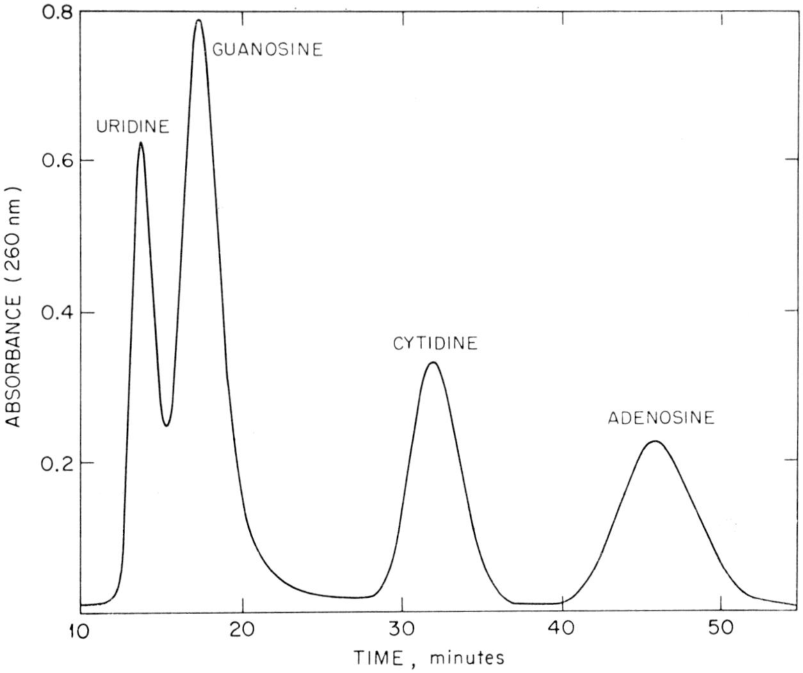

FIG. 2. Separation of uridine, guanosine, cytidine, and adenosine. Conditions same as in Table 2.

N NH_4OH is a convenient eluting agent. Retention volumes are listed in Table 2 and some of the separations possible are shown in Figures 2, 3, and 4.

Bases. The bases are more strongly retained on the column than the

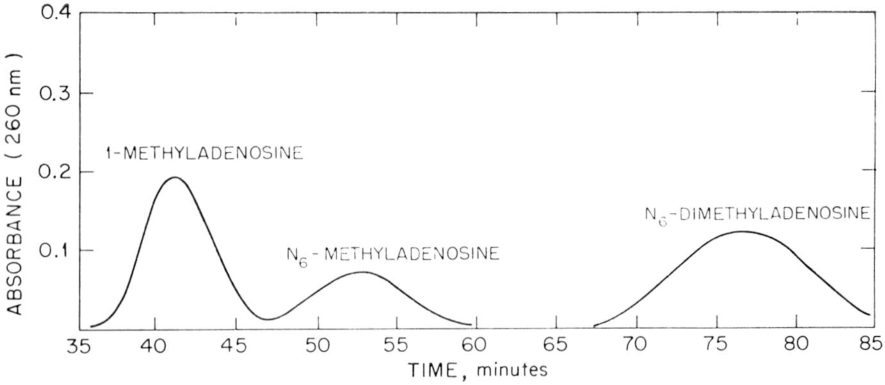

FIG. 3. Separation of methylated adenosine derivatives. Conditions same as in Table 2.

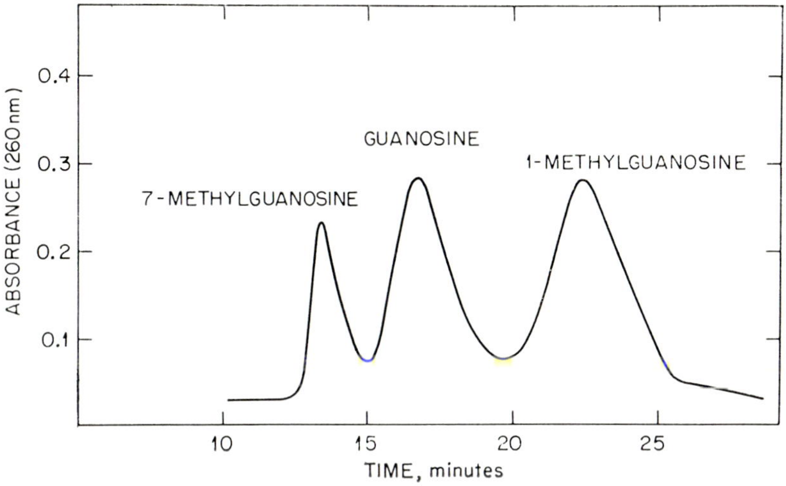

FIG. 4. Separation of guanosine and methylated guanosine derivatives. Conditions same as in Table 2.

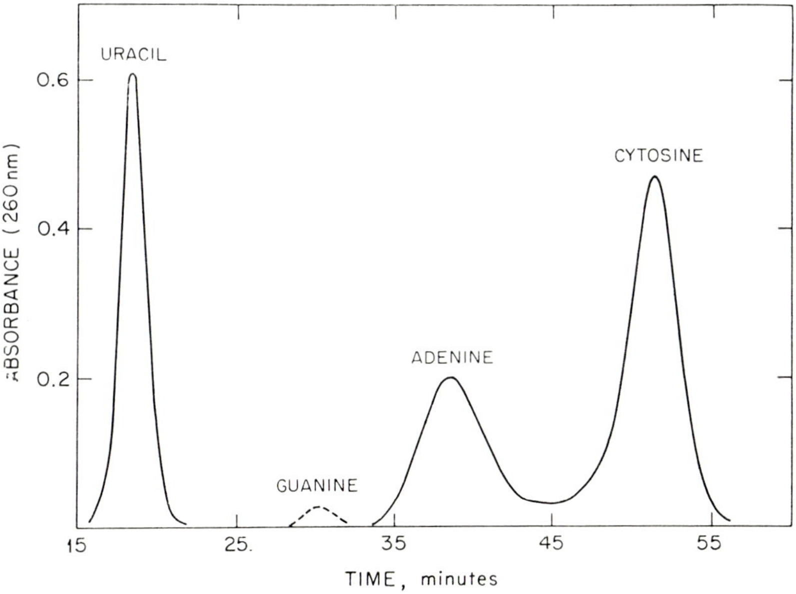

FIG. 5. Separation of nucleic acid bases by elution with 2.5 N NH_4OH. Conditions same as in Table 3. The guanine peak has been multiplied by a factor of 10.

TABLE 3
Retention Volumes of Nucleic Acid Bases[a]

Base	Peak		Corrected retention volume
	Time, min	Vol., ml	V'_R, ml
Nucleotides	13.0	10.0	—
Guanine	30.5	23.2	13.2
Adenine	39.0	29.6	19.6
5-Hydroxymethylcytosine	42.5	32.3	22.3
Cytosine	52.0	39.5	29.5
5-Methylcytosine	55.5	42.2	32.2

[a] 33 × 0.9 cm column; flow rate, 0.76 ml/min; 2.5 *N* NH_4OH elution.

nucleosides, but can be eluted with more concentrated NH_4OH. The major nucleic acid bases are easily separated by elution with 2.5 *N* NH_4OH (Fig. 5), although guanine is only slightly soluble in this medium. Retention volumes are shown in Table 3. Uracil and its derivatives can be eluted with water.

DISCUSSION

It is apparent that ligand-exchange chromatography is an extremely useful technique for the separation of nucleic acid components. Nucleotides, nucleosides, and bases are easily separated from each other and isolation of individual nucleosides or bases is easily accomplished. This technique has some distinct advantages. Separations are unusually rapid (rarely longer than 1 hr) and the product can be obtained in a small volume of water or ammonia solution free of buffers or salts. One possible disadvantage is the tendency of some compounds to hydrolyze in the ammoniacal medium. We have studied the stability of nucleosides in 1 *N* NH_4OH at 37° by repetitively scanning the ultraviolet absorption spectrum over a 24 hr period and found that 7-methylxanthosine and 7-methylinosine decompose rapidly, and 1-methyladenosine slowly changes to N_6-methyladenosine. 7-Methylguanosine decomposes almost instantaneously; however its decomposition product has a definite chromatographic position and can be used in place of the parent compound. None of the other compounds listed in Tables 2 or 3 showed any change in ultraviolet absorption.

The copper-loaded resin column is reasonably stable over a period of several months. There is little or no leaching of copper or ultraviolet-absorbing impurities into 1 *N* NH_4OH after the initial equilibration period. The main problem we have encountered is that halide salts and acidic solutions leach copper from the resin. Column sizes and eluant flow rates were chosen as a reasonable compromise between resolution desired and time of analysis. Longer columns and/or slower flow rates give better resolutions.

Studies with this column are continuing. Preliminary experiments indicate that it may be possible to separate deoxyribonucleosides from their corresponding ribonucleosides. Gradient elution with increasing ammonia concentration has so far been unsuccessful apparently because of the pH gradient which is simultaneously generated, but further tests should be made. Ligand-exchange separation is useful in the quantitative determination of ribonucleic acid end groups and base ratios and we will report this work shortly.

SUMMARY

Ligand-exchange chromatography, with a copper-loaded chelating resin (Chelex 100), is a useful technique for the rapid separation of nucleic acid components. Nucleotides are not retained on the column and are eluted with water. Weakly basic nucleosides and bases are only weakly retained and can be resolved by elution with water. More basic nucleosides can be separated by elution with 1 N NH_4OH. Nucleic acid bases are more strongly retained but can be eluted and separated with 2.5 N NH_4OH.

ACKNOWLEDGMENTS

The author is indebted to K. B. Green and Dr. C. A. Burtis for their assistance with some of the experimental work.

REFERENCES

1. Helfferich, F., *Nature* **189,** 1001 (1961).
2. Helfferich, F., *J. Am. Chem. Soc.* **84,** 3237 (1962).
3. Helfferich, F., *J. Am. Chem. Soc.* **84,** 3242 (1962).
4 Walton, H. F., and Latterell, J. M., *in* "Analytical Chemistry 1962" (P. W. West, A. M. G. MacDonald, and T. S. West, eds.), p. 356. American Elsevier, New York, 1963.
5. Latterell, J. J., and Walton, H. F., *Anal. Chim. Acta* **32,** 101 (1965).
6. Hill, A. G., Sedgley, R., and Walton, H. F., *Anal. Chim. Acta* **33,** 84 (1965).
7. Shimomura, K., Dickson, L., and Walton, H. F., *Anal. Chim. Acta* **37,** 102 (1967).
8. Siegel, A., and Degens, E. T., *Science* **151,** 1098 (1966).

ANALYTICAL BIOCHEMISTRY 20, 484–494 (1967)

Evaluation of Gas and Other Chromatographic Separations of Indolic Methyl Esters[1]

CLAUS GRUNWALD,[2] MIGUEL VENDRELL,[3] AND BRUCE B. STOWE

Department of Biology, Yale University, New Haven, Connecticut 06520

Received March 8, 1967

Gas chromatographic (5, 13, 16, 19, 20), thin-layer (1, 4, 7, 9–12, 15, 17), and gradient elution (13) chromatographic methods have been published for the separation of acidic indoles, but no single method is entirely satisfactory for the gamut of substances likely to be present in biological extracts, nor has a quantitative comparison of methods been made. Furthermore, the more labile indole acids pose special problems of handling that have not been satisfactorily solved.

For instance, Stowe and Schilke (16) reported the gas chromatographic retention volumes of a series of alkyl esters of indole-3-acetic, indole-3-propionic, and indole-3-butyric acids ranging from the methyl to the 2-butyl derivatives and concluded that on a single substrate the *n*-propyl esters were the first to be adequately separated. However, the BF_3 catalysis esterification technique they used decomposed indole-3-carboxylic, indole-3-glyoxylic, indole-3-lactic, and indole-3-pyruvic acids, for which they suggested diazoalkylation would be more suitable. Diazopropane (18) would provide the propyl derivatives with the desirable range of retention volumes. But as generation of diazopropane is more complex and requires less readily available starting material, diazomethylation has been used in this study. Diazomethylation already has been employed successfully by several workers for esterifying a limited number of acid indoles (5, 7, 13, 19, 20).

Eleven closely related simple indole acids, including most of the labile acids most likely to be encountered in biological materials, were selected

[1] This work was supported by research grants from the U. S. Public Health Service (GM-06921) and the Whitehall Foundation to B. B. Stowe.

[2] Present address: Department of Agronomy, University of Kentucky, Lexington, Kentucky 40506.

[3] Recipient of Fulbright Travel Award from Committee on International Exchange of Persons between the U. S. and Spain. Present address: Division of Food Preservation, C. S. I. R. O., P. O. Box 43, Ryde, N. S. W., Australia.

for esterification by the diazomethylation method. Four gas chromatographic column substrates, expected from our own experience and from recommendations in the literature to be most suitable for indole methyl esters, were compared quantitatively as to theoretical plates and resolution values. Tables of relative retention volumes for these compounds were compiled to permit selection of the best substrate for a particular separation. In addition, thin-layer and gradient elution column chromatographic methods that might permit prepurification of indolic methyl esters prepared from biological extracts were investigated.

METHODS

Gas Chromatography

The gas chromatograph was a Research Specialties model 600 equipped with an ionization detector (^{90}Sr). The columns were 1.83 m U-shaped glass, 6 mm i.d. They were packed with Anakrom ABS 70/80 mesh (Analabs, Hamden, Conn.) coated with 3% Versamid 900 (an ethylenediaminelinoleic acid polyamide resin, General Mills, Inc.), 4.8% SE-52 (methyl phenyl vinyl silicone rubber, General Electric Co.), 7.3% SE-30 (methyl vinyl silicone rubber, General Electric Co.), and 3% HI-EFF 8 BP (polycyclohexanedimethanol succinate, Applied Science Laboratories, State College, Pa.). The column temperature was between 190 and 210°C and the vaporizing block temperature was kept 50–100° above that of the column. Argon was used as the carrier gas at a flow rate of 110 ml/min at 20–25 lb/in^2 pressure. Injected were 2–10 μg samples of indole esters dissolved in acetonitrile.

Thin-Layer Chromatography (TLC)

The TLC of the indole esters was carried out on silica gel G (Brinkmann Instruments) with and without carboxymethylcellulose (No. 70, premium grade, Hercules Powder Co.) (10) and on Eastman Chromagram Sheets No. TK-301 R. The plates of the former were activated at 115° for 1 hr. A number of solvents were tested: *n*-hexane/2-butanone (3/1), *n*-hexane/2-butanone (85/15), *n*-hexane/2-butanone/benzene (75/25/10), *n*-hexane/benzene (3/1), *n*-hexane/carbon tetrachloride (3/1), and cyclohexane/isopropanol (3/1); however, none was as useful as *n*-hexane/2-butanone (3/1). All TLC runs were carried out at room temperature and in the light.

Elution Gradient Column Chromatography

The column chromatography of the indole esters was based on the method developed in this laboratory by Powell (13). Silicic acid (Mallinckrodt) was washed with 3 N HCl, then with distilled water until a pH of about 6 was obtained, rinsed with acetone, and dried at 100°. Twelve grams of a 100 to 200 mesh fraction was activated for 1 hr at 115° and treated with 7.5 ml 0.5 N formic acid, mixed, and made to a slurry with n-hexane that had been saturated with 0.5 N formic acid. The slurry was poured into a 12.5 mm i.d. column. The first and second elution chambers each contained 112.5 ml ethyl acetate saturated with 0.5 N formic acid. The indole sample was dissolved in 0.25 ml acetone and then 1 ml n-heptane was added and the acetone was finally evaporated. The n-heptane mixture was transferred to the column and 4.1 ml fractions were collected.

For most of this work 2–10 μg of the indole derivative was sufficient. The elution pattern was determined by taking the fractions to dryness, dissolving in 1 ml water, and adding to this 2 ml Ehrlich reagent (10 gm p-dimethylaminobenzaldehyde dissolved in 100 ml concentrated HCl).

Esterification

Volatility of acidic indoles must be increased by esterification before they can be used in gas chromatography. The esterification was via the micro method as outlined by Schlenk and Gellerman (14) and adopted for indoles by Powell (13). The setup consisted of three test tubes in series; the first tube contained about 3 ml methylene chloride, the second tube contained 2.0 ml practical-grade 2-(2-ethoxyethoxy)ethanol (Carbitol) and 2.0 ml 40% KOH, and the third tube contained the indole sample dissolved in 10 ml methylene chloride/methanol (9/1). The diazomethane was generated by adding to test tube 2 about 150 mg N-methyl-N-nitroso-p-toluenesulfonamide (Diazald, Aldrich Chemical Co.) dissolved in 2 ml methylene chloride.

A stream of nitrogen was passed through the methylene chloride in the first tube and carried into the second, where the nitrogen picked up the generated diazomethane and passed it into the third tube, where the indole esterification took place. Small-diameter Teflon tubing and rubber stoppers were used to connect the three test tubes.

The following acidic indoles from diverse commercial sources were used as starting materials for the synthesis of the methyl esters. The melting points of the methyl esters obtained from them follow each compound: indole 3-carboxylate (ICA) 151–2°, indole 3-acetate (IAA) 50.5–51°, indole 3-propionate (IPA) 79.5–80°, indole 3-butyrate (IBA) 73–74°, indole 3-glyoxylate (IGlyoxA) 224–6°, indole 3-lactate (ILA), indole 3-acrylate (IAcryA) 150–152.5°, indole 3-pyruvate (IPyA) 155.5–158°, indole 3-carboxylate (I2CA) 153.5–154.5°, indole 5-carboxylate (I5CA) 127–8°, and 5-hydroxyindole 3-acetate (5OH-IAA). Hexane was found to be the best solvent for recrystallization and was used for all of these esters except 5OH-IAA and IPyA. Methyl IPyA was recrystallized from a small volume of chloroform, while methyl 5OH-IAA was used without recrystallization as only small quantities were available.

RESULTS AND DISCUSSION

Preparation of Methyl Esters

Methyl esterification by this method proved to be simple and a large number of samples could be handled in a relatively short time. With care, recovery of microgram quantities easily exceeds 95%. The esterification of up to 10 mg of acidic indole was complete within 10 min and no breakdown products were observed in any of the indoles tested, except IPyA. Methyl IPyA showed a complex pattern of peaks which varied with the time between dissolving in acetonitrile and injection into the gas chromatograph column, in part due to the tautomerism of the compound and in part due to the formation of indole 3-carboxaldehyde, indole-3-acetic acid, and other products. This decomposition has been the object of a separate study which will be reported elsewhere.

The corrected melting points of the indole esters are listed above; all are within one degree of previously published values except those for ICA, I2CA, and I5CA methyl esters for which the above melting points are 4°, 2.5° and 2° higher than those reported earlier. Methyl ILA was found, as has been previously reported (2), to be a glass melting indefinitely at a low temperature. Since methyl 5OH-IAA was not isolated crystalline, there could be a question whether it had been methoxylated during diazomethylation. However, this has been reported to require much longer exposure to diazomethane (18), and the presence of a free phenolic group is confirmed by the relatively low R_f values obtained with our sample (Table 3).

Relative Value of Gas Chromatography Substrates

The four liquid phases used for gas chromatography of these indole esters were selected because of our experience with Versamid 900 (16), recommendations in the literature for SE-30 (5, 19, 20), and SE-52 (5), while HI-EFF 8 BP was used because it was expected to be superior to the chemically similar polyneopentyl glycol succinate (5, 16). No claim is made that completely optimum conditions were obtained for each substrate. Obviously, different column loadings, support sizes, temperatures, flow rates, and other variables might have changed the absolute values. Indeed, we have reported higher effective plate values for Versamid 900 columns operated at a higher temperature earlier (16).

However, the results reported here are representative of our experience with these substrates and they were tested under roughly comparable conditions which should permit evaluation of relative merits.

The results for the ten indole methyl esters on each of the four substrates are in Table 1. Relative retention values r are given with respect to ethyl indole acetate, previously suggested to be the most suitable standard (5, 16); r and the effective plate number N were calculated according to Ettre (6).

TABLE 1
Comparison of Relative Retention Times and Effective Plate Values of Various Indole Methyl Esters on Four Gas Chromatography Column Substrates
N = effective plate value, r = relative retention time (6)

Column characteristics	Substrates: Versamid 900		HI-EFF-8BP		SE-52		SE-30	
% substrate on column	3.5		3.0		4.8		7.3	
Column temperature, °C	205		190		210		208	
Detector temperature, °C	300		210		300		300	
Column pressure, psi	25		21		20		23	
Flow rate, ml/min	110		110		110		110	
t'_R, ethylindole 3-acetate, min	8.04		7.28		2.27		1.67	
Indole ester	r	N	r	N	r	N	r	N
Ethylindole 3-acetate	1.00	174	1.00	1025	1.00	400	1.00	484
Methylindole 3-carboxylate	2.26	502	1.79	764	0.84	52	0.99	331
Methylindole 3-acetate	0.96	385	1.02	698	1.09	117	0.99	400
Methylindole 3-propionate	1.09	666	1.25	924	1.23	77	1.05	538
Methylindole 3-butyrate	1.48	947	1.78	1158	1.53	147	1.47	727
Methylindole 3-glyoxylate	1.21	584	1.30	876	1.24	479	1.29	807
Methylindole 3-lactate	2.72	461	3.60	853	1.79	66	1.91	449
Methylindole 3-acrylate	7.19	37	6.29	1368	2.65	138	2.53	638
Methylindole 2-carboxylate	0.33	400	0.35	520	0.40	119	0.45	100
Methylindole 5-carboxylate	1.49	694	1.34	830	0.87	81	0.84	528
Methyl-5-hydroxyindole 3-acetate	2.16	974	2.82	1131	1.72	298	1.76	408

The substrates SE-30 and SE-52 under our conditions gave short retention times, none longer than 13 min, which caused crowding at the beginning of the chromatogram. In our experience, higher column loadings or lower flow rates did not improve the separation, while at lower temperatures the substrates are insufficiently volatile (16). Dedio and Zalik (5) have reported higher N values for the indoles they tested on SE-52, which we could not attain. Under our conditions, it consistently gave the lowest values among these four substrates. Ironically, they also found that under their conditions Versamid 900 was one of the least satisfactory substrates while for us it has been one of the best. Other than different instrument geometries, the only obvious explanation may be that Versamid 900 is a difficult resin to apply uniformly to support material. The results here confirm that Versamid 900 provides excellent separations of these ten indole esters, even for the IAA, IPA, and IBA group previously reported as difficult to separate. The only two indole esters not adequately separated were IBA and I5CA, but these can be separated on HI-EFF 8 BP.

The substrate HI-EFF 8 BP gave the highest effective plate numbers and also very good separation for most of the tested indole esters. However, HI-EFF 8 BP did not separate ICA from IBA and it only poorly separated IPA from IGlyoxA, and IGlyoxA from I5CA; but all these indole esters can be separated using Versamid 900 as the liquid phase. The methyl esters of ICA and IBA are also easy to distinguish by other means, since the ester of ICA does not react, at any concentration, with Ehrlich reagent while IBA in the presence of this reagent gives a purple color (Table 3). Judging from the above data it should be possible to identify any methyl esters of the common acidic indoles by use of these two column substrates, Versamid 900 and HI-EFF 8 BP.

Up to this point only the separation of synthetic acidic indoles has been discussed. The possibility of using this method with biological extracts and of collecting the individual indoles for further analysis also must be considered. In order to use any of the collected samples for chemical analysis, the sample must be of relatively high purity. Comparison of relative retention times (t_R) gives only the separation between two peak maxima, and does not indicate how clearly the peaks are separated from each other. In order to calculate completeness of separation, or resolution (R), one must also take peak width at the base (W_b) into account (6). The equation:

$$R = \frac{2(tR_1 - tR_2)}{Wb_1 + Wb_2}$$

was used to calculate the R values of Table 2. If $R = 1$, the two peaks are only 95% resolved and, if $R = 1.5$, the two peaks are better than 99% resolved from each other.

If a criterion for a single-step purification method be established as $R \geqslant 1$, the four tested liquid phases may be compared directly. SE-52 is undesirable as a substrate for indole esters analysis because the resolutions are very poor. With SE-52 the resolution of consecutive peaks of only two of the indole ester derivatives went above 95%, the lowest acceptable limit. The other three substrates meet the criterion. HI-EFF 8 BP shows the best resolution, Versamid 900 is slightly less effective, and SE-30 has somewhat lower resolution. None of the substrates has a resolution of at

TABLE 2

Gas Chromatographic Resolution of Indole Methyl Ester Pairs by Various Substrates

Column characteristics as in Table 1, abbreviations as in text. *R* = resolution of adjacent peaks arranged in order of retention volumes on each substrate.

Methyl ester of	*R* on HI-EFF 8 BP	Methyl ester of	*R* on Versamid 900	Methyl ester of	*R* on SE-30	Methyl ester of	*R* on SE-52
I2CA		I2CA		I2CA		I2CA	
	6.15		4.39		2.34		1.43
IAA		IAA		I5CA		ICA	
	1.32		0.95		1.68		0.06
IPA		IPA		ICA		I5CA	
	0.44		0.61		0.00		0.58
IGlyoxA		IGlyoxA		IAA		IAA	
	0.16		1.36		0.80		0.28
I5CA		IBA		IPA		IPA	
	1.83		0.05		1.30		0.03
IBA		I5CA		IGlyoxA		IGlyoxA	
	0.35		2.52		0.91		0.80
ICA		5OH-IAA		IBA		IBA	
	3.47		0.35		0.97		0.41
5OH-IAA		ICA		5OH-IAA		5OH-IAA	
	0.76		1.00		0.46		0.01
ILA		ILA		ILA		ILA	
	5.81		1.81		1.62		0.97
IAcryA		IAcryA		IAcryA		IAcryA	

least 95% for all nine adjacent pairs of the ten tested indole esters. At 95% resolution Versamid 900 and HI-EFF 8 BP resolved five, and SE-30 resolved four pairs of the 10 indole derivatives. If near 100% resolution of adjacent pairs is required, HI-EFF 8 BP could resolve four, while Versamid 900 and SE-30 resolved three of the nine ester pairs. The closest pairs are IAA and IPA, and IPA and IGlyoxA, for both of which the best resolution was 1.3. But all other possible pairs of the ten derivatives can be better than 99% resolved on one or another of the three columns. Thus these three substrates are likely to meet any needs encountered in indole esters analyses.

Gradient Elution Column Chromatography

However, it has been assumed so far that no interfering substances are present, not a realistic assumption when working with biological material. Powell (13) has developed a method to partially purify crude extracts by preliminary fractionation into the following four major groups: (*1*) acidic, (*2*) basic, (*3*) neutral, and (*4*) water soluble. This is followed by a silica gel partition column chromatography procedure which offers a mild and convenient way to eliminate many nonindoles and also effectively separates many indoles from each other. But the method with this group of acidic indoles gives poor resolution and crowding. An attempt was made to overcome the crowding and resolution problem by using the methyl esters instead of the free indole acids.

The acid fraction was methylated via the diazomethane procedure, taken to dryness, and either put on the column directly, or partitioned between methylene chloride and 2% sodium bicarbonate. The latter step eliminated any nonesterified substances and made a cleaner separation. The methylene chloride containing the methyl esters was then taken to dryness and put onto the column, and the eluted fractions collected (Fig. 1). The ester derivatives still showed some crowding, especially between

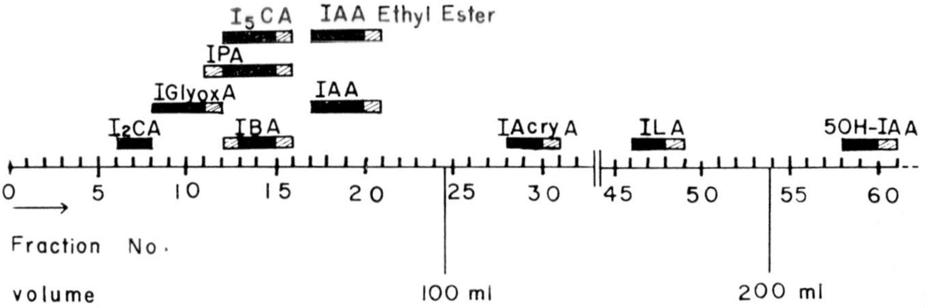

FIG. 1. Fractionation of indole methyl esters by gradient elution column chromatography. Conditions and abbreviations in text. Hachure indicates presence of small quantity in adjacent fraction.

fraction numbers 12 to 16; however, these indoles could be separated and distinguished by means of gas chromatography. Generally this gradient elution column procedure gave a highly purified sample which could be run directly by gas chromatography. However, two problems were encountered: (*1*) as the methyl ester derivative of ICA does not give a color reaction with Ehrlich or Salkowski reagent it was difficult to follow this compound, and (*2*) since recovery after the silica gel column chromatography was only 60–80% at 2–10 μg levels depending on the indole involved, larger quantities of tissue are required for extraction.

Thin-Layer Chromatography

Thin-layer chromatography also was tested as a prepurification method (Table 3). As expected, most of the closely related indole esters cannot be separated adequately by this method; however, these indoles can be resolved sufficiently by gas chromatography. A number of solvents were tested for indole ester separation, but none was as useful as *n*-hexane/2-butanone (3/1). The other solvents gave either poor resolution and/or very much indole diffusion. But again, recovery drops to the 70–90%

range when elution of 2–10 μg samples is attempted. However, for free IAA, Tafuri (17) reports special elution methods can improve the recovery to 95% or better, while Owaki (11) recommends TLC on cellulose, with which he reports quantitative recoveries of 10–300 μg. Thus, it may be desirable to carry out TLC of free indole acids before esterifying them for gas chromatography.

The problem of spot spreading can be minimized somewhat for these substances, as for others reported earlier, by using carboxymethylcellulose as a binder with the silica gel G (10). Smaller spots were obtained and R_f values were generally increased with the addition of carboxymethylcellulose; also the separation between closely related indole esters was improved. It was found that 1 gm of carboxymethylcellulose per 29 gm of silica gel G was sufficient to obtain these desirable characteristics. On the other hand, 1.5 gm of carboxymethylcellulose per 28.5 gm of silica gel G, while not further increasing the desirable characteristics, did increase running time. Indole esters were too weakly adsorbed on Eastman TK 301 R sheets, as almost all R_f values were too high to be useful.

TABLE 3
R_f Values of Indole Esters Using Various Thin-Layer Media in n-Hexane/2-Butanone (3/1)
(see text for details)

	Support				
Methyl ester of	Silica gel (G)	Silica gel G/cellulose gum 29.0:1.0	Silica gel G/cellulose gum 28.5:1.5	Eastman sheet TK 301 R	Ehrlich reagent color
Indole 3-acetate	0.35	0.52	0.59	0.91	Purple
Indole 3-propionate	.39	.60	.60	.94	Purple
Indole 3-butyrate	.39	.63	.65	.96	Purple
Indole 3-glyoxylate	.49	.67	.74	.97	Purple
Indole 3-lactate	.10	.17	.13	.50	Purple
Indole 3-acrylate	.24	.39	.36	.78	Golden
Indole 2-carboxylate	.55	.73	.77	—	Pink-red
Indole 5-carboxylate	.34	.55	—	.90	Red
5-Hydroxyindole 3-acetate	.10	.15	—	.34	Blue
Ethylindole 3-acetate	.35	.61	—	.95	Purple

Ultraviolet and Spectrophotofluorometry

Once a suspected acidic indole is separated and purified, UV and spectrophotofluorometric methods can be employed to confirm the indole structure. Spectrophotofluorometric methods for indoles in plants have been described by Stowe and Schilke (16) and Burnett and Audus (3). As anticipated, the UV and spectrophotofluorometric spectra of the methyl esters studied here were found to be almost identical to the indole acid spectra themselves; only minor peak shifts occur and these are generally to a higher wave number, except for ICA and I2CA, which exhibit a slight shift to a lower wave number. At liquid nitrogen temperatures, with the indoles dissolved in the glass-forming PPR solvent, characteristically higher wave numbers and about 50% higher absorption coefficients were noted, but again in most cases no marked differentiation of individual substances was obtained. The principal value, then, of the ultraviolet techniques lies in confirming the indolic nature of an isolated substance, and in measuring its concentration. Actual identification of the compound rests most securely on the chromatographic properties cited above.

SUMMARY

Diazomethylation esterified all tested acidic indoles without appreciable loss. A group of ten methyl ester derivatives were obtained in crystalline form. These were used to test the relative values of four gas chromatographic substrates. Quantitative comparisons led to the selection of Versamid 900, HI-EFF 8 BP, and SE-30 as permitting complete separation of all indole esters, while SE-52 was unsatisfactory. Gradient elution column and thin-layer chromatography as pre- and post-purification techniques for these indole esters were also compared, as was the usefulness of UV spectroscopy and spectrophotofluorometry in acidic indole analysis.

ACKNOWLEDGMENTS

We are much obliged to Professor Saul Zalik for his courteous criticisms of this manuscript, and to Mr. Robert E. Kaplan whose preliminary studies of the thin-layer chromatographic system under a U. S. National Science Foundation Undergraduate Research Participation grant were helpful to us.

REFERENCES

1. Ballin, G., *J. Chromatog.* **16,** 152 (1964).
2. Bentley, J. A., Farrar, K. R., Housley, S., Smith, G. F., and Taylor, W. C., *Biochem. J.* **64,** 44 (1956).
3. Burnett, D., and Audus, L. J., *Phytochem.* **3,** 395 (1964).
4. Collet, G., Dubouchet, J., and Pilet, P.-E., *Physiol. Vég.* **2,** 157 (1964).
5. Dedio, W., and Zalik, S., *Anal. Biochem.* **16,** 36 (1966).
6. Ettre, L. S., *J. Gas Chromatog.* **1,** 36 (1963).
7. Glombitza, K.-W., *J. Chromatog.* **25,** 87 (1966).
8. Kaper, J. M., Gebhard, O., van den Berg, C. J., and Veldstra, H., *Arch. Biochem. Biophys.* **103,** 475 (1963).
9. Leung, A. Y., Smith, A. H., and Paul, A. G., *J. Pharm. Sci.* **54,** 1576 (1965).
10. Obreiter, J. B., and Stowe, B. B., *J. Chromatog.* **16,** 226 (1964).
11. Owaki, Y., *Botan. Mag. (Tokyo)* **79,** 200 (1966).

12. Perley, J. E., and Stowe, B. B., *Biochem. J.* **100,** 169 (1966).
13. Powell, L. E., *Plant Physiol.* **39,** 836 (1964).
14. Schlenk, H., and Gellerman, J. L., *Anal. Chem.* **32,** 1412 (1960).
15. Schmid, E., Laudi, B., Krautheim, J., and Tautz, N. A., *Z. Klin. Chem.* **4,** 250 (1966).
16. Stowe, B. B., and Schilke, J. F., in "Régulateurs Naturels de la Croissance Végétale," *Colloq. Intern. Centre Natl. Rech. Sci.* (*Paris*) **123,** 409 (1964).
17. Tafuri, F., *Phytochemistry* **5,** 999 (1966).
18. Wilcox, M., *Anal. Biochem.* **16,** 253 (1966).
19. Williams, C. M., *Anal. Biochem.* **4,** 423 (1962).
20. Williams, C. M., and Sweeley, C. C., in "Biomedical Applications of Gas Chromatography" (H. A. Szymanski, ed.), p. 225. Plenum Press, New York, 1964.

ANALYTICAL BIOCHEMISTRY 20, 495–501 (1967)

A Brief Method for the Identification of the α_1-Acid Glycoprotein Variants

KÄTHI HUNZIKER AND KARL SCHMID

Department of Biochemistry, Boston University School of Medicine, Boston University Medical Center, Boston, Massachusetts 02118

Received March 13, 1967

Recent studies on α_1-acid glycoprotein (1, 2), a well-characterized globulin of normal human blood (3, 4), showed that this protein exhibits polymorphism in the native state (5) and two variants after removal of its sialyl residues (6). For the identification of these variants by the technique hitherto used (5, 7), it was necessary to isolate α_1-acid glycoprotein from a relatively large volume of blood by several complex and time-consuming steps. Therefore, a simple method presented in this paper was developed for this purpose.

METHODS

The new method for the isolation and identification of the α_1-acid glycoprotein variants involves the following three steps:

1. *Fractionation with $HClO_4$:* 5 ml of serum pipetted into an appropriate centrifuge tube was diluted with 15 ml of 0.85% NaCl, cooled to —2°C and placed in a —2° bath. Perchloric acid (2.5 ml, 1.8*N*, —2°) was added to the dilute serum with stirring. The formed precipitate was immediately centrifuged off at —2° and 3,500 rpm for 15 min (8). The supernatant solution was poured into a precooled test tube (2.3 × 20 cm) and adjusted to pH 1.45 to 1.55 at —2° by addition af a previously determined volume (about 8 ml) of 0.5 *N* NaOH precooled to —2°. After the solution was brought to room temperature, the pH was adjusted to exactly 1.60 (9).

2. *Hydrolysis at pH 1.6:* The above-mentioned solution was heated in a water bath at 80°C for 1 hr. The resulting hydrolyzate was immediately cooled to room temperature, neutralized with 0.05 *N* NaOH to pH 6 to 7, dialyzed against several changes of cold distilled water for two days, and lyophilized. The yield of protein was 4 to 5 mg.

3. *Identification of α_1-Acid Glycoprotein Variants:* (*a*) *By starch gel electrophoresis at pH 5.1 followed by staining with amido black.* Starch

gel electrophoresis was performed in pH 5.1 Γ/2 0.02 sodium acetate buffer using a 24 × 10 × 0.3 cm starch gel plate. The protein samples were dissolved in this buffer to give a 20% solution. Aliquots (0.01 ml) were taken up in Whatman 3 MM paper strips (1.0 × 0.3 cm) which were inserted in the gel on one line and 1 cm apart. Ten samples and a reference (sialyl-free α_1-acid glycoprotein) could be analyzed simultaneously. The electrophoresis was performed at 4°C and at 300 V (~60 mA) for 6 hr. The direction of the electrical movement was parallel to

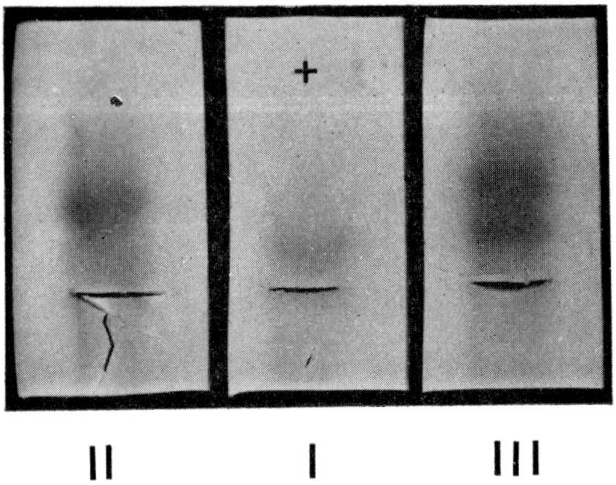

FIG. 1. Starch gel electrophoretic analysis at pH 5.1 of the variants of human serum α_1-acid glycoprotein. Note that the minor components present in these protein fractions migrated in the direction opposite that of the α_1-acid glycoprotein variants (+).

the shorter edges of the starch gel plate. During this period of time, the faster moving variant migrated 2 cm. After electrophoresis the gel was cooled for 30 minutes, cut into two slices, and stained with amido black (Fig. 1). The amount of protein required for analysis could be halved if the length of the paper strips was reduced to 0.5 cm. Hence, the minimum volume of serum needed for this procedure is 2.5 ml.

(b) *Auxiliary procedure for identification of the variants by immunoprecipitin reaction.* Starch gel electrophoresis at pH 5.1 was carried out in the same size gel plate as described above, but the direction of the electrophoretic migration was parallel to the longer side of the plate so that the two variants could be separated from one another by a greater distance (17 hr, 150 V, 35 mA). Thus, only five samples could be analyzed simultaneously. After electrophoresis, an appropriate piece (0.8 × 6 cm) containing the protein variant(s), was cut out from one of the two starch gel slices and placed on an agar plate (2% agar in

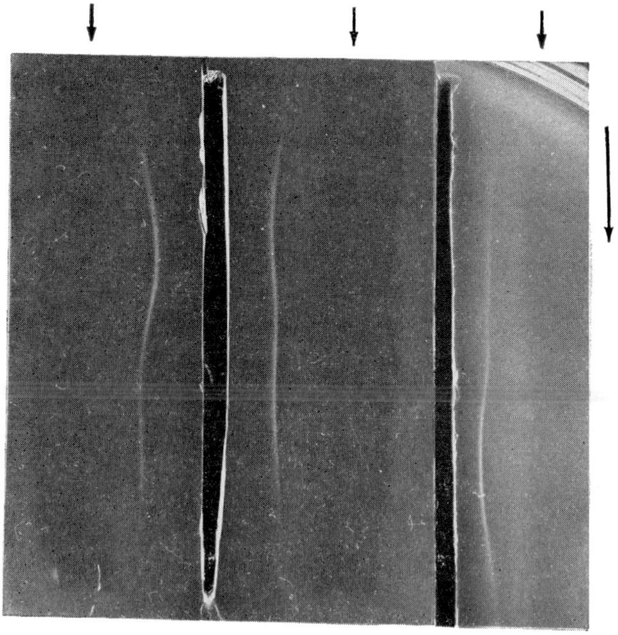

FIG. 2. Immunoelectrophoretic identification of the α_1-acid glycoprotein variants. The long vertical arrow indicates the direction of the electrophoretic migration in the starch gel. The three short vertical arrows point to the dark rectangles where the starch gel slices were placed. Before the photographs were taken these starch gel slices were removed from the agar plate. The formed precipitin lines (white) correspond to types I, II, and III, respectively.

pH 8.6 borate buffer, $24 \times 10 \times 0.5$ cm) (10) which served for the simultaneous identification of five samples. The distance between two such starch gel cuts was 2 cm. After 6 hr, 1 mm wide troughs were made into the agar at a distance of 1 cm from the longer edge of the starch gels. These troughs were filled with an antiserum active against pooled normal α_1-acid glycoprotein(Hyland Laboratories, Los Angeles, California, and Behringwerke, Marburg/Lahn, Germany). The agar plate prepared in this fashion was then wrapped in a transparent plastic sheet (Saran) and kept at room temperature. After 24 to 48 hr the formed precipitin lines allowed the best identification of the variants (Fig. 2).

CORRECTED INVESTIGATION

1. *Paper and Starch Gel Electrophoretic Analysis:* The $HClO_4$-soluble serum protein fraction revealed on paper electrophoresis at pH 8.6 and 5.1 four bands (α_1-, α_2-, β-, and γ-globulins), of which α_1-acid glycopro-

tein used as control was one of the two major components. On starch gel electrophoresis at these two pH values, a resolution into five bands was obtained, and α_1-acid glycoprotein represented the major component.

After mild acid hydrolysis the $HClO_4$-soluble protein fraction revealed on paper electrophoresis at pH 8.6 a major peak in the β-globulin region corresponding to desialized α_1-acid glycoprotein. At pH 5.1 a resolution into four well-separated bands was noted, one of which migrated with the electrophoretic mobility of desialized α_1-acid glycoprotein. Starch gel electrophoresis at pH 8.6 (Fig. 3) also revealed one major band in the position of the sialyl-free α_1-acid glycoprotein (Fig. 3g). A faster moving trace component was noticed, which probably represented α_1-acid glycoprotein that still contained a small amount of sialic acid (5). Starch gel electrophoresis at pH 5.1 (Fig. 3) showed two well-separated

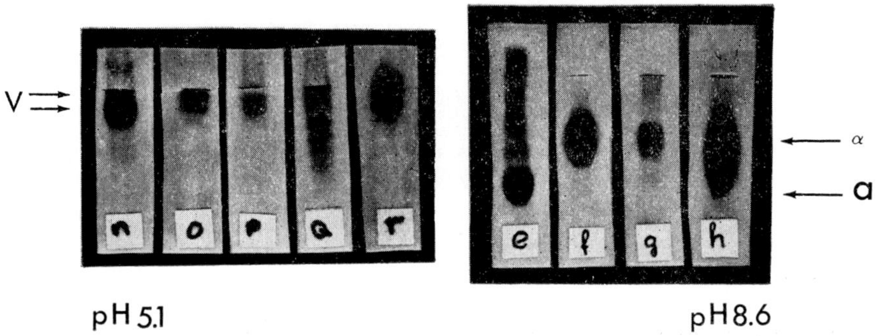

FIG. 3. Starch gel electrophoresis at pH 8.6 and 5.1 of the perchloric acid-soluble proteins of normal serum after acid hydrolysis at pH 1.6 (g, p). Sialyl-free α_1-acid glycoprotein prepared by neuraminidase (f, o) or mild acid hydrolysis at pH 1.6 (r), normal serum (e, n) and Cohn fraction VI obtained after mild acid hydrolysis at pH 1.6 (h, Q) were included as references in this analysis. The relative positions of albumin (a), sialyl-free α_1-acid glycoprotein (α) and the two variants of this glycoprotein (V) are indicated by arrows.

bands in the position of the two α_1-acid glycoprotein variants prepared by cleaving off the sialyl residues either with neuraminidase or by mild acid hydrolysis. The minor proteins present in this fraction migrated in the opposite direction. Cohn fraction VI, an intermediate of the original method, and known to contain α_1-acid glycoprotein, resolved into at least eight bands after hydrolysis at pH 1.6, but could not be utilized directly for the identification of the variants of this protein by the staining techniques because its albumin migrated at the same rate as the variants.

2. *Effect of the Perchloric Acid Precipitation and Mild Acid Hydrolysis on Sialic Acid Content and Specific Optical Rotation of α_1-acid*

Glycoprotein: Native α_1-acid glycoprotein, homogeneous as judged by classical criteria of purity, was subjected to the conditions of the $HClO_4$ precipitation. The sialic acid content of the resulting preparation, determined by the Warren procedure[1] (11), was 10.6% as compared with 10.8% of the native protein, the difference probably being due to the error of this method. α_1-Acid glycoprotein when measured before and after the $HClO_4$ step revealed the same electrophoretic mobility on paper and starch gel electrophoresis and the same specific optical rotation ($[\alpha]_{546} = -26°$). After hydrolysis at pH 1.6, the sialic acid content was reduced to 0.5% and the specific optical rotation increased to −20°.

APPLICATION OF THIS METHOD TO INDIVIDUAL SERA

1. *α_1-Acid Glycoprotein Variants of Four Caucasian Adults:* Serum from four normal Caucasian adults, whose α_1-acid glycoprotein variants had been determined by the original technique, was taken three times at

TABLE 1
Identification of the α_1-Acid Glycoprotein Variants of Four Normal Adults

Individual	Blood taken	α_1-Acid glycoprotein variants identified by	
		Staining	Immunochemical reaction
KS	May 5	Type I	Type I
	May 12	I	I
	May 16	I	I
HK	May 5	Type I	Type I
	May 12	I	I
	May 16	I	I
RN	June 21	Type II	Type II
	June 25	II	II
	June 29	II	II
KH	May 5	Type III	Type III
	May 12	III	III
	May 17	III	III

5 to 7 days intervals and analyzed by the new procedure. The results obtained by both the staining and immunoprecipitin techniques (Table 1) were identical with those obtained by the original procedure.

2. *Relative Percentage of α_1-Acid Glycoprotein Variants in Nyambaanese:* Sera from 50 normal Nyambaanese adults (South Africa) were analyzed by the new method. The α_1-acid glycoprotein variants were determined from the stained starch gels. The results are summarized in

[1] For the complete liberation of the protein-bound sialic acid the glycoprotein was hydrolyzed with 0.1 N HCl at 80°C for 1 hr.

TABLE 2

Relative Percentage of the Three Patterns of the α_1-Acid Glycoprotein Variants of Normal Nyambaanese

α_1-Acid glycoprotein variants, type	Nyambaanese		For comparison, relative %[a]	
	Number of analyses	Relative %	Japanese	Caucasian
I	10	20	17	11
II	15	30	63	46
III	25	50	20	43

[a] Data from reference 6.

Table 2 and are compared with the corresponding analyses of Caucasians and Japanese determined by the original method. (5, 7).

DISCUSSION

For the determination of the variants of human serum α_1-acid glycoprotein a short method was developed which consists of three simple steps. By contrast, the original method required five complex and time-consuming steps (5, 7). It should be added that, although each of these three steps has been utilized earlier for different purposes (6, 8, 9), in this paper it is shown for the first time that it is possible to combine these steps to determine the variants of α_1-acid glycoprotein. The new procedure has the additional advantage that only one dialysis and lyophilization is required, whereas the earlier method required dialysis and lyophilization three times. Mild acid hydrolysis, replacing the neuraminidase step of the original method, did not lead to denaturation of the $HClO_4$-soluble proteins which would impair or even prevent identification of the α_1-acid glycoprotein variants. Independent investigations revealed that under the latter conditions α_1-acid glycoprotein undergoes only minute changes in its conformation, as judged by optical rotation measurements.

The composition of the perchloric acid soluble serum protein fraction proved to be such that, after hydrolysis at pH 1.6, the desialized α_1-acid glycoprotein migrated on starch gel electrophoresis at pH 5.1 in the direction opposite that of the several minor components. Therefore, it is possible to determine the α_1-acid glycoprotein variants by the simple staining technique, and the immunochemical determination represents a valuable adjunct.

The analysis of individual serum specimens whose α_1-acid glycoprotein variants were typed by the original method demonstrated the feasibility and validity of the new technique.

SUMMARY

A brief method for the identification of the α_1-acid glycoprotein variants of human serum is presented. This technique consists of three simple steps: (*1*) Precipitation of the bulk of the protein from diluted serum with $HClO_4$ in the cold, (*2*) hydrolysis of the perchloric acid soluble proteins at pH 1.6, 80°C, for 1 hr, and (*3*) starch gel electrophoresis at pH 5.1 followed by staining with amido black. The minimum volume of serum required is 2.5 ml. The immunochemical identification of the variants represents a valuable adjunct to this method. The validity of the procedure was demonstrated by the analysis of sera that had been typed by the original technique. The new method was applied to determine the relative percentage of the α_1-acid glycoprotein variants in normal Nyambaanese.

ACKNOWLEDGMENT

The authors are very grateful to Dr. A. Zoutendyk, The South African Institute for Medical Research, Johannesburg, for his most valuable gift of serum specimens of Nyambaanese.

This study was supported by grants from The Lilly Research Laboratories, Eli Lilly Company, Indianapolis, and the U. S. Public Health Service, National Institute of General Medical Sciences (GM-10374 and 1-K3-GM-32, 160).

REFERENCES

1. Weimer, H. E., Mehl, J. W., and Winzler, R. J., *J. Biol. Chem.* **185,** 561 (1950).
2. Schmid, K., *J. Am. Chem. Soc.* **75,** 60 (1953).
3. Jeanloz, R. W., *in* "Glycoproteins" (A. Gottschalk, ed.), p. 362. Elsevier, Amsterdam- New York, 1966.
4. Gottschalk, A., and Graham, E. R. B., *in* "The Proteins" (H. Neurath, ed.), Vol. 4, p. 96. Academic Press, New York, 1966.
5. Schmid, K., Binette, J. P., Tokita, K., Moroz, L., and Yoshizaki, H., *J. Clin. Invest.* **43,** 2347 (1964).
6. Schmid, K., Tokita, K., and Yoshizaki, H., *J. Clin. Invest.* **44,** 1394 (1965).
7. Tokita, K., Burke, J., Yoshizaki, H., and Schmid, K., *J. Clin. Invest.* **45,** 1624 (1966).
8. Schultze, H. E., Heide, K., and Haupt, H., *Clin. Chim. Acta* **7,** 854 (1962).
9. Schmid, K., Polis, A., Hunziker, K., Fricke, R., and Yayoshi, M., *Biochem. J.*, in press.
10. Debray-Sachs, M., Antoine, B., and Fine, J. M., *Rev. Franc. d'Etudes Clin. Biol.* **6,** 435 (1961).
11. Warren, L., *J. Biol. Chem.* **234,** 1971 (1959).

ANALYTICAL BIOCHEMISTRY 20, 502–516 (1967)

Microenzymic Method for the Quantitative Analysis of Acetyl Groups in Proteins and Peptides[1]

LEWIS D. STEGINK

Childrens Research Unit, Department of Pediatrics, The University of Iowa, Iowa City, Iowa 52240

Received January 16, 1967

Interest in methods for the quantitative determination of acetyl groups in proteins and peptides has grown rapidly since Narita (1) isolated and characterized the acetyl peptide from the amino-terminal position of tobacco mosaic virus protein. Prior to this, acetyl groups were felt to be associated with the carbohydrate portion of glycoproteins, occurring mainly as *N*-acetylhexosamine derivatives. Since Narita's work, a large number of other proteins have been shown to possess *N*-acetyl groups, including: cytochrome *c* (2), turnip yellow mosaic virus protein (3), cucumber virus protein (4), α-melanocyte stimulating hormone (5), beef fibrinogen (6), ovalbumin (7, 8), chicken globin (9), fetal hemoglobin (10), calf thymus histones (11), enolase (12), myosin (13), actin (14, 15), apoferritin (16), tropomyosin (17), carbonic anhydrase (18), collagen (19), α-glycerophosphate dehydrogenase (20), luteinizing hormone (21), lactate dehydrogenase (22), pyruvate kinase (see Table 4), and likely many others.

Several analytical methods are available for the determination of acetate (21–34), and a number of these (1, 7, 10, 21–26) have been utilized for the analysis of acetyl groups in protein samples. When this investigation was initiated, the procedures available for the analysis of acetyl groups required fairly large quantities of protein (0.5–10.0 μmoles), and we hoped to find a more sensitive method. This led to the development of a microenzymic assay for acetate described briefly in connection with earlier studies on the amino-terminal sequence of lactate dehydrogenase (22). This method possessed good sensitivity, but was difficult to use because inhibitors to the enzymic reactions develop on hydrolysis. These inhibitors were extracted with the acetic acid; thus the quantity of inhibitor carried into the assay cuvet increases with increasing aliquot size, and markedly lowers the amount of acetate converted to citrate. This required the aliquot assayed

[1] This investigation has been supported by funds from the Public Health Service General Research Support Grant to the University of Iowa College of Medicine and from Grant NB-05489 from the National Institutes of Health.

to be of such a size that increasing or decreasing the size produced a linear response in the assay. Since only very small aliquots could be assayed, the method was difficult to use. We felt that, if either hydrolysis or extraction conditions could be found which would eliminate these inhibitors, the assay would be of much greater value, especially with small samples. This report describes a revision of the earlier method which fulfils these requirements and provides an extensive improvement over the previous method.

MATERIALS AND METHODS

The diethyl ether was purchased from Mallinckrodt Chemical Company. Propyl ether, isopropyl ether, and *tert*-butyl ethyl ether[2] were purchased from Distillation Products Industries. Anhydrous sodium sulfate was purchased from Fisher Chemical Company.

Diphosphopyridine nucleotide, reduced diphosphopyridine nucleotide, and adenosine triphosphate were purchased from Sigma. L-Malic acid, dithiothreitol, and alumina C_γ gel were purchased from Calbiochem. Coenzyme A was purchased from Calbiochem and Pabst. Tris buffer was purchased from Mann Laboratories.

Malate dehydrogenase (pig heart) and citrate condensing enzyme were purchased from Calbiochem. Ovalbumin samples were purchased from Calbiochem, Sigma, and Pierce Chemical Company or were the gift of Professor H. B. Bull, Department of Biochemistry, The University of Iowa. Horse heart and beef heart cytochrome *c* were purchased from Sigma. Rabbit muscle pyruvate kinase was the generous gift of G. L. Cottam and M. J. Coon, Department of Biological Chemistry, the University of Michigan. Rabbit muscle aldolase was the gift of G. Lehrer and R. Barker, Department of Biochemistry, The University of Iowa. Rat liver malate dehydrogenase was the gift of K. G. Mann, Department of Biochemistry, The University of Iowa.

Acetyl-CoA synthetase was prepared from yeast by the method of Berg (35) with the modifications described below: 400 gm of fresh baker's yeast were suspended in 400 ml of 0.1 *M* cold dipotassium phosphate, and this paste was pressed in a thoroughly chilled French Pressure Cell (American Instrument Company). In our hands, extracts prepared by sonication contained considerably fewer units than those described by Berg. Toluene autolyzates and phosphate buffer extracts of yeast cells frozen in liquid nitrogen were unsatisfactory. The crude extract from the French Pressure Cell closely resembled the crude extract described by Berg.

[2] The abbreviations used are: *t*-BEE, *tert*-butyl ethyl ether; ATP, adenosine triphosphate; DPN^+, diphosphopyridine nucleotide; DPNH, reduced diphosphopyridine nucleotide; CoA, coenzyme A; DEAE-cellulose, diethylaminoethylcellulose; PPi., pyrophosphate.

The broken cell suspension was centrifuged at 10,000g for 15 min and the supernatant solution was purified as described by Berg (35) through the first ammonium sulfate step. The alumina C_γ gel step which follows this ammonium sulfate step was the most difficult step to reproduce, largely because of wide variations in the adsorptive properties of the alumina C_γ gels. This step worked best if the protein solution was dialyzed for 4 hr against 100 vol of 0.001 M 2-mercaptoethanol prior to addition of the gel. Usually two to three times more alumina C_γ gel was required than the amount described by Berg (35). The step works best if just enough C_γ gel is added to completely absorb all the acetyl-CoA synthetase. This requires that the C_γ gel be added stepwise, first with the amount Berg recommends, and then, if necessary, by doubling or tripling the amount of gel if the enzyme is not absorbed. The recovery and specific activities of this preparation agreed well with the figures given by Berg (35).

Occasionally, usually as the result of a poor alumina C_γ gel step, the enzyme isolated by this procedure contained quantities of lactate dehydrogenase. Since this enzyme could interfere with the assay, it was removed by chromatography on DEAE-cellulose, when necessary, as follows: The enzyme was dialyzed against 0.005 M phosphate buffer, pH 8.0, containing 0.001 M dithiothreitol and applied to a DEAE-cellulose column (1 × 10 cm) previously equilibrated with this buffer. The protein was washed into the column with the same buffer and eluted with a phosphate buffer gradient prepared by placing 300 ml of 0.005 M phosphate buffer, pH 8.0, containing 0.001 M dithiothreitol in the mixing chamber, and 300 ml of 0.2 M phosphate buffer, pH 7, containing 0.001 M dithiothreitol in the other chamber of the gradient apparatus. The acetyl-CoA synthetase was usually found in the first peak eluted from the column, appearing at about 400 ml of eluate. A large number of units were lost in this step, but a 5- to 10-fold purification was obtained. The protein eluted from the DEAE-cellulose column was precipitated with ammonium sulfate and dissolved in 0.1 M phosphate buffer, pH 7.5, containing 0.001 M dithiothreitol.

Acetyl-CoA synthetase purified from bovine heart mitochondria by the method of Webster (36) may also be used. This crystalline enzyme has been well characterized by Webster (36–38), but the preparation is longer than that from yeast (35), and the resulting enzyme is less stable. Since it had no great advantage over the less pure yeast preparation, the yeast enzyme was utilized in these experiments.

The acetyl-CoA synthetase was assayed using the conditions of the microenzymic assay described in this paper with the exception that 10 μmoles of potassium acetate and 50 μmoles of potassium fluoride were added, and acetyl-CoA synthetase was made rate-limiting.

Reference standards of potassium acetate were prepared by dilution of glacial acetic acid with the appropriate quantity of water containing a slight molar excess of potassium hydroxide.

Hydrolysis and Extraction

The protein sample to be studied was assayed before hydrolysis for the presence of any acetate remaining from the purification procedure. If any acetate was found, the sample was extensively dialyzed and reassayed for acetate. Protein samples calculated to contain between 0.10 and 0.60 μmole of acetic acid after hydrolysis were placed in 1.0 ml hydrolysis vials. Samples containing 0.05 μmole can be assayed, but since the change in optical density is small a larger error results. Samples containing 0.10 μmole are easily assayed. The sample was dissolved in 200 μl of 18 *N* H_2SO_4 by gentle mixing on a Vortex mixer. The protein sample may be lyophilized upon the surface of the hydrolysis vial, or the lyophilization step may be omitted if the protein sample is concentrated, and an equal volume of concentrated H_2SO_4 added directly. The hydrolysis vial was flushed with nitrogen and sealed.

The protein samples were hydrolyzed in an oil bath at 105°C for 2 hr. After hydrolysis the vials were thoroughly chilled in ice and briefly centrifuged at low speeds to remove any liquid adhering to the vial walls. During all subsequent manipulations, the hydrolyzate was chilled to prevent the loss of acetic acid. After chilling, the vials were opened, the contents carefully removed with a Pasteur pipet which had been drawn to a fine tip, and transferred to a chilled 10 × 75 mm test tube placed in an ice bath. The vial was carefully washed with a 0.10 ml portion of cold water, which was removed and added to the hydrolyzate, and the washing step was repeated with an additional 0.10 ml aliquot of cold water.

The acetic acid was extracted from the hydrolyzate as follows: 150 mg of anhydrous sodium sulfate and 500 μl of *tert*-butyl ethyl ether (extracted prior to use with an equal volume of 0.5 *N* KOH) were added to each tube. The tubes were carefully mixed several times on a Vortex mixer, and allowed to stand for 3 min in an ice bath to allow the layers to separate. If the organic and aqueous layers do not separate quickly, the tubes may be briefly centrifuged to facilitate the separation. The *t*-BEE layer was carefully removed with a Pasteur pipet which had been drawn to a fine tip, and transferred to a 10 × 75 mm chilled test tube containing 0.20 ml of 1 *M* Tris buffer, pH 8.2, and 0.10 ml of 1.0 *N* KOH. The acetic acid was extracted from the organic layer into the alkaline Tris layer by mixing several times on the Vortex mixer. The *t*-BEE was removed from the alkaline Tris solution under vacuum while carefully shaking the tube on a Vortex mixer. This was accomplished by placing a one-holed stopper containing a T tube into the 10 × 75 mm test tube. One section of the T was attached to a water aspirator, and the remaining section of the T was used to control the vacuum by closing or releasing the system to the atmosphere. At this stage it is not necessary to completely remove the *t*-BEE. The protein hydrolyzate was re-extracted with 500 μl of fresh *t*-BEE, the acetic acid in the organic layer was extracted into the alkaline Tris solution, and the *t*-BEE was removed under vacuum as before. This extraction sequence was carried out a total of 4 times.

After the last extraction had been completed, the alkaline Tris mixture was quickly brought to room temperature in a 25° water bath and the last remaining traces of *tert*-butyl ethyl ether were removed by briefly evacuating the tube while mixing the solution on a Vortex mixer.

After removal of the *t*-BEE, 0.10 ml of 1.0 *N* HCl and 0.10 ml of cold water were added to the alkaline Tris extract, bringing the pH to about 8 and the volume to 0.50 ml. Any residue or droplets remaining on the side of the test tube were carefully mixed with the rest of the Tris extract using a glass rod, and if necessary, centrifugation. After careful mixing, aliquots of the Tris-acetate solution were assayed in the microenzymic assay described below.

Microenzymic Assay for Acetate

The basic components of the microenzymic assay system are similar to those described in the earlier method (22). In this method, added acetate is quantitatively converted to citrate with the production of an equivalent quantity of DPNH. The enzymic reactions involved in this assay are shown below:

$$\text{acetate} + \text{ATP} + \text{CoA} \overset{Mg^{++}}{\rightleftharpoons} \text{acetyl-CoA} + \text{AMP} + \text{PP}_i$$
$$\text{L-malate} + \text{DPN}^+ \rightleftharpoons \text{oxalacetate} + \text{DPNH} + \text{H}^+$$
$$\text{acetyl-CoA} + \text{oxalacetate} + H_2O \rightarrow \text{citrate} + \text{CoA}$$

In this procedure, acetate is converted to acetyl-CoA in the presence of acetyl-CoA synthetase, CoA, $MgCl_2$, and ATP. The acetyl-CoA formed is coupled with oxalacetate to form citrate in the presence of citrate-condensing enzyme. Oxalacetate in turn is formed from L-malate in the presence of malate dehydrogenase and DPN^+, and the appearance of DPNH is followed spectrophotometrically at 340 mμ. If the precautions recently described by Pearson are followed (39) (see "Discussion"), the amount of DPN^+ reduced to DPNH is equivalent to the amount of acetate added. The optical assay was carried out in 1.4 ml silica cuvets with a 1 cm light path.

The complete reaction mixture (in a total volume of 1.05 ml) contained:

200 μmoles Tris buffer, pH 8.2; 5 μmoles magnesium chloride; 10 μmoles adenosine triphosphate; 1.0 μmole dithiothreitol; 0.10 μmole

CoA; 1.0 μmole potassium L-malate; 1.4 μmoles DPN^+; malate dehydrogenase (5 μg of protein; specific activity 39); citrate-condensing enzyme (20 μg of protein; specific activity 70); acetyl-CoA synthetase (50 μg; specific activity 50); and 0.06 μmole potassium acetate.

A cuvet without CoA or without acetyl-CoA synthetase, but containing 0.05 μmole of DPNH, served as a control. In the previous method, 0.10 μmole of DPNH had been added to satisfy the equilibrium considerations between oxalacetate and DPNH as discussed by Pearson (39). However, even under optimal conditions, commercial DPNH rapidly develops an inhibitor to the over-all reaction in aqueous solution; thus, in this method, the proper quantity of DPNH was generated in the cuvet by the addition of 0.06 μmole of potassium acetate. When this system had reached equilibrium, the aliquot containing the unknown quantity of acetate was added to the assay mixture, and the appearance of DPNH was followed spectrophotometrically at 340 mμ until the system reached equilibrium. At this time, the change in absorbance was noted and the quantity of DPNH produced was calculated from its molar extinction coefficient (40). The change in absorbancy was followed using a Beckman DB spectrophotometer equipped with a Photovolt Varicord model 43 Recorder at a chart speed of 6 in./hr.

All the stock solutions which required such treatment were neutralized with KOH prior to use in the optical assay. The use of NaOH should be avoided since acetyl-CoA synthetase is inhibited by sodium ions (35, 38). The stock solutions should be made fresh every week and should be frozen between use.

The response of the assay is always slightly below 100% (usually 96–99% of the added acetate is converted to citrate and DPNH) and a standard is run each day with a known quantity of acetate to obtain a correction factor. This correction factor is then used in subsequent assays. A sample calculation follows:

Standard:

0.05 μmole acetate standard added.
Change in absorbancy at 340 mμ = 0.270.
Final volume = 1.10 ml.
Total absorbancy = (0.27 × 1.10) = 0.297.
μmole DPNH = 0.0479.
% recovery = 96%.

Unknown:

0.05 ml aliquot of an unknown sample with a total volume of 0.40 ml added.
Change in absorbancy at 340 mμ = 0.170.

Final volume = 1.10 ml.
Corrected total absorbancy = 0.187.
μmole DPNH = 0.0305.
Corrected for 96% recovery = 0.0314 μmole.
Amount of acetate per aliquot = 0.0314 μmole.
Total amount per sample = (0.0314 × 8) = 0.25 μmole.

RESULTS AND DISCUSSION

Hydrolysis and Extraction Steps

The relatively large volume of 6 *N* hydrochloric acid utilized in our previous procedure (22) made handling and quantitative extraction difficult. Following the suggestion of Ward *et al.* (26), we found that optimal hydrolysis conditions for our assay were obtained using small volumes of either 12 or 18 *N* sulfuric acid. Hydrolysis times greater than 2 hr at 105° did not increase the amount of acetate released from the sample, in agreement with the findings of Ward *et al.* (26). Alkaline hydrolysis conditions should be avoided because various amino acids, especially serine and threonine, decompose to form acetate under such conditions. This occurs both in synthetic mixtures of amino acids and in bovine serum albumin, which contains no acetyl residues (22). In addition, *t*-BEE was employed as the extracting solvent instead of the diethyl ether used previously (22) because of its lower volatility.

The quantity of inhibitor carried from the hydrolysis mixture into the assay cuvet is minimal in this method, and a linear response to aliquot size is obtained. The hydrolysis volume must be kept as small as possible, since the quantity of acetate extracted into the *t*-BEE decreases with increasing hydrolysate volume. Both protein hydrolyzates and mixtures of synthetic amino acids inhibited the enzymic reactions of the assay, making it impossible to assay the hydrolyzate directly as originally hoped.

Four extractions with *t*-BEE will quantitatively remove up to 0.90 to 1.0 μmole of acetate, but the efficiency decreases past this point (see Table 2). Protein samples with an acetyl content higher than this level should be reassayed at a lower level. The *t*-BEE must be extracted with an equal volume of 0.5 *N* KOH just prior to use to remove an acidic impurity which interferes with the optical assay.

In general two sources of error can be anticipated. First, the removal of *t*-BEE from the aqueous layer may not be complete. This error will be minimal with a little practice since the final *t*-BEE extract usually contains negligible quantities of acetate. This source of error can be eliminated by the addition of a fifth extraction with *t*-BEE if relatively high quantities of acetate are expected. The second source of error is a possible loss in volume from the alkaline Tris layer when the *t*-BEE is removed under vacuum. However, control experiments indicate this loss represents less than 5% error.

Conditions of the Microenzymic Assay

The basic components of the microenzymic assay are similar to those described in the earlier version of this method (22), and the reader is referred to that paper for a more detailed discussion of the assay variables. The most troublesome of these conditions is the need for an initial 10:1 ratio of DPNH to oxalacetate, noted first by Pearson (39) for the acetyl-CoA assay of Ochoa, Stern, and Schneider (41), and which is also necessary in this assay (22). The data shown in Figure 1 demonstrate the variable response of this assay to changing ratios of DPNH to oxalacetate.

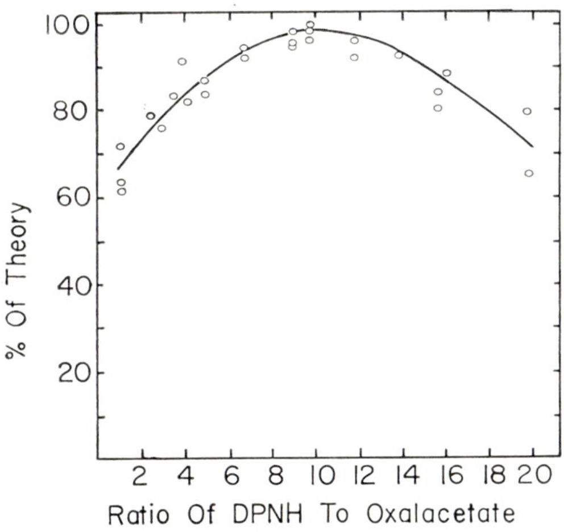

FIG. 1. Effect of varying ratios of DPNH to oxalacetate on the quantitative conversion of added acetate to citrate.

Commercial DPNH rapidly develops an inhibitor to the enzymic reactions of this assay in aqueous solution, presumably similar to those encountered by Fawcett *et al.* (42). The present method generates the required amount of DPNH in the assay cuvet by the addition of 0.06 μmole of acetate. If desired, DPNH can be substituted for the acetate if added in sufficient quantity to give a 10:1 initial ratio of DPNH to oxalacetate, but a fresh sample must be prepared for each assay.

Specificity of Assay

The microenzymic method described is quite specific for acetate. The following compounds were found to be inactive when tested at final concentrations of 50 or 250 μM in the assay system: potassium formate, potassium trichloroacetate, potassium propionate, potassium lactate, potassium pyruvate, potassium butyrate, potassium α-hydroxybutyrate, potassium α-hydroxyisobutyrate. Acrylate and propionate are substrates of the acetyl-CoA synthetase, although only one-third as active as acetate (43), but propionyl-CoA, butyryl-CoA, malonyl-CoA, and glycolyl-CoA are not substrates for the citrate-condensing enzyme.[3] Thus the specificity of the assay is not surprising.

Quantitative Response of the Assay to Added Acetate

Under the conditions described, the microenzymic assay gives a linear response to added acetate as shown in Figure 2. As little as 0.01 μmole of

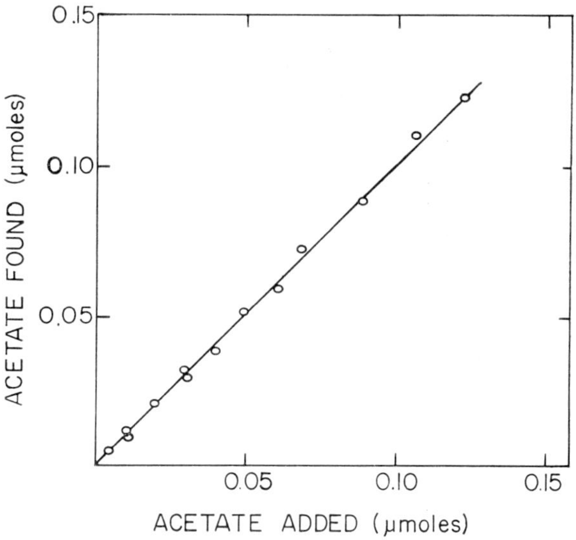

FIG. 2. Response of microenzymic assay to added acetate (see "Methods" for description).

acetate is easily assayed. Aliquots found to contain quantities of acetate greater than 0.10 to 0.12 μmole should be reassayed at greater dilution since accurate absorbancy readings are difficult to obtain in this range.

Application of the Assay to Protein Hydrolyzates

The data in Table 1 show the response of the assay system to bovine serum albumin hydrolyzates containing known quantities of acetate. Each sample containing 0.20 μmole of bovine serum albumin and the designated quantity of acetate was dissolved in 200 μl of 18 N H_2SO_4, hydrolyzed for

[3] P. Srere, personal communication.

TABLE 1
Replicate Analysis of Bovine Serum Albumin Hydrolyzates Containing Known Quantities of Acetate

Components	Acetate, μmole		Per cent recovery
	Theoretical	Found	
Bovine serum albumin	0.00	0.01	
+ 0.05 μmole acetate	0.06	0.07	116
+ 0.10 μmole acetate	0.11	0.12	109
+ 0.15 μmole acetate	0.16	0.15	93
+ 0.20 μmole acetate	0.21	0.20	95
+ 0.20 μmole acetate	0.21	0.21	100
+ 0.25 μmole acetate	0.26	0.25	96
+ 0.40 μmole acetate	0.41	0.40	97
Mean ± standard deviation		101 ± 8%	

2 hr at 105°, and carried through the entire assay procedure. The results show good recovery of the added acetate, and demonstrate the absence of acetyl groups in bovine serum albumin as expected. The mean average recovery was 102% with a standard deviation of ±6%.

The data contained in Table 2 show the results obtained by applying this procedure to samples of ovalbumin, a protein which has been shown to contain four acetyl groups per molecule of 45,000 molecular weight (7). The ovalbumin used was the gift of Professor H. B. Bull, and had been freshly prepared by a slight modification of the method of Kekwick and Cannan (44). Some samples of ovalbumin contained a quantity of acetate added prior to hydrolysis as indicated. The samples were dissolved in 200 μl

TABLE 2
Replicate Analysis of Ovalbumin for Acetyl Groups

Components	Acetate, μmole		Per cent recovery
	Theoretical	Found	
1.28 mg ovalbumin	0.11	0.11	100
1.28 mg ovalbumin + 0.2 μmole acetate	0.31	0.28	90
1.71 mg ovalbumin	0.15	0.14	93
1.71 mg ovalbumin + 0.2 μmole acetate	0.35	0.34	97
2.56 mg ovalbumin	0.23	0.24	104
2.56 mg ovalbumin + 0.2 μmole acetate	0.43	0.43	100
5.13 mg ovalbumin	0.46	0.47	102
5.13 mg ovalbumin + 0.2 μmole acetate	0.66	0.66	100
10.25 mg ovalbumin	0.91	0.98	108
10.25 mg ovalbumin + 0.2 μmole acetate	1.12	1.11	99
20.5 mg ovalbumin	1.82	1.09	60
20.5 mg ovalbumin + 0.2 μmole acetate	2.02	1.11	56
Mean and standard deviation of samples containing 1.1 μmole or less = 99.3 ± 5%			

of 18 N H_2SO_4, hydrolyzed for 2 hr, and carried through the entire assay procedure.

The results obtained are in excellent agreement with the theoretical values based on the data of Johansen, Marshall, and Neuberger (7), and also show an excellent recovery of the added acetate. The data also show that, as the quantity of acetate in the sample exceeds 1.0 μmole, the acetate is no longer quantitatively extracted from the hydrolyzate. This was confirmed by extracting such samples with additional quantities of *t*-BEE and assaying the acetate remaining in these samples. This places an upper limit of 0.9 to 1.0 μmole of acetyl groups per protein sample on the method.

Although the samples of ovalbumin used contained the expected quantity of acetyl groups, certain commercial preparations varied widely in acetyl content. Preparations containing 2, 3, and 4 acetyl groups per mole were obtained from various commercial sources. The acetate content of the various ovalbumin samples was checked by the method of Phillips (24), and the results obtained in this manner were in good agreement with those obtained by the microenzymic method.

The data in Table 3 show the results obtained by applying this procedure

TABLE 3
Replicate Analysis of Horse Heart Cytochrome *c* for Acetyl Groups

Protein assayed, μmole	Acetate added, μmole	Acetate found, μmole	Acetyl groups, mole/mole protein	Acetate, μmole, theor.[a]	Per cent recovery of added acetate
0.09	—	0.08	0.89	—	—
0.09	—	0.09	1.00	—	—
0.12	—	0.11	0.91	—	—
0.15	—	0.14	0.93	—	—
0.15	—	0.13	0.87	—	—
0.15	—	0.14	0.93	—	—
0.09	0.05	0.13	—	0.13	100
0.09	0.10	0.19	—	0.18	105
0.11	0.05	0.16	—	0.15	107
0.11	0.10	0.18	—	0.20	90
0.11	0.15	0.27	—	0.25	108
0.15	0.05	0.17	—	0.19	89
0.15	0.10	0.24	—	0.24	100
0.15	0.10	0.25	—	0.24	104
0.15	0.15	0.29	—	0.29	100
0.18	0.08	0.25	—	0.25	100
0.18	0.10	0.27	—	0.27	100
0.18	0.15	0.30	—	0.32	94

Mean number of acetyl groups per mole ± standard deviation = 0.92 ± 0.04
Mean recovery of added acetate ± standard deviation = 99.8 ± 5.7%

[a] Theoretical calculations are based on actual acetyl analysis of 0.92 mole per mole.

to commercial samples of horse heart cytochrome *c*. The protein concentration of the cytochrome *c* was measured by its extinction coefficient at 280 mμ (45). Each sample contained the indicated quantity of protein, and where indicated, an additional quantity of acetate added prior to hydrolysis. The hydrolysis and extraction steps were carried out as described earlier. The data show the presence of 0.92 mole of acetyl groups per mole of protein in this preparation, in good agreement with the expected value of 1 mole per mole (2). The data also show good recovery of added acetate with a mean average recovery of 99.8% with a standard deviation of ±5.8%.

The various commercial cytochrome *c* preparations assayed showed the same wide variation (0.30 to 0.95 mole per mole) in the number of acetyl groups noted in the ovalbumin samples. However, the recovery of added acetate was excellent in all cases, indicating the low values obtained were due to hydrolysis of the amino-terminal *N*-acetyl bond of this protein during preparation or storage.

Commercial preparations of cytochrome *c* contain substantial quantities of acetate which are not covalently bound. This acetate undoubtedly arises from the purification procedure which utilizes an acetic acid extraction and acetate buffers. This acetate was not completely removed either by dialysis against buffer or 8 *M* urea, or by chromatography of the protein on Sephedex G-25 or Bio Gel P-2 resins. Thus, the protein samples were carefully assayed for the presence of noncovalently bound acetate before hydrolysis. Direct analysis for acetate in protein samples is difficult, since, as noted earlier, the microenzymic assay is inhibited at higher protein concentrations, giving a nonlinear response to added sample. However, this noncovalently bonded acetate was completely extracted from the acidified protein sample into *t*-BEE. Accordingly, samples of the protein dissolved in 0.4 ml of 6 *N* sulfuric acid were extracted before hydrolysis using the usual *t*-BEE and alkaline Tris buffer procedure, and the extracted acetate was assayed in the microenzymic method. All the data in Table 3 have been corrected for these values.

The data in Table 4 show the results obtained by applying this procedure to a variety of protein samples. The values for bovine serum albumin, ovalbumin, and horse heart cytochrome *c* are average values taken from Tables 1, 2, and 3. Samples of beef heart cytochrome *c* assayed showed the presence of 0.62 mole of acetyl group per mole of protein. Although this figure is lower than the expected value of 1 mole per mole (2), the recovery of added acetate from these samples was excellent, indicating partial hydrolysis of the *N*-acetyl bond had taken place during storage. Rat liver malate dehydrogenase (mitochondrial form) contained no acetyl groups. Rabbit muscle aldolase, a preparation of specific activity 10, contained

0.29 mole of acetyl groups per mole. This finding is of interest in view of the current discussions concerning the number of polypeptide chains in this protein (46–54), but may be due to the presence of other proteins in the sample assayed. A freshly prepared sample of rabbit muscle pyruvate kinase provided by G. L. Cottam and M. J. Coon was found to contain an

TABLE 4
Acetyl Group Analysis of Several Protein Samples

Sample	Protein assayed, μmole	Acetate found, μmole	Acetyl groups, mole/mole protein
Bovine serum albumin	0.200	0.01	0.05
Ovalbumin	0.114	0.47	4.1
Cytochrome *c* (horse heart)	0.150	0.14	0.93
Cytochrome *c* (beef heart)	0.160	0.10	0.62
Malate dehydrogenase (rat liver)	0.132	0.01	0.07
Aldolase (rabbit muscle)	0.140	0.04	0.29
Pyruvate kinase	0.039	0.16	4.1
(rabbit muscle)	0.046	0.17	3.7

average of 3.9 moles of acetyl groups per mole. This figure agrees well with the other physical and chemical data for this protein obtained by these investigators (55). Commercial preparations of rabbit muscle pyruvate kinase usually contained substantially fewer acetyl groups, while retaining enzymic activity.

General Discussion

Although a variety of methods are available for the determination of acetate (21–34), the methods available for the determination of acetyl groups in proteins (1, 7, 10, 21–26) require fairly large quantities of protein (0.5 to 10 μmoles). Even the excellent method of Ward *et al.* (26) requires 0.5 to 2.0 μmoles of protein or 0.33 to 1.6 μmoles of acetate. The micro-enzymic method described in this paper has an advantage in sensitivity over the other methods, using only 0.05 to 0.90 μmole of protein or an equivalent quantity of acetate. This procedure has eliminated the disadvantages due to inhibitors present in an earlier version of the assay (22), making it easier to use, and giving greater reproducibility with small samples.

The present method does not differentiate between *N*-acetyl and *O*-acetyl residues, and for such work the differential hydrazinolysis technique of Phillips (24) must be utilized.

In these studies, it has been noted that the number of acetyl groups found on proteins containing such groups varied widely from preparation to preparation. The effect of this variation on the biological activity of such proteins as ovalbumin and cytochrome *c* is difficult to access, but it now appears that enzymes like pyruvate kinase may also be isolated in varying acetylation states. Additional studies are being carried out in an attempt to clarify the relationship of the acetyl groups to the biological activity of the protein.

SUMMARY

A micro method for the determination of acetyl groups in proteins and peptides is described. The procedure involves acid hydrolysis, extraction of the liberated acetic acid from the hydrolyzate with *tert*-butyl ethyl ether, extraction of the acetic acid from the *tert*-butyl ethyl ether into Tris buffer, and assay by enzymic means. The procedure requires only 0.10 to 0.90 μmole of protein or an equivalent quantity of acetate. Application of the method to simulated hydrolyzates, known acetylated proteins, and several proteins which have not previously been studied is described.

ACKNOWLEDGMENTS

The author wishes to express his appreciation to Dr. L. T. Webster, Jr., for making available his data on the beef heart acetyl-CoA synthetase prior to publication, and to Dr. C. S. Vestling for his helpful comments and suggestions.

REFERENCES

1. Narita, K., *Biochim. Biophys. Acta* **28,** 184 (1958).
2. Titani, I., Narita, K., and Okunuki, I., *J. Biochem. (Tokyo)* **51,** 350 (1962).
3. Harris, J. I., and Hindley, J., *J. Mol. Biol.* **3,** 117 (1961).
4. Narita, K., *Biochim. Biophys. Acta* **31,** 372 (1959).
5. Harris, J. I., *Biochem. J.* **71,** 451 (1959).
6. Folk, J. I., and Gladner, J. A., *Biochim. Biophys. Acta* **44,** 383 (1960).
7. Johansen, P. G., Marshall, R. D., and Neuberger, A., *Biochem. J.* **77,** 239 (1960).
8. Narita, K., and Ishii, J., *J. Biochem. (Tokyo)* **52,** 367 (1962).
9. Satake, K., Sasakawa, S., and Maruyama, T., *J. Biochem. (Tokyo)* **53,** 516 (1963).
10. Schroeder, W. A., Cua, J. T., Matsuda, G., and Fenninger, W. D., *Biochim. Biophys. Acta* **63,** 532 (1962).
11. Phillips, D. M. P., *Biochem. J.* **87,** 258 (1963).
12. Winstead, J. A., and Wold, F., *Biochemistry* **3,** 791 (1964).
13. Offer, G. W., *Biochim. Biophys. Acta* **90,** 193 (1964).
14. Gaetjens, E., and Barany, M., *Biochim. Biophys. Acta* **117,** 176 (1966).
15. Alving, R. E., and Laki, K., *Biochemistry* **5,** 2597 (1966).
16. Suran, A. A., *Arch. Biochem. Biophys.* **113,** 1 (1966).
17. Alving, R. E., Moczar, E., and Laki, K., *Biochem. Biophys. Res. Commun.* **23,** 540 (1966).

18. Marrig, C., *Biochim. Biophys. Acta* **105,** 606 (1965).
19. Hörmann, H., and Joseph, K. T., *Biochim. Biophys. Acta* **100,** 598 (1965).
20. Van Eys, J., Judd, J., Ford, J., and Womack, W. B., *Biochemistry* **3,** 1755 (1965).
21. Ward, D. N., and Coffey, J. A., *Biochemistry* **3,** 1575 (1964).
22. Stegink, L. D., and Vestling, C. S., *J. Biol. Chem.* **241,** 4923 (1966).
23. Augustyniak, J. Z., and Martin, W. G., *Can. J. Biochem.* **43,** 291 (1965).
24. Phillips, D. M. P., *Biochem. J.* **86,** 397 (1963).
25. Ludowieg, J., and Dorfman, A., *Biochim. Biophys. Acta* **38,** 212 (1960).
26. Ward, D. N., Coffey, J. A., Ray, D. B., and Lamkin, W. M., *Anal. Biochem.* **14,** 243 (1966).
27. Von Korff, R. W., *J. Biol. Chem.* **210,** 539 (1954).
28. Rose, I. R., *in* "Methods in Enzymology" (S. P. Colowick and N. O. Kaplan, eds.), Vol. I, p. 591. Academic Press, New York, 1959.
29. Bartley, W., *Biochem. J.* **53,** 305 (1953).
30. Lundquist, F., Fugmann, U., and Rasmussen, H., *Biochem. J.* **80,** 393 (1961).
31. Medzihradsky, F., and Lamprecht, W., *Z. Physiol. Chem.* **343,** 35 (1965).
32. Bergmeyer, H. U., and Moellering, H., *Biochem. Z.* **344,** 167 (1966).
33. Jackson, R. B., *J. Chromatog.* **16,** 306 (1964).
34. Kaplanova, B., and Janak, J., *Mikrochim. Acta* **2,** 119 (1966).
35. Berg, P., *in* "Methods in Enzymology" (S. P. Colowick and N. O. Kaplan, eds.), Vol. V, p. 461. Academic Press, New York, 1962.
36. Webster, L. T., Jr., *J. Biol. Chem.* **240,** 4158 (1965).
37. Webster, L. T., Jr., *J. Biol. Chem.* **240,** 4164 (1965).
38. Webster, L. T., Jr., *J. Biol. Chem.* **241,** 5504 (1966).
39. Pearson, D. J., *Biochem. J.* **95,** 23c (1965).
40. Horecker, B. L., and Kornberg, A., *J. Biol. Chem.* **175,** 385 (1948).
41. Ochoa, S., Stern, J. R., and Schneider, M. C., *J. Biol. Chem.* **193,** 691 (1951).
42. Fawcett, C. P., Ciotti, M. M., and Kaplan, N. O., *Biochim. Biophys. Acta* **54,** 210 (1961).
43. Jones, M. E., and Lippman, F., *in* "Methods in Enzymology" (S. P. Colowick and N. O. Kaplan, eds.), Vol. I, p. 585. Academic Press, New York, 1959.
44. Kekwick, R. A., and Cannan, R. K., *Biochem. J.* **30,** 227 (1936).
45. Margoliash, E., and Frohwirt, N., *Biochem. J.* **71,** 570 (1959).
46. Drechsler, E. R., Boyer, P. D., and Kowalsky, A. G., *J. Biol. Chem.* **234,** 2627 (1959).
47. Winstead, J. A., and Wold, F., *J. Biol. Chem.* **239,** 4212 (1964).
48. Edelstein, S. J., and Schachman, H. K., *Federation Proc.* **25,** 412 (1966).
49. Ginsburg, A., and Mehler, A. H., *Federation Proc.* **25,** 407 (1966).
50. Castellino, F. J., and Barker, R., *Biochem. Biophys. Res. Commun.* **23,** 182 (1966).
51. Stellwagen, E., and Schachman, H. K., *Biochemistry* **1,** 1056 (1962).
52. Deal, W. C., Rutter, W. J., and Van Holde, K. E., *Biochemistry* **2,** 246 (1963).
53. Kawahara, K., and Tanford, C., *Biochemistry* **5,** 1578 (1966).
54. Penhoet, E., Rajkumar, T., and Rutter, W. J., *Proc. Natl. Acad. Sci. U. S.* **56,** 1275 (1966).
55. Hollenberg, P. F., Cottam, G. L., and Coon, M. J., *Federation Proc.* **26,** 60Z (1967).

ANALYTICAL BIOCHEMISTRY 20, 517–524 (1967)

Correction for Cross-Contamination in AutoAnalyzer Analysis

VOLNEY WALLACE

Chemical Division, Test Operations Directorate, Dugway Proving Ground, Dugway, Utah, 84022

Received January 19, 1967

A particular problem in AutoAnalyzer analysis is the masking of weak samples by strong samples. Weak samples sometimes appear on the recorder strip chart as distorted or hidden peaks at the base of a major peak. Rerunning the sample by itself gives a lower reading indicating positive interference. The solution to this problem has been to decrease operating rate to the point that reruns are seldom needed. The situation is undesirable because of the expense of rerunning samples, the arbitrary nature of the decision to rerun a sample, and the limitation it places on operating rate.

The problem of carryover or cross-contamination in AutoAnalyzer analysis can be blamed on the analyst for using standard curves and data processing methods designed for assays free of cross-contamination. When cross-contamination is relatively consistent it can be evaluated and corrected for in data processing with consequent gain in reliability and operating rate.

One laboratory reported carryover correction at a recent symposium (1). Carryover error was treated as proportional to the concentration of the preceding sample. This treatment is simple and practical but not always applicable as this paper will show.

SIMPLE CROSS-CONTAMINATION

The AutoAnalyzer operating at 60–120 samples per hour commonly shows cross-contamination resulting from sample tailing. The contamination appears to be constant on a volume basis as equations based on this assumption fit the usual case of cross-contamination. The basic equation based on this assumption and on a linear absorbance/sample concentration relationship is:

$$A_n = (1 - m)ac_n + mA_{n-1} + b \qquad (1)$$

where A = absorbance,

c = concentration given no cross-contamination,

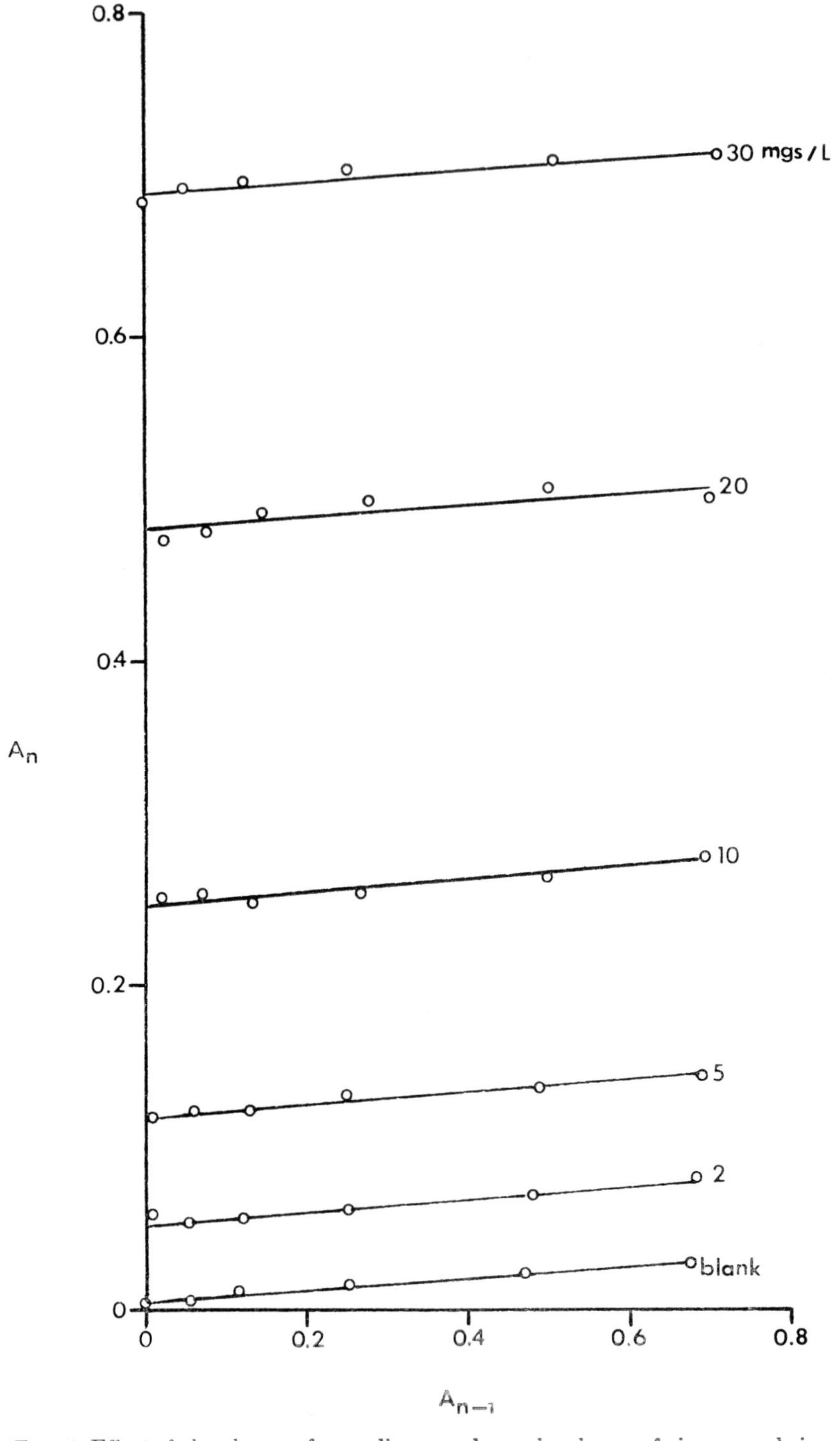

FIG. 1. Effect of absorbance of preceding sample on absorbance of given sample in an AutoAnalyzer method for atropine.

a = absorptivity,
m = proportion of sample $n - 1$ in sample n,
b = reagent and/or instrument blank, and n, $n - 1$ denote sample sequence.

This is rearranged to a form convenient for data reduction

$$c_n = \frac{A_n - mA_{n-1} - b}{(1 - m)a} \tag{2}$$

To test the applicability of equation 1, data are plotted according to this equation first for constant values of c_n and then for zero values of A_{n-1}. This is illustrated in Figures 1 and 2, respectively, with data from the

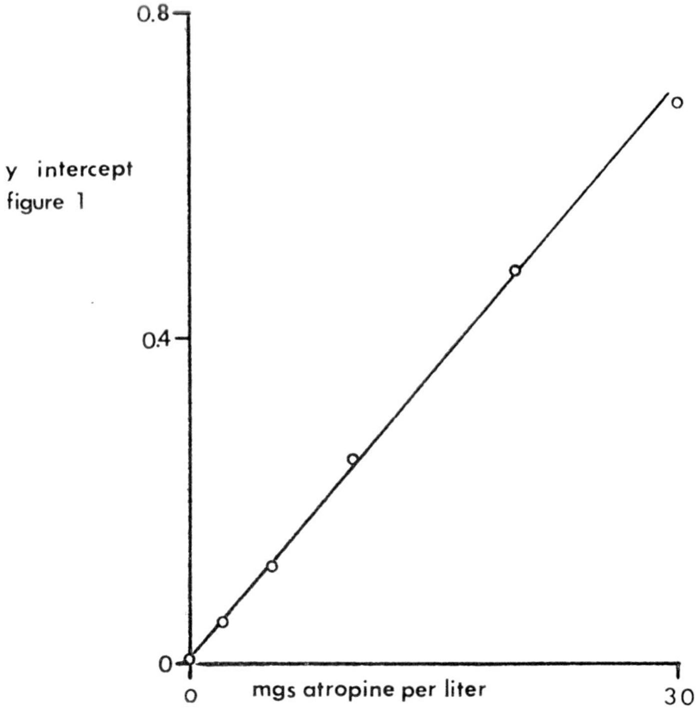

FIG. 2. Absorbance vs. concentration given. $A_{n-1} = 0$.

preceding article (2). In the first plot the slope of the concentration contours equals m. If m is positive there is contamination by the preceding sample. If the contours are linear and parallel then m is independent of c_n and c_{n-1}. In the case in hand the slope is positive, indicating contamination, and the contours are for practical purposes linear and parallel.

In Figure 2 a straight line indicates a linear relationship between absorb-

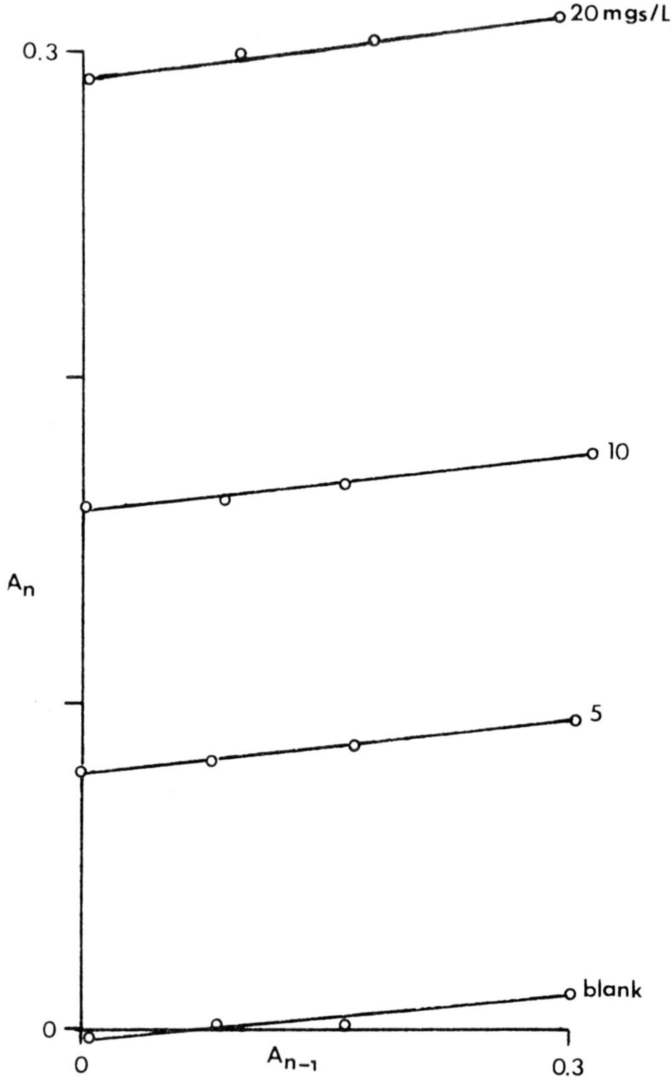

FIG. 3. Effect of absorbance of preceding sample in analysis of *o*-chlorobenzalmalononitrile.

ance and sample concentration. The slope of the line is absorptivity and the *y* intercept is the value of the blank.

Not all cases are this simple. One may find nonlinear relationships and there may be cross-contamination from more than one other sample. The following section describes one such case.

COMPLEX CROSS-CONTAMINATION

A moderately complicated case of cross-contamination was encountered in a trial method for *o*-chlorobenzalmalononitrile. The method, which is not recommended, consisted in mixing without incubation (A) 0.05% aqueous sodium 1,2-naphthoquinone-4-sulfonic acid, (B) 0.05% NaOH in a 1:9 mixture of water and isopropanol, and (C) sample in isopropanol in the sequence (A + B)+C and in the volume ratio of 1:1:2. The sample program was continual intake of sample with samples being changed every 30 sec.

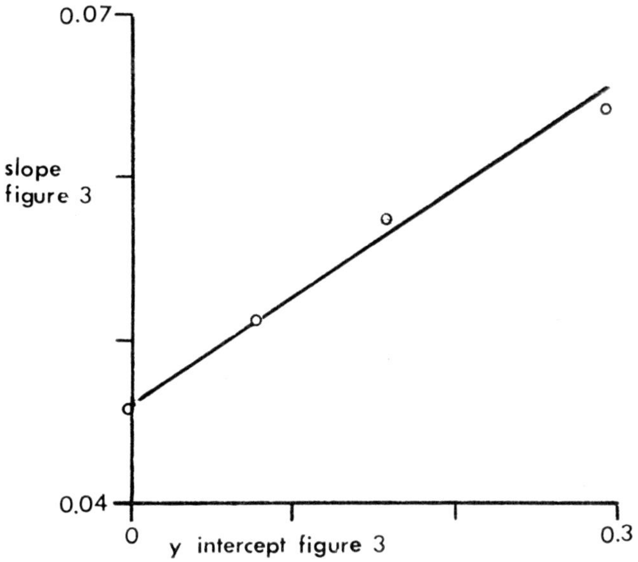

FIG. 4. Variation in slope in Figure 3.

In this assay it was observed that a given sample was contaminated by both the preceding and the succeeding samples. The contamination from the preceding sample did not behave as a constant volume contamination.

For simplicity of presentation this case is treated by "correcting" the observed absorbance for cross-contamination. The correct absorbance is taken as the value obtained when the given sample is contaminated by samples of the same absorbance. Data obtained under other conditions is corrected to this norm on the basis of observed relationships.

Graphs of data from this method of analysis are shown in Figures 3–5. Figures 3 and 4 show that there is carryover from the preceding sample with an interaction such that high concentration of the given sample boosts the effect of the carryover. The cause of this is not known. It is treated

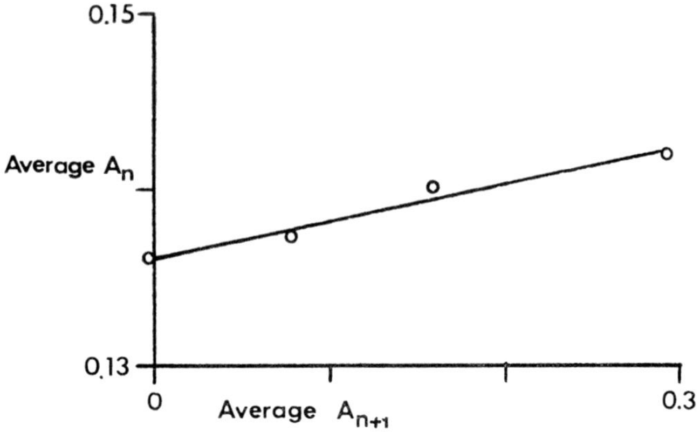

FIG. 5. Data grouped according to concentration of the $(n + 1)$th sample.

simply as a variable value of m. Figure 5 shows that there is contamination of the given sample by the succeeding sample.

The cross-contamination shown by Figures 3 and 5 is assumed to be additive, which leads to equation 3:

$$(A)_{\text{corr}} = A_n + m_1(A_n - A_{n-1}) + m_2(A_n - A_{n+1}) \tag{3}$$

where m_1 is the slope in Figure 3
m_2 is the slope in Figure 5, and
$(A)_{\text{corr}}$ is the corrected value of A_n.

Substituting observed values, we arrive at equation 4:

$$(A)_{\text{corr}} = A_n + (0.0457 + 0.0614A_n)(A_n - A_{n-1}) + 0.0215(A_n - A_{n+1}) \tag{4}$$

Equations for corrected absorbance can be tested by comparing the variance of data before and after correcting for cross-contamination. The corrected data should have the lower variance, as the correction should remove cross-contamination as a contributing cause of variance. Equation 4 is tested thus in Table 1. This table shows that the corrected data are indeed lower in variance.

TABLE 1
Correction for Cross-Contamination in Analysis of *o*-Chlorobenzalmalononitrile
(average and standard deviation for eight samples)

Standard sample concn., mg/liter	Observed absorbance	Corrected absorbance
Blank	0.0026 ± 0.0056	−0.0034 ± 0.0060
5	0.0860 ± 0.0063	0.0821 ± 0.0020
10	0.1673 ± 0.0071	0.1695 ± 0.0019
20	0.3015 ± 0.0075	0.3135 ± 0.0038

Absorbancy and the blank relative to $(A)_{corr}$ are derived from the data of Table 1 and substituted into equation 4 to give:

$$c_n = \frac{A_n - 0.006 + (0.0457 + 0.0614A_n)(A_n - A_{n-1}) + 0.0215(A_n - A_{n+1})}{0.0155} \quad (5)$$

Note that corrected absorbance does not appear in the final equation. The concept of a true or correct absorbance is merely a convenience. One could have arrived at the same equation correcting to zero values of A_{n-1} and A_{n+1}. The derivation is a little simpler but the interpretation of the norm is a bit involved.

ECONOMY OF EFFORT

The routine analyst and the research chemist developing a method are interested in economy of effort, but different circumstances prevail and different economies are in order.

In method development, the chemist is faced with the task of defining comprehensively the pattern and magnitude of cross-contamination. In terms of Figure 1, the area bounded by the limits of the assay should be adequately sampled. As a matter of economy the number of samples run should be minimal and the processing of the resultant data should be simple. To this end it is recommended that a standard sample sequence be used which has the following characteristics.

(1) A low number of standard sample concentrations, say 5 or 6.
(2) All permutations of two sample concentrations present in consecutive samples.
(3) No duplication of these permutations.

Figure 6A illustrates individual sequences of two samples given five standard sample concentrations. In Figure 6B these individual sequences are connected into one long sentence. In connecting individual sequences one can inadvertently omit individual sequences as in Figure 6C. This is easier to correct than to avoid, and correction consists of breaking the main sequence and inserting the stranded sequences. Both the main sequence and the correction can be randomized if a random sequence is desired.

This sample sequence permits the plotting of Figure 5 and an analogous plot for testing contamination by the preceding sample. The latter plot yields an average value for m (Fig. 1 or 3) which is a convenience. The property of this sequence, which permits these plots, is that samples of a given standard concentration are both preceded and followed once and once only by each of the standard sample concentrations. When values are grouped according to a given concentration of preceding or succeeding sample, the averages are comparable because the groups are equal with respect to sample concentrations included in the groups.

The foregoing sequence is useful in routine standardization of a procedure if the laboratory has prompt computer service. Lacking this, shortcuts are in order and the particular shortcuts available depends on how much the analyst can assume. If the analyst can assume linear relationships as

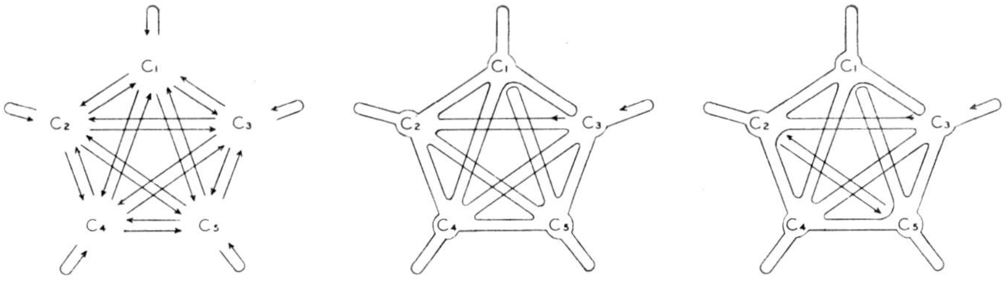

A B C

FIG. 6. (A) Permutations of sample sequence for five samples, C_1 . . . C_5. (B) An over-all sequence containing these individual sequences once and once only. (C) A trial sequence in need of correction.

described by equation 1 and adequate accuracy in his observed or averaged data, he can find the constants of equation 1 with three data points in Figure 1. If only cross-contamination can be assumed to be constant, one can determine its value with a single concentration contour.

SUMMARY

Figures 1, 3, and 5 are graphic demonstrations of cross-contamination in AutoAnalyzer analysis. Equations which express sample concentration as a function of the absorbance of both the given sample and the contaminating sample can be derived from graphs such as these. Insofar as cross-contamination is consistent and the equations are properly derived, these equations eliminate cross-contamination as a source of error in the assay.

Cross-contamination error in AutoAnalyzer analysis is normally avoided by use of a sufficiently slow operating rate. If this error is avoided by data reduction techniques, the AutoAnalyzer can operate at higher rates with attendant economies in time and equipment.

REFERENCES

1. BLAVIS, M. A., AND MENCZ, A., Technicon Symposium, "Automation in Analytical Chemistry," New York, Oct. 1966.
2. WALLACE, V., *Anal. Biochem.* 00, 000 (1967).

ANALYTICAL BIOCHEMISTRY **20**, 525–532 (1967)

A Graphic Method for the Determination and Presentation of Binding Parameters in a Complex System[1]

HANNAH E. ROSENTHAL

Roswell Park Memorial Institute, Buffalo, New York 14203

Received March 15, 1967

Basic information on the association of small molecules with macromolecules can be obtained from equilibrium dialysis or ultrafiltration. It is customary to conduct a series of such experiments by varying the concentration of the small molecule or ligand while the concentrations of the binding macromolecules are held constant. Different graphic methods have been used to plot the experimental results. These methods have in common that they yield a straight line in a graph with rectangular coordinates for the simplest case of one ligand and one group of mutually noninteracting binding sites. The two parameters for binding—the number of binding sites per macromolecule, n, and the intrinsic association constant, k—are obtained from the geometry of these graphs.

The two most widely used graphic presentations are the reciprocal plot and the Scatchard plot (1). In the reciprocal plot, $1/r$ is plotted against $1/[u]$, where r is that fraction of available binding sites on a macromolecule that is occupied by a ligand, and $[u]$ is the concentration of free ligand. The plot follows the equation:

$$\frac{1}{r} = \frac{1}{n} + \frac{1}{nk} \cdot \frac{1}{[u]} \qquad (1)$$

In the Scatchard plot, $r/[u]$ is plotted against r. The plot follows the equation:

$$\frac{r}{[u]} = kn - kr \qquad (2)$$

If the macromolecule has more than one group of binding sites, a curved line is obtained rather than a straight line in either graphic presentation. The coordinates as given above are not suited for presenting a system that contains one ligand and more than one species of binding macromole-

[1] This study has been supported in part by a grant (AM-01240) from the National Institutes of Health, U. S. Public Health Service.

cules that differ in their concentration. In order to include binding macromolecules of differing concentrations in one graph, it is necessary to choose coordinates that are independent of the concentrations of the macromolecules.

In a complex system of one ligand and one or more macromolecules with one or more binding sites each, all moieties are in mutual equilibrium. Specifically, the amount of free ligand is in equilibrium with all species of ligand bound to the various available groups of binding sites. It is, therefore, propitious to choose a graphic presentation that will conveniently locate not only the various n and k values but also the concentration of the free ligand.

A complex equilibrium system may contain more than one ligand competing for binding sites. In this system too, all moieties must be in equilibrium with each other. The following analysis deals only with the simpler case of one ligand in equilibrium with various groups of binding sites in the absence of any competitor for the same sites.

GRAPHIC ANALYSIS

Let $[b]$ be the concentration of a monovalent ligand bound to a macromolecule M with n equivalent and noninteracting binding sites, and let $[u]$ be the concentration of the free ligand; then the intrinsic association constant, k, is given by:

$$k = \frac{[b]}{[u] \cdot [\text{concentration of free binding sites}]} \tag{3}$$

or

$$\frac{[b]}{[u]} = k \cdot [\text{concentration of free binding sites}] \tag{4}$$

Upon replacing the concentration of free binding sites in expression (4) by the difference of the concentration of available binding sites and the concentration of occupied binding sites, the following equation is obtained:

$$\frac{[b]}{[u]} = k(n \cdot [\mathrm{M}] - [b]) \tag{5}$$

where [M] is the concentration of the macromolecule. This equation, which is similar to equation 2, is applied by plotting $[b]/[u]$ as a function of $[b]$ (see Fig. 1). Thus, the two coordinates are independent of the concentration of the macromolecule.

Equation 5 is a straight line with a slope of $-k$, an intercept on the ordinate of $k \cdot n \cdot [\mathrm{M}]$, and an intercept on the abscissa of $n \cdot [\mathrm{M}]$. The product $n \cdot [\mathrm{M}]$ is the concentration of binding sites in this coordinate system. If [M] is known, n can be computed.

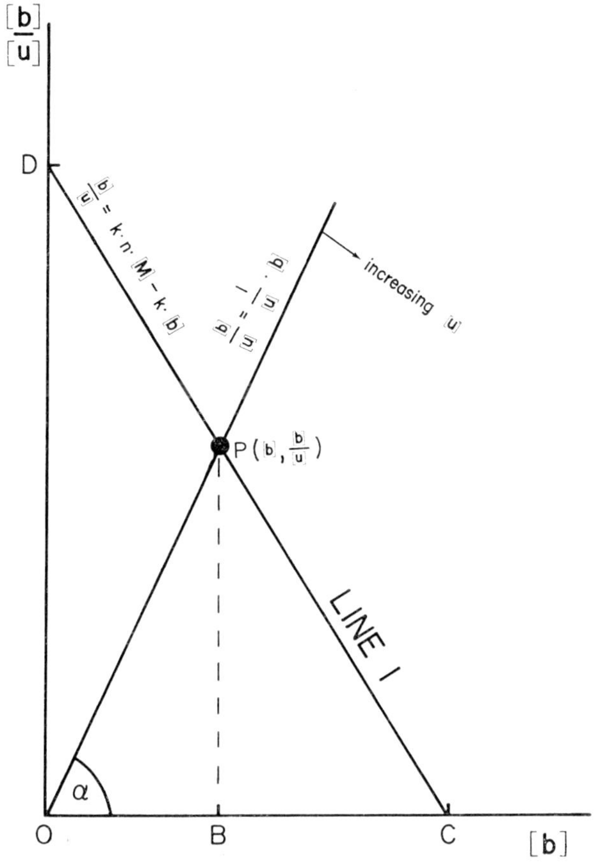

FIG. 1. Binding curve for one ligand and one group of binding sites.

On this plot, as well as on the Scatchard plot, the values for the concentration of free ligand, $[u]$, are on straight lines going through the origin of the coordinates (see Fig. 1). The slope of these lines is $1/[u]$, or $[u] = \cot \alpha$. For any point P on the binding curve (line 1 in Fig. 1), $[b] = \overline{OB}$ and $[u] = \overline{OB}/\overline{PB}$. The concentration of free binding sites is also represented in this graph. It is the difference between the total concentration of binding sites ($\overline{OC}$ in Fig. 1) and the concentration of binding sites occupied by the ligand ($\overline{OB}$ in Fig. 1). Thus, the concentration of free binding sites is represented by $\overline{BC} = \overline{OC} - \overline{OB}$.

In a system with two groups of noninteracting binding sites, where $n_1 \cdot [M_1] \neq n_2 \cdot [M_2]$ and/or $k_1 \neq k_2$, a plot of $[b]/[u]$ against $[b]$ gives a curved line (curve 1 in Fig. 2). At each point P of curve 1 the concentration of the free ligand is in equilibrium with the concentrations of ligand bound

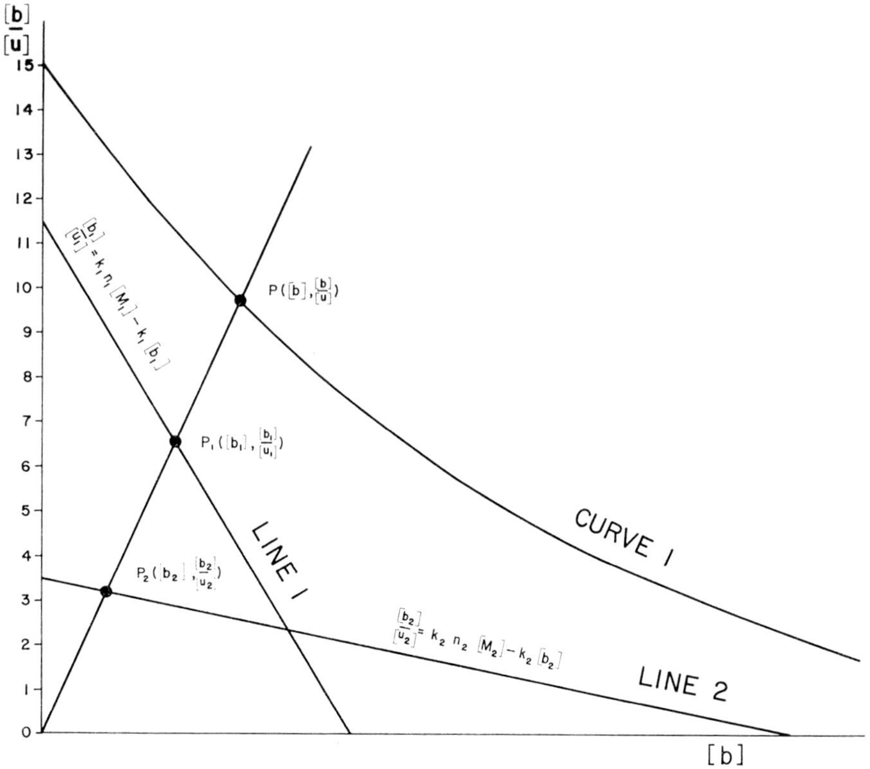

FIG. 2. Binding curve for one ligand and two groups of binding sites.

to each of the two groups of binding sites. Thus, $[b]/[u]$ (or $[b]$) at point P is the sum of $[b]/[u]$ (or $[b]$) taken for each group of binding sites at a constant value for $[u]$. The algebraic expression relating $[b]/[u]$ to $[u]$ is given, for two binding sites, by:

$$\frac{[b]}{[u]} = \frac{n_1k_1[\mathrm{M}_1]}{k_1[u] + 1} + \frac{n_2k_2[\mathrm{M}_2]}{k_2[u] + 1} \tag{6}$$

The algebraic procedure to obtain the association constants (k_1, k_2) and binding capacities ($n_1[\mathrm{M}_1]$, $n_2[\mathrm{M}_2]$) from equation 6, or from an expanded equation for a more complex system with more than two groups of binding sites, has been worked out by Hart (2).

Figure 2 demonstrates the graphic presentation. If line 1 in Figure 2 represents one binding system and line 2 a second binding system, then curve 1 is the resultant curve found experimentally. Any point P ($[b]$, $[b]/[u]$) on curve 1 is the sum of the binding coordinates of system 1 at point P_1 ($[b_1]$, $[b_1]/[u]$) and of system 2 at point P_2 ($[b_2]$, $[b_2]/[u]$). Points P_1, P_2, and P are chosen to lie on the same straight line through the origin and are thereby points of constant $[u]$. Equations 7 to 9 summarize these relations:

$$[b] = [b_1] + [b_2] \tag{7}$$

$$\frac{[b]}{[u]} = \frac{[b_1]}{[u]} + \frac{[b_2]}{[u]} \tag{8}$$

$$\overline{\mathrm{OP}} = \overline{\mathrm{OP}}_1 + \overline{\mathrm{OP}}_2 \tag{9}$$

In order to resolve an experimentally obtained binding curve (curve 1 in Fig. 2) into its components (lines 1 and 2 in Fig. 2), straight lines are drawn under curve 1 so as to satisfy the relation expressed by equation 9. Sometimes, it will be necessary to introduce a third straight line representing a third binding system in order to explain the experimental results satisfactorily. Experimental results will rarely be precise enough to justify the introduction of more than three binding systems.

The distribution of a ligand between its free form and various bound forms may be represented graphically on a plot similar to that shown in Figure 2. A slight change of definitions of the coordinates permits the inclusion, in Figure 2, of a third straight line that shall represent the free (i.e., unbound) ligand. The free ligand shall be redefined as "solvent-bound" ligand. Thus:

$$\text{"solvent-bound" ligand} \equiv \text{free ligand} \equiv u \tag{10}$$

For the free ligand, $[b]/[u]$ becomes

$$\frac{[\text{"solvent-bound" ligand}]}{[\text{free ligand}]}$$

and by the definition of equation 10 this term equals 1. Thus:

$$\frac{[b]}{[u]} = 1 \tag{11}$$

is the equation for the straight line that represents free ligand in the binding system (see line 3 in Fig. 3). As in Figure 2, curve 1 in Figure 3 is the experimental curve obtained in a system with two groups of non-interacting binding sites. By adding to the coordinates of every point on this curve the coordinates from points on line 3 such that P_3 and P lie on a straight line going through the origin of the coordinates, curve 2 is obtained. For curve 2:

$$[b] \equiv \text{total ligand} \tag{12}$$

and

$$\frac{[b]}{[u]} \equiv \frac{[\text{total ligand}]}{[\text{free ligand}]} \tag{13}$$

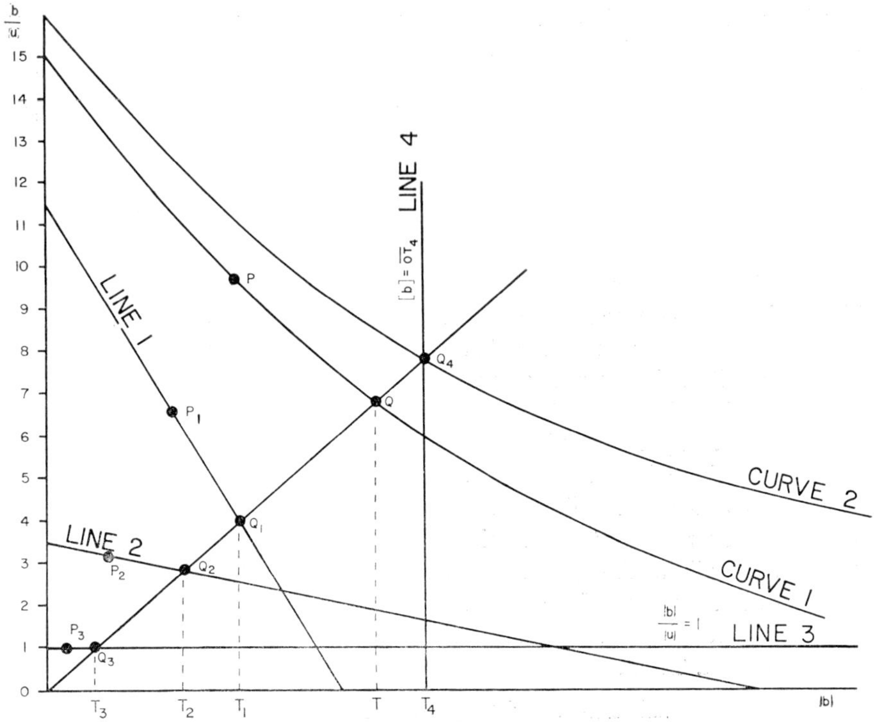

FIG. 3. Binding curve for one ligand and two groups of binding sites plotted with coordinates that are defined so as to include unbound ligand.

Owing to the newly defined coordinates, the distribution of the total ligand can now be determined by the simple geometry of this plot. Let the concentration of the total ligand be equal to $\overline{OT}_4$ on the abscissa, then this concentration is represented in Figure 3 by line 4, which follows the equation:

$$[b] = \overline{OT}_4 \tag{14}$$

Point Q_4 on curve 2 is the point that represents the binding system at a total concentration of ligand equal to $\overline{OT}_4$. The distribution of the ligand is made at a constant concentration of free ligand, which is represented by a straight line passing through Q_4 and the origin O. This line cuts the experimentally obtained binding curve (curve 1 in Fig. 3) at point Q, line 1 representing binding system 1 at point Q_1, line 2 representing binding system 2 at Q_2, and line 3 representing free ligand at Q_3. The abscissas to these points represent the values of the concentration of ligand bound to the two binding systems and the concentration of free ligand. Thus, if $\overline{OT}$ is the concentration of bound ligand, then $\overline{OT_1}$ is the concentration of ligand bound to binding system 1, $\overline{OT_2}$ is that bound to system 2, and $\overline{OT_3}$ is the concentration of free ligand. Other relations are:

$$\overline{OT} = \overline{OT_1} + \overline{OT_2} \tag{15}$$

and

$$\overline{OT_4} = \overline{OT_1} + \overline{OT_2} + \overline{OT_3} \tag{16}$$

In practice, the binding curve for the total ligand does not have to be drawn. To the plot of Figure 2 is added a horizontal line through $[b]/[u] = 1$ and a vertical line through $[b]$ = total ligand. A ruler is placed with one end at the point of origin of the graph and rotated around this point as shown in Figure 4 until $\overline{OQ_3}$ equals $\overline{QQ_4}$. A straight line is then drawn through O and Q_4, and T, T_3, T_2, and T_1 are read off the graph.

The method described has been employed by us (3) in studies on the interaction of steroid hormones with plasma proteins.

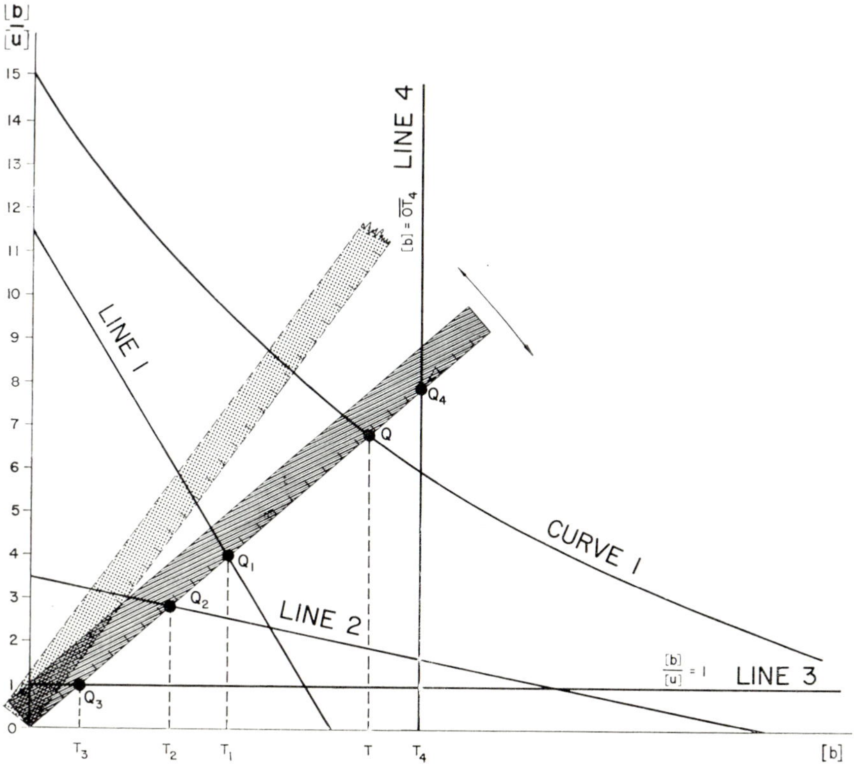

FIG. 4. Distribution of the total ligand from the plot of the binding curve.

SUMMARY

A graphic method is presented which correlates on a single graph the physicochemical parameters of a binding system consisting of one ligand and one or more binding macromolecules each having one or more groups of mutually noninteracting binding sites. Experimental data from equilibrium dialysis or ultrafiltration are plotted to obtain the number of equivalent binding sites and the corresponding association constant for each group of binding sites. This plot is then further extended to obtain information on the distribution of the ligand among the various groups of binding sites and on the concentration of its free form.

REFERENCES

1. SCATCHARD, G., *Ann. N. Y. Acad. Sci.* **51,** 660 (1949).
2. HART, H. E., *Bull. Math. Biophys.* **27,** 87 (1965).
3. SANDBERG, A. A., ROSENTHAL, H., SCHNEIDER, S., AND SLAUNWHITE, W. R., JR., *in* "Steroid Dynamics" (G. Pincus, T. Nakao, and J. F. Tait, eds.), p. 1. Academic Press, New York, London, 1966.

ANALYTICAL BIOCHEMISTRY 20, 533–544 (1967)

The Determination of Transfer Ribonucleic Acid by Aminoacylation

I. Leucine and Phenylalanine Transfer Ribonucleic Acid from *E. Coli* B[1]

I. B. RUBIN, A. D. KELMERS, AND G. GOLDSTEIN

Analytical Chemistry and Chemical Technology Divisions, Oak Ridge National Laboratory, Oak Ridge, Tennessee 37830

Received January 16, 1967

During recent years there has been considerable interest in the study of the transfer ribonucleic acids (tRNA), and programs for the separation, purification, and characterization of these compounds are in progress in many laboratories.[2] There is an obvious need for accurate and precise analytical data, particularly for the assay of individual, purified, or partially purified tRNA's. Consequently we have begun a critical evaluation of the available analytical techniques in order to establish the optimum conditions for quantitative determinations. This report describes the determination of picomolar quantities of purified phenylalanine- and leucine-accepting tRNA's by aminoacylation using a crude synthetase enzyme preparation.

The aminoacylation reaction was first described by Hoagland, Zamecnik, and Stephenson (1). Previous studies of this reaction are reviewed by Brown (2) and Zachau and Feldmann (3). The tRNA is incubated with a ^{14}C-labeled amino acid and a mixed synthetase preparation, in the presence of ATP and other cofactors, to form a tRNA-amino acid ester linkage according to the over-all reaction.

$$\text{tRNA} + \text{aa}^* + \text{ATP} \xrightarrow[\text{cofactor}]{\text{enzyme}} \text{tRNA}\cdot\text{aa}^* + \text{AMP} + \text{pp}_i$$

[1] Research sponsored by the U. S. Atomic Energy Commission under contract with Union Carbide Corporation.

[2] Abbreviations used in this paper are: tRNA, transfer ribonucleic acid; AMP, adenosine 5'-monophosphate; ATP, adenosine 5'-triphosphate; aa, amino acid; Tris, tris-(hydroxymethyl)aminomethane; GSH, glutathione; ME, 2-mercaptoethanol; TCA, trichloroacetic acid; PPO, 2,5-diphenyloxazole; dimethyl POPOP, 1,4-bis-2-(4-methyl-5-phenyloxazolyl) benzene; EDTA, disodium or dipotassium salt of ethylenediaminetetraacetic acid; ODU, optical density unit; BSA, bovine serum albumin; pmole, 10^{-12} mole; pp_i.

The aminoacylated tRNA is then precipitated by acid, excess amino acid washed away, and the precipitate counted. We have adapted the paper disc technique of Mans and Novelli (4) in which a portion of the assay mixture is precipitated onto a filter paper disc by immersion in TCA. A rigorous study was made of the effects of pH and buffer, metal ions, ATP, enzyme, and amino acid concentration on the determination, using both crude (unfractionated) and purified tRNA preparations. The effects of a few enzyme-stabilizing agents and extraneous salts were also examined.

METHODS

A. Materials

Preparation of the purified $tRNA^{Phe}$ and $tRNA^{Leu}$ from *Escherichia coli* B used in most of this work has been reported (5, 6). Crude soluble RNA was from General Biochemicals, Chagrin Falls, Ohio.

Tris(hydroxymethyl)aminomethane, cacodylic acid (sodium salt), ATP (disodium salt), and glutathione (reduced form) from Sigma Chemical Co., St. Louis, Mo.; 2-mercaptoethanol, from Eastman Organic Chemicals, Rochester, N.Y.; streptomycin sulfate, U.S.P., from Calbiochem, Los Angeles, Calif.; PPO and dimethyl POPOP from Packard Instrument Co., Downers Grove, Ill.; ^{14}C-L-phenylalanine and ^{14}C-L-leucine, 321 and 223 mc/mmole, respectively, from New England Nuclear Corp., Boston, Mass.

The liquid scintillator was composed of 4 gm of PPO and 0.1 gm of dimethyl POPOP per liter of toluene.

The aminoacyl-tRNA synthetase mixture was prepared from *Escherichia coli* B as described by Kelmers, Novelli, and Stulberg (7). The protein content was determined by the Lowry method, using BSA as the reference (8).

B. Procedures

1. Amino Acid Acceptor Activity. The standard incubation mixture consisted of 0.10 ml of tRNA solution, 50 μmoles of buffer, 5 μmoles of magnesium acetate, 2.5 μmoles of potassium chloride, 1 μmole of ATP, and 750 picomoles of ^{14}C-labeled amino acid in a volume of 0.40 ml. To this was added 0.10 ml of the enzyme preparation (~ 1 mg of protein/ml) in 0.05 *M* ME, and the mixture was incubated at 37°C. After a specific length of time, a 50 μl aliquot was withdrawn and pipetted onto a 2.3 cm Whatman 3MM paper disc. The disc was dried in a stream of warm air and dropped into a beaker of cold 10 w/v% TCA. The disc was washed in the 10% TCA, twice in cold 5% TCA, in 50 v/v% absolute ethanol and ether, and finally in ether, with the latter two washes being at room temperature. Each washing period was 10 min. The disc was dried under an infrared lamp for

10–15 min, placed in a scintillation vial which contained 5 ml of the scintillator, and counted in a Packard Tri-Carb scintillation spectrometer for 10 min. A blank with no tRNA was processed along with the sample.

II. Half-Life Studies. Optimum pH and concentrations of reagents for the formation of the aminoacyl-tRNA were used in the incubation mixture in a total volume of 1 ml. The aminoacyl-tRNA was precipitated at 0°C after the incubation period by the addition of 0.25 ml of 5 *M* NaCl and 6.5 ml of ethanol. A 2 ml portion of an *E. coli* tRNA solution, 1 mg/ml, was added as a carrier. The precipitate was allowed to flocculate at least 2 hr, and was then centrifuged for 30 min at 30,000*g*. The product was dissolved in water, precipitated twice more, and finally dissolved in 1.6 ml of the incubation mixture from which ATP was omitted. This solution was divided into two equal portions. To one portion, 0.20 ml of water was added, while 0.20 ml of the enzyme solution was added to the other. The tubes containing the solutions were placed in a water bath at 37°C, and aliquots were taken out at intervals and processed as described above.

RESULTS AND DISCUSSION

pH and Buffer

The quantitative esterification of tRNA with an amino acid depends not only on pH but also on the kind of buffer used. Preliminary data indi-

TABLE 1
Effect of Buffers on Aminoacylation

		^{14}C-aa charged (pmoles/ODU tRNA)			
Buffer	pH[a]	7.8	8.2	8.6	9.0
A. $tRNA^{Leu}$					
Na glycinate		1020	1130	1110	1040
Na cacodylate		1210	1260	1210	1210
Tris HCl		870	860	900	890
Na carbonate		1180	1130	1170	1110
Na borate		1030	1030	990	980
B. $tRNA^{Phe}$					
Na glycinate		1300	1360	1360	1330
Na cacodylate		640	740	870	920
Tris HCl		1210	1280	1290	1210
Na carbonate		1250	1250	1140	—
Na borate		1150	1070	980	810

[a] pH measured at 23°.

The reaction mixture was the same as for Figure 3. Glycinate, cacodylate, and Tris buffers, 50 μmoles; carbonate and borate buffers, 10 μmoles.

cated that maximum incorporation of leucine and phenylalanine into their respective purified tRNA's took place over a pH range of 6 to 9 for the former and 7 to 9 for the latter. There was a decided buffer effect, with phosphate being inhibitory in both systems and Tris being inhibitory in the leucine system. The data presented in Table 1 compare the effect of several buffer solutions. Highest values of aminoacyl-tRNA formation were obtained by the use of cacodylate buffer for the leucine system and glycinate buffer for the phenylalanine system. The pH values were measured at 23°C, while the reaction was carried out at 37°C; thus, for the buffer solutions chosen—cacodylate at pH 8.2 and glycinate at pH 8.4—the pH values obtained at 37°C were 8.1 and 8.0, respectively. When solutions of crude tRNA were studied a similar pH effect was noted, but the pH range for maximum incorporation of leucine was 7 to 8.5 and for phenylalanine, 6 to 9.5. In this test the buffer effect was not so pronounced.

In two recent studies with purified aminoacyl-tRNA synthetases, phenylalanyl and lysyl, rather than with a crude enzyme mixture, it was also concluded that pH 8 was the optimum for these specific systems (9, 10).

ATP Concentration

ATP is a necessary cofactor in the aminoacylation of tRNA, but the optimum concentration for aminoacylation of the two purified tRNA's is different, as shown in Figure 1. For the formation of Leu-tRNA, the optimum ATP concentration was in the range of about 0.5 to 2 μmoles per 0.5 ml when 5 μmoles of magnesium was present, and about 0.5 to >5 μmoles per 0.5 ml at the 10 μmole magnesium level. For the formation of Phe-tRNA, the optimum ATP concentration range was from 0.3 to 0.8 μmoles per 0.5 ml with both levels of magnesium. Similar curves were obtained with crude tRNA, but in the leucine system the maxima were in the ATP concentration ranges of about 1.3 to 4 μmoles and 1 to >5 μmoles per 0.5 ml, respectively, for the 5 and 10 μmole levels of magnesium, while in the phenylalanine system, the maxima were almost identical for both magnesium levels, ranging from about 0.2 to 1 μmole of ATP.

Aminoacyl-tRNA Synthetase Concentration

The relationship between quantity of crude aminoacyl-tRNA synthetase mixture, added as total protein, and the amount of aminoacylation is shown in Figure 2. For this quantity of $tRNA^{Phe}$, 0.058 ODU, the optimum concentration of protein was 70 to 120 μg per assay mixture, while for the $tRNA^{Leu}$, 0.034 ODU, it was 20 to 70 μg per assay. When larger quantities of enzyme were added, the amount of amino acid incorporated decreased. When the enzyme requirement of crude tRNA was studied, the curves were similar to those in Figure 2; however, for $tRNA^{Phe}$, the optimum protein

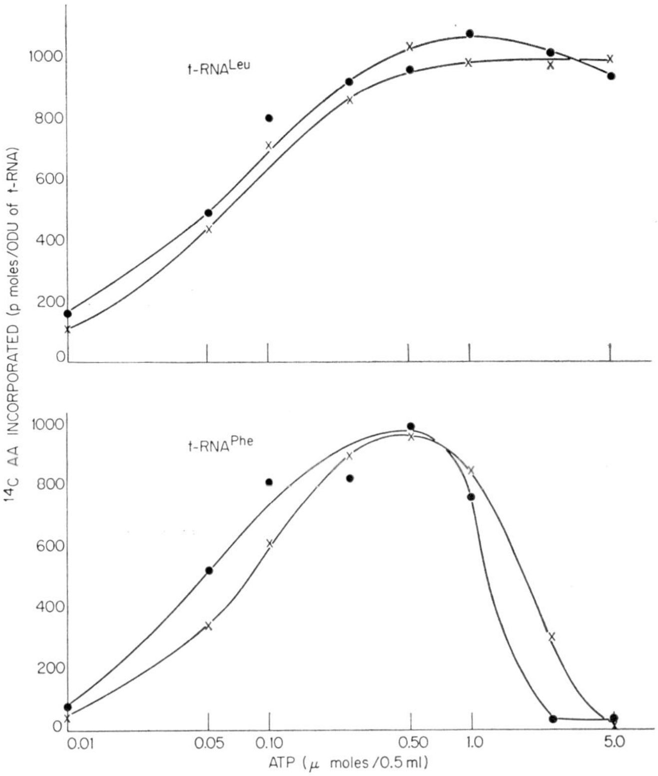

FIG. 1. Effect of ATP concentration on aminoacylation of purified tRNA's. The reaction mixture contained: $tRNA^{Leu}$, 0.034 ODU, or $tRNA^{Phe}$, 0.018 ODU; buffer, 50 μmoles (cacodylate, pH 8.2 for Leu; glycinate, pH 8.4 for Phe); ^{14}C-AA, 750 pmoles; K^+, 2.5 μmoles; ME, 5 μmoles; aminoacyl-tRNA synthetase, 55 μg of protein; Mg^{++} (●) 5 μmoles, (×) 10 μmoles.

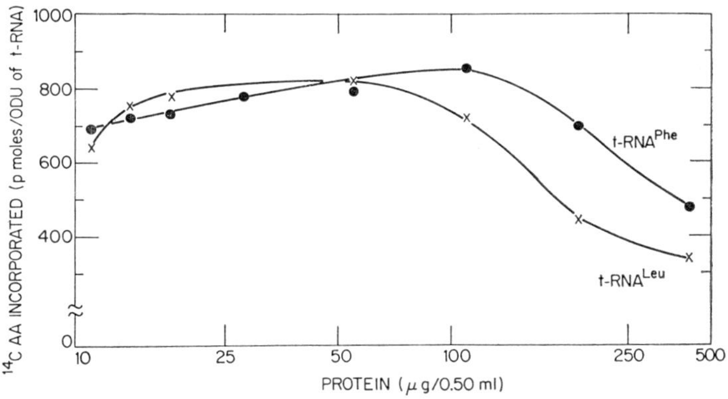

FIG. 2. Crude aminoacyl-tRNA synthetase requirement. The reaction mixture contained: $tRNA^{Leu}$, 0.034 ODU, or $tRNA^{Phe}$, 0.058 ODU; ^{14}C-aa, 750 pmoles; buffer, 50 μmoles (cacodylate, pH 8.2 for Leu; glycinate, pH 8.4 for Phe); ATP (2 μmoles for Leu, 0.5 μmoles for Phe); Mg^{++}, 10 μmoles; K^+, 2.5 μmoles; ME, 5 μmoles.

concentration was 10 to 100 μg per assay while, for $tRNA^{Leu}$, the optimum increased to 70 to 150 μg per assay. These values were for samples of about 1.8 ODU of crude tRNA. In the optimum range of enzyme concentration formation of Leu-tRNA reached a maximum in 15 min, and Phe-tRNA in 20 min. Total aminoacylation decreased after about 20 min in the leucine system, but was still maximal after 30 min in the phenylalanine system.

Divalent Metal Ions and Incubation Time

The effects of various divalent cations on the aminoacylation of tRNA from several sources have been reported (10–14). Results of the present study confirm that the presence of a divalent metal ion is necessary to effect formation of Leu- and Phe-tRNA, and these results indicate that Mn^{++} is as effective as Mg^{++} for this process. The time-metal ion con-

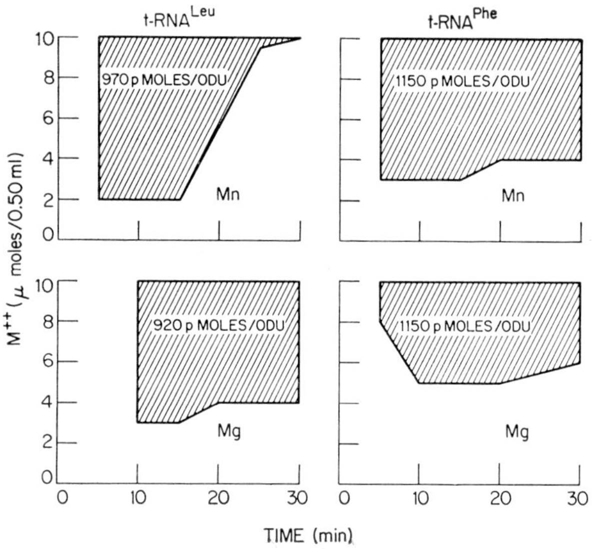

FIG. 3. Effect of incubation time and divalent metal ion concentration. The reaction mixture contained: $tRNA^{Leu}$, 0.034 ODU, or $tRNA^{Phe}$, 0.016 ODU; Tris, pH 7.4, 50 μmoles; ^{14}C-AA, 750 pmoles; ATP, 1 μmole; K^+, 2.5 μmoles; GSH, 1 μmole; and aminoacyl-tRNA synthetase, 100 μg of protein.

centration relationships for the leucine and phenylalanine systems are shown in Figure 3. Within the cross-hatched areas, aminoacylation is maximal and equal at all points on the metal concentration-time coordinates. For example, when manganese was used in the leucine system, maximum incorporation took place within incubation times of 5 to 15 min over a manganese concentration range of from 2 to at least 10 μmoles per test solution but, with a 20 min incubation period, at least 6 μmoles of manganese was required. The limits of the test were 10 μmoles of cation and a 30 min incubation. For the incorporation of leucine in its tRNA, the minimum requirements for either magnesium or manganese differed but slightly and the use of manganese seemed to increase total aminoacylation by about 6%. Manganese also allowed the reaction to go to completion in a shorter minimum time. For the incorporation of phenylalanine in its tRNA, the minimum magnesium requirement was somewhat higher than that for manganese, but the maximum aminoacylation was the same in both cases. The minimum incubation times were the same at the higher metal ion concentrations. In both systems, the results were more consistent when 10 μmoles of the cation was present and, at this concentration, incubation time was less critical. A drawback to the use of manganese is that it tends to precipitate at the pH chosen for the assay.

Co^{++} and Ca^{++} were also tested with the purified tRNA's; the results are shown in Table 2. Co^{++} precipitated when ME was used but not with GSH.

TABLE 2
Effect of Divalent Metal Ions

Metal	^{14}C-aa Charged (pmoles/ODU tRNA)	
	Leu	Phe
None	30	10
Mg	880	1020
Ca	640	130
Co	ppt	130

The reaction mixture contained: 0.034 ODU $tRNA^{Leu}$, or 0.016 ODU $tRNA^{Phe}$; Tris, pH 7.4, 50 μmoles; ^{14}C-aa, 750 pmoles; ATP, 1 μmole; K^+, 2.5 μmoles; aminoacyl-tRNA synthetase, 100 μg of protein.

Results obtained with crude tRNA were comparable, relatively, to those in Table 2. The presence of Cu^{++} and Ni^{++} completely inhibited the reaction, and precipitates formed when Fe^{++} and Zn^{++} were added.

Monovalent Metal Ions

Potassium ion is generally added to the reaction mixture for the aminoacylation of tRNA, although its usefulness depends on the specific system under investigation (10, 11). Results of the present study indicate that a monovalent cation may be a necessary cofactor in the leucine and phenylalanine systems in *E. coli*. Both tRNA and ATP are added to the assay mixture as sodium salts, and the quartz-distilled water and the magnesium solution were found to contain minute quantities of sodium and potassium, so the solution is never free of these cations. However, when 2.5 μmoles potassium or ammonium chloride was added to the solution, the incorporation of phenylalanine was enhanced by about 7%; sodium decreased incorporation by a like amount, and lithium had no effect. In the leucine system, the addition of 2.5 μmoles of potassium, lithium, or sodium ions had no significant effect, while the additional ammonium ion caused an enhancement of about 10%. More alkali ion up to 10 μmoles caused no further change. Tris buffers, with the pH adjusted by hydrochloric acid, were used in these tests.

Amino Acid and tRNA Concentration

The degree of incorporation of amino acid into $tRNA^{Leu}$ and $tRNA^{Phe}$ is dependent upon the molar ratio of amino acid to tRNA as indicated in Figure 4. In the leucine system, a minimum of a 10-fold molar excess of

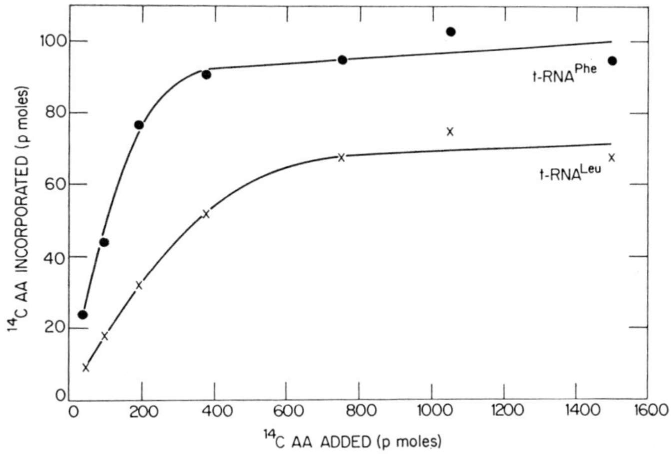

FIG. 4. Effect of amino acid concentration. The reaction mixture contained: $tRNA^{Leu}$, 0.068 ODU, or $tRNA^{Phe}$, 0.08 ODU; buffer, 50 μmoles (cacodylate, pH 8.2 for Leu; glycinate, pH 8.4 for Phe); Mg^{++}, 10 μmoles; ATP, 1 μmole; K^+, 2.5 μmoles; GSH, 1 μmole; aminoacyl-tRNA synthetase, 100 μg protein.

amino acid was needed for maximum aminoacylation, while in the phenylalanine system, the minimum amino acid requirement was a 6-fold molar excess.

Recommended Conditions

The recommended conditions for the determination of purified $tRNA^{Leu}$ and $tRNA^{Phe}$ are summarized in Table 3. For the determination of these tRNA's in crude tRNA, the same conditions are used, but total aminoacylation is less sensitive to minor changes in solution variables.

TABLE 3
Recommended Conditions for Determination of $tRNA^{Leu}$ and $tRNA^{Phe}$ [a]

Condition	$tRNA^{Leu}$	$tRNA^{Phe}$
tRNA, ODU	0.01–0.08	0.01–0.08
AA, pmoles	750–1000	750–1000
pH[b]	8.2	8.4
Buffer, μmoles	Cacodylate, 50	Glycinate, 50
ATP, μmoles	2	0.5
Mg^{++}, μmoles	10	10
M^{+}, μmoles	NH_4, 2.5	K, NH_4, 2.5
Reductant, μmoles	ME, 5	ME, 5
Aminoacyl-tRNA synthetase, μg protein	20–70	70–120
Incubation time, min	15	20

[a] Incubation temperature 37°C; volume 0.5 ml.
[b] pH measured at 23°C.

Under the conditions specified in Table 3, aminoacylation of $tRNA^{Leu}$ and $tRNA^{Phe}$ increases linearly with the tRNA concentration in the range shown in Figure 5. Assuming the optical density of a solution of 1 mg tRNA/ml in water to be about 20, these quantities would represent con-

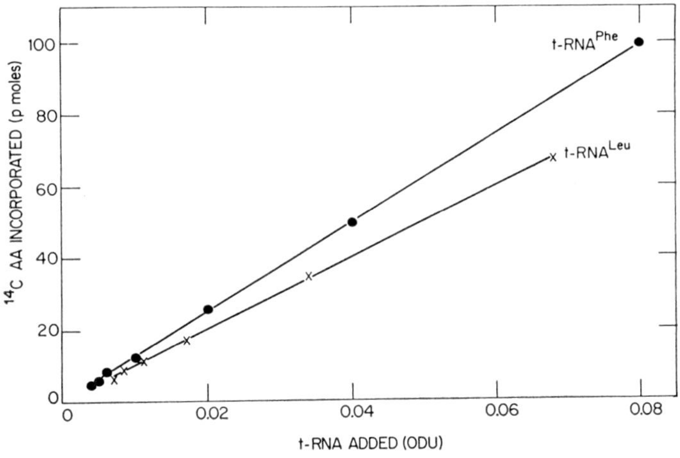

FIG. 5. Calibration for tRNA determination. The reaction mixture was the same as for Figure 4 with 750 pmoles of ^{14}C-AA.

centrations of about 0.2 to 4 μg of tRNA per assay mixture. At the highest concentrations of tRNA noted in this figure, the excess amino acid is approaching the minimum requirement reported above while, at the lowest concentrations of tRNA, the molar excess of amino acid is about 100-fold for leucine and about 180-fold for phenylalanine.

The relative standard deviation for routine sample analysis of chromatographic fractions, i.e., partially purified material, is 5 to 10%, but for purified samples a relative standard deviation of 1% can be attained. Precision will of course depend on counting rate and counting time. Since there are no purified tRNA's available for use as standards, we judge accuracy by finding no additional incorporation of amino acid in the presence of inorganic pyrophosphatase, under the conditions outlined in Table 3, and by comparing maximum aminoacylation with the determination of adenosine end groups. One sample of $tRNA^{Phe}$ accepted 1340 pmoles of phenylalanine per ODU, while 1320 pmoles of terminal adenosine per ODU were found (5). This same figure of 1340 pmoles/ODU was also obtained under different conditions using purified synthetase (9). One sample of $tRNA^{Leu}$ accepted 1000 pmoles of leucine per ODU, while 1070 pmoles of terminal adenosine per ODU were found. This sample also accepted 20 pmoles of phenylalanine per ODU.

Salt Effects

Gradient elution with salts is commonly used in chromatographic fractionation of tRNA (7, 15). The $tRNA_4^{Leu}$ and $tRNA^{Phe}$ fractions are eluted from quaternary amine columns at a sodium chloride concentration of 0.7–0.8 *M* (7). In the routine analysis of these fractions, the portion of the sample taken for analysis is diluted 5-fold in the assay mixture; thus, the sodium chloride concentration of the assay mixture is 0.14–0.16 *M*. This quantity of sodium chloride inhibits aminoacylation of both tRNA's by about 12%. When these tRNA's are purified by gel filtration the initial sodium chloride content is 0.4 *M* (5, 6), and the concentration in the assay mixture is 0.08 *M*, which is still inhibitory in the phenylalanine system, but not seriously so in the leucine system.

When the tRNA is fractionated on a hydroxyapatite column, the fractions contain phosphate (16). The $tRNA^{Phe}$ fraction is eluted at a phosphate concentration of about 0.17 *M*, which is then diluted to about 0.034 *M* in the assay mixture. This quantity of phosphate strongly inhibits the formation of Phe-tRNA. The $tRNA^{Leu}$ fractions are eluted at lower concentrations of phosphate, and the formation of Leu-tRNA is not significantly affected by as much as 0.05 *M* phosphate. Consequently, samples of purified $tRNA^{Leu}$ and $tRNA^{Phe}$ are usually dialyzed against water prior to analysis.

Enzyme Stabilizing Agents

Both GSH and ME as well as EDTA were tested for their usefulness in the assay solutions. The results were comparable in both the leucine and phenylalanine systems. The presence of 0.1 μmole of either GSH or ME had no effect on the incorporation of the amino acids into tRNA; however, the addition of 0.5 μmole of GSH to the solution was inhibitory, while the addition of 1 μmole of ME enhanced incorporation of phenylalanine about 5%, and of leucine about 15%. The use of additional ME, up to 10 μmoles, did not increase aminoacylation significantly. The presence of EDTA concentrations of up to 0.5 μmole per assay mixture caused no significant changes in aminoacylation, while greater amounts were inhibitory.

Half-Life Studies

Hydrolysis studies of tRNA-amino acid esters prepared from crude tRNA have been reported (3). The hydrolytic half-lives of leucyl- and phenylalanyl-tRNA prepared from highly purified $tRNA^{Leu}$ and $tRNA^{Phe}$ have now been determined. The half-life of the phenylalanine ester is 23 to 24 min, and the half-life of the leucine ester is about 7 min, under the designated conditions. The hydrolyses were carried out under conditions which were optimum for formation of each aminoacyl-tRNA, except that the ATP and the synthetase were omitted from the final solution.

SUMMARY

A study was made of the aminoacylation of purified and partially purified transfer ribonucleic acids by ^{14}C-labeled amino acids using a crude synthetase enzyme preparation, and the optimum conditions have been established for the quantitative determination of purified leucine and phenylalanine accepting transfer ribonucleic acids from *E. coli* B. An analytical procedure was developed for the determination of picomolar quantities of these two nucleic acids, based on a filter paper disc technique and scintillation spectrometry. Relevant solution parameters have been investigated, including: pH, type of buffer, incubation time, concentrations of transfer ribonucleic acid, amino acid, adenosine triphosphate, and aminoacyl-tRNA synthetase, as well as concentration of divalent metal ion cofactors. The optimum pH for the aminoacylation reaction is 8–8.5; cacodylate and glycinate buffers were preferred, respectively, for the formation of the leucyl- and phenylalanyl-tRNA's. Magnesium and manganese appeared to be equally effective as cofactors, while sodium chloride and phosphate used in chromatographic separation of the tRNA's had inhibiting effects. The hydrolytic half-lives of the two tRNA esters at the pH of optimum formation were 23–24 min for the Phe-tRNA and 7 min for Leu-tRNA.

ACKNOWLEDGMENTS

The authors would like to acknowledge the constructive advice and criticism of Dr. G. D. Novelli. This work was supported partially by a grant from the National Institute of General Medical Science.

REFERENCES

1. Hoagland, M. B., Zamecnik, P. C., and Stephenson, M. L., *Biochim. Biophys. Acta* **24**, 215 (1957).

2. Brown, G. L., *in* "Progress in Nucleic Acid Research and Molecular Biology" (J. N. Davidson and W. E. Cohn, eds.), Vol. II, pp. 259–310. Academic Press, New York, 1963.
3. Zachau, H. G., and Feldmann, H., *in* "Progress in Nucleic Acid Research and Molecular Biology" (J. N. Davidson and W. E. Cohn, eds.), Vol. IV, pp. 217–230, Academic Press, New York, 1965.
4. Mans, R. J., and Novelli, G. D., *Arch. Biochem. Biophys.* **94,** 48 (1961).
5. Kelmers, A. D., *J. Biol. Chem.* **241,** 3540 (1966).
6. Kelmers, A. D., *Biochem. Biophys. Res. Commun.* **25,** 562 (1966).
7. Kelmers, A. D., Novelli, G. D., and Stulberg, M. P., *J. Biol. Chem.* **240,** 3979 (1965).
8. Lowry, O. H., Rosebrough, N. J., Farr, A. L., and Randall, R. J., *J. Biol. Chem.* **193,** 265 (1951).
9. Stulberg, M. P., *J. Biol. Chem.* **242,** 1060 (1967).
10. Kalousek, F., and Rychlik, J., *Collection Czech. Chem. Commun.* **30,** 3909 (1965).
11. Schweet, R. S., and Allen, E. H., *J. Biol. Chem.* **233,** 1104 (1958).
12. Devi, A., and Sarkar, N., *Biochim. Biophys. Acta* **68,** 254 (1963).
13. Allende, J. E., Mora, G., Gatica, M., and Allende, C. C., *J. Biol. Chem.* **240,** PC 3229 (1965).
14. Berg, P., and Ofengand, E. J., *Proc. Natl. Acad. Sci. U. S.* **44,** 78 (1958).
15. Cherayil, J. D., and Bock, R. M., *Biochemistry* **4,** 1174 (1965).
16. Pearson, R. L., and Kelmers, A. D., *J. Biol. Chem.* **241,** 767 (1966).

ANALYTICAL BIOCHEMISTRY **20** (1967)

SHORT COMMUNICATIONS

A Versatile Apparatus for Membrane Transport Studies

One of the critical problems in biology today is an understanding of the mechanisms operative in transmembrane transport of various molecules and ions. The development of the short-circuit technique by Ussing and his collaborators (1) provided a valuable tool for such investigations. A variety of devices have been designed to utilize the short-circuit technique, each specifically adapted to the tissue studied. We present the design for a simple and versatile apparatus for measuring membrane transport and attendant electrical properties in a variety of different tissues. The instrument is easily constructed, and has proved quite durable. Its ease of operation has permitted wide application in research as well as teaching laboratories.

An expanded schematic drawing of the apparatus is shown in Figure 1. All parts of the instrument are drawn to scale, and direct measurements can be taken from the figure for construction. The solution chambers are milled and drilled from Lucite blocks. A 1 mm inlet port is drilled into each chamber and fitted with a stainless-steel tubing adapter. This port is used to introduce the desired gas phase, which simultaneously provides effective mixing. Rapid withdrawal and exchange of the entire contents of each chamber can also be effected through these ports. The most important single feature of the device is the inexpensive interchangeable membrane holder which fits into the appropriate space between the Lucite chambers. The size and shape of the opening can be varied over a wide range to comply with the dimension of the tissue studied. Stainless-steel pins mounted on one of the Lucite panels position the membrane over the opening, which is sealed by a recessed O-ring gasket. Additional recessed O-ring gaskets in the main chambers provide an effective seal with the membrane holder in the assembled apparatus. Threaded insert plugs either solid (not shown) for open-circuited systems or drilled to accommodate Ag/AgCl electrodes and agar bridges for short-circuit systems are also sealed by O-rings. Fritted discs of glass or plastic can be fitted on the chamber-facing side of these plugs to minimize the diffusion interface between the agar bridges and the solution without interfering with current density distribution across the membrane.

Once the membrane has been mounted, the two chambers can be rapidly bolted together, filled with the desired bathing solution, and aeration commenced. The model, as shown, will accommodate from 7 to 16 ml in each chamber. Lucite holders for electrical potential measuring bridges are positioned using set screws which permit adjustment of the height of

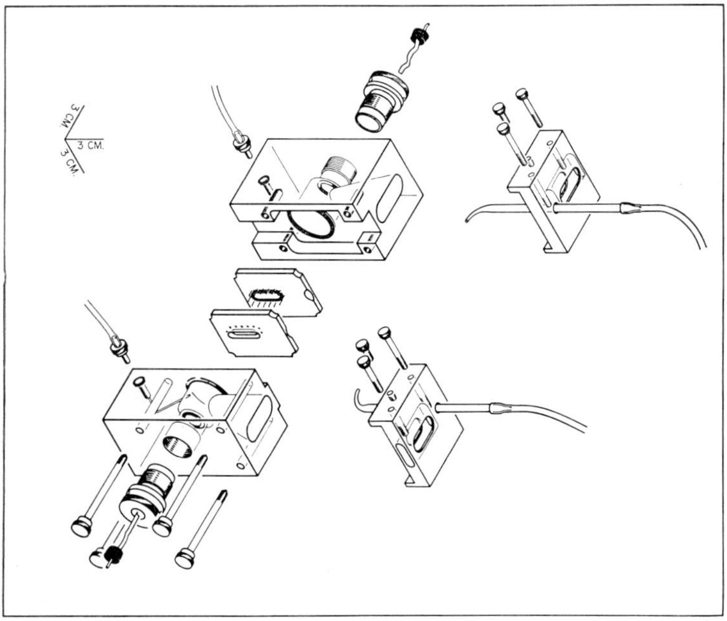

FIG. 1. Expanded drawing of apparatus, drawn to scale indicated.

the measuring bridge as well as its distance from the membrane. Openings in the holders permit the removal of aliquots for analysis, the addition of reagents of specific interest, and the introduction of other electrodes. A third set screw is provided to hold a plastic insert (not shown) in the opening to minimize exchange of the internal gas phase with the atmosphere.

The bridges used for the measurement of the transmembrane potential consist of glass tubes with 0.5 mm diameter tips, fitted with a flexible tubing, and filled with 2.5% agar/4 M KCl. The agar bridges make contact with a suitable high impedance potentiometer through calomel cells in 4 M KCl solution. The external current is applied through the Ag/AgCl electrodes[1] mounted into the Lucite plugs filled with 2.5% agar made up

[1] Heavy silver wire or ribbon is chlorided electrolytically in 0.1 N HCl using the silver wire as the cathode by passing 1 mA of current for 30 min.

in a solution containing the principal ions of the bathing medium. Various circuit diagrams are available for the application of a short-circuit current. These include either simplified, manually operated circuits (1, 2) or more sophisticated apparatus capable of maintaining a constant voltage across the membrane by various feedback networks (3, 4).

This instrument has been successfully applied to transport studies using rabbit gall bladder, small intestine from rats and chicks, and gastric mucosa from dog, frog, tadpole, and rabbit (5).

Summary. An instrument is described for transport studies in a short-circuited system which can be easily and inexpensively adapted to accommodate the physical limitations of size and shape imposed by a variety of biological membranes.

ACKNOWLEDGMENTS

We thank Mr. V. Fryckman and Mr. C. Lafors for their skill and workmanship. Miss Maryellin Reinecke rendered the drawing. The apparatus is now available from Frickie Instruments Company, 4118 4th Avenue, Los Angeles, California 90008.

Paul Saltman is a Research Career Development Awardee of the U. S. P. H. Service. Grants from the John A. Hartford Foundation and the U. S. P. H. Service supported this work.

REFERENCES

1. Ussing, H. H., and Zerahn, K., *Acta Physiol. Scand.* **23**, 110 (1952).
2. Crane, E. E., Davies, R. E., and Longmuir, N. M., *Biochem. J.* **43**, 321 (1948).
3. Menninger, J. M., Snell, F. M., and Spangler, R. A., *Rev. Sci. Instr.* **31**, 519 (1960).
4. Candia, O. A., *I. E. E. E. Trans. Biomed. Eng.* **13**, 189 (1966).
5. Wheeler, H., personal communication. Norman, A., personal communication. Helbock, H. J., Forte, J. G., and Saltman, P., *Biochim. Biophys. Acta* **126**, 81 (1966). Forte, J. G., *Federation Proc.* **26**, 274 (1967).

John G. Forte

Department of Physiology
University of California, Berkeley 94720

Harold Helbock
Paul Saltman

Graduate Program in Biochemistry
University of Southern California
Los Angeles 90007
Received March 14, 1967

Ultrasensitive Detection of Certain Microbial Metabolites by Gas Chromatography

It has been reported that the electron capture detector (ECD) employed in gas chromatography is sensitive to certain organic compounds, such as compounds containing conjugated carbonyls, halogens, sulfur, or nitro groups (1, 2). In an investigation of the possible use of gas chromatography for the detection and identification of microorganisms, it was found that ECD is highly sensitive to a number of common products of microbial metabolism.

Several compounds known to be produced during microbial growth (3) were selected. The chemicals were of the highest purity available commercially, and were not purified further. The instrument used was an Aerograph model 200 dual-channel gas chromatograph with flame ionization and electron capture detectors.[1] The apparatus was fitted with a Wilkens H_2 generator, model 650, and a model LD 11A dual-pen recorder[2] operating at a speed of 40 in./hr. Each pen was adapted to swing freely along the full 11 in. scale of the recorder with an input signal of 2.2 mV. The column was stainless steel, 6 ft long, ⅛ in. o.d., and it was packed with Chromosorb W treated with HMDS 60/80 mesh and 10% Carbowax (20M). The flow rate of the carrier gas, N_2, was 40 ml/min through the column and 20 ml/min through each detector. A 3.0 μl sample containing the test substance was injected into the instrument, each detector thereby receiving 1.5 μl. The operating temperatures were column 100°, detectors 120°, and injector 150°C. The quantity of chemical reaching the detector is designated as the charge.

The sensitivity of the gas chromatograph with electron capture detector to some common products of microbial metabolism is shown in Table 1. The quantity of a compound that can be detected by ECD varies considerably. The sensitivity limit was defined as the quantity of a compound necessary to give a peak area of 10 mm² at range 1 and attenuation 1 of the instrument. This detector is most sensitive to acetoin, 1 pg giving a peak area of 10 mm² in the chromatogram. Henis, Gould, and Alexander (4) observed the extreme sensitivity of the ECD to acetoin and diacetyl produced during the growth of a variety of bacteria. The sensitivity limit

[1] Wilkens Instrument and Research, Inc., Walnut Creek, California.
[2] Westronics, Inc., Fort Worth, Texas.

herein noted for diacetyl, 14 pg, is similar to that recently reported by Shilman and Schaper (5). Pyruvic acid, another carbonyl-containing compound, is also detectable in concentrations of less than 1 ng.

The detector is also quite sensitive to acrylic acid, crotonic acid, acetone, phenol, and isobutyric acid; in each instance, less than 10 ng is required for detection by ECD. It should be noted that these sensitivity

TABLE 1
Sensitivity of Gas Chromatograph to Some Microbial Metabolites

Compound	Retention time, sec	Charge, μg	Sensitivity limit, ng
Methanol	15	7.5	130.
Acetone	20	7.5	5.8
Ethanol	25	12.5	29.
Diacetyl	35	0.033	0.014
n-Propanol	40	7.5	100.
n-Butanol	80	7.5	150.
Crotonic acid	110	12.5	5.9
Methylamine	115	37.5	34.
Acetoin	150	0.003	0.001
1,4-Butanediol	170	60.	110.
Ethylamine	410	75.	270.
Acetic acid	425	37.5	39.
Phenol	510	7.5	5.8
Formic acid	535	75.	16.
Propionic acid	680	37.5	180.
n-Butyric acid	700	37.5	36.
Pyruvic acid	705	7.5	0.43
Valeric acid	710	37.5	14.
Isobutyric acid	765	37.5	7.9
Acrylic acid	1170	37.5	4.6

values are calculated from peak areas produced by the charge. By contrast with the marked sensitivity to these carbonyl and unsaturated compounds, only moderate sensitivities to certain normal fatty acids and generally low sensitivities to short-chain alcohols were observed.

The data indicate that the ECD is an extremely sensitive means for the detection of certain common microbial metabolites. Further studies on the use of ECD for the detection and identification of various microorganisms are in progress.

ACKNOWLEDGMENTS

The authors thank Mrs. S. S. Presnell for able technical assistance. This investigation was supported by the U. S. Air Force Office of Scientific Research under Contract AF49(638)-1737.

REFERENCES

1. Lovelock, J. E., *Anal. Chem.* **35**, 474 (1963).
2. Oaks, D. M., Hartmann, H., and Dimick, K. P., *Anal. Chem.* **36**, 1560 (1964).
3. Miller, M. W., "The Pfizer Handbook of Microbial Metabolites." McGraw-Hill, New York, 1961.
4. Henis, Y., Gould, J. R., and Alexander, M., *Appl. Microbiol.* **14**, 513 (1966).
5. Shilman, A., and Schaper, L. W., *J. Gas Chromatog.* **4**, 486 (1966).

B. M. Mitruka
M. Alexander

Laboratory of Soil Microbiology
Department of Agronomy, Cornell University
Ithaca, New York 14850
Received March 28, 1967

Electrophoretic Separation of Soluble Rat Liver Cell Proteins on Gelatinized Cellulose Acetate

Soluble rat liver cell proteins have been separated by electrophoresis on filter paper (1, 2) cellulose acetate (3), and starch gel (4) and by the Tiselius method (5). Although each of these approaches has its disadvantages, the main problem with cellulose acetate is drying of the strips during sample application and electrophoresis at higher voltages. Recently, a new type of gelatinized cellulose acetate, Cellogel, became available (Colab Laboratories, Chicago Heights, Illinois). This product is not prone to drying, and gives superior separations of liver cell proteins when compared with four other types of cellulose acetate.

METHODS

Male Sprague-Dawley rats were anesthetized with Nembutal and their livers were perfused through the portal vein with 0.14 *M* sodium chloride containing 0.01 *M* trisodium citrate at the rate of 5 ml/min for 5 min at 5°C. The liver was removed from the rat and forced through 1 mm diameter holes in the base plate of a tissue press to separate parenchymal from stromal components. The parenchymal exudate was homogenized with a Teflon pestle driven at 1000 rpm for ten complete, rapid passes in an ice bath. The homogenate was then transferred to a 2 ml nitrocellulose centrifuge tube and centrifuged at 105,000 *g* (av. rad.) for 1 hr at 4°C. The resulting supernatant fluid was aspirated from beneath the lipid layer with a syringe fitted to a hypodermic needle which was inserted through the wall of the centrifuge tube.

Strips of Cellogel (3.5 × 20 cm) were soaked in barbital buffer, pH 8.6, $\mu = 0.05$, for 15 min. They were blotted lightly, and 10 to 15 μl of the liver supernatant fluid was applied with a Beckman paper electrophoresis sample applicator 2 cm from the cathode. The strips were then placed across the 10 cm wide gap of an electrophoresis tank. Both buffer compartments contained barbital buffer of the same composition as that used to soak the strips. A constant voltage of 20 V/cm length (200 V)

TABLE 1
Fixing and Staining Mixture

Formaldehyde (37 to 40%)	50 ml
Distilled water	300 ml
Saturated solution of mercuric chloride	50 ml
1% solution of fast green FCF	100 ml
Trichloroacetic acid	15 gm

was applied for 3 hr. After electrophoresis, the strips were fixed and stained for 30 min in the mixture described in Table 1. Excess stain was removed by washing in three 10 min changes of 5% acetic acid, followed by two 10 min changes of the mixture indicated in Table 2. The strips were then rendered transparent by placing them on glass plates and heating at 75°C for 20 min.

TABLE 2
Destaining and Clearing Mixture

Methyl alcohol	1050 ml
Distilled water	1500 ml
Glacial acetic acid	210 ml
Diacetone alcohol (4-hydroxy-4-methyl-2-pentanone)	240 ml

RESULTS AND DISCUSSION

A typical electropherogram of soluble liver proteins is seen in Figure 1. With this technique, 17 bands were reproducibly obtained. To determine the amount of protein in each band, the strips were scanned with a densitometer or individual bands were cut out, dissolved, and quantitated by spectrophotometry (6). Good separation of protein samples on any type of cellulose acetate requires that the sample be applied in a neat, straight line. In this respect, the Beckman sample applicator was superior to micropipets or capillary tubing.

The accepted procedures for homogenization and centrifugation of rat liver usually require addition of sucrose or salt solutions to the tissue (7–11). Although these solutions are necessary for the isolation of various subcellular fractions, the result is a supernatant fluid that is highly dilute with respect to soluble proteins. Subsequent concentration of this

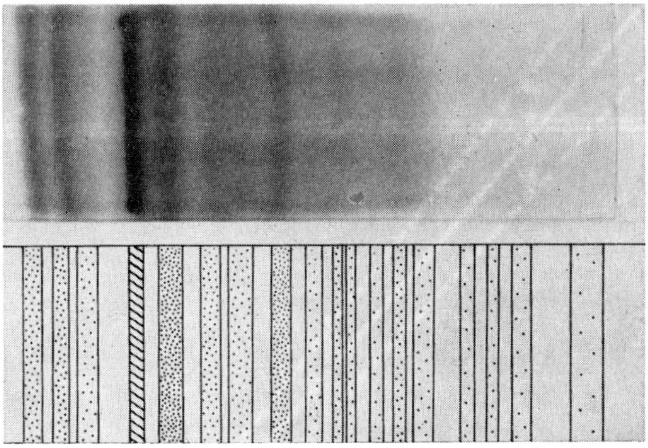

FIG. 1. Photograph and drawing of a typical electropherogram of soluble rat liver cell proteins. The fourth band from the left (cathode) is the origin.

fluid by dialysis, lyophilization, or other means, usually denatures many of its constituent proteins, especially lipoproteins (12). The method described in this report yields about 1 ml of concentrated soluble liver cell proteins from a 10 gm (wet weight) rat liver, which can be electrophoresed approximately 75 min after opening the animal's peritoneal cavity. If the subcellular fractions are still desired, the sediment from the initial centrifugation could be rehomogenized and then subjected to differential centrifugation.

REFERENCES

1. ADJUTANTIS, G., *Nature* **173**, 539 (1954).
2. DISABATO, G., *Experientia* **12**, 385 (1956).
3. MULLAN, F. A., HANCOCK, D. M., AND NEILL, D. W., *Nature* **194**, 149 (1962).
4. KLEIN, A. E., *Naturwiss.* **50**, 669 (1963).
5. ANDERSON, N. G., AND SWANSON, H. D., *Exptl. Cell Res.* **23**, 58 (1961).
6. SCHERR, G. H., *Trans. N. Y. Acad. Sci.* **23**, 519 (1961).
7. POTTER, V. R., AND ELVEJHEM, C. A., *J. Biol. Chem.* **114**, 495 (1936).
8. CLAUDE, A., *J. Exptl. Med.* **84**, 51 (1946).
9. CLAUDE, A., *J. Exptl. Med.* **84**, 61 (1946).

10. Hogeboom, G. H., Schneider, W. C., and Striebich, M. J., *J. Biol. Chem.* **196,** 111 (1952).
11. Anderson, N. G., *Exptl. Cell Res.* **8,** 91 (1955).
12. McFarlane, A. S., *Nature* **149,** 439 (1942).

A. V. LeBouton

Department of Anatomy
The Center for the Health Sciences
University of California
Los Angeles, California 90024
Received April 11, 1967

On the Identification of Some Naturally Occurring Hydroxycinnamic Acid Derivatives[1]

Hydroxycinnamic acids are widely distributed in plants, often in the form of water-soluble derivatives. 4-Hydroxycinnamic (*p*-coumaric), 3,4-dihydroxycinnamic (caffeic), and 3-methoxy-4-hydroxycinnamic (ferulic) are the commonest such acids; generally they occur free, esterified to glucose, esterified to quinic acid, or as glucosides. Because of similarities in such properties as fluorescence and absorption spectra, the identification of these derivatives in extracts can be somewhat difficult. This note reports some methods convenient for systematically isolating and identifying the twelve compounds of Table 1 from small amounts of plant material.

Beginning with the hot-water soluble components of the plant, the free acids were first removed by ether extraction and separated by paper chromatography in BzAW (benzene/acetic acid/water, 125/72/3). The remaining aqueous solution was chromatographed in BPW (*n*-butanol/pyridine/water, 14/3/3) to separate glusose esters (R_f region 0.55–0.75) from glucosides and quinic acid derivatives (R_f region 0.10–0.30). The glucose esters were than eluted and resolved by chromatography in BAW (*n*-butanol/acetic acid/water, 20/5/11).

Separation of the remaining glucosides and quinic acid esters was accomplished by descending chromatography in BADW (butyl acetate/dioxane/1% aqueous formic acid, 68/30/2) after the paper had been equilibrated overnight over BADW (2/37/61). In this solvent all three

[1] Issued as NRC No. 9686.

glucosides had R_f values between 0.10 and 0.15 while *p*-coumaroylquinic acid (R_f 0.40), caffeoylquinic acid (R_f 0.31), and feruloylquinic acid (R_f 0.43) ran well ahead. The glucosides could then be eluted and resolved in BzAW, and the quinic esters in KFW (methyl isobutyl ketone/formic acid/water, 14/3/2). For survey purposes quinic acid derivatives and glucosides of phenolic acids need not always be separated as such; glucosides can be hydrolyzed by treatment with 0.1% emulsin for 3 hr and the free acids ether-extracted, in which case the quinic acid esters can then be resolved in either BAW or KFW. Alternately, the quinic derivatives can be selectively cleaved by treatment with 2.5 *N* NaOH at 25° for 1 hr, their aglycones removed by neutralization of the solution and ether extraction, and the residual glucosides differentiated by careful chromatography in BzAW.

Table 1 shows R_f values for twelve compounds in five solvents. Most of these compounds could be readily located by their fluorescence colors as listed in Table 2. Their identification could be further confirmed by measurement of the absorption maxima, first in dry ethanol, then after addition of a drop of 1% $AlCl_3$ in methanol, and finally after further addition of 3 drops of 1% aqueous NaOH. Alkali is of course a usual reagent for the detection of phenolic groups by means of the higher wavelength of the absorption maxima of the resulting phenolate ions.

TABLE 1

R_f Values of Some Hydroxycinnamic Acids and Derivatives

Compound	BPW	BAW	BzAW	KFW	HOAc
p-Coumaric acid	0.78	0.88	0.70	0.89	0.45(0.73)[b]
Caffeic acid	0.61	0.84	0.31	0.82	0.35(0.65)
Ferulic acid	0.78	0.88	0.81	0.88	0.39(0.66)
3-*p*-Coumaroylquinic acid	0.30	0.76	0.15	0.72	0.68(0.77)
3-Caffeoylquinic acid[a]	0.28	0.62	0.09	0.38	0.63(0.76)
3-Feruloylquinic acid	0.28	0.71	0.17	0.52	0.64(0.78)
p-Coumaroylglucose	0.74	0.71	0.09	0.49	0.73(0.80)
Caffeoylglucose	0.71	0.57	0.05	0.31	0.65(0.73)
Feruloylglucose	0.68	0.64	0.19	0.46	0.67(0.75)
Glucosido-*p*-coumaric acid	0.28	0.62	0.16	0.32	0.71
4-Glucosidocaffeic acid	0.19	0.58	0.11	0.25	0.59
Glucosidoferulic acid	0.26	0.62	0.25	0.32	0.72

[a] Chlorogenic acid.

[b] R_f values in parentheses are for *cis* forms.

Solvents used: BPW = *n*-butanol/pyridine/water (14/3/3); BAW = *n*-butanol/acetic acid/water (20/5/11); BzAW = benzene/acetic acid/water (125/72/3); KFW = methyl isobutyl ketone/formic acid/water (14/3/2); HOAc = acetic acid/water (1/49).

Chromatography was carried out on Whatman #1 paper at 24° without equilibration, all descending except HOAc and KFW.

TABLE 2
Fluorescence Colors and Absorption Maxima of Some Hydroxycinnamic Acids and Derivatives

Componnd	Fluorescence colors[a]				Absorption maxima, mμ		
	254 mμ + NH_3		366 mμ + NH_3		C_2H_5OH	+$AlCl_3$	+NaOH
p-Coumaric acid	dk VI	VI	f	VI	310	317	332
Caffeic acid	BL-VI	BL	BL	BL-WH	324	366	349
Ferulic acid	BL-VI	bBL-VI	BL	bBL	322	330	344
3-*p*-Coumaroylquinic acid	dk VI	VI	f	BL-VI	312	316	365
3-Caffeoylquinic acid	BL-VI	GN	BL	GN	328	357	376
3-Feruloylquinic acid	BL-VI	BL-GN	BL	BL-GN	325	327	375
p-Coumaroylglucose	dk VI	VI	f	BL-VI	316	316	371
Caffeoylglucose	BL-VI	GN	BL	GN	333	344	382
Feruloylglucose	BL-VI	BL-GN	BL	BL-GN	329	329	383
Glucosido-*p*-coumaric acid	abs.	abs.			287,301[b]	298[b],307	275
4-Glucosidocaffeic acid	BL-VI	OR	BL-VI	YW-OR	284,314	294,324	285,332
Glucosidoferulic acid	VI	VI	BL-VI	BL-VI	284,310	297,320	276,324

[a] VI = violet; BL = blue; GN = green; WH = white; YW = yellow; OR = orange; dk = dark; b = bright; f = faint; abs. = absorbing spot.

[b] Shoulder. Derivatives of caffeic and ferulic acids generally have inflections in the region 290–300 mμ.

Aluminum chloride, which has been used in the characterization of flavonoids (1) and free phenolic acids (2), produces spectral shifts in molecules capable of chelating it. Thus the carboxyl groups of the free cinnamic acids and their glucosides respond to this reagent strongly; the carboxyl of quinic acid derivatives, being removed from the aromatic portion of the molecule, produces only a slight shift; and glucose esters show none at all. The *o*-dihydroxy group of caffeic acid also chelates aluminum chloride, so an additional degree of shift is apparent in this acid and its esters. These shifts are summarized in Table 2.

All the spectra of Table 2 were obtained using natural mixtures of *cis* and *trans* isomers but may be taken to represent the *trans* compounds. Such mixtures can be resolved if necessary by chromatography in 2% aqueous acetic acid (Table 1) (3).

The glucosides used here were prepared synthetically by procedures described elsewhere (4). The glucose esters were isolated from tobacco plants after feeding of the aglycones.

ACKNOWLEDGMENTS

Thanks are extended to Dr. O. L. Gamborg for the use of authentic samples of 3-*p*-coumaroylquinic acid (from Dr. E. Haslam) and 3-feruloylquinic acid (from Dr. J. Corse); and to Mr. B. K. Bailey for technical assistance.

REFERENCES

1. JURD, L., *in* "The Chemistry of Flavonoid Compounds" (T. A. Geissman, ed.), p. 119. Macmillan, New York, 1962.
2. NAKAGAWA, Y., SHETLAR, M. R., AND WENDER, S. H., *Anal. Biochem.* **7**, 374 (1964).
3. CHALLICE, J. S., AND WILLIAMS, A. H., *J. Chromatog.* **24**, 357 (1966).
4. STECK, W., *Can. J. Biochem.* **45**, 889 (1967).

WARREN STECK

Prairie Regional Laboratories
National Research Council of Canada
Saskatoon, Canada
Received May 17, 1967

The Hazards of Knotting Dialysis Bags

Tappan's simple dialysis method (1), although possibly a useful improvement over the classically knotted dialysis bag, still has one

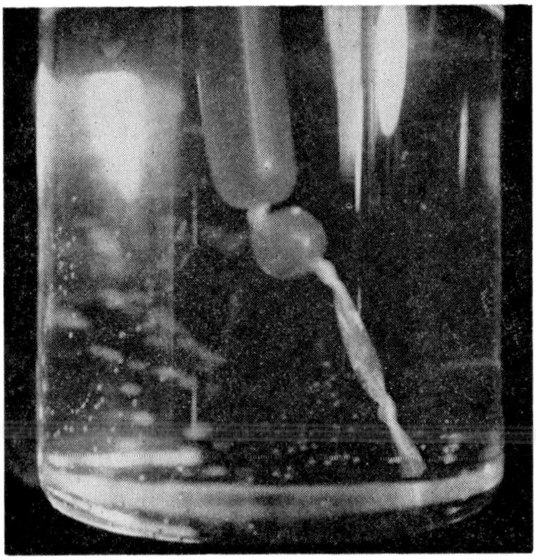

FIG. 1. Dialysis of normal pooled human plasma (containing 5% dextrose) against distilled water, after a 22 hr dialysis and two changes of water. Note how the solution has forced itself past the first knot and is in the process of passing the second one. The other end was similarly knotted and had very much the same aspect.

important flaw. That flaw is the other knot. The vast majority of workers using dialysis likes to believe that a knot in cellophane tubing is impermeable to solute as well as to solvent.

It is not. When a dialysis bag is closed with several knots (with about 1 in. interval) on each side, it quickly becomes apparent that the liquid to be dialyzed very easily passes the first knot and often also the second one (see Fig. 1). *Three knots at each end* (or when used as a U-tube, three knots with both ends knotted together), *are the minimum safeguards for the prevention of large, but generally unnoticed, losses of solution* (2, 3).

It would be interesting to learn if there are data about the impermeability of Tappan's clamp system (1). If these clamps are really impermeable, his system (1) could be used to clamp off *both ends* of the cellophane simultaneously and thus not only facilitate repeated sampling but also assure the integrity of the dialysis bags.

REFERENCES

1. TAPPAN, D. V., *Anal. Biochem.* **18,** 392 (1967).
2. VAN OSS, C. J., *in* "Seminars in Immunogenetics" (T. J. Greenwalt, ed.), p. 1, Lippincott, Philadelphia, 1967.

3. VAN OSS, C. J., *in* "Advances in Separation and Purification," (E. S. Perry, ed.), Wiley, New York, 1967.

CAREL J. VAN OSS

Serum and Plasma Departments, Milwaukee Blood Center and Department of Biology, Marquette University Milwaukee, Wisconsin 53233
Received May 23, 1967

Thin-Layer Chromatographic Separation of Hexitols and Corresponding Hexoses

The hexitols, sorbitol and galactitol, have become of increasing biological importance, the former because of its accumulation in nervous tissue of diabetic animals (1) and the latter because of its presence in the tissues and urine of patients with congenital galactosemia (2) and in the tissues of animals fed a high galactose diet (3). Galactitol has been considered the etiological factor in galactose cataract formation (4).

Metabolic studies with galactitol have necessitated a convenient method of separation of this polyol from galactose as well as from other common hexitols. Paper chromatographic procedures have failed to achieve the desired results (5). Gas chromatography has resolved this difficulty but requires laborious procedures and expensive equipment (6). Recently Nemec *et al.* (7) employed silica gel G on glass plates to separate sorbitol, galactitol, and mannitol from their related aldoses but were unable to separate these hexitols from each other. This communication describes the use of borate impregnated silica gel G on thin layer to effect the separation of these polyols from their corresponding hexoses and from each other.

Materials and Methods. 0.02 *M* borate buffer, pH 7.85, was made up fresh as a 3% solution of 0.02 *M* sodium borate, pH 9.2, in 0.02 *M* boric acid, pH 6.6; 120 ml of the resulting solution was added to 60 gm silica gel G, according to Stahl (Brinkmann Instruments). The mixture was shaken manually for 90 sec and spread onto 20 × 20 cm glass plates to a thickness of 250 μ using the Desaga spreader. After drying overnight the plates were placed into a 126°C oven for 60 min, then stored at room temperature in a wooden box with desiccant. Before using, the plates were reactivated for 30 min in the 126° oven.

Unlabeled sugars were obtained from Phanstiehl Laboratories, Inc.

Galactitol-1-^{14}C 2.26 μc/mg, was provided by the National Bureau of Standards and galactose-1-^{14}C obtained from New England Nuclear was diluted with unlabeled galactose to 2.26 μc/mg.

With a 2 μl pipet, 2 μl of each of the unlabeled 30 mM solutions was spotted 3.5 cm above the bottom of the plate. The plates were run in a glass tank. The solvent, 80% isopropanol in water, was run at room

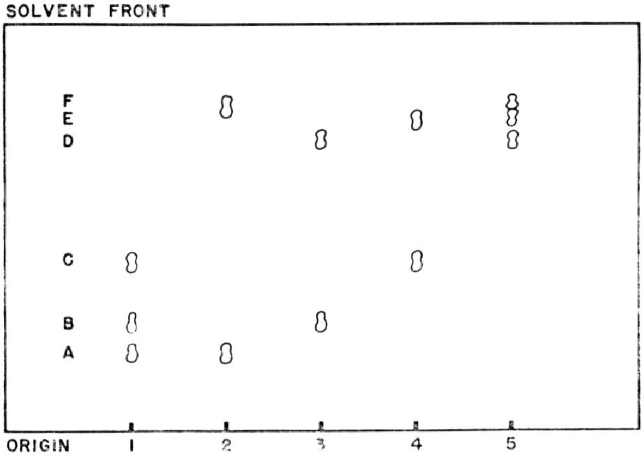

FIG. 1. Representation of chromatogram in which three hexoses had been run with their respective sugar alcohols on borate-impregnated silica gel G. Applications were made as follows: (1) galactitol, sorbitol, mannitol; (2) sorbitol, glucose; (3) galactitol, galactose; (4) mannitol, mannose; (5) galactose, glucose, mannose. Resulting R_f values were as follows: (A) sorbitol, 0.192; (B) galactitol, 0.269; (C) mannitol, 0.415; (D) galactose, 0.711; (E) mannose, 0.750; (F) glucose, 0.788.

temperature to a predetermined solvent front 13 cm above the origin (approximately 4 hr). After the plates were removed and dried at room temperature, the procedure was repeated twice using the same solvent. To detect the sugars, the plates were sprayed with a 10% solution of sulfuric acid in methanol and dried at 126° for 40 min. All of the sugars appeared as deep charcoal spots after 15 min and the polyols were noted after 30 min as light brown spots.

When labeled galactose and galactitol were used 2 μl of 30 mM galactitol or 1 μl of 100 mM galactose was applied and after development of the plate the area above the origin was divided into 1 cm portions, 3 cm in width. The 1 cm portions were scraped from the plates into small glass counting vials; 10 cc of liquid scintillator, made as 5% solution of Liquifluor (New England Nuclear Co.) in toluene was added to each counting vial. Samples were counted in the Packard model 3365 liquid scintillation counter.

Results and Discussion. Figure 1 is a representation of a chromatogram in which each of the three hexoses was run with its respective sugar alcohol. Also, the three sugars were run as a mixture, as were the three polyols. A series of thin-layer experiments indicated that the separation of the hexoses and polyols was reproducible and the separation and relative positions of the three polyols were also constant in these studies.

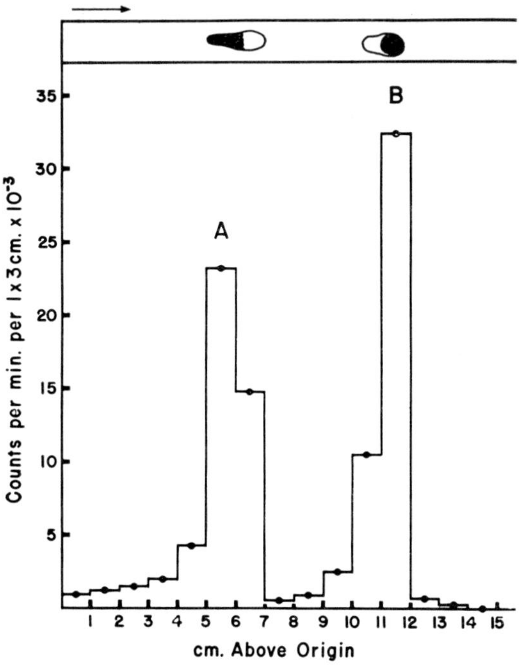

FIG. 2. Sketch of chromatograph analyzed by spraying as well as scraping. 2 μl of 30 m*M* galactitol (2.26 μc/mg) and 1 μl of 100 m*M* galactose (2.26 μc/mg) were spotted together as a mixture, in duplicate at the origin. The bar graph represents the radioactivity recovered in the 1 × 3 cm sections scraped; circles indicate the spots visualized after spraying. Identity of peaks are: (A) galactitol; (B) galactose.

Application of this method has also been made to the separation of pentoses from their corresponding pentitols. Resulting R_f values were as follows: D-arabitol, 0.469; D-arabinose, 0.692; L-arabitol, 0.476; L-arabinose, 0.684; ribitol, 0.561; ribose, 0.500; xylitol (two resulting spots), 0.453 and 0.253; and D-xylose, 0.669. Although it was possible to separate D- and L-arabinose and D-xylose from their respective polyols, it was only possible to separate ribitol from the other three pentitols. The method, however, can be employed to separate the pentitols and the hexitols. (See R_f values in Figure 1).

Figure 2 shows the results of a chromatograph of a mixture of galactose-1-^{14}C and galactitol-1-C^{14}, applied as adjacent spots, where, after running, one of the chromatographs was analyzed by spraying and the other by counting. The sketch indicates that the sugar and the polyol are clearly separated by this system and that the radioactivity peak for both migrates to the same position on the plate as the visual spot.

Borate-impregnated silica gel G has proved to be a simple means for the detection of galactitol in the urines of patients given labeled galactitol and in various animal tissues which had been incubated with labeled galactitol in metabolic experiments (8), thus eliminating the need for complicated analysis by gas chromatography.

ACKNOWLEDGMENTS

This work was supported by a grant from the John A. Hartford Foundation and grant AM 10894 from the National Institutes of Health.

REFERENCES

1. Gabbay, K. H., Merola, L. D., and Field, R. A., *Science* **151**, 209 (1966).
2. Quan-Ma, R., Wells, H. J., Wells, W. W., Sherman, F. E., and Egan, T. J., *Am. J. Diseases Children* **112**, 477 (1966).
3. Quan, R., and Wells, W. W. *Biochem. Biophys. Res. Commun.* **20**, 486 (1965).
4. Bannon, S. L., Higgenbottom, R. M., McConnell, J. M., and Koan, H. W., *Arch. Opthalmol.* **33**, 224 (1945).
5. Stahl, E., and Kaltenbach, U., *in* "Thin Layer Chromatography," pp. 461–469. Academic Press New York, 1965.
6. Wells, W. W., Pittman, T. A., and Egan, T. J., *J. Biol. Chem.* **239**, 3192 (1960).
7. Nemec, J., Kefurt, K., and Jary, J., *J. Chromatog.* **26**, 116 (1967).
8. Weinstein, A. N., and Segal, S., in preparation.

Adrienne N. Weinstein
Stanton Segal

Division of Biochemical Development and Molecular Diseases
Children's Hospital of Philadelphia
Philadelphia, Pennsylvania 19146
Received May 23, 1967

Erratum

Vol. **19**, No. 1 (1967), in the article entitled, "Detection of *N*-Methylated Ethanolamines in Phosphatide Hydrolyzates by Thin-Layer Chromatography," by W. Reissmann and Th. Wieske, pp. 46–49:

Due to a technical error, the legend to Figure 1 was omitted. The figure and legend are printed below:

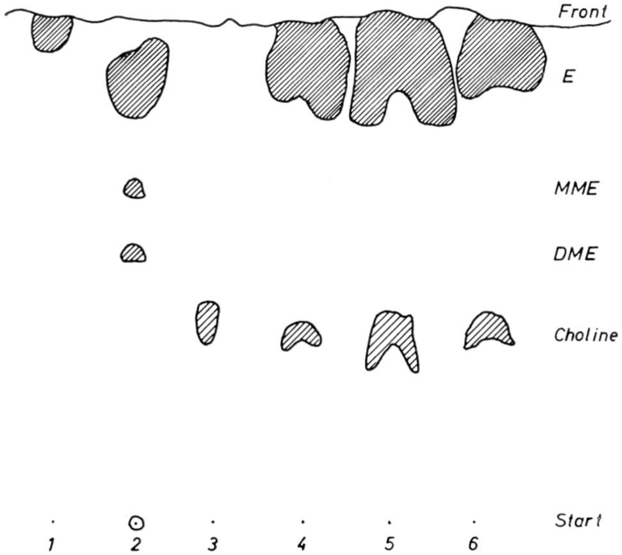

Start No.	Substance	Amount μg/μl
1	Glycerol	20
2	Ethanolamine (E)	300
	MME and DME; of each:	3
3	Choline chloride	10
4	Egg yolk hydrolyzate	0.04 ml
5	Egg yolk hydrolyzate	0.1 ml[a]
6	Soybean phosphatide hydrolyzate	0.07 ml[b]

Sorption layer: silica gel G
Thickness of layer: 0.25 mm
Plate size; 20 × 20 cm
Solvent: methanol/conc. HCl (95:5)
Staining: alkaline 0.5 *N* $KMnO_4$
Substance dissolved in: C_2H_5OH/H_2O
Travelling time: about $2\frac{1}{2}$ hr

[a] Corresponding to 453 μg E.
[b] Corresponding to 1528 μg E.

AUTHOR INDEX

A

Ajl, Samuel J., 335
Alexander, M., 548
Attal, J., 394
Aung-Than-Batu, 432

B

Baldwin, T., 58
Bartosik, D. B., 233
Bauer, Š., 387
Beinert, Helmut, 40, 325
Benson, J. V., Jr., 51
Bentley, Ronald, 312
Biely, P., 387
Bleiweis, Arnold S., 335
Bogdonoff, Morton D., 466
Bon, W. F., 37
Booth, Robert A., 198
Botlock, Nancy, 312
Brentani, M., 361
Brentani, R., 361
Brodbeck, U., 58
Brown, Ronald D., 358
Burger, Charles L., 373
Busch, Harris, 439

C

Carlson, Don M., 195
Chambers, Cecil W., 321
Chandelier, E. L., 419
Chartrand, A., 224
Chauhan, U. P. S., 155
Chen, Raymond F., 339
Chrambach, A., 150
Clarke, Norman A., 321

D

Davis, John Gorton, 363
Dietz, Albert A., 246
Dorfman, Ralph I., 294

E

Ebner, K. E., 58
Efron, Mary L., 299
Eik-Nes, K. B., 394

F

Feeney, J., 1
Forte, John G., 545

G

Glebko, L. I., 16
Goldstein, Gerald, 477, 533
Grunwald, Claus, 484

H

Hamman, Bette L., 423
Hansen, Raymond E., 40
Haraguchi, K. H., 167
Hathaway, Paul W., 466
Helbock, Harold, 545
Hemming, F. W., 1
Hendeles, S. M., 394
Hla-Pe, U, 432
Holt, Charles E., 358
Hunziker, Käthi, 495
Hurst, A., 24

I

Ingram, L., 24
Ipata, P. L., 30

J

Jakoi, Laszlo, 466
Jansen, J. C., 167
Johnson, W. J., 224

K

Kalal, Theodore T., 40
Karmen, Arthur, 102
Kato, J., 233
Kekwick, R. G. O., 171
Kelmers, A. D., 533
Khan, W. A., 58
Kim, Je. H., 258
Knox, R. J., 282
Ko, Howard, 205

L

Laskowski, M., Sr., 94
LeBouton, A. V., 550
Liao, Ta-Hsiu, 258

LISBOA, B. P., 77
LUBRANO, TINA, 246
LUST, JEAN, 65

M

MARTIN, MALCOLM M., 423
MAURITZEN, CHARLES M., 439
MCCARTHY, TIMOTHY E., 275
MCCLIMANS, CAROLYN, 439
MCEWEN, C. R., 114
MECHANIC, GERALD L., 299
MILLER, WARREN W., 181
MITRUKA, B. M., 548
MONDER, CARL, 215

N

NELSON, GARY J., 198
NERENBERG, CLINTON A., 294
NISHIMURA, JONATHAN S., 275

O

OHMS, J. I., 51

P

PALMER, R. F., 77
PATTERSON, J. A., 51
PIERCE, JOHN G., 258

R

RAW, I., 361
REEVES, HENRY C., 335
REISFELD, R. A., 150
RICHARDS, VICTOR, 65
RIEGELMAN, S., 463
RIZACK, MARTIN A., 192
ROGERS, CHARLES J., 321
ROMANOFF, E. B., 233
ROSENTHAL, HANNAH E., 525
ROWLAND, M., 463
ROYER, MAX E., 205
RUBIN, I. B., 533
RUSHIZKY, GEORGE W., 181

S

SALASOO, I., 200
SALTMAN, PAUL, 545
SARKAR, B. C., 155
SCHMID, KARL, 495
SCHUEL, HERBERT, 86
SCHUEL, REGINA, 86
SEGAL, STANTON, 558
SELLS, NEWELL, 215
SHARMA, DINESH C., 294
SHIH, VIVIAN E., 299
SHOME, BASUDEV, 258
SIEGEL, B. V., 167
SIELE, MARY, 363
SKILLETER, D. N., 171
SLATER, GARY, 365
STARBUCK, WESLEY C., 439
STAVRIC, B., 224
STECK, WARREN, 553
STEGINK, LEWIS D., 502
STOWE, BRUCE B., 484
SULKOWSKI, E., 94

T

TOMBS, M. P., 24
TROYER, WILLIAM G., JR., 466

U

ULKINA, J. I., 16

V

VAN DE BOGART, MILDRED, 325
VAN OSS, CAREL J., 556
VASKOVSKY, V. E., 16
VEIGA, L. A., 419
VENDRELL, MIGUEL, 484

W

WALLACE, VOLNEY, 411, 517
WARD, MARTHA A., 275
WATSON, D. J., 233
WEINSTEIN, ADRIENNE N., 558
WINKELMAN, JAMES, 365
WISE, C. DAVID, 369
WYCKOFF, M., 150

Z

ZACCARI, J., 150
ZAUGG, W. S., 282
ZEC, J., 51

SUBJECT INDEX

A

N-acetylgalactosaminitol, assay for, Carlson, 195
Acetyl groups, in proteins and peptides, quantitative analysis of, Stegnik, 502
α_1-Acid glycoprotein variants, identification of, Hunziker and Schmid, 495
Acrylamide-gel electrophoresis, mobility-molecular weight relationships of small proteins in, Ingram *et al.*, 24
Actinomycin amino acids, gas-liquid chromatography of, Ward *et al.*, 275
Activation analysis, Rushizky and Miller, 181
Adenosine 3′,5′-phosphate derivatives, separation of, Rizack, 192
Amino acid analysis data, computer program for, Starbuck *et al.*, 439
Amino acids, rapid short-column chromatography of, Shih *et al.*, 299
Aminoacylation, for determination of transfer ribonucleic acid, Rubin *et al.*, 533
p-Ansidine periodate reaction, for sugar detection, Veiga and Chandler, 419
Atomic absorption spectrophotometry acids and analysis by, Monder and Sells, 215
Atomic absorption spectrophotometry for phosphate determination, Zaugg and Knox, 282
Atropine, by a Prudhomme method, Wallace, 411
Autoanalyzer analysis, correction for cross-contamination in, Wallace, 517

C

Δ^{16}-C_{19}-steroids, isolation, Lisboa and Palmer, 77
Calcium, acids and atomic absorption spectrophotometry of, Monder and Sells, 215
Calcium, in biological materials, micro determination, Sarkar, 155
Carbon disulfide, as a solvent for carboxylic acid silylation, Rowland and Riegelman, 463
Carboxylic acids, silylation of, Rowland and Riegelman, 463
Carboxylic acids, thin-layer chromatography of, Bleiweis *et al.*, 335
Char sprays, increasing sensitivity of, Nelson and Booth, 198
Column chromatography, of sugars, Ohms *et al.*, 51
Continuous free-flow electrophoresis for nucleotide separation, Sulkowski and Laskowski, 94
Copper, micro determination, Van de Bogart and Beinert, 325
Corticosteroids, measurement of, Hamman and Martin, 423

D

2-deoxy-*D* glucose 6-phosphate, determination, Biely and Bauer, 387
Dialysis bags, hazards of knotting, van Oss, 556
α-ϵ-diaminopimelic acid, spectrophotofluorometric determination, Rogers *et al.*, 321
Disc electrophoresis of lactic dehydrogenase isoenzymes, Dietz and Lubrano, 246

E

Ecteola cellulose, for separation of cyclic-AMP derivatives, Rizack, 192
Electron capture detection, for determination of free estrone, Attal *et al.*, 394
Electron paramagnetic resonance sample, temperature control for, Hansen *et al.*, 40
Electrophoresis, of liver proteins, LeBouton, 550
Estrone, in blood plasma, determination, Attal *et al.*, 394

F

Forminoglutamic acid, in urine, determination of, Hla-Pe and Aung-Than-Batu, 432

G

Gas chromatography, detection of microbial metabolites, MITRUKA AND ALEXANDER, 548

Gas liquid chromatography, of actinomycin amino acids, WARD *et al.*, 275

Gas liquid chromatography, of mutarotase, BENTLEY AND BOTLOCK, 312

α-*D*-glucose, 1,6-diphosphate, chemical synthesis of, KAHN *et al.*, 58

Gradient sedimentation, tables for, MCEWEN, 114

H

Hexitols, thin layer chromatographic separation, WEINSTEIN AND SEGAL, 558

Hydroxycinnamic acid derivatives, identification, of STECK, 553

I

Indolic methyl esters, chromatographic separations, GRUNWALD *et al.*, 484

Ion-exchange chromatography, of mevalonate derivatives, SKILLETER AND KEKWICK, 171

Iron, micro determination, VAN DE BOGART AND BEINERT, 325

L

Lactic dehydrogenase isoenzymes, disc electrophoresis of, DIETZ AND LUBRANO, 246

Ligand-exchange chromatography, of nucleotides, GOLDSTEIN, 477

Liquid-liquid extraction, WALLACE, 411

Liquid scintillation mixture components, chemiluminescence of, WINKELMAN AND SLATER, 365

Liver proteins, electrophoresis of, LEBOUTON, 550

M

Magnesium, acids and atomic absorption spectrophotometry of, MONDER AND SELLS, 215

Membrane-gas detector, KARMEN, 102

Membrane transport studies, apparatus for FORTE *et al.*, 545

Mevalonate derivatives, chromatography of, SKILLETER AND KEKWICK, 171

Microbial metabolites, detection by gas chromatography, MITRUKA AND ALEXANDER, 548

Microsomal ribonucleic acids, liver, buffers, and phenol extraction of, LUST AND RICHARDS, 65

Mutarotase, gas liquid chromatography of, BENTLEY AND BOTLOCK, 312

N

Nitrogen determination, using thymolhypobromite reaction, GLEBKO *et al.*, 16

Nonpolar acids, submicromolar assay for, KO AND ROYER, 205

Nucleic acids, activation analysis, RUSHIZKY AND MILLER, 181

5′-nucleotidase, optical assay for, IPATA, 30

Nucleotide contents of tissues, after wholebody X-irradiation, BURGER, 373

Nucleotides, electrophoresis of, SULKOWSKI AND LASKOWSKI, 94

P

Paper chromatography, device for adding solvents, NERENBERG *et al.*, 294

Parameters, binding, determination and presentation, ROSENTHAL, 525

Phenol extraction of liver microsomal ribonucleic acids, influence of buffers on, LUST AND RICHARDS, 65

Phosphate determination, ZAUGG AND KNOX, 282

Polyacrylamide gel electrophoresis, protein staining, CHRAMBACH *et al.*, 150

Polyprenols, nuclear magnetic resonance spectrometry of, FEENEY AND HEMMING, 1

Progesterone, in biological specimens, determination of, WATSON *et al.*, 233

Protein determination, in presence of sucrose, SCHUEL AND SCHUEL, 86

Protein staining, of polyacrylamide gels, CHRAMBACH *et al.*, 150

Proteins, small, in acrylamide-gel electrophoresis, mobility-molecular weight relationships, INGRAM *et al.*, 24

R

Rabbit serum proteins, distribution, SALASOO, 200
Rapid short-column chromatography, of amino acids, SHIH *et al.*, 299
Ribonucleic acid, transfer, determination, RUBIN *et al.*, 533
RNA, zone sedimentation analysis of, BRETANI *et al.*, 361

S

Serotonin, brain, fluorometric determination, WISE, 369
Spectrophotofluorometer, Aminco-Bowman, calibration, CHEN, 339
Spectrophotometric column monitoring system, multiple-wavelength selector for, HARAGUCHI *et al.*, 167
Steroid chromatograms, direct spectrophotometric quantitation, HAMMAN AND MARTIN, 423
Sucrose density gradients, tables for, MCEWEN, 114
Sugars, column chromatography of, OHMS *et al.*, 51
Sugars, detection and differentiation on paper, VEIGA AND CHANDELIER, 419

T

Thin-layer chromatograms, sensitivity of char sprays for, NELSON AND BOOTH, 198
Thin-layer chromatography, for separation of Δ^{16}-C_{19}-steroids, LISBOA AND PALMER, 77
Thin-layer chromatography, of carboxylic acids, BLEIWEIS *et al.*, 335
Thymine-dimer-pyrimidine separation BROWN AND HOLT, 358
Thymol-hypobromite reaction, for determination of nitrogen, GLEBKO *et al.*, 16
Thyrotopic hormone, sugars of, gas chromatography of, KIM *et al.*, 258

U

Ultracentrifuge, simultaneous analysis in, BON, 37
Ultrafilter, for concentration of high molecular weight solutes, DAVIS AND SIELE, 363
Uridine diphosphate-2-deoxy-*D*- glucose, determination, BIELY AND BAUER, 387
Urinary catecholamines, differential analysis of, HATHAWAY *et al.*, 466
Urinary DDA excretion in humans, determination, STAVRIC *et al.*, 224

V

Volatites, dissolved, measuring concentration of, KARMEN, 102

W

Whole body X-irradiation, nucleotide content of tissues, BURGER, 373